Los Angeles
The Complete **Residents'** Guide

Los Angeles Explorer 1st Edition ISBN 978-9948-8585-2-2

Front Cover Photograph – Pete Maloney

Printed and bound by Emirates Printing Press, Dubai, United Arab Emirates.

Explorer Publishing & Distribution
PO Box 34275, Dubai
United Arab Emirates
Phone   +971 (0)4 340 8805
Fax   +971 (0)4 340 8806
Email   info@explorerpublishing.com
Web   www.explorerpublishing.com

Welcome

You've just made living in Los Angeles a whole lot easier. In the following pages you'll find out everything you need to know to get settled into – and then get the most out of – your new life in one of the world's most exciting cities. From finding a house to watching the Lakers, we can tell you how and where to do it.

General Information (p.1) fills you in on Los Angeles' history, geography and culture, and provides details of how to get around and where to stay when you first arrive.

The **Residents** chapter (p.37) takes away all the headaches involved in setting up your new home. With information on visas, residential areas in and around LA, schools, healthcare and red tape, this section will tell you how to deal with all the formalities.

After settling in, take a look at **Exploring** (p.139). This chapter lifts the lid on the LA areas that are worth a visit, and then lists the city's essential attractions, including galleries, museums, parks and beaches. You'll also find some suggestions for holiday getaways.

If you've still got time on your hands, move on to **Activities** (p.209). Whether it's canoeing clubs or comedy classes you're after, this chapter will help you find something to keep you occupied. And if all that exertion leaves you exhausted, wind down with a selection of the city's best spas.

Now that you're living in Los Angeles, you'll have full access to some of the finest **Shopping** in the world (p.255). We've got a whole chapter dedicated to helping you discover the best malls, markets and designer boutiques in which to splash the cash.

Don't spend it all in the shops though – save some for the evening. Our **Going Out** chapter (p.313) gives you a detailed run-down on the premier places for eating, drinking and partying in LA.

Places of interest listed in the book have references that correspond to the detailed **Maps** (p.365) in the back of the book. Use these for everything from finding a bar on Sunset Strip to avoiding traffic on the 101. Many places have colour-coded icons too, making it even easier to locate the restaurant, park, shop or club you're looking for. There's also a Metro map inside the back cover.

And if you think we've missed something, whether it's a hot new hidden-away bar or the best surf school in SoCal, please tell us. Go to www.explorerpublishing.com, fill in the Reader Response form, and share the knowledge with your fellow explorers.

The Explorer Team

Explorer's LA

There are so many things to get excited about in Los Angeles. Here are just a few of them: take a Universal Studios tour (p.187); amble round the Botanical Gardens at The Huntington (p.174); get some culture in The Getty (p.172); enjoy the many concerts at the Hollywood Bowl (p.182); admire the views from the Griffith Observatory (p.182); see fossils at La Brea Tar Pits (p.177).

Alexander Maksik Alexander has lived off and on in LA for 20 years. He's a regular contributor to *The Nervous Breakdown* website and the travel section of the *San Antonio Express-News*, and his work has recently been published in *Crate* magazine and *Nerve* website. While Alexander has worked in LA as a writer, bartender, teacher, actor and creative executive, it was, above all, his short-lived career as a pizza delivery person that taught him the most about this great city. **Favourite LA cultural experience:** The Museum of Tolerance (p.176).

Amanda Knoles Amanda grew up in Texas and arrived in Los Angeles after a 10 year stint as a magazine editor in New York City. She has more than 15 years' experience as a travel writer and frequently profiles shops, restaurants and spas for the *Citysearch* website. She has also written a book on shopping in Las Vegas. She enjoys weekend getaways to San Diego and Palm Springs. **Favourite daytrip:** Taking the ferryboat to Santa Catalina Island (p.160). It's only 22 miles from Los Angeles but seems a world away.

Benjamin Eachus Ben is originally from New Jersey, and moved to Los Angeles after graduating from Princeton. He has no plans to ever leave. When he's not writing, Ben also enjoys taking improv comedy classes, going to movies, hiking, playing basketball, and embarrassing himself at the gym. **Favourite LA restaurant:** Moonshadows in Malibu (p.324) sits right on the Pacific. You can watch the waves crash under the restaurant while you eat.

Deanna Barnert Deanna is an internationally published writer and journalist. She has seen the world and lived in New York City and Madrid, but always comes back to her hometown, LA. She just can't live without the sunshine, the Hollywood Bowl and her local peeps. **Best city memories:** Being serenaded by Mos Def on stage at the Hollywood Bowl, wave diving with dolphins in Malibu, running into friends while biking in Venice and people-watching just about anywhere in the city.

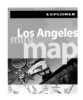

Having trouble navigating your way around sprawling LA? Look no further than the **Los Angeles Mini Map**, an indispensable pocket-sized aid to getting to grips with the roads, areas and attractions of this mega-metropolis.

Elizabeth Borsting Elizabeth is a freelance writer and public relations consultant for the hospitality industry. Her writing credits include *Celebrity Weddings & Honeymoon Getaways*, *California's Best B&Bs*, *LA With Kids*, and her work has appeared in the *Los Angeles Times* and *National Geographic Traveler*. She lives with her family in Long Beach. **LA must-do**: Read the headstones of the famous at Hollywood Forever Cemetery (p.182).

Gwen Helene Kleist A freelance travel writer, Gwen also owns a company specialising in public relations and marketing communications writing. She has lived in Southern California for more than 12 years, and has written for such publications as *Sunset Magazine*, *Huntington Beach Magazine*, *San Diego Family* and the *Los Angeles Times*. **Favourite daytrip**: Being able to take her 3 year old son to Disneyland (p.186) any time she wants.

Hayley Fox After leaving her heart in San Francisco (well, at school in Berkeley), LA-born Hayley returned home and traded in a steady income to pursue her love of independent film. Along the way, she found where her passions merged, as film and music became sources for writing. **Best view:** From the Getty Museum (p.172). You can see the clean air of the ocean on one side, and the settling layer of smog on the other. Overall, a 360 degree view of the city.

Jed Maheu Jed is a writer, actor, comedian and musician living in Los Angeles. A native of the Northwest, he enjoys muscle cars, guitars, food and freedom. Writing credits include *The OC Weekly*, *Seattle Weekly*, *SF Weekly* and *Helio Magazine*. Having an intense passion for food and music, he is equally qualified to write about both. **Favourite restaurant**: Mayflower in Chinatown (p.324). Not the greatest food in the world, but there's a good vibe and the roast duck is spectacular.

Now that you've moved to LA, it won't be long before you're playing host to wave upon wave of visiting family and friends – and we've got the perfect guide to help them get the most out of their sightseeing. Packed with info on the city's shops, restaurants and tourist spots, you can't go wrong with the **Los Angeles Mini Explorer**.

Jonathan Jerald Jonathan has contributed to *California Magazine* and *Vanity Fair*, and is the co-author, with David Reid, of *Pure Silver: The Second-Best of Everything*. He has produced more than a dozen documentaries for The History Channel, including the award-winning *History of LSD*. Jonathan is the former managing editor of *Citizen LA* and is currently editor-in-chief of *Bedlam*, a new magazine about the Los Angeles arts scene. **Best thing about living in LA**: The lively Downtown arts scene.

Michal Lemberger When she moved to LA in 1995 to start graduate school at UCLA, Michal took advantage of LA's famous nightlife. Since then, she has joined the ranks of the married with children and come to see a whole other side of this city – mainly playgrounds, and more children's clothing stores than seems humanly possible. In between, she got a dog, finished her PhD in English and left academia to become a freelance writer, editor and lecturer. **LA Must-Do**: Go down to Little Tokyo (p.155) and eat.

Peter Darchuk Peter is a freelance writer and video artist who has called Los Angeles home for more than 10 years. Curiosity fuels his voracious appetite for experiential living. Late at night you may spot Peter squirrelling across the city in search of the next puzzle piece that will help complete his existential journey. Or he may just be looking for tacos. **Best city memory**: Running into Ronald Reagan and Gregory Peck in the same day. Where else can something like that happen?

Shannon Dunn Over 13 years, Australian Shannon Dunn has honed her journalism and photography skills in newspapers, magazines and the publicity industry in Australia, New Zealand and the United States. After filing the Going Out chapter of the *Sydney Explorer Residents' Guide* in 2006, Shannon moved to Los Angeles with her actor husband. She currently lives in Studio City. **Best view**: Driving down Ventura Boulevard at sunset with swaying palm trees either side.

BLAN
K
SPAC
ES ᴡᴏʀᴋ
ᴡɪᴅᴇ
ᴏᴘᴇɴ

YOUR PROFESSIONAL INDEPENDENCE IS OUR NEW WORK ORDER

Introducing BLANKSPACES, a modern environment of flexible workspaces as adaptive and talented as you are where well-designed form meets well appointed function. A community where creative entrepreneurs and independent professionals foster collaboration. Our inspiring workspaces are available by day, month, or year, based on your specific needs.

A work bar, high-tech conference room, inventive workstations, and private offices are all at your disposal, supported by modern amenities including Wi-Fi, VoIP and color laser printing.

BLANKSPACES is specifically designed to meet your individual work needs and change how you think about where you work. You define the space, we make room for your opportunities. At BLANKSPACES, Work Wide Open!

DAILY WORK SPACE

This certificate is good for
40 HOURS at the WORK BAR or
20 HOURS at a WORK STATION.

Call to reserve your work space today.
At BLANKSPACES we invite you to WORK WIDE OPEN!

offer expires 05.31.09 / code EPD

5405 WILSHIRE BLVD. LOS ANGELES, CA 90036 **BLANKSPACES.COM** 323 330 9505

Where are we exploring next?

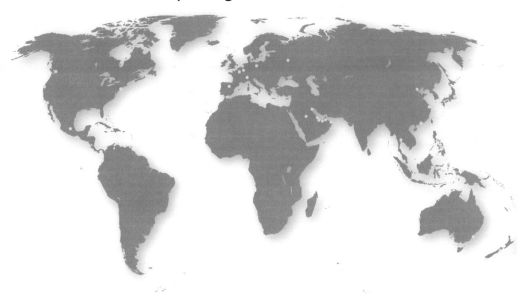

- Abu Dhabi
- Amsterdam
- Bahrain
- Bangkok*
- Barcelona
- Beijing
- Berlin
- Brussels*
- Dubai
- Dublin
- Geneva
- Hong Kong
- Kuala Lumpur
- Kuwait
- London
- Los Angeles
- Mexico City*
- Moscow*
- New York
- New Zealand
- Oman
- Paris
- Qatar
- San Francisco*
- Saudi Arabia*
- Shanghai
- Singapore
- Sydney
- Taipei*
- Tokyo
- Vancouver

* Available 2008/2009

Where do you live?
Is your home city missing from our list? If you'd love to see a residents' guide for a location not currently on Explorer's horizon please email editorial@explorerpublishing.com.

Advertise with Explorer...
If you're interested in advertising with us, please contact sales@explorerpublishing.com.

Make Explorer your very own...
We offer a number of customisation options for bulk sales. For more information and discount rates please contact corporatesales@explorerpublishing.com.

Contract Publishing
Have an idea for a publication or need to revamp your company's marketing material? Contact designlab@explorerpublishing to see how our expert contract publishing team can help.

Online

Life can move pretty fast, so to make sure you can stay up to date with all the latest goings on in your city, we've revamped our website to further enhance your time in the city, whether long or short.

Keep in the know...

Our Complete Residents' Guides and Mini Visitors' series continue to expand, covering destinations from Amsterdam to New Zealand and beyond. Keep up to date with our latest travels and hot tips by signing up to our monthly newsletter, or browse our products section for info on our current and forthcoming titles.

Make friends and influence people...

...by joining our Communities section. Meet fellow residents in your city, make your own recommendations for your favourite restaurants, bars, childcare agencies or dentists, plus find answers to your questions on daily life from long-term residents.

Discover new experiences...

Ever thought about living in a different city, or wondered where the locals really go to eat, drink and be merry? Check out our regular features section, or submit your own feature for publication!

Want to find a badminton club, the number for your bank, or maybe just a restaurant for a hot first date?

Check out city info on various destinations around the world in our Residents' info section – from finding a pilates class to contact details for international schools in your area, or the best place to buy everything from a spanner set to a Spandau Ballet album, we've got it all covered.

Let us know what you think!

All our information comes from residents which means you! If we missed out your favourite bar or market stall, or you know of any changes in the law, infrastructure, cost of living or entertainment scene, let us know by using our Feedback form.

Contents

Contents

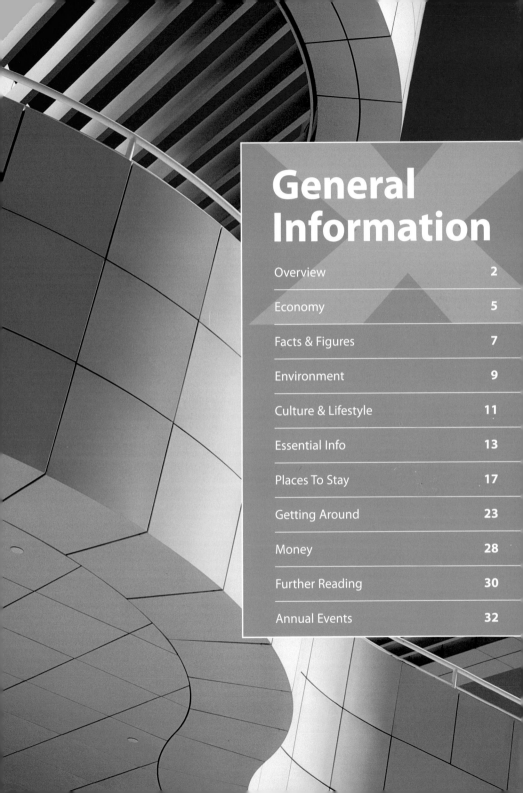

General Information

General Information

Geography

Los Angeles sits on a coastal plain with the Pacific Ocean to the south and west, the San Gabriel Mountains to the east and the Santa Monica Mountains to the north. The sprawling city covers nearly 500 square miles, and is the only city in the US bisected by a mountain range. Geologically unstable, LA offers its residents some 10,000 earthquakes per year.

LA is in the state of California, the third largest and most populous state of the United States, bordered by Oregon to the north, Mexico to the south and Nevada and Arizona to the east. The majority of California's population lives within one of five different metropolitan areas, Los Angeles, San Francisco, Riverside, San Diego and Sacramento.

With a coastline 1,300km long (800 miles), the state is tremendously diverse, encompassing gorgeous mountain ranges, sweeping desserts and wide sandy beaches. California's Central Valley is one of the most productive agricultural areas in the world and the largest of any US state. The Yosemite Valley, 56km (350 miles) north of LA, is famous for its breathtaking landscapes and incredible rock domes. There is also Sequoia National Park, home to the largest living organisms on Earth, the massive giant sequoia trees. Mount Whitney, the highest point in the contiguous United States, is in California, as is the hottest place in the western hemisphere, Death Valley.

But despite all the physical wonders of the state, it is Los Angeles and mythical Hollywood which captivates the world's attention.

Fact File
Longitude: 114° 8′ W to 124° 24′ W
Latitude: 32° 30′ N to 42° N

History

Thousands of years ago the area now known as Los Angeles was a paradise of pristine beaches, mountains and desert. Back then the coastal region was inhabited by the Chumash and Tongva tribes. It wasn't until 1542 that Joao Cabrilho, a Portuguese explorer, speaking for the Spanish, declared the area 'City of God'. Cabrilho soon left and it wasn't until a Franciscan missionary named Juan Crespi came riding into town on 2 August 1769 that the place really began its life as a city. A few years later another Franciscan, Junipero Serra, built the San Gabriel Mission in what is now the San Gabriel Valley. Were he alive, Junipero might be dismayed to know that the site of his mission is now home of the porn industry.

In September of 1781, 44 settlers of Native American, Filipino, African American and Spanish blood founded 'El Pueblo de Nuestra Señora la Reina de Los Angeles del Rio de Porciuncula' (The Town of Our Lady the Queen of the Angels of the River of Porciuncula). The majority of the settlers had some African ancestry and all of them were of mixed race, beginning the city's multicultural tradition. Their original pueblo remains today on historic and touristy Olvera Street (p.155), where you can presently purchase an excellent taco and an overpriced sombrero.

When Mexico took its independence from Spain in 1821 the little pueblo went along with it and the Queen of the Angels remained under Mexican rule until the end of the Mexican-American war in 1848.

The Southern Pacific Railway rolled into town, and in 1876 completed its line to Los Angeles. Californians soon discovered oil, and by 1923 the city was producing 25% of the world's black gold. Along with the oil industry, the film and aviation industries began to flourish.

With a booming economy and a war abroad, people began to pour in – both exiles from Europe, and African American labourers from the gulf states. By 1932, when Los Angeles hosted its first summer Olympics, there were more than one million people living in the city.

In 1965, LA exploded in violence as the Watts Riots tore the city apart, and Angelenos continue to struggle with a complicated and wide variety of racial tensions. In the 80s, gang violence, in concert with the introduction of crack cocaine, and corruption in the

Santa Monica Pier

Another LA sunset

View from Griffith Observatory

Community Service
Check out the Communities section on www. explorerpublishing.com, where you can post comments, join groups, network with other expats and search for updates.

Los Angeles Police Department, lay the groundwork for what would be known as the Rodney King riots.

Although Los Angeles is plagued by pollution, racial tension, earthquakes and violence, people continue to move to the city. The beaches, the weather and the promise of fame and fortune lure people from around the world. The city is rapidly gentrifying and, despite the recently cooled market, housing is breathtakingly expensive.

Today, more than 10 million people live in Los Angeles County. They live in 88 cities and in 140 'unincorporated areas.' While the city is famous for blonde starlets and the Hollywood sign, Los Angeles is home to one of the most ethnically and culturally diverse populations in the world.

Los Angeles Timeline

1542   Portugese explorer Joao Cabrilho declares what was not yet a city as The City of God.

1781   Settlers from the San Gabriel Mission concisely name the city El Pueblo de Nuestra Señora la Reina de Los Ángeles del Río de Porciúncula (The Town of Our Lady the Queen of the Angels of the River of Porciuncula).

1850   The city becomes incorporated and a law is passed which states: 'No black or mulatto person, or Indian, shall be permitted to give evidence in favor of, or against, any white person. Every person who shall have one-eighth part or more of Negro blood shall be deemed a mulatto and every person who shall have one-half of Indian blood shall be deemed Indian.'

1876   Southern Pacific Railroad finishes its line to LA.

1892   Oil is discovered.

1900   Harvey Wilcox purchases 160 acres of land to form a conservative community. He calls it Hollywood and prohibits the sale of alcohol.

1911   The first film studio in Hollywood is created, Nestor Film Studio.

1917   The Charlie Chaplin film studios are created just south of Sunset Boulevard.

1923   The Hollywood sign is erected. It reads Hollywoodland, an advertisement for a new housing development.

1941   The Colorado River Aqueduct is completed.

1943   Riots break out in Venice after a soldier is stabbed by a Pachuco, a young Mexican man wearing a 'zoot suit'. Racial violence continues between soldiers, police and Mexicans, who are singled out and randomly attacked and arrested. Eleanor Roosevelt gets involved and speaks out on behalf of the Mexicans. She's accused of being a communist.

1947   The first Los Angeles television station, KTLA, is launched.

1958   The Hollywood Walk of Fame is created; Joanne Woodward is honoured with the first star in 1960.

1965   The Watts Riots break out. Five days later 34 people are dead and $200 million worth of property has been destroyed.

1968   Robert Kennedy is shot dead in the kitchen of the Ambassador Hotel.

1971   The San Fernando Earthquake rocks the city killing 58 people and causing $500 million worth of damage.

1987   The Whittier Earthquake kills eight people.

1992   When the verdict in the Rodney King case is read, riots explode across the city.

1994   The Northridge Earthquake kills 57 people and becomes the costliest earthquake in US history.

2003   Arnold Schwarzenegger assumes office as Governor of California.

2007   Fires rage across Los Angeles county. Mudslides follow.

USA Overview

In both size and population, the US is the third largest country in the world. Despite recent disasters, including the 9/11 attacks, Hurricane Katrina and the bungled adventure in Iraq, the United States' economy is still relatively strong. However, the massive credit woes of the country have started a major economic landslide.

With a gross domestic product of $13.21 trillion, the country has the world's largest economy. Given the nation's level of wealth, newcomers may be disappointed to discover that American streets are rarely paved with gold. The widening gulf between rich and poor has left the country distinctly separated. Those with money have access to the world's best healthcare, infrastructure and education. Those without are increasingly left uninsured and poorly schooled by a crumbling public education system. According to the United Nations, 17% of the US population lived below the poverty line between 1999 and 2002.

The United States is host to some 15 million illegal immigrants (these numbers vary enormously depending upon sources), most of whom are from Mexico and Central American countries. These illegal immigrants contribute enormously to the US economy, providing cheap labour and, subsequently, inexpensive produce and high profit margins. The question of what to do about illegal immigration is being asked more and more often, with a variety of answers. Ultra-conservatives want the borders closed and illegals sent home, while the president of Mexico is arguing for an open border between Mexico and the United States.

Los Angeles Overview

While Los Angeles is most famous for Hollywood and its film industry, the city's booming economy reveals a far more complex and varied city. The television, film and music industries play a major role in the city's economy, but aerospace, technology, petroleum, fashion, finance, law, medicine, transportation and tourism are also major economic contributors. The city is the largest centre of manufacturing in the United States and, combined with Long Beach, is one of the world's busiest ports.

After manufacturing, steel fabrication and the production of fashion apparel are the city's largest industries. Newcomers are often surprised to discover that more cars are built in Los Angeles than in any city in the country, other than Detroit.

The large population of immigrants provides the bulk of the city's labour pool, with most working in agricultural or service-oriented jobs. There are an estimated one million illegal immigrants living in Los Angeles County alone.

New Developments

In recent years the city has focused on bringing new life to the once derelict Downtown area of the city, as well as in Hollywood. Frank Gehry's Walt Disney Concert Hall (p.184) was completed in 2001 and is now home to the LA Philharmonic. An enormous Catholic cathedral (p.184) was built in 2002 and a new film studio, Center Studios (www.lacenterstudios.com), has undergone yet another expansion. Efforts to turn decrepit old Downtown buildings into Manhattan-style lofts have improved the area, though some streets remain dead and dangerous at night.

In Hollywood, the city has invested millions to return the area around Hollywood Boulevard to its glamorous origins. The new Kodak Theatre (p.183), home to the Academy Awards, is the centrepiece of an enormous new shopping centre – the Hollywood and Highland (p.308).

Gross Domestic Product

- Wholesale trade 7%
- Agriculture, forestry, and fishing 1%
- Construction 5%
- Transportation and public utilities 8%
- Finance, insurance and real estate 20%
- Services 22%
- Government 13%
- Retail trade 9%
- Mining 1%
- Manufacturing 14%

Tourism

In 2006 25.4 million people visited Los Angeles, spending $13.5 billion. Throughout the Los Angeles Metropolitan Area, more than half a million people were employed in the tourist industry making it the second largest in the city after international trade.

Drawn to Los Angeles by beaches, business, Hollywood, or a combination of the three, tourists have made the city a major year-round destination. Los Angeles hotels have the fourth-highest occupancy rate in the nation. The average visitor to the city is white and college educated with a median income of $70,000. The average room rate in Los Angeles is $120 with a 75% occupancy rate.

Grauman's Chinese Theatre

The Governor

Following a successful career as a bodybuilder and then an actor, Arnold Schwarzenegger moved into politics as a Republican, and surprised many by becoming governor of California in October 2003, despite never holding public office before. He was then re-elected for another term starting in 2007. His governorship has been a moderate one and Schwarzenegger surprised Republicans when he chose a Democrat as his Chief of Staff.

International Relations

Nearly every major nation maintains consular offices in Los Angeles. More than140 different countries are represented in the LA area, by people speaking more than 200 different languages. The city's mayor was born in Mexico, and his citizens make up a population more likely to speak a language other than English. The city has an inextricable link to Mexico and Central American countries. Every year, thousands of immigrants pour into Southern California looking for work on farms, in hotels and in private homes and restaurants.

Government & Politics

There are three main branches of the US government; the legislative, judicial and executive. The legislative branch includes Congress (split into the Senate and the House of Representatives) and government agencies, and is responsible for drafting and creating legislation that, if passed by the president, becomes law.

The judicial branch, including the Supreme Court, holds the power of judicial review. It interprets the law and decides how it should be applied.

The president, vice president and independent agencies make up the executive branch, and concentrate on enforcing laws passed by Congress. The powers of the president include: declaring war and overseeing treaties (with the approval of Congress), suggesting bills and then, once approved, signing them in as laws, and appointing judges and heads of government departments.

The City of Los Angeles is governed by a mayoral council system, presided over by the present mayor, Antonio Villaraigosa. The City Council consists of 15 members, each representing one district. These members are elected by voters every four years. Residents also elect the city attorney, who is responsible for prosecuting crimes within the city limits.

The County of Los Angeles is governed by the Los Angeles County Board of Supervisors – a group of five supervisors who are elected in regular county elections.

In general, LA tends toward the left but there are strong and wealthy bastions of right Republicanism;

Population

According to the latest available data from the US Census Bureau, Los Angeles City had an estimated population of 3,819,951 in 2003, and that number is rapidly increasing. The 2006 population estimate for LA County was 9,948,081, and 36,457,549 for the state of California. Visit http://quickfacts.census.gov to explore the census figures. There is a large Latino population in LA, and it is just as likely to hear Spanish being spoken as any other language. The Asian community is growing quickly and tensions between the African-American and Korean communities has run high in recent years, most famously during the Rodney King riots. The general problem is that Korean families own a large percentage of the small businesses in traditionally African-American neighbourhoods. West Los Angeles (from West Hollywood to Santa Monica and north) remains nearly entirely white. The city has a long history of racial tension, but, for all that, Los Angeles is one of the most culturally and racially rich cities on the planet.

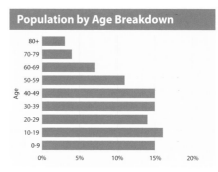

Population by Age Breakdown

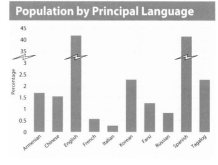

Population by Principal Language

Downtown lights

National Flag

The flag of the United States of America is composed of 13 horizontal red and white stripes, one for each of the original British colonies. In the upper left corner there's a blue rectangle with 50 five-pointed stars, one for each of the states. The flag is often referred to by its nickname, Old Glory.

Visitors to the United States are often struck by the prominence of the flag in daily life. The flag is displayed not only on public buildings and landmarks, but in front of many private residences. This is particularly true on Memorial Day (the last Monday in October) and Independence Day (4 July) when Old Glory seems to flutter everywhere – from sea to shining sea.

Time Difference	
Dallas	+2
Dubai	+11
Frankfurt	+8
Honolulu	-3
London	+7
Mumbai	+12.5
Moscow	+10
New York	+3
Shanghai	+15
Tokyo	+16

The American flag flies without fail from many public buildings including, of course, the White House. There are six American flags (one for each successful Apollo mission) flying weightlessly on the moon. California's flag is known as the Bear Flag, and shows the now extinct California grizzly along with a single red star and the words 'California Republic'.

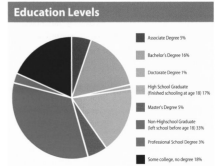

Education Levels

- Associate Degree 5%
- Bachelor's Degree 16%
- Doctorate Degree 1%
- High School Graduate (finished schooling at age 18) 17%
- Master's Degree 5%
- Non-Highschool Graduate (left school before age 18) 33%
- Professional School Degree 3%
- Some college, no degree 18%

Local Time

Los Angeles is on Pacific Standard Time (PST), which is eight hours behind UTC (formerly known as GMT). Daylight saving begins on the second Sunday in March and ends on the first Sunday in November, putting the clocks forward by one hour. During daylight saving, LA is seven hours behind UTC.

As a guide, when it is midday in LA, it is 15:00 in New York, 20:00 in London, 01:30 the next morning in Delhi, and 05:00 in Tokyo.

Social & Business Hours

While it's true that Los Angeles is certainly less formal than New York, Boston or Chicago, a great deal of work is done over the course of a year – in fact, quite a bit more than in any of those eastern cities. The workday begins at 10:00 in certain sectors and dawn in others. Given the vast scope of industry in the city, it's impossible to provide an absolute rule. Hollywood generally gets up later than investment bankers. If you're moving to the city to work in the mail room at a talent agency then you'll be up early and going home late. People come to Los Angeles hungry, and the competition for any job, whether it is actor or fruit picker, is as fierce as anywhere in the world. Don't let all those surfers bobbing around in the ocean at 08:00 on a Monday morning fool you, people work very hard in Los Angeles and many of them would happily sell a parent for a chance to be employed.

Incredibly, bars, clubs and restaurants close their doors at 02:00, which means that things start early in the city. Lunch is an important social meal, particularly for wealthy 'industry' people. Happy hours are popular, and on the weekends you'll find the beach bars packed with people as soon as the sun drops into the Pacific.

Public Holidays

If you're moving to Los Angeles from a wealthy European country, prepare yourself: Americans live to work. If you're used to six weeks of vacation per year, you might consider another country. The United States is a nation of many cultures, religions and languages, but 'work' is the nation's true religion and unifying cult; your fellow immigrants are there because they too believe that in the United States, 'anything is possible if you work hard

Public Holidays	
New Year's Day	1 Jan
MLK Birthday	3rd Mon in Jan
President's Day	3rd Mon in Feb
Memorial Day	Last Mon in May
Independence Day	4 Jul
Labor Day	1st Mon in Sep
Columbus Day	2nd Mon in Oct
Veterans Day	11 Nov
Thanksgiving	Last Thurs in Nov
Christmas Day	25 Dec

enough'. And nowhere else in the United States is that more true than in Los Angeles. If you're lucky, you'll have two weeks off per year. Usually less. Enjoy!

Climate

The winters are mild; the summers warm (brutally hot, inland). In autumn, the city is at its best when the Santa Ana winds blow out the smog and temperatures begin to drop into the sixties fahrenheit. There is a dramatic difference between the weather at the beach and the weather inland. On any given July day there can be a difference of nearly 7°C (20°F) between Santa Monica and Hollywood. On those terribly hot days it's far more pleasant to live at the sea. On the other hand, in June, the June Gloom (or May Grey) keeps the beaches foggy and cool while a few miles inland the sun shines and the sky is clear.

The median temperature in January is 14°C (57°F) and 23°C (73°F) in August. Unfortunately, for a city with an ongoing water crisis (see Polanski's *Chinatown*) there's very little rain; only 15 inches per year. February is the wettest month.

The city is regularly used by environmentalists as an example of what's wrong with the world.

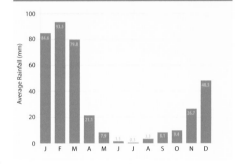

Los Angeles is located in a dry and arid desert basin. But Angelenos insist on watering their lawns with water from as far away as Colorado. The basin geography retains the smog generated by the millions of cars and factories, and pollution is a terrible problem. The American Lung Association (www.lungusa.org) ranks the city as the most polluted in the United States.

Flora & Fauna

Coastal sage covers the low-lying hills and mountains that surround Los Angeles. The California poppy and coastal live oak are also both indigenous and abundant throughout the city, as are the iconic date palms that line neighbourhood pavements. Those tall palms that have become so much a part of the image of the

LA's prized palms

city are now reaching the ends of their lives. While there are tens of thousands of the trees spread out across the city, it may be that in a generation there will be few left. Thanks to the Las Vegas casinos paying anything for them, the cost of date palms have become increasingly expensive and the city plans to plant trees with wider canopies, like jacarandas, ficus and oaks, to fight pollution.

While LA may appear at first to be nothing but beach, pavement and asphalt, there is a wide variety of wild animals living on the edges of the cities. Coyotes often slip down out of the canyons and help themselves to house hamsters, cats and puppies. Deer still show up in backyards. Snakes, scorpions and the odd mountain lion live among the rocks and dry sage of the Santa Monica Mountains and the San Fernando Valley. Despite the polluted ocean, it is not uncommon to see dolphins and even whales cruising along the coastline.

Environmental Issues

Los Angeles leads the nation in air pollution and has been condemned by the American Lung Association for its disregard for air quality. Not surprisingly, there are more vehicles in Los Angeles than in any other state in the country. Due in part to the California Clean Air Act, pollution levels have dropped over the last few years, but only minimally. There remains one car for every two people living in the city and more than 32,000km (20,000 miles) of roadways. The car industry has enormous power and little is being done to improve what appears to be an untenable situation.

Nonetheless, there are more than 60,000 acres of state and national parkland in Los Angeles County. The Santa Monica Mountains National Recreation Area (p.179) covers 17,615 acres, or about 11% of the Santa Monica Mountains.

Palos Verdes

Huntington Gardens

Culture

Although LA's culture is more complex than many imagine, many of the stereotypes do hold true. Actors here do become movie stars, musicians do become rock stars and blonde women with surgically enhanced breasts do stroll Rodeo Drive. Every waiter in West Los Angeles wants to be an actor, or a model, or a screenwriter, or a director. Or a model's assistant. Bikini-clad women rollerblade along the beach, and inflated men lift weights in the sunshine in Venice.

Los Angeles is a city of people from everywhere else. It's a city that has, since its inception, drawn people escaping one life and looking for another. That sensibility continues today. Los Angeles, like New York, offers limitless possibilities for the determined, the talented and, above all, the lucky. The story of actress Lana Turner being discovered at a Schwab's drugstore on Sunset Boulevard may be a legend (she was actually discovered at the Top Hat Café across the street from Hollywood High), but the city is full of people who imagine that in one way or another, they too will be discovered.

From afar, Los Angeles appears to be a promised land and people from hundreds of different cultures, countries and backgrounds arrive in droves in hope of a better life. Most of them will have little or no contact with Hollywood, but nearly all of them are seeking 'the American Dream'. Aside from New York, no other city in the nation embodies that dream the way Los Angeles does.

Los Angeles is a progressive, liberal city with a minority of wealthy, powerful and conservative pockets.

The steady flow of mostly poor immigrants to the Los Angeles area combined with an undermanned police force, plagued by corruption, has driven tensions high. From the 'Zoot Suit' riots to the Rodney King riots, the city has a long history of violent racial conflicts exacerbated by interracial tensions, deep poverty, and what has been, at times, institutional racism.

Language

Other options **Language Schools** p.226

While the United States doesn't have an official language, 82% of the population speaks American English and 12% of the population speaks Spanish. In Los Angeles, 41% of the population speaks Spanish and 42% speaks English.

Religion

The largest religious communities are, in descending order, Catholic, Jewish, Baptist, Mormon and Muslim.

Places Of Worship

Name	Area	Phone	Web
7th Day Adventist Church	Compton	323 774 0181	www.tamarindavenue.com
Angelus Temple	Echo Park	213 816 1119	www.angelustemple.org
Bel-Air Presbyterian Church	Bel-Air	818 788 4200	www.belairpres.org
Beth Shir Sholom	Santa Monica	310 453 3361	www.bethshirsholom.com
Cathedral of Our Lady of the Angels	Downtown	213 680 5200	www.olacathedral.org
First Congregational Church UCC	Long Beach	562 436 2256	www.firstchurchlb.org
Islamic Center of Reseda	Reseda	818 996 9116	na
Islamic Center of Southern California	Westlake	213 382 9200	www.islamctr.org
Khandakapala Buddhist Center	Elysian Park	323 223 0610	www.meditateinla.org
Los Angeles California Temple	Westwood	310 474 5569	www.ldschurchtemples.com/losangeles
University Synagogue	Brentwood	310 472 1255	www.unisyn.org
Westwood Hills Christian Church	Westwood	310 208 8576	www.westwoodhillschristianchurch.org

Angelus Temple

Catholicism is the predominant religious group in Los Angeles with the largest archdiocese in the country based Downtown in the new Cathedral of Our Lady of the Angels (p.184), which serves the vast Latino community. The second largest Mormon temple in the country was built in 1956 on Westwood Boulevard and serves the expanding Mormon community. The Jewish community in Los Angeles is the second largest in the United States. The Church of Scientology maintains its famous Celebrity Center in Hollywood and a growing collection of historically important buildings. California has been, for decades, a magnet for cults, religions, semi-religions, spin-offs and new age spiritualists, and welcomes any follower of any faith.

Tacoway

Some of the best, most authentic and least expensive Mexican food is served from the taco trucks parked around the city. If you see a long line of people waiting on some corner, pull over and join them. You won't be sorry.

National Dress

Styles vary widely depending upon the neighbourhood you're in, but generally speaking, Los Angeles' style is one of studied messiness and careful carelessness. LA style has been influenced dramatically by surfing, skateboarding and rock cultures as well as gang culture. Perhaps the most globally dominant and universally present LA designer is Dov Charney, whose environmentally friendly, sweatshop-free and hyper-hip American Apparel boutiques have spread across the world.

Food & Drink

Other options **Eating Out** p.314

LA's venues serve nearly every international cuisine imaginable, and the standard is high. From grand, architecturally stunning restaurants to roaming taco trucks, the choice is breathtaking. If you're determined and passionate, you will find authentic, inspired and exciting food here. Because of the city's proximity to Mexico and its huge Latino population, there are excellent Mexican, Honduran and Salvadoran restaurants throughout the city. The Asian population in Los Angeles has contributed significantly to the culinary traditions of the city and to the nation as a whole. There's not a city in the country that doesn't have a sushi bar, and America's willingness to eat raw fish and rice began, as so many national and international trends do, in California.

Because of California's culturally diverse and generally progressive population there is an openness here to experimentation and the fusing of flavours and influences that simply doesn't exist in other cities. What is now known as California cuisine began with Alice Waters' Chez Panisse in Berkeley (www.chezpanisse.com). Waters emphasised locally grown and seasonal produce, and cooked accordingly. As the 'slow food' movement has gained international steam and the popularity of organic, boutique produce becomes more mainstream, Alice Waters has become even more famous.

As influential in the developing of California cuisine as Waters is Wolfgang Puck, who became almost as famous as the celebrities he cooked for at his landmark restaurant Spago. It was Puck who pioneered what is now known as fusion cuisine, the 'fusing' of international influences in a unified dish. His Santa Monica restaurant, Chinois, blends Chinese and French cooking (www.wolfgangpuck.com).

In Los Angeles County alone there are more than 100,000 acres of farmland, and independent organic farms are being developed throughout the state. The easy access to inexpensive, high quality produce, combined with an international and adventurous population, makes the food scene in Los Angeles vibrant, exciting and ever-changing.

Emergency Number

24 Hour Pharmacies	
CVS	888 607 4287
Longs Drugs	www.longs.com
Sav-On	877 728 6655
Walgreens	800 925 4733
Emergency Services	
Ambulance	911
Fire	911
Police	911
Hospitals	
Cedars Sinai	310 423 3277
Huntington Hospital	626 397 5000
Saint Johns	310 829 5511
UCLA	310 825 9111
USC University Hospital	888 700 5700

In Emergency

Accidents and emergencies can never be predicted, but Los Angeles is well-equipped to deal with events that come up. Like most places in the US, Los Angeles uses the 911 system. Should you find yourself in any kind of emergency, you can call 911 from any phone to connect with fire, police or ambulance departments. This is true for landlines as well as domestic cell phones. There are also many hospitals, fire stations and police departments scattered throughout the city, so getting to know which is closest, as well as the fastest, route to get there, is always a good idea. If you are travelling from abroad, it is also a good idea to know the phone number of your local consulate, which can be of assistance should you find yourself facing legal obstacles. Make sure to have a list of phone numbers for credit card companies set aside in case you lose your wallet.

Gay & Lesbian

Although San Francisco is more famous for being home to a large population of gay and lesbian residents, Los Angeles can boast an equally robust scene. One entire municipality – West Hollywood – is even known as 'boy's town', where on any given night, gay-owned, frequented and friendly cafes, nightclubs and performances abound. Perhaps because of the prominence of the entertainment industry, in which gay men and lesbians have both found acceptance and played prominent roles, attitudes toward homosexuality tend to be very liberal, and gay culture is accepted as one of the many that make up the tapestry of life in LA.

Women

Generally speaking, LA is a safe city. It has its share of crime, as does any big metropolis the world over. Women travelling alone in Los Angeles would be wise to take the same precautions as anywhere else. As in most American cities, catcalling or other forms of street-side harassment are rare, but it is still a good idea to stride confidently and always act like you know where you're going, even when you don't. Most areas can empty out at night, and those that don't can be some of the rougher neighbourhoods, so try to

Embassies & Consulates

Argentina	323 954 9155
Australia	310 229 4800
Austria	310 444 9310
Bangladesh	323 932 0100
Belize	323 469 7343
Brazil	323 651 2664
Britain	310 481 0031
Canada	213 346 2700
China	213 807 8088
Colombia	323 653 9863
Costa Rica	213 380 7915
Croatia	310 477 1009
Czech Republic	310 473 0889
Denmark	818 766 0003
Ecuador	323 658 6020
Finland	310 203 9903
France	310 235 3200
Germany	323 930 2703
Greece	310 826 5555
Guatemala	213 365 9251
Israel	323 852 5500
Italy	310 820 0622
Japan	213 617 6700
Korea	213 385 9300
Mexico	213 351 6800
Netherlands	310 268 1598
New Zealand	310 207 1605
Pakistan	310 441 5114
Paraguay	310 417 9500
Peru	213 252 5910
Philippines	213 639 0980
Poland	310 442 8500
Romania	310 444 0043
Saudi Arabia	310 479 6000
South Africa	323 651 0902
Spain	323 938 0158
Sri Lanka	213 387 0210
Sweden	310 445 4008
Switzerland	310 575 1145
Thailand	323 962 9574
Turkey	323 937 0118

have a companion with you if you have to walk after dark. That said, LA rightly has a reputation for ostentatious self-display, so women can freely wear expensive jewellery or whatever style of clothing they like, from conservative to extremely revealing, in most areas without feeling unsafe or self-conscious.

Children

Los Angeles is a wonderful place to be a child. Granted, parents or guardians have to drive their little ones all over, but there are so many activities here to amuse, from beaches (p.189) and parks (p.190) to museums (p.170) and world-famous theme parks (p.186), such as Disneyland and Magic Mountain. Most restaurants are happy to provide high chairs or booster seats, while you'll generally find that the more upscale a hotel is, the more accommodating it will try to be, regarding children, pets or anything else. One thing to keep in mind, though, is that California law requires that all children who weigh less than 36kg (80lbs) must be seated in the back seat of a car, and those under 6 years of age and 27kg (60lbs) must be strapped into an appropriate car seat or booster. Luckily, domestic car rental agencies are equipped to provide car seats should you need them.

People With Disabilities

The Americans with Disabilities Act, signed into law in 1990, changed the way those with physical or mental limitations experience life all over the US. As a result, all public transportation and public services must be wheelchair accessible. In Los Angeles, that means that buses and municipal buildings are equipped with ramps and, where appropriate, wide doorways and accessible facilities. Restaurants, hotels, movie theatres – essentially any public space – must also conform to these rules. Generally speaking, LA is an easy place to live and get around for those with disabilities. There are some older buildings that won't be able to accommodate those with extra needs, so it's always a good idea to call ahead and inquire about any concerns.

Casually Cool ◀

*Don't let the ultra-
hipness of LA intimidate
you. Fashionistas
only make up a small
percentage of the
population and in
everyday life people
are rarely judged on
their style choice. Also,
don't worry about
being under-dressed:
jeans and a T-shirt are
perfectly acceptable at
all but the poshest
of venues.*

What To Wear

The warm, sunny conditions are one reason that people flock to the city at all times of the year. Even though you may encounter a balmy 27°C (80°F) day in the middle of January, there are seasons here, and it sometimes rains in the winter. The rule of thumb in Los Angeles is to wear layers, as it gets cold at night, even during the summer months, so take a sweater or light jacket with you when you go out. You'll be prepared for the day and for any trips to malls or movie theatres, which tend to blast the air-conditioning to compensate for the heat outside.

Dos & Don'ts

Some of the laws to which Angelenos have grown accustomed may surprise international visitors. Seat belt and drink driving laws are rigidly enforced, for example. The national legal BAC limit for alcohol consumption is 0.08 so don't get behind the wheel after imbibing. Rather than risk arrest or an accident, you can call one of the multiple car and taxi services to pick you up, or AAA of Southern California (800 400 4222) for a tow home. And remember that open containers of any alcoholic beverage are prohibited within any vehicle, even if held by a backseat passenger. Smoking is banned in all restaurants, bars and clubs, so head outside to huddle with the other smokers if you must light up. And although it may seem silly, the LAPD periodically binge on enforcing jaywalking laws, which is no joke when you get stuck with a hefty fine.

Photography

The paparazzi have become so commonplace in LA that nobody seems to notice when cameras are pointed in their direction. It's always polite to ask people if they mind being a part of your composition, but you'll rarely run into trouble if you forget to do so. As in other US cities, photography is prohibited in some parts of the airport, in government buildings and near any military compounds. Surprisingly, most malls discourage photography, even with small point and shoots. Outdoors, even tripods rarely draw attention. Indoors, however, security guards will sometimes ask you to move along if they see you setting up a steady shot.

Crime & Safety

Other options **In Emergency** p.13

Like all big cities, Los Angeles has its share of crime. Although rates have fallen over the last decade, LA still struggles with gang-related violent crimes. This should not be ignored, but the truth is that gang activity is often concentrated in specific neighbourhoods and does not affect outsiders. Still, don't take your safety for granted. Always act like you know where you are and where you're going. Be aware of your surroundings. Don't walk down empty streets by yourself at night. Make sure you lock your car every time you leave it.

Traffic Accidents & Violations

Of more immediate concern than violent crime to those who are not gang members is the high number of car crashes in Los Angeles. With so many people driving, accidents are bound to happen. Although an accident can happen at any time, a good rule of rule of thumb is to stay out of your car if at all possible in the early morning hours, when drunk drivers tend to hit the streets after a night out. More importantly, don't cause an accident. It is easy to find out the rules of the road at www.dmv.com (also see p.136), so learn and live by them. If you do get pulled over, for anything from speeding or ignoring a stop sign to drunk driving or being involved in a hit-and-run, expect to have 'points' assigned to your licence. Your licence can be suspended with as little as

Mural on N Gower Street

four points acquired in a 12 month period, so be careful. In addition to seeing your insurance rates go up, you can be arrested if you are found to be at fault in an injury or fatal crash, or if you leave the scene of an accident. Best, then, not to break the law in the first place.

Getting Arrested

Movies and television shows have made the 'Miranda warning', a list of the rights enjoyed by all people arrested in the United States, famous. It grew out of a Supreme Court case that questioned a criminal suspect's ability to maintain the right against self-incrimination. The list includes the right to remain silent so as not to say anything that can be used against you in a courtroom, the right to an attorney, whether privately hired or appointed by the court, and in California, the right to contact your consulate before being questioned. In all but the most severe situations, or in cases where there is a fear that a person will flee the state or country, a judge will set bail. Once paid, you will be free to leave, but will have to return to stand trial at the time assigned.

Death Penalty
For all of its progressiveness, California still enforces the death penalty. There are currently over 600 people on death row at the San Quentin prison. Since 1976, the state has executed 13 people. There is a strong opposition against the death penalty and several groups have formed to bury the practice.

Prison Time

California has long struggled with the problem of its overcrowded prisons which, in addition to violent or intransigent criminals, are stuffed with many non-violent drug offenders. As in the rest of the US, prisons in California have the reputation of being dangerous, gang-infested places. And although news comes out periodically about abysmal medical treatment or harsh conditions, prisoners do have constitutional rights to fair and human treatment and those who will fight to ensure them. On the other hand, once convicted of a crime, certain rights, like the vote, are revoked, until the completion of parole or forever.

Police

Live in Los Angeles for long enough and you will get to know the sound and sight of helicopters chasing suspects or hovering over crime scenes. LA does not have the ideal number of street cops for the size of its population, so the police have taken to the skies to get a better view. This does not mean that there are no patrol cars driving the streets. Each municipality has its own force, and then there is the California Highway Patrol, made famous in the 1970s television series *CHiPs*, and the Los Angeles Sheriff's Department, the largest in the world. You can tell the difference between them by noting that the police wear dark blue, while CHP officers and sheriff's deputies have khaki-coloured uniforms. While CHP officers stay on the road, police officers and sheriff's deputies can be called upon in an emergency, to help settle a minor dispute, or give directions. Members of all three departments can and do give out speeding tickets.

City Information

Although you won't find too many tourism offices or kiosks (Santa Monica has one on Main Street), many of the municipalities that make up LA County have excellent web resources for visitors, residents and business owners. These can provide you with information about government, local happenings, business opportunities and regulations and a host of other services, from hotel recommendations to directions.

Information Websites
www.lacity.org
www.visitlosangeles.info
www.beverlyhills.org
www.santamonica.com
www.visitwesthollywood.com
www.pasadenacal.com
www.valleyofthestars.org

Places To Stay

Los Angeles has no shortage of accommodation; from opulent to grungy, the options are seemingly endless. Hotels are spread far and wide from the ocean to the desert; there are missions, motels, hotels, residences and hostels in every neighbourhood you'd want to visit (and quite a few in places you wouldn't).

Hotels

Perhaps the most expensive accommodation is found on Ocean Avenue in Santa Monica, Sunset and Wilshire Boulevards in Beverly Hills and Sunset Boulevard in West Hollywood where rooms at the most prestigious hotels – Shutters, The Viceroy, The Beverly Hills Hotel, The Mondrian to name a few – begin at their cheapest at around $400 per night. On the other hand there is plenty of cheap, safe and clean accommodation throughout the city and often not far from the expensive hotels. The Seashore Motel on Main Street in Santa Monica is perfectly located – a block from the beach, great bars and restaurants on all sides – and profoundly less expensive than anything in the neighbourhood. Unless of course you're looking to rent by the hour, in which case head down Lincoln Boulevard a few miles. In Hollywood, the USA Hostels Hollywood is noisy, wild, young, clean and perfect for those in search of a party and a safe place to sleep. The Farmer's Daughter hotel on Fairfax is centrally located, across the street from CBS and the Farmer's Market, newly refurbished and ironically designed in country chic denims, wood panelling and barnyard bird wallpaper.

For details of LA's landmark hotels, see the reviews starting on the next page.

Main Hotels

Name	Phone	Web	Map Ref	
Beverly Hills Hotel	310 276 2251	www.beverlyhillshotel.com	4 E1	1
The Fairmont Miramar	310 576 7777	www.fairmont.com/santamonica	3 B4	13
The Farmers Daughter	323 937 3930	www.farmersdaughterhotel.com	7 B1	14
Four Seasons Los Angeles at Beverly Hills	310 273 2222	www.fourseasons.com/losangeles	4 F2	5
Hotel Bel-Air	310 472 1211	www.hotelbelair.com	2 C1	
Mondrian	323 650 8999	www.mondrianhotel.com	5 B2	15
The Park Hyatt	310 277 1234	www.hyatt.com	4 E4	16
The Peninsula	310 551 2888	www.peninsula.com	4 E3	17
Raffles L'Ermitage	310 278 3344	www.raffles-lermitagehotel.com	4 F2	18
Ritz Carlton Huntington	626 568 3900	www.ritzcarlton.com	2 E1	
Ritz Carlton Marina del Rey	310 823 1700	www.ritzcarlton.com	3 F3	19
Seashore Hotel on Main	310 392 2787	www.seashoremotel.com	3 D4	20
Shutters On The Beach	310 458 0030	www.shuttersonthebeach.com	3 C4	21
The Standard	213 892 8080	www.standardhotel.com	5 C2	22
The Viceroy	310 260 7500	www.viceroysantamonica.com	3 C4	23

Hotel Apartments

Fully furnished hotel apartments are available throughout the city and can be rented on a daily, weekly and monthly basis. As with all other accommodation in Los Angeles the range is tremendous, from single burner basement dens to massive penthouse lofts, whatever you want, or at least whatever you can afford, is available. Most hotels provide similar services, so if you have a favourite check with them – the city's hotels are used to people checking in for extended stays.

Hotel Apartments

Name	Area	Phone
Cresecent Legacy	Westwood	310 858 5517
Hollywood Orchid Suites	Hollywood	323 874 9678
The Oakwood Apartments	Various Locations	310 478 1021
YourStay Wilshire	Park La Brea	310 478 1021

Landmark Hotels

Artists' Inn & Cottage

1038 Magnolia St
Pasadena
Map 2 E1

626 799 5668 | *www.artistsinns.com*

Originally a chicken ranch built in 1895, the Artists' Inn is now a quaint B&B tucked into a neighbourhood of classic California Craftsman homes. In desperately hip Los Angeles, cosy and charming hotels are hard to come by, but this one has fireplaces, rosebushes and rocking chairs on the porch.

Beverly Hills Hotel

9641 Sunset Blvd
Beverly Hills
Map 4 E1 1 **1**

310 276 2251 | *www.beverlyhillshotel.com*

The 'Pink Palace' opened in 1912 and has since hosted kings, presidents, athletes and movie stars. Humphrey Bogart helped make the hotel's bar, the Polo Lounge, famous by spending his time drinking there. Today, the hotel maintains its reputation as a discreetly luxurious oasis.

Beverly Wilshire

9500 Wilshire Blvd
Beverly Hills
Map 4 E3 **2**

310 275 5200 | *www.fourseasons.com/beverlywilshire/*

Maintaining a place of grand prominence on Wilshire Boulevard, smack in the centre of Beverly Hills, the Beverly Wilshire offers more elegance and style than many of the passers by – here you'll find understated wood-panelled common rooms and crystal chandeliers. Should you need a ride across the street to Gucci, the hotel offers a complimentary Rolls.

Chateau Marmont

8221 Sunset Blvd
West Hollywood
Map 5 C2 **3**

323 656 1010 | *www.chateaumarmont.com*

As discreet as the Beverly Hills Hotel, the Chateau Marmont caters to a hipper, younger and wilder crowd. The Chateau sits on Sunset Boulevard and offers everything from cottages to penthouses. Jim Morrison slept here and famously jumped from a balcony into the swimming pool. Some say the hotel relies more on its reputation than the quality of its rooms and service.

The Crescent

403 N Crescent Dr
Beverly Hills
Map 4 E2 **4**

310 247 0505 | *www.crescentbh.com*

Silent-film actors in the 1920s used to stay here when The Crescent was just a simple dormitory. The hotel has become slicked up in recent years and now has a jumping bar scene. It was built in 1926 which makes it profoundly historic among the disposable buildings of Los Angeles.

300 S Doheny Dr
Beverly Hills
Map 4 F2 5

Four Seasons Los Angeles at Beverly Hills

310 273 2222 | *www.fourseasons.com/losangeles*
Though less famous than the Beverly Wilshire, this is
one of the most luxurious hotels in upscale Beverly Hills.
The expert staff and subtly decorated rooms and suites
warrant the mile-high price tag, and most rooms come
with exquisite views of Los Angeles. Don't be surprised
to see A-list celebs strutting through the halls on their
way to a shopping spree.

1415 Ocean Ave
Santa Monica
Map 3 B4 6

Georgian Hotel

310 395 9945 | *www.georgianhotel.com*
In the 1920s, the Georgian was a hangout (and
speakeasy) for Clark Gable and Carole Lombard, where
they would sit on the oceanfront terrace, drink and listen
to jazz. The hotel was built in 1933, and has preserved
its art deco charm. The Georgian is perhaps the most
interesting building on Ocean Boulevard – aqua green
and facing the sweeping coastline.

7000 Hollywood Blvd
Hollywood
Map 6 A1 7

Hollywood Roosevelt

323 466 7000 | *www.hollywoodroosevelt.com*
In 1929, the Roosevelt hosted the very first Academy
Awards. In the 50s, Marilyn Monroe was a frequent guest
and back then it was the hippest spot in the city. While
the hotel has been beautifully renovated, The Roosevelt
seems determined to follow the lead of so many
Hollywood hotels that make the mistake of creating an
exclusive nightclub rather than a hotel serving its guests.

701 Stone Canyon Rd
Bel-Air
Map 2 C1

Hotel Bel-Air

310 472 1211 | *www.hotelbelair.com*
The gorgeous Bel-Air has been a legendary bastion
for the rich and famous since it opened in 1940. The
man behind the hotel and the Bel-Air estates, oil baron
Alphonso E Bell, originally constructed the building
to serve as his offices. Today the hotel's buildings and
bungalows are quiet and luxurious, spread over 12 acres
of some of the city's most expensive real estate.

1910 Ocean Way
Santa Monica
Map 3 C4 8

Hotel Casa Del Mar

310 581 5503 | *www.hotelcasadelmar.com*
Casa Del Mar began as a chic beach club in 1926,
providing a place to drink and lie in the sun when Santa
Monica was little more than a village by the beach. Since
then, the building has served as a military hotel and then
as rehab centre, before a $60 million renovation created
the present Spanish-style luxury hotel with wonderful
views of the ocean.

939 S Figueroa St
Downtown
Map 10 C2 **9**

Hotel Figueroa

213 627 0305 | www.figueroahotel.com
With a great location across the street from the Staples Center and near the Convention Center, the beautifully restored Figueroa often hosts awards events. The Spanish tiles, moody lighting and billowing curtains add to the Arabian feel, and the deep colours of the rooms are perfect for romantic evenings.

506 S Grand Av
Downtown
Map 10 D2 **10**

Millennium Biltmore

213 624 1011 | www.millenniumhotels.com
Perhaps the most beautiful building in the city, the beaux-arts Biltmore has hosted Academy Awards ceremonies and was home to the 1960 Democratic National Convention. John F Kennedy spent time wandering the lobby before he was president of the United States. The lobby alone is worth a trip. If you stay Downtown, stay here.

1126 Queens Hwy
Long Beach
Map 2 D4

Queen Mary

562 435 3511 | www.queenmary.com
The liner Queen Mary made its maiden voyage in 1936. It served as a personnel carrier during the second world war, transporting more than 700,000 troops. After crossing the Atlantic 1,001 times, it was retired to Long Beach in 1967 and has sat there ever since. The ship serves as a hotel composed of 365 staterooms, a spa, restaurants and all the other amenities you'd expect to find.

8358 Sunset Blvd
West Hollywood
Map 5 C2 **11**

Sunset Tower

323 654 7100 | www.sunsettowerhotel.com
Built in 1929, the hotel has gone through various incarnations and was, until recently, known as The Argyle. Now, after a $60 million renovation, this spectacular art deco building, once home to Marilyn Monroe, Howard Hughes and Bugsy Siegel, is elegant and hip, with some of the best views in the city.

930 Hilgard Av
Westwood
Map 4 B2 **12**

W Los Angeles

310 208 8765 | www.starwoodhotels.com
Well-off hipsters flock to W for its futuristic design and attentive staff. The service is sometimes described as pretentious, but for those who seek to impress, it's hard to beat this popular brand. Don't let its obsession with the namesake letter distract you, W's minimalist decor and signature beds are worth the kitschiness.

When you're lost what will you find in your pocket?

Item 71. The half-eaten chewing gum

When you reach into your pocket make sure you have one of these miniature marvels to hand… far more use than a half-eaten stick of chewing gum when you're lost.

Explorer Mini Maps
Putting the city in your pocket

Motels & Rest Houses

In a transient city full of cars and endless roads, motels are everywhere. The best of them are adorned with classic 50s and 60s facades. Neon signs and swimming pools in the courtyard lure immigrants of all shapes and sizes, from wannabe rock stars to day labourers. Sunset Boulevard, from West Hollywood east, is lined with classics, and the further east you go the seedier they become.

Motels & Rest Houses			
Name	Area	Phone	Web
Brentwood Motor Hotel	Brentwood	310 476 9981	www.bmhotel.com
Cal Mar Hotel Suites	Santa Monica	800 776 6007	www.calmarhotel.com
Inn at Venice Beach	Venice	800 828 0688	www.innatvenicebeach.com
Saharan Motor Hotel	Hollywood	323 874 6700	www.saharanmotel.com

Guesthouses & Bed & Breakfasts

While Los Angeles isn't the New England countryside, you'll find a fair share of B&Bs and guesthouses around. Accommodation ranges from the luxurious to the spare and, as with hotels, there's no official rating system. The Automobile Club of America reviews all forms of accommodation and its diamond system is fairly reliable when searching for clean accommodation. The BedandBreakfast website lists B&Bs all over the city (www.bedandbreakfast.com/los-angeles-california).

Guest Houses & Bed & Breakfasts				
Name	Address	Area	Phone	Web
Brentwood Motor Hotel	12200 W Sunset Blvd	Brentwood	310 476 9981	www.bmhotel.com
Channel Road Inn	219 W Channel Rd	Santa Monica	310 459 1920	www.channelroadinn.com
Elaine's Hollywood Bed & Breakfast	1616 N Sierra Bonita Ave	Hollywood	323 850 0766	www.elaineshollywoodbedandbreakfast.com
Su Casa at Venice Beach	431 Ocean Front Walk	Venice	310 386 7466	www.sucasaatvenicebeach.com
The Venice Beach House	15 30th Ave	Venice	310 832 1966	www.venicebeachhouse.com

Hostels

There are plenty of youth hostels here – from Venice to Hollywood and everywhere in between. The Banana Bungalow gets consistently rave reviews, looking more like a funky boutique hotel and offering fun events such as barbecues and film evenings.

Hostels				
Name	Area	Phone	Web	Map Ref
Banana Bungalow	West Hollywood	323 655 2002	www.bananabungalow.com	5 D4
HI-Los Angeles	Santa Monica	310 393 9913	www.hilosangeles.org	3 B4
USA Hostels Hollywood	Hollywood	323 462 3777	www.usahostels.com	6 B1

Campsites

Other options **Camping** p.216

For a massive metropolis, Los Angeles offers surprisingly good camping options. The best spots are along the coast where you'll pay very little to stay on priceless property across the street from beautiful beaches. Malibu has several campsites where you can wake up in the morning and go for a surf. All LA County camping is operated by the California State Parks (www.parks.ca.gov). Highly recommended is Leo Carrillo State Park, which offers great camping, great surfing, and even Wi-Fi access.

Getting Around

Other options **Exploring** p.146

Los Angeles can be a bewilderingly difficult place to get around. For one thing, it is immense, stretching from the Pacific in the west all the way to the San Gabriel Mountains in the east. And, unlike most cities, there is no true 'centre' around which everything else seems to revolve. On the other hand, there is so much to see and do in so many of those far-flung spots that it's worth braving the freeway system – or becoming very familiar with Google maps – to get there.

It wasn't always this way. For years, Los Angeles boasted one of the most extensive railway and streetcar systems in the country. These 'Red Cars' and 'Yellow Cars' connected urban, suburban and exurban areas, stretching from Santa Monica east to Pasadena and south to Orange County. The extensive system grew throughout the second world war, when workers poured into the area following the jobs created by the war effort. Soon thereafter, though, a consortium of three companies invested in the growth of the automobile industry. General Motors, Standard Oil and Firestone Tires started buying up streetcar lines all over the US, dismantling them and replacing them with buses. This marked the beginning of the end of light rail service in the greater Los Angeles region, which limped on until the last streetcar made a final run in 1963. Ironically, the average speed on today's freeways is about the same as the slowest running time of the Red Line connecting Santa Monica and Hollywood: 13mph. Today, the landscape is crisscrossed with freeways, which have become so integral to the lives of Angelenos that they are generally referred to with definite articles. Calling the main east-west artery I-10, as you would anywhere else, is to mark yourself immediately as a newcomer. Natives always say 'the 10'.

Air Travel

Securiosity

Thanks to new safety regulations, waiting times at US airports seem to constantly increase. In an effort to help travellers prepare for their flight, the Transportation Security Administration maintains a website of average and maximum security wait times at each US airport. See http:// waittime.tsa.dhs.gov.

The main airport serving Los Angeles is LAX, which handles both domestic and international traffic. It is one of the busiest airports in the world, through which more than 60 million passengers pass each year. It is also the second busiest point of entry for international travellers to the US, behind only JFK airport in New York. As the pace of air travel has grown, so have the calls to expand and renovate LAX, which hasn't been updated since the 1984 Los Angeles Olympics. In fact, a master plan to reconfigure the airport has been in the works for years, with politicians and local residents sparring about the details. Add to that the delays caused by security checks that have become much more rigorous since 9/11, and braving the LAX experience can be a challenge. Still, it is the only major international airport and it has the benefit of being ideally situated in the neighbourhood of Westchester, only 26 km (16 miles) from Downtown. When leaving, give plenty of extra time to get through security, whose lines can snake across entire terminals. When you do get up to the metal detector, remember to remove all shoes, jackets, cell phones, loose change and belts, and to take your laptop from its bag. All these items must go through the x-ray machine. If you do fly in from overseas, expect to go through customs and immigration, where you will present your entry form and have your passport stamped. Be sure to have your visa, which you must obtain in your country of origin (for more information on visas, see p.40).

LAX is not the only option available in the greater Los Angeles area, which is served by a group of smaller airports that may prove more amenable to your travel plans. The largest of these are located in Burbank, Ontario and Long Beach, which may take longer to get to, but once there, the time from check-in to gate may be much shorter. From these airports, airlines fly various routes across the US and to a few international destinations, so it may be worth checking to see if one of these can serve your needs.

You will still have to go through security before boarding any flight, and if you fly in from another country, immigration and customs will still be awaiting you, but you may find the experience more to your liking than the chaos of LAX.

Airport Transport

Public transport is available to and from LAX, although most people will be dealing with short or long-term parking, rental car pick-up or drop-off or hotel shuttle buses. While short-term parking, appropriate for dropping off or picking up passengers, is located within the airport itself, there are three lots, labelled A, B and C, for longer term parking located around the perimeter of LAX. Shuttles run regularly to and from all the terminals at the airport. All the major car rental agencies have offices nearby. Again, shuttles run between the airport itself and the lots where travellers can pick up their cars after they've landed or drop them off before they fly out. You can take a taxi to the airport, too, but a more economical option may be to arrange for a share van to pick you up at your residence or hotel, or at the airport to take you home. Make a reservation at www.supershuttle.com or www.primetimeshuttle.com, and you will have door-to-door service, often at half the price of a taxi. Public transportation is also available. There is a Metro Bus Center located in parking lot C, at which bus number 6 of the Culver City Bus Line, number 3 of the Santa Monica Big Blue buses and number 8 of Torrance Transit make stops. A shuttle bus to and from the Aviation Metro Rail Station also makes stops there. Each ground transportation option is clearly marked outside the terminals, with different coloured signs guiding passengers there. As for the smaller airports, cars, taxis or share vans are the best options for getting there and back.

Bicycle

Other options **Cycling** p.219

Los Angeles actually has some progressive laws regarding bicycle use. While cyclists are bound by the same rules as other drivers, they are also entitled to parking and showers in any new construction over 10,000 square feet. Additionally, all city buses are equipped with bike racks. Whether those perks are put into place is another matter. In fact, cycling in LA is not for the faint of heart. Bicycle lanes are few and far between, motorists don't pay much attention to them and even police officers are ignorant enough of cyclists' legal rights to penalise them instead of drivers in minor traffic incidents. If you do decide to pedal around the city, keep off the sidewalks, remember your helmet, make sure your bicycle has brakes and night-time reflectors, and get a licence from your retailer – they're required by law.

Bus

Los Angeles boasts a huge fleet of buses, up to 2,000, covering over 3,625 sq km (1,400 square miles) of street at peak hours every day. Run by the Los Angeles Metropolitan Transit Authority, or Metro, most buses are a distinctive orange colour and run on 189 routes around all of Los Angeles County. In addition, Rapid Red lines offer limited stops along more crowded surface streets. Green Culver City buses and Santa Monica Big Blue buses also run through the city, crossing over the boundaries of their own municipalities into adjacent neighbourhoods to provide even more options in surface transportation. Fares ranging from 50 cents to $1.50 make the buses a good way to get around town without breaking the bank. Schedules and route information are available on board as well as at www.metro.net, www.bigbluebus.com or www.culvercity.org/bus. Although class distinctions in LA are most readily apparent to bus riders – those who can afford to drive usually do – taking the bus can also be a nice way to sightsee, since many routes meander through different

Surface To Say
You'll often hear Angelenos suggest 'surface streets' as shortcuts. A surface street is any street that isn't a freeway.

Bike riding in Santa Monica

Union Station

LA's freeways

Hollywood/Highland Metro Station

LA Metro

Los Angeles St →

parts of LA, rather than travelling on a straight route. Of course, buses are at the mercy of the flow of traffic, so getting places can be a slow process. If you have the time, they can be a good alternative to driving and can show you a whole side of life in LA that cannot be seen from the inside of an automobile.

Car

Other options **Transportation** p.132

Angelenos have taken the American love of the automobile to a new level. Status, both real and perceived, is closely bound up with the kind of car that a person drives, so streets are full of all the latest high-end models. The pride and joy that people take in their cars, though, has a downside. Los Angeles consistently has the some of the worst traffic in the entire country, from bottlenecks on local freeways to intersections where gridlock can add up to an hour to a short ride. Still, in a city as spread out as Los Angeles, most people come to the conclusion that driving is the only reasonable mode of transport. A wide network of services has been developed to deal with the inevitable snarls of the daily commute; foremost among them is the SigAlert. Named after the man who created a device to get traffic information from the police department to local radio stations, a SigAlert (www.sigalert.com) refers to any unplanned event that closes one lane of a freeway for at least 30 minutes. The Department of Transportation has also set up a website, http://trafficinfo.lacity.org, with a colour-coded system to show real-time traffic conditions.

Driving on surface streets is often the easier route, although during peak hours major roads and intersections will get backed up too. Almost all streets, including narrow, winding residential roads high up in the hills, run two ways. The exception lies in Downtown, which is laid out in a grid of alternating one-way streets. Many streets have restricted parking during daytime hours, but others require permits to park at any time, day or night, and almost all streets have designated cleaning days, so pay careful attention to street signs. Los Angeles has not instituted a congestion charge, and the freeway system remains free of tolls, so it depends upon the revenue created by enforcing parking violations. Members of the Parking Violations Bureau regularly patrol the streets in their signature white cars, looking for expired meters, cars parked in front of driveways or red kerb zones, or any other infringement of parking rules.

BRT

LA's Orange line Metro is a form of Bus Rapid Transport. The system, which is being promoted throughout the country, uses buses on traffic-free roadways. BRTs tend to work much like light rail or metro lines; buses conform to a strict schedule, rarely encounter car traffic and stop at covered metro-like pavilions.

Metro

The Red Car trolley lines vanished in the early 60s, but by the 1970s there were calls to create another form of mass transit other than the bus system. The first light rail borne of that campaign opened in 1990, and currently there are six lines of light rail, subway and Bus Rapid Transport (BRT). Beginning in Downtown and working outwards (see the Metro map inside the back cover), the subway consists of two lines: the Red line, which runs between Downtown and North Hollywood, and the Purple line, which runs between Downtown and Koreatown. Connected to the subway lines are the Orange BRT line, running from North Hollywood into the Valley and ending at Warner Center; the Gold light rail line, running east to Pasadena; and the Blue light rail line, running south towards Long Beach. There is also the Green light rail line, which runs east-west from Redondo to Norwalk and bisects the Blue line. There are endless calls for an expansion of the subway system to the Westside, and after years of wrangling, ground was finally broken on an Exposition line of light rail, which will finally bring rail service to those in Culver City and the surrounding neighbourhoods.

Motorcycles

Although cars dominate the road, it is not uncommon to see motorbikes and scooters zipping through traffic in LA. Generally speaking, all traffic rules apply equally to cars and motorcycles: speed limits, stop signs and yielding for pedestrians. Motorbike riders have to pass a special test and hold a motorcycle licence, their bikes must be registered and they must wear helmets at all times. Special parking is sometimes available but, mostly, motorbikes are restricted by the same rules that apply to cars.

Taxi Companies	
Bell Cab	800 666 6664
	888 235 5222
Beverly Hills Cab Company	800 273 6611
Checker Cab	800 300 5007
City Cab	800 750 4400
	818 252 1600
Independent Taxi	323 666 0050
	800 521 8294
United Checker Cab Company	310 834 1121
United Independent Taxi	800 411 0303
	213 483 7660
	310 821 1000
United Taxi of San Fernando Valley	800 290 5600
	818 780 1234
Yellow Cab	800 200 1085
	310 808 1000

Taxi

Unlike other cities around the world, Los Angeles is not crawling with taxis roaming the streets in search of the outstretched arm of a potential rider. Rather, taxis and car services can be called upon to send a car upon request. There are nine taxi franchises that operate more than 2,300 cars. Sanctioned cars will display an official City of Los Angeles Taxicab seal, which means they carry insurance, have trained drivers and are regularly inspected by the city. Riders in authorised cars will encounter meters that charge $2.65 for the first 1/7 of a mile travelled and then $0.035 for each additional 1/7 of a mile or 47.5 seconds of waiting time. There is a fixed price of $42.00 between LAX and Downtown, with a $2.50 surcharge for any ride originating at LAX, which is one of the only places where a taxi can be found by simply going out to the kerb. More information about the rights of taxi riders and other services can be found at www.taxicabsla.org.

Train

For those travelling farther afield, Los Angeles does provide access to intercity Metrolink trains and to Amtrak, the national passenger train company. These, as well as the subway and many bus lines, can be accessed at LA's historic Union Station. Located in the heart of Downtown, Union Station is a beautiful building, with elements of Dutch revival, mission revival and streamline moderne styles. Surrounded by gardens, it was once a bustling hub for the entire area, although now some of the rooms are shuttered. These days, travellers wishing to use the Metrolink regional system can find buses and rail lines to Orange County, Riverside and Antelope Valley, among others. Union Station is also the only place in the city to get direct rail service to Burbank Airport, as well as the FlyAway Bus service to LAX. Amtrak provides long-distance services both within California and towards the rest of the country, via Chicago and New Orleans. More information on Union Station and train and bus routes and schedules can be found at www.mta.net, www.metrolinktrains.com and www.amtrak.com.

Walking
Other options **Hiking** p.224

Although many business and shopping districts are teeming with pedestrians, walking is not an efficient way to get around Los Angeles, which sprawls out for miles on end. Some areas have sidewalks while others don't, stop lights are often placed very far apart, which benefits car traffic but can strand pedestrians, and most neighbourhoods don't have small groceries or other shops that make it possible to avoid taking a car to stock up on essentials. However, there are small pockets such as parts of Santa Monica, Pasadena, or even Downtown, that are well-maintained and amenable to walkers.

Money

The use of credit cards is widespread and popular. People use their cards for everything, limits are rarely in place, and no one will blink when you use one to buy a pack of gum. Cash is also accepted but in a city devoted to cars, the drive-through is far more conducive to plastic than it is to cash. Most gas stations offer a speed pass option, which allows the customer to wave a magnetic keychain at the pumps and fill up without even having to worry about opening their wallet. In the United States, and particularly in Los Angeles, easier is always better.

Local Currency

One dollar is equal to 100 cents. Regardless of denomination, each bill is green and exactly the same size. George Washington graces the $1 bill, Thomas Jefferson the $2, Abe Lincoln the $5, Alexander Hamilton the $10, Andrew Jackson the $20, Ulysses S. Grant the $50 and Benjamin Franklin the $100. Coins are available in denominations of one cent (a penny), five cents (a nickel), 10 cents (a dime), 25 cents (a quarter), 50 cents and one dollar.

Pershing Square

Banks

There's a lot of money in Los Angeles – hence, there are a lot of places to put it. You don't have to go far to find a bank; from small local operations to massive internationals. Not surprisingly most branches have drive-through windows where you don't have to leave your car or turn off your engine to do your banking. Major banks in Los Angeles include Wells Fargo, Bank of America, Washington Mutual, Citibank and HSBC.

ATMs

ATMs are plentiful. You'll find ATMs in liquor stores, supermarkets, country clubs, gyms, bars and attached to banks. Unless you use the ATM at your own bank, you'll be charged a minimum of $1.50 for accessing your money. Withdrawing money from small, independent groceries or kiosks is likely to incur a higher fee. Be careful when withdrawing money from ATMs; scams have become increasingly frequent and sophisticated. Make sure that what you're typing your PIN into is, in fact, a legitimate ATM and not a facade created to steal your card and record your number.

Material Value

The current incarnation of the dollar bill is printed in three stages on special paper made by the Crane Paper Company. The paper is a type of 'rag' that incorporates cotton, linen and silk into the weave. This combination makes the bills last longer.

Money Exchanges

The best way to assure the fewest complications and a competitive rate when exchanging money is to use your ATM card. Your bank may provide exchange services, but fees can be high and usually the branch will need to order foreign currencies. American Express and Thomas

Tax Tip Off

Even if your waiter isn't up to par, remember that in the US, waiters aren't subject to the same minimum wage as others. Unlike the rest of the country, waiters can't rely on the federal minimum wage of $5.85. Instead, their minimum wage is $2.13. Plus, when the IRS looks at their income taxes, they compare their reported tips to the restaurant's nightly earnings. So when you short a waiter, they still have to pay taxes on the money you didn't give them.

Cook both offer reasonable rates but when combined with fees, an ATM is usually your best bet.

Credit Cards

Americans love their credit cards, and living with debt is a part of American life. As soon as you start receiving mail in the United States, you'll start receiving credit card offers. Every major credit card is accepted everywhere, as are many cards you've never heard of. Debit cards are more and more popular but there's no question that the credit card is king. If you suspect that your credit card has been stolen, contact the credit card company immediately. Depending upon your card and your credit, you may or may not be responsible for charges made to your account.

Exchange Rates		
Foreign Currency (FC)	1 Unit FC = x$	$1 = x FC
Argentina (peso)	0.32	3.16
Australia (dollar)	0.94	1.07
Brazil (real)	0.59	1.68
Canada (dollar)	1.02	0.98
China (yuan renminbi)	0.14	7.15
Egypt (pound)	0.18	5.56
Euro	1.52	0.66
Hong Kong (dollar)	0.13	7.79
Iceland (kronur)	0.01	68.37
India (rupee)	0.02	40.45
Israel (new shekel)	0.28	3.63
Japan (yen)	0.01	106.90
Jordan (dinar)	1.41	0.71
Mexico (peso)	0.09	10.73
New Zealand (dollar)	0.80	1.25
Saudi Arabia (riyal)	0.27	3.75
Singapore (dollar)	0.72	1.40
South Africa (rand)	0.13	7.46
United Arab Emirates (dirham)	0.27	3.67
United Kingdom (pound)	1.99	0.50
Rates correct at time of going to print		

Tipping

Tipping is common, expected, encouraged and relied upon. Tip everyone – waiters, bartenders, taxi drivers, bell people, anyone who is likely to be working for minimum wage and depending on tips to make their rent. The bare minimum at a restaurant where someone takes your order (you don't need to tip at fast food joints where you order from the counter) is 15%. A tip of 20% is good, but certainly not outrageous. A bartender will expect a $1 per drink minimum. Bellhops will expect at least a dollar per bag and, in a good hotel, they'll expect quite a bit more. Keep in mind that those working in the service industry make very little on their monthly paycheques, that the government taxes them on their tips, and that they work very hard. Besides, in Los Angeles, the odds are good that the person delivering your food will someday be more famous than you are.

Sunset Boulevard

Newspapers & Magazines

Los Angeles is an international city with an extremely diverse population. Each of the groups that make up its mosaic, from Europeans and South Americans to east Asians and Africans, has easy access to the most up-to date news from back home via periodicals found at the large newsstands dotted throughout the city. There, they share shelf space with the local English language paper, *The Los Angeles Times* ($0.50 Monday to Saturday and $1.50 on Sundays). The *LA Times* is one of the most well respected newspapers in the country and its Sunday edition contains the *Los Angeles Times Magazine*, complete with what's on listings and a knowledgeable style guide. LA also has a number of free weeklies, foremost among them being *LA Weekly*, which provides excellent local listings of movies, restaurants, club happenings and concerts, in addition to a slightly different take on news coverage. *Los Angeles CityBeat* is another 'alternative weekly,' covering local news, events, arts and entertainment, and *Citizen LA* is a monthly arts and lifestyle magazine that can be picked up for free around Downtown and neighbouring communities. *LA's The Place* is a free magazine with news and features aimed at residents, and an emphasis on entertainment and celebrity. A smaller selection of magazines can be found in most supermarkets and pharmacies, and individual vending boxes containing some of the papers with larger circulations are almost everywhere. You can also have a paper delivered to your doorstep every morning. LA Inc, the Los Angeles Convention and Visitors Bureau, produces a comprehensive visitors' guide twice a year, and travellers need not go without their news fix, either, as most hotels will provide a paper in the morning.

Great Scott

For a trip into the filmmaking world, F Scott Fitzgerald's great unfinished novel, The Last Tycoon, *is a thinly veiled portrait of Irving Thalberg, the MGM wunderkind who died young enough to be immortalised as a perfect Hollywood producer.*

Books

Other options **Websites** p.31

The film industry really put LA on the map, and it is through the lens of movies that most people know anything about this town. There are plenty of books that cater to the ongoing fascination with Hollywood, such as *Hollywood: The Movie Lover's Guide* by Richard Alleman. But there's more to LA than that. Many coffee table and photography books highlight the city's history. Rosemary Lord has compiled two books, *Los Angeles Then And Now* and *Hollywood Then And Now* that juxtapose photographs from the past and present, to sometimes exhilarating, sometimes depressing, ends. Los Angeles has also been at the vanguard of architectural developments over the years, with some of the world's

Los Angeles Times building

foremost architects living here at one time or another. Sam Waters has put together two books that chronicle specific periods, *Houses of Los Angeles, 1885-1919* and *Houses of Los Angeles, 1920-1935*, while *An Architectural Guide To Los Angeles* by Robert Winter and David Gebhard takes the reader through areas of LA, highlighting notable structures. For a unique experience of the city, take a look at *City Walks Los Angeles*, a deck of cards with 50 walks around the city, or for those who want to escape the pavement, *Day Hikes Around Los Angeles* by Robert Stone will direct you to some of the gorgeous natural landscape that Angelenos have access to all year long. Readers looking into the workings of the city should thoroughly enjoy *City of Quartz: Excavating the Future in Los Angeles* by Mike Davis. The book looks at many of the problems facing the city and includes an interesting dissection of LA's many social and economic groups. Finally, *Los Angeles A to Z: An Encyclopedia of the City and County* by Leonard and Dale Pitt is a thick compendium that can answer just about any question you may have about this town.

Websites

Los Angeles is a pretty wired city, from wireless access in coffee shops to the plethora of online resources available to residents and visitors alike. The *LA Weekly* and *Zagat* sites are good for finding restaurants, bars and clubs, and newcomers to the city should keep Craigslist (http://losangeles.craigslist.org) in mind, with its warehouse of listings advertising apartments, furniture, jobs and more. The table below offers a selection of sites that should be of interest to residents.

Websites	
Los Angeles Information	
www.culturela.org	Los Angeles Department of Cultural Affairs
www.experiencela.com	Cultural calendar and trip planner
www.golosangeles.about.com	Multi-faceted tourist information
www.lacity.org	Official site of the City of Los Angeles
www.lapdonline.org	Official site of the LA Police Department
www.latourist.com	Tourist information for visitors to Los Angeles
www.losangeles.craigslist.org	Online marketplace for buying, selling and services
www.seemyla.com	Los Angeles Convention and Visitors Bureau
www.visitcalifornia.com	Multilingual California tourism site
Leisure	
www.artscenecal.com	Museum and gallery listings
www.gocitykids.com	Information about activities for children
www.losangeles.citysearch.com	City info, with user reviews
www.zagat.com	Restaurant reviews and listings
Online Publications	
www.laist.com	Blog covering local news and happenings
www.latimes.com	Online edition of the newspaper
www.laweekly.com	Online edition of the newspaper
Transport	
www.ladottransit.com	City of Los Angeles Department of Transportation
www.metro.net	Metropolitan Transportation Authority site
www.metrolinktrains.com	Southern California Commuter Rail Service
Work & Education	
www.calstatela.edu	California State University
www.lapl.org	Los Angeles Public Library site
www.ucla.edu	Official site of UCLA
www.usc.edu	University of Southern California

Annual Events

Pasadena
January

Tournament Of Roses
www.tournamentofroses.com
Since 1890, a parade has been held on 1 January in Pasadena to celebrate the mild weather that Southern California enjoys all year long. The event quickly became known as the Tournament of Roses. Featuring elaborately designed floats covered entirely in flowers, the Rose Parade is watched by television viewers around the country, and is followed by the Rose Bowl Game, one of college football's premier events.

Santa Monica
January

Los Angeles Art Show & Art LA
www.laartshow.com & www.artfairsinc.com
These annual exhibitions of fine art showcase high-end artwork from around the world. Held on the last week in January, the shows cater to international buyers with very deep pockets. Galleries participate by invitation only, but anyone can stop in and look. Lectures and presentations on art and interior design are held in conjunction with the exhibits.

Various Locations
January-February

Restaurant Week
www.dinela.com/restaurantweek
LA's reputation as a haven for food lovers has recently gained traction, and the city is crowded with wonderful eateries. Take advantage of this week by going to one of the many restaurants that offer fixed price three-course lunch and dinner menus. Lunches range from $15-$22, and dinners are only $25-34. Be sure to make a reservation, and remember that these prices don't apply on Saturday night, the busiest of the week.

Hollywood
February/March

Academy Awards
www.oscar.com
Millions of TV viewers tune in every year to watch glamorous celebrities head into the Kodak Theatre for the film industry's biggest awards ceremony. Star-spotters also attend in person, lining the sides of the red carpet to catch a glimpse of the rich and famous as they descend from their limousines.

Downtown
March

Los Angeles Marathon
www.lamarathon.com
Thousands of runners (and cyclists) make their way through streets cleared of traffic in this annual event. The course winds its way through LA, past some of the town's famous landmarks. Spectators are encouraged to come out and lend their support. There are entertainment centres set up along the route with live performances, making the marathon a festive event for participants and viewers alike.

UCLA
April

LA Times Festival Of Books
www.latimes.com/extras/festivalofbooks
For one weekend of the year, the main plaza of UCLA turns into a tented city devoted to books, books and more books. Author panels, vendor exhibits, publishers and performances attract over 140,000 people. Readings are scheduled throughout the weekend, and there are two areas devoted to children.

Lancaster
Antelope Valley
April

California Poppy Festival
www.poppyfestival.com
This is a two-day festival in Antelope Valley that celebrates the annual blooming of California's state flower. Take in the entertainment, food and crafts while surrounded by hills of wild orange poppies.

El Pueblo de Los Angeles

Rodeo Drive

Wall mural in Hollywood

Santa Monica Beach

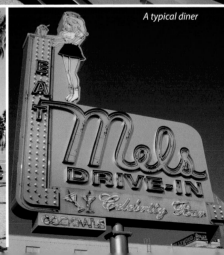

A typical diner

Cinco De Mayo

Various Locations
May

www.olvera-street.com

Celebrated by Mexicans and Mexican-Americans to commemorate a military victory in 1862, Cinco de Mayo festivities take place all over the city, but traditional cultural activities can be found at El Pueblo de Los Angeles Historic Monument on Olvera Street. Visitors can take in the folk dancing, traditional Mexican songs and try the delicious food on sale.

Memorial Day

Various Locations
May

While it is customary for Americans to light up the barbecue with friends and family on this national holiday, there are also various festivals to entice people out of their backyards and into the streets. One example is the Garden Grove Strawberry festival (www.strawberryfestival.org), offering family fun and entertainment.

LA Pride

West Hollywood
June

www.lapride.org

Organised by Christopher Street West (named after the street in New York where the Stonewall Riots ushered in the gay-pride era), this festival has developed into a major event in West Hollywood. Featuring marchers dressed in all sorts of ecstatic and wild costumes, the parade draws spectators from across the city.

Los Feliz Street Fair

Los Feliz
June

www.losfelizstreetfair.com

One of the biggest street fairs in the city, this event in the neighbourhood of Los Feliz has been held for the past 15 years. With a petting zoo, performance stages, tonnes of food kiosks as well as a wine and beer garden, this street fair has something for everyone.

Playboy Jazz Festival

Hollywood Bowl
June

playboy.com/arts-entertainment/features/jazzfest2008

Sponsored by Playboy Enterprises, this world-class jazz festival, which features some of the genre's most famous artists as well as promising newcomers, is held every year at the Hollywood Bowl. Bill Cosby MCs the two-night event.

LA Film Festival

Various Locations
June/July

www.lafilmfest.com

Held at venues across LA, the film festival screens domestic and international movies, but also sponsors panel discussions, seminars, family events and free outdoor screenings.

Hollywood Bowl Summer Concerts

Hollywood Bowl
June-September

www.hollywoodbowl.com

Nestled in the Hollywood Hills, the Bowl (p.182) is the largest outdoor amphitheatre in the United States. The summer months, when the weather is especially balmy, is high season, with concerts of all sorts, from classical and world music to contemporary pop and rock, scheduled almost every night of the week. Bring a picnic and a bottle and enjoy the music.

Independence Day

Various Locations
July

July fourth celebrations can be found all over LA County, from firework displays at the Rose Bowl in Pasadena, over the water in Marina Del Ray and at the Queen Mary in Long Beach to the body building competition, Mr & Mrs Muscle Beach, in Venice.

Echo Park
July

Lotus Festival
www.laparks,org/grifmet/lotus.htm
If you've always been curious about Asian and Pacific Island culture, this is the place to go. For 31 years, the LA Parks and Recreation department has put on this festival, which highlights the art, cuisine, music and dance of the Far East.

Laguna Beach
July/August

Pageant Of The Masters
www.foapom.com
Since 1932, when the tiny artists' colony of Laguna Beach staged its first festival of the arts, the 'living

Hollywood Bowl

pictures' show has played a central role. Minutely detailed recreations of famous artworks, with people posed to look like their artistic counterparts, are displayed in this elaborately choreographed spectacle.

Hollywood
October

Dia De Los Muertos (Day Of The Dead)
www.ladayofthedead.com
The Hollywood Forever Cemetery (p.182), in which notables such as Rudolph Valentino, Douglas Fairbanks and Peter Lorre are buried, holds an annual Mexican Day of the Dead celebration. Open for two nights, the aisles of the park are lined with intricate altars and shrines to commemorate those who have passed away, while songs, dance and revelry joyfully celebrate the spirits of those who have given inspiration to their friends and loved ones.

West Hollywood
October

West Hollywood Halloween Carnival
www.weho.org
Every year, Santa Monica Boulevard in West Hollywood is taken over by an outrageous and raucous costume carnival. Over 300,000 people come to celebrate on 31 October.

Various Locations
October-November

AFI Fest
www.afi.com
The oldest movie festival in Los Angeles, the AFI Fest showcases international films and filmmakers. Showing features, documentaries and shorts, the festival also hosts evening galas where journalists and attendees get a chance to mix with hundreds of filmmakers.

Griffith Park
November-December

Holiday Light Festival
www.dwplightfestival.com
Organised by the Department of Water and Power, this event sees a one-mile strip of Griffith Park set aglow with thousands of light displays. More than half a million people drive through to witness the spectacle, and 'walk only' nights are set aside during the first week.

Marina Del Rey
December

Marina Del Rey Holiday Boat Parade
www.mdrboatparade.org
The parade of boats features vessels vying for honours such as best lights, best theme, and even best animation. Boat owners go all out when it comes to decorating their craft, and then glide slowly through the water, much to the delight of the spectators who line the route.

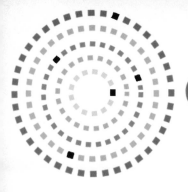

austra USA

where australia mee

connecting australians

cultural event

social networks

+1 310 980 5907
www.austraUSA.com

Residents

Residents

Overview

The City of Angels may be home to the glitz, glamour and gaffes of Hollywood, but few of the 10 million angels here actually live in the paparazzi's glare. Hopeful writers, actors, rockers and artists move here in droves, but LA is also the nation's largest international trade and manufacturing centre and a magnet for fashionistas, digital techies, finance gurus, tourism professionals and surf bums alike. Professionally, it pays to speak English. With immigrants from over 140 countries, however, the streets and even some offices hum with languages such as Spanish, Korean and Farsi. Thanks to this diversity – and contrary to a sometimes lowbrow reputation – LA claims some of the top cultural, medical and educational facilities in the world. Due to the city's sprawling nature, it can be difficult for newcomers to manoeuvre, both geographically and socially. This section will help get you started.

Considering The City

With a warm climate, gorgeous beaches and active pace, there is little question about the appeal of LA. Unfortunately, the cost of living here can be astronomical and housing is a major factor. The key is finding which neighbourhoods and housing styles fit your bank account, as accommodation here ranges from a $600 rental share in Los Feliz to a multimillion dollar mansion in Beverly Hills. The added cost of LA's car culture, however, is less avoidable, especially when the 'LA' job hunt can take you from San Diego to Santa Barbara. The LA Metro Area includes the four surrounding cities, making it larger than all but four US states, and locals often work at least an hour from home. Relying on the bus and growing rail systems could cost you an interview if you don't do your research and allow time for mishaps. As for landing the job, the toughest thing is the sheer number of people who arrive in Los Angeles daily. That's why it pays to start your hunt as soon as you are considering the move, using job boards such as http://losangeles.craigslist.org or www.careerbuilders.com. Also be sure to have your working papers in order. LA is infamous for employing illegal workers, especially for low-paid manual labour, but going this route could get you thrown out of the country for up to 10 years.

Before You Arrive

Moving is one of life's most stressful undertakings, especially when crossing continents. The better prepared you are before you leave, the easier the transition will be.

- **Get your documents in order** – in addition to procuring travel documents such as your visa and travel tickets, have important documents like marriage licences and children's birth certificates attested in your country. This could be a lengthy procedure, so put it high on your checklist.
- **Feel out the job market** – as well as perusing online job listings, make contact with a few real employment leads. Whether or not you land the jobs, you will garner helpful information about your field of interest. You may also make headway with online networking sites like www.linkedin.com and www.mediabistro.com (a site for media professionals).
- **Tidy up your financial affairs** – check with your banks, mortgage providers, pension company and tax officials how to prepare for your move and how your move will affect your finances.
- **Close up house** – look into shipping your belongings early in the game to accommodate handling requirements and transit time. If you own property, you may want to hold onto it while you test the waters in LA, so start by renting it out. If all goes well, you can put it on the market in a year or two.

- **Neighbourhood watch** – research LA neighbourhoods to see which is best for you. If you are moving with children, investigate public and private school options and remember your child's public school will probably be defined by your address.

When You Arrive

You've made it, but it is going to take a while to get settled in. Here are some tips to get you started:

- **Residency and visas** – take the necessary steps outlined by your visa. If you land a job while here on a visitor's visa, you may have to head back to your country of origin to manage the paperwork.
- **Find housing** – even if you have done the research, choosing housing without seeing it first is dangerous. Set up something short term through sites like http://losangeles. craigslist.org, and give yourself time to shop around.
- **Set up house** – once you have a place, furnish for less by perusing craigslist, local flea markets and Ikea. Find decorative fabrics and more in Downtown's fashion district. See p.105 for information on connecting your utilities.
- **Transportation** – car is king in LA, so you are likely to need one. For info on buying, leasing, registration and licensing, see Transportation on p.132.
- **Get social** – register with your embassy and consider joining social groups such as EuroCircle (www.eurocircle.com). You can also jump into local life with a free issue of *LA Weekly* magazine and websites like www.flavorpill.com and www.citysearch.com.

When You Leave

Closing up shop in the US should be a tad easier than coming in was. Here are some things to remember:

- **Tidy up your financial affairs** – be sure your landlord knows you are leaving and that you have had your utilities disconnected. Keep any financial institutions informed of your move as well.
- **Get organised** – book ahead when arranging for your goods to be shipped to your next destination.
- **Sell, sell, sell** – sites like craigslist and ebay turn your trash into gold, but an old-fashioned yard sale is another great way to clean house, make a few bucks and save on those shipping costs. Just pay attention to yard sale regulations in your local area, as some neighbourhoods prohibit them.

Welcome to the neighbourhood

Documents

Sanctuary City
A hotbed of immigrant activism and protest, LA is a 'sanctuary city', which means police are banned from asking about your immigration status. If you are already in LA and feel you are being mistreated, or you just want to get involved, contact the Coalition for Humane Immigrant Rights of Los Angeles (888 624 4752, www.chirla.org), an organisation that has campaigned for the immigrant community for over 20 years.

With millions of foreigners coming to the US each year, rules and regulations regarding entry and residency often become confusing. The post 9/11 climate and the political backlash against illegal immigration have only exacerbated this by creating a system of ongoing updates and changes. The saying goes, 'even immigration lawyers go to immigration lawyers', but rest assured, this process is not impossible. After all, the 2006 census reported that 3,516,970 foreign-born immigrants have successfully made it to LA, so with patience and perseverance, you can too.

As you venture through this process, www.unitedstatesvisas.gov is an invaluable source for determining what type of visa applies to you and how to proceed and locate the forms you will need to file. In addition, you can request all necessary forms by calling 800 870 3676.

Many procedures require 'essential documents', which include but are not limited to:
• Original passport
• Residence card or visa
• Passport photos
• Passport copies

Confirm such requirements before beginning any procedure, as you may also need copies of your employment offer, a salary certificate and a tenancy contract. Be sure to store copies of all your essential documents somewhere safe and separate from the originals, in case of emergency. It is also wise to have to hand your birth, marriage or divorce certificates, high school or college diplomas, and any certificates of special training or skills

Entry Visa

Family Ties
Several visitors' visas have provisions for your family to join as a subset of the same category as you, or vice versa. For example, if you enter the US on an H-1 visa (Temporary Worker), your spouse and children can enter on H-4 visas.

Generally, a citizen of a foreign country who wishes to enter the United States must first obtain a non-immigrant or immigrant visa. An immigrant visa is a permanent visa or 'green card', while there are numerous types of non-immigrant, or temporary visas, which are lettered from A to Z. The procedure, application process and waiting times vary depending on your reason for entry and how long you intend to stay.

Below are explanations on how to get your green card, as well as business, pleasure and student visas. Other visitor visa categories include:

A: Foreign officials and immediate family.
C: Aliens in transit.
H: Temporary workers and immediate family.
J: Exchange students, cultural groups and immediate family.
K: Spouse or fiance(e) of US citizen and young children.
L: Inter-company transferees and selected family members.
M: Vocational and language students and immediate family.

Student Visa

Non-resident student visas are available to academic and vocational foreign students. To qualify, you must apply and be accepted to a full-time school approved by US Citizenship and Immigration Services (USCIS), be proficient or studying for proficiency in English, show proof of sufficient funds to support yourself while in the US, and have full-time residency abroad. The academic visa (F-1) lasts as long as you continue matriculating full-time towards completing your course of study, while the vocational visa (M-1) covers either one year or your course of study. Provisions allow your spouse and children to join you during your studies, and academic students are also eligible for work permits after one year of study. Pay attention to regulations on exit and re-entry and extending your stay.

Visa Waiver

Visitors from certain countries and adjacent islands can enter the US for short visits without a visa, through the Visa Waiver Program. If your country is on the list, you may visit the US for 90 days or less for business or pleasure. To enter, you must present a machine-readable passport that is valid for six months past your expected stay in the US, and a return ticket for travel to a non-US destination. Upon entry, an immigration inspector will provide you with form I-94W (or you may get one on the plane), which records the duration of your stay. This must be kept with your passport during your visit. Short trips to Canada, Mexico or surrounding islands are permissible, as long as you return within your visa duration period and prove you continue to be eligible.

The hitch in this clearly convenient visa process is two fold. First, if your application is denied for any reason, there is no right to appeal (unless you are applying under the Convention Against Torture and Other Cruel, Inhuman or Degrading Treatment or Punishment). Second, if you decide to stay in the US, you cannot change or extend this visa. You will have to leave the country to begin the process.

Visa Waiver Countries

The 27 countries on the visa waiver list (at the time of going to press) are Andorra, Australia, Austria, Belgium, Brunei, Denmark, Finland, France, Germany, Iceland, Ireland, Italy, Japan, Liechtenstein, Luxembourg, Monaco, Netherlands, New Zealand, Norway, Portugal, San Marino, Singapore, Slovenia, Spain, Sweden, Switzerland and the United Kingdom. Although Canada and Mexico are not on the list, you may be able to cross the border under the waiver, but regulations regarding these borders are currently under heated debate. For a complete and current list, visit the US Department of State website (www.travel.state.gov).

Stopped At The Border
If your friend or family member arrives in the US to visit and does not qualify for a visa on arrival, there is little you can do to assist them. You can, however, lend him or her a hand with obtaining a tourist visa beforehand. For example, if there is a wedding in the works, send an invitation, a short-form affidavit for support (I-134), along with a letter saying something to the effect of 'Please come to Joe Smith's wedding and stay with us for a couple of months'.

Spouse Or Child Of A US Citizen

Immediate family can enter the US on a temporary visa while awaiting approval of Form I-130 (relative petition) or the availability of an immigrant visa. The spouse of a US citizen is eligible for a K-3 visa, while children of US citizens or K-3 visa holders are eligible for K-4 visas as long as they are under 21 and unmarried. To apply for a K visa with an I-130 already filed, the US citizen spouse files Form I-129F (petition for alien fiancee) with the US consulate in the country of marriage or, if that country is the US, in the alien spouse's country of residence. The USCIS will continue the process by sending Form I-797 to the US citizen. A K-3 or K-4 non-immigrant receives his or her green card when both Form I-130 and Form I-485 (Application for Adjustment to Permanent Residence) have been approved. This process can take three to six months. If you enter on a non-immigrant visa and wish to work, you must file Form I-765 (Application for Employment Authorization) with USCIS, along with a $340 application fee.

Humanitarian Parole

'Parole' is available to foreigners outside of the US who are in immediate peril or offer significant public benefit to the US. Requests are considered by the Secretary of the Department of Homeland Security on a case by case basis within 60 to 90 business days. If you are awarded entry, the length of your stay is defined by the reason for your request, but limited to one year. Such a request may be made by anyone, including the prospective parolee or a concerned organisation. Forms I-131 and I-134 need to be sent to the Department of Homeland Security. Be specific and include evidence of your claimed circumstances. There is no process of appeal, but you may reapply (and repay the fee) if more information comes to light. Humanitarian relief can also be found through Temporary Protected Status and Asylum and Refugee programmes. These are each defined to address specific issues and nations, so you must review the criteria to determine if one of these applies to you.

Extending Your Visit

It may be possible to extend your non-immigrant visa, assuming you apply for an extension before it expires (see the date indicated on your arrival and departure Form I-94) and your passport is still valid. You must file Form I-539 (Application to Extend or Change Non-immigrant Status), along with a $300 fee, or have your employer file Form I-129 (Petition for a Non-immigrant Worker). If your request is denied, you cannot appeal to a higher office. Your case will be reconsidered only if new facts come to light. If you miss the deadline, you will have to prove the delay was beyond your control and reasonable and that there are no deportation orders against you. Extension is not available if you are in the US on the Visa Waiver Program or a D, C, K or S class visa.

Applying With Children

If you apply to enter the country with your children, but not their other parent(s), you must present evidence you have that right as the custodial parent. Step-children are eligible for entry as your children as long as they became your step-child before turning 18. Adopted children are eligible as long as an adoption is recognised by the country of origin, occurred before the age of 16, and the child has lived with you for at least two years. The Child Citizenship Act of 2000 allows certain foreign-born children of US citizens to acquire citizenship automatically upon entering the US.

Residence Visa

Millions set out to make the US their permanent home and the first step in achieving this is applying for Lawful Permanent Resident status (LPR), or a 'green card' (Form I-551), which gives non-US citizens the right to live and work in the US indefinitely. Once you obtain this, you must carry the card as proof of your status and it must be renewed after 10 years (by filing Form I-90). In most cases, obtaining a residence visa requires you to be sponsored by a US citizen, such as a family member or prospective employer who files an immigrant petition on your behalf. You will know you have been granted a visa once you are provided a visa number, but with limited visas available, you may end up waiting several years. When researching which type of visas apply to you, pay attention to how high you might rank in each application pool.

There are two parallel systems for applying for a green card, one for those who are in the US already and one for those applying from outside of the US. If you are outside the country, you must apply through the US State Department (www.state.gov) by visiting the US consulate in the country you are in. If you are already in the US on a temporary visa or illegally, you must apply through the Department of Homeland Security's Citizenship and Immigration department (www.uscis.gov).

Family Visa

Family visas are available to relatives of US citizens and green card holders, and are a popular means of entry into the US. If you are applying for entry this way, the length of the process will vary based on your relationship to your sponsor and his or her citizenship. The parent, child or spouse of a US citizen, for example, can enter as quickly as the papers are processed, but if you are applying from Afghanistan to join your sister in the States, it could be over 10 years before you receive your visa number. Your eligible spouse, parent, offspring or sibling in the US sponsors you by filing Form I-130 (Petition for Alien Relative) with the USCIS and submitting proof of your relationship, his or her own LPR or citizenship and the ability to support you financially. All US citizens can sponsor their spouses and offspring, but citizens must be over 21 to sponsor their parents or siblings. Those with green cards are limited to sponsoring their spouse and unmarried offspring.

Once the petition is accepted, the National Visa Center (NVC) is informed and you may be eligible to apply to immigrate, but if you are not a spouse, unmarried child under 21 or parent of a US citizen, this is where the waiting game begins. You will be placed in line among others who are approved and waiting for a visa number based on the same qualifying relationship as yours. Distribution of visa numbers functions in a three-tier preference system, so be sure to review where your particular relationship and country of origin fits into the spectrum, as that will affect the time it takes. Once your wait is over, the NVC will invite you and your qualifying dependants to apply for immigrant visas. Those already in the US legally must change their status by filing Form I-485, while those not in the US must visit their local consulate service office.

Documents

Front Of The Line

If you have questions about a pending immigration case or are concerned something that should have been completed was not, avoid queuing up by making an appointment through INFOPASS (www.infopass.uscis.gov). You will probably be directed to the Federal Building at 300 N Los Angeles St, but your zip code may land you in an office in the surrounding areas.

It Takes A Village

If your family sponsor has limited funds and cannot support you alone, it is possible for household members to pool their financial sponsorship by filing Form I-864A.

The Visa Grandfather Clause

According to the 'Registry' provision of the Immigration and Nationality Act, if you have been in the US since 1 January 1972, you may be eligible to obtain LPR even if you are in the US illegally. Be prepared to prove you have 'continuously resided in the US since entry,' are of 'good moral character' and have no history of terrorist or Nazi participation.

Employment Visa

Foreign citizens are eligible for employment visas once they are offered a job in the US. There are four levels of preference for Employment Based Immigration, each correlating to decreasing levels of professional training and ability. In other words, the more advanced your training and ability, the easier this process becomes. You and your prospective employer must first determine if and where you fit the criteria of those categories. From there, filing requirements vary, but in most cases, your employer must file the paperwork, including the US Department of Labor Form ETA 750 (labour certification request) and USCIS Form I-140 (Petition for Alien Worker). Visit the USCIS website (www.uscis.gov) for more information and updates on the preference categories and procedures to follow.

If you are approved for this visa, the US Department of State will assign you a visa number. Those in the US legally cannot begin work until they adjust to permanent status by filing Form I-485. Those outside the US must go to their local consulate office.

The Visa Lottery

The Diversity Visa Lottery Program issues 50,000 immigrant visas a year to citizens from any country that has not sent over 50,000 immigrants to the US in the past five years. To enter, you must have completed a 12 year course of elementary and secondary education or have two years' experience in an occupation that requires training. Randomly selected winners are permitted to apply for permanent residence, and if LRS is granted, you may bring your spouse and any unmarried children under the age of 21. Find information on deadlines and procedures at www.travel.state.gov, and be sure to follow the annually published rules to the letter.

Same-Sex & Common-Law Couples

If you are a common-law or same-sex spouse, immigration statutes do not recognise you as a spouse. This means you are not eligible to enter as each other's family and the law is unlikely to change anytime soon, but you can research progress or get involved by visiting The Immigration Equality LA website (www.immigrationequalityla.org).

Health Requirements

Everyone applying for a residency visa must be examined by a doctor designated by the consular officer, and submit a completed Form I-693 (Medical Examination). Beyond that, health rules and regulations vary based on the type of visa for which you are applying.

Labour & ID Card

If you are in the US with a green card or on an H-1b visa for temporary workers, that document serves as your labour card and ID card wrapped in one, and you are ready to work in the US. If you are here already and petitioning for a work visa, you may receive a short-term work permit, or employment authorisation card (EAD), while awaiting your appointment for your final green card. Family members of an applicant for LPR are eligible to apply for this card as well. To apply, look into the requirements, which include submitting Form I-765 and a $340 fee to the USCIS.

Citizenship

The decision to become a US citizen is not taken lightly and an immigration attorney will come in handy. You are qualified to apply once you have resided in the US for five years as a green card holder, or only three years if you entered the country through marriage and are still married. To qualify, you must be a person of good moral character who believes in the US Constitution, is loyal to the country and, unless here through marriage, you must also prove a working knowledge of the English language.

Driving Licence

Other options **Transportation** p.132

Other options **Transportation** p.132

DMV Queue Cutter

The DMV is infamous for long queues, followed by even longer waits (especially the Hollywood office), so whether you are registering your car, transferring your licence or picking up a local ID, save at least an hour with the Online Appointment Scheduler at www. dmv.org or by calling 800 777 0133.

It may be true nobody walks in LA, but in order to drive in California you need a class C driving licence or permit, as well as insurance for the vehicle you are driving. If you are just here for a visit and are over 18, you can use a valid licence from your home country, but California does not recognise the International Driving Permit (IDP). Once you become a California resident (by voting in an election, procuring paid employment, paying resident tuition or availing yourself of any other benefit not ordinarily extended to non-residents), you have 10 days to apply for a California licence through the Department of Motor Vehicles (DMV). The DMV offers licences to those over 16 years old. To get yours, visit a DMV office and complete application form DL 44 (note that in signing this form, you consent to future drug or alcohol testing by an officer of the law). You will have to provide verification of birth date and legal presence (such as a green card or a US border crossing ID card and visa with valid I-94), your social security number, your full name and a $27 application fee. You must also pass a driving test (see below).

The DMV rates your driving record on a point system and your licence may be revoked or suspended if you acquire four points within a 12 month period, six points in a 24 month period or eight points in a 36 month period (these points also affect your insurance rates). You earn one point for being at fault in an accident or receiving a minor moving violation, and two points for reckless driving, a hit-and-run accident, driving on a suspended or revoked licence, or driving under the influence of drugs or alcohol (DUI). Points usually remain on your record for three years, but there are exceptions and you can often erase one moving violation point a year by attending an approved California traffic school, onsite or via the internet.

Officers of the law cannot pull you over without cause, unless you encounter a sober driving checkpoint. If you are pulled over, you will need to provide your licence, as well as the vehicle's registration document and proof of insurance.

Driving Test

You must pass vision, written and road tests before being given a driving licence. As long as you can see clearly with or without corrective lenses or glasses you will pass

Driving in LA

the vision test, and many foreigners find the DMV road test easy. But the written test can be more taxing as it requires knowledge of traffic laws, road signs and driving safety rules. It is administered in an assortment of languages, as well as via audio, but you must be able to understand English signage. There are 36 questions taken directly from the *California Driver Handbook* and you have three chances to pass. Once you pass, you then have three chances to pass the driving test, with each re-test costing $6, after which point you will have to make a new appointment to try again.

Provisional Licences

Teenagers under 18 but over 15 and a half must acquire provisional licences, or 'permits', before taking their driving test to earn the full rights of a driving licence. To maintain their permits, provisional teen drivers must obey traffic laws and avoid collision and cannot get behind the wheel unless accompanied by a licensed adult who is 25 or older. After completing six months of permit driving, along with a driver education course, six hours of professional driver training, and 50 hours of practice with an adult 25 or older, permit drivers are eligible to take the driving test.

Adults who have never driven before and are not prepared to take the driver's test may also be issued with a permit after passing the written test. When practising behind the wheel, these adults must have an accompanying licensed adult aged 18 or older.

Motorcycle Licence

In order to ride a motorcycle in California, you must acquire a class M motorcycle licence or instruction permit. The application process parallels that of the Class C licence, with testing requirements focused on motorcycle safety knowledge and on-cycle skill. If you are over 21 and currently have a California driver's licence, you can bypass taking the on-cycle test by completing a 15 hour California Highway Patrol (CHP) course and submitting a certificate of Completion of Motorcycle Training (DL 389). If you are under 21, this training course is mandatory and fulfils the testing requirements.

Driving Schools

Allied Driving School	323 660 7355	www.allieddrivingschool.net
California Driving School Inc	800 522 5374	www.california-driving-school.com
Community Driving & Traffic School	323 222 3333	www.communitydriving.com
Dollar Driving School	310 275 0189	www.dollardrivingschool.com
Driveby LA	888 559 8378	www.hometrafficschool.com
DriversEd.com	877 233 3977	www.driversed.com
Improv Comedy Traffic School	800 775 5233	www.mrtraffic.com/improvts.htm
Inter-American Driving School	323 773 7483	www.cardrivered.com

Birth Certificate & Registration

Naming Ceremonies
In a city with so much religious and cultural diversity, there is no 'norm' for baby-naming ceremonies. Whatever your custom, you will find a religious or cultural organisation that can accommodate your beliefs.

Any baby born in the US or its territories is automatically an American citizen with all rights of citizenship. When a mother gives birth, her physician, midwife or a hospital administrator is responsible for preparing and filing the official birth certificate. If you do not have a provider to file the paperwork for any reason, contact Los Angeles County Vital Records on 213 240 7812. They will walk you through the process, but be aware the certificate must be filed at least 24 hours before the baby's first birthday.

If the birth parents are not legally married, according to state law the father's name cannot go on the certificate. To be added to the certificate, parents must complete and file a Declaration of Paternity form (CS 909) with the Department of Child Support Services (866 249 0773; www.childsup.ca.gov) and then submit a copy of that form, along with Form VS 22 (Application to Amend the Record) and a $20 fee to the California Department of Health Services' Office of Vital Records (916 445 2684; www.dhs.ca.gov). If you intend to travel internationally, you must first obtain a passport in your baby's name. Your baby must be present when you file Form DS-11 and you must have his or her certified birth certificate, Form DS-3053 (Statement of Consent: Issuance of a Passport to a Minor Under Age 14), two passport photos and payment of $85. Hospital issued souvenir birth certificates, which usually include footprints of the newborn, are not legally accepted as proof of age or citizenship. To find the nearest passport agency, visit www.iafdb.travel.state.gov.

You can apply for your baby's social security number as soon as he or she is born or at a later time, but sooner is probably better, as this number allows you to claim your child as a dependant on income tax returns, open bank accounts or buy savings bonds in his or her name and obtain medical coverage or apply for government services for your child.

If you would prefer your child retain citizenship from your country of origin, you may usually take or send a certified US birth certificate to your country's embassy and the embassy will assist you in getting a new certificate from your country. However, rules and regulations vary by country. If either parent is British, for example, the baby is born a US citizen and a British citizen by descent. Your child is eligible for dual citizenship. You may get him or her a UK passport directly and you may also want to file a 'Registration of a Birth in the USA' with the consulate, which costs about $250. If the father is the UK citizen and the parents are unmarried, however, the procedure becomes more involved. For more information, contact the British embassy on 202 588 7812.

Take note that if you plan to remain in the States, it is recommend you obtain and retain a US passport for your child, as this will make his or her travel, re-entry and residency experience go smoother.

Adoption

Any adult can petition to adopt a child in California, but the process can be surprisingly lengthy and difficult when you take into account the number of children in the childcare system. If considering adoption, you must first determine whether to proceed through agency adoption or independent adoption. In an agency adoption, the birth parents' rights are forfeited to the agency, which then studies and approves adoptive applicants and supervises each child's placement for at least six months before the court approves the adoption. In independent adoptions, birth parents place their children directly with adoptive parents with the assistance of a lawyer, physician or referral service, retaining their parental rights until 30 days after signing an Independent Adoption Placement Agreement (AD 924).

Specific procedures vary, but as a prospective parent, you must prove you can support the child and offer a safe, stable environment with private sleeping quarters. You are certain to be vetted with interviews, homestudy visits and criminal checks and will attend pre-adoption counselling and education. This process can take up to a year in an agency adoption, after which you and the child will go before a judge who will review your case and hopefully approve and finalise your adoption with an Adoption Decree. Independent adoption times vary based on when the biological parent makes her choice, but they must be investigated within 180 days of filing the petition.

California's maximum fees for public adoptions are $500 for agencies and $2,950 for independent adoptions. Private adoption costs can range between $1,000 and $50,000, depending on a host of factors, including the child's age, nationality, ethnicity or special needs and your willingness to wait. Once you adopt, your child is your financial responsibility, but there are means of financial assistance such as The Adoption Assistance Program and the state's medical insurance, Medi-Cal.

For a list of California adoption agencies, call 800 KIDS 4 US (800 543 7487). You can also start the adoption process or research local support groups by contacting the Department of Children and Family Services (888 811 112; adoptions@dcfs.lacounty.gov).

International Adoption

The procedures and costs for international adoption vary depending on which country you are working with, but as long as the foreign adoption is valid under the home country's laws, the adoption is recognised by the US. Children who have immigrated to the US to be adopted become citizens as soon as the adoption decree is final.

If you and your spouse are not US citizens, however, you will run into a major snag here. The visa programme recognises adoptive children who have lived with the parent for at least two years, before or after the adoption. This means you may have to leave the US for two years in order to bring your new child back with you, or if you recently adopted outside the US, will have to be with the child for two years before applying for your family visas.

LA Confidential

LA offers two marriage licences, one of which is confidential. This means your marriage records are permanently sealed from public view and even you must get a court order to view them or purchase additional certified copies at a later date. Some theorise this licence was created to protect Hollywood stars and starlets – back when they actually had some privacy to protect.

Marriage Certificate & Registration

To get legally married in California, you and your fiance must first visit an LA County registrar-recorder or county clerk office together to obtain a marriage licence. You will be asked to provide your California driver's licences or passports, proof of divorce (if either of you was divorced in the last two years) and a joint fee of $70. Same day licensing takes at least an hour at most LA offices, but if you time it right, you can be married the day you get your licence. If you do not get your licence 'solemnized' with a marriage ceremony within 90 days, your licence expires and you will need to apply for a new one. Your ceremony must be led by an 'officiant', who is defined as an adult priest, minister or rabbi of any religious denomination, an active or retired judge, commissioner or assistant commissioner of a court of record or justice court, or a deputy commissioner of civil marriages. You can also pay $35 to get anyone deputised to perform your ceremony on the day of your wedding (call 562 462 2081 for info on the 'deputy commissioner for a day' programme).

According to state law, your officiant must ask each of you whether you want to marry the other and you must each say 'I do'. Then your marriage licence is signed by the officiant and at least one adult witness, and the officiant files it with the recorder's office. Your licence should make its way through the system in four to six weeks, at which point your marriage is recorded and your $70 payment will be deposited. If you have not ordered copies of your licence, you should not hear from the recorder's office again, but if your paperwork gets caught in the system, you may receive warnings that your licence is going to expire. Generally, as long as you have had the ceremony within the 90 day period allotted, you need not worry. For information on licensing procedures or filing locations, call 562 462 2137.

Several offices of the registrar-recorder/county clerk also offer civil marriage by appointment for $25, but you must provide your own witness. The cost for a religious official is self-determined and therefore varies, but it can be several hundred dollars. A husband or wife can choose to take the other's last name or create a hyphenated name during the licensing, but if you have filed for any type of immigration status adjustment, it is best to wait to change you name until the procedure is complete. There is no residence or citizenship status requirement for marriage in the US, but if you are a foreign citizen who marries a US citizen and then applies for a visa or change in status (form I-485), your visa will be provisional for two years and the validity of your marriage may face enquiry during that time. In addition, if you are not in the US at the time of the marriage, there will likely be delays in joining your citizen spouse in the US (see p.42).

This vigilance is to discourage marriage for green card, which is not legal. To prepare for the bureaucratic task ahead, be sure to order extra official copies of your marriage licence when you file.

Domestic Partnership

Though same-sex couples still cannot get legally married, California has a registry for domestic partnerships that serves to assist couples in sharing employment benefits. Filing a Statement of Domestic Partnership does not, however, authorise your partner to make medical or financial decisions for you, nor will it give your partner the rights to make arrangements in case of your incapacity or death. Talk to an attorney about preparing legal documents that will protect the additional rights you and your partner would like to share. The fee for filing a Statement of Domestic Partnership is $20 and includes a certificate, while termination of partnership costs $15. For more information about the rights and procedures, contact the Registrar's office on 562 462 2060.

Taxes & Financial Planning

Once you are married, you must change your tax status to 'Married Filing Joint' or 'Married Filing Separate'. Most couples decide to file jointly to take advantage of tax benefits and credits, but there are cases were filing separately could save you money. Your best bet is to consult with an accountant about your options. If you change your name, inform Social Security by filing Form SS-5. Also be sure to add your spouse as a beneficiary in any life insurance policies you hold, as well as your 401(k) and IRA retirement accounts (p.55).

Certified Copies
You can order certified copies of LA County death ($12), birth ($14) and marriage ($13) certificates by mailing the appropriate application and fee to the registrar, along with a notarised sworn statement confirming your right to make the request. Find filing information at www.lavote.net or by calling 562 462 2137.

Death Certificate & Registration

In the unfortunate event you lose a friend or family member in LA, the manner of death will determine what steps you must take. You should always dial 911 for emergency service if you believe someone is dying, so that a licensed medical expert will be dispatched to either help the person or confirm the death and issue a death certificate. Inform 911 if you are confident the person has already passed, and they will send the police and a medical examiner to assist you. The examiner will release the body to the next of kin for burial service as soon as any necessary investigation is completed.

In cases where a death clearly requires no investigation, such as the death of someone terminally ill or infirm, your first call can be to the funeral home instead. If the deceased has not already made a 'pre-need' agreement with a funeral home regarding interment of his or her body, you can search the phone book or internet for one that caters to the deceased's personal beliefs. They will pick up the body from wherever it is and assist you with the next steps, including coordinating with the cemetery.

If your loved one's body is viable for donation and they have indicated they are donors, you may be contacted regarding donation (see p.112).

Cause Of Death

Heart disease, which includes stroke, high blood pressure and heart failure, continues to be the leading cause of death in the US and most of the world. Recent studies show an increase in survival thanks to improvements in healthcare, but project the associated price tag for this care to be $448.5 billion in 2008. Smoking and obesity, which are fighting for the top spots of avoidable causes of death, are both linked directly to heart disease.

Registering A Death

A death certificate is filed by a funeral director after the coroner has determined the cause of death. Certified copies of the certificate can be ordered through your funeral director or purchased from the registrar's office (562 462 2137).

In order to avoid identity theft, cancel all credit cards and charge accounts, cancel your loved one's licence at the Department of Motor Vehicles, and refuse any requests for duplicates; send copies of the death certificate to the credit-reporting bureaus Equifax, Experian and TransUnion. Do not include month and date of birth or home address in any obituary or release regarding the death.

Investigation & Autopsy

In cases of violent, sudden, or unusual deaths where a physician has not seen the deceased 20 days prior to death, an investigation, including autopsy, will be deemed necessary. This process usually takes no more than three days, but it is recommended you do not set a date for the funeral until the body is released. You can, however, contact a funeral home and inform them of your situation.

If the police do not deem an autopsy necessary, you may request one from the coroner's office for a charge of about $5,000. In addition, if a case is closed and the death is deemed natural, you can hire a private investigator or pathologist to investigate further.

Returning The Deceased To Country Of Origin

If your loved one would prefer to be laid to rest in his or her country of origin, it is wise to choose a funeral home that is experienced with the procedures that may entail. Its guidance will be invaluable as you navigate the logistics, which vary based on the country of origin. Also be aware that the additional cost, including first-class airfare for your loved one's remains, can add up to several thousand dollars.

The Finances Of Death

Death can be a very costly event. You'll likely pay nearly $5,000 for a full funeral, which may include transfer of remains, embalming and other preparation, use of ceremonial and viewing facilities, hearse, limousine and casket. The burial site could add another few thousand dollars. Cremation, which costs about $500, is a cheaper option and the remains can be scattered at sea (over 500 yards off the coast), on private property with written permission, kept at home or released to a cemetery. If you are next of kin and can prove you are unable to afford the cost of burial, contact the Department of the Coroner (323 343 0775) to apply for county disposition of remains.

LA does not have a 'blood money' system per say, but if your loved one had life insurance and did not commit suicide, the policy's noted beneficiary will receive money. In addition, you may receive insurance money as next of kin if a death was related to a work or car accident. You can also sue for wrongful death in civil court if you believe an individual or organisation was responsible due to wilful neglect, recklessness, misfeasance (commission of an illegal act), malfeasance (inadequate or improper performance) or non-feasance (failure to perform a required task). It is highly recommended you find a personal injury attorney specialising in your circumstances before taking any legal action.

Exposition Rose Garden

Happy Hours ◀

Many restaurants host a weekday happy hour to lure the workforce from the office to the bar. Typically, happy hours are held Monday to Friday from 15:00 to 18:00 with a menu of drink specials and half-price appetisers. It's one way to unwind with co-workers and can be a source of networking.

Working In Los Angeles

Los Angeles is no stranger to foreign workers. In fact, the city and surrounding areas were built and settled by a cross section of immigrants: English, French, Mexicans and Germans, just to name a few. Chinese labourers were brought to the city to help build the railroads and they, just like the Japanese, Russians and European Jews, created their own ethnic communities, many of which still exist today. Within the last 10 years, LA has succeeded New York City in becoming the nation's major port of entry for immigrants. LA is recognised as one of 11 US global cities boasting more than 20 'Fortune 1000' company headquarters within the city. Skilled and educated workers who arrive in Los Angeles with a work visa can find employment in a breadth of industries, from aerospace and agriculture to entertainment and tourism. LA is also the largest manufacturing centre in the western United States, according to the LA County Economic Development Corporation.

Salaries

It comes as no surprise that Los Angeles is an expensive place to live. According to the HR and financial consultancy firm Mercer, LA ranks second behind New York City as the nation's most expensive city. As a result, wages tend to be significantly higher than other parts of the country; in fact, the hourly minimum wage is over two dollars more than the $5.85 the federal government requires.

Work Ethic

America has always had a strong work ethic; one that can be credited to the Puritans. At one time the 'American Work Ethic' meant staying with the same company until retirement, putting in a full day's work for a full day's pay and calling in sick only when you were practically on death's doorstep. While career employees are rare these days and the occasional 'mental health' day is perfectly acceptable, Americans haven't strayed far from their roots. Unlike many other countries, where employees are given midday breaks, put in less than 40 hours a week and enjoy a month-long summer holiday, Americans are working harder than ever. It's not unusual to work 50 to 60 hours per week, and Americans have never been privy to midday breaks. As for summer holidays, the typical American is usually allotted a two-week vacation. With the invention of mobile phones, laptop computers and the ever-efficient Blackberry, many workers are finding themselves tethered 24-7 to electronic leashes.

Business Councils & Groups

Asian American Economic Development Enterprises	www.aaede.org
British American Business Council Los Angeles	www.babcla.org
California Chamber of Commerce	www.calchamber.com
California-Asia Business Council	www.calasia.org
Foreign Trade Association of Southern California	www.ftasc.org
Inland Empire Economic Partnership	www.ieep.org
Iranian Trade Association	www.iraniantrade.org
Italian Trade Commission	www.italtrade.com
Japan Business Association of Southern California	www.jba.org
Latin Business Association	www.lbausa.com
Los Angeles Business Council	www.labusinesscouncil.org
Los Angeles Urban League	www.laul.org
Orange County Business Council	www.ocbc.org
Singapore American Business Association	www.saba-usa.org
Sustainable Business Council	www.sustainablebc.org
Trade Commission of Mexico	www.mexico-trade.com

Working Hours

A typical working week is Monday to Friday from 08:00 to 17:00 or 09:00 to 18:00. Certain industries, along with salaried positions known as non-exempt status, often require more than a traditional 40 hour working week. Hourly employees who work overtime, either more than eight hours in a day or 40 hours per week, are paid time and a half as mandated by federal and state law. Full-time employees working in the private sector and those with government positions typically receive major holidays off, such as Thanksgiving and Christmas, plus an annual two-week paid vacation after one full year of employment. People in other industries, such as finance and securities, as well as entertainment and hospitality, can expect to work non-traditional hours.

Advance Your Career ◀
Networking is one of the most productive ways to advance your career. Expats often join social groups focused on their homeland in order to make connections within their industry. Once such group, Advance, helps Australians make business connections through events like performances and meet-ups. See www.advance.org.

Finding Work

There are plenty of jobs in LA waiting tables or working as a barista at one of the countless coffee houses, but landing your dream job in a more competitive field takes some finesse and determination. People from all over the world flock to Los Angeles to chase their professional dreams, and maybe more often to take advantage of the enviable climate.

While most think of LA as the 'entertainment capital of the world', many might be surprised to learn that it is the largest manufacturing centre in the western United States, boasts one of the world's busiest ports, is a major financial and banking centre and has the largest retail market in the nation.

Seasoned professionals, as well as those holding advanced degrees or with bilingual capabilities, are at a greater advantage than those with lesser skills and experience. Because of LA's large Latino population, fluency in Spanish is a plus; especially if you plan on securing work in the hospitality industry or with a government agency. And with the vibrant business dealings that take place between Southern California and nations across the Pacific, Mandarin, Japanese and Korean language skills are highly valued.

Finding Work Before You Come

When considering a job, keep in mind that a company willing to sponsor a foreign employee must essentially convince the government that no US resident could be found to fill the job. Applying for a green card on behalf of a foreign employee can be a long and difficult process that may involve several government agencies and lots of red tape. Still, don't be discouraged. With access to the internet, finding work prior to arriving in Los Angeles eases the burden of having to hit the pavement once you arrive.

Finding Work While You're Here

It's easy to set up job interviews and appointments if you're already in Los Angeles. One way to find employment and meet in person with company representatives is by

Hollywood & Highland Center

attending a scheduled career fair in the Los Angeles area. These 'job junkets' are held throughout the year and bring together several companies at one location, usually at a conference hotel or on a college campus. They're promoted in major newspapers, such as *The LA Times* and *Orange County Register*, as well as on local television and radio.

Foreigners already enrolled at one of Southern California's major universities should also visit the campus career centre, which can lead to many additional resources from local firms seeking talent.

Job Sites
• www.monster.com
• www.losangeles.
craigslist.org
• www.career
builder.com
• www.hotjobs.com
• www.jobing.com

Networking is another way to make contacts. You may want to frequent areas and establishments where people from certain industries tend to congregate. Entertainment movers and shakers, along with wannabes, are found inside hotel bars and lounges on the Westside of town (West Hollywood, Beverly Hills, Century City and Santa Monica). Downtown restaurants and lounges cater to financial workers from Monday to Friday after work. In general, bars and restaurants in areas with large workforces, such as Downtown, Santa Monica's downtown, Hollywood and West Hollywood, will have a surge of business people once the work day is over.

Seasonal Work

There are many opportunities to secure seasonal work in Los Angeles. Hotels, amusement parks, local attractions, and beach-area retailers often hire additional staff in April and May in preparation for the summer tourist season. Major retailers and parcel service companies (such as UPS, FedEx and DHL) are in need of seasonal employees during the Christmas holiday rush and begin their hiring processes in October.

Action!
A fun and interesting way to earn some money while you job hunt is to do some work as a film or television extra. Central Casting in Burbank hires people for non-speaking, 'background' roles for crowd scenes. Visit www.centralcasting. org for details of how to register.

Recruitment Agencies

Registering with a recruitment agency or temp agency is simple and can often lead to full-time work. You'll need to call and set up an appointment to meet with a representative, and you'll likely be asked to bring a copy of your resume as well as ID. General employment placement is available through a number of agencies, including AppleOne and Manpower, which typically look to staff office workers, typists, receptionists and warehouse workers.

Third Party Recruiters & Headhunters

To lessen the burden of your job search, consider enlisting the help of a fee-based headhunter or search firm. A headhunter works much in the same way as an agent does for an actor. Their main focus is to find you the right job. Headhunters don't get paid unless you are hired, at which point they earn a commission (paid by you) equal to about 20% to 30% of your first year's salary. Firms often specialise in a specific field, such as PeopleConnect (recruiting for the high-tech industry), Global Medical Staffing (healthcare), and Account Temps and Robert Half (finance and accounting).

Recruitment Agencies

Account Temps	800 803 8367	www.accounttemps.com
AppleOne Employment Service	310 477 0021	www.appleone.com
Blaine and Associates	310 785 0560	www.blainepersonnel.com
Career Strategies, Inc	213 385 0440	www.csi4jobs.com
Express Personnel Services	310 571 2200	www.expresspersonnel.com
Global Medical Staffing Inc.	800 697 9652	www.lagms.com
Manpower Incorporated	310 629 2686	www.manpower.com
Office Team	310 209 6811	www.officeteam.com
PeopleConnect	800 693 5430	www.peopleconnectstaffing.com
Robert Half Finance & Accounting	213 629 4602	www.roberthalffinance.com

Voluntary & Charity Work

As a major metropolis, Los Angeles has an abundance of volunteer opportunities. Hopeful helpers usually find opportunities in non-profit organisations, churches and synagogues and other charitable causes that provide outreach to those in need. Waiting lists vary, and typically a work visa is not necessary. A good place to begin is at www.volunteermatch.org and www.volunteerlosangeles.com, both of which offer large lists of volunteer opportunities.

Working As A Freelancer Or Contractor

Freelancing opportunities continue to grow, as many employers opt to outsource to avoid having to offer full-time benefits such as healthcare and paid vacation. The benefit to you, the freelancer, is flexibility. Should you be hired as a freelancer, you may then apply for a work visa as long as you are working full time and can provide a letter from your client (or employer) confirming the length of your assignment. Applying for membership of the Freelancers Union (www.freelancersunion.com) can help you find job opportunities in your field. Other websites that may be of use when looking for freelance work are www.craigslist.com and www.losangelesfreelancers.com.

Labour Law

California has one of the most stringent sets of labour laws in the nation. They are designed to protect the rights of workers and, as a result, you'll find that most employers in Los Angeles will not enter into a written contract with employees. Instead, most employees work 'at will', which means they can be terminated at any time and for any reason as long as it's not illegal (race, sexual orientation, etc). Employer responsibilities are outlined within the laws and disputes are typically settled through the courts or state agencies. Many of these workplace requirements are administered through the California Labor and Workforce Development Agency (www.labor.ca.gov), a department within the state government. Some companies may ask that you sign a contract, in which case you should review the document carefully and consider taking legal advice.

Equal Employment
Equal opportunity for employment is the law. An employer cannot discriminate against any individual based on race, colour, sexual orientation, religion, sex, national origin, age, disability, political affiliation or belief.

Wages

As of 1 January 2008, the California minimum hourly wage was $8.00. This is significantly higher than the federal level of $5.85 per hour. If you are hired on an hourly basis and work more than eight hours in a single day or more than 40 hours per week, you must be paid time and a half for additional hours worked. If you work more than 12 hours in a single day, you must be paid twice the standard rate. In addition, employees working seven consecutive days must be paid time and a half for the first eight hours of the seventh day, and double time for any additional hours after that. The seventh consecutive day law applies regardless of how many hours an employee worked in the preceding six days.

Pension Plans

A pension plan is a qualified retirement plan established by an employer, labour union, government or other organisation as a benefit to employees. It could be offered as a profit-sharing plan, 401(k) plan, stock bonus plan, an employee stock ownership plan (ESOP), or some other type of benefit that would provide retirement income or defer income until termination of covered employment or beyond. Although such plans are not guaranteed by law, the Employee Retirement Income Security Act is an American federal statute that establishes minimum standards for pension plans in private industry. For more information, see Financial Planning on p.55.

Health Plans

Many companies will offer health benefits to full-time employees (and their dependants) through a group health plan. If healthcare is not entirely covered by the employer, and it rarely is, an employee has the option of participating in the company's group plan by contributing a certain amount of money each month. The Consolidated Omnibus Budget Reconciliation Act (COBRA) is a scheme that allows workers to keep their group health benefits under certain circumstances, such as if they lose their job. See www.dol.gov/ebsa for details. For more information on health insurance see p.111.

Family & Medical Leave

The Family and Medical Leave Act (FMLA) and the California Family Rights Act (CFRA) allow eligible employees to take up to 12 weeks of paid or unpaid job-protected leave per year. During the approved leave, the employee's health, dental and vision benefits are maintained. In order to be eligible, a full-time employee must have been employed for a total of 12 months and have worked a minimum of 1,250 hours in the year prior to the date in which the leave is to begin. The two acts are for employees unable to work due to a serious health condition, those caring for a family member with a health condition, or for the birth, adoption, or foster care placement of a child.

Holiday Time

California law does not require employers to provide employees with paid holidays, close its doors on any holiday or give the day off to employees on any particular holiday. Hours worked on holidays, Saturdays and Sundays are treated like hours worked on any other day of the week. In a typical nine-to-five, 40 hour a week job, most businesses do provide paid holidays to their employees even though it is not a requirement.

Unemployment Benefits

California's Employment Development Department (EDD) offers an Unemployment Insurance programme for people who have lost their job through no fault of their own. To see if you qualify for Unemployment Insurance (UI), which is intended to be temporary assistance for qualified jobless workers, visit www.edd.ca.gov.

Unions

Most labour unions in the United States are members of one of two larger umbrella organisations: the American Federation of Labor-Congress of Industrial Organizations (AFL-CIO) or the Change to Win Federation. They are made up of working people with a goal to bring social and economic justice to the workplace. Depending on your vocation, you may be required to join the union, which requires dues. Many industries have unions, including those protecting the interests of law enforcement officers, sanitation workers, firefighters, culinary workers and even screenwriters.

Changing Jobs

The most common working visa used in the US is the H-1B visa, which is reserved for specialised professionals who already have a job offer from a company willing to sponsor them. If an employee with an H-1B visa wishes to change jobs while living in the US, he or she must obtain a new H-1B from the new employer. The L1 visa programme (intra-company business visa) does allow employees to transfer or change jobs as long as the US Citizenship and Immigration Services are notified of any such changes. Those working under a different visa programme should closely review the specific terms and conditions to see if changing employers is permitted. For more information visit the US Citizenship and Immigration Services website at www.uscis.gov.

Company Closure

The Worker Adjustment and Retraining Notification (WARN) act requires certain employers to give their workers 60 days' advance notice of any company closure or mass layoffs. The law is designed to give employees the chance to find another job. There are exceptions, so check www.edd.ca.gov/eddwarn.htm for specifics.

Bank Accounts

Establishing Credit ◄

If you've just landed in the United States, you'll want to establish credit as soon as possible. Even if you don't care for a credit card, having one in America is almost a right of passage. More importantly, it is a necessity when renting or buying a home, purchasing a car, and arranging utilities. First open a bank account and apply for a credit card. Then use the card to begin establishing credit. Make sure you pay the bill on time, and always pay more than the minimum amount required.

LA has plenty of local and national banks, as well as a few international institutions. Those banks with multiple branches include Washington Mutual, Bank of America, Wells Fargo and Downey Savings & Loan. Look for a bank that offers conveniences such as online banking, ATMs that are part of a larger network, and extended banking hours. It's advisable to choose a bank that is insured by the Federal Deposit Insurance Corporation (FDIC). Nearly all banks provide the same basic account options, including checking (current) and savings accounts. Some banks also offer 'Christmas' accounts where you set aside a certain amount to be spent on shopping during the holiday season. Most banks require a minimum monthly balance to avoid paying a penalty fee, and most offer overdraft protection. Even with overdraft protection, you'll likely pay a fee of around $10 to $25 to the bank for bouncing a cheque. In order to open a bank account you'll need two forms of identification. For US citizens it would be a driver's licence and social security card; for non-citizens, a passport and foreign licence is required along with another form of ID showing the person's name. A residence visa is not necessarily needed. US citizens can open an account online with most banks, while non-citizens must apply in person at a local branch. Most banks also have custodial savings accounts where the custodian, usually a parent or guardian, controls the account for the benefit of a minor.

Banks are open Monday to Friday from 09:00 to 18:00, and until 16:00 on Saturdays (some banks close earlier on Saturdays). Banks are becoming more competitive, so it pays to shop around.

Financial Planning

Independent Advisor? ◄

A broker who represents funds where a commission is earned (by the broker themselves) may try to convince you to purchase the funds they represent, thus making them more of a sales person than a true financial advisor.

The most common form of retirement savings is the 401(k). This investment package is usually set up by an employer and added to with a percentage of each paycheque. Taxes are withheld on the deposited amount until the money is taken out of the account. Often, the employer will match the employee's contribution to his or her 401(k). Another popular savings scheme is the ROTH IRA, which allows individuals to set up an investment package that takes money after it's been taxed. The advantage here is that when the investor is ready to withdraw, the money earned will be tax free. Keep in mind that most high-yield investments like those mentioned have penalties for withdrawing the money before a certain time.

If you plan to return to your home country after a few years, check to make sure that your financial institution permits withdrawals from non-US citizens that are not living in the country. Most do.

Considering the current state of the US economy, both citizens and expats might want to consider investing their money in overseas markets. Just make sure you're working with an experienced financial planner.

Banking Comparison Table

Name	Phone	Web	Online Banking	Telebanking
Bank of America	800 622 8731	www.bankofamerica.com	✗	✓
Capital One Direct banking	na	www.capitalone.com/directbanking	✓	✗
Citibank	800 374 9700	www.citibank.com	✗	✓
ING Direct	na	www.ingdirect.com	✓	✗
Union Bank of California	800 796 5656	www.uboc.com	✗	✓
US Bank	800 872 2657	www.usbank.com	✗	✓
Wachovia	800 922 4684	www.wachovia.com	✓	✓
Washington Mutual Bank	800 788 7000	www.wamu.com	✗	✓
Wells Fargo Bank	800 869 3557	www.wellsfargo.com	✗	✓
World Savings	866 467 3776	www.worldsavings.com	✗	✓

Financial Advisers

Ameriprise Financial	800 297 7378	www.ameriprise.com
Charles Schwab	866 232 9890	www.schwab.com
Merrill Lynch	800 637 7455	www.ml.com
T. Rowe Price	877 804 2315	www.troweprice.com

Taxation

According to the US Constitution, Congress has the power to 'lay and collect taxes', which are then used to pay debts and provide for the welfare of citizens. The tax rates tend to be lower in the United States than other developed countries throughout Europe and Asia, but nearly everyone – citizen or not – pays taxes either as a homeowner, consumer, employer, employee or all of the above. If you live or work in LA County, you can expect to pay federal, state, city and county taxes. Federal and state income taxes are deducted from your paycheque, and the amount is determined by how much you make and how many dependants you claim. You must file a tax return with the Internal Revenue Service (IRS) on or before 15 April each year. This involves a series of forms to show proof of your earnings along with any tax deductions you may be entitled to. A certified public accountant (CPA) or tax attorney can help you, as each year the government seems to alter the rules just enough to drive you mad.

Sales Tax

Sales tax generally applies, but is not limited, to the following items:
• Drug sundries, toys, hardware, and household goods
• Alcoholic beverages
• Carbonated soft drinks and mixers
• Carbonated and effervescent water
• Tobacco products
• Dietary supplements
• Medicated gum
• Petrol (gasoline)
• Soaps or detergents
• Cameras and film
• Clothing
• Ice
• Sporting goods
• Nursery stock
• Pet food and supplies

Restaurant Tipping

When dining at a restaurant, a 15 to 20% gratuity is the going rate. The best way to figure this out in Los Angeles County is to double the tax, which would be a 16.5 % tip.

Additional Taxes

Aside from income tax, you'll also have to pay sales tax on many purchases. In Los Angeles County, sales tax is currently 8.25%. Clothes, toys, most household goods, books and publications, over-the-counter medicines and cosmetics are all taxable. Groceries you buy in a shop are not taxed, but food consumed on the premises, such as at a restaurant, comes with a generous side order of tax. Also, if you make an online purchase from a retailer that has outlets located anywhere in California, you will have to pay sales tax on those items. If the retailer does not have a shop anywhere in the state, then no sales tax is charged. Even celebrities who are accustomed to being lavished with gifts are told they now have to pay up. Gift baskets, also known as swag, are as much a part of the awards hoopla as red carpets and air kisses. However, a recent law requires that anyone who receives more than $27,000 in swag must count it as additional income.

You'll also pay property taxes twice a year (December and April) if you own a home or real estate. Unless you have an impound property tax account (in other words, they are part of your monthly mortgage), you will receive an invoice for both 'payments'. The LA County Tax Collector usually mails these out in late October or early November.

Cost Of Living

Apples (per pound)	$2.00
Aspirin (24)	$3.00 - $5.00
Bananas (per pound)	$0.70
Beef (fresh, per pound)	$5.50
Beer (six pack)	$6.00
Bottled Water (1 litre)	$1.50
Bread (loaf)	$2.50
Burger (fastfood, takeaway)	$2.00
Bus fare (day pass)	$5.00
Camera film	$5.00
Can of dog food	$1.00
Can of soft drink	$1.00
Cappuccino	$3.50
Car Rental (small, per day)	$45.00
Carrots (per pound)	$1.25
Chicken (fresh, per pound)	$3.00
Chocolate bar	$1.00
Cigarettes (pack of 20)	$5.00
DVD (new release)	$20.00
Eggs (dozen)	$2.00
Fish (fresh, per pound)	$3.00 - $10.00
Gasoline (per gallon)	$3.00 - $4.00
Milk (per gallon)	$3.00 - $4.00
Movie Ticket (adult)	$10.00
Newspaper (international)	$4.00
Newspaper (local)	$0.50 - $1.50
Pizza (large, take away)	$15.00 - $20.00
Postage Stamp	$0.42
Postcard	$0.50 - $1.00
Potatoes (per pound)	$3.00
Rice	$1.00
Soup (can)	$2.00
Sugar (per pound)	$3.00
Toothpaste (per tube)	$3.00 - $5.00

Legal Issues

Every statute, court decision or government action is upheld by the Constitution. The California judicial system reviews cases that occurred within the state. If a crime happened in more than one state, it is usually tried in a federal court. California has both elected and appointed judges. The US judicial system also allows the option to appeal, and these cases are always tried under a different judge and jury. Resident expats fall under the same laws as citizens. The most pressing legal issue that a non-national might face is the immigration process. Subtleties in immigration law change quite often. If you plan on becoming a citizen or obtaining permanent residency, you should look into getting an immigration lawyer. Finding one is always a daunting task and most people rely on recommendations. If you're still unsure, the State Bar of California website (www.calbar.co.gov) maintains a legal specialist search.

Making A Will

The state of California recognises any foreign will that is deemed valid in the place it was drafted and signed. If you plan on drafting a will while in California, your options vary depending on the size of your estate. If you don't own much, but would still like to stipulate where your assets go when you pass away, the State Bar of California offers a fill-in-the-blanks will form. Go to www.calbar.ca.gov and search for 'statutory will form'. Not all wills are simple, however, and drafting a more complex will usually requires the help of a lawyer. For a will to be legal, it must be signed by two non-affiliated witnesses.

Divorce

Nobody's Fault
California was the first state to champion 'no-fault' divorce when the Family law Act of 1969 was signed by Governor Ronald Reagan. It took effect on 1 January 1970, abolishing the old common law action for divorce and replacing it with the proceeding for the dissolution of marriage on the grounds of irreconcilable differences.

Under state law in California, couples can divorce on two grounds: irreconcilable differences or incurable insanity. Most opt for the former, as the latter requires medical proof. The only residency requirements are that either you or your spouse have lived in California for six months and your county for three months before filing for divorce. If you do not meet these requirements, you could still be eligible for a legal separation or annulment. The length of proceedings varies, depending on how quickly both parties agree to the terms, but a judgment cannot be passed until at least six months after the initial request for divorce. Assets are divided depending on whether they are communal (such as property acquired during marriage, and divided equally) or separate (such as personal gifts, which are not usually included in the hearing). It is worth noting that debt (including credit card debt) often falls under community, so although your name may not be on the card, you could be liable for half of any outstanding debt. If you have children, after filing for divorce there may be restrictions placed on taking them out of the state, or relocating them without court permission. Child support, or spousal support as it is known in California, is determined by a number of factors including the length of marriage, income and even the amount of time a parent usually spends with their child. For more information on the process and links to legal teams, the State Bar of California website (www.calbar.ca.gov) is very comprehensive.

Crime

As you'd expect, the more affluent areas of the city tend to have low crime rates while the opposite holds true for low-income areas. Much of the crime is gang related. Petty offences could result in monetary fines, while more serious violations (misdemeanours) could require time in the local jail. Breaking a state law or committing a felony is likely to lead to detention in a state or federal prison (depending on the severity of the crime) and, for expats, possible deportation. Each tier of the legal system has its own unique set of judicial processes based on the specific statutes within that tier of government. The accused has rights, including trial by a jury of their peers, access to legal counsel either hired by the defendant or appointed by the courts, and the right to appeal.

Housing

The housing market has finally levelled off, though it remains expensive compared with most other parts of the country. Until recently, houses were selling before they hit the market, even in some of the more dismal areas. The seller had all the power and serious buyers couldn't afford to hesitate. The roles are starting to reverse. Housing prices have dropped, and listings typically stay on the market much longer. The upside to house hunting in Los Angeles is that it's a huge city. There is a lot of inventory and all kinds of choices, from brand new tract homes or vintage bungalows to classic Spanish-style architecture and lofts housed in historic buildings. Your choice of location also depends on how much you are willing to spend. You can live by the beach, in one of the many revitalised downtown areas, in a suburban neighbourhood, near the foothills, or on a ranch. If you're going to rent a house or apartment, you may be asked to sign a one-year lease. You may also be required to pay the first and last month's rent and a cleaning deposit at the time of signing. Usually, the cleaning deposit is returned at the end of the contract along with the last month's rent, as long as the property is in good condition. Also, don't hesitate to negotiate the monthly rent, especially if the rental market is soft and saturated.

Your Right To Privacy
Your landlord's right to enter your accommodation is limited. It is legal in the case of emergencies, for necessary or agreed-upon improvements, in order to show the unit to prospective tenants, buyers, lenders or hired workers, or with a court order.

Renting In Los Angeles

In a city this diversified by area, common factors in choosing where to live tend to be price, view and the general vibe of the area. Many locals commute over an hour each way so they can live by the ocean and enjoy the funky, laid back pace of Venice Beach (p.93), while others make similar commutes for the gritty, artsy city life of Downtown (p.73). Those with the funds commute from more exclusive areas like the winding, lush Hollywood Hills (p.76) and Bel-Air (p.68) or the beach escape of Malibu (p.78).

Many Angelenos would love to make any of those commutes, but are relegated by budget to the less expensive San Fernando Valley. There are, however, tricks to getting into a more exclusive area without breaking the bank. If you are flying solo, for example, a guest house may be your ticket into an exclusive area. Another option is to choose more affordable areas nearby the area you like. As you get to know LA, you will find rents can change with the crossing of a street. Venice Beach is a strong example, as the entire area is a mesh of expensive and inexpensive blocks. This intermingling may allow you to live in an area that seems out of your price range, but be aware of safety if you go this route. If you are interested in an area but are concerned about safety, check with the local police department or even chat to a local officer.

If you are hoping to get your child into a particular public school, this may trump any reason to choose a neighbourhood. As mentioned in the Education section (p.124), the LA public school your child attends is determined by address. With new schools currently being built, however, be sure to do some research about expected boundary changes.

If you come to the US on a work visa through a large corporation, it may offer you the services of a relocation broker, in addition to a relocation reimbursement. If you are here for a short visit, the company may even supply a fully furnished short-term apartment, like those in the Oakwood complexes in the Marina, Woodland Hills and Burbank (see www.oakwood.com).

Finding A Home

Most newcomers start their hunt by signing up with an internet service such as Westside Rentals (www.westsiderentals.com) and visiting www.craigslist.com. If you already have a neighbourhood in mind, you may do just as well driving around and looking for rental or lease signs and calling on the places you like. If you have any friends in LA, put the word out, especially if you are looking to set up a share. Shares will often be listed on the rental sites and Craigslist, but you may prefer a match made through personal referral.

Almost endless housing options

PETS O.K.
NO LEASE REQ.
EASY MOVE-IN

Be aware of how you present yourself when you see an apartment and meet the landlord. If you see something you like, you are wise to jump on it fast and it will help your case if the landlord takes you seriously.

The LA Housing Department (LAHD) monitors and finances 'affordable housing' by reducing rents in private housing for low-income tenants and public housing for low-income families, the elderly and people with disabilities. There are several providers to consider and you may apply to more than one, but the Department of Housing and Urban Development (HUD) provides access to more affordable rentals than any of its competitors and has one waiting list for all of its properties. Public housing options are described at length on www.hud.gov and you can find more information by calling the Housing Authority of LA (HACLA) at 213 252 2500.

Rent Disputes

If you find yourself in a dispute with your landlord, it is not advisable to hold your rent payment as ransom. That may give him or her the right to charge you late penalties and evict you, which can create problems when procuring another lease. Review The California Tenants Book (available online at www.dca.ca.gov/publications/landlordbook), which outlines your rights, your landlord's obligations and what steps you may take. If you and your landlord cannot work out the dispute and you are legally in the right, you may decide to take it up in a small claims court. If you want to stay in your rental, however, this may not be the best course of action. If you feel you have been discriminated against for reasons such as race, colour, sex or religion, however, you can get information about your rights and lodge a complaint with the Housing Rights Center at 800 477 5977.

Real Estate Agents

With so many rental websites and services covering LA, most locals only turn to a real estate agent when they are ready to buy. Even then, it is possible to complete your search without an agent by using the *LA Times Sunday Edition*, online listing services and even driving around. Unless you find a home that is 'For Sale by Owner', you will ultimately encounter an agent. A real estate agent must pass an exam to be licensed by the state, and will often work with a brokerage company. The agent is paid commission by the seller, at a negotiable 6% rate. Seller's agents are paid to sell a home, not find you one, but in helping you, they help themselves. You may feel more comfortable shopping with a buyer's agent, who has agreed to represent you instead of the seller. Most agents specialise in certain areas or neighbourhoods, so if you meet one through a house you are interested in, you may end up sticking with them. If you are not seeing anything you like on your own, however, your best reference for an agent will be a friend or colleague. There are also several reputable national brokerage firms who can pair you with one of their agents.

Snapshot Averages
These average monthly two-bedroom rents allow a snapshot view of how area can affect your rent, but be advised that a two-bedroom in Downtown is most likely an apartment, while in Studio City it could be a duplex, apartment or house.
Van Nuys (central Valley): $1,483
Koreatown: $1,541
Granada Hills: $1,676
Culver City: $1,891
Pasadena: $1,896
Hollywood: $1,997
Silver Lake: $2,115
Studio City (east Valley): $2,138
Calabasas (west Valley): $2,143
West LA: $2,240
Santa Monica: $2,447
Downtown: $2,483
W Hollywood: $2,661
Beverly Hills: $3,063
Bel-Air: $3,400
Malibu: $4,567

Real Estate Agents			
Alison Winston	310 277 0461	www.alisonwinston.com	Residential
Anna Solomon	310 820 9306	www.larealtor4u.com	Residential
Anne Austin	323 462 0867	www.coldwellbanker.com	Residential
Century 21	877 221 2765	www.century21.com	Major Broker
Coldwell Banker	800 500 4053	www.californiamoves.com	Major Broker
Marcia Glow	310 404 4807	www.hiltonhyland.com	Residential
Marcus & Millichap	818 907 0600	www.marcusmillichap.com	Commercial Agency
Maurice Kozak	818 325 8261	www.osterandkozak.com	Residential
Todd Nathanson	818 380 9966	www.cbm1.com	Commercial Leasing

Month-To-Month Living ◀

If you find a month-to-month or even week-to-week rental, you will probably encounter a periodic rental agreement instead of a lease. This agreement outlines your tenancy rights much as a lease does, but differs in that it does not have an end date. Instead, each payment made extends your agreement for one more cycle and you or your landlord must give each other at least one pay-cycle's notice before breaking the agreement.

The Lease

A rental lease is a binding legal agreement between the tenant and landlord, and you will rarely encounter a landlord willing to negotiate the terms of your lease. If you have a roommate, he or she must also sign the lease. Most leases cover a one-year period, though you may find shorter or longer term leases. Rent is usually due on the first of each month, with penalties for late payment. Unless your lease specifies early outs, your landlord may hold you to the entire length of the contract.

Your lease will identify the premises being rented and which utilities and maintenance will be covered by the landlord. It will also outline limits on use and occupancy, length of rental, payment of rent, security deposit, utilities, subletting and extended absence, pets, the landlord's right to access the premises and grounds for termination of contract. When you sign the lease, you will give your landlord the predetermined deposit, often equal to one month's rent if you have reasonable credit history. If you have not yet built credit in the US, you will be asked for a larger deposit. When you move out, your landlord will inspect the premises again and, barring any undue wear and tear, should return that deposit within 21 days.

Many areas in LA are rent controlled, which means your annual rent increase is controlled by the city; currently this is held at 5%. You must be given at least 30 days' notice before any changes take affect. In addition, your landlord can only terminate your residency for an approved reason. If you are not in a rent-controlled area, your landlord can make any increase or terminate your residency, but must give you 30 days' notice for a 10% (or less) increase and 60 days' notice if the increase is greater than 10%.

Housing Abbreviations

1/2 bath	no shower or bath
3+1, 2+1, etc	bedrooms + bathrooms
a/c or air cond	air conditioned
adj	adjacent
aoc	on approved credit
apt	apartment
ba or bth	bathroom
balc	balcony
bldg	building
bmt, bsmt	basement
br, bd, bdr or bdrm	bedroom
cbl	cable
dep	deposit
dr or din	dining room
dup	duplex
elev	elevator
f/p	fireplace
furn	furnished
gar or grg	garage
gdn	garden
hdwd	hardwood floors
kit	kitchen
lndry	laundry
ocnfrnt	ocean front
off or offc	office
oh	open house
ren or renov	renovated
rf	roof
st	studio apartment
swm pool	swimming pool
terr	terrace
w/d	washer/dryer
w/w	wall to wall
wic	walk in closet

Main Accommodation Options

The amount locals spend on rent varies greatly in LA, and there is more to determining price than type of rental. Location and condition of the rental are major factors, so while paying more for an apartment than a house may seem counterintuitive, you may find yourself choosing to do just that.

Apartment/house sharing: It is not uncommon for locals to team up with friends or strangers to get more bang for their buck. Whether it's a duplex, an apartment or a house, a one-room will often be less than half the rent of a two-bedroom in the same area. In other words, instead of spending $1,000 on a Santa Monica studio the size of your bathroom back home or $2,000 on a one-bedroom with more amenities (like a kitchen), you might prefer sharing a two-bedroom for $2,400. You may even find a share where your family uses a four-bedroom house and someone else is in the guest house. Just be sure to define which rooms are public spaces and remember that everyone living in rented property must be on the lease.

Apartment: As in all cities, LA flats come in all shapes and sizes. Studios, bachelors and lofts are the most basic rental, offering a bathroom and main room that may or may not have a kitchen space. You will find high-rise apartment buildings in areas such as Downtown or The Wilshire Corridor, as well as smaller complexes in West Hollywood, Santa Monica or The Valley that have two floors situated around a pool or common area. The latter tend to be slightly more social. Your apartment complex will likely offer shared amenities such as coin-operated washing machines, a carpark, swimming pool, roof deck, central air conditioning and a doorman.

Duplex or Quad: These split properties can be a divided home or multiple freestanding buildings, with each portion being rented by different people. They are very popular in Beverly Hills Adjacent, West Hollywood, Miracle Mile and certain parts of Hollywood and Los Feliz. They certainly offer more independence than an apartment, but you may find yourself living above your landlord. Prices vary, with an 'upper' (second floor) three-bedroom ranging from $2,800 to $4,000. 'Lowers' are usually a few hundred less. These often require at least a one-year lease.

Condo/Townhouse: LA does offer its share of condos, but many have rules about how many years the owner may rent out their units, making apartment rentals more common. You will usually find condo listings mixed in with apartments and prices are comparable.

Lease Law
Subletting, or renting all or part of your rented accommodation to someone else, is illegal without the express permission of your landlord, and it is wise to get that permission in writing. Your lease may even include penalties for hosting overnight guests for longer than a specified period, because no landlord wants the responsibility of a tenant who has not signed on the dotted line.

Guest house: Freestanding rentals near a main house afford you the opportunity to live alone on a budget – if you can land one. Though you are on a shared property, the extent of your relationship with the main house occupants depends on the space and your choice. Most are comparable to a studio, but some offer multiple rooms, a patio, a city view or a shared pool. This is one way to live in a swanky area like the Hollywood Hills or on a fancy estate in Beverly Hills. Some are fully furnished. Prices start at around $900 but can get up into the thousands.

House/villa: The price and size of a house varies enormously by area. A two-bedroom with one bathroom might be as much as $6,000 monthly in Malibu or $2,400 in Venice, while you can find a four-bedroom with three baths in Woodland Hills for $4,000. That $4,000 will barely cover a two-bedroom in Beverly Hills 90211, let alone in Bel-Air, where the monthly tag may exceed $21,000. Some may even come furnished.

Other Rental Costs

Your monthly rental fee is not the only cost associated with your new digs. Before you move in, your landlord will usually request a deposit, normally equal to one month's rent, that should be returned when you move out, barring undue damage to the property. If you or your roommate has a pet, the deposit may be higher. Once you move in, you will likely be responsible for set up, maintenance and monthly payment on utilities such as electricity, phone, internet and cable. Water and gas services, which include municipal service charges, are sometimes covered by your landlord, but not always. Your landlord is, however, always responsible for gardening fees and covering wear and tear maintenance of the property, which means taking care of repairs unless the damage is caused by your irresponsibility. LA is unique in that you may also be responsible for procuring your own refrigerator and, if there are hook-ups, a washing machine and dryer. If you live in an apartment complex, there may be a coin-operated washer and dryer onsite, but many people have to use local laundromats. Depending on your neighbourhood, you may also have to pay a monthly parking fee to your landlord or purchase an annual street parking permit from the city. Your lease should address the majority of the issues.

Buying Property

If you can afford the initial investment, buying is certainly more cost effective than renting. Instead of losing your money to rent, you are investing money in your future, and home ownership will also avail you of tax deductions. That said, LA has not been a buyers' market for some time. In fact, about twice as many locals rent as buy. Monthly payments may be as much as twice your rent, while the initial downpayment and closing costs alone may be prohibitive. Your downpayments may cover 10% or 15% of the cost and can easily surpass 25%. That means if you can somehow find a $300,000 home, you may need $30,000 or even $75,000 to buy it.

Of course, if you are looking to buy a house, the toughest part in this scenario will be finding a $300,000 home. For some time, new families have flocked to the San Fernando Valley and outskirts like Valencia, which can be more reasonably priced and offer more space for less money than high-demand areas like Santa Monica or West Hollywood. But as LA grows, so does the distance to affordable prices. Those who once looked to Valencia, which is about 30 miles from West Hollywood, may now have to look twice as far.

Community Service
Check out the
Communities
section on www.
explorerpublishing.
com, where you can
post comments, join
groups, network with
other expats and
search for updates.

The currently unstable market may create interesting opportunities for those on the cusp of being able to afford buying. The mortgage system has returned to more stringent and conservative loan requirements, which has slowed sales. Also, many foreclosed homes are returning to the market. You can already find deals on foreclosed property for auction and regular selling prices may also start to fall, especially in recently developed areas like Downtown, where some fear all the exciting new loft complexes will remain empty.

Anyone can buy property in the US and if you have the cash, you can pay in full, but mortgage purchases are more common and pose hurdles for anyone without a good US credit history. Property can mean a parcel of land, a house and the land it is on, a condo and its shared property or an apartment in a complex. Many areas have building ordinances that might specify things such as the number of permissible storeys or the style of home you may build. Occasionally, you will find an owner who is willing to lease to you until you are ready to buy, but that is rare.

With a bit of digging, you can find public assistance programmes for home buyers, each with its own assistance plans and eligibility requirements. While some may assist with downpayments, others offer preferred loans. The California Housing Finance Agency (CalHFA) works with lenders to provide below-market interest rate mortgage programmes to low income, first-time homebuyers. If you are not a US citizen, contact one of its lenders who will then help determine if you are an 'eligible alien'. CalHFA (310 342 1250; www.calhfa.ca.gov) also offers information on a handful of other assistance programmes.

The Process

The first step towards buying a new home is figuring out your credit and financial situation. As a guideline, some experts recommend your house cost one and a half to two and a half times your annual salary, with monthly mortgage payment at less than 30% of your monthly income. This is easier said than done in LA, so be wary of overextending yourself. Once your finances are in order, contact your local bank about getting pre-approved for a loan. The bank will review your finances and issue a pre-approval letter that confirms your buying capabilities. You will want your deposit money ready for use at least 60 days before you start Escrow and the mortgage process (p.65). With the pre-approval letter in hand, you can begin your house hunt, which starts with determining the area and housing that suit your budget. Once you find the house you want to buy, you work with your agent to make an offer. You may decide to offer more than the asking price if the house is clearly in high demand, or less if you know the sellers are anxious to get out. A written offer includes the address and description of the property being purchased, your offered price, terms of payment, a seller's promise to provide clear title (ownership), your target closing date, plans for the proration (division) of utilities and payment of closing costs, specifics of your downpayment and an expiration date for the offer. It will also leave room for physical and legal contingencies and include a provision for a final walk-through inspection right before closing. The seller does not have to accept your offer, but if he or she does not, you may be able to negotiate and come to agreement on another offer. Your offer will have more weight if you are able to include the loan pre-approval letter from your bank or are paying cash. Once your written offer is accepted by the seller, it becomes a binding sales agreement. You will pay the agreed deposit, usually 3%, and the house goes into 'escrow'.

Your offer will define the length of escrow, which is the term in which the sale is pending. During this time, it is your right to inspect the house and the seller's obligation to make or provide for any necessary repairs on the roof or operating systems, though you may decide to take the house 'as is'. Your agent will likely have contacts for inspectors, but you can also find information and referrals on the California Real Estate Inspection Association website (www.creia.org). You will also use this time to get your mortgage in order, which will run much more smoothly if your downpayment has already been in your bank account for at least 60 days. Finally, if you are buying a condo, the seller must provide co-op documents for your approval. If something goes wrong, you can back out during escrow for any reason, but you will probably lose your deposit. If all goes well, however, your escrow agent will have you and the seller sign on the dotted line about 50 times on your closing date and will then file your Deed of Trust with the County Recorder. You will be the proud owner of a new home, with the keys to prove it.

A Helping Hand
Los Angeles Utilities (www.losangelesutilities. com) is a fee-based service that allows you to compare and order utilities and home services – perfect if you're short of time or want to arrange things before you arrive in LA.

Buying To Rent

If you are buying residential property to rent, it is considered a residential purchase for a 'non-owner'. When you set up your financing, there will be slightly increased rates and fees. If your new purchase has multiple units and you plan on living in one and renting out the other, that would be a 'two-unit owner occupied unit' and there would be no additional fees. Be warned that as the owner you are responsible for your property and those on it. That means covering maintenance issues, but also presents an insurance issue. If you are buying commercial property such as an apartment complex, you should work with a commercial agent and comply with a different set of procedures compared to residential buying.

Selling Property

The resale value of your property depends on many of the factors that matter to you as a buyer, including the surrounding area, local schools and property taxes, government services, view and the state of the home.

You may decide to sell your home without an agent to save yourself around $10,000 in fees. About 20% of sales are 'For Sale By Owner' and it is doable, but there are advantages to having an agent. In addition to knowing how to price your home, an agent will handle advertising and multiple listing services (MLS), which means other agents can see your listing. They also serve as your middle man with the buyer, weeding out candidates and negotiating price. With or without an agent, the first steps in selling your home are doing a professional pre-sale inspection, making any home improvements you can afford, pricing your home and then preparing your seller disclosures. Once that is completed, the marketing, showcasing and negotiations begin. Selling your home can have major federal and state tax implications, but there are also several stipulations to guard your money. Your best bet is to review your sale with a tax specialist to learn what you will be facing.

Don't Borrow Trouble ◀

Los Angeles Housing Department's 'Don't Borrow Trouble' campaign is geared at protecting home buyers and owners from predatory lenders. Some lenders will not hesitate to take advantage of your naivety about loans, perhaps charging excessive fees with high interest rates you may not be able to afford. Be sure to understand the terms and conditions of your loan before you sign on the dotted line. For free advice, call 800 477 5977.

Mortgages

The mortgage industry is facing a major upheaval and may be completely different by the time you arrive. To qualify for a mortgage, you must meet certain credit and finance standards. In past years, these standards suddenly became much looser. Many 'sub prime' lenders were offering riskier mortgages to borrowers with credit problems, which ultimately didn't work out for anyone. Now, overextended buyers are losing their homes to foreclosure at astonishing rates, while their loan providers are not recouping their investment. Even large providers like Countrywide are going out of business or being bought out.

Criteria are once again becoming tougher. If you are looking for a competitively priced financing package, you must have a strong credit score based on your US credit history and be able to document your income for at least the last two years. Unfortunately for newly arrived expats, having no credit history is not the same thing as having good credit. Before you start house hunting, review your score by visiting www.freecreditreport.com and be sure to file any corrections to your history with all three credit websites (www.equifax.com, www.experian.com and www.transunion.com), which takes 30 days to process. Lenders today are looking for a credit score above 660. If your score is below 620, expect a major challenge. That said, you may still be able to procure a loan with poor credit or without proving your earning history, but you will pay substantial penalties in terms of higher rate and fees.

The standard fixed-rate loan is 30 years, with the entire balance paid off over that time in regular, fixed payments. Longer and shorter term loans are available as well. In an Adjustable Rate Mortgage (ARM), your interest rate is adjusted according to current national interest rates, which means your monthly payments fluctuate with the market. In most cases there is no penalty for paying off your loan early, but if you miss payments on your loan your house will be repossessed and become the property of the bank.

Securing the best loan for you will take research. You can keep abreast of what brokers and local banks are offering in the *LA Times Sunday* real estate section and by shopping around, but you can also get competing offers from websites such as www.lendingtree.com.

Mortgage Providers

Change My Rate	866 869 9992	www.sevarghomeloans.com
Lending Tree	800 555 8733	www.lendingtree.com
Marc Cohen	310 777 5401	www.cohenfinancialgroup.com
Orion Finance Corp	909 418 8868	www.carloslending.com
Roger Gertz, Fallbrook Financial Services	818 657 2100	www.fallbrookfinancialservices.com
Terri Shnitzer	818 773 6170	http://countrywide.dorado.com/terrishnitzer

Other Purchasing Costs

When your sale closes, you will have to pay a closing cost of 2% to 5% of the sale, payable in cash. The payment is often tied into your mortgage and may cover loan fees, prepaid interest, inspection fees, appraisal, mortgage insurance, hazard insurance, title insurance and documentary stamp. The seller may be responsible for covering the broker's commission of about 6%, transfer taxes, documentary stamps, title insurance and prorated property taxes. Your offer will outline the breakdown of these payments. Once you buy your home, everything in it is your responsibility. You are responsible for paying your portion of the prorated taxes, all utilities, basic maintenance and monthly mortgage payments, which include monthly interest, taxes and the home owner's and mortgage insurance. Some of these expenses will be recouped in tax deductions.

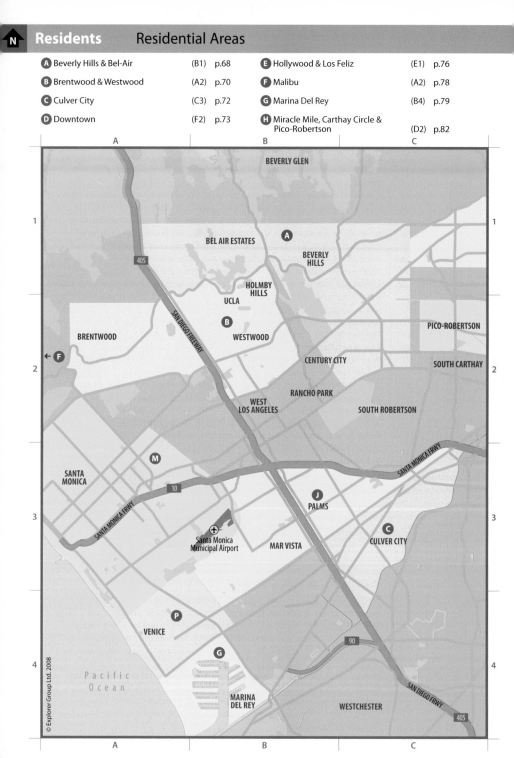
© Explorer Group Ltd. 2008

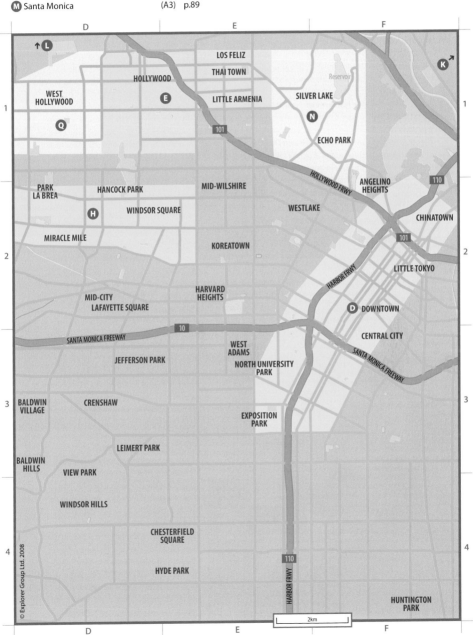

© Explorer Group Ltd. 2008

Area **A** *p.66*
See also Map 4

Best Points
Quiet, suburban lifestyle in a lush, mountainous environment offering amazing views.

Worst Points
Prices are prohibitive. The secluded, suburban lifestyle is not for everyone.

Beverly Hills & Bel-Air

Once dubbed the 'Golden Triangle', the super swank Beverly Hills, Bel-Air and Holmby Hills have since been promoted to the 'Platinum Triangle'. This is where you will find the homes of the rich and famous and all the shopping, nightlife and action to keep them – and tourists – happy. Even though traffic curves through residential areas, many neighbourhoods have a decidedly suburban feel, especially in the hills and foothills.

Accommodation

Many homes in this area offer private driveways, backyards, pools, tennis courts and unbelievable views. Some, like Hugh Hefner's famous Playboy mansion, are concealed by property walls and foliage. If you do not need all the space and amenities of a Hugh Hefner, however, you may find homes in this area selling for only a few million or even under a million, though they are few and far between. Beverly Hills in particular offers less pricey areas with condos, small homes and duplexes located just south and east of its infamous Rodeo Drive shopping area. This area has a strong art deco flair and a duplex unit around Doheny may rent for as much as $3,000 to $4,000 a month, while the whole duplex may sell for $1.5 to $3 million. As with buying, rental prices depend on location, view, style and amenities, among other things. You will pay a pretty penny, for example, to lease one of the fully furnished mansions frequented by stars and power players coming to LA for long or short-term stays.

Shopping & Amenities

The further up into the hills you move, the less convenient shopping for necessities will become. There are a few fancy mini-malls with grocery stores and other amenities tucked into the residential areas, like The Glen Center on Beverly Glen, but many locals find their nearest grocers around thoroughfares like Wilshire and Santa Monica or even 'over the hill' in the San Fernando Valley. Those on the Westside in Bel-Air may find the Westwood and Brentwood shopping areas most convenient, but Beverly Hills has its own famed shopping scene just east of the Wilshire and Santa Monica intersection. In the sometimes pretentious area surrounding the Rodeo Drive pedestrian block, you will find mainstream shops like Gap and Victoria's Secret now intermingle with the upscale designer boutiques, speciality shops and department stores for which the area has always been known. You will also find a Ralphs and Rite-Aid in the neighbourhood, with the Sunday farmers' market at the nearby Civic Center. It is of note that the famed Beverly Center (p.307) is not actually in Beverly Hills, but rather on Beverly Drive in WeHo.

Entertainment & Leisure

If you are not in the mood for shopping, The Beverly Hills Civic Center often has music and family events going on, and The Museum of Television and Radio (www.mtr.org) hosts regular events and series about the business. If it is a beautiful day, you might enjoy having tea and a tour at Greystone Mansion (www.greystonemansion.org) or just finding a spot on the lawns to sit and enjoy the sun. Franklin Canyon Park is so natural you might forget you are in the city, until you follow the main trail to find an amazing

Bel-Air

Beverly Hills homes

city view. Beverly Hills has about 175 restaurants to choose from, but fastfood is less easily found. In addition to posh restaurants like Spago's and Maestro's around the Rodeo area, you will find an active hotel bar and restaurant scene at the likes of The Peninsula (p.17) and Beverly Hills Hotel (p.18). For the most part, those in the hills of Bel-Air come down the hill to play in Westwood and Brentwood or The Valley, but the secluded Bel-Air Hotel (p.19) has a bar and restaurant, while The Glen Center near Mulholland is home to cool spots like Vibrato Grill Jazz (p.324).

Healthcare

Beverly Hills is near the Cedars-Sinai Medical Center (p.113), while Bel-Air residents may find themselves closer to UCLA Medical Center (p.114). There are countless doctors' offices throughout commercial Beverly Hills, which is the epicentre of plastic surgery.

Education

These areas are served by LAUSD, with Beverly Hills schools ranking quite well. There are also several prominent private schools, including Marymount High School, The Mirman School for the Gifted, Berkeley Hall, The Westland School, Hillel Hebrew Academy and Milken Community High School. While there are several preschools in Beverly Hills, including Beverly Hills Presbyterian Nursery School and Temple Emanuel Preschool, Bel-Air locals may have look to neighbouring areas.

Transport

Beverly Hills is not close to any freeways, but is accessible via commercial thoroughfares like Wilshire, Santa Monica, Melrose and Sunset. The Sunset entrances to residential Bel-Air are located just off the 405. Both Beverly Hills and Bel-Air are accessible by car, but there is little bus access north of Sunset Boulevard, which traces the area's foothills. Canyons like Crescent Heights, Benedict Canyon and Beverly Glen traverse the residential areas, while also serving as major access points to and from the San Fernando Valley. This can cause major traffic in the canyons and along Sunset during rush hour. If you get lost, you will likely spot someone on Sunset selling a map to the stars' homes.

Safety & Annoyances

This area is relatively safe, especially behind the gates of Bel-Air or your own private mansion. You may find life in the hills inconvenient, as you have to go down the hill to do anything, while city lovers are sure to find it too suburban and quiet. If you buy a star home or there is a mistake on a map, tourists may end up gawking at your house. Beverly Hills' more urban neighbourhoods have a slightly lower safety rating, while offering a more convenient lifestyle. Rainstorms have been known to cause mudslides in the canyons, leading to road closures and the destruction of homes.

Area **B** p.66
See also Map 4

Brentwood & Westwood

Brentwood and Westwood may not share the international recognition of Beverly Hills, Bel-Air or Malibu, but these areas are no less exclusive. Brentwood is largely residential and attracts families and celebs with healthy bank accounts. Westwood is also family friendly, but as home to UCLA and its college town environs, you will also find a healthy mix of students, professors and the like. Though not beachside, these Westside areas enjoy the cooler beach climate, with a tendency for late night and early morning fog that burns off by midday.

Best Points

These areas combine the best points of a college town, suburb and city, offering many educational and cultural opportunities, as well as great views and proximity to the beach.

Accommodation

Brentwood homes average in the $2 million range, but you will also find high-end mansions priced into the multi millions, and homes for under a million south of San Vicente. Prices in Westwood are not much lower and you will have to travel further south, past Santa Monica Boulevard, to find anything for under a million. Westwood is also home to Wilshire Corridor, a two-mile strip of high-rise condos just east of UCLA, nicknamed Millionaire's Mile. As the moniker suggests, these luxurious condos may easily put you into the mega millions, with or without a scenic view to the ocean. Apartments are prevalent in Westwood, where student shares are popular and prices start at around $1,500 for a one-room apartment. Brentwood apartments tend to be smaller, yet more expensive, with few options on the low end, while condo rentals in Wilshire Corridor lean toward the astronomical.

Worst Points

Housing prices are steep. Traffic and parking can be brutal.

Shopping & Amenities

Though some portions of this area can be entirely residential, you will find your local grocers and mini-mall fare on major streets like Wilshire and Santa Monica. You may, however, find yourself closer to the Brentwood Country Mart at 26th and San Vicente Boulevard, which offers a general store, as well as upscale boutiques and a post office. You will also find a host of shopping along San Vicente, including Duttons (a book lover's paradise), and north into Barrington Village. Westwood Village below UCLA offers all the shopping of a college town, from chain retailers to Textbooks Plus, Birkenstocks and the gag and party store Ahhs. That said, many locals prefer the shopping in neighbouring Santa Monica and Century City. The Westwood farmers' market is at the VA's Vets Garden on Thursdays from 13:00 to 19:00, with the Brentwood Market at South Gretna Green Way and San Vicente on Sundays from 09:00 to 13:00. You should have no trouble tracking down your local gym, but you are also a skip from beachfront exercise, not to mention hiking and biking in the gorgeous hills north of Brentwood. Barrington Recreation Center, Crestwood Hills Park, Westwood Recreation Complex and Westwood Park each offer basketball courts and ball fields, among other athletic facilities and activities. Barrington in particular offers a dog park, while the massive Westwood complex offers a pool and tennis courts. The nearby Holmby Park also offers the Armand Hammer Golf Course.

Entertainment & Leisure

In addition to all the fun to be had outdoors, this area has a lot going on, especially around Westwood Village. You will find expansive arts, sports, educational and cultural programmes and events at and around UCLA, including performances and exhibits by local and international superstars. There are also several cinemas in the area, with many major movie premieres held in Westwood. Of the local museums, the free Getty (p.172) is notable for its fantastic views, gardens and architecture, not to mention funky events like the live 'Fridays Off the 405' DJ nights during the summer. With over 150 restaurants, you will find no shortage of dining options in the shopping areas and along the major thoroughfares, with a prevalence of Asian and Persian cuisines. Westwood offers about twice as many choices, including much of the local fastfood fare, while Brentwood is known for its upscale spots. San Vicente in particular specialises in pricey hot spots where celeb spotting is a normal occurrence. If you are just looking for a drink, you will find some interesting options, including the W Hotel's funky bar (p.20), the casual Westwood Brewing Co or the Brentwood Restaurant's clubby lounge where you can catch a game. While there is enough nightlife to keep you busy, locals often venture out to meet friends in more happening areas of LA.

Healthcare
The local UCLA Medical Center (p.114) continuously ranks as 'The Best in the West,' or the top hospital west of the Mississippi. There is also a major Veteran's hospital centre associated with the medical school.

Education
As home to UCLA (p.130), is it no surprise this area has strong educational opportunities for young and old alike. It is served by LAUSD, including the local Brentwood Science Magnet and Paul Revere Middle School Math/Science Magnet. Preschools include the Early Childhood Learning Center, Brentwood Presbyterian Preschool, Sinai Temple Nursery School and Sunshine Preschool. There are several local private schools, including Brentwood School, Mirman School for Gifted Children, Berkeley Hall School and Marlborough School for Girls. In addition to UCLA and its professional schools, there is a local branch of Mount St Mary's College.

Transport
The basic mode of transportation in Brentwood is the Mercedes or BMW, while locals in Westwood often get around via bike or even on foot. Both Westwood and Brentwood are accessible via the 405 Freeway's Montana, Sunset, Wilshire and Santa Monica exits. Additional thoroughfares in Brentwood include San Vicente, Barrington, Montana and Bundy Drive, while Westwood's include Westwood, Sepulveda and Beverly Glen. Buses travel the major thoroughfare, offering more access to Westwood than residential Brentwood. The only thing more taxing than the rush hour traffic may be finding parking on the metered streets. You will also find restricted permit parking in residential areas.

View over Westwood

Safety & Annoyances
Westwood offers the safety of any college town, while Brentwood locals quip that if you walk the streets after dark, you are more likely to get stopped by the police than be confronted by actual crime. You will find that even the few commercial areas in Brentwood quiet down after early evening. Traffic in the area can be intense, with congestion on the 405 and the main thoroughfares, especially around the freeway exits and during rush hour. Parking for a night out can be impossible to find, though you may be able to rely on valet at many restaurants.

Area **C** p.66
See also Map 2

Best Points
This centrally located, up-and-coming area offers reasonable prices, great schools and lots of recreational fun.

Worst Points
Prices are already skyrocketing.

Culver City

Culver City, aka 'The Heart of Screenland', is still home to several movie and television lots and studios, including the massive Sony Pictures. It is also home to several new business parks and five major car dealerships, but these days the largely commercial city is becoming the hip and happening place to live and play, while remaining family friendly. Many are attracted by the affordable housing and the central location, not to mention the burgeoning art scene, fantastic restaurants and great schools. Also attractive is Culver City's local government, which provides outstanding area services, as well as a pedestrian-friendly downtown area. This is being expanded to include a new Town Plaza that will accommodate exhibitions, movie screenings, antique shows, book fairs and more.

Accommodation

Culver City is known for its neighbourhoods of simple, two or three-bedroom single family homes, but you will also find apartments and condos, especially on the west side. Climbing prices run the gamut, but you may find better deals here than in much of LA. You may even see a small single-family home for as low as $400,000 in less gentrified areas, but don't be surprised when your tastes pass the million dollar mark. Average rents on a house, condo or townhouse are around $2,225, with apartment averages closer to $1,080. This is one area where you may find a studio for well under a thousand dollars.

Shopping & Amenities

There are grocers, banks and mini-malls on the main roads like Venice Boulevard, but downtown Culver City offers a Trader Joe's and an Albertson's, as well as a local farmers' market on Main Street from 15:00 to 19:00 on Tuesdays. You will also find assorted funky stores and galleries throughout the area, while the nearby Helms Furniture District (www.helmsfurniture.com) offers mostly upscale furniture, design and appliance shops. The Foxhills Mall on the south side of La Cienega offers the standard mall chains, as well as lesser known boutiques. The area is also home to discount megastores like Costco, Staples and Target. Culver City's Recreation Division is expansive, offering athletic, educational and social programmes for toddlers, children, teens, adults and seniors. Its public parks include a skate park and the 'Boneyard' dog park. The Municipal Plunge at 4175 Overland Avenue offers an assortment of pool activities. Find out what else you can get into by visiting www.culvercity.org.

Entertainment & Leisure

As mentioned above, Culver City provides plenty of recreational activities for locals. You can also get swinging nearby at Rancho Park Golf Course (p.223). If you are feeling less active, you may prefer walking around the downtown area for dinner and a movie or catching a live performance at The Kirk Douglas Theater (p.361) or some tunes at The Jazz Bakery (www.jazzbakery.org). There is a city orchestra, playhouse, public theatre and symphony orchestra to check out. In addition to standard mini-mall eateries and pavement cafes, restaurants like Wilson's and Beacon are pumping up the area's reputation with foodies. An impressive list of annual events includes an Art Walk and Music Festival, the Mercedes-Benz Fashion Week, George Barris Culver City Car Show and Taste of the Nation food fest.

Healthcare

The new Century City Doctors Hospital (p.113) at 2070 Century Park East offers a 24 hour emergency service, but locals may find themselves closer to hospitals that are technically in other areas. Residents may also prefer making the small commute to visit prestigious UCLA or Cedars-Sinai, which are both about 10 minutes north of Culver City. There is also a large Kaiser facility just outside the La Cienega border.

Education

Culver City ranks well in education and has its own public school district, CCUSD. It is also home to a Help Group Child and Family Center (www.thehelpgroup.org) and The Kayne Eras Center Diagnostic and Therapeutic Services Agency (www.kayneeras. org), both of which provide testing, specialised education services and educational therapy. Culver City is convenient for a selection of small private schools, with local preschools including Happyland Preschool, La Playa Cooperative Nursery School, Montessori Preschool and Culver Palms Family YMCA. It is also central to many higher and adult education centres, including CCUSD's Culver City Adult School, West LA College, Yo San University of Traditional Chinese Medicine, Debbie Allen Dance Academy and The New School of Cooking.

Transport

The area is accessible via the 10 and 405 freeways and major east-to-west thoroughfares like Venice, Washington and Culver, and north-south roads like La Cienega and Sepulveda. Culver City's bus line, which has service to the beach, has ranked in the top 10 bus fleets in the US, while a new 15.4km (9.6 mile) light rail line into Downtown is currently in the planning phase. There is plenty of metered parking and paid and free carparks in busy areas, while some areas require residential parking permits.

Safety & Annoyances

Culver City touts itself as one of the safest areas to live and work in LA. While the major commuter freeways are conveniently located, you may be wise to avoid rush hours by taking surface streets.

Area **D** p.66
See also Map 10

Downtown

One of the few LA areas with the skyscrapers, exhaust and human bustle to feel like a real city, Downtown has revitalised in recent years. It is home to LA's Financial District, Bunker Hill, Historic Downtown, Fashion District, Artist District and South Park, not to mention touristy Chinatown, Little Tokyo and Olvera Street. The local businesses, court houses, museums, music halls, posh hotels, discount and wholesale shopping and incredible architecture and design have long made this area a hotbed of activity during the week, but in recent years it has also hit a residential boom. High-end lofts in new and renovated Downtown buildings have popped up, attracting an artsy, hip, professional community of locals. With that came new restaurants and bars, not to mention the area's first major grocery store, Ralphs. To make room for this influx, the homeless who have long characterised the area are being pushed out, but that doesn't mean you won't see them around.

Best Points

This newly inspired area has all the culture and entertainment of big city living. It has a prominent, avant-garde art community, amazing transportation and cool, new housing.

Accommodation

Downtown is almost entirely comprised of new and renovated lofts in both historic and new buildings. The state of the building, its amenities, location and your floor level will affect the cost as much as the size. Rents on a small loft might start as low as $1,000 and a one-bedroom condo with about 700 to 900 square feet may easily sell for $400,000. That said, you may end up paying a lot more for a lot less space in one of the renovated, historic art deco buildings or paying a lot less for more space closer to the Staples and Convention Center. As with most parts of LA, you will also find lofts and apartments that go well into the millions. The area offers senior and low income affordable housing rentals. Recent zoning changes have opened the door to new construction, assuming the market can sustain it. If the boom slows due to the current market conditions, however, some of the area's brand new and newly renovated properties may stay empty, which is likely to lower prices.

Shopping & Amenities

Downtown is all about the shopping. Deals abound at the jewellery mart, Sante Alley, the fabric district and the uber-hip Fashion Institute of Design and Merchandising. The MOCA gift shop (p.175) offers funky fare and you will also find shopping malls tucked into the Bonaventure, The Water Plaza and California Plaza. You can do some damage at The Brewery Art Colony or any number of local galleries. Downtown is also a step away from the Chinatown, Little Tokyo and Olvera shopping scenes. The area is full of banks and there is a Gold's Gym (p.212) at Macy's Plaza. Perhaps most useful to locals, the area recently opened its first major grocery store, Ralphs (p.310).

Entertainment & Leisure

If you feel like walking, you can tour the historic architecture or check out dazzling historic hotels like the Biltmore (p.20). The modern Standard has an amazing rooftop pool and bar, but get there before the crowds at weekends. You may enjoy spending a free Thursday evening at The Museum of Contemporary Art (p.175) or checking out the current trade show or event at the Convention Center. There's also the Natural History Museum, African-American Museum, California Science Center (see Exposition Park, p.179), LA Central Library (p.226) and Brewery Art Colony (see I-5, p.169) to investigate. When you are ready to eat, Downtown has all the fastfood options you can imagine, as well as extravagant dining spots like The Water Grill, landmark eateries like Philippe (p.320) and new, hip everyday restaurants and bars like Pete's Cafe and Bar (p.327). After an early dinner, you can hit a concert at the brand new Disney Hall (p.184) or catch an opera, play or musical at the Music Center (p.361). If you are a sports fan, you will enjoy having the Staples Center and Dodger Stadium in your backyard.

Healthcare

There are eight massive health facilities in the immediate vicinity and some of the top programmes and faculties in the US. The California Hospital Medical Center (www.chmcla.org) operates one of the busiest 24 hour ERs in LA at 1401 South Grand Avenue. Other area providers include the Good Samaritan Hospital (p.113), USC University Hospital (p.114) and the Children's Hospital of LA (p.113).

Education

In addition to nearby USC, one of the nation's top 30 graduate and undergraduate universities, Downtown is home to Loyola Law School (www.lls.edu). Local LAUSD schools include the Santee Education Complex, Downtown Magnets High School, Belmont High School and Miguel Contreras Learning Complex. Local preschools include the Joy Picus Child Development Center, Garden Co-op Nursery School, Ketchum-Downtown YMCA's Montessori Preschool and Day Care Center and LA Smile Preschool.

Transport

Downtown is easily accessible by car, bus or even Metro, with the Blue, Red and Gold Metro line stops in Pershing Square, the Civic Center and Staples Center. Traffic on the nearby 10, 110 and 101 freeways can be shocking, especially during rush hour or around a major event. This is one of the few areas with one-way streets, and those too can become congested during business hours. Even foot traffic is likely to be heavy. The Dash bus system will get your around Downtown for 25 cents a ride. There is limited metered street parking, with several parking lots that charge $25 to $40 a day or a few hundred dollars a month. Many buildings offer one or two parking spots to residents.

Safety & Annoyances

Living in Downtown you will run into all the hazards and annoyances of city life. Safety has increased, but the area is still more dangerous than most of the city and many Angelenos shy away from it because of the homeless population. Traffic during business hours and before and after major events can be a nightmare.

Chinatown

Olvera Street

Corner of 5th and Broadway

Downtown highrise

Area **E** *p.66*
See also Map 6

Hollywood & Los Feliz

LA's trademark entertainment centre is in the midst of a renaissance, with hundreds of millions of dollars going into shining its world famous tinsel. Downtown Hollywood, the Walk of Fame and the new Hollywood & Highland Complex in particular have been revitalised. In addition to the Paramount movie studio and Prospect Studios, you will find countless movie and television studios and soundstages, as well as record labels and concert venues, theatres and performance halls. The Los Feliz area to the east has a truly 'Old Hollywood' feel and is home to the country's largest municipal park and urban wilderness area, Griffith Park (p.191). It is also of note that Hollywood is the centre of action for the Church of Scientology. In addition to the Celebrity Centre mansion on Franklin, you will actually find an L Ron Hubbard Way on Sunset near Vermont.

Best Points
The area offers both old Hollywood charm and the glitz and glamour of Hollywood today. The hills offer gorgeous homes, with views and seclusion. It is centrally located, especially if you are looking to work in the entertainment business.

Accommodation

Hollywood offers a true variety of accommodations, from low and high-rise apartments to one-family homes in the Hollywood Hills and Los Feliz. This is another area where prices can be astronomical, with the average price per square foot ranging from $550 to $650, yet there are still low rates in the sketchier neighbourhoods. Rent on a one-bedroom apartment starts at around $1,100 and skyrockets from there, while the average home in the hills rents for about $5,000. Buyers may find a two-bedroom condo for $532,500, while houses can go into the millions. With all the new transplants heading straight for this area, you will find many shares or rooms available in both the Hollywood Hills, Los Feliz and the more inexpensive flatlands.

Worst Points
Much of the area is unsafe, with heavy traffic and homelessness, drug and prostitution problems. The local education system is weak.

Shopping & Amenities

Hollywood's main thoroughfares offer the usual grocery stores and mini-malls, as well as boutiques, rock and roll supplies and more, with much action on Hollywood and Sunset Boulevards. Those in the hills may have to come down to Sunset for groceries, though there is a local market midway up Laurel Canyon. The Hollywood & Highland Center (p.308) is a $615 million retail centre with clothes, accessories and more, but due to it being a tourist hotspot with expensive parking, you won't find many locals doing their shopping there. That area is also packed with memorabilia and T-shirt shops, as well as sexy lingerie and stripper shops. You may prefer walking the Los Feliz or Beachwood areas' eclectic boutiques and trinket shops along northern Vermont and Franklin respectively, or hitting funky Melrose or a nearby neighbourhood mall. If you get sick of your local gym, you can get your workout in Runyon Canyon or Griffith Park.

Hollywood apartments

Entertainment & Leisure

There are often free events going on, like summer movies at the Hollywood Forever Cemetery (p.182). Across from Grauman's Chinese Theatre (p.181), with its pavement of famous handprints, you will find the gorgeous El Capitan and Egyptian Theatres (p.179). Further east, the infamous Cinerama Dome has been expanded into the Arclight multiplex (p.357), which

Homes in the hills

offers the occasional 21 and over showings where alcohol is allowed. The area is also ripe with live theatres, like the historic Pantages. You may be more interested in checking out the concert and club halls, not to mention the countless places to catch an outdoor show, the most impressive being the Hollywood Bowl (p.182) and Greek Theater (p.360). Hollywood also has a hopping bar scene, especially along Cahuenga Corridor, as well as a host of strip clubs. For a taste of Old Hollywood nightlife, head towards Los Feliz for drinks at The Dresden Room (p.346) or swing dance at The Derby (p.354). Franklin near Beachwood Canyon also has a strip of cool restaurants, not to mention the Bourgeois Pig coffee shop. When you need a break from city life, Griffith Park (p.191) offers camping, hiking, horseriding, swimming, golf and the world famous Griffith Observatory, while Runyon Canyon is loved for its dog-friendly hiking trail and view.

Healthcare
There are several hospitals, including Good Samaritan Hospital, Children's Hospital of Los Angeles and Hollywood Presbyterian Hospital (all p.113). Hollywood is also home to the massive Kaiser Sunset Medical Center (p.113), but only the ER is open to non-Kaiser patients.

Education
Hollywood and Los Feliz are served by LAUSD, but this not a great area for students. Fortunately, its central location makes many LA private and charter schools easily accessible. You will also find several local schools directed at the Hollywood crowd, including the renowned Stella Adler Academy & Theatres, Musicians Institute, Joe Blasco Make-up Center and Dvorak & Co Acting Studio.

Transport
In addition to being accessible via car or bus, Hollywood is one of the most metro-friendly areas of LA, with several Red line stops along Vermont, down Hollywood and into The Valley. There is, however, little metro and bus access to the hill areas. For drivers, Laurel Canyon, Highland and Cahuenga are major thoroughfares into and out of The Valley, causing bottleneck traffic during rush hours. The busy 101 traces through Hollywood, with Los Feliz near the 2 and 5 freeways. Finding metered street parking in these areas can be rough, especially during hours of business and play. There are private carparks throughout, ranging in price from $5 to $20, depending on the time of day. The Hollywood & Highland carpark costs a maximum of $10.

Safety & Annoyances
Hollywood is still not very safe. The money flooding in to clean it up has done little to decrease the area's homelessness, prostitution and drug problems, and you will still find several seedy areas throughout, even right off the main drag of downtown Hollywood. It is wise to be aware of your surroundings and watch for street cons. Traffic can be brutal and you will also encounter the expected annoyances of living in a major tourist destination.

Area **F** p.66
See also Map 2

Malibu

Tucked between 21 miles of breathtaking Pacific Ocean coastline and mountainous canyons, Malibu is an oasis from city life and home to the most expensive, exclusive property in LA. Celebs and industry folk have long turned to areas like Malibu Colony and Broad Beach to create 'normal' lives out of the Hollywood glare. Unfortunately, the arrival of young newsmakers like Britney Spears has made the local grocery store a paparazzi hang out; but occasional sightings aside, Malibu life is about as peaceful and beautiful as it comes, and is enjoyed by surf bums, LA locals and tourists alike.

Best Points
Malibu is undeniably one of the most beautiful places on earth; somewhere you can catch a wave with dolphins and celebs. It is a safe, quiet, suburban oasis.

Accommodation

Multimillion dollar houses line the beaches, perch on cliffs and tuck back into the canyons. You may find interesting mobile home or apartment deals for under a million in the canyons, but even an old trailer on a prime plot of land is likely to go for a few million. A fixer-upper might set you back as much as eight or nine million, while Barbara Streisand's mansion has been priced at $30 million.

Worst Points
Astronomical housing prices are prohibitive. Fires, floods and rockslides destroy property and cause road closures and evacuations. It is at best a 30 minute drive to the rest of LA and at least 45 minutes to Downtown. Road closures and weekend beach traffic can increase travel times greatly.

Shopping & Amenities

The Pacific Coast Highway is lined with fastfood, fine dining, surf shops, boutiques, salons, banks and doctors' offices, but the focal points are the Malibu Country Mart and Malibu Colony Plaza. The Mart is a trendy, laid-back mall with over 60 shops, restaurants and galleries, as well as health and service providers and outdoor areas. It's also home to the farmers' market on Sundays from 10:00 to 15:00. The Plaza houses a Ralphs grocery store, as well as boutiques, fastfood and fine dining.

Entertainment & Leisure

If you are looking to fill up, you can enjoy the view in your swimsuit at Malibu Seafood on the Pacific Coast Highway, or go for broke at Taverna Tony Greek Eats & Sweets at the Mart. You can grab a beer with a view at Moonshadows (p.324) or Dukes (p.318) or catch legendary and local performers at Malibu Inn (www.malibu-inn.com). The selling point of Malibu, however, is the endless outdoor fun. Not only is the coastline gorgeous, but it offers some of LA's cleanest waters, best surf and living tide pools. Surf and boating rentals are available in the area and the Leo Carrillo beach allows camping. Up in Malibu Creek, you can go hiking, fishing, birdwatching or horseback riding. There are also seasonal outdoor events, like the annual Labor Day Chili Cookoff (September), with carnival rides, games and a petting zoo. For a bit of historic beauty, locals visit the J Paul Getty Villa (www.getty.edu) and Serra Retreat (www.serraretreat.com).

Healthcare

Malibu is known for its many exclusive, luxury residential rehab clinics. Nearby medical centres are Los Robles Regional Medical Center, Simi Valley Hospital & Health Care and Santa Monica UCLA Medical Center (p.114), although none of these are less than 21 kilometres (13 miles) away. Malibu Urgent Care (23656 Pacific Coast Highway; 310 456 7551) is open from 09:00 to 19:00, seven days a week. Round the clock emergency care is available about 10 kilometres (six miles) from Malibu at Westlake Outpatient Medical Center (4415 Lakeview Canyon Rd, Westlake Village; 818 706 8000).

Education

Malibu is home to Pepperdine University (p.130), a top US graduate and undergraduate school with a hilltop view of the ocean. Local preschools include Malibu Methodist Nursery, St Aidan's Preschool, Malibu Jewish Center and the Children's Creative Workshop. The area's public elementary schools are Juan Cabrillo,

Point Dume Marine Science and Webster Elementary. The public high schools are Malibu High School and Santa Monica-Malibu Unified School District. Local private schools include Our Lady of Malibu School (grades K to 8), Odyssey School (4 to 8) and Colin Mcewen High School (7 to 12).

Transport

In perfect conditions you can get in your car or catch the 534 Express bus and travel the Pacific Coast Highway from Santa Monica to Malibu in about half an hour. Winding, scenic thoroughfares like Topanga Canyon, Malibu Canyon and Kanan Dume Road connect the PCH to the western San Fernando Valley and take about the same time. Weekend beachcomber traffic can turn these drives into an hour or longer, but the area's major transportation issue is the weather. Fires, rock slides and the like have been known to close down the PCH, the main thoroughfare between much of LA and Malibu. If you are on the wrong side of a PCH closure, you may have to go inland to The Valley or even north and then inland in order to get around the closure. This could add hours to your drive. There are street parking spots and paid carparks lining PCH. Neighbourhood parking varies, but the area has several gated communities and homes.

Safety & Annoyances

Malibu's main safety issue is natural disasters. Area homes are lost every year to fires, while rains cause flooding and landslides. Area evacuations are not unheard of. It's wise to take precautions in the ocean and beware of local wildlife, especially in the canyons and plains. The weekend beachcomber traffic can be a nuisance as well, and you may get stuck behind the occasional mob of paparazzi.

Area **G** p.66
See also Map 2

Marina del Rey

Marina del Rey is all about pleasure boating, fresh air and ocean views. It boasts one of the largest ma-made small-craft harbours in the world, with six local yacht clubs and 19 anchorages, as well as prime beachfront property. The actual marina is leasehold property, however, owned by LA County. This means Marina del Rey is predominantly a rent-based community composed of young professionals and industry folk.

Best Points

You have a harbour and beach in your backyard and the rest of LA is around the corner. The area is easily accessible for commuters.

Accommodation

The land in the actual marina, bordered by Lincoln, Washington and Via Marina and including the boat slips, is unincorporated LA County land, which is leased out to private leaseholders on long-term agreements. That means the high and low-rise apartments and boat slips in this area are rental only, except for the condos in Marina City Club, which can be purchased on a leasehold basis. Rentals in this area start at $1,750, or $1,995 with a view. You are not likely to find much for under $1,500 in the greater Marina area, especially with a marina view. The rest of Marina del Rey is incorporated and thus you may find homes, condos and apartments for rent and sale. A single-family home may go as low as $720,000, but the average is over $2 million, with some homes reaching $7 million. The beachfront homes on Silver Strand, for example, are multimillion-dollar affairs. Condo prices here may come in below $550,000, but views and amenities can easily put you into the millions. The Oakwood Apartments (www.oakwood.com) offer both unfurnished and furnished apartments.

Worst Points

Rent prices run high. LA County owns most of the land. Parking can be very difficult.

Shopping & Amenities

The Marina Beach Shopping Center offers the essentials and local service, while The Waterside at Marina del Rey (www.shopwaterside.com) and Villa Marina Marketplace (www.villamarinamarketplace.com) each offer a pharmacy and 24 hour market. You will also find groceries and necessities along the main streets, including the Ralph's on Admiralty Way and Costco at Washington and Lincoln. The revamped Waterside offers upscale boutiques, while the larger Marketplace offers 70 shops and restaurants, including mainstream spots like Gap, Bath & Body Works and Barnes & Nobel. Some great boutiques are tucked around the main streets and you will find great shopping in neighbouring Venice, Culver City and Santa Monica. If you have your boat docked here, your local marina will likely provide several amenities, from showers and mail service to laundry room and pool, though there may be a 'membership' fee to use them. You can get your exercise on the water, beside the water or by hiking in the Ballona Wetlands, but you may also find facilities in local gyms, yacht clubs or even in your own building.

Safety & Annoyances
This area is pretty safe, but it may be unwise to hang out on the beach after dark. Parking can be difficult to find or pricey in some residential and commercial areas.

Entertainment & Leisure

Marina del Rey offers all sorts of fun on the water, including a Saturday Dinner Dance Cruise with Hornblower (p.192). Fisherman's Harbor is a great place to find a cruise, class or a rental. During summer weekends there is often live music here and at Waterside. Nearby Chase Park also offers a free summer classical and pop concert series, as well as guest boat docks, outdoor adventure programmes and a fishing pier. If you want to take a swim and the Pacific waves are too much for your child, go to kid-friendly Mother's Beach. Also be sure to keep your eye out for area events, including the fantastic boat show, Fourth of July fireworks and the Christmas boat parade. As for eating out, the marina boasts 60 full-service restaurants, many of which can be found in the shopping areas and at the end of Washington Boulevard. To dine in style and with a view, check out the Ritz-Carlton or Café del Rey (www.cafedelreymarina.com). C&O Cucina (www.cocucina.com) is family friendly, while Baja Cantina (www.bajacantinavenice.com) has a hopping happy hour, but you may prefer grabbing a beer and turtle race at Brennan's Irish Pub (www.brennanspub-la.com). For a quieter night, catch a movie at the Marketplace.

Healthcare

In addition to the Centinela Freeman Medical Center (310 823 8911), this area is home to a collection of UCLA doctors' offices. You will also find yourself about four miles from St John's Health Center (310 829 5511) and Santa Monica UCLA Medical Center (p.114).

Education

Marina del Rey offers reasonable schooling options, especially if your child is in middle school. Served by LAUSD, the marina is home to Westside Leadership Magnet and Marina del Rey Middle School & Performing Arts Magnet Center, but your child may end up schooling in Venice. Local preschools include Kid's Pointe Pre School, Gan Israel Preschool of Marina Del Rey, Morning Glory Preschool and Montessori Academy of Culver City. The Marina is also home to Loyola Marymount University, with its college and professional schools, as well as the USC Information Sciences Institute.

Transport

In addition to being accessible by car via the 90 freeway and major thoroughfares like Washington, Culver and Lincoln, Marina del Rey is served by three bus lines. During the summer, a water bus makes six stops in the Marina. You can also rent boats for water travel or catch a day cruise to Catalina Island. Many locals enjoy getting around via bikes or skates once they are in the neighbourhood and a path runs along the coastline. Sky rise apartments, condos, shopping centres and some restaurants have private carparks, while the large, flat-rate beach parking lot at the end of Washington Boulevard is open until 01:00, but street parking in Marina del Rey can be difficult to nonexistent.

Is getting lost your usual excuse?

Whether you're a map person or not, this pocket-sized marvel will help you get to know the city like the back of your hand – so you won't feel the back of someone else's.

Los Angeles Mini Map
Fit the city in your pocket

Area **H** p.66
See also Map 7

Miracle Mile, Carthay Circle & Pico-Robertson

The areas south of Wilshire and north of the 10 offer less expensive and potentially less-maintained residential neighbourhoods with a strong Spanish colonial and art deco flair. Carthay Circle, Miracle Mile and Pico-Robertson are examples of these areas, with Miracle Mile also stretching north to the massive La Brea Park apartment complex (www.parklabrea.com). These conveniently located areas are popular with families and singles alike, creating a diverse community with a strong Jewish presence. It is also home to Little Ethiopia, LA's Museum Row and the bustling Farmers' Market and Grove Mall.

Best Points

These residential areas are conveniently located. The accommodations are relatively spacious and attractive while being more affordable than in neighbouring areas.

Accommodation

These areas are known for pretty duplexes and triplexes, but you will also find mid-sized apartment building scattered throughout, as well as streets and neighbourhoods where homes have not been split. As a general rule, property values decrease as you move south of Pico, while the Carthay neighbourhoods are better maintained and therefore pricier. South Carthay, between Olympic and Pico, is a Historic Preservation Zone and very well maintained. Rents on an upper duplex with a shared back garden may cost from $2,700 to $4,000. A two-bedroom apartment may be around $2,000 and a studio apartment could go for $1,000. There isn't much for sale under one or two million, but you will tend to get more bang for your buck than in neighbouring areas like West Hollywood or Beverly Hills. The massive Park La Brea is an apartment community with over 4,000 art deco rentals in high rise and garden-style buildings. A one-bedroom costs from $1,700 to $2,200, while a two-bedroom is $2,200 to $2,800.

Worst Points

Safety and congestion may be a concern in many areas. Properties are not always well maintained.

Shopping & Amenities

The main roads like Pico and Wilshire all have supermarkets, gyms and everyday amenities. Speciality food shopping includes Little Ethiopia and the kosher Pico area, as well as the permanent Farmers' Market on Fairfax and Third (p.180). There are a handful of 99 cent stores north of Wilshire as well. The Grove (p.308) next to the Farmers' Market is a relatively new upscale, outdoor mall with many recognisable chains. Some locals find they are quite close to the Beverly Center mall or Culver City Downtown. Third Street and Beverly Boulevard offer some cute, hip boutiques and there are some less expensive boutiques on Pico and Venice. The Robertson Recreation Center offers community programmes, as well as floodlit basketball and handball courts, a children's play area, indoor gym and picnic tables. The nearby EG Roberts Swimming Pool (4526 W Pico Boulevard) offers swimming classes and several other activities.

Entertainment & Leisure

The highlight of this area has long been Miracle Mile, which is named for the stretch of museums on Wilshire between Fairfax and La Brea, including LA County Museum of Art (p.174), Petersen Automotive Museum and kid-favourite La Brea Tar Pits (p.177). There are several hip spots for brunch or dinner on nearby Beverly and Third, east of Fairfax. Locals enjoy the swanky A.O.C. (p.321) and cool Cobras and Matadors. There is less going on south of Wilshire, where it is more residential, but there are interesting restaurants throughout the area, with many fastfood, Ethiopian, kosher and Mexican options. You can also get a beer at Tom Bergin's Tavern (p.351), the oldest Irish establishment in LA. The strength of these areas is their central location, often only a short jaunt to Downtown, Culver City, West Hollywood, Hollywood or even the beach.

Healthcare

These areas are conveniently located for access to top-ranking Cedars-Sinai Hospital (p.113) in West Hollywood.

Education

This family-friendly area boasts a large selection of preschools. It is served by the LAUSD public school system, but your child may attend a neighbouring school like John Burroughs Middle School or Fairfax High. It is also home to the Hollywood Actors Studio and a number of Jewish schools, including the orthodox Yeshiva University High (YULA).

Transport

These areas are central and convenient for most other parts of the city. They are bordered by or near the 10 freeway, but traffic often runs faster on east-west thoroughfares like Pico or Olympic. Other major thoroughfares include Wilshire, La Cienega, Robertson, Fairfax and La Brea, which can get congested during rush hours. Bus routes cover many of these major streets, but the Metro has not yet made it to this area. Streets in the residential pockets tend to be narrow, with limited or permit-only parking. Commercial areas have metered street parking, with a massive private carpark at The Grove and Farmers' Market.

Safety & Annoyances

Safety here is growing on the whole, but there are still some unsavoury spots around. As a general rule, safety plummets in the less well-maintained residential areas, many of which are south of Pico. Some of the tight residential streets can be a bit stressful for drivers, especially during rush hour.

Apartments with character

Miracle Mile houses

Park La Brea

Area ❶ p.66
See also Map 3

Palms & Mar Vista

Palms and Mar Vista offer relatively affordable living with proximity to the beaches and the rest of LA, attracting a mixed bag of families, young singles and retirees. The lines between these areas and Culver City or Marina del Rey often become fuzzy, but one line that remains firm is the price difference – these areas are usually cheaper than both their beachfront and citified neighbours.

Best Points
These residential neighbourhoods are adjacent to LA hot zones and major commuter thoroughfares. Housing prices are more reasonable than in neighbouring areas and you may land an amazing view.

Accommodation

Mar Vista still holds much of its 1930s charm, while parts of Palms have been rebuilt to create a haven of affordable housing, so the area is now very apartment heavy. The area around National and Palms, in particular, is popular with those more concerned with price, space and location than aesthetics. Mar Vista's apartments and multi-family units are found in the flatlands south of Venice, while single-family units are more prevalent in the hilly, landscaped neighbourhoods north of Venice, some with amazing views of the beach or city. Prices vary based on accommodation, location, upkeep of the neighbourhood and view. You may, for example, find a small three-bedroom starter house for under a million, but a renovated home in Westside Village or a Mar Vista Hill mansion could set you back well over $3 million. As a renter, you can find a small studio apartment for under $1,000, while singles start at around $1,100. Rental on a three-bedroom hilltop home with a view, however, may come in closer to $4,500. As with all areas, prices here are climbing, but you are still likely to get more space for your money than in Marina del Rey, Santa Monica or Culver City.

Worst Points
Safety may be a concern. Some Palms neighbourhoods lack aesthetic charm.

Shopping & Amenities

The shopping is better and easier in neighbouring areas, but the main roads have the usual groceries, banks and necessities. You can buy bulk amenities and food at the Costco on Washington and Lincoln. The Mar Vista farmers' market is at Grand View Boulevard on Sundays from 09:00 to 14:00. Nearby malls include the Fox Hills and Third Street Promenade. The Mar Vista Recreation Center offers a good range of sporting facilities and classes, as does the Palms Recreation Center.

Entertainment & Leisure

There's a handful of ethnic restaurants in the area, especially along Venice. With Santa Monica, Venice, Culver City and Marina del Rey close by, you will have no shortage of activities and things to see and do.

Healthcare

Both areas are close to Centinela Freeman Medical Center (310 823 8911), Century City Doctors Hospital (p.113), St John's Health Center (310 829 5511) and Santa Monica UCLA Medical Center (p.114). The main ULCA hospital in Westwood is also straight up Sepulveda.

Safety & Annoyances
These areas are relatively safe, with Palms being slightly less safe than Mar Vista. Traffic can become congested.

Education

Local LAUSD schools, including Pacifica Community Charter School, score quite well. Local privates include Winward, Le Lycee Francais de Los Angeles, Westwood Prep and Wildwood School. For a change of pace, Peach Tree Pottery offers private and group classes for young and old. You will also find classes available at the local recreation centres.

Transport

One of the major benefits of living here is its accessibility via the 405 and the 10, as well as major thoroughfares like Venice, Sepulveda, National and Centinela. Bus access is on main thoroughfares only, but can get you just about anywhere in the city. There has been little action following talk of extending a Metro line to the area. Parking can be competitive.

Area **K** *p.66* ◀
See also Map 2

Best Points ◀
*Suburban living
with all the perks
and culture of city
life, combined with
outdoor mountain fun.*

Worst Points ◀
*Not centrally located.
Awful commuter traffic.
Nearest ER may be as
far as 10 kilometres (six
miles) away.*

Pasadena

It's tempting to describe Pasadena as an LA suburb, but the massive city actually offers as much variety as the rest of Los Angeles put together. Tucked into the San Gabriel Mountains about 20 minutes from Downtown, Pasadena's streets are lined with striking turn-of-the-century architecture and a host of museums, gardens and cultural centres. The sun often shines here throughout the winter and you cannot beat the average year round temperature of 24°C (76°F). NASA and CalTech University's Jet Propulsion Laboratory (JPL) puts Pasadena at the centre of jet propulsion and space travel research and advancement. The gorgeous Ritz-Carlton Hotel and nearby convention centre are just two reasons why the area is popular for conventions, tours and the like.

Accommodation

This area is known for its 'Old Hollywood' mansions, which can set you back many millions, but savvy house hunters could find a three-bedroom home or condo for under a million. In fact, the average price for a three-bedroom home here is around $860,000, or $700,000 for a three-bedroom condo. Renters will also find more for their money, with some homes renting for as little as $1,500. Prices skyrocket for deluxe accommodations, but even those will be less expensive than their counterparts in the city centre.

Shopping & Amenities

The area is known for its shopping, and you will have no problem finding a local grocers, bank or gym. Weekly farmers' markets are at Meridian Avenue and Mission Street on Thursday, from 16:00 to 20:00, and at Pasadena High School on Saturday, from 08:30 to 12:30. The Old Pasadena shopping centre hosts art galleries, trendy boutiques and vintage clothing shops, while the upscale South Lake Avenue is known for its designer boutiques. One Colorado, with its funky one-of-a-kind shops, and the more mainstream Paseo Colorado Village, are also popular. The Pasadena Antique Center is famed for its variety, while the massive Rose Bowl Flea Market (p.307) takes over the football stadium on the second Sunday of every month.

Entertainment & Leisure

For some fresh air, go biking or hiking in the 132 acre Arroyo Seco, or hit Brookside Park for a picnic and swim. When in need of culture, there is a long list of museums to explore, including Huntington Library, Art Collections and Botanical Gardens (p.174) and the Norton Simon Museum (p.177). Schedule a tour of JPL (818 354 9314), which includes NASA's Space Flight Operations and Assembly Facilities. You may enjoy a performance around the Pasadena Playhouse District, or check out what's happening at the elegant Civic Center, which hosts the People's Choice Awards and Pasadena Symphony. Most of the shopping centres listed above are also entertainment centres. Go to these areas to find cinemas, bars and dance clubs. Over 500 local restaurants offer all levels of service and cuisine, from people-watching patio brunches to fine dining. Local favourites include the Tuscan Gale's, the sophisticated Parkway Grill and tasty Il Capo. Popular nightspots include the infamous Ice House Comedy Club and speakeasy Magnolia Lounge. Beer lovers take note that Yard House (www.yardhouse.com) boasts the world's largest selection of draught beers.

Healthcare

Huntington Memorial (626 397 5000) in west Pasadena currently offers the only 24 hour emergency trauma centre in the San Gabriel Valley, with Methodist Hospital in Arcadia (626 898 8000) being the closest for some locals in east Pasadena. Huntington Memorial is also a leader in cancer research and treatment, among other specialities, and the Ronald McDonald House across the street provides support to families of critically or terminally ill children. Las Encinas (800 792 2345) offers mental health and addiction treatment.

Education

The Pasadena Unified School District offers 20 elementary schools, three middle schools, two high schools and one charter school, in addition to a continuation school. While some of these rank quite well, others fall behind. The area has around 41 private schools, including The Waverly School, Westridge School, Pasadena Montessori, Pasadena Christian School and Pasadena Waldorf. Higher education centres include the renowned California Institute of Technology (CalTech) and Art Center College of Design, as well as the California School of Culinary Arts, Fuller Theological Seminary in California and Pasadena City College.

Transport

Pasadena touts itself as pedestrian friendly and there are several fun areas where you won't need your car. In commercial areas there's a mixture of public and private carparks, as well as metered parking. Traffic in and out of the city on the 110, 134 and 210 freeways can be very congested. You can avoid this by hopping the Gold line Metro, which travels between Pasadena and Downtown, with six stations in Pasadena. The Burbank Airport is more convenient for Pasadena than LAX.

Safety & Annoyances

Pasadena is a relatively safe spot, though it pays to be mindful of your belongings in busy shopping and entertainment areas. Many locals must brave a difficult commute into the city, San Fernando Valley or beyond for work. You will also find that many of your friends in the city and The Valley will be reluctant to come to you for a visit, which means social commutes as well.

Accommodation options in Pasadena

Area **L** p.66
See also Map 2

San Fernando Valley

'The Valley' is considered by many the suburbs of LA. This area north of Mulholland Drive and west of Hollywood is in fact largely residential and quiet in comparison with the citified areas 'over the hill', but there is still plenty going on. Back in the 1950s, orange groves still flourished all the way to Lauren Canyon, but LA steadily pushed west and north until homes and businesses took over the entire basin. It is now home to much of the entertainment industry, with over a hundred soundstages in Burbank, Studio City, Canoga Park and other areas. It is also a centre for aerospace and defence technologies, financial services, healthcare and high-tech manufacturing. Tucked between five ranges of mountains and hills, the enormous community has even more neighbourhoods and personalities than LA proper. Depending on which grocers you hit, you may find yourself in line with an A-list celeb, a struggling single mom, an underpaid manual labourer, or a young publicist who works in the city. The Valley has long been a haven for families in search of backyards and pools, or even just enough space to survive at reasonable prices, but there are as many singles and young professionals, particularly in the areas closest to Hollywood. This younger population has increased as general housing prices have gone up, leading to a bit of a renaissance in Eastside neighbourhoods like Studio City and North Hollywood. At the same time, LA's climbing prices have reached The Valley, making it less of the affordable haven it once was.

Best Points
Quiet, suburban and convenient family-friendly living that is close to the city, but with more space. There are still some affordable areas.

Worst Points
Prices are becoming prohibitive. The Valley has zero cool factor, though NoHo and Studio City are making great strides. Summer temperatures can be brutal without air conditioning. Traffic is often congested, especially during rush hours.

Accommodation

About 50% of Valley housing is free-standing homes, but there are also apartments, condos and townhouses. Pricing is difficult to describe across the board, and it is determined as much by location as by housing type and amenities. As The Valley gets extremely hot in the summer, it is important to note that a swamp cooler is not nearly as affective as air conditioning. Average rents in large complexes are around $1,600 a month, but Central Valley neighbourhoods like Reseda and Van Nuys average closer to $1,000, while prices climb for upscale areas and those closer to the city. In western areas like Calabasas and Woodland Hills, or Studio City and Burbank to the east, for example, prices start closer to $2,000. The housing market for buyers is competitive. The 2007 median price for housing in The Valley was about $630,000. Average prices in the North and Central Valley were about $100,000 less, while Glendale and Burbank and the upscale West Valley averaged about $100,000 more. Keep in mind that these averages take into account all types of accommodation and you are not likely to find a free-standing home for less than a million, unless you venture into a questionable neighbourhood. Once you get into the foothills and hillside, you may be talking multi and mega millions.

Entertainment & Leisure

Locals revel in hosting social barbecues and poolside weekends, but if you want to get out of the house, there are countless local parks, with Balboa Park in Encino worth a mention for its amazing recreational facilities, three-kilometre (five-mile) bike path and lake with paddle boating. The variety of restaurants is vast, covering just about every ethnicity and price level, from fastfood chains and takeaway joints like Thai and I to sophisticated spots like Max and Café Bijou. You will also find more sushi bars than you can count, including the LA favourite Katsu Ya. That said, many of the restaurants don't quite measure up to their counterparts over the hill. If you are looking to be entertained, cinemas and live theatres abound, but you can make a night of it by visiting Universal Studios' bustling City Walk (p.187) for dinner, a movie and drinks. You may also enjoy spending a day touring the studios. If you are looking for a night on the town, the fashionable Cahuenga Corridor actually starts on Ventura Boulevard and continues into Hollywood, but you may prefer east Valley hotspots like Match or the kitschy Blue Room. There are also several places to catch a live band, from the local bar or jazz club to the Universal Amphitheatre, which features major performers. The nearby Hollywood Bowl (p.182) is a five-minute shuttle ride from Studio City.

Shopping & Amenities

Major east-west and north-south commercial streets are strewn with mini-malls and strip malls offering everything from high-end boutiques and second-hand clothes to nail salons and pool products. The Valley is also known for its major shopping malls, including the mammoth Northridge Fashion Center (www.northridgefashioncenter.com) and upscale Westfield Topanga (p.309). 'The Alley in the Valley' is a discount area, known for great deals on handbags and dresses for the mother of the bride or cocktail partiers. You can also find big-name discounts on everything from clothes and shoes to homewares at The Camarillo Outlets (www.premiumoutlets.com) off the 101. The renaissance in the east side of The Valley has also led to a funky art scene centred in and around the NoHo Arts District.

Healthcare

There are several hospitals in The Valley, including Encino-Tarzana Regional Medical Center (p.113), Valley Presbyterian Hospital (p.114) and Los Angeles County-Olive View (p.113), in addition to a large Kaiser facility in Woodland Hills. The Valley is also home to the Motion Picture & Television Fund Hospital (www.mptvfund.org) and there are countless clinics and doctors' offices.

Education

Many local LAUSD schools are highly rated, especially at the elementary school level, and some locals in areas like Calabasas and beyond even claim the money saved by using the strong public school system offsets the high cost of homes. However, some Valley schools simply do not pass muster, so research is recommended. The Valley is also home to several prominent private schools, including Harvard-Westlake, Oakwood and Pinecrest. There are several opportunities for higher education, including California State University, Northridge, Pepperdine University's Encino Graduate Campus, and Valley, Glendale, Pierce and Mission Community Colleges.

Transport

The Valley is serviced by several freeways that intersect at various points, with the 101-405 interchange in Sherman Oaks being the most travelled in the world. The freeways are conveniently located, but there is often traffic, especially during commuter hours. The Valley streets are essentially a grid of major thoroughfares, with access to the city via the 405 and 101 freeways, as well as through the busy canyons, including Lauren, Coldwater and Beverly Glenn. You can also take Ventura Boulevard straight into Hollywood. In addition to using cars and buses, The Valley can be accessed through the Metro. The Red line travels as far as Universal City and North Hollywood, with a major commuter carpark by the Universal stop. The new Orange line makes 14 stops across The Valley, starting in North Hollywood. The area also has two airports, in Van Nuys and Burbank.

Safety & Annoyances

As you'd expect in such a big area, some parts of The Valley are very safe, while others are markedly less so. There is often traffic on the freeways and the canyons, and freeways are choked during rush hour. Though it may only be a 15 minute trip over the hill, many locals have difficulty motivating themselves to go out in the city, while most of your friends from the city will rarely come out to visit.

Area **M** *p.66*
See also Map 3

Best Points
Santa Monica is a beach and mountain playland, with many pedestrian areas, a strong art community and fantastic educational opportunities. It has a vibrant but laid-back bar and club scene.

Worst Points
Housing prices can be prohibitive. It has a major homeless problem.

Santa Monica

Starting at the beach town and stretching inland, Santa Monica attracts a mix of residents, including a community of British expats. It offers a more laid-back attitude than you might find in WeHo, Hollywood and the like, but there are plenty of yuppies and Hollywood power players mixed in with the hippies, surfer types and the third largest homeless population in LA. Most locals are involved in their community, with the Santa Monica government at the forefront of social, environmental and health trends. It was one of the first to ban restaurant smoking, for example, and has since expanded the campaign to local beaches. In recent years, this area has also become a centre for entertainment, high-tech and software companies. This trend has increased property values and interest in the area, which has long been a favourite for singles, couples and families.

Accommodation

Santa Monica is comprised primarily of low-rise apartment buildings, many with little architectural personality. There are also neighbourhoods with single-family homes, which can be quite small in some areas. As Santa Monica stretches from the five-kilometre (three-mile) beachfront area, neighbourhoods become slightly less expensive, with few luxury condos to speak of. About three quarters of locals are renters and the area is rent controlled, but a one-bedroom apartment may still cost at least $2,000 or $2,500 a month. The average price for home buyers is around the million dollar mark, but you could find beachfront spots in the multi-millions or an inland 'fixer upper' for closer to $700,000.

Shopping & Amenities

The area's famous farmers' market is on Wednesdays and Saturdays on Arizona and 3rd Street. Locals here prefer outdoor shopping areas like Main Street and the pedestrian-only 3rd Street Promenade. The Promenade offers over 200 shops, covering recognisable chains like Gap, Zara, Mac and Borders, as well as cool speciality boutiques like Hennessy + Ingalls' bookstore (www.hennesseyingalls. com) or Shiva Imports (310 394 1191). Just off the drag are the trendy Fred Segal shops, which are very Hollywood and worth a look. Montana Avenue's 150 high-end boutiques offer the hippest fashions, antiques and fine art, while Bergamot Station is brimming with art galleries. In addition to private gyms, there are several adult sports leagues and two local pools: Santa Monica Swim Center and Lincoln Pool. For info on city services and leagues, visit www.smgov. net. In addition, the social athletic group Fit Club (www.thefitclub.org) meets on the beach before work and on Sundays.

Rooms with a view

Entertainment & Leisure

Santa Monica's beachfront offers ocean and beach sports, the Santa Monica Pier and Pacific Park (p.168) and a bike and jogging path. You can also get physical in the Santa Monica Mountains, a hiker's dream. There is also a host of inland parks, including the new Airport Park with playground, dog park and sports field. The Civic Auditorium always seems to have new events. You may prefer

Santa Monica

strolling pricey Montana Avenue and doing lunch at one of the local restaurants or going a bit more mainstream with an entertaining day at Third Street Promenade, where you can shop, eat, drink, see a film and get caught up in a host of street performances. Main Street is also a fun outdoor spot for dining, and there are several movie and live theatres in the area. Note that some local restaurants will add a mandatory tax that is split between the city and the restaurant, and essentially covers your gratuity.

Healthcare

Santa Monica is home to two reputable, state-of-the-art hospitals with emergency rooms: St John's Health Center (310 829 5511) and Santa Monica UCLA Medical Center and Orthopaedic Hospital (p.114). The St John's ER boasts new rapid diagnosis, treatment and charting systems and UCLA also has several medical offices in the area.

Education

Santa Monica is home to Santa Monica College (SMC), Art Institute of California-Los Angeles, Emperor's College of Traditional Oriental Medicine, and Mount St Mary's College. Public school education from preschool to graduation is provided by the Santa Monica-Malibu Unified School District (SMMUSD), with the LAUSD's Canyon Elementary School being the only local charter. Local private schools include the prominent Crossroads School, in addition to the Delphi Academy of Santa Monica, New Roads School, and several others. Preschools include Santa Monica Montessori School, Westside Waldorf School, The Growing Place and countless others.

Transport

Santa Monica is easily accessible by bus or car via the 10 and 405 freeways, as well as thoroughfares like Wilshire, Pico, Olympic and Santa Monica Boulevards. But it is no stranger to traffic, especially on gorgeous, sunny days. Many locals prefer to ditch their cars once home, especially if they live near major pedestrian areas like Third Street, Main Street or Montana. These areas offer ample paid parking at reasonable rates, but finding metered street parking can be a challenge. Many residential neighbourhoods, especially those closer to the beach, offer permit parking only. You will see more cyclists in this area and some locals make use of Santa Monica's Big Blue Bus system (www.bigbluebus.com), which has routes into LAX and Downtown. You can also get around Santa Monica on the electric Tide Shuttle bus. In addition to being only 13 kilometres (eight miles) from LAX, Santa Monica has its own one-strip airport.

Safety & Annoyances

Santa Monica is a relatively safe area, with a strong but relaxed police presence in the tourist hotspots. With gentrification has come a decrease in gang activity, but you will note some areas are still unsafe, especially at night. The area has a huge homeless population and perhaps due to the liberal nature of the residents, locals have long discussed how best to handle this with little actual outcome. If you live closer to the beach, you may feel trapped or frustrated by the influx of tourists and weekend visitors.

Area **N** p.66
See also Map 8

Silver Lake & Echo Park

Silver Lake has long been home to locals looking to escape the hustle and bustle of LA proper, without losing the city vibe. Just east of Hollywood and a skip from Downtown, this hilly, green area with its own reservoir lake was once less expensive and even a bit grimier than its neighbours, making it ideal for gay and straight LA hipsters and creative types, who got along with the local Latino community. Like much of LA, however, Silver Lake has experienced gentrification. The area has so far managed to maintain its cool factor, while less expensive Echo Park has come into its own as the newest, hippest re-energised eastside area. Unsurprisingly, prices there have gone up as well, with nearby Highland Park and Mt Washington following suit.

Best Points
This is a hip and hilly area where you get more bang for your buck.

Accommodation

Architecture lovers have taken an interest in these areas as they reflect well over a century of building history – a rarity in LA. You will find much of the Spanish flair that characterises LA's oldest areas, but you will also find homes in the French Normandy, English Tudor, Gothic and post-modern styles. While you may find a condo for as low as $500,000, a house will probably cost about a million dollars. If you are eyeing the hills or a lake view, you may be looking at $2 million or $3 million. That said, you will probably get more for your money than you would in areas like Bel-Air, Beverly Hills and nearby Los Feliz, in terms of space and views. If you have the time and the skills to take on a fixer upper, this area offers some opportunities. As a renter, you may find a one-bedroom for around $1,000, but you are likely to pay quite a bit more. As with most areas facing a renaissance, you will find prices and safety levels can change with the crossing of the street.

Worst Points
Relatively unsafe in certain areas, with a history of gangs and homelessness. Prices are skyrocketing.

Shopping & Amenities

Silver Lake and Echo Park are predominantly residential areas, but you can find everyday necessities like groceries, banks and gyms on main streets like Glendale

Silver Lake reservoir

Echo Park suburbs

Boulevard, Hyperion Avenue, Sunset Boulevard and Silver Lake Boulevard in Silver Lake; or on Sunset or Echo Park Avenue in Echo Park. As you get to know the area, you will discover interesting boutiques and galleries hawking artsy wares. Local farmers' markets are in Silver Lake at 3700 Sunset Boulevard on Saturdays from 08:00 to 13:00, and in Echo Park on Logan Street on Fridays from 15:00 to 19:00. In addition to local gyms and trainers, you can get some exercise at nearby Griffith and Elysian Parks.

Down The Drain
Silver Lake's reservoir was drained and cleaned in 2008 after elevated levels of bromate were detected. Bromate is formed when sunlight interacts with bromide and chlorine in the water; one suggestion put forward to stop the problem recurring was to cover the reservoir with millions of floating plastic balls.

Entertainment & Leisure
The area is not flooded with restaurants or nightlife, but locals will tell you it's about quality, not quantity. Far too hip for chains, most locals love their neighbourhood coffee shops and cafes. You will also find a few choice dining spots, like Blair's (p.317) in Silver Lake. Echo Park's Taix French restaurant (p.327) offers fine food without the fine prices, making it a local favourite for some 70 years. If you are looking to get some sun, Echo Park has opened its former reservoir for recreational use. Go fishing, paddle boating or picnicking and you may be surprised by the gorgeous view of Downtown. The Vista Theater brings modern films to an Old Hollywood haunt, but make sure you know which movie is playing before you head over. You will find many galleries and boutiques have a social element to them, both formally and informally. Echo Curio (www.echocurio.com), for example, occasionally hosts screenings, musical events and lectures. When you are ready for a drink, spots like Cha Cha Lounge (p.346) are packed with hipsters, and Mixville caters to a more adult crowd. Akbar is the local gay spot, but this area tends to shy away from segregation. Annual events include the Sunset Junction Street Festival, The Silver Lake Film Festival and the Lotus Festival.

Healthcare
This area has no major hospital, but Good Samaritan Hospital (p.113) is only two miles away, with Los Angeles County Hospital (USC, p.113) about twice as far. Silver Lake is home to the Braille Institute and The Salvation Army Alegria, a one-of-a-kind, low-density village-style community for homeless and low-income families affected by HIV and AIDS.

Education
This area is not the best for education, though that is improving. It is served by LAUSD, with local private schools including Immaculate Heart, St Theresa of Avila Catholic School and Our Lady of Loretto Elementary School. Local preschools include Echo Park-Silver Lake People's Childcare Center, Silver Lake-Los Feliz Jewish Community Center, Rose Sharlin Co-op Nursery School and Neighborhood Nursery School. There is also the local non-profit Conservatory of Music (p.230).

Transport
These areas are accessible via the 101, 2, 5 and 110 freeways as well as major thoroughfares like Sunset Boulevard, but their proximity to Downtown and Dodger Stadium makes for serious congestion. The area lies between the Red and Yellow Metro lines, with the nearest station in Chinatown. Bus lines access Silver Lake, but skirt Echo Park.

Safety & Annoyances
Home to the infamous LAPD Ramparts district, this area has a serious history of gang problems. It is not the safest part of LA and you may feel quite unsafe in certain areas, particularly at night, but locals are struggling to change that. Traffic can be awful, especially when there is an event at nearby Dodger Stadium. As these areas are perceived as far out, your friends in the city are not likely to visit often.

Area ➋ p.66
See also Map 3

Venice

Built around narrow canals and single-lane bridges inspired by its namesake, Venice is famous for its lively Ocean Walk Drive boardwalk. To LA locals, it is known for being a laid-back, eclectic beach community with artsy and gritty elements, although the recent gentrification has wiped away some of the grit. The area also has a strong reputation for being 'green' and is pedestrian and biker friendly. Residents include artists, surfers, burn-outs, urban professionals and families. Almost 75% of locals are white, with Latinos being the second biggest group.

Best Points
Voted one of the country's funkiest cities, eclectic, green Venice pairs incredible beach town living with the best of city living. It has a notable art scene and is one of the few pedestrian and biker friendly communities in LA.

Accommodation

While the average home price is about $1.3 million, price, building type and safety factors vary greatly by neighbourhood. The majority of locals are renters and choose from bungalows, new condos, apartments and single-family homes. Housing along the canals, in swank duplex apartments or along the pedestrian streets often sells for several million dollars. Just about every area has seen gentrification, which means increases in safety and prices.

Worst Points
The area pairs high property prices with a higher crime rate than much of LA. Tourist traffic can be frustrating.

Shopping & Amenities

Along the Venice boardwalk, vendors in temporary and permanent structures hock sunglasses, T-shirts, bikinis, shoes, smoking paraphernalia, tattoos, piercing and even massages. The Abbot Kinney area, named after Venice's founding father, is full of hip galleries, furniture stores and boutiques, while Main Street is more mainstream, with boutiques and international brands like Gap and Armani Exchange. Lincoln Boulevard is a commercial thoroughfare, offering the general mini-mall fare, including chain groceries, drugstores and nail salons. You will also find scattered local markets offering a range of amenities and a prevalence of bike, skate and surf shops for renting and buying. Venice has a bustling farmers' market on Friday mornings at Venice Boulevard and Ocean Avenue, and galleries often host flea markets featuring local artists, designers and jewellers. In addition to private gyms throughout the area, you'll find impressive public sports facilities at the beach.

Canalside living

Entertainment & Leisure

Second only to Disneyland as LA's top tourist destination, Venice Beach can easily keep you occupied. You can enjoy the scene on the boardwalk on foot, or watch the procession from a seat at one of the boardwalk restaurants or bars. If you are feeling more active, there are basketball and handball courts, a bike path, beach volleyball, and waves for swimming and surfing. You can fish off the piers or sunbathe on the widest beach in the South Bay. Closer to Lincoln Boulevard, Penmar Park offers public tennis courts and a golf course. Once the sun goes down, Venice offers a decent nightlife. Abbott Kinney and Main Street are great for making a night of dinner, drinks and window shopping, but for dinner and a movie you will have to hit the nearby Santa Monica or Malibu theatres. In

Houses in Venice

addition to special events like the annual Art Walk & Auctions, you can usually find an art opening or local show happening just about any night of the week.

Healthcare

The Venice Free Clinic (310 392 8636), which offers primary healthcare, mental health services, health education and child development services by appointment, is the largest free clinic in the country. The nearest 24 hour ER is at the nearby Marina Campus of the Centinela Freeman Regional Medical Center (310 823 8911; www.centinelafreeman.com). You will also find several good doctors at the UCLA Marina professional building on the corner of Admiralty and Bali.

Education

There is a host of nursery school and childcare options in Venice, but your child's LAUSD school may be slightly outside the Venice limits. Local public schools are Coeur D'Alene Avenue Elementary, which ranks quite well, Broadway Elementary, Westminster Avenue Elementary, Venice Senior High School, and Animo Venice Charter High School. Private schools include First Lutheran School of Venice (K-8) and St Mark's School (K-8). Venice Skills Center offers career advancement training and courses.

Transport

Tucked between Santa Monica and Marina del Rey, Venice is near the 10, 90 and 405 freeways and easily accessible via surface streets, including major thoroughfare Lincoln Boulevard, but the closer you get to the water, the more congested the streets become. Many locals commute to work in other parts of the city, but once back home they park their cars and travel via bicycles, skateboards, skates and good old-fashioned walking. When Angelenos and tourists flock to the beach for weekends and holidays, some Venice locals feel trapped by the influx of people and traffic. Parking in most neighbourhoods is limited or restricted, with many carparks offering unfixed rates that can go as high as $30 during peak hours at the weekend.

Safety & Annoyances

Venice has a long history of local gangs and is not as safe as other areas of LA, with a Sperling's crime rating of seven out of 10 (see www.bestplaces.net). The boardwalk and beaches, in particular, are not considered safe after dark, but even Oakwood, an infamously rough area on Sixth Avenue, is seeing improvement. Many locals will insist the Venice Beach ocean is safe, while others will refuse to go in it. It may be cleaner than neighbouring Santa Monica, but thanks to a combination of the boardwalk action and storm drains emptying into the ocean, the National Resource Defense Council (www.nrdc.org) reported over half of the water tested in 2006 failed their hygiene standards. This area also has the expected nuisances of being a major tourist centre, including traffic and tourist traps.

West Hollywood

Area ❼ p.66
See also Map 5

Nestled between Beverly Hills, the Hollywood Hills and Hollywood, West Hollywood is a hip and happening area overflowing with new and historic nightclubs, restaurants, hotels, spas and boutiques. In fact, WeHo is so happening, the population tends to double or triple during evenings and weekends. The infamous rock 'n' roll lifestyle of the Sunset Strip lives on, but you will also find quieter areas, like the Avenues of Art & Design district near Robertson. WeHo is a liberal community predominantly composed of singles and couples, with a strong homosexual and Russian presence. The west side of Santa Monica Boulevard serves as the centre of LA's gay life, which is why many call the area 'Boys' Town'. You will find more families in the nearby Fairfax District, which shares an orthodox Jewish community with WeHo.

Best Points

One of the most happening areas in LA, WeHo is centrally located, with easy access to the fun and business of Hollywood. There are several pedestrian-friendly neighbourhoods and areas. Many homes have fantastic views and art deco styling.

Accommodation

WeHo is peppered with small residential neighbourhoods offering apartments, condos, small starter homes and even a few duplexes. This area is one of the most expensive, with the average costs for one square foot coming in at $500 to $600. This is why almost 80% of locals are renters. The area is rent stabilised, but due to its stellar location rates start high, at about $1,500 for a one-bedroom. As a buyer, you will be hard pressed to find a home on the market for under a million, but you may get lucky and find a tiny one-bedroom condo for $430,000 or a two-bed, two-bath for $740,000. Add a view, an extra bathroom, or renovated art deco flair, however, and you will easily breach the million dollar mark. It is of note that the west side of Santa Monica Boulevard in is a primarily gay area, while the east side has a heavy Russian presence.

Worst Points

Housing is expensive and relatively small. The population can triple during the evenings and weekends, and traffic and parking can be dire during rush and party hours.

Entertainment & Leisure

There are over 140 restaurants to choose from, although fastfood pickings are slim compared to the rest of LA. The area is flush with cute brunch spots like Hugo's, where you are sure to spot a celeb or two, as well as chic, trendy nightspots like Koi. Sunset Plaza and Boys' Town offer a great selection of patios for eating well and watching the parade of locals. You can also cruise into Fairfax Village at any hour for some Canters' Deli fare (www.cantersdeli.com). If shopping and eating isn't your idea of leisure, you can spend your days working your own plot at the Community Gardens or taking advantage of the area's four parks, softball field, swimming pool (on San Vicente), and tennis and paddle courts. The area also maintains a buzzing nightlife, especially over in the Boys' Town side of Santa Monica Boulevard, where you can actually go bar hopping on foot for a change. Eastern spots tend to have queues after 22:00. If concerts are your thing, hit Sunset Strip or the Troubadour. The pool and bar scenes at hotels like The Standard and The Mondrian can get crowded at the weekend; most offer phenomenal views, day or night. Wherever you are heading, take note of dress codes as some spots don't allow trainers (sneakers), flipflops or jeans. The annual Pride Parade and WeHo Halloween Carnival are must-see events that bring in hundreds of thousands of people.

Read the signs

Shopping & Amenities

You will have no trouble finding your local grocery store in WeHo, and the West Hollywood Gateway at Santa Monica and La Brea is home to discount shops like Target and Best Buy. There are plenty of delis and bakeries, including kosher outlets, in the Russian area and Fairfax Village. A local farmers' market takes place on Mondays from 09:00 to 14:00 at Plummer Park (1200 N Vista Ave), and then of course there is *the* Farmers' Market (p.180) at the corner of 3rd and Fairfax. For high-end clothes shopping, you may enjoy Sunset Plaza and Sunset Millennium, while Robertson Boulevard offers that and more for a hipper, younger crowd. The Grove (p.308) offers plenty of shopping and eating in a pleasant outdoor setting. Turn up at Melrose and Beverly for LA's hottest design showrooms, shops and galleries, or visit Melrose, west of Fairfax, for cheaper, funkier apparel and jewellery – not to mention smokers' shops. There is no shortage of gyms, banks and beauty salons in this area, with much found on the main drags like Sunset or Santa Monica. The city has also added a four-kilometre (2.5 mile) walking path between West Hollywood Park and Plummer Park.

Healthcare

WeHo is home to Cedars-Sinai Medical Center (p.113), one of the top US hospitals. Its 24 hour Emergency and Trauma Care facility is one of the largest and most advanced in LA, and is located in the North Tower on Gracie Allen Drive. You will also find a host of health and social services offered by the city.

Education

The area is served by LAUSD, with Fairfax High being a prominent local school. Public preschools include Rosewood Children's Center, Laurel Children's Center, and West Hollywood Preschool. Private preschools include ABC Little School, Beverly Hills Montessori, Center for Early Education, Institute of Jewish Education and Just Like Mom's Day Care Center, with several of these teaching up to grade eight or 12.

Transport

WeHo is among the few foot-friendly areas in LA. Locals tend to park and walk in areas such as the Avenues of Art & Design, Sunset Strip, Sunset Plaza and Boys' Town. There is no immediate freeway access, but the area is centrally located and easily accessible by a grid of major thoroughfares. Traffic can get rough during rush hour and party hours. If you are heading up to Sunset Boulevard on a Friday or Saturday night, for example, be prepared for stop-and-go traffic. Interestingly, in order to avoid cruising and to decrease traffic, some WeHo residential areas do not allow you to make turns on small streets at night. During the busy hours, parking can also be tough. Paid carparks and street spots are scattered around populated areas, but if you come in on a busy night, you may have to pay $5 to $25 for parking. Several residential areas offer permit parking for locals only. The CityLine/DayLine bus will get you around WeHo for 25 cents a ride. The City Hall offers MTA and DASH bus route maps and MTA passes in its Commuter Center (8272 Santa Monica Boulevard).

WeHo condos

Safety & Annoyances

Crime rates in WeHo tend to be higher than in much of LA. The sheer number of weekend partiers causes serious crowding, traffic and parking issues. Being that close to the action may be a boon or a bane, depending on your lifestyle.

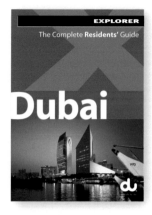

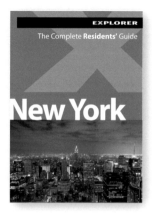

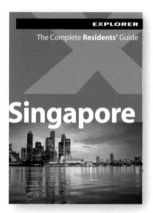
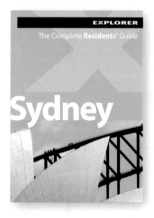

Other Residential Areas

From Hollywood to Downtown, LA's neighbourhoods are constantly transforming themselves, and areas that were once considered off limits to new arrivals are now gaining in popularity. Koreatown, Mt Washington and Highland Park are three examples of the new wave of gentrification. These areas are considered hip alternatives to their pricier counterparts like Echo Park or West LA. Although prices are already starting to rise in these neighbourhoods, development is just starting to get underway and many housing options are still sub-standard.

Koreatown

This urban area between Downtown and Mid-Wilshire has long offered affordable housing in a good, central location, but the options are small and often not well maintained. It is also common to find several families living in one apartment, which sometimes gives the area the unpleasant feeling of a labour camp. Safety remains questionable as well. However, with rents still as low as $500 to $1,200, it has become popular with students from USC and UCLA. As with any surge, this has led to gentrification and now hundreds of millions of dollars are going into redevelopment and clean up, with several upscale condos in the works.

Mt Washington & Highland Park

For whatever reason, locals have long preferred the Westside and beaches to the hilly retreats of Northeast LA, or NELA, but that trend is changing. Historic Mt Washington and Highland Park (aka 'HP' or 'Old LA'), in particular, are two of the newest areas to be hit by the LA hip wave. A surge of artists and professionals who cannot afford the funky suburban life of Silver Lake and Echo Park are flocking to this area, which is just minutes from Downtown. You may actually find a small fixer upper with a view for well under a million. In addition to agreeable pricing, these areas are convenient for major freeways and the Gold Line Metro. If you act fast enough, you may even beat the skyrocketing prices that are sure to come.

Housing options in Koreatown

Smooth Move

Having the correct amount of storage boxes, bubble wrap, packing peanuts and packing tape can make moving a lot easier. Old newspapers, blankets, pillows and clothing can also serve as a shock absorber for breakable items.

Moving Services

Finding a moving company to schlep your belongings to your new home shouldn't be a problem. There is page after page of companies listed in the yellow pages of the phone book. Working in your favour is the weather and the many choices of reputable moving companies. If you do some research, the transition should go smoothly.

Narrow your search by asking friends and co-workers for recommendations. Next, start making calls to the companies on your list to learn about their specific fees, insurance coverage, and scope of services. Pricing for movers depends on several factors, including the amount and weight of goods to be transported, the distance between locations, whether you will need packing services, and if there are flights of stairs involved. Once you've narrowed your search to a few select companies, call the Department of Transportation (202 366 4000) to verify they are properly licensed. You should also enquire at the Better Business Bureau (www.bbbonline.org) to see if any complaints have been filed against the company by other consumers. When you settle on your final choice, provide a detailed and accurate inventory of items to be moved, and request that any price quotes be binding and put in writing.

Removal Companies

American Best Moving	888 236 9939	www.americanbest.net
American Trusted Movers	888 226 0105	www.americantrustedmovers.com
Atlas Van Lines	800 638 9797	www.atlasworldgroup.com
Bekins Moving and Storage	877 680 8076	www.bekinsms.com
California Moving Service	818 256 1949	www.californiamovingservice.com
Mayflower	800 325 3863	www.mayflower.com
Melrose Moving	800 431 3920	www.melrosemovinginc.com
Moving Market	800 856 7196	www.movingmarketplace.com/losangeles
PODS Moving	866 229 4120	www.pods.com
Sterling Van Lines	800 264 6313	www.sterlingvanlines.com
U-Haul	800 468 4285	www.uhaul.com
U-Pack Moving	800 355 1696	www.upack.com

You can save money by working with a moving or storage company that offers an 'in-between option'. This flexible service doesn't require you to handle the entire move on your own, but it's not a full-service move either. Another option to consider if you're on a tight budget is the 'self-move service.' This can save you up to half the cost of your move by having the moving company equip you with a truck, container and driver. You load and unload the belongings, and the company does the actual transporting. Moving containers can be delivered to you well in advance of moving day, thus allowing you to load up at your leisure. Many of these container services have ground-level loading where no loading ramps or excessive lifting are needed.

When The Sky's The Limit

The award-winning Pacific Design Center (p.177) is the west coast's leading resource for home furnishings. This high-end emporium only sells to industry professionals, but if you're working with a designer you can accompany them to choose pieces. The centre can refer designers as well.

Furnishing Your Home

Most rentals in Los Angeles, whether a single-family dwelling, duplex or apartment, come with four walls, a roof and little else. Kitchens are usually equipped with major appliances such as refrigerators and ovens. Some newer units may also have microwave ovens, dishwashers and washer and dryers. It's unusual to find furnished or semi-furnished apartments for rent. Those that are advertised as 'furnished' tend to be filled with mismatched pieces left behind by former tenants.

What's nice in leasing an unfurnished space is that you can decorate it the way you want, and you'll find Los Angeles has many home-furnishing shops eager to help. There's a seemingly endless supply of sofas, beds and bedding ensembles, tables, and chairs. There are also many options for nearly every taste and budget. You might want to read the Thursday *Home* section of the *LA Times*, which features a column called 'The Scout' profiling unusual home decor shops and unique finds within the city. For listings of popular home-furnishing outlets, see the Shopping section, p.256.

Discount Retailers & Second-Hand Stores

There are a number of discount retailers offering inexpensive home furnishings, including Target (www.target.com), HomeGoods (www.homegoods.com) and IKEA (www.ikea.com). Local discounters include Larry St John (www.larrystjohn.com), which makes Pottery Barn-style furniture for much less, Just Like The Model (www. justlikethemodel.com), which carries furniture and artwork used for staging model home interiors, and Hotel Furniture Outlet (www.hotelsurplus.com), which stocks a warehouse full of new and mostly used furniture and accessories from hotels, including many four and five-star properties. Here you can find microwave ovens starting at $15, and 20 inch colour televisions starting at $40. For flea market finds, check out the monthly Rose Bowl Flea Market (www.rgcshows.com) held on the second Sunday of every month in Pasadena, or try the Long Beach Outdoor Antique & Collectible Market (www.longbeachantiquemarket.com) at Veteran's Stadium in Long Beach on the third Sunday of the month. Both have a modest admission price, and items run the gamut from reasonable to ridiculously expensive.

Curtain Call

In the United States a tailor is typically a person who alters clothing. If you want someone who makes or supplies window treatments, search the internet or look in the phone book under 'window treatments', 'draperies' or 'curtains.'

Tailors

Other options **Tailoring** p.296

Los Angeles may be the land of nip and tuck, but the knife cuts more than just skin deep. There are tailors, those who can create window treatments and curtains with a needle and a thread, and upholsterers – craftsmen who can create and adjust furniture with a big needle and lots of thread. The choices range from proprietors offering interior design services to companies that carry a wide array of options, from valances and floor-length curtains to privacy blinds. Smith + Noble (www.smithnoble.com) is an online company that offers an array of styles and fabrics for windows. It provides tips for measuring, too. The company recently introduced its 'Shop at Home' service, where a consultant will come to your residence to help you select styles and fabrics.

If it's time for your furniture to go under the knife, LA has many re-upholstering shops listed in the yellow pages of the phone book. Most will come to your house, take a look at the piece you want to have re-upholstered, bring samples of fabric, and give you an estimate of what it will cost to do the job. Once you have made your selection, the upholsterer will usually remove and deliver your furniture as part of the service.

Tailors		
Angela's Custom Upholstery	West Adams	323 737 2771
Budget Blinds	Various Locations	800 214 9124
Galaxy Draperies	San Fernando Valley	818 782 1660
Interstate Custom Reupholstry	North Hollywood	323 875 2741
Jacoby Company	Various Locations	310 476 3291
Orantes Upholstery	Mid Wilshire	323 464 4251

Household Insurance

In Los Angeles, renters' insurance can buy you peace of mind from property loss due to a robbery, fire or some other unfortunate incident. A policy for $30,000 property coverage and $100,000 liability coverage will cost as little as $25 to $30 per month. Rates will vary and are based on your personal inventory of belongings. You'll want to carefully review the terms and conditions of your policy, from specific areas of coverage to items that may be excluded. Losses that occur due to fire or theft are normally covered, but other losses, such as earthquake or flood damage, may not be covered or require a separate policy. You may want additional coverage added for specific claims, such as guest medical coverage should someone be injured while inside your home. Items such as fitness or data-processing equipment may require additional policies; even wedding gifts may warrant additional coverage. As always, the higher the deductible, the lower the premium costs.

While renters' insurance is completely optional, homeowners' insurance is mandatory in California. A separate policy, such as earthquake coverage, is also available for homeowners at an additional cost. You'll find that these policies typically have a higher deductible. Once coverage is secured, you should record and date stamp the contents of your home or apartment digitally or on video tape, and then store the tape in a safe and separate location. This will help prove you owned any claimed assets prior to a loss.

Household Insurance

AIG	877 638 4244	www.aig.com
Allstate	866 621 6900	www.allstate.com
CIG-Home Insurance	866 318 7227	www.cig-home.com
Farmers Insurance	208 239 8400	www.farmers.com
Liberty Mutual Insurance	877 665 7173	www.libertymutual.com
Nationwide	877 669 6877	www.nationwide.com
State Farm Insurance	323 462 1096	www.statefarm.com
Union Bank Insurance Service	800 530 2512	www.uboc.com

Laundry Services

If you're living in a large apartment complex, you'll probably have a central laundry room with coin-operated washers and dryers. Buildings with only a handful of units may not have this convenience, so you'll have to visit a laundromat (launderette). There are countless laundromats throughout Los Angeles that are open either round the clock or daily with extensive hours. You'll need a roll of quarters on hand as one load of laundry typically costs between $1.50 and $2.00, with drying time costing an average of 50 cents per load, per 15 minute cycle – so, you'll need $1.00 to $1.50 to dry the average load.

While doing laundry is not likely to top your list of favourite activities, some laundromats have got creative in trying to attract customers by offering wireless internet service, television viewing areas and even espresso bars to help pass the time. You'll also find 'fluff and fold' services available for about $1.50 per pound. Some fluff and fold services offer pick-up and delivery too.

Domestic Help

You don't need to be rich or famous to have domestic help. Many middle-class people, from singletons to those married with children, have their lawns mowed weekly, get their homes cleaned on a regular basis, or employ nannies to look after the children. No matter what your needs may be, personal recommendations are the best bet for finding dependable, honest help. Housecleaning services, either performed by an individual or cleaning crew, will cost anywhere from $50 a visit for a one-bedroom apartment, to $125 per visit and upwards for a 3,000 square-foot home. Gardeners, or 'mow and blows', usually spend 10 minutes mowing the lawn and blowing off leaves, and cost about $10 to $15 per week depending on the size of the yard or garden. These types of gardeners advertise their services in the local paper. As for nannies, they can make anywhere from $8 to $20 per hour and up depending on their skills, the number of children you have and the scope of the work. If room and board is included, the pay can be much less.

Domestic Help Agencies

Amaidzing	310 287 1878	www.amaidzing.com
Buckingham Nannies & Domestics	818 784 6504	www.buckinghamdomestics.com
Distinguished Domestic Services	818 884 0400	www.distinguisheddomestics.com
Domestic Affairs	310 552 4444	www.domesticaffairs.com
Elite Domestic Agency	310 651 1994	www.elitedomesticagency.com
ISA International Services Agency	310 278 4470	www.isastaffing.com
Maid Pro	909 593 6690	www.maidpro.com/losangeles
Mission Maids	323 302 5493	www.mission-maids.com
Molly Maid	213 745 9955	www.mollymaid.com
The Help Company	888 435 7880	www.thehelpcompany.com

Aside from friends and co-workers, you can also turn to a professional agency to aid in your search. Typically the agency will screen potential help, conduct interviews and do thorough background checks of all candidates. You'll find out more than you'd ever need to know about the potential employee: credit reports, driving records and any evidence of federal, state or local misconduct relating to their skill. If money is no object, there are many agencies that specialise in staffing entire households, from estate managers to personal chefs and professional chauffeurs. They'll even help employ pilots and flight attendants for your Gulfstream.

Many people who employ domestic help without going through an agency do not bother to check whether the person is legally permitted to work in the country, nor do they report the nanny's salary to the government. Both are required. You can visit www.4nannytaxes.com to learn how you can satisfy your tax requirements. Legal Nanny (www.legallynanny.com) located in Orange County offers one-stop, hassle-free, flat-rate solutions for all your legal and tax needs relating to hiring and paying a nanny legally.

Nanny State
I Saw Your Nanny is a new service that allows people to report bad nanny behaviour when they witness it in public spaces. The website lets people leave physical descriptions of both the nanny and children, take photos of the nanny and describe in detail her bad behaviour (www.isawyournanny. blogspot.com).

Babysitting & Childcare

The best and probably most reliable way to find a babysitter or childcare centre is to ask someone you trust – a friend or co-worker who uses childcare, your paediatrician or obstetrician, other mothers or neighbours. Be sure to get as much information as you can from these sources, then narrow the list and interview some of the people yourself. Have your kids there, too, to see how they react to the potential sitter and vice versa. Always ask for local references. Many middle school, high school and college students like to babysit as a means of making a little extra money. You can expect to pay a non-driving sitter (these are usually middle school and high school students) $5 to $7 per hour. You'll need to pick them up, bring them to your house, and drive them home at the end of the evening. College students usually charge about $10 per hour and have their own transportation. If you have more than three kids, the rate increases. Cultural Care Au Pair (www.culturalcare.com) is an exchange programme that has provided families with flexible, affordable childcare for almost 20 years. You could also browse through *LA Parent* magazine or *Kids Guide*, both free publications found at medical and dental offices as well as newsstands throughout the area. Both have resources sections that include childcare and babysitting services. If your needs are more extensive, www.enannysource.com helps locate qualified nannies. Other options, though less ideal, are craigslist, the classified section of the newspaper and the *PennySaver*, a free, ad-filled weekly paper delivered by mail.

Domestic Services

If you're renting and the bathroom springs a leak or you blow an electric fuse, the solution is typically to call the landlord, building superintendent or apartment manager. If you own your home, all the responsibility falls on you to find help. Don't wait for an emergency; instead, start compiling a list of reliable sources now. Ask neighbours and friends who they use regularly. You'll also find pages of contract workers in the phone book. A good rule of thumb is typically this: the larger the ad, the more expensive the company. Before inviting a worker into

Domestic Services			
A-1 Carpenter Service	Hollywood	323 656 8698	Carpentry
Bob's Rooter & Plumbing	Hollywood	323 284 7915	Plumbing
Delight Electric	West LA	818 720 0784	Electrical
Handyman	Brentwood	310 923 5321	Handyman
Jeff Hiatt – Termite Professionals	West LA	800 691 5207	Termite Service
One Hour Heating & Air Conditioning	Culver City	866 354 1441	Heating & Air
Pete's Plumbing	Long Beach	562 986 5353	Plumbing
Terminix	West LA	310 536 0600	Pest Control

your home, ask if the company offers free estimates, how they bill (by the hour or by the job), if they guarantee their work and for what length of time, and ask for recent references. Also, get it all in writing before you agree to anything. Realtors are not allowed to recommend specific vendors, but most usually have a referral list, and yours may be willing to tell you who they personally use at their own homes.

DVD & Video Rental

Once the kings of the rental game, popular retailers like Blockbuster Video (www. blockbuster.com) and Hollywood Video (www.hollywoodvideo.com) are getting a run for their money. Many grocery stores now have small DVD sections. Red Box vending machines (www.redbox.com) are found in convenient locations like McDonald's and outside mini-malls. The crimson-coloured boxes dispense first-run movies for only $1 per rental, per night. There is also NetFlix (www.netflix.com), which charges a low monthly fee for unlimited DVD rentals which you select online. The movies are then quickly mailed to you, and you return them in the prepaid envelope provided. There are no late fees, so you can keep them for as long as you wish.

DVD & Video Rental		
Amoeba Music	Hollywood	323 245 6400
Broadway Video	Long Beach	562 438 8919
Video Star	Beverly Hills	310 585 8453
Video West	West Hollywood	310 659 5762

You'll also find individually owned video shops around town where you can rent the latest DVD or video game, though these are slowly vanishing. Each outlet has its own policies but most require a major credit card, limit rentals to one night for new releases and charge late fees for not returning DVDs on time.

Pets

Pet Taxi
If your pet needs to get somewhere and you can't take them, call the Pet Taxi (310 575 1985; www.lapettaxi.com). This service provides both emergency and non-emergency transportation for your pet 24/7 throughout Los Angeles and Southern California. Affordable transportation is available to the vet's, kennels, groomers and even the airport.

Dogs are quite popular in the city, but there are also plenty of cats, exotic birds, domestic rodents, rabbits, amphibians and fish. For the most part, exotic and farm animals are in violation of city health codes, so it is illegal to keep these as pets. Visit www.laanimalservices.com for more information.

Los Angeles has several dog parks (or 'bark parks' as they're commonly called) including one at Griffith Park and another in Laurel Canyon. Visit www.laparks.org for additional locations. Both Long Beach and Huntington Beach in Orange County have off-leash beaches where dogs can frolic in the surf. For those who work, you can entrust your dog to one of the many 'doggy daycare' facilities, or hire a dog walker to come in and exercise your pooch while you're at the office. There are even 'pooper scooper' services that come to your house and rid you of the canine waste in your yard. The Poop Butler (www.poopbutler.com) in Orange County is one such service and We Do Doo Doo (www.wedodoodoo.com) is another company serving most of LA County. We Do Doo Doo also has a cat box exchange service.

The County requires dogs four months of age and older to be licensed. Licences, which are valid for one year from 1 July to 30 June, are available through the LA County Department of Animal Care & Control (www.animalcare.lacounty.gov). Dogs are also required to be vaccinated against rabies for the entire licensing period, and reduced licence fees are offered when a dog has been spayed or neutered. You'll need to present a Certificate of Sterility and rabies vaccination certificate when purchasing a licence.

LA County also requires all dogs to be on a lead (leashed) on any public street, park (unless otherwise noted) or on private property other than that of the dog's owner. The dog's leash can't be longer than 1.8 metres (six feet) and the animal must be under the supervision of a competent person. Also, keep in mind that animals aren't allowed

Pets Boarding/Sitting

Adele's Pet Sitting Service	323 463 5593
Doggie Central	310 390 3645
LA Cat Sitter	310 573 3702
My Doggy Diva	310 430 3660
The Kennel Club	310 338 9166
The Pet Staff	310 273 5600

to do their business on private property other than the owner's. If Fido can't hold it, you must immediately pick up your pet's waste or prepare to be fined. Visit www.lapublichealth.org for more tips on keeping your pets safe and legal. If you are renting and thinking of having a pet, make sure you first check with your landlord to see if it is permitted. Many places have a 'no pet policy' while others may allow a small dog or cat.

Lost & Found

The Dog Detective (www.dogdetective. com) is an online network that helps reunite owners with their missing pooches. If your dog is lost or stolen, you can post an alert which is then sent to registered animal shelters, law enforcement agencies and pet shops.

Puppy Buying

Beware of small-breed puppies for sale on street corners, in carparks and at flea markets. The sellers could be part of a puppy-smuggling ring, where smugglers purchase puppies at rock-bottom prices in Mexico, then bring them illegally into California. Owners discover too late that their new dog is either too sick or too young to survive on its own, and by the time they do, the seller is long gone.

Kennels & Vets

If you want to leave your pet at home you can hire a petsitter, like Adele's Petsitting Service, to come in twice a day to feed, walk and play with your pet. Another option is to board your pet either at your vet's or at a kennel. Ask if the kennel is a member of the American Boarding Kennels Association (719 667 1600). Also check with the Better Business Bureau (www. bbbonline.org) to see if any complaints have been filed against a kennel you may be considering. Make a personal visit to see if the kennel looks and smells clean, if the staff seem caring, and if each dog has adequate accommodation for its size.

Bringing Your Pet To Los Angeles

Typically it's the Centers for Disease Control and Prevention (CDC), part of the Federal Department of Health and Human Services, which regulates the importation of pets into the United States. General health certificates are not required by the CDC, although certain airlines and states may require such documentation. Pet dogs

Pets Grooming/Training

Belmont Pets & LaunderPet	562 433 3605
Chateau Marmutt	323 653 2062
Dog Remedy	310 390 0380
Doggy Manners	877/ 736 4443
Euphoria Pet Salon	818 760 2110
Muttropolitan	213 626 8887
Pampered Pets Mobile Salon	323 653 0917

Veterinary Clinics

Best Friends Animal Hospital	818 766 2140
Brentwood Pet Clinic	310 473 0957
Cahuenga Pet Hospital	323 462 0660
California Animal Hospital	310 479 3336
Hollywood Cat & Dog Hospital	323 469 3616
Los Altos Animal Hospital	562 421 3749
Steven John Smith DMV, Home Pet Doctor	323 469 3442
Valley Animal Hospital	818 785 5483
VCA Wilshire Animal Hospital	310 828 4587

and cats are subject to inspection upon arrival at ports of entry for evidence of zoonotic diseases (those which can be transmitted to humans). Dogs and cats appearing to be ill upon arrival with a disease that may be transmissible to humans, are subject to veterinary medical examination, treatment or quarantine. For more information on restrictions or requirements, visit the CDC website at www.cdc.gov. If you plan to export your pet from the United States, contact the embassy or consulate of the country your pet is going to.

Pet Shops

California has some strict laws when it comes to pet dealers. They must give purchasers of cats or dogs a written paper that recommends early-age spaying or neutering, vet wellness visits, and compliance with registration laws. A written history of the pet's health, vaccination, and ownership must also be included. The Pet Lemon Law further protects would-be owners by offering recourse to those who purchase sick or diseased animals from a pet shop.

Give A Dog A Home

LA County's many animal shelters house hundreds of adoptable pets, and the fee to adopt can be much less expensive than going through a private owner or pet shop. See http://animalcare.lacounty.gov.

Electricity & Water

The Los Angeles Department of Water & Power (LADWP) oversees the city's water and electrical needs and serves nearly four million residents. Other utility companies, such as Southern California Edison, provide electricity to incorporated cities within LA County. Some cities within the county, such as Pasadena and Burbank, operate their own water and power companies. Ever since the now infamous California Water Wars at the turn of the 20th century, when Los Angeles and the Owens Valley were at odds over water rights, arid LA has been plagued with water shortages. The lack of adequate rainfall creates continuous drought-like conditions, and residents and businesses are constantly being asked to conserve water. There are eight storage reservoirs along the LA Aqueduct, with 99 reservoirs and tanks located within the city. The water is distributed through more than 11,500 kilometres (7,200 miles) of pipes. According to the LADWP, Angelenos use an average of 135 gallons per person, per day.

In recent years, Los Angeles has also had some electrical woes and, during periods of peak demand, has been prone to rolling blackouts. The term comes from the practice of shutting off power in a specific area and then restoring it when additional power is obtained or the power is turned off in another area. Typically, these blackouts happen during the summer months when people tend to blast their ACs.

Utility bills are usually on a 30 day cycle and arrive each month in the mail. Users can pay by US mail, in person, by wire transfer, or by credit card via the phone or internet. You can enrol with each utility company to have your bill paid using direct debit. Once set up, this service is free and you will still receive a monthly statement.

Meter Readers
Each home or apartment complex is equipped with electric, water and gas meters, which are checked each month by meter readers. If you are a homeowner, your meters are usually located in an accessible, outdoor area, but if they're behind a gate, make sure the gate is unlocked and unfriendly pets are locked away.

Electricity

To get juiced, you'll first need to determine which company serves your area. If you live in LA proper, call the LADWP (818 342 5397; www.ladwp.com). For other cities within LA County, contact Southern California Edison (800 990 7788; www.sce.com). You can also visit the California Energy Commission website (www.energy.ca.gov) to see if your city uses a company other than the two mentioned. You will need to arrange for your electricity to be turned on before you move in, and typically you can do this online. Most utility companies offer discounts for low-income families and disabled citizens. Some, including SCE, offer billing options such as the Level Pay Plan, which allows customers to spread the cost of high summer or winter bills over an entire year.

Dollar Bills
The cost of monthly utilities obviously depends on many factors, but a couple living in a one-bedroom apartment can expect to pay an average of $70 a month. In peak winter and summer months, when the heater is running or the AC is blasting, those rates can soar.

Water

Assuming you're not building from the ground up, your new dwelling will already have pipes ready to dispense running water, but you may need to have the supply turned on when you move in. In the case of the LADWP, you can sign up online. Be sure you request this service early, as it takes at least two business days to get connected. If a deposit is required, you will receive a separate bill in the mail. A new account service charge of $13 for the first meter and $2.50 for each additional meter will also be payable. The tap water is safe for drinking and cooking, but many people prefer the taste of bottled or filtered water. The City of Los Angeles Water Services produces an annual Water Quality Report available online at www.ladwp.com. To find out who your city's water supplier is, visit the Metropolitan Water District of Southern California (www.mwdh2o.com) and click on 'member agencies' at the top.

Water Suppliers

Central Basin Municipal Water District	323 201 5500
Foothill Municipal Water District	818 790 4036
Las Virgenes Municipal Water District	818 251 2100
Los Angeles Department of Water & Power	818 342 5397
Three Valleys Municipal Water District	909 621 5568
Upper San Gabriel Valley Municipal Water District	626 443 2297
Western Basin Municipal Water District	310 217 2411

Gas Suppliers	
Long Beach Gas & Oil	562 570 2000
Southern California Gas Company	800 427 2200

Gas

Some appliances such as stoves, water heaters, furnaces and dryers may use natural gas instead of electricity. You may also have a gas-burning fireplace instead of a wood-burning one. Should this be the case, you should call the Southern California Gas Company (800 427 2200; www.socalgas.com) to activate this utility. SCGC services most of LA County with the exception of Long Beach, which has its own gas company (562 570 2000; www.longbeach.gov/lbgo). In addition to turning on your gas, the technician will also light and test any pilot lights you may have. If there is a gas leak, the homeowner or landlord is responsible for having it fixed.

Sewerage

Rubbish Tip

Different cities within LA have different rules regarding how you dispose of your recyclables. Some allow the collection to mingle while other areas may require you to physically separate items (such as glass from plastic). You may also be required to rinse containers.

LA operates and maintains one of the nation's largest waste-water collection systems. There are some 6,500 miles of public sewers, transporting 550 million gallons of flow per day to four waste-water treatment and reclamation plants. The city is currently initiating a decade-long sewer construction programme which will see the production of 150 new sewer-related projects. Residents pay for sewer usage through their water bills; it is itemised on the monthly statement.

Rubbish Disposal & Recycling

Rubbish and recyclable goods are usually collected on a designated day of the week, usually Monday to Friday. The City of Los Angeles Bureau of Sanitation (www.lacity.org/san) collects rubbish from residents and businesses, while unincorporated areas of LA County are serviced by the Garbage Disposal Districts (http://ladpw.org/epd/gdd). The GDD contracts private waste haulers to provide rubbish collection. Most incorporated cities, such as Santa Monica, Long Beach and Pasadena, manage their own disposal services. Both the city's Bureau of Sanitation and the GDD manage a comprehensive recycling programme that collects glass containers, newspapers and other recyclable objects from the kerb, along with the rubbish. Independent cities have similar programmes, and most city services provide residents and businesses with a container for rubbish and another for recyclable goods. Where you put your rubbish varies by area. Some cities collect from containers that line alleys, while others retrieve rubbish from the kerb. If you live in a large apartment building, taking out the trash may mean walking to the end of the hall to a 'garbage shoot' or outside to a dumpster.

Telephone

Contain Your Excitement

In 1986, Californian legislation was introduced to promote the recycling of beverage containers. A tax was added to the price of recyclable drink containers purchased from retail outlets, returnable to consumers who brought the used items to recycling centres. Today the rate is 10 cents for containers of 24 oz or more, and five cents for smaller containers. See www.conservation.ca.gov for your nearest centre.

Although more and more people are choosing to drop their landline and use only their mobile, there is still some healthy competition between landline providers. Verizon Communications is the largest supplier of landlines in Los Angeles. You can also opt to use other companies, like Vonage, which offers local and long-distance calling with many features, including unlimited calls to certain European countries. Verizon, along with some of LA's cable companies (like Charter Communications), has what is called 'bundle' packages that combine cable, phone and internet services. Also included in these packages are all sorts of extra features, such as call waiting, caller ID, call forwarding, voicemail and blocking options. Pre-paid calling cards are another

Codebreaker

Currently Los Angeles County has seven area codes:
213 – Downtown
310 – West LA, Santa Monica & South Bay
323 – Hollywood
562 – Long Beach & south-east LA
626 – Pasadena & San Gabriel Valley
661 – Santa Clarita Valley
818 – San Fernando Valley
Ten-digit numbers beginning with 800, 877, and 888 are usually toll-free from anywhere in the country.

option for local and international calls. In many cases, the rates can be much lower than a telephone company's basic

Telephone Companies

AT&T	800 331 0500	www.wireless.att.com
Charter Communications	888 438 2427	www.charter.com
Verizon	800 483 4000	www.verizon.com
Vonage	800 975 5270	www.vonage.com

international rates. However, it's a 'buyer beware' situation. Purchase your pre-paid card from a reputable retailer, such as Costco, and not the corner liquor store. Some common complaints include access numbers that don't work, card issuers that go out of business, and undisclosed user fees. If you feel you've been taken advantage of, contact the Better Business Bureau (www.bbbonline.com) or the FTC (877 382 4357). As for the iconic payphone, in the last decade the number in the United States has gone from over two million to just about one million. AT&T announced it would stop owning and operating payphones by the end of 2008. It's possible that some private companies will purchase and operate the existing payphones deserted by AT&T.

Don't Call Us
The national 'Do Not Call' list (www. donotcall.gov), managed by the Federal Trade Commission (FTC), bans pesky telemarketers from bothering you. If you're still getting calls 31 days after registering, file a complaint via the website.

Mobile Phones

Most mobile phone companies will lure you with great offers, such as $39.99 a month with a certain number of minutes and unlimited calls during designated hours and at the weekend. Some will even throw in a free phone. The catch is that you will usually have to sign a two-year contract, with penalties for early termination. Read the small print, as there is usually a list of restrictions such as additional roaming or text messaging charges. You may even have to pay an activation fee. Also keep in mind that phones bought through a mobile carrier are often locked to that company, and can't be used with other providers (see p.286 for more details).

Mobile Service Providers

AT&T	www.wireless.att.com	Both
Boost Mobile	www.boostmobile.com	Prepaid
Net10	www.net10.com	Prepaid
Sprint	www.sprint.com	Contract
STI Mobile	www.stimobile.com	Prepaid
T-Mobile	www.t-mobile.com	Both
TicTalk Mobile	www.mytictalk.com	Prepaid
Tracfone	www.tracfone.com	Prepaid
Verizon Wireless	www.verizon.com	Both
Virgin Mobile	www.virginmobile.com	Both

If contracts and catches sound a bit risky, there are also prepaid options where you purchase a certain amount of minutes that will expire if not used by a certain date. You can top up your minutes whenever you run out, and you'll receive a message on your phone when the minutes are running low. Prepaid minutes are purchased in $25, $50 and $100 increments and often expire one year from the date issued. There are also several plans for children which offer parental controls, allowing you to restrict and programme the phone with incoming and outgoing numbers. You can put limitations on the amount of time the phone can be used, such as certain days and hours. This way, your kid isn't calling anyone and everyone. The TicTalk Mobile from Leapfrog uses prepaid phone cards with no activation fee. Coverage is limited.

Cheap Overseas Calls

If you plan on making frequent international calls, your long-distance carrier can help recommend the best plan for you. If you're getting broadband, you might want to forget a long-distance plan altogether. VoIP (Voice over Internet Protocol) services let you make cheap international calls over the internet. Skype (www.skype.com) is the most popular of these services, and calls to any computer that has Skype are free, no matter where they are located. Skype can also call international mobiles and landlines for significantly lower costs. Qwest offers a similar take on VoIP that uses a phone connected to the internet.

Cheap Overseas Calls

Qwest	800 860 1020	www.qwest.com
Verizon	800 922 0204	www.verizonwireless.com
Vonage	800 975 5270	www.vonage.com

Internet

Almost every Los Angeles household has access to either a broadband, wireless or dial-up internet service, and there are several companies competing for your business. Verizon, with its fibre-optic technology, is making a real effort in LA's neighbourhoods to persuade customers to sign on and 'bundle' their collective services (phone, TV, long-distance and mobile). Charter Communications also offers an internet service, as do EarthLink, AOL, and smaller companies such as USA Connex and High-Speed Solutions. Rates typically start at $9.95 for dial-up and $12.95 for high-speed internet.

Internet Service Providers	
America Online	www.aol.com
Charter Communications	www.charter.com
EarthLink	www.earthlink.net
High-Speed Solutions	www.1800high-speed.com
USA Connex	www.usaconnex.com
Verizon	www.verizonwireless.com

If you have a wireless device, many municipalities such as Downtown and Long Beach offer free Wi-Fi to everyone. Many restaurants and cafes also offer Wi-Fi, but typically charge a fee for the service. The Los Angeles Central Library (p.226) in Downtown, one of the city's architectural gems, has 55 one-hour internet stations for library card holders and eight 15 minute internet stations available for non-card holders.

Bill Payment

The quickest way to ruin your credit rating is to not pay your bills on time. Utility bills, whether bundled or not, must be paid monthly. The same rule applies to credit cards and any other service where you're invoiced. Most companies these days make it easy to pay on time through the internet, provided you have money in the bank. If you fail to pay your bills on time, expect to pay a late fee. Utility companies might shut off services until payment is received, and you may also have to pay a reactivation fee.

Postal Services

Restricted Mail

Packages over 32 kilograms (70 pounds) need to be taken to the post office, as a mail carrier will not pick them up. Hazardous and restricted items, such as aerosols, firearms, lottery tickets and flammable materials are usually banned or only permitted in very small quantities. Alcoholic beverages, ammunition, drug paraphernalia and fireworks are never permitted in the mail. If in doubt, call 800 275 8777.

The government-owned United States Postal Service (USPS) has a monopoly on non-urgent, first-class mail. Aside from everyday letters, postcards and bills, the post office has become more competitive with its other services, thanks to the success of private-sector companies like FedEx, UPS and DHL Worldwide. USPS now offers Express and Priority Mail, Media Mail and Parcel Post, along with online tracking and several options for overseas parcels. Many tasks that once required a trip to the post office can now be done online at www.usps.com. The web service lets customers locate zip code information, purchase stamps, calculate postage (a first-class letter costs 42 cents to mail), confirm delivery, request a mail hold while on holiday and schedule a pick up. About the only thing you can't do is retrieve your mail, which is delivered to your home once a day, from Monday to Saturday. If you feel your home delivery isn't secure enough or you are frequently out of town, you can rent a post office box at the post office, or from a private postal retailer such as Mailboxes Etc (www.mbe.com). Post offices are abundant in Los Angeles and you'll usually find them open Monday to Friday from 08:00 to 17:00, with limited hours on Saturdays. Letters that need to be mailed can either be left halfway out of the mailbox for the carrier to pick up, deposited in blue collection boxes found throughout the city or taken to the post office in person.

Courier Services

All the usual big-name couriers have a presence in LA, and there are plenty of local companies as well. Most offer a pick-up service and online tracking. As mentioned above, the USPS has a monopoly on non-urgent first-class mail, but courier and messenger companies can be used for urgent mail, including overnight delivery. The law states that only the USPS is permitted to place mail in private mailboxes, so a courier or messenger company will have to leave the item by the front door, place it in a separate mailbox dedicated to that company or deliver it directly to the recipient.

Courier Services

A-1 Courier	310 450 9000	www.a-1courier.com
A1Express	323 657 5917	www.a1express.com
Classic Couriers	323 461 3741	www.classic-couriers.com
DHL Worldwide	213 225 5345	www.dhl-usa.com
Federal Express (FedEx)	800 463 3339	www.fedex.com
Midnite Express Messenger	310 330 2300	www.mnx.com
Premier Eagle	323 969 0000	www.premiereagle.com
Rapid Express Delivery	909 923 1000	www.rapid-express.com
United Parcel Service (UPS)	800 742 5877	www.ups.com
Zip It Express	213 388 0700	www.zipitexpress.com

Radio

In addition to TV, Los Angeles has perhaps one of the best radio selections in the country. The top talk radio stations are KFI 640 AM, 97.1 FREE FM and KABC 790 AM. If you're more musically inclined, JACK FM 93.1 plays a mix of classic tunes, while 98.7 STAR FM and KROQ 106.7 FM play alternative rock. KOST 103.5 FM broadcasts soft rock and easy listening, and KIIS FM 102.7 pumps mostly urban and hip hop. INDIE 103.1 FM is an alternative music station with a popular show called *Jonesy's Jukebox*, hosted by Sex Pistols guitarist Steve Jones. The city's main classical station is K-MOZART 1260 AM. KUSC, a broadcast service of the University of Southern California campus, is a public radio station that also plays classical music on the FM dial at 91.5. With the large Latino population, there are also some Spanish-language stations, including KLVE 107.5 FM, which plays a mix of Spanish adult and contemporary music. Satellite radio, which is becoming increasingly popular, has two providers: Sirius Satellite Radio (www.sirius.com) and XM Satellite Radio (www.xmradio.com). Both services have an array of channels blasting music, sports, news and talk shows. Service starts at about $13 a month, and the price can drop to as low as $10 a month if you commit to 12, 24 or 36 months of service.

Television

Local network affiliates in Los Angeles are KCBS, KNBC, KABC and FOX, which show local programming (including news) and national network programming, which includes talk shows, soap operas and primetime shows. There is also CW (formerly 'The WB'), known as KTLA Channel 5, and UPN Channel 13, both of which air local news and original network programming. The Public Broadcasting Service (PBS) is also known as KCET in Los Angeles, and is a member-supported and commercial-free station, although 'sponsorship' announcements are often sandwiched between shows. On weekday mornings and afternoons the station shows educational programmes for kids.

Cable & Satellite

Having landed in the entertainment capital of the world, you'll find Los Angeles is blessed with endless viewing options. There are two companies offering satellite television: DIRECTV and the DISH Network. If you don't already have cable lines connected through your house, the company will install them at no charge and connect a small satellite dish to your home. If you're renting, you'll probably need permission from your landlord to install a satellite dish. Verizon currently provides select areas with fibre-optic television (FIOS), which has a small, external box to hold the wiring. In addition to basic cable channels, you can choose premium movie channels and international channels so you can stay connected to your homeland. A basic package for satellite, Verizon FIOS or cable television starts at around $40 a month, depending on the provider, for approximately 200 local and national cable channels as well as some foreign networks such as the BBC. You can build on your package to include movies, sports, and even karaoke.

Satellite & Cable Providers

Charter Communications	866 499 8080	www.charter.com
DIRECTV	877 238 3214	www.directv.com
Dish Network	888 356 8833	www.dishnetwork.com
Time Warner	800 356 6605	www.timewarnercable.com
Verizon	800 922 0204	www.verizon.com

Dial 911 ◀

*If an emergency
medical situation
leaves you unable
to transport yourself
to the ER, call 911.
An operator will
confirm your location,
immediately dispatch
an ambulance and
inform you of your
expected waiting time.
You can also use this
service when you need
police or fire assistance,
but do not use it for
non-emergencies. That
is a misdemeanour
offence that bumps up
to a felony if someone
dies due to your call.
Call 800 582 2258
for non-emergency
ambulance care.*

General Medical Care

While you can find the highest standard of care in the US and Los Angeles, the cost of that care is a highly controversial issue. In short, this country is one of the only major industrialised nations lacking universal healthcare, which means it does not guarantee medical care to its citizens or visitors. The exception is emergency room care centres (ERs), which are federally required to treat those in need of emergency attention, regardless of their ability to pay. Outside of emergencies, most individuals rely on private health insurance, which is often but not always provided and subsidised by their employer. Others rely on flawed but helpful government programmes such as Medicare, Medicaid and the State Children's Health Insurance Program.

The majority of your medical experiences will be outpatient appointments with a primary care physician for checkups, prescriptions, treatment of common illnesses and, if necessary, references to specialist doctors. Angelenos often rely on word of mouth to choose their doctors or call renowned medical care providers like UCLA (800 825 2631) and Cedars-Sinai (800 233 2771) for referrals. Most insurance companies, however, will only subsidise treatment with pre-selected doctors, so if you have insurance be sure your doctor is on this list before your appointment. Women will find the majority of their gynaecological and maternity care is covered by insurance as well, but dental care does not fall under regular insurance plans. There are separate plans available to help cover the cost of your once or twice a year visits for cleaning and checkups.

If you are in the market for plastic surgery, you have come to the right city, but your insurance only covers plastic surgery if it is deemed necessary to your medical well-being or as a direct result of a disfiguring accident or illness.

Government Healthcare

The government-subsidised medical assistance programmes face major challenges, including poor access to speciality care and rising healthcare costs, but they provide relief to many. In the US, seniors over 65 years and individuals with long-term disabilities are eligible for Medicare, the underprivileged can apply for Medicaid, and low-income children whose parents don't qualify for Medicaid are aided by the State Children's Insurance Program (SCHIP). California's Medicaid scheme, Medi-Cal (ww.medi-cal. ca.gov), provides coverage to 6.5 million low-income and disabled Californians. Some immigrants are eligible for full benefits, while others may only be eligible for a limited

*Cathedral Of Our Lady
Of The Angels*

set. The City of LA also has a handful of reputable free clinics and hospitals (see the tables over the page) and many will help determine what sort of assistance you can receive.

Private Healthcare

With two major medical schools, the city boasts some of the top medical professionals and facilities in the nation. UCLA Medical Center, for example, is consistently noted as 'The Best of the West' and ranked third in *Newsweek*'s report on 'America's Best Hospitals' in 2007, with Cedars-Sinai coming in at 18. Where your treatment is provided, however, is usually determined by your physician's affiliation. If you are new to LA and need a doctor or would like to find a doctor associated with a specific hospital, your local hospital likely offers a referral service. Just be sure to match your doctor with your insurance provider too, if necessary.

Pharmacies

Most LA pharmacies are located in 'drug stores' such as CVS, Walgreens or Rite-Aid, which also stock food and household items, but may prefer an independent pharmacy to these mass market chains. Either way, your pharmacy will offer over-the-counter first aid and medicine such as aspirin and mild cold and allergy relievers, as well as controlled, prescriptive medicines that are distributed by the pharmacist, such as antibiotics, strong pain killers and birth control pills. Prescriptions are provided by your doctor and can only be filled at a pharmacy. While insurance often assists with prescription costs, the exorbitant price of these drugs is a key component in the healthcare controversy. Save money by asking your pharmacy if your prescription is available in generic form. Most pharmacists are happy to discuss your prescriptions and even over-the-counter treatments.

In LA, you can find a pharmacy any time of the day. Most are open at least 12 hours on weekdays, with fewer hours on the weekend, but you are sure to have a 24 hour chain location in the neighbourhood, such as the Downtown Rite Aid (334 S Vermont Avenue) and a few CVS stores (3010 S Sepulveda Boulevard, and 13171 Mindanao Way). Call around to find one close to you, but be sure to ask about hours for the pharmacy itself, as apposed to the drug or grocery store, which may stay open longer.

Out-Of-Pocket ◀
The term 'out-of-pocket' describes healthcare costs that are not covered by your insurance, meaning you have to pay for these yourself.

Health Checkups

It is recommended you get health checkups annually, though not everyone in LA does. When most locals with insurance need a checkup, they simply make an appointment with their family doctor or primary care physician. If you do not have insurance or do not qualify for Medi-Cal or Medicaid, many local private and public community clinics provide free or sliding scale services. You can find one by calling 211 or contacting your local Department of Public and Social Services office (http://dpss.lacounty.gov).

Your employer will probably not require that you take a medical exam, but some may insist that you pass a drug test. Your child's school will require his or her immunisations to be up to date before beginning classes and may also require complete health and immunisation records.

Healthy City ◀
Pick up the phone and dial 211 for an often overlooked but very informed medical resource. Operators offer 24 hour guidance, advocacy and referrals to community health and human services. You can also search their database online at www.healthycity.org.

Health Insurance

Many point to large insurance companies as a central cause in the US healthcare crisis, but in a country where a bypass may come in at $57,000 and removing a tough splinter can somehow skyrocket to $700, health insurance is a virtual must. Your monthly or annual insurance premium payment will cover most of your necessary medical expenses, minus a set deductible and $5 to $45 co-pays on all visits to the doctor and prescription medication, which you must cover out-of-pocket. You may purchase a family or individual plan on your own, but your employer is likely to offer you insurance coverage, and will sometimes shoulder much of the cost of the yearly or monthly premium.

The average insured American spent $4,000 on coverage in 2006, but your premium and out-of-pocket expenses will depend on the type of plan you purchase, your age and a host of other factors. Websites such as www.ehealthinsurance.com offer personalised comparison quotes from multiple carriers, as well as detailed explanations of the different types of insurance plans, including Preferred Provider Organisations (PPO) and Health Maintenance Organisations (HMO). When comparing plans, it is important to consider the premium and what care is (or isn't) covered. Also note any limitations on access to doctors, hospitals and other providers, and after-hours

Health Insurance Companies

Aetna	800 592 3711	www.aetna.com
Blue Cross	888 777 0799	www.bluecrossca.com
CIGNA	800 244 6224	www.cigna.com
eHealthInsurance	800 977 8860	www.ehealthinsurance.com
Health Net of California	800 522 0088	www.healthnet.com
Kaiser Permanente	800 464 4000	www.kaiserpermanente.org
PacifiCare	800 577 0001	www.pacificare.com
Western Health Advantage	888 563 2250	www.westernhealth.com

and emergency care. Finally, don't forget to take into account those out-of-pocket expenses, which can quickly add up.

If you are unable to keep up with your premium payments, you might consider a lower premium but higher deductible 'emergency insurance' plan, just in case you need that bypass. If you, like millions of Americans, cannot make that work either, see Government Healthcare on the previous page.

Donor Cards

A third of US patients awaiting organ donation will die waiting. If you are at least 18 years old, you can make a difference by donating your body, body parts or pacemaker after your death. The easiest way to become a donor is to designate your decision on your driving licence application when you renew or obtain one. The DMV will then provide you a donor card (DL 290) and print the pink donor symbol on your licence or ID card. In addition, you can sign up with California's non-profit Organ and Tissue Donor Registry (www.donatelifecalifornia.org). Both resident and non-resident expats can donate and receive organs. Harvested organs are given to patients according to medical need, not citizenship. If you become a donor, be sure to inform your family of your decision. For more information, contact 800 243 6667 or visit www.organdonor.gov.

Giving Blood

A Quick Pint
For information about blood and platelet donation, the Southern California Red Cross site (www. socalredcross. org) will direct you to your nearest donation centre.

Hospitals and clinics are desperate for blood donations, especially type O. You can donate blood in LA as long as you are healthy, at least 17 years old, weigh at least 110 pounds and have not donated blood in the last eight weeks or double red cells in the last 16 weeks. With drives sponsored by hospitals, schools, employers and the government, you can find a place to donate just about any day of the week.

Giving Up Smoking

LA is a decidedly non-smoking town these days, and that can only help your task. You can start nicotine replacement therapy for about $55 with an over-the-counter patch, lozenge or gum, or a prescriptive inhaler. The doctor-prescribed cessation drugs Zyban (bupropion) and Chantix (varenicline) are more expensive, but may ease your transition to non-smoker. For support and information, contact The California Smokers Helpline (800 662 8887; www.nobutts.org), which offers self-help materials, a referral list of other programmes, and one-on-one counselling over the phone. You will also find a wealth of cessation techniques available, from acupuncture to hypnotherapy.

Hospitals

Below is information on some of LA's major hospitals. In most cases, they offer emergency services and physician referral programmes, as well as community

Health Centres & Clinics

Arroyo Vista Family Health Center	Various Locations	323 254 5221	www.arroyovista.org
Health Care Partners	Various Locations	310 354 4200	www.healthcarepartners.com
Los Angeles County Mental Health Services	Downtown	323 669 2350	http://dmh.lacounty.gov
Los Angeles Free Clinics	Hollywood	323 653 1990	www.lafreeclinic.org
Northeast Valley Health Corporation Centers	Various Locations	818 340 3570	www.nevhc.org
South Bay Mental Health Center	El Segundo	323 241 6730	www.sccc-la.org
Southern California Counseling Center (SCCC-LA)	West LA	323 937 1344	www.southbaymentalhealth.com
UCLA Health System	Various Locations	310 208 7777	www.uclahealth.org

Hospitals

Century City Doctors Hospital	310 772 4000	Private
Good Samaritan Hospital	213 977 4190	Private
Harbor-UCLA Medical Center	877 726 2461	Public
Henry Mayo Newhall Memorial Hospital	661 253 8000	Private
Hollywood Presbyterian Medical Center	213 413 3000	Private
Mission Community Hospital	818 787 2222	Private
Olive View-UCLA Medical Center	818 364 1555	Public
Rancho Los Amigos National Rehabilitation Center	562 401 7111	Public
West Hollywood Urgent Care	323 851 4777	Private
White Memorial Medical Center	323 881 8811	Public

outreach and educational programmes such as support groups and maternity classes. If you'd like to know how your local hospital fares in comparison to the rest of the nation, *The US News & World Report* publishes a yearly ranking of the nation's top hospitals. The results can be found online at www.usnews. com by clicking the 'Health' tab at the top of the page.

8700 Beverly Blvd
West Hollywood
Map 7 A1 **1**

Cedars-Sinai Medical Center
800 233 2771 | www.csmc.edu
Famous for catering to Hollywood's glitterati, Cedars is consistently cited as the best by LA locals. It is also the largest non-profit hospital in the western US, with 900 beds and many top doctors. The hospital offers inpatient, outpatient and emergency services, as well as a leading programme for digestive disorders.

4650 Sunset Blvd
Hollywood
Map 8 A1 **2**

Children's Hospital Los Angeles
323 660 2450 | www.chla.org
This private, non-profit teaching hospital is affiliated with the Keck School of Medicine of USC and boasts some of the top doctors in LA. It offers emergency, inpatient and outpatient paediatric and adolescent care, with 85 sub-specialities. Home to the Saban Research Institute, it is a leader in the treatment of heart disease, cancer and blood disease.

18321 Clark St
Tarzana
Map 2 C1

Encino-Tarzana Regional Medical Center
818 881 0800 | www.encino-tarzana.com
One of San Fernando Valley's most respected hospitals, Encino-Tarzana has two locations with a host of speciality centres. Its San Fernando Valley Heart Institute is considered the best heart treatment centre in The Valley. Both locations offer inpatient, outpatient and 24 hour emergency services. Other location: 16237 Ventura Blvd, Encino.

Various Locations

Kaiser Permanent
800 954 8000 | www.kaiserpermanente.org
Kaiser hospitals are not accessible unless you are a Kaiser patient. Legally, however, they cannot reject anyone requiring emergency care in their ERs, including the ones at 1526 N Edgemont Street in Hollywood and 6041 Cadillac Avenue in Culver City.

1200 N State St
East LA
Map 2 D1

Los Angeles County-USC Medical Center (County USC)
323 226 2622 | www.lacusc.org
This 800 bed facility is the largest single healthcare provider in LA County and the largest public hospital in the US. It offers emergency, inpatient and outpatient care to anyone. As it's a teaching hospital, it is staffed by faculty from neighbouring medical school, Keck.

18300 Roscoe Blvd
Northridge
Map 2 B1

Northridge Hospital Medical Center
818 885 8500 | www.northridgehospital.org
Northridge houses one of the only trauma units in the Valley, and with nearly 400 beds, it's one of the largest in the area. It offers speciality centres in cancer, diagnostic

imaging, trauma, surgical, rehabilitation and cardiovascular care. It also houses a reputable inpatient psychiatric unit.

1250 16th St
Santa Monica
Map 3 B2 **7**

Santa Monica UCLA Medical Center

310 319 4000 | www.uclahealth.org
As another branch of the UCLA Health System, the 337 bed Santa Monica centre has a strong reputation for primary and speciality care and is internationally renowned for its Rape Treatment Center and Stuart House for sexually abused children. UCLA announced that an adjoining Orthopaedic Hospital would be opening in 2009.

4929 Van Nuys Blvd
Sherman Oaks
Map 2 C1

Sherman Oaks Hospital

818 981 7111 | www.shermanoakshospital.com
This 153 bed community hospital is home to the renowned Grossman Burn Center (www.grossmanburncenter.com). The hospital's moderate size provides patients with a sense of personal attention. Other services include inpatient and outpatient services, as well as a 24 hour ER.

10833 Le Conte Ave
Westwood
Map 4 B3 **9**

UCLA Medical Center

310 825 9111 | www.uclahealth.org
UCLA's campus hospital is routinely touted as the 'Best in the West' and ranks third, nationally, according to *US News & World Report*. It is a centre for research and a teaching hospital associated with David Geffen School of Medicine, offering inpatient, outpatient and emergency services. The 11 storey building was recently renovated, and an additional building is being constructed across the street.

1500 San Pablo St
East LA
Map 2 D1

USC University Hospital

888 700 5700 | www.uscuh.com
This ultra modern, private, 265 bed research and teaching hospital is staffed by faculty from Keck. Boasting a large list of specialities, it consistently ranks high for ophthalmology and gynaecology. Its online screening tool lets patients review their symptoms to find possible causes.

15107 Vanowen St
Van Nuys
Map 2 C1

Valley Presbyterian

818 782 6600 | www.valleypres.org
Often referred to as 'Valley Pres', this 350 bed, non-profit, acute care hospital boasts more than 50 specialities and offers inpatient, outpatient and ER services. The hospital remains on the cutting edge in maternal and child health, cardiac care, orthopaedics and critical care services.

Dermatologists		
Daniel Taheri	Various Locations	818 789 6296
Darlene D Sampson	Inglewood	310 673 3582
Dr Alan Mantell	Glendale	818 790 3588
Dr Glynis Ablon	Manhattan Beach	310 727 3376
Dr Jack Silvers	Brentwood	310 826 2051
Dr Mary Lee Amerian	Santa Monica	866 811 7986
Gennady (Gene) Rubinstein	San Fernando Valley	818 505 9300
Joyce N Fox	Beverly Hills	310 385 3366
Tommy H Chen	Montebello	323 727 0163
UCLA Dermatology Center	Westwood	310 825 6911

Maternity

Other options **Maternity Items** p.285

Post Partum Depression

Two out of 10 new mothers experience post partum (postnatal) depression, but most try to hide it. If you recognise signs like detachment from your baby, persistent crying, anxiety, insomnia or an inability to concentrate, you may find relief through therapy, support groups or medicinal intervention. For support and information, contact your doctor and connect with LA-based Postpartum Support International (www.postpartum.net; 800 944 4773).

Most expats stay in the US to give birth not only for the high standard of care, but also because babies born in the US are born US citizens. In LA, an obstetrician, obstetrician/gynaecologist (OB/GYN), family practitioner, certified nurse midwife (CNM) or direct entry midwife (DEM) can legally deliver your baby at home, at a free-standing birth centre or as part of a hospital team. Fathers, family and friends are all welcome in the birthing room, though there may be exceptions at your birthplace of choice, so be sure to review the rules before your baby's birth. You and your care provider will likely create a birth plan that outlines your preferences on issues such as pain relief, which may range from epidural anaesthetic to natural delivery.

Your plan should also address your preferences on c-section. Many US maternity advocates question the rapidly growing national rate of caesareans, which is why you will find a wide range of OB/GYNs and alternative care specialists who are dedicated to natural childbirth or at-home births. Hospitals like UCLA and Good Samaritan also offer natural childbirth options, but be sure to discuss these issues with your birthing professional, who will already be affiliated with specific hospitals.

While health insurance covers most maternity care costs, only recently have some providers started covering at-home births, and Medi-Cal will only cover the cost of a doula or midwife in a hospital setting. Without insurance, a midwife-assisted birth, including prenatal care, delivery and postnatal visits, may cost about $2,000 to $3,500. You can also hire a doula for non-medical assistance during and after childbirth, with fees ranging between $300 and $1,000. For more on assisted birthing options, visit www.socalbirth.org or www.mybirthteam.com.

Antenatal Care

It is important to start your prenatal care as early as possible. You and your doctor will outline a care plan, but as an expectant mother, you can expect to see him or her about once a month for the first six months, every two weeks during the seventh and eight month and then every week until the baby is born. If you are over 35 or at high risk because of health problems (like diabetes or high blood pressure), you will probably see your doctor more often. In fact, your best bet is to consult with a doctor before becoming pregnant, when possible. If money is a significant factor, contact the Maternal and Child Health Bureau (800 311 2229) to find out about low or no-cost prenatal programmes in LA. When choosing a doctor, remember that unless you elect a home birth, the hospital you give birth at will be determined by the affiliation of your delivery specialist.

Maternity Care In Private Hospitals

If you are insured, your provider will cover the majority or all of your maternity care. If you do not have insurance, you can advance purchase 'cash packages'. At Cedars-Sinai (p.113), for example, a one day hospital stay with vaginal delivery will cost around $5,400, including anaesthesia. An extra day will bump the cost to about $6,900. Additional costs may crop up if there are complications and you need a c-section or surgery. Your hospital will likely accommodate any birth plan that does not endanger the hospital – so no mood candles.

Maternity Care In Public Hospitals

Public hospitals will take both insurance and Medi-Cal to cover your maternity costs, but also offer packages for those without any cover. At USC County, for example, you can pay for seven prenatal visits at $50 each and then pay $1,500 for the delivery, with no hidden costs. If you do not pay within seven days of the birth, however, you will be responsible for the full, actual cost of your treatment. After the birth, you must also immediately apply for medical cover for your new baby. You will not be denied access if you are in labour, but a private room is unlikely and if available will certainly require an additional fee.

Abortions

First trimester abortions are legal for any reason, but after 24 weeks, abortions are only legal for serious health reasons, such as developmental defects in the foetus or endangerment to the mother. The cost is usually $350 to $700, out-of-pocket. For abortion counselling, services or referral, contact Planned Parenthood (800 230 7526; www.plannedparenthood.org).

Postnatal Care

As soon as your baby is born, he or she will be given an APGAR test, which checks the newborn's colour, heart rate, reflex, muscle tone and respiratory effort to determine their health. Your baby will also be measured, weighed and then, after some bonding time with you, he or she will be given a bath, a range of tests and possible vaccinations. You have a say over every step of your new baby's healthcare, including the testing and immunisations, so discuss all options with your doctor before birth. In most cases without complication, mothers spend one to two days in the hospital. Before you take your new addition home, you will have to sign his or her birth certificate (p.45). He or she will also receive a newborn screening blood test to identify any diseases that require treatment during early infancy, such as PKU (phenylketonuria) or congenital hypothyroidism. Many hospitals have a lactation consultant to help with feeding, but you will also be offered pamphlets and information about caring for your new baby and support groups and classes in your area. New mums will also schedule a checkup for around six weeks after the birth or sooner if delivery was more complicated.

Maternity Leave

Many working women take about three months' maternity leave after having a child in the US, and short paternity leaves are becoming more common. According to the country's Family and Medical Leave Act (FMLA), your employer must hold your job for up to 12 work-weeks after the birth or adoption of a new child. The law only pertains to those who have worked for a company for at least 12 months and at least 1,250 hours over the previous 12 months. The company must also have at least 50 employees that are employed within 75 miles. If the company is too small, however, FMLA may not apply.

Many employers offer paid maternity leave and will define the terms you must adhere to, which may or may not include stipulations on returning to work. If your employer does not offer pay, you are likely eligible for six weeks of benefits through California's Paid Family Leave and Disability Insurance programme. Discuss your options with your human resources department, noting that in order to be protected by FMLA, you must do this before your leave begins.

Maternity Hospitals & Clinics

Cedars-Sinai Medical Center	8700 Beverly Blvd	West Hollywood	800 233 2771	Private
Children's Hospital Los Angeles	4650 Sunset Blvd	Downtown	323 660 2450	Private
Encino-Tarzana Regional Medical Center	18321 Clark St	Tarzana	818 881 0800	Private
Good Samaritan Hospital	1225 Wilshire Blvd	Downtown	213 977 2121	Private
Hollywood Presbyterian Medical Center	1300 North Vermont Ave	Hollywood	213 413 3000	Private
The Natural Birth and Women's Center	14140 Magnolia Blvd	Sherman Oaks	818 386 1082	Private
Providence Saint Joseph Medical Center	501 S Buena Vista St	Burbank	818 843 5111	Private
Santa Monica UCLA Medical Center	1250 16th St	Santa Monica	310 319 4000	Private
White Memorial Medical Center	1720 Cesar E Chavez Ave	Downtown	323 881 8811	Public
Women & Children's Hospital at County USC	1200 N State St	Downtown	323 226 2622	Public

Gynaecology & Obstetrics

Most LA locals select their gynaecologists or obstetricians by word of mouth referral, but you may also select one from your insurance provider's list of approved doctors or your local hospital's referral programme. You may also look after your gynaecological health by visiting an LA free clinic, women's clinic or family planning clinics such as Planned Parenthood (www.plannedparenthood.org). Whomever you select, do not hesitate to change doctors if he, she or the environment makes you uncomfortable.

Contraception & Sexual Health

In addition to providing regular checkups, your gynaecologist can provide information about sexual health and prescriptions for the contraceptive pill, implant, patch, ring or shot, as well as IUDs and cervical barriers. These prescriptions are also available through doctors at free clinics and family planning clinics. Barrier contraceptives like condoms, spermicidals and sponges are available over the counter at drug stores, pharmacies, grocery stores and convenience markets like 7/11.

Your gynaecologist or clinic doctor can also provide testing for sexually transmitted diseases. In the interest of your privacy, however, it is best to get HIV testing done somewhere that provides anonymous testing. Search for a testing clinic at www.hivla.org.

Gynaecology & Obstetrics		
Dr Frederick M Kohn	5525 Etiwanda Ave, Tarzana	818 344 0960
Dr Mark Dwight	637 Lucas Ave, nr Good Samaritan Hospital	213 977 4190
Dr Michaelyn Wilson	8641 Wilshire Blvd	310 659 6210
Dr Paul Crane	415 N Crescent	310 659 5810
Dr Robert Katz	8920 Wilshire Blvd, Beverly Hills	310 657 1600
Dr Ronald Wu	435 Arden Ave, Glendale	818 244 3572
Dr Sharon Pushkin	10921 Wilshire Blvd, Westwood	310 208 3111
Dr Stephen Schmones	2625 West Alameda Ave, Burbank	818 843 2826

Fertility Treatments

Fertility therapy can be a financially and emotionally taxing journey, but you will find the most advanced treatments available in LA, as well as alternative treatments such as acupuncture. Most US doctors will recommend giving the body a year to conceive on its own if the hopeful mother is under 30, but you may want to start sooner if she is over 30 and right away if she is over 40. Your insurance may cover the majority of the costs, depending on your plan, but will not cover in vitro fertilisation (IVF), which can cost about $12,400. For more information or support, call the Resolve of LA hotline (877 203 7773).

Paediatrics

Most new parents in LA consider word of mouth, their insurance's approved doctor list or doctor referral in choosing a paediatrician. It is recommended your baby be checked by one within 24 hours of birth. If you have not selected one yet, one will be on hand at the hospital, but it is your choice whether to stick with that doctor once you leave.

The decision about which vaccinations your child will receive is also ultimately yours. Immunisations have become a controversial issue in the States. Not only are vaccines like MMR getting a bad rap, but a small group of advocates oppose vaccinations altogether. Many doctors consider these movements an unfortunate result of misinformation and will recommend you follow the US suggested immunisation schedule (found at www.cispimmunize.org). It is wise to make your decisions about immunisation before your baby arrives, as the first Hepatitis B shot is recommended at birth, with follow ups over the first four months. Another round of vaccinations is recommended between six and twelve weeks and then again at 12 months. Your doctor may also recommend flu shots for the whole family.

In most cases, your private insurance or Medi-Cal will cover the costs of regular visits and recommended vaccinations.

Paediatrics

Dr Andre Vanderhal	8700 Beverly Blvd	Beverly Hills	310 423 4434
Dr Aviva Biederman	8635 W 3rd St	Beverly Hills	310 652 3324
Dr Dave Michelis	601 Dover Dr	Newport Beach	949 645 4670
Dr Evelyn Henar	1111 Sixth St	Downtown	213 975 9626
Dr Jeannette Levenstein	16550 Ventura Blvd	San Fernando Valley	818 783 3110
Dr Marshall Sachs	2122 Wilshire Blvd	Santa Monica	310 829 9935
Dr Pejman Salimpour	15477 Ventura Blvd	Sherman Oaks	818 907 0322
Dr Richard Feuille	1530 E Chevy Chase Dr	Glendale	818 246 7260
Dr Richard Levy	1245 16th St	Santa Monica	310 453 9010
Dr Robert Hamilton & Dr Jenna Roberts	2216 Santa Monica Blvd	Santa Monica	310 264 2100
Dr Sonya Sethi Gohill	11633 San Vicente Blvd	Brentwood	310 826 5513
Dr Sung Jeen Hong	955 S Western Ave	Koreatown	213 733 1122

Dentists & Orthodontists

California is the state of cosmetics. Your dentist will certainly provide regular checkups for teeth and gums, along with occasional rehab work to restore the damage of decay or trauma, but chances are, he will also offer or suggest cosmetic services such as veneers, tooth whitening, dental implants and bridges and tooth reshaping to make your smile shine. It is recommended your children have their first dental appointment by their first birthdays, with bi-annual checkups.

Dental insurance can help shoulder the bill and some dentists provide financing, as well. Without insurance, an exam, cleaning and fluoride alone might cost $350. A root canal can come in as high as $1,000 and dental implants start at a few thousand, but can total up to $30,000.

Orthodontics is extremely common for children and also popular with adults, especially as modern advances can make braces virtually invisible. Your dental insurance may cover orthodontic care for your minor children, but not for any adults, who can expect to pay around $5,000 for basic braces.

Dentists & Orthodontists

1-800-DENTIST	na	na	800 336 8478
Arthur Alex Kezian	443 N Larchmont Blvd	Hollywood	310 467 2777
BabyTeeth Children's Dentistry	10921 Wilshire Blvd	Westwood	310 443 9596
Children's Dental World	3932 Wilshire Blvd	Koreatown	213 381 5437
Dr Bradley Matthew	8540 S Sepulveda	West LA	310 670 0659
Dr Donald Eslick	10921 Wilshire Blvd	Westwood	310 208 4072
Dr Kari Sakurai	1304 15 St	Santa Monica	310 458 6222
Dr Thomas Stelmach	8920 Wilshire Blvd	Beverly Hills	310 659 5399
Robert Wong	23111 Ventura Blvd	Woodland Hills	818 225 7744

Opticians & Ophthalmologists

You can pick up a new pair of prescription glasses or sunglasses just about anywhere in LA, from your local mall to your eye doctor's office. While your doctor's office may offer a more traditional exam environment, vendors such as LensCrafters and superstores like Target may offer a one-hour lens service, not to mention the occasional promotion for free eye exams with purchase of glasses. Once you have your prescription, you can order contacts from your doctor, vendor or the internet. You can purchase reading glasses and most contact solutions and eye drops without prescription at grocery stores, pharmacies and convenience stores. Medical insurance often covers a portion of your eye care, but exam and lens prices vary. If you require a specialist, The Doheny Eye Institute in East LA (323 442 6300) is a leading centre for research and patient care. In addition, it is recommended your child receives his or her first eye exam by the age of six months, but if you detect a problem, see a doctor as soon as possible. The Children's Hospital (p.113) has several of the nation's top doctors on hand.

Many people forgo the upkeep of exams and lenses by opting for the virtually painless laser or Lasik surgery. You can usually be back at work the same day, but the price tag may be as high as $3,200 per eye. Most offices offer finance programmes, as this is elective surgery and your insurance is not likely to assist you.

Opticians & Ophthalmologists			
Andrew Caster / Caster Eye Center	9100 Wilshire Blvd	Beverly Hills	310 274 1221
Dr Marshall Field	18429 Sherman Way	Reseda	818 344 4012
Dr Robert Maloney	10921 Wilshire Blvd	Westwood	877 999 3937
Dr Simon Cheng	2109 Hillhurst Ave	Hollywood	323 660 2020
John E Maanum	9701 Pico Blvd	West LA	310 553 7011
Jonathan Gording	2035 Westwood Blvd	Westwood	310 470 4289
Kenneth W Wright	520 S San Vicente Blvd	Beverly Hills	310 652 6420
LensCrafters	na	Various Locations	310 470 9669

Forever Young

Botox and Restylane remain two of the hottest non-surgical temporary anti-wrinkle aids, but new products are hitting the market constantly. The newest FDA approved injectable, ArteFILL, is used as a filler in the side of the nose and mouth and is reported to last up to five years. Prices may adjust as this treatment becomes more mainstream, but don't be surprised if it costs up to $3,000.

Cosmetic Treatment & Surgery

It is not unusual to see a 70 year-old woman in LA without a single wrinkle or laugh line, and it's a common occurrence to come across a skinny mini with breasts the size of her head. Cosmetic enhancement is LA's fountain of youth, with Beverly Hills at the epicentre. Many advertised clinics offer the latest surgical and non-surgical techniques, from surgical breast augmentation and cellulite removal to the ever popular anti-wrinkle injections such as collagen, botox, restylane and juvederm. Laser skin resurfacing and hair removal are also very popular.

Your insurance will not cover cosmetic therapy unless it is deemed medically necessary, such as a breast reduction to protect your back or a 'nose job' for a deviated septum. Prices vary by service and provider. Depending on where you go and how much you have done, liposuction, for example, may cost as little as $1,000 or more than

Cosmetic Treatment & Surgery		
Bernard Markowitz	Beverly Hills	310 205 5557
Douglas Hamilton	Woodland Hills	818 884 7150
Dr Gary J Alter	Beverly Hills	310 359 8528
Dr Grant Stevens	Marina Del Rey	866 588 7507
Helen Elliott, Plastic Surgery Consultant	na	888 433 9091
Malcolm Lesavoy	Encino	818 986 8270
Norman Leaf	Beverly Hills	310 274 8001
Rodeo Drive Plastic Surgery	Beverly Hills	310 550 6300
UCLA Cosmetic Surgery Center	Westwood	310 829 0391

$3,000. You may pay by credit card and financing is often available. You may also find safe and less expensive services at UCLA Cosmetic Surgery Center, as it is a teaching environment. Wherever you go, be sure to check the provider's reputation with friends, professionals or even on the internet to avoid botched treatments.

Finding Holistic Care

If you are searching for a practice or specialist not listed here, do not lose faith. It more than likely exists in LA. Visit the Holistic Health Network at www. holisticnetwork.org for more information on practitioners, schools and local events.

Alternative Therapies

LA's diverse immigrant population and rich history in alternative living go hand in hand with an openness to alternative healthcare and therapies. Your employer may bring in reflexologists to boost worker morale and productivity, while your insurance may even cover chiropractic care and acupuncture. Some practitioners offer a traditional approach to these therapies, but many medical professionals couple the most modern advances with alternative, traditional or eastern practices. Cancer experts, for example, often prescribe acupuncture or medical marijuana as secondary treatments. Rule of thumb: if you have heard of it, someone in LA is probably doing it.

Acupressure/Acupuncture

Acupuncture and acupressure are extremely common in LA and are often available in conjunction with chiropractic care. The specialists and doctors in Koreatown are likely to offer a more traditional approach and are also known to have strong hands. Just make sure the doctor you choose speaks your language.

Healing Meditation

Perhaps because the majority of the city's meditation centres have Buddhist affiliations, many in LA view the practice as a lifestyle or religious activity. In spite of this perception, meditation is another alternative practice and a respected tool in psychotherapy, pain management and healing.

Reflexology

Reflexology treatments are found mostly in wellness, massage and beauty spas, but your acupuncturist or chiropractor may incorporate the technique as well. It is also not uncommon to see practitioners set up along the Venice Beach boardwalk or at local fairs and festivals.

Homeopathy

You could live your whole life in LA without hearing anyone talk about their local homoeopathist, but they do exist here. If you are interested in finding a practitioner or pharmacy, the Los Angeles School of Homeopathy (310 772 8235; www. lahomeopathicschool.com) might be of assistance.

Massage Therapy

Few in LA will turn down a good massage. Whether you are searching for Thai, Swedish, shiatsu, lymphatic or deep-tissue relief, there is a massage parlour, spa or medical

Alternative Therapies		
The Clinic at Emperor's College	310 453 8383	Acupuncture & Herbology
Dr Evan Ross	310 659 1883	Acupuncture
Golden Cabinet Medical	310 575 5611	Integrative medicine combines Eastern and Western practices
Marvin Portner	310 454 6226	Medical Doctor
Pure Center	323 878 2600	Colonics & colon cleansing
Willow Spa	310 453 9004	Wellness spa
Wilshire Oriental Medical Center	323 931 3663	Medical centre

office catering to your budget and your style. Some masseuses even make house calls. Depending on where you go, prices can range from virtually free (through insurance) to hundreds of dollars. Also see Massage in the Activities chapter, p.250.

Medical Marijuana

California was the first state to legalise medical marijuana back in 1996, but marijuana 'dispensaries' did not start popping up until recently and their future remains highly controversial and uncertain. California's Medical Marijuana ID Program, which is only active in 36 counties including LA, registers and issues photo ID cards to patients who are prescribed marijuana for a variety of ailments, including chronic pain, AIDS, mood disorders and cancer. These IDs give you the right to purchase marijuana from a dispensary and use it in a responsible manner. The problem is that the federal government still categorises marijuana as illegal. If this therapy interests you, learn more at www.medicalmarijuanaoflosangeles.com.

Physiotherapy

Most LA hospitals offer sports-medicine centres, such as Cedars' Spine Group, which are essentially consortiums of doctors with a similar speciality. In addition, LA is home to Kerlan-Jobe Orthopaedic Clinic, an industry leader in treating and diagnosing all orthopaedic injuries. You may also find great trainers and physical therapists ready to work with you in the gym, your home or an office setting, but many doctors still consider these professionals the gardeners, rather than landscapers, of healing. In other words, while your 'gardener' can help you work your problem, a doctor should identify the problem first. This difference is slowly changing and it is now possible to find doctors of physical therapy who are able to diagnose most ailments. Your doctor may refer you to a licensed professional, but you can also find them through friends or advertisements. Your insurance may assist with costs, which vary based on treatment and provider.

Physiotherapy

Beyond Physical Therapy	2903 Washington Blvd	Marina Del Rey	310 578 5960
Cedars-Sinai Institute for Spinal Disorders	444 San Vicente Blvd	West Hollywood	310 423 9900
Joel Scherr Physical Therapy	8635 W 3rd St	Beverly Hills	310 657 8591
Kerlan-Jobe Orthopaedic	301 North Lake Ave	Pasadena	626 568 9030
KOR Health & Fitness	815 N La Brea Ave	Hollywood	323 933 3744
Southern California Sports Medicine Institute	5900 W Olympic Blvd	Fairfax	310 657 5900
STAR Training	409 N Crescent Dr	Beverly Hills	800 850 7487

Back Treatment

Back care in LA comes in more flavours than icecream. The city offers experts in chiropractic care, acupuncture, physiotherapy, therapeutic massage, Pilates, craniosacral therapy and just about any treatment you can think of. In addition, your doctor may offer one specific treatment, such as chiropractic adjustments, while clinics like Live Well Pilates & Chiropractic blend services for an integrated approach. You may even find chiropractic care in an office focused on skin care or beauty. Interestingly, you will not find as many osteopaths, who can prescribe medicine, but they are available. If treatment is medically prescribed, your insurance might assist with the costs.

Back Treatment

Cedars-Sinai Institute for Spinal Disorders	444 San Vicente Blvd	West Hollywood	310 423 9900
Live Well Chiropractic & Pilates Center	5553 W Pico Blvd	Fairfax	323 930 9355
Ole Henriksen	8622 W Sunset Blvd	Hollywood	310 854 7700

Nutritionists & Slimming

Weight loss and health are big business in LA and the US at large. If you're looking to get in shape, this city offers countless gyms, weight loss programmes, nutritionists and fad alternatives such as the uber-hip fitness boot camps (p.246). If you are battling serious digestive disorders like IBS or Crohn's disease, however, Cedars' Digestive Diseases programmes are ranked as the top in the US.

Nutritionists & Slimming		
Barry's Bootcamp	1106 La Cienega Blvd	310 360 6262
Bryan Abel	984 Monument St	310 428 1215
Carolyn Katzin	12011 San Vicente Blvd	310 471 0529
Cedars-Sinai Center for Digestive Diseases	8700 Beverly Blvd	800 233 2771
Diet Designs	9040 Lindblade St	310 253 9079
The healthXchange	9300 Wilshire Blvd	866 632 9972
NutritionBite	1901 Avenue of the Stars	310 526 7872
Ultra Body Fitness	828 N La Brea Ave	323 464 5300
Weight Watchers	Various Locations	800 651 6000

Counselling & Therapy

No matter how serious your psychological problem, you can find a psychiatrist, psychologist or clinical social worker with the skill set to help you. Outpatient therapy and services are available in government-sponsored clinics, private practices and most hospitals, while inpatient care is reserved for those with more intense psychiatric needs. If your child is grappling with behavioural issues, The Child and Family Development Center at St John's Hospital (www.stjohns.org) has a reputable early childhood programme, while UCLA's Resnick Neuropsychiatric Hospital (www.uclahealth.org/nph) is a leader in treating neuropsychiatric and behavioural disorders for people of all ages. Your psychologist, social worker or psychiatrist may provide talk therapy or behavioural training, but only your internist or psychiatrist may prescribe psychotropic aids, including anti-depressants and ADHD medications. If your depression is a component or response to culture shock, it may help to connect with expats (see Social Groups, p.236) or even cook up your favourite dish from back home, but it is important to recognise that severe depression or mental instability requires medical intervention. Many clinics, hospitals and private therapists provide counselling on a sliding scale fee (based on your financial means) if your insurance does not assist with the costs.

Counsellors & Psychologists				
AJ Barnert	San Fernando Valley	818 594 4152	na	Hypnosis and EMDR
Cheryl Arutt	Beverly Hills	310 273 2755	www.drcherylarutt.com	Clinical and forensic psychology
Craig Hands	Beverly Hills	310 271 7702	www.doctorhands.com	Anxiety, depression and self destructive life patterns
David W Scott	Beverly Hills	310 423 9618	www.csmc.edu/2830.html	Pain management
Deborah Buckwalter	South Pasadena	626 449 2484	www.personagroup.com	Neuropsychological and psychodiagnostic assessment and treatment
Don Etkes	Westwood	310 979 0245	www.sexesteem.com	Sex therapy
Gregory Cason	West Hollywood	877 437 4734	www.drgregcason.com	Cognitive-behavioral therapy
Neil B Haas	Westwood	310 475 5532	www.csmc.edu	Addiction psychiatry
Pamela Perry-Hunter	Santa Monica	310 582 2290	pperryhunt@aol.com	Attention deficit disorder and mood disorders
Peggy Bailey	San Fernando Valley	818 728 8480	www.blvd.pediatrics.com	Paediatric

Addiction Counselling & Rehabilitation

With extravagant facilities in Malibu that can cost as much as $85,000 per stay, and the constant hum of starlets checking in and out of rehab, LA has become synonymous with overpriced addiction services, but don't let the hype scare you away from getting the help you need. In addition to more affordable residential and inpatient treatment, you can find outpatient detox, counselling and support centres throughout LA. In fact, several treatment centres, including those listed below, offer both inpatient and outpatient services. Visit www.drugtreatment.tv for a full list of reputable low and no-cost programmes. The National Council on Alcoholism and Drug Dependence (NCADD), a non-profit organisation partially funded by the state, is another great resource for information and referrals. You can also find the 12 step appraisal at Alcoholics Anonymous, Narcotics Anonymous, Gamblers Anonymous and Overeaters Anonymous. These organisations are listed online and in the yellow pages of the phone book.

Addiction Counselling & Rehabilition

Alcoholics Anonymous	Various Locations	323 936 4343	www.lacoaa.org
Cri-Help	Various Locations	818 985 8323	www.cri-help.org
Insight Treatment Programs	14156 Magnolia Blvd	818 501 3512	www.insighttreatmentprograms.com
National Council on Alcoholism and Drug Dependence	6640 Van Nuys Blvd	818 997 0414	www.ncadd-sfv.org
Promises Treatment Centers	Various Locations	866 783 4287	www.promises.com
Sober Living By The Sea Treatment Centers	2811 Villa Way	866 323 5609	www.soberliving.com
Tarzana Treatment Centers	Various Locations	800 996 1051	www.tarzanatc.org

With many drugs, including alcohol and methamphetamines, detox is a vital step in recovery, and it is important it's done with medical supervision. Withdrawal symptoms can be dangerous and quitting 'cold turkey' without the proper medication and supervision can be deadly. After graduating from a detox or residential programme, a patient might be referred to a 'sober living house', an alcohol and drug free environment where housemates are making a similar transition.

Support Groups

Finding your place in a city as sprawling and diverse as LA can be daunting, and not just for expats. If you are grappling with a social or physical hurdle and cannot find the support you need in friends, family or your spiritual advisor, rest assured that LA offers an endless variety of support groups. You may find them locally, with or without facilitators, through your healthcare organisation or by contacting your local hospital or clinic. UCLA (p.114) hosts disease-specific support groups for those battling everything from multiple sclerosis to bipolar disorder, while Northridge Hospital has three pages of groups on its website (www.northridgehospital. org). You may also find support or references by connecting with other expats through organisations such as EuroCircle (www.eurocircle.com) and Expat Contact Los Angeles (www. expatcontact.com). For more on Social Groups, see p.236.

Support Groups

Bereavement Group	818 885 5351
Cedars-Sinai (for new mothers, children & families)	310 423 1510
Chronic Pain Support Group	818 885 8500
Compassionate Friends of LA	310 474 3407
Depression & Bipolar Support Alliance, Pasadena	323 255 4478
Depression after Delivery (info request line)	800 944 4773
Haven Hills (victims of domestic violence)	818 887 6589
Jewish Family Service of LA (hosts a variety of groups)	323 761 8800
LA Gay & Lesbian Center	323 860 7302
The Men's Center	818 348 9302
The Ted Mann Family Resource Center (Cancer Support)	310 794 6644
UCLA TIES for Adoption	310 825 6110

Education

Rarely is there a political battle in the US where the state of the education system is not a hot topic. Issues raised are not only about quality of learning, but also about standardised testing, access to materials, and safety. Determining how to best ensure your child receives the education he or she deserves can be daunting, but you are likely to meet with success if you take the time to understand what LA has to offer, including public, private and homeschooling.

If you have documentation regarding your child's previous school performance, such as report cards, transcripts or testing information, that can only help, especially if you are entering mid-year or your child has special needs. Regardless of what you supply, the school might suggest or require you child enrol at a grade lower than you anticipated. If you and your child decide to head back to your country of origin, be sure to ask your school for a copy of report cards and any other academic information they can provide.

After-School Specials

Once your child reaches secondary school, competitive sports are a fantastic way to keep him or her busy and supervised, as practices, meetings and games take place after school and at weekends. Your child's school may offer other extra-curricular activities, such as performance, social or academic clubs that meet in the afternoons for rehearsals, meetings or competitions.

Public Education

No matter what their residency status – permanent, visitor or illegal – all children in LA are entitled to a free education, which is provided by the Los Angeles Unified School District (LAUSD), and funded through federal, state and local taxes. In the majority of the LAUSD's 424 elementary schools, 72 middle schools and 49 high schools, curriculum and budget are controlled by the state, with learning measured through standardised testing in maths, English, reading, writing, science and history. There are also physical education requirements. Schools with the allocated budget will offer programmes in music and art, but many struggle against serious financial restraints. You may often find the wealth and quality of a public school correlates with its neighbourhood, but be warned that is a generalisation, not a rule.

If your child is from a non-English speaking country, the school may test his or her English and will provide the necessary ESL (English as a second language) classes. In addition, there are two levels of bilingual teaching, but if your child speaks English well enough, the regular curriculum is preferable and you may have to ask for it. In California, school size is limited until the end of third grade, but after that there is no guarantee on the class size or student-teacher ratio, which is why many locals believe the disparity between public and private schools becomes apparent in middle school. It is of note, however, that LAUSD is currently in the process of adding several schools to the district in order to combat overcrowding and improve the learning environment. A $19.3 billion construction programme is already under way, with145 new schools anticipated by 2012.

In most cases, the LAUSD school your child attends is determined by your address. Unless you are considering an alternative programme listed on the next page, your first step is to determine your child's school of residence using the LAUSD School Finder (213 241 5437; www.lausd.net). You can then learn how the school measures up by visiting www.greatschools.net, an independent, non-profit organisation that rates schools. To enrol your child in your local school, you must fill out the paperwork provided by the school to get him or her registered. Any child with an address in LA will be accepted, regardless of residency status, but you must provide proof of the child's age (birth certificate and passport) and residence address (utility bill), in addition to complete health and immunisation records. All immunisations, including polio, chickenpox, DTP, MMR, hepatitis B and tuberculosis, must be up-to-date before your child may attend class. Your school can direct you to the nearest free immunisation clinic if necessary.

Private Education

If you elect to send your child to a private school, you will pay heavily for that decision. One year's tuition may cost more than your car, unless of course your child qualifies for a scholarship or grant. Tuition at the prestigious Harvard-Westlake school (p.128), for example, is $26,000 a year, plus out-of-pocket expenses of about $3,000. Many schools, especially those with religious affiliations, may be cheaper.

Parents decide to shoulder this cost for a variety of reasons, but most believe they are simply ensuring a better education for their children. Not only do private schools have impressive campus facilities and control class size and student-teacher ratio, but they also have more independence from state regulations regarding curriculum and budget, which allows for diversity that goes beyond the 'basics' of the LAUSD. Detractors argue the weakness of this freedom is that most private schools do not require teachers be certified beyond a college degree.

Your child must apply to private school, and acceptance will take into account both academic and social factors. He or she will face a process that includes school tours, testing, an interview and getting teacher recommendations. Testing for elementary school might include examination in a group setting, but if your child is in grade five to 12, he or she will likely need to take the Independent School Entrance Examination (ISEE), which costs $78. Most LA private schools will not assist you in getting a student visa for your child, but once he or she is here, they are not likely to ask you to show his or her residency papers either.

In most cases you will find private school admission highly competitive, with certain grades noted as 'main entry points', which means those are the years the school admits a bulk of the student body. This, however, is one place where being a newly arrived expat can come in handy. If a school is accepting as few as eight students to your child's grade, LA newcomers are often considered first. In addition, most private schools are constantly struggling to enrol a diverse population – a foreign passport can only help those numbers. If you arrive in town mid-term or mid-year, your school of choice may even make a special case of your child. Many feel the selective process (and the money) of private schools ensures a safer and better environment. For better or worse, it may also create a relatively homogenous group of peers for your child. Boarding schools are not very popular in LA, but there are some on the outskirts of the county. If you choose this option, it can cost an additional $10,000.

Public Alternatives

If you are concerned or dissatisfied with your neighbourhood school, you may apply for a transfer through programmes such as Permits With Transportation (PWT) and

Hollywood High School

Open Enrolment. If your child is academically advanced, he or she may also qualify for transfer to a Magnet School or Centre. Magnets are still run through LAUSD, but enrolment is not defined by geography. Students must apply. Most magnet schools centre their curriculum on a theme like maths, language or the arts. To review your options, visit the LAUSD E-choices website (http://echoices.lausd.net). You may also consider sending your child to a Charter school, which can best be described as a hybrid of the public and private school systems, though LAUSD might not approve that comparison. These 104 schools are open to all children from all neighbourhoods and receive more freedom in curriculum and class size. Unlike privates, however, they must be non-sectarian and free, though many encourage parental contribution. In order to remain active, Charters must maintain a high standard of learning and many surpass their LAUSD counterparts. Enrolment is mostly conducted by lottery, but the student body must reflect the racial and ethnic balance of the district population. You can learn about the Charter system on the LAUSD website (www.lausd.net) or by contacting the Charter School Division (213 241 2665). These schools are also rated and evaluated at www.greatschools.net.

Home Schooling

Home schooling, which can actually take place at home or in an alternative setting, was once seen as a sideline solution for child actors, but it is becoming an increasingly more popular choice. Those who opt for homeschool often site a frustration with both the public and private school systems. There are several ways to set up your child's homeschool environment and make it work legally, but the central concept is that you, as the parent, control your child's education and learning. That said, if your child will be applying to university in the future, there are standards his or her education must meet. If this interests you, find out more by contacting the Homeschool Association of California (www.hsc.org) or the California Homeschool Network (www. californiahomeschool.net).

After-School Services

You child's school, public or private, will likely offer after-school programmes. Many public schools only offer these on a lottery basis as they don't have enough room for all pupils. This is made worse by the fact that schools may make additional money by enrolling students from another school.

If your child cannot join a programme, look into the possibility of getting on the waiting list for the following year. In the meantime, you can find reasonable after-school activities at your local park or YMCA (www.ymcala.org). They may be interest based, academic or purely social. The costs vary and may include some financial assistance, but, for example, a YMCA programme could cost $25 a day, instead of the $100 you will pay for a babysitter.

Nurseries & Preschools

While preschool is not mandatory in the US, many educators feel attending one gives your child a leg up in learning and social skills. For a recently arrived expat, it may also help in finding friends for your little one, as well as yourself. LA offers every form of preschool, including public, co-op, religious, Montessori, Waldorf and Reggio Emilia schools, and most welcome children over 3 years old, though some will go down to two and a half. If your child's preschool programme is associated with a full-time school, it may offer full daycare, but many programmes only offer classes for a few hours a day, or will only have room for your child in one part of the day. The State Preschool Programme, for example, only provides preschool for three hours. Thus, some parents sign up with multiple programmes to cover more hours.

Whether going public or private for preschool, expect to encounter a waiting list that is months, if not years, long. It may help to apply to several schools, but many locals simply decide to get started with the application process early. Another tip is to get involved with an organisation. If you are interested in a specific preschool, for example, sign up with that school's 'mommy and me' class. If you are looking at a religious school, connect with the affiliated church or temple.

Private school entry may be highly competitive, as well as pricey. The Center for Early Education in Westwood (323 651 0707; www.centerforearlyeducation.org), which is

Fight For Your Rights ◀

The law protects your right as a parent to be an informed participant in your child's education. If you are going to send your child to public school, it is highly recommended that you take an active role. LAUSD is a bureaucracy and sometimes you have to fight to get your child what he or she is due.

considered a feeder school for Harvard-Westlake, can cost up to $15,400. Religious and co-op schools will be cheaper, and the LAUSD offers a host of free educational programmes to your toddler or preschooler, including The State Preschool Programme (www.lausd.net), but be sure to pay attention to eligibility requirements. In addition to space issues, most LAUSD programmes require parent involvement, which can be difficult to accommodate in a one-parent household or if both parents have to work. Co-op schools also require parent involvement.

Also of note is Los Angeles Universal Preschool (213 416 1200; www.laup.net). It is dedicated to providing education to all 4 year olds and several income groups by offering half-day preschool programmes. Parents pay a one-time fee based on zip code that may be markedly lower than private schools rates. If you were in Woodland Hills, for example, you would pay $900 for the year and if you cannot afford this fee, you may apply to have it waived.

Primary & Secondary Schools

Search For A School
As you begin your search, there are several helpful tools. For example, www. savvysource.com and www.greatschools.net rate and review schools in your area. The Whitney Guide – The Los Angeles Pre School Guide, reviews more than 70 top LA preschools and costs just under $40.

Legally, your child must be enrolled in full-time education from the age of 6 to 18, but he or she will be welcomed into an LAUSD kindergarten if he or she turns 5 on or before 2 December of the year of registration. Private schools often cite the same age limit, but may make exceptions. The LAUSD school year is 180 days, while private schools may have more vacation days and average a bit lower. LAUSD tried implementing a 'year-round system', but is already rolling that back to the normal September to June schedule that you will find in private schools. The school week is Monday to Friday, sometimes ending early on Fridays. The elementary school (grades K to 5) day often runs approximately 06:45 to 14:15, while middle and high school days tend to run from around 08:00 to 15:30.

Classrooms and facilities differ from school to school, relying greatly on a school's budget and whether it is private or public, but in each classroom, your child will likely be given his or her own desk or a longer table to share with another student. You are bound to find a campus auditorium, if not a fully fledged theatre, and most LA campuses provide students ample outside space and sports facilities, as well as competitive sports in secondary schools.

Brentwood School

100 S Barrington Place
Brentwood
Map 4 A3 **12**

310 476 9633 | *www.bwscampus.com*
With a student-to-teacher ratio of eight to one and less than 1,000 students, this college prep school covers grades K to 12. The elementary and secondary schools are separated into two campuses. K to 6 costs $22,500 annually and 7 to 12 $26,200. The curriculum encompasses arts and fine arts, computer science, English, maths, physical education, science, social science and social studies with history. Admission is highly competitive, with 14% of applicants successful. Kindergarten and grades 7 and 9 are the main entry points.

The Buckley School

3900 Stansbury Ave
Sherman Oaks
Map 2 C1

818 783 1610 | *www.buckleyla.org*
Serving K to 12 students, The Buckley School has one of the smallest student-to-teacher ratios at seven to one, and capacity for 750 students. The curriculum covers arts and fine arts, computer science, English, foreign language, humanities, mathematics, performing arts, physical education, science and social science. Admission is competitive, with about 29% of applicants accepted, and kindergarten and 7th and 9th grades being the main entry points. Tuition at the lower school (K to 5) is $23,100, while the middle school (grades 6 to 8) and upper school (9 to 12) come in at $26,000.

Campbell Hall

4533 Laurel
Canyon Blvd
North Hollywood
Map 2 C1

818 980 7280 | *www.campbellhall.org*

This co-ed prep school is affiliated with the Episcopal Church. Its curriculum covers arts and fine arts, computer science, English, foreign languages, mathematics, physical education, science, and social studies with history. It has a student-to-teacher ratio of eight to one. Tuition is $18,440 for elementary and $23,460 for secondary.

Crossroads School for Arts & Sciences

1714 21st St
Santa Monica
Map 3 C2 15

310 829 7391 | *www.xrds.org*

The K to 12 Crossroads educates 1,100 students at two campuses, with the elementary school (and athletic facility) located on the Norton Campus (1715 Olympic Blvd). The curriculum covers visual arts, literature, language, music, maths, drama, history, science, dance, athletics, computer science and environmental and experiential education, with a student-to-teacher ratio of 17 to one. Admission is competitive, with about 11% of applicants accepted. Kindergarten and grades 7 and 9 are the main entry points. Tuition is $22,030 for elementary and $26,100 for grades 6 to 12.

Harvard-Westlake

700 N Faring Rd
Holmby Hills
Map 4 C1 16

310 274 7281 | *www.hw.com*

The popular Harvard-Westlake only serves middle and high school students, starting in grade 7. There are approximately 1,600 students and a student-to-teacher ratio of eight to one. The middle school (grades 7 to 9) is located in Holmby Hill, while the Upper School (grades 10 to 12) is located in Studio City. The curriculum covers arts and fine arts, English, foreign languages, history, human development, mathematics, physical education and science. Impressive facilities include an athletics field, two pools, music and dance studios and art labs. Admission is competitive, with 20% of applicants admitted. Grades 7 and 9 are the main entry points. Tuition is $25,000.

Marlborough School

250 S Rossmore Ave
Hollywood
Map 7 E1 17

323 935 1147 | *www.marlboroughschool.org*

This all-girl prep school offers approximately 800 students (grade 7 to 12) a curriculum that includes arts and fine arts, computer science, English, maths, physical education, science and history. The student-to-teacher ratio is six to one. It boasts an impressive sports programme that includes equestrian training. Annual tuition is $26,750 and admission is highly competitive, with about 13% of applicants successful.

The Mirman School for Gifted Children

16180 Mulholland Dr
Santa Monica Mountains
Map 2 B1

310 476 2868 | *www.mirman.org*

Mirman is a co-ed school that serves remarkably gifted students between the ages of 5 and 14. The lack of grade levels reflects the school's curriculum and style of teaching, which is geared toward the special needs of gifted children who often suffer under traditional methods. Mirman's two campuses are located above the Sepulveda Pass, overlooking the San Fernando Valley. Admission is highly competitive. Tuition for the lower school (ages 5 to 9) is $19,000, while the upper school (ages 10 to 14) is $20,300.

Oakwood School

11230 Moorpark St
North Hollywood
Map 2 C1

818 752 5277 | *www.oakwoodschool.org*

Oakwood's curriculum covers arts and fine arts, computer science, English, languages, mathematics, physical education, science and social studies. There are 1,200 students with a student-to-teacher ratio of 10 to one. The upper campus has seen impressive expansion, including several new buildings. About 44% of applicants are accepted, with kindergarten, and grades 7 and 9 being the main entry points.

11350 Palms Blvd
West LA
Map 3 F1 20

Windward School
310 397 7127 | www.windwardschool.org

The curriculum at this co-ed prep school covers English and literature, social studies, maths, science and foreign languages, in addition to alternative courses. The school serves 800 students from grade 7 to 12 and there is a small student-to-teacher ratio of seven to one. Only 19% of applicants are accepted and tuition is $24,884.

Keep Learning
You may find continuing and higher education courses and programmes through LAUSD's Division of Adult and Career Education (http://adultinstruction. org) and most major LA universities. Programmes such as UCLA Extension (www.uclaextension. edu) are geared to help working professionals, but are usually open to F-1 visa students as well. Each programme has its own set of requirements, fees and procedures, with university programmes likely to cost the most.

University & Higher Education

While LA is far too big to be considered a college town, it is home to 200 private and state campuses. UCLA and USC, which share a well-known rivalry, are top US universities, while Pepperdine University also ranks well.

However, many students are drawn to LA's speciality schools, such as California Institute of Technology (CalTech), California Institute for the Arts (CalArts) and the Fashion Institute of Design and Merchandising (FIDM). This city is also host to a multitude of prestigious graduate schools where those with a bachelor's degree may study towards their masters, doctoral or professional degrees, as well as advanced certification in various fields. You will find top medical, dental and law schools here, many offering both undergraduate and graduate studies. UCLA's law, business, medical and education graduate schools, for example, each rank in their respective top 20s. Most Los Angeles universities are thrilled to welcome expats and international students and most will have a special office to assist you with this process. You may also find guidance in the Student Visa section (p.40). Undergraduate application requirements vary by school and programme, but in most cases, you must be a high-school graduate or GED holder (high school equivalency certificate) and you will probably have to prepare an admission package that includes your application fee, application form, high school transcript, letters of recommendation, ACT or SAT admissions test scores, personal essays and, if you are from a non-English speaking country, TOEFL or ELTS scores. Artistic programmes may also require a portfolio, audition tape or in-person audition. If you make the first cut, you will likely be interviewed by a representative from the school. If you have already begun your undergraduate education in your own country, look into transfer applications or semester exchange programmes. Graduate school admission usually requires an undergraduate degree and your application package is similar to the above, but with graduate admissions tests. Your school of choice will outline its own requirements.

Community College & Continuing Education

The Los Angeles Community College District (LACCD) offers nine two-year community colleges that may serve as a stepping stone for transferring into a four-year school such as UCLA or CSUN. Whether you are looking to transfer up, advance your professional training or simply learn a new skill or language, you are likely to find the necessary art, science or vocational course or curriculum here. You may enrol full-time or just sign up for one course if you are a high school graduate or over 18 and 'able to benefit from instruction'. International students pay $189 per course, as well as an $11 health fee. Students on an F-1 visa also pay a $25 per semester processing fee. Find more information at www.laccd.edu.

1200 E California Blvd
Pasadena
Map 2 E1

California Institute of Technology (Caltech)
626 395 6811 | www.caltech.edu

One of the world's leading research institutes, Caltech is a private mathematics, science and engineering university serving 2,000 graduate and undergraduate students. It has graduated several Nobel laureates in physics. This is a highly selective school, with a rigorous curriculum that promotes group work.

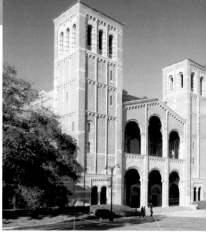

UCLA

24700 McBean Parkway
Valencia
Map 1 A3

California Institute of the Arts (CalArts)
661 255 1050 | www.calarts.edu
With 1,300 graduate and undergraduate students. CalArts' art, critical studies, dance, film and video, music, and theatre schools offer BFAs (Bachelor of Fine Arts) and MFAs (Master of Fine Arts). The school was set up by Walt Disney to promote the talent of the future. Study is full-time and entrance requirements are based on artistic merit.

Various Locations

California State University (CSU)
www.calstate.edu
Touted as one of the most affordable systems in the country, CSU has 23 campuses, including LA (www.calstatela.edu), Northridge (www.csun.edu) and Long Beach (www.csulb.edu), and serves 450,000 students. There is a separate application process for international students and some campuses may restrict enrolment of non-residents.

24255 Pacific
Coast Hwy
Malibu
Map 2 A2

Pepperdine University
310 506 4000 | www.pepperdine.edu
Though overshadowed by UCLA and USC, and slightly less selective, Pepperdine is a top-ranking school. Affiliated with the Churches of Christ, it serves 3,000 undergraduate students and offers four professional schools. The campus lies in the hills above Malibu and overlooks the Pacific.

405 Hilgard Av
Westwood
Map 4 B2 **24**

University of California–Los Angeles (UCLA)
310 825 4321 | www.ucla.edu
Ranked 25th best university by *US News & World Report*, UCLA is an enormous state school with approximately 25,000 undergraduate students and 12,400 graduates, boasting theatres, museums and research centres. The school offers 151 science and liberal arts majors and 11 professional schools, many of which rank well. Selection is very competitive, with preference given to LA and California residents.

University Park
Downtown
Map 9 B3 **25**

University of Southern California (USC)
21 740 1111 | www.usc.edu
UCLA's rival school was ranked 27th by *US News* and is quite pricey. A highly competitive private research university, it is home to 25 doctoral programmes and offers around 6,400 undergraduates a science and liberal arts education. The extremely competitive USC Film School offers graduates an unparalleled network to get into the business.

Universities & Colleges

Art Center College of Design	Pasadena	626 396 2200	www.artcenter.edu
The Claremont Colleges	Various Locations	na	www.claremont.edu
The Fashion Institute of Design and Merchandising	Downtown	800 624 1200	www.fidm.com
Los Angeles Community Colleges	Various Locations	213 891 2000	www.laccd.edu
Loyola Marymount (LMU)	Westchester	310 338 2700	www.lmu.edu
Otis College of Art & Design	Westchester	310 665 6800	www.otis.edu

Student Life

LA is home to students from all over the world and small 'college town' communities sometimes exist near individual campuses, such as Westwood Village near UCLA. On campus, your university is likely to foster a community feeling, offering a multitude of health and social services. Most have extensive mental and physical healthcare services or at least offer students obligatory medical coverage.

Socially, you may choose to get involved in countless ways, including competitive or recreational athletics, community activism, campus groups or performing arts. While you may attend or be involved in student performances or art shows, schools such as UCLA and CalArts host events showcasing renowned international performers, artists, politicians and intellectuals.

Many universities have limited on-campus housing, so it is quite common for students to set up local digs through college listings, craigslist or local roommate ads.

If you need financial assistance, you may be eligible for a student loan from your school or bank, but if you are not a citizen or green card holder, scholarships or financial aid at certain universities may not be available.

If you are planning to apply for a student visa, you will need to show your ability to support yourself while studying in the US. Your school of choice is certain to have an international students' office that can assist you during the application process, as well as provide information and social support after you have arrived.

Once enrolled, you will receive a student ID that may get you discounts at restaurants, theatres, museums, and amusement parks, as well as deals at STA Travel (800 781 4040, www.statravel.com). If you travel outside of the city or country, look into getting an international student ID card and you may be eligible for similar discounts.

Pleased To Meet You
If you're new to LA and want to connect with people in the same boat, check out the Communities section on www.explorerpublishing.com, where you can join groups, post comments and share your news and views.

Special Needs Education

LAUSD is required to provide the necessary services to accommodate and teach your school-age child (between the ages of 5 and 22), whatever his or her special needs, but as a parent, you'll need to know how to navigate the system.

LAUSD's Division of Special Needs (http://sped.lausd.net) offers programmes for children with a variety of needs and disabilities. Most children with special needs will be diagnosed when teachers or staff notice something is amiss, but you may request testing yourself. Early intervention is available for some children whose disabilities are picked up before the age of 3.

LAUSD may put you in touch with The Help Group (877 943 5747, www.thehelpgroup.org), which offers a 'non-public' dayschool. While some parents pay to send their children here, most are funded through their local school district. It can be a complicated process, but your LAUSD school should assist you in applying and with funding. The Help Group also provides outpatient services at its four campuses.

If you suspect your child or a loved one under the age of 18 has a developmental disability, The Department of Developmental Services Regional Centers is a very helpful resource. It has seven offices serving LA County, including the Westside centre, supporting Culver City, Inglewood, and Santa Monica (310 258 4000, www.westsiderc.org); the Lanterman centre, overseeing Central, Glendale, Hollywood-Wilshire, and Pasadena (213 383 1300, www.lanterman.org); the North LA centre, for San Fernando and Antelope Valleys (818 778 1900, www.nlacrc.org) and the South Central office, covering Compton and Gardena (213 744 7000, www.sclarc.org). These offices do not provide services directly, but rather coordinate with support groups and other resources. California Children's Services (800 288 4584) might be of assistance if your child has certain physical limitations, chronic health conditions or diseases. The Department of Children and Family Services (213 351 5602) and the Department of Mental Health (800 854 7771) can also help.

Public Transportation
More than 400 million people use LA's public transport system each year, which includes some 200 bus lines and five light rail lines. You can easily plot your route by visiting the Los Angeles County Metropolitan Transportation Authority website at www.mta.net.

Transportation

Other options **Car** p.26, **Getting Around** p.23

There's an old saying that nobody walks in LA. In spite of all the wasted hours spent sitting in traffic, darting across town, or clocking miles on the freeway, Angelenos remain obsessed with their cars. Even though there have been many campaigns to encourage ride-sharing among residents and co-workers, driving remains the preferred mode of transportation. Don't be misled, though. There are also city buses, mini shuttles that operate in specific business districts, and a light rail system that fans out across the city and into neighbouring counties. Taxis can be seen lining up outside hotels and restaurants, but they're not as commonly used as in other cities. And, yes, there are pedestrians in LA, but walking the city streets is less common simply because the region is so sprawling.

Freeway Numbers & Names	
2	Glendale
5	Golden State/Santa Ana
10	Santa Monica/San Bernardino
14	Antelope Valley
22	Garden Grove
57	Orange
60	Pomona
71	Corona
90	Marina
91	Gardena/Artesia/Riverside
101	Ventura/Hollywood
105	Glen Anderson
110	Pasadena/Harbor
118	Simi Valley/San Fernando Valley (Ronald Reagan)
134	Ventura
170	Hollywood
405	San Diego
605	San Gabriel River
710	Long Beach

Driving in Los Angeles

Driving in Los Angeles usually means a mix of city streets and five-lane freeways that will take you from one side of town to the other. The term 'surface streets' is often used when referring to roads other than the freeway. LA's traffic problems are well documented, but driving remains the most popular mode of transport. For information on driving licences, see p.44.

Freeways

For most newcomers, the Los Angeles freeway system may seem daunting. It's an intricate tangle of roadways punctuated with heavy traffic, brisk speeds of 65mph or more, merging lanes, on ramps and off ramps, and sometimes erratic drivers who impatiently weave in and out of traffic. Learning the freeway system can also be something of a challenge. The first rule of thumb is that all freeways have both a name and a number. The name should indicate the road's final destination, but this is not always the case. For example, the San Diego Freeway, also known as the 405, doesn't end in San Diego but rather merges with the Interstate 5 Freeway in Orange County. It is the 5 Freeway – the Santa Ana Freeway – that actually takes you to San Diego.

Slow going on the 101

The table above gives the names and numbers of LA's major freeways.

Rush Hour

Traffic patterns, once so predictable, seem to no longer exist. There is congestion seven days a week, at all hours of the day, and sometimes for no apparent reason. For weekday commuters, queues start somewhere around 06:00 and last until about 09:30. Evening rush hour can start as early as 16:00 (earlier on Friday afternoons) and last well past 19:00. If you're travelling on a freeway that leads to a weekend destination (such as the I-15 towards Las Vegas, Highway 101 to Santa Barbara, or the I-5 or 405 Freeways heading south to San Diego), expect a much longer commute on a Friday afternoon. The website http://trafficinfo.lacity.org has details of current and planned road closures, as well as real-time traffic updates. To encourage people to travel together, LA County's freeways have more than 200 miles of High Occupancy Vehicle (HOV) lanes that are reserved for cars carrying two or more people. If you're keen to cut down on LA's traffic problem, www.erideshare.com is a carpool community where people can advertise and search for lift-sharing opportunities.

Cutting Corners
LA-based company A-1 Courier has kindly shared some of its favourite time-saving shortcuts. Visit www.a-1courier.com/lashortcuts.htm and learn how to shave precious minutes off your journey.

Petrol Stations

Petrol stations are abundant in Los Angeles: you'll find them on corners, near freeway off ramps, in town, on desolate highways, and just about everywhere else. Petrol (gasoline) prices have risen in recent years in line with the price of oil, and prices in California are often higher than elsewhere in the US (local laws call for cleaner fuel than in other states). Despite this, fuel prices in LA are still considerably cheaper than many European countries. Petrol stations located within the city typically tend to have higher prices than those located in suburban areas, and the difference in price from station to station can be as much as 50 cents per gallon. Check out www.losangelesgasprices.com, which has daily updates on the cheapest and most expensive fuel around town. There are three grades of petrol available at the pumps – regular (87 octane), midgrade (89 octane) and premium (91 octane) – plus diesel. Most petrol stations (with the exception of a few like ARCO which only take cash or debit cards) accept major credit cards which can be inserted at the pump for added convenience. Many stations are open 24 hours a day, seven days a week.

Full service, which once meant an attendant who would fill your tank, wash the windows, check the oil and air in your tyres, now means a guy just fills the tank. You'll pay quite a bit more for this service, which is becoming almost obsolete.

Parking

Most business districts within LA County have either parking garages or lots, where you pay an attendant as you exit, or metered street parking which requires you to insert quarters into the machine to buy time. Typically, 25 cents buys you 15 minute increments, so metered parking is only advisable for short-term parking. Depending on what part of the city you're in, metered parking can be enforced from 08:00 to 21:00, seven days a week; in other parts of the city it might be 10:00 to 19:00, with free parking on Sunday. It's important that you read the signs posted either on the street or on the meter to determine when parking is enforced in that area or neighbourhood. Parking on residential streets and walking a few blocks may seem like a good idea, but keep in mind that many neighbourhoods and cities, such as West Hollywood, require residential permits for street-side parking. If you do find free parking, be sure to avoid tow away zones, and check for signs indicating the day and hours for street sweeping.

Vehicle Leasing

In the United States, 'leasing' and 'renting' are two different practices. A lease is a contract for a specified term. Unlike car rental, which is usually no more than a two-week commitment in which you pay a daily rate, a car lease is usually through a dealership, and typically requires a minimum two-year contract with monthly instalments. You are also responsible for the maintenance of the vehicle and, usually, you are given an annual mileage allowance. If you surpass the allowance, you may face steep penalties.

Should you decide to lease rather than buy a vehicle, your monthly payments simply entitle you to use or drive the vehicle, and you won't own the car once the lease expires because it is returned to the dealer. Car leases usually appeal to people who don't like the long-term commitment of a car loan, or who prefer to change their car every few years. Many of the upfront costs of a lease are less than those involved with a purchase. However,

Vehicle Leasing Agents		
Absolutely Ugly	310 696 2310	www.uglyrentacar.com
Atwest	310 417 9050	www.atwest-rentacar.com
Beverly Hills Rent A Car	310 670 2020	www.bhrentacar.com
Budget	310 820 9899	www.budget.com
Dollar	310 274 0001	www.dollar.com
Enterprise	213 627 1487	www.enterprise.com
Hertz	310 568 5100	www.hertz.com
Thrifty	626 449 0012	www.thrifty.com

payments on leased cars tend to be higher than payments on car loans. There may be some restrictions to the lease, so read the fine print and ask questions before signing on the dotted line. If you are not a citizen, you'll need to show a passport and valid US work visa along with proof of employment. You'll also need to be approved for credit if borrowing from the dealer's lender.

Short-Term Rents

In cities where most residents don't own cars, but still yearn to get behind the wheel on a weekend, short-term rentals certainly make sense. In Los Angeles, where driving is a necessity, there aren't many short-term vehicle programmes available. Absolutely Ugly Rent-A-Car in West LA specialises in monthly car rentals, but a better bet for securing a car for the weekend or longer is through one of the many car rental companies. You'll find the usual suspects when trying to rent a car, such as Enterprise or Hertz, but there are also some rental companies where you can drive off in a convertible Jaguar or swanky Rolls Royce. You can likely strike an excellent deal, depending on the dates and type of car you're willing to negotiate, through priceline.com, which is a clearinghouse for travel-related companies. You might also try comparing prices through www.travelocity.com. For an additional fee you can request a car with a Global Positioning System (GPS) to assist you with city and freeway navigation. You can also purchase insurance from the car rental company, or check with your credit card company to see if this service is already provided for cardholders.

Buying A Vehicle

Los Angeles' addiction to the automobile has created a market that provides for everyone's needs. The many shiny showrooms and second-hand lots offer everything from Jaguars to jalopies. Although petrol prices are still well below the rest of the world, they are on the rise and manufacturers have reintroduced the economic compact car. New compacts start at around $10,000. The area's obsession with environmental care has prompted the sale of hybrid cars, the most popular of which is the Toyota Prius. Hybrids

New Car Dealers			
Acura	Santa Monica	800 432 2872	www.santamonicaacura.com
BMW	Beverly Hills	866 849 3816	www.bmwofbeverlyhills.com
Chevrolet/Cadillac	Exposition Park	800 599 8302	www.felixchevrolet.com
Chrysler/Jeep	Park La Brea	800 651 9584	www.labrea.fivestardealers.com
Ford	Hollywood	323 663 9999	www.hollywoodford.net
Honda	Hollywood	866 632 4180	www.hondaofhollywood.com
Mercedes-Benz	Beverly Hills	310 659 2980	www.bhbenz.com
Nissan	Santa Monica	310 998 2200	www.santamonicanissan.com
Porsche	Beverly Hills	310 557 2472	www.beverlyhillsporsche.com
Subaru	Santa Monica	877 289 7822	www.santamonica-ca.subaru.com
Toyota	Hollywood	877 216 5966	www.hollywoodtoyota.com

tend to be more expensive, but the state rewards those who buy them with discounted parking. Many people choose to purchase a late model second-hand car. Dealers often sell returned lease cars at massive discounts and with a warranty. Many dealerships offer 'certified pre-owned' vehicles that have passed extensive tests before going on sale. The *Kelley Blue Book* (www.kbb.com) is the industry standard when it comes to new and used vehicle pricing. Do your research and make sure you're getting a good deal, whether it's new or second-hand.

Before buying from a dealership, be sure to review the fine print and any details pertaining to the warranty. If you're buying from a private dealer, don't hesitate to have the vehicle checked out by a mechanic of your choosing before making a down payment.

Kerb Colours ◀

To avoid receiving a parking ticket or having your vehicle towed (or both) you'll need to know what each kerb colour signifies:

Red Zone
No parking under any circumstance. These red zones are reserved for emergency vehicles.

White Zone
For passenger loading and unloading only. A five-minute time limit usually applies, and the driver must remain in the vehicle.

Green Zone
This is for limited, short-term parking not exceeding 30 minutes. If it's a metered area, you still need to buy time if the parking hours are enforced.

Yellow Zone
This is for commercial vehicles that are actively loading or unloading.

Blue Zone
Only for vehicles with a valid disabled parking permit.

Used Car Dealers

Advantage Lincoln Mercury	626 359 9689	na
Bozzani Motors	626 736 4275	www.bozzani.com
Car Max	310 568 9272	www.carmax.com
Enterprise Car Sales	888 556 3323	www.enterprisecarsales.com
Nick Alexander Imports	310 583 1901	www.alexanderbmw.com
South Bay Chrysler Jeep Dodge	310 542 0900	www.southbaycpj.com

Vehicle Finance

Unless you have enough cash for a vehicle purchase, you'll probably have to finance your new wheels. You might want to secure a copy of your credit report so you can correct errors and know exactly what creditors will be viewing. You can request a free report at www.annualcreditreport.com if you have established credit in the United States. Next, you'll want to compare annual percentage rates and financing terms from multiple sources, such as banks, finance companies and credit unions. The most common type of vehicle financing, and possibly the most convenient, is through the dealership. The length of a loan can vary, typically from 36 to 60 months, and the dealer typically 'sells' the loan to a third-party financer, such as a bank or credit union.

Vehicle Finance

Car Loans Los Angeles	na	www.carloanslosangeles.com
CT Loans	213 624 2815	www.ctloanscenter.com
EZ Access Auto Loan	213 622 4220	www.ezaccessautoloans.com
Lending Tree	800 956 7684	www.lendingtree.com
Washington Mutual	888 800 8738	www.wamu.com
Wells Fargo Bank	213 483 2681	www.wellsfargo.com

Vehicle Insurance

In order to register a motor vehicle in California, you need to provide proof of financial responsibility to the DMV, and there are four ways to go about this: show a motor vehicle liability insurance policy, make a deposit of $35,000 with the DMV, show proof of a security bond obtained from a company licensed to do business in California, or have a DMV-issued self-insurance certificate. Out of all of these options, purchasing auto insurance is the most popular. You must show your insurance card each and every time you renew your vehicle's registration or register a new car. All motor vehicle insurance must be provided by a state-approved insurance carrier; check the DMV

Vehicle Insurance

Allstate	866 621 6900	www.allstate.com
Nationwide	877 669 6877	www.nationwide.com
Progressive Auto Insurance	800 776 4637	www.progressive.com
State Farm	323 478 9346	www.statefarm.com
Wawanesa Insurance	800 640 2920	www.wawanesageneral.com

website (www.dmv.ca.gov) for approved carriers. The minimum liability insurance required in California – the 15/30/5 rule – is $15,000 for injury or death of one person; $30,000 for injury or death of more than one person; and $5,000 for damage to property. This amount, $35,000, is the absolute minimum required, but most people insure for much more. Your insurer may even recommend coverage in the range of 100/300/100. If there is a lien on your car (meaning you borrowed money to buy it), you may be required by the lender to carry full-coverage on the vehicle as well. This will, of course, be more extensive and expensive than basic liability because it covers any outstanding balance due on the loan of the vehicle in the case of a total loss. Proof of coverage is required in the event you are pulled over by a police officer or involved in a car accident. Not having proof of insurance may result in steep fines, a suspended driving licence or having your vehicle impounded.

Registering A Vehicle

Selling A Vehicle
If you sell or transfer a vehicle, it must be reported to the DMV within five days of the transaction. The necessary form, Notice of Release of Liability (REG 138), can be downloaded at the DMV website (www.dmv.ca.gov) and mailed to the DMV office.

If purchasing a new or used vehicle from a licensed California dealer, they will collect all the necessary taxes and fees to register and title the vehicle. This includes submitting the fees and documents to the DMV and providing you with temporary operating authority. It usually takes between six and eight weeks to receive your registration card, licence plates, stickers and a Certificate of Title. Buying from a private seller is a bit more involved and requires you to transfer ownership within 10 days of the purchase. You'll also have to submit a completed and endorsed Certificate of Title or Application for Duplicate Title. Other requirements may include a seller-provided smog certification, odometer mileage disclosure statement and appropriate DMV fees. Vehicles registered in another state or foreign country must be registered in California within 20 days after you either become a resident or secure a job. The only exception to this is non-resident military personnel who, along with their spouses, can operate their vehicles in California with valid home state licence plates or until the plates issued from their last duty station expire. For more information on registering a vehicle, visit www.dmv.ca.gov.

Traffic Fines & Offences

Back To School
Some traffic tickets can be resolved by attending traffic school, and in LA County you can even attend online. In addition to the ticket fine you will also be charged a traffic school fee, but it is a way to avoid points on your licence.

At some point in your driving career, you're likely to see the flashing red lights from a police vehicle in your rear-view mirror. When signalled to pull over, do so at the next safe spot, either along the shoulder or roadside. The officer will approach the passenger side of your vehicle and ask for your licence, vehicle registration and proof of insurance. Keep all of these documents with you, as you could face fines if they're absent. If you've done something wrong, the officer will write you a traffic ticket and ask you to sign it before he gives you your copy. By signing, you are not admitting guilt. You are simply agreeing to appear in court. The appearance date is noted on the front of the ticket, which can be paid either online or via mail. Less serious offences are called infractions and include things such as speeding and not stopping at a stop sign. In these cases, going to court isn't necessary unless you plan on contesting the charge. More serious offences like drag racing or reckless driving are called misdemeanours and require that the driver appear in court. The penalty for misdemeanours might include jail time, and the help of an attorney may be needed. Tickets can be handled online or via mail.

Driving Under The Influence Of Alcohol (DUI)

It is a serious offence to drive intoxicated in California. The blood alcohol limit in the entire state is 0.08%, but you can still be charged regardless of the blood alcohol amount if the police can prove that you were affected by alcohol. Periodically, random sobriety check points are set up around town. To determine if a driver is under the influence, an officer may ask the driver to walk a straight line or do a number of other such exercises. If it appears that the driver is intoxicated, the officer will administer a breathalyser test, although the suspect can ask for a blood test instead. If you are caught driving under the influence, penalties can carry a $2,000 fine or more, or even jail time.

Rules Of The Road ◀

• The driver and all passengers must wear seat belts.
• All children under 6 or less than 60lbs must be in approved child-restraint seats or holders.
• Driving under the influence of alcohol (DUI) is a serious offence in California, with criminal penalties and drastic consequences.
• In most cases, it is legal to make a right turn at an intersection even against a red light. Look for signs that say otherwise.
• Don't move into an intersection if there's a chance you'll end up blocking it after the lights have changed.
• You must stop for pedestrians who have entered a crossing (crosswalk).
• Carpool, High Occupancy Vehicle (HOV), or Multiple Occupancy Lanes are for cars carrying two or more people.
• Emergency vehicles have right of way when using sirens or flashing lights. You must pull over and let them pass.

Breakdowns

If your vehicle stalls in a traffic lane, turn on your emergency (hazard) lights immediately. If you're able to steer the car, move it to the shoulder of the road and remain inside with seat belts fastened while you wait for help. Don't try to cross freeway lanes on foot. If you have a mobile phone, dial 911 and tell them your location. If not, call boxes are located every quarter of a mile on the freeway and operators can connect you to AAA, a family member or your insurance company. Always face traffic, and be aware of oncoming vehicles when making such calls. Also, if you're driving with pets, leave them in the car as it will be much safer for them and you. LA County is part of the Freeway Service Patrol (FSP), a joint venture involving the highway patrol and local transportation agencies, which provides emergency roadside assistance during peak commute periods. The FSP programme is a free service. While the FSP won't tow your car, they will help jump start dead batteries, provide you with a gallon of gas should you need it, refill your radiator, tape cracked or broken hoses and change flat tyres.

Recovery Services/Towing	
Brothers Towing	951 817 0380
Charlie's Towing	626 279 5530
Eddie's Towing Service	323 973 4208
G&R Towing Services	323 734 2258
M&M Towing	818 774 2233
Redondo Beach Towing	310 530 0140

Traffic Accidents

If you're involved in an accident, regardless of who is at fault, you must stop or you could be convicted of a 'hit and run', which carries punishments. Be prepared to show your licence, registration card, insurance card with policy number and provide your current address to the other driver or the responding officer. You or your insurance agent or representative must report the accident to the police or California Highway Patrol within 24 hours if someone was injured or killed, and within 10 days to the DMV if there is more than $750 in property damage or anyone was injured or killed. If you hit a parked vehicle or other property, be sure to identify yourself before leaving the scene. If you can't find the owner, leave a note with all pertinent information so they can contact you.

Vehicle Repairs

There are a number of auto repair and body shops within Los Angeles County. The Automotive Service Councils of California (ASCCA) is an organisation supported by approximately 1,350 automotive repair facilities. Its goal is to promote goodwill and service between motorists and mechanics. To find out if a shop is an ASCCA member, look for the logo displayed prominently at a repair shop, or search on the organisation's website at www.ascca.com. You may also want to visit the Better Business Bureau (www. bbbonline.com) to see if any complaints have been filed against a company. Most new car dealerships have service and repair shops on the premises.

Vehicle Repairs		
Advanced Auto Clinic	Los Feliz	323 462 7855
Long Automotive	Los Feliz	323 668 0810
One Stop Auto Shop	West Hollywood	323 954 6811
Sato's Auto Repair	Hancock Park	323 734 6766
Soto Auto Repair	Boyle Heights	323 980 9220

Exploring

Exploring

Outsiders often degrade Los Angeles with nicknames such as LaLaLand and Forty Suburbs In Search Of A City. Nonetheless, the city constantly and vigorously re-invents itself. Even its harshest critics concede LA is in the midst of a dramatic renaissance that is revitalising surrounding communities and reshaping its urban core (take a walk down Grand Avenue between Temple and 5th and see for yourself). Of course, there are also the miles of beaches, a mild Mediterranean climate and the largest urban park in the country (Griffith Park, p.191). Add to that some of the finest museums, restaurants and bars on the planet and you'll understand why Angelenos love their city so much.

The city's architecture is familiar to movie and television audiences worldwide. More than 800 feature productions were shot on city streets in 2007, and on any given day a visitor cruising Downtown will likely encounter a location production. The city's near future was famously realised in *Blade Runner*.

In the 1930s, Hollywood became a favoured destination for exiles who fled pre-war European tensions, among them Bertolt Brecht, Aldous Huxley and Thomas Mann. Their enduring legacies continue to undermine the views of those who claim the only culture in LA is in the yogurt. The 1930s also saw the rise of the movie palaces, and two of the finest in the country are Grauman's Chinese Theater (p.181) and the Egyptian (p.179), both of which have been restored to their full glory on Hollywood Boulevard.

The city's core decayed in the waning decades of the 20th century but Los Angeles' stunning comeback is perhaps best symbolised by the Gehry-designed Disney Center (p.184), which has become an instant urban icon. Downtown also features a vibrant new nightlife scene that rivals the fabled Sunset Boulevard.

At just shy of 500 square miles Los Angeles is big. It is divided into dozens of townlets annexed as the city expanded. Within these massive boundaries lie shopping centres such as Rodeo Drive and unique institutions that don't fit easily into a single category, such as The Huntington gardens and library (p.174). LA can also boast the best performing arts west of New York, whether it is among the temples to high culture atop Bunker Hill (at the Dorothy Chandler, p.361 and the Ahmanson, p.361) or at new venues such as the Kirk Douglas Theater (p.361). Despite all of that, it is the family destinations for which Los Angeles is most well-known, and Disneyland (p.186) and Universal Studios (p.187) are the most obvious. Thankfully, there are more thoughtful attractions, such as the Page Museum at the La Brea Tar Pits (p.177), that offer experiences to satisfy everyone.

California Science Center, Exposition Park

Checklist

Take A Grand Stroll
The powers that be have promised to transform Grand Avenue into the Champs Élysées of LA. They're about halfway there – or so they claim. The Disney Hall (p.184) is indeed an architectural marvel and an hour spent at the Museum of Contemporary Art (p.175) is time well spent. There are also the computer-controlled fountains around California Plaza. Maybe the city planners are onto something.

Go On A Surfin' Safari
This is the land of *Baywatch* and the Beach Boys. Research your destination first, however, so you know where to park and how to access the beach of your choice (p.189). Amp up your street cred and find a way onto the 'private' beaches in front of Malibu's bungalows (p.152).

See A Movie
Go catch the latest blockbuster at Grauman's Chinese Theater (p.181) or see a classic at the Egyptian (p.179). These two ornate, fully restored and digitally enhanced movie palaces are just a couple of blocks apart on Hollywood Boulevard.

Cycle Into The Sunset
Rent a bicycle in Venice Beach (p.153) and see if you can find the southern end of the coastal pathway. Take water and be prepared for a long ride. If you really feel adventurous (and you don't mind looking silly at first) rent a pair of rollerblades and really get into the swing of things. No one will laugh. Honest.

To Die For
The Hollywood Forever Cemetery (p.182) is the final resting place for many of Hollywood's most legendary stars. On warm summer nights, classic films (zombie movies are favourites) are projected onto the wall that separates the cemetery from Paramount Studios. This is one of those uniquely LA experiences that you really should try to catch.

Time For Tea
Call for reservations and enjoy high tea in a solarium on the grounds of The Huntington (p.174). Oscar Wilde will not show up, but the cucumber and watercress sandwiches served with tea and cakes will make you feel almost as witty as one of his characters.

Get Lost In Space
Griffith Observatory (or Jor-El's laboratory to fans of the *Superman* TV series) has a big new planetarium projector that takes visitors at light-speed on a journey across space and time. You can also check out the Zeiss telescope, and snack at the Café at the End of the Universe. See p.182.

Enjoy The Music

There is nothing quite so magical as live music under the stars on a warm summer night at the Hollywood Bowl (p.182). Take a picnic basket and experience one of the great pleasures of Los Angeles. Don't miss the amazing Los Angeles Philharmonic, which plays here throughout the summer.

Pick A Theme Park

Whether you get thrilled through blockbuster sets of Universal Studios (pictured, p.187) or relive your childhood at Disneyland (p.186), your time in LA won't be complete without trying one of the major themeparks. Day passes aren't cheap, and the crowds are usually a pain, but this is a slice of Americana that everyone needs to experience.

You Can Lead A Mammoth To Culture...

Museum Row is an intense hotspot of art, natural science and popular culture on Wilshire. The Los Angeles County Museum of Art (p.174) has pieces from across the full spectrum of European and American art, as well as a whole building dedicated to Japanese art. Next door is the Page Museum (p.177), with its paleontological exhibits based on the fossils that bubble up out of the nearby La Brea Tar Pits.

It's Not Just Raw Fish

There's lots to see in Little Tokyo (p.155), and even more to eat. This is a great place for Japanese food, from the very best sushi at R23 (pictured, p.330) to ultra thin meat at Shabu Shabu House (p.331), or at any of the more traditional joints around the area.

Savour The View

The hills above the city are renowned for their views. Around sunset, drive west on Sunset (it's named for the view) from the Cahuenga Pass to Coldwater. There's a handful of turnoffs where you can pause and contemplate the view of Los Angeles laid out in front of you.

Listen To Acoustic Perfection

Frank Gehry's Disney Hall (p.184) is not just a remarkable work of architecture and the ultimate icon of the Downtown renaissance, it just may be one of the most perfect acoustic spaces in the world. There are no bad seats, as the audience is wrapped right around the orchestra so they can see the musicians and hear every note with almost uncanny clarity. Give it a listen.

Go For Gold

The Gold Line Tram between Union Station and Pasadena (p.157) is a delightful ride along elevated tracks by Chinatown (p.155) and through lush Mt Washington and Highland Park (p.154). It is a beautiful, dreamy ride that transports passengers back through time, and at $1.25 it is one of the best bargains in town. If you're lucky, you may even get a conductor who narrates a little history on the way.

Shop With The Stars

For the real bling and guaranteed authentic name-brand accessories, head for Rodeo Drive (p.300) in Beverly Hills and check out Bvlgari, Gucci, Saks Fifth Avenue and the various boutiques that dress the stars. You can even opt for a guide (p.196) to show you the ins and outs of this shopaholic's dream. Don't forget to bring your gold card.

Hug A Dinosaur

The Natural History Museum of Los Angeles County (p.176) is one of the most impressive institutions of its kind in the world. If you love dinosaurs, the exhibits make the prehistoric past come alive. Walk a few metres to the south and let your child's mind roam free at the California Science Center (p.171).

Have A Big Night Out

Dress fashionably and hit the nightspots on Sunset Strip (p.162). Hang out at the sidewalk cafe at the Cajun Bistro, grab a hot dog at Carney's (p.317), then see who's playing at the House of Blues.

Soak Up Some Greenery

If it's a hot weekend, cool off in a paddleboat at Echo Park (p.190) or go for a stroll on the pathways that ascend to the hills overlooking the city in Elysian Park (p.191). Even better, get a couple of sandwiches to go and dine alfresco at MacArthur Park (p.166).

Walk The Walk

Head for Hollywood (p.150) and hit the pavement around Hollywood and Vine, then just follow the stars beneath your feet to see where they lead you. Along the way, hit the tacky-but-fun Ripley's Believe It Or Not! (p.178), Hollywood Wax Museum (p.174) and Guinness World Records Museum (p.172).

Go Lakers!

Catch a Lakers game at the Staples Center (p.183) and watch one of the best teams in the NBA perform their magic. There are no bad seats and the giant screen suspended above mid-court lets you see every move up close and personal – and that includes watching Jack Nicholson leaping up from courtside to offer his invaluable assistance to the coaching staff.

Get High At The Getty

Catch the electric tram from the carpark off Sepulveda and ascend to one of the world's leading high art museums. In addition to the Getty's peerless collection of antiquities, there are regular shows with more contemporary themes, as well as special theatre, music and dance events. The view from on high is also one of the best in LA. See p.172.

BEVERLY GLEN

A B C

1

BEL AIR ESTATES

BEVERLY HILLS

HOLMBY HILLS

UCLA

A

PICO-ROBERTSON

BRENTWOOD

WESTWOOD

P

2

F
←

CENTURY CITY

SOUTH CARTHAY

RANCHO PARK

WEST LOS ANGELES

SOUTH ROBERTSON

M

SANTA MONICA

10

PALMS

3

Santa Monica Municipal Airport

MAR VISTA

B
CULVER CITY

VENICE

F

90

4

Pacific Ocean

MARINA DEL REY

WESTCHESTER

SAN DIEGO FRWY

405

© Explorer Group Ltd. 2008

↓ **L**

↓ **F**

↓ **E**

A B C

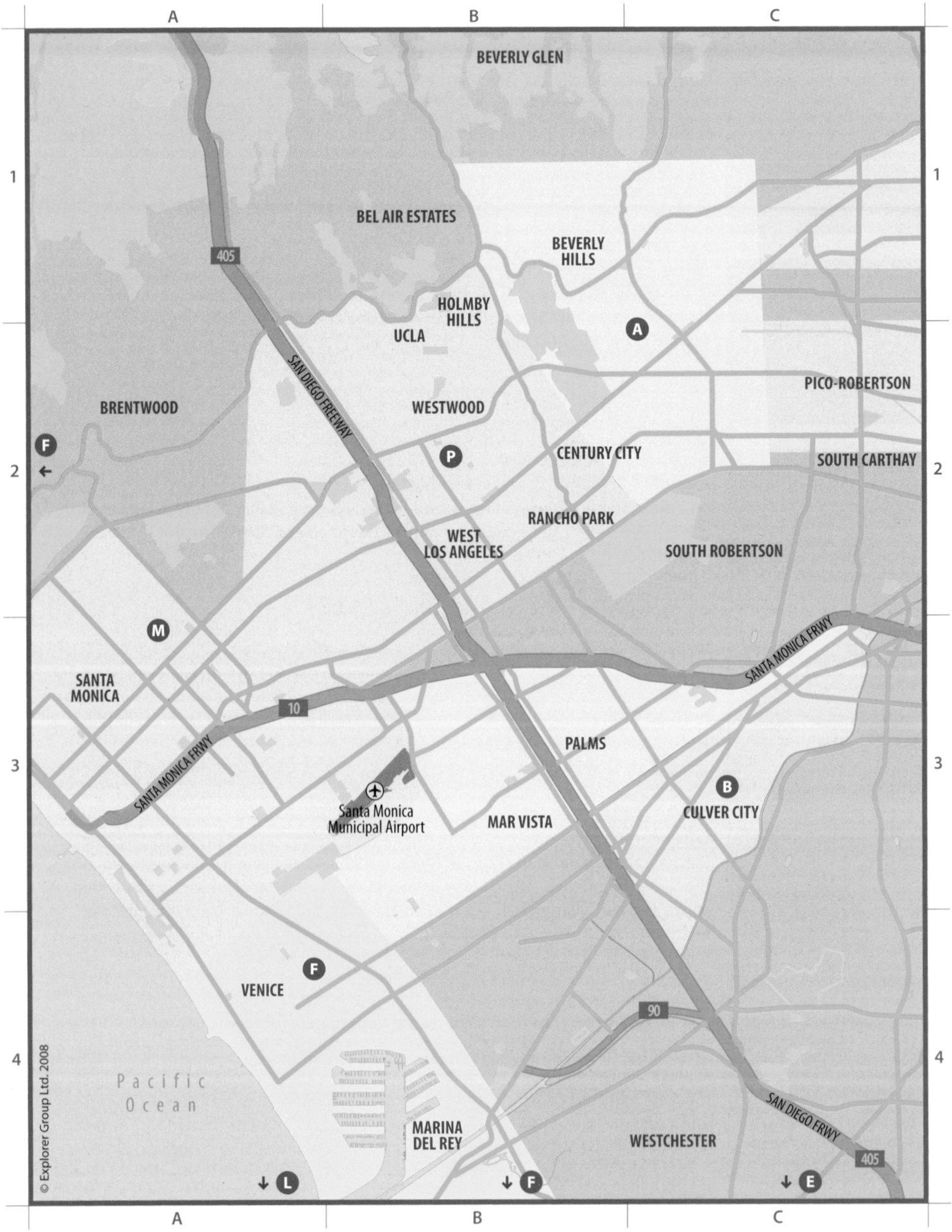

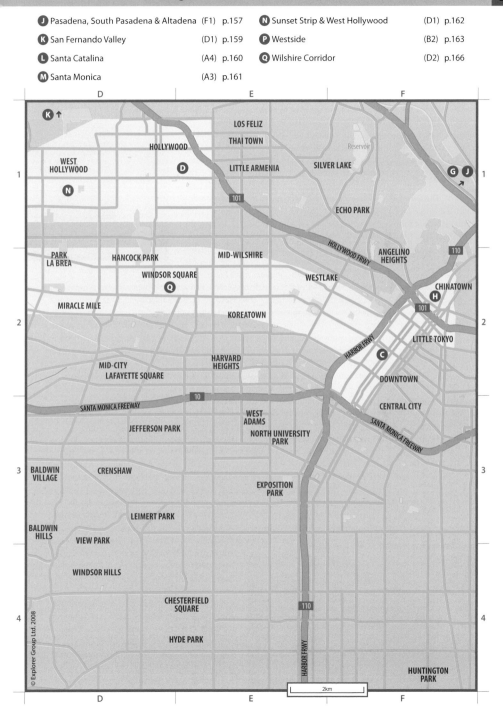
K ↑

LOS FELIZ

THAI TOWN

HOLLYWOOD

WEST HOLLYWOOD

LITTLE ARMENIA

SILVER LAKE

Reservoir

D

G **J**

101

ECHO PARK

N

PARK LA BREA

HANCOCK PARK

MID-WILSHIRE

HOLLYWOOD FRWY

ANGELINO HEIGHTS

110

WINDSOR SQUARE

WESTLAKE

CHINATOWN

Q

H

MIRACLE MILE

KOREATOWN

101

LITTLE TOKYO

HARVARD HEIGHTS

HARBOR FRWY

C

MID-CITY LAFAYETTE SQUARE

DOWNTOWN

10

SANTA MONICA FREEWAY

CENTRAL CITY

WEST ADAMS

SANTA MONICA FREEWAY

JEFFERSON PARK

NORTH UNIVERSITY PARK

BALDWIN VILLAGE

CRENSHAW

EXPOSITION PARK

LEIMERT PARK

BALDWIN HILLS

VIEW PARK

WINDSOR HILLS

CHESTERFIELD SQUARE

110

HYDE PARK

HARBOR FRWY

HUNTINGTON PARK

2km

© Explorer Group Ltd. 2008

Area Ⓐ p.144
See also Map 4

The Lowdown
This is the tasteful, upscale playground of the rich and famous and it is appropriately green, well-groomed and architecturally pleasing.

The Good
Rodeo Drive is a mecca for shoppers in search of the latest fashions and the most exclusive brands.

The Bad
There's no public transport through the hills. If you don't have a car, you'll have to take a bus tour or hire a cab.

The Must-Dos
The most fashionable meal of the day here is lunch. Indulge yourself at Crustacean or the Beverly Hills Hotel.

Ritzy Rodeo Drive

Beverly Hills

Together Beverly Hills, Holmby Hills and Bel-Air comprise the 'Platinum Triangle', where you'll find, according to Coldwell Banker, the priciest real estate in the US – including, of course, the Beverly Hillbillies Mansion. In the centre of Beverly Hills is the 'Golden Triangle', one of the most expensive shopping districts in the world, bordered by Rodeo Drive, Wilshire Boulevard and Santa Monica Boulevard. This is where you can shop for bling at Bvlgari, bags and shoes at Gucci and the rest of your high-end wardrobe at Saks Fifth Avenue (see Shopping, p.256). You can then skip down the Spanish Stairs and dine at some of the best restaurants on the west coast, such as Crustacean (p.338) and Wolfgang Puck's flagship restaurant, Spago (310 385 0880; www.wolfgangpuck.com). Some of the finest art galleries on this side of the confederation are here as well, in particular Galerie Michael (p.169), which regularly features work by Picasso, Rembrandt, Chagall, Matisse and other masters. Just a few blocks

Paley Center For Media

north up Beverly on Sunset (and theoretically within walking distance, if anyone bothered to walk in Beverly Hills), is the Beverly Hills Hotel (p.18). Surrounded by 12 acres of lush tropical gardens, it is home to the famed Polo Lounge, a favourite breakfast spot and watering hole for generations of stars and Hollywood deal-makers. The Sunday brunch, featuring live jazz, is, as you might expect, one of the best in town. Although Benjamin 'Bugsy' Siegel lived some blocks away, he came to the hotel every morning for a shave and a trim. The spa treatments are still popular and more affordable than you might think.

The largest Iranian population outside Tehran lives in and around Beverly Hills in an area that has been dubbed 'Tehrangeles'. One recent report put the number of Iranians in Beverly Hills as high as 20% of the total population. As a result, there are a number of excellent restaurants specialising in Iranian fare; notable among them is Aram (138 S Beverly Drive, 310 859 8585), reputed to serve the best Iranian cuisine in town.

Beverly Hills is, of course, home to the stars and has been ever since 1919, when Douglas Fairbanks and Mary Pickford bought land on Summit Drive and built Pickfair, the first and most celebrated of the many grand residences in the community, at number 1143. A tour of the mansion-studded hillsides is a must. One of the best and most economical ways to explore is on the Beverly Hills Trolley, which offers a 40 minute narrated tour every Saturday and Sunday (www.beverlyhills.org). Greystone Mansion, formerly the Doheny Mansion, is nestled in its own 18.5 acre park at 905 Loma Vista Drive (310 550 4654). The gardens and courtyard are open to the public, and you can even rent the whole thing for your wedding. Much of the area is familiar to audiences around the world thanks to several popular TV shows

and films set here, including the *Beverly Hills Cop* movies and hit series *Beverly Hills 90210*. The Paley Center For Media (formerly known as the Museum of Television & Radio; 310 786 1025, www.mtr.org) offers lectures, screenings and special events of particular interest to anyone infatuated with the past, present and future of the ever-expanding electronic media. For a nightcap, try one of the cool subterranean bars at Aqualounge (424 N Beverly Drive, 310 275 8511). Order a mermaid and see what happens.

Culver City

Area **B** p.144
See also Map 2

The Good
Everything is within walking distance of the corner of Washington and La Cienega.

The Bad
You can get there by bus only if you can interpret the Metro bus schedule. Good luck with that.

The Must-Dos
The Kirk Douglas Theater. The Museum of Jurassic Technology is just around the corner and if you enjoy being pleasantly baffled, check it out.

Culver City's signature is 'The Heart of Screenland', and with some justification. It was built by MGM and Hal Roach Studios (now Culver Studios) which moved there in the 1920s, and the Hughes Aircraft Company, which established its headquarters there in 1932 so that founder Howard Hughes could work within commuting range of his hobby, Hollywood. Hughes left in 1985 but MGM and Culver Studios remain and have been joined by massive Sony Pictures Entertainment and National Public Radio West, making it one of the primary media nodes in LA. Parts of the city still retain a sort of main street, small-town quality that has attracted sidewalk cafes, a score of small galleries and a new population of youthful artists. It's a dizzying eruption of culture that is attracting attention from across the country. Sony is the sponsor of an annual Culver City Art Walk, which takes place early in June (www.culvercity.org).

During the prohibition era, nightclubs and speakeasies crowded along a swank, honky-tonk Washington Boulevard; that era was also Culver City's golden age of the silver screen with *The Thin Man, Gone with the Wind, Citizen Kane*, and the original *King Kong* all produced at this time. The original yellow brick road from *The Wizard of Oz* is still preserved on Stage 27 of Sony Studios. The well-preserved 1950s era residential streets of Culver City are in continuous demand for production shoots – fans of *The Wonder Years* may recognise some of the locations from the series.

Culver City isn't known for conventional attractions. The best reason to explore the area is to check out the architecture and hip lifestyle. Museum lovers shouldn't miss the unusual Museum of Jurassic Technology (p.175), which strives more for amazement than pure education. Also worth a visit is the relatively new (2004) Kirk Douglas Theatre (p.361). The tiny space features original plays by the popular Center Theatre Group.

Culver City is also home to some of the most remarkable and revolutionary architecture in Los Angeles. There are now more than a dozen futuristic structures designed by renowned architect Eric Owen Moss, running through Culver City mainly concentrated around Hayden Avenue. For building buffs in search of the cutting edge, these structures are well worth seeking out.

The Lowdown
This community still has the American small-town, main street look it created for itself when it served as home for the workers at MGM and Hughes aircraft – but the sleepy main drag has lately come alive with art galleries and chic little bistros.

Eastern Columbia Building

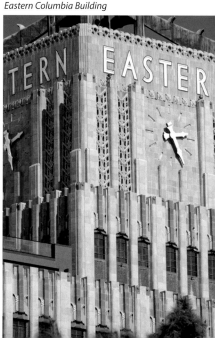

Downtown

Area **C** p.144
See also Map 10

The Lowdown
A renaissance has re-awakened the old urban core and made it one of the most vibrant and intriguing districts in the city.

Downtown Los Angeles has dramatically re-invented itself over the past decade – and changes continue to alter the city at a remarkable rate. What was once a grim and decaying urban core is today a lively, vibrant and colourful inner city attracting a new generation of urban pioneers to the fastest growing residential area in LA. The extensive renovation has forced greater public

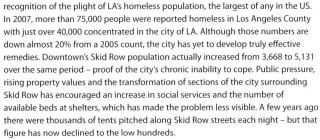

The Good
Hundreds of older buildings have been renovated and works of world class architecture are lighting up the skyline.

The Bad
There's still a shamefully large homeless population crowded up against newly fashionable areas.

The Must-Dos
So many to choose from: The Gallery Row artwalk, an architectural tour down Grand Avenue from Fifth to Temple, a martini at The Edison or a meal at e3rd or R23 in the Arts District.

recognition of the plight of LA's homeless population, the largest of any in the US. In 2007, more than 75,000 people were reported homeless in Los Angeles County with just over 40,000 concentrated in the city of LA. Although those numbers are down almost 20% from a 2005 count, the city has yet to develop truly effective remedies. Downtown's Skid Row population actually increased from 3,668 to 5,131 over the same period – proof of the city's chronic inability to cope. Public pressure, rising property values and the transformation of sections of the city surrounding Skid Row has encouraged an increase in social services and the number of available beds at shelters, which has made the problem less visible. A few years ago there were thousands of tents pitched along Skid Row streets each night – but that figure has now declined to the low hundreds.

In the historic core adjacent to Skid Row, scores of older structures have been transformed to accommodate lofts, condos, restaurants, galleries and retail space and shiny new world-class architectural marvels are rising all around. The new icon of the LA renaissance is unquestionably Frank Gehry's Disney Hall on Grand Avenue near 1st Street. It is the crown jewel of the Music Center, which includes the Dorothy Chandler Pavilion, the Ahmanson Theatre and the Mark Taper Forum, as well as outdoor theatres, plazas and gardens (p.361). Ironically sited beneath Disney Hall and accessed around the corner (and attracting a very different audience) is the REDCAT (the name, baffling to many, is actually an acronym for Roy and Edna Disney CalArts Theater), a post-avant-garde venue dedicated to artistic risk in theatre, film, video, dance (p.362). Across from Disney Hall, the Museum of Contemporary Art (MOCA) has become a global centre for post-modernism (p.175). Adjacent to MOCA is California Plaza. From June to September (and on some holidays at other times of year) free concerts attract thousands of urban picnickers each week to enjoy world-class music during long, lingering, moonlit summer nights (www.grandperformances.org). Attending one of these Grand Performances should be on every visitor's list of must-do activities.

Sculpture outside MOCA

Down the hill from the Grand Avenue citadels of high art, the formerly mean and ragged stretches of Main and Spring Streets (roughly between 1st and 9th) is Gallery Row in the Old Bank District, a lively quarter of galleries, restaurants, bars and cafes in ornate, lovingly restored buildings dating as far back as the first decade of the 20th century. On the second Thursday of every month the galleries stay open into the evening for an art walk featuring live street music, performance art and other enticements. A free bus service circles through the art zone. This is another activity not to be missed (www.downtownartwalk.com). Anchoring one corner of the district is Pete's Bar and Café, featuring dark wood panelling, floor-to-ceiling windows, bistro-style sidewalk seating and a reasonably priced cosmopolitan menu (213 617 1000; www.petescafe.com). A half block up from Pete's on 4th Street is the cosy little Warung Café, which serves tapas-type hot and cold dishes with an Asian accent. It's affordable, intimate and a big favourite among locals (213 626 0662;

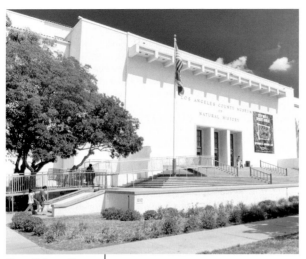
Natural History Museum

www.warungcafela.com). A few blocks northwest, at the corner of 5th and Figueroa, is Ciudad, specializing in Cuban, Spanish, Portuguese and South and Central American cuisine, and boasting the finest rum bar in town. This is also treasured by locals who pack the place on Tuesdays for 'Paella on the Patio' night (213 486 5171; www.ciudad-la.com). Close by is Wolfgang Puck's LA Bistro. This is the newest creation of the famed celebrity chef and it is just as good as his umpteen other venues, serving inventive nouveau cuisine at surprisingly affordable prices (213 614 1900; www.wolfgangpuck.com/bistro). There is a lively nightlife throughout the area – but a couple of places in particular stand out. The aptly named Edison is a former power plant, built deep beneath the city's streets more than a century ago. The dynamos and other Victorian-era electrical artefacts have been artfully preserved in the huge cavern-like space beneath the Higgins building. The entrance, off an alley, is hard to find so check the website for directions (p.346). Perhaps the ultimate LA bar experience, if you can afford it, is the roof bar of The Standard (p.350) at the corner of 6th and Flower, which features spectacular views, an outdoor fireplace, a heated pool, sculpted topiary and, of course, vibrating waterbed pods. Those who crave a hard rock, hip-hop or DJ scene should check out Crash Mansion (p.358) at the intersection of South Grand and West Olympic. Located in a former 1930s ballroom, it features one of the biggest stages in town plus smaller, more intimate performance spaces and half a dozen bars. Other Downtown bars worth checking out include The Broadway Bar (830 Broadway, thebroadwaybar.net/main.html), The Golden Gopher (417 W 8th St, www.goldengopherbar.com) and of particular note, 410 Boyd (410 Boyd St), a favourite hangout of the Downtown arts crowd, it also features a reasonably priced and elegant menu, ever-changing artwork by Downtown artists and a patio for smokers.

A dozen blocks or so southwest of Gallery Row are temples to commerce and popular culture, including the Convention Center (www.lacclink.com) and the Staples Center (p.183) home of the National Basketball Association's Los Angeles Lakers and LA Clippers, the National Hockey League LA Kings and the American Football Association's Avengers. Across the street is the Nokia Theatre LA Live (p.360), one of the premier concert venues in Southern California.

Further out and in the north-west quadrant of downtown – and a pleasant escape from the urban hustle and bustle – is Exposition Park, a graceful and spacious complex of gardens and museums, the grandest of which is the Natural History Museum of LA County (p.176). Now almost a century old, it is one of the finest museums of its kind in the US, well known for creating groundbreaking (and crowd-pleasing) exhibitions. Towering 'Duelling Dinosaurs,' complete skeletons of a Tyrannosaurus rex and Triceratops in battle, greet visitors when they enter the majestic Grand Foyer. This is an ideal destination for families – or anyone awed by the wonders of the natural world.

Area ❶ p.144
See also Map 6

Hollywood

In 1910, legendary director DW Griffith wrestled a Ford model T along a dusty maze of dirt roads from his provisional studio in a Los Angeles hotel to an orange grove at the base of the Santa Monica Mountains to scout locations for the movie *In Old California*. He found the perfect spot in the sleepy little village of Hollywood (the origin of the name has been traced to the native California Holly that covers the hillsides with clusters of bright red berries each winter), bought a ranch, built a bungalow for interior photography and more or less invented the filmmaking capital of the world. Although most of the major studios have long since relocated to larger tracts in neighbouring communities such as Burbank and the Westside, Paramount, with its distinctive gates (most memorably depicted in *Sunset Boulevard*) remains on Melrose Avenue, where it has absorbed the old RKO studio. For the best tour of a working studio, check out its website (www.paramount.com). Advance reservations are required. Of course, the sidewalk along Hollywood Boulevard is strewn with stars celebrating the directors, writers and, well, stars, whose collective contributions to film, music and television comprise the history of much of modern media. A few traces of Old Hollywood still remain, among them Musso and Frank Grill at 6667 Hollywood Boulevard (p.320) which has been around for so long that Douglas Fairbanks and Charlie Chaplin are rumoured to have raced there on horseback. History does not record who won, but undoubtedly the loser paid for a round of the fabulous martinis still poured there. Just up the street is Grauman's Chinese Theater (p.181), which opened in 1927, and where towering, lotus-shaped fountains and intricate tile work flank the footprints of Hollywood's elite. Across the street is the Roosevelt, one of Hollywood's legendary hotels and now restored as one of its hippest hangouts. Just down the street is the El Capitan, now owned by Disney and another great movie palace that has been lovingly restored. At Hollywood and Highland, the fairly new Kodak theatre complex (p.183), home of the Academy Awards, is a great place to shop for Hollywood memorabilia or catch the latest flick. A few blocks into the hills is the justly famed Hollywood Bowl (p.182) if you are in town on a summer night, call for tickets for whatever is playing and take a picnic basket for a once-in-a-lifetime experience.

Across Highland from the Bowl is the Ford Amphitheater (p.180), one of the premier venues for live theatre this side of the Hudson River. Nearby, back down on Hollywood Blvd, is the Pantages Theater (www.pantages-theatre.com), where the latest live musicals are staged months before they appear on Broadway. Right next door is a tiny little bar called the Frolic Room (www.bobsfrolicroom.com) that is famed for its Al Hirschfield mural dating back to the late 1940s, which depicts pretty much the entire panoply of Hollywood stars from that heady era. Have a drink and see how many you can identify. For a true taste of working Hollywood, try the Cat and the Fiddle restaurant and pub (www.thecatandfiddle.com) a couple of blocks south, at 6530 Sunset Boulevard, where you can sit around a tiled fountain among moviemaking's working class of grips, stuntmen, extras and many of the other 'little people' who are the industry's backbone. They also serve the best fish and chips this side of Liverpool.

The Lowdown
Most of the studios are long gone but Hollywood remains the glitzy entertainment capital of the world.

The Good
The grand old movie palaces and shiny new pedestrian-friendly attractions on Hollywood Boulevard make exploring on foot a treat.

The Bad
It can get crowded and there are still some seedy corners and shady characters to avoid.

The Must-Dos
In the summer, there are few pleasures greater than an evening at the Hollywood Bowl. It's also a rare treat to catch a movie at Grauman's or the Egyptian. Musso and Frank's serves the most famous martinis in town.

The lights of Hollywood Boulevard

Area **E** p.144
See also Map 2

The Lowdown
Long Beach is a huge
commercial port with
a thriving marina
crammed with pleasure
craft. This area is all
about the sea.

The Good
The annual Long Beach
Grand Prix is one of
the great events of
the racing world. The
marina, the aquarium
and the Queen
Mary are all within
walking distance in a
clean, well-groomed
downtown area.

The Bad
It's a bit of a freeway-
jammed drive from
Los Angeles (about 45
minutes), but you can
get there on a metro
tram if you don't have
a car.

The Must-Dos
The Aquarium of the
Pacific is one of the
finest in the world
– and after a few hours
petting sharks, you
can dine and enjoy a
cocktail aboard the
Queen Mary.

Long Beach

There's the aquarium, a beautiful marina,
the Queen Mary, galleries, bars and
restaurants but let's face it, the overwhelming
attraction of Long Beach is the three days of
testosterone, high-octane gas and alcohol
that fuel the cars and the crowds during the
Long Beach Grand Prix (www.gplb.com) in
early April of each year, and if a long weekend
of Champ Car World Series (similar to Formula
1) racing through sinuous curves along the
waterfront and city streets weren't enough,
there are a few side events to capture your
attention. Fans of *The Fast and the Furious*
can watch people flinging their autos
around curvy courses in the Formula Drift
Championship, which has grown into one of
the main events of the LBGP. Another draw
is the Toyota Pro Celebrity Race. Among past

Aquarium of the Pacific

drivers are Cameron Diaz, Gene Hackman, Clint Eastwood and Jay Leno. At night, crowds
foam through the city, particularly along Pine Avenue, and pack the bars and restaurants to
exchange tales of the day's thundering events. The races drew 180,000 spectators in 2007.
If you visit Long Beach on any of the other 362 days of the year, don't miss the Queen
Mary (p.20). Launched in 1934, she is one of the last of the great pre-war luxury liners
that plied the chilly Atlantic between Southampton and New York. During the second
world war she served as a troop carrier and in 1942, on a voyage from New York to Great
Britain with a passenger manifest of 16,000 troops, she encountered heavy seas 700
miles from Scotland. In *Age of Cunard*, maritime historian Daniel Allen Butler describes
what happened next: 'A rogue wave, measuring perhaps 92 feet, hit the ship broadside,
breaking windows on the bridge, 90 feet above the waterline, and pushing her so far over
(an estimated 52 degrees) that she paused just on the brink of capsizing – then righted
herself'. The incident was long a wartime secret and the inspiration for Paul Gallico's novel
The Poseidon Adventure (made into a film, twice, although once was enough). Butler's
is just one of the many stories that thrill visitors to her Art Deco lounges and dining
rooms. The ship is now a permanently moored floating hotel where guests bunk down in
restored luxury suites and dine and drink at six on-board venues.
If you prefer the natural world to man-made marvels, visit the Aquarium of the Pacific (562
590 3100; www.aquariumofpacific.org), one of the world's largest ocean aquariums, where
you can pet a shark or sign

The grand Queen Mary

up for a two-hour whale-
watching cruise.
Also in Long Beach is the
Museum of Latin American
Art (562 437 1689; www.
molaa.org), which showcases
contemporary art by Latin
American artists. Located in
the trendy East Village Arts
District, the museum has
received incredible buzz for
creating and exchanging
break-out exhibits.

*Area **F** p.144*
See also Maps 2 & 3

Malibu, Venice & The Beach Cities

Malibu

The Lowdown
The beaches and the coast near Los Angeles are spectacular. The surf, sun, seafood and exhilarating vistas are great for body and mind.

Don't let the constant threat of brush fires and landslides stop you from frolicking in the waves along some of the most enticing beaches in California – as long as you can solve the two riddles that confront all who are not residents: where to park and how to get to the beach. From the coastal highways, the beachfront looks like an unbroken wall of multi-million dollar bungalows. Before you commence your Malibu surfin' safari, visit the Urban Rangers website (www.laurbanrangers.org), click on 'events' and then 'Malibu public beaches' where you can download a copy of the Malibu Beaches Owners Manual. It lists access points, many of which are well hidden. The most obviously accessible sections of the beach, abutting Pacific Palisades, will look familiar to fans of *Baywatch*, while the Malibu Surfrider Beach offers some of the best boarding on the coast. La Piedra State Beach is popular with fishermen and divers, and the kelp beds ensure favourable conditions for surfers even when the sea is choppy elsewhere. The Malibu beaches extend for about 21 miles and are best explored by car. All the television weather people include a surf report in their segments of the local news. Of course, Malibu is also known for its beachfront bistros, seafood restaurants and most intriguing of all, the Getty Villa (310 440 7300; www.getty.edu).

The Good
There are so many miles of beaches that even on the hottest summer days you can find an uncrowded stretch of sand and sea.

Manhattan Beach

The Bad
Some of the best beaches are in Malibu and property owners have made it difficult to find an access point and parking can be a nightmare. You must have a car to truly explore the coastal towns.

Manhattan Beach, just south of Dockweiler (p.189), features a 928 foot pier at the end of Manhattan Beach Boulevard that offers fishing all year. At the end of the pier is Roundhouse Marine Studies Lab and Aquarium (www.roundhouseaquarium.org), which is free to the public. It includes a huge shark tank and a touch tank featuring native tide-pool flora and fauna. Also of note is the newly built Manhattan Beach Studios, which is worth a drive-by to see where they really shot *The OC*.

Marina del Rey

South of Venice is Marina del Rey, where high-rise condos surround a bustling marina for pleasure craft. On Wednesday afternoons from mid-April to early September, you can watch from the decks of waterfront restaurants or the Fisherman's Village boardwalk as scores of sailors race across the clear waters in a weekly mini-regatta. There's also a quiet little family beach, locally known as Mothers' Beach, facing the lagoon and within strolling distance of restaurants and hotels.

The Must-Dos
Stroll along Venice Beach boardwalk and rent a bicycle. The Getty Villa is one of the most spectacular destinations on the Southern California coast.

Newport Beach

Newport Beach is the Martha's Vineyard of the Southern California coast, the second home of celebrities and the well-heeled. It is built on seven islands, the largest of which is Balboa Island, ringed by a scenic walkway. The main strip, Marine Avenue, houses tiny shops and restaurants. Keep an eye out for the famous 'balboa bars' and frozen bananas that are dipped in a variety of toppings. One of the most famous surf spots is here as well, a jetty called 'The Wedge' where even the best surfers are challenged. The area gained popularity with the US television drama *The OC*, but there's more to the town than designer teen drama. Visitors can take advantage of the Balboa Pavilion, harbour cruises and boat rentals. This is also one of the main departure points for trips to Catalina Island (p.160). The Hyatt Newporter plays host to an annual line up of jazz artists in concerts each May. The several public golf courses include Newport Beach Golf Course (www.npbgolf.com), Hyatt Newporter Golf Course (http://newportbeach.hyatt.com) and the Pelican Hills Golf Course (www.pelicanhill.com). Nearby, popular Corona del Mar State Beach sits in picturesque splendour below protective cliffs. If you just want a nice bit of sand, this is your spot.

San Pedro

San Pedro is one of the largest deep-water ports in the country. Visitors can fish for free off the 1,200 foot Cabrillo Beach Pier (3730 Stephen White Dr). Anglers sometimes find mackerel, white croaker and occasionally even halibut. Ports O' Call, a New England-style village, features restaurants, shops and boat excursions around the bay. The Red Car Trolley ride takes visitors on a one-and-a-half-mile journey on a replica of the Red Cars that once served passengers throughout Southern California. Connecting the Red Car to Cabrillo Beach is a shuttle that runs Friday to Monday. Parking is available at a free lot on Harbor and 22nd Street. The Los Angeles Maritime Museum (310 548 7618; www.lamaritimemuseum.org) near Harbor and 6th Street is filled with historic displays, including a remarkable collection of model ships from across the centuries. Other attractions to see in San Pedro include the Cabrillo Marine Aquarium (www.cabrilloaq.org), and the Point Fermin Lighthouse, built in 1874 (www.pointferminlighthouse.org).

Seal Beach

'Cute' is an adjective often applied to this coastal community, named for the seals that once thronged the beaches. Old Town Seal Beach is a faded but charming remnant of a once-popular resort. It features a shady, tree-lined Main Street, reminiscent of small town America during the mid 1900's. The Red Car Museum (562 683 1874) on Electric Avenue near Main Street sits in a rare version of the old Red Cars, built in 1925. The area is also home to renowned sand sculptor Gerry Kirk, who claims the sand at Seal Beach is some of the best in the world since it compacts well, and its colour provides contrast.

Venice Beach

Heading south along the beach from Santa Monica, you'll come to Ocean Park, a pleasing stretch of broad white sand. One beach south lies Venice Beach, with its crowded, boisterous, colourful boardwalk that includes a short stretch known as Muscle Beach, immortalised by Arnold Schwarzenegger in the classic 1974 documentary, *Pumping Iron*. Street performers provide entertainment amid sidewalk cafes, shops and stalls selling everything from surfboards to incense. You can rent a bike or rollerblades, both of which are a great way to cover a lot of territory. A few blocks inland are upscale restaurants, galleries and chic shops along Abbot Kinney Boulevard. A couple of blocks east of the beach, between Virginia Court and Sherman Canal, are the residential waterways that inspired the community's name.

A Starry Night in Venice

A Venice star

Area **G** *p.144*
See also Map 2

Mt Washington & Highland Park

Just to the north-east of Downtown are two of the oldest settled areas in Los Angeles, Highland Park and Mt Washington. The Gold Line light rail tram connects them to the inner city and they are bordered on the south-west by the Pasadena Freeway, constructed in 1940, and the oldest superhighway in the US. This is one of the most scenic areas in LA, centred on an oak-filled valley, the Arroyo Seco, and strewn with sprawling parks, wooded hills and Victorian architecture. The Gold line, which runs between Union Station Downtown to Pasadena, bisects the area, and there are stops for two of the most intriguing attractions in Southern California: Heritage Square and the Southwest Museum of the American Indian. Even the tram ride itself is a worthwhile trip; the tracks are elevated from Union Station to Chinatown and pass through wooded communities, cross dramatic bridges and stop at quaint shopping areas (where antiquing opportunities abound).

Heritage Square (p.172) is a living history museum featuring eight structures built between the civil war and the early 20th century, and includes some true marvels of Victorian architecture. Southwest Museum (p.178) currently holds one of the nation's most important collections related to Native American culture. However, the galleries are currently closed due to the poor condition of the building, with the collection slated to move to improved premises in 2009. Check the website for details before visiting.

The area has experienced a wave of gentrification sparked by a new generation of renovation-minded home buyers searching for bargains in a wildly-fluctuating market, who found what they were looking for in the dilapidated craftsmen-style and river rock homes of the area. Many former dive bars and small family businesses have been snatched up by canny entrepreneurs and the main drag is taking on a distinctly hip new look.

One of the best ways to explore Mt Washington and Highland Park (www.nelaart.com) is on the monthly Northeast Los Angeles Arts Organization art walk on the second Saturday of each month, when home studios and lofts throughout the area open their doors to visitors.

The Good
Time has stood still in some neighbourhoods that look as they did 50 years ago.

The Bad
Developers insist on tearing down many older single-family dwellings to erect cheap multiple-family condos and apartments, and no one seems to have the political will to stop them.

The Must-Dos
Take the Gold Line from Union Station and get off wherever the fancy strikes you – though the Southwest Museum stop and Heritage Square might be the best.

The Lowdown

Among the oldest residential communities in LA, beautiful old craftsman-style and river stone homes are scattered on green hillsides and among the densely wooded arroyos.

Heritage Square

Area **H** p.144
See also Maps 8 & 10

The Lowdown
These three communities retain their ethnic flavour in spite of the touristy gloss.

The Good
Chinatown is a new centre for the arts scene with little galleries popping up in unexpected places; Olvera Street is the frequent host to festivals that host the best mariachi music outside a concert hall and the history of Little Tokyo is written in the sidewalk on 1st Street, be sure to look down and decipher the code.

The Bad
Olvera Street and Chinatown souvenir vendors can obscure the history all around you.

The Must-Dos
In Chinatown, seek out the Grand Star on weekend nights for some extraordinary jazz; in Olvera Street, look for the Siqueiros mural and in Little Tokyo, visit the Geffen, eat some sushi and look for the 2nd Street Jazz Club.

Olvera Street, Chinatown & Little Tokyo

These adjacent colourful Downtown communities offer a window on the true multicultural character and history of LA. In all three you'll find museums, galleries, restaurants, bars, sidewalk bistros and event venues where there is almost always something happening. They are within walking distance of one another, and the DASH bus service is available during the day.

Olvera Street (or El Pueblo de Los Angeles Historic Monument) is celebrated as the birthplace of LA. Directly across from Union Station, it is a block-long quaint Mexican-style market place flanked by historic structures, including Avila Adobe, built in 1818, fully restored and open for tours, and Italian Hall, a late 19th century structure that features a massive mural painted by the great Mexican artist David Siqueiros in 1932. 'American Tropical' features a Mexican worker crucified on an inverted cross representing the forces of capitalism that was whitewashed into oblivion by the conservative powers-that-were almost as soon as it was unveiled. Recently uncovered by the Getty, it is visible from the street. An enormous bandstand dominates the plaza that is the focal point for fiestas and frequent music and dance performances. Midway down the street is La Golondrina. At 80 something it is the oldest restaurant in El Pueblo, famed for its margaritas, premium tequilas and traditional Mexican cuisine (213 687 0800; www.lagolondrina.com). Across the pedestrian passage is El Paseo Inn (213 626 1361; www.elpaseoinn.com), which features equally excellent Mexican dishes and patio dining. For more modest budgets, La Luz del Dia (213 628 7495), situated on the plaza, offers cafeteria-style dining, hand-made tortillas and a patio with a view of the bandstand. On Cinco de Mayo (5 May), Olvera Street and its plaza are the epicentre of one of Los Angeles' most colourful annual events.

Although most of Chinatown is directly to the northeast of Olvera Street, the two communities overlap historically. The original Chinatown, which began with a few settlers around 1852 and grew to 3,000 residents by 1890, was located southeast of Olvera Street until it was demolished to make way for a new railway station. The forced relocation was bitterly resented by the Chinese community and a long, curving line set in stone in the plaza adjacent to Union Station marks the border of the original community and memorialises its inhabitants. After a period of decline and much celebrated corruption, local Chinese Americans in the 1930s embarked on a building campaign to create a new Chinatown – a process that continues to this day. Featuring shopping plazas, restaurants, bars, nightclubs and a new generation of art galleries, it is a lively destination, day or night, with an exotic architectural and culinary charm that was considerably enriched in the 1970s and 80s with the influx of Vietnamese immigrants. The most celebrated Chinatown eatery is the Empress Pavilion (988 Hill St; 213 617 9898; www.empresspavilion. com), a self-proclaimed 'dowager of dim-sum' that is a favourite of locals, famed for a Hong Kong-style menu characterised by an astonishing variety of dim sum dishes wheeled around the huge dining hall on carts. It is particularly recommended for Saturday brunch. More affordable but just as celebrated for its cuisine, particularly its myriad of seafood dishes, is ABC Seafood (708 New High Street; 213 680 2887). The decor may be modest, but this is a favourite among diners who prize authenticity. For pure fun, there is nowhere in LA quite like the Grand Star Jazz club (943 N Broadway; 213 626 2285; www.grandstarjazzclub.com). Remember the bar in the original *Star Wars* movie? This could have been the model. There is excellent live jazz with frequent performances by visiting elite performers and a standing invitation for anyone to step up to the mic for some karaoke with a live band. An upstairs club features hip-hop and DJ events. Just around the corner, tucked into a neon pagoda is the ultra-cool Hop Louie Bar. It cultivates a deceptive

Japanese Village Plaza

seediness that might discourage casual visitors – but those who stick around discover it is the preferred hangout of musicians, artists and other interesting Downtown residents, many of whom go there just for the jukebox that features an eclectic mix of vinyl stretching across half a century and a couple of continents. In early February, the Chinese New Year is celebrated in Chinatown with a traditional Dragon Parade that is one of the largest and most spectacular in the US (www.lagoldendragonparade.com). Watch out for the firecrackers.

Little Tokyo (or Sho-Tokyo) is about 10 blocks south of Chinatown. It is one of three official Japantowns left in the United States. The area was a magnet for immigrating Japanese from the late 19th century until the Exclusion Act of 1924 slammed the door. In the 1930s the population grew to 30,000 but the community was emptied during the second world war when the residents were sent to detention camps. The stretch of pavement along the north side of First Street between Central and Judge John Aiso Street is embedded with images and legends in brass that recall where the buses came to take away the residents and identify the businesses lost to intolerance. Today the area is one of the most popular cultural destinations in LA, featuring world-class museums, fine dining, lively bars, one of the best jazz clubs in California and an authentic medieval Japanese watchtower. The Japanese American National Museum (p.174) exhibits the work of the finest Japanese artists and features a permanent display of the rigours experienced by Japanese Americans who were sent to the high desert detention camp of Manzanar – including a complete barracks building that housed several families. The Japanese American Cultural and Community Center (p.183) is a showcase for traditional arts such as bunraku, the astounding Japanese puppet theatre, as well as classic Japanese cinema and exhibitions. One recent exhibit featured Bugu: The Spirit of the Samurai Warrior. The Far East Café is unmistakably noted by its somewhat incongruous 'Chop Suey' neon sign. It's a classic 1930s style LA eatery that has been lovingly restored to its original glory, and features an eclectic, moderately priced menu and a narrow, brick-enclosed outdoor bar that is a particularly engaging spot on warm summer nights (347 E 1st St, 213 617 9990). For a true fusion of Japanese, Korean and American cuisine, there is probably no place better in California than e3rd Steakhouse & Lounge (p.322), which features adaptations of traditional sushi and tofu dishes with Korean and nouveau cuisine twists (try the ribs marinated in pear juice). Reasonably priced, and decorated in industrial loft chic, it is among the best LA dining experiences. Of course sushi is the top of the list, and one of the best joints this side of Tokyo is R23 (p.330). Tucked away off an alley in an old industrial building converted to lofts and hidden galleries, it's not cheap but it is very good and it features some of the best art in town. Call for dinner reservations. If you are on a modest budget, splurge for lunch. Jazz aficionados swear by the 2nd street Jazz Club (213 680 0047; 366 E 2nd St). In August, Little Tokyo hosts two events: the annual Tofu Festival (www.tofufest.org) where you will learn there is virtually no food this crafty bean curd can't mimic, and Nisei Week, a culture and food festival unparalleled on this side of the Pacific (www.niseiweek.org).

Area ❶ *p.144*
See also Map 2

Pasadena, South Pasadena & Altadena

Pasadena is one of the most physically charming and historically entertaining areas in Los Angeles. It is a traditionally conservative, old-money (by California standards, anyway) community of leafy boulevards graced by large, craftsman-style homes fronted by emerald lawns and shaded by towering native oaks. The residential streets meander among lush green parks and reveal sudden, breathtaking glimpses of the purple San Gabriel Mountains towering to the east. It's also where L Ron Hubbard switched from science fiction to scientology in the late 40s while he was sharing quarters with a rocket scientist and follower of Alistair Crowley, and where, in 1963, Eve Babitz played nude chess with Marcel Duchamp (in what is now the Pacific Asia Museum, p.177).

The Lowdown
Colorado Boulevard, the main street of this staid community of leafy avenues and towering oaks, has been intensely gentrified to good effect. The old town is a delightful pedestrian-thronged area of excellent boutiques, shops and restaurants.

On 1 January each year Pasadena is host to the Tournament of Roses parade (p.32), a fabulous spectacle of marching bands and floats, each of which must be made of natural materials and that take up to a year to build. After the parade, the best college football teams in the nation are matched in the Rose Bowl, the culminating event in the collegiate football season and occasionally a pretty good game.

The main drag, Colorado Boulevard (famously terrorised by the *Little Old Lady from Pasadena* in the Beach Boys song), bisects the old town, now one of the hottest shopping, dining, movie-going and bar-hopping locales in the area, following one of the most extensive urban revitalisations in California. Of course, some of that resulted in the predictable ratio of 2.3 Gaps for every six Starbucks – but there are enough eclectic eateries, independent bistros and chic boutiques to please the crowds that throng the sidewalks every night and at the weekends. The public art and alfresco dining in broad plazas, enclosed by restored brick structures turned into galleries and cafes make Old Town Pasadena a particularly appealing getaway for Angelenos and visitors. If you are looking for interesting bar talk, this is definitely the place to hang out. The California Institute of Technology is within staggering distance of Old Town

The Good
The Norton Simon Museum, the Pacific Asia Museum and a short drive up Colorado, The Huntington.

The Bad
It's crowded.

and the bars are often abuzz with discussions of string theory or Bose-Einstein condensates, a refreshing change from the usual film industry gossip that permeate most of LA's watering holes. Before Old Town was subjected to upmarket restoration, the late Nobel Laureate Richard Feynman used to frequent a strip joint where he would sketch the performers.

The Must-Dos
Call The Huntington and make reservation for high tea. The Norton Simon's Picassos are also worth a look and an interlude in the garden courtyard at the Pacific Asia Museum is good for your karma.

Just across the freeway, a block or two west from the Old Town district on Colorado, is the Norton Simon Museum (p.177), which houses seven centuries of European art from the Renaissance to the 20th century, including paintings by van Gogh, Picasso, Rembrandt, and Fragonard. The museum also features an astounding collection of Buddhist sculpture from throughout Asia and a sculpture garden with works by Rodin. Half a dozen blocks or so east on Colorado and half a block north on North Los Robles

Pacific Asia Museum

Avenue is the Pacific Asia Museum (p.177). Artfully housed in a Chinese mansion built in 1929, it consists of six galleries surrounding a garden courtyard.

A few miles further east is the entrance to one of the most remarkable attractions anywhere in California – or anywhere else, for that matter: The Huntington (p.174) is an oasis of art and culture set amid 150 acres of breathtaking gardens. The library features a vast collection of literary works, including an original Gutenberg Bible and Chaucer's *Canterbury Tales,* on public display in a vast and magnificent hall, as well as meticulously maintained private collections, stored in temperature, humidity and light-protected vaults but available to scholars from around the world. Three art galleries showcase 18th and 19th century British and French masterpieces, including the 'Blue Boy' and 'Pinkie.' Fifteen gardens feature 14,000 species of plants. High tea is served daily in a light and airy space surrounded by windows on all sides that overlook gardens that seem to stretch endlessly into the distance. You must make a reservation. It is surprisingly affordable and the teas and cucumber and watercress sandwiches and various sweets are on a par with what you would expect at London's finest hotels.

Just north of Pasadena in the foothills of the San Gabriels is Altadena. At the far eastern edge, tucked up against the mountain canyons and ridges, is NASA's Jet Propulsion Laboratory (818 354 9314; www.jpl.nasa.gov). The JPL is mission control for the Mars Rovers and a dozen or so other unmanned space craft whizzing through the solar system and beyond. Remarkably, the JPL offers public tours, and for the cosmically minded, this is a once-in-a-lifetime experience.

In South Pasadena, a couple of dozen blocks down Fair Oaks from Old Town Pasadena, is the Rialto, one of the last remaining single-screen movie palaces in Los Angeles. Built in 1925, the interior is a blend of Spanish Baroque and Egyptian, the sort of exuberant, over-the-top design only found in old movie theatres (this was featured in *The Player*). It is highly recommended for anyone in search of an authentic cinematic time-travel experience.

The Huntington

Colorado Boulevard

Norton Simon Museum

Area **K** *p.144*
See also Map 2

The Lowdown
A vast suburban sprawl with several isolated islands of popular culture.

The Good
The Metro subway stops at Universal Studios.

The Bad
It gets incredibly hot in the summer.

The Must-Dos
Don't miss the Universal City Studios Tour and the Valley side of Griffith Park, particularly the Museum of the American West. Yippee yi yo ki yay!

San Fernando Valley

The 'Valley of the Stars' is the nickname given to the home of the much-maligned valley girl and vast middle-class residential communities. It is to The Valley that Universal Studios Hollywood, Warner Bros Studio and Walt Disney Studios fled when they outgrew their original Hollywood quarters. It is also home to TV network studios including ABC, CBS and NBC. Just over the Cahuenga Gap from Hollywood, at the gateway to The Valley, Universal Studios (p.187) offers tours and Universal CityWalk (p.188) presents bizarre landscapes that feature abbreviated versions of attractions in LA's many communities. Although it was much derided when it originally opened as a theme park that was virtually a caricature of its host city, it has since become immensely popular, second only to Disneyland as a family destination. Other studios, such as Warner Bros and NBC, offer tours and free tickets to TV show tapings, such as the *Tonight Show with Jay Leno*. Warner Bros also offers tours (www.warnerbros.com) of a real working studio, which are highly recommended.

Aside from the studios, there is the hip and still funky NoHo Arts District in North Hollywood which has more than 20 little theatres and is home to Oscar's cousin, Emmy, produced annually at the Academy of Television Arts And Sciences (www.emmys.tv). Quirky, independent coffee shops, galleries and bistros make this an excellent area for a stroll.

Griffith Park (p.191) is near the gateway to the valley, just where it opens and drops down into the LA Basin. At more than 4,100 acres, it is the nation's largest municipal park and offers picnicking, hiking, cycling, horseback riding and other activities. The park also features the LA Zoo and Botanical Garden (p.188). Although it tends to be compared unfavourably with the amazing San Diego Zoo, it is still one of the top facilities in the country, thanks to new exhibits, including a highly rated reptile and amphibian house. Other must-see attractions include the The Museum of the American West (p.176), an enchanting window onto the Wild West, the Greek Theatre (p.360) and the recently renovated and restored Griffith Observatory (p.182), which is worth the trip if only for the spectacular view of the city. Griffith Park is also home to the Los Angeles Equestrian Center (www.la-equestriancenter.com), which hosts several companies that offer lessons you can even ride through The Valley to discover pockets that have stubbornly resisted development.

In the triangle formed by the 5, 405 and 118 freeways, you can still catch a glimpse of the Mission San Fernando Rey de Espana (www.missiontour.org/sanfernando), one of the 21 original California missions, founded in 1797 and featuring a spectacular altar. High up in La Canada Flintridge is the enchanting Descanso Gardens (www.descanso.com), which features an authentic Japanese tea house and a dazzling display of seasonal blooms. It is a wonderful getaway, particularly during the hot summer months. The Valley also has its own commercial airport: Bob Hope Airport in Burbank. It is linked to Hollywood and Downtown by the Metro Red line, which also stops at Universal City.

Universal CityWalk

Area **L** p.144 ◄

Santa Catalina

The Lowdown ◄
The local island getaway that is as good, if not better, than its publicity.

The Good ◄
It's an island paradise.

The Bad ◄
You have to cross water to get there. You can catch a boat from Newport Beach, Long Beach or Marina del Rey.

The Must-Dos ◄
Go there, snorkel, and dance at the Avalon Ballroom.

Getting There ◄
Catalina-Marina del Rey Flyer (310 305 7250; www.catalinaferries.com), Catalina Classic Cruises (800 641 1004; www. catalinaclassiccruises.com), Catalina Express Ferry (800 481 3470; www. catalinaexpress.com), Catalina Explorer (877 432 6276), Catalina Flyer (949 673 5245; www.catalina-flyer.com)

As the island of romance, Santa Catalina is aptly named. It was her second European discoverer, the Spanish explorer Sebastian Vizcaino, who dubbed her thus on the eve of St. Catherine's Day in November of 1602. St. Catherine of Alexandria is celebrated for refusing to wed unless it would be to someone better than her in all things. She was promptly transported to heaven and married to Christ. If that cosmic connection weren't enough, the sister-in-law of George Shatto, the island's owner in the late 19th century, designated the main town Avalon, the name of paradise in Arthurian legend. It is indeed a pleasant place, renowned for its climate, turquoise waters and relaxed lifestyle. Situated just 35 km (22 miles) off the coast, there's almost no traffic and so little crime that the island's only judge works just one day a week. Avalon's resident population is just 3,500, but in late summer that number swells to 10,000 or more. Even then, there's plenty of beach to go around and you can always find a secluded cove if you rent or hire a boat to the deserted, opposite side of the island.

Avalon is nestled in the green hillsides above a graceful bay. The local waters are so translucent and swarming with marine life that it has been called Southern California's largest aquarium. It's a favoured destination for divers, kayakers, and fishermen and one of the most popular attractions is the semi-submersible sub tour run by Catalina Adventure Tours (310 510 2888; www.catalinaadventuretours.com).

The town is ringed by rugged hills, beyond which lie pristine open ranges. Nearly all of the island is wild – and likely to remain so, thanks to the Wrigley family (of chewing gum fame) who entrusted it to the Santa Catalina Island Conservancy in 1975. Wrigley also turned Avalon into a fabled resort for Hollywood's elite. Several films were shot on the island, including *Mutiny on the Bounty* and *The Ten Commandments*. It was in 1925 that *The Vanishing American* was filmed here – and although the movie is long forgotten, it left on the island a living legacy of 14 American bison. The herd has grown to more than 200 and you can hike into the island's interior in search of them, or take a Jeep Eco-Tour (310 510 2595; www.catalina.com/jeeptours).

As the owner of the Chicago Cubs, Wrigley built the team a hacienda-style clubhouse that is now the Catalina Country Club (310 510 7404), which today features the island's finest and most elegant dining. But it was Wrigley's Casino, opened in 1929, that drew the greatest crowds. An elegant 12 storey masterpiece of art deco, the circular casino is built on its own jetty in the little bay. The top floor is the country's largest circular ballroom and at its centre hangs an enormous Tiffany crystal chandelier. This was one of the great homes of the big bands, led by the likes of Benny Goodman and Glenn Miller, and it is from here that big band music was broadcast across the country in the 1930s and 1940s. The Avalon, as it is simply called, with its mythically themed art deco murals, is so stunning that it remains a favourite among Hollywood types who still go there to get married, some of them two or three times.

Those wanting to spend a weekend on the island can choose from the luxurious Inn at Mt Ada (310 510-2030, www.catalina.com/mtada), the stylish, in-town Motel Metropole (800 300 8528, www.hotel-metropole.com) or the historic Glenmore Plaza Hotel near the beach (800 422 8254, www.glenmorehotel.com).

Several ferry companies service the island and regularly scheduled trips leave from Marina del Rey, Newport Beach and Long Beach. Contact one of the companies to the left to see which service best suites your needs. Those with private boats can also access the island. Avalon and Two Harbors both have mooring facilities and services. There are also many coves around the island that have moorings or anchorages. The Catalina website (www.catalina.com) has more details. To get there even faster, you might want to splurge and take the 15 minute Island Express Helicopter trip (www.islandexpress.com).

Santa Monica

Area **M** *p.144*
See also Map 3

The Lowdown
Despite a reputation for being 'the home of the homeless', this charming coastal community has one of the best pedestrian shopping districts in LA, and is beautifully situated on a bluff above the Pacific.

The Good
The Third Street Promenade, the Santa Monica Pier and the beach.

The Bad
It's the 'home of the homeless'.

The Must-Dos
After lunch at the Third Street Promenade or a day at the beach, catch an art opening at Bergamot Station, particularly if there's something happening at Track 16.

Santa Monica, created by land speculators in 1875, is the original Los Angeles coastal resort community. It stretches nonchalantly along alarmingly eroding seaside bluffs above quarter-mile wide swaths of beach and the azure Pacific. The city has grown from a scruffy, laid-back coastal village, once notorious for the gambling ships anchored just off shore, into a fanatically manicured, politically liberal community.

The carnival rides and souvenir booths on the pier below are the slightly funky remnants of an amusement park built in the 1920s when the city was the end of the line for the Red Cars (the long-lost public trolley system that was dismantled by a gang of oil producers, tyre manufacturers and car dealers in the 1940s). The town was also home to several amateur aviators in the 1930s and 1940s who pushed their planes from garages down city streets to the local airfield, which remains a popular private airport. Today, Santa Monica is better known locally for its strictly enforced rent control policies and its delicate, politically correct treatment of the poor, which has earned it the ironic title 'the home of the homeless'.

The beaches and the recently refurbished Santa Monica Pier are still the main attractions. Also recommended is the UCLA Ocean Discovery Center (www.odc.ucla.edu), just below the pier where you can fondle sea anemones and starfish. The grand beach houses along the broad beach to the north of the pier made up Hollywood's 'Gold Coast'. Among them is the Sand and Sea Hotel, once the servants' quarters for a long gone 120 room Victorian monstrosity built by William Randolph Hearst. In the 1960s the Kennedy brothers were rumoured to have 'entertained' Marilyn Monroe in an oversized bungalow next door, originally owned by Louis B Mayer (of MGM).

The city's most interesting locales are within strolling distance of Palisades Park, an intertwining series of palm and cypress tree-lined pathways that meander precariously along the cliffs overlooking the beach. The Third Street Promenade, a few blocks east, is a growing and lively pedestrian shopping zone menaced by topiary dinosaurs and popular with street vendors, musicians, performance artists and soapbox preachers. Although the predictable chain stores and fastfood franchises have replaced many (but not all) of the independent bookstores and boutiques, it remains one of the best people-watching venues in town.

A few blocks further inland is Bergamot Station, a former Red Car stop and now Southern California's largest gallery complex and cultural centre, featuring contemporary art galleries, The Santa Monica Museum of Art (310 586 6488; www.smmoa.org) and architecture and design firms. In particular, look for events at the Track 16 Gallery (p.170), perhaps the most intriguing privately owned gallery in the city.

Santa Monica Beach

Third Street Promenade

Area **N** *p.144*
See also Map 5

Sunset Strip & West Hollywood

Where Sunset Boulevard rises into the foothills of the Santa Monica Mountains west of Crescent Heights Boulevard, it enters West Hollywood, and from there to Phyllis Street on the border with Beverly Hills, it is known as Sunset Strip, one of the most legendary stretches of roadway in the world. The giant billboards, nightclubs, chic shops and sidewalk bistros along The Strip constitute a long, sinuous community unto itself, undoubtedly the greatest people-watching place in LA. At night, when The Strip explodes in a blaze of neon and paparazzi flashes, it seems to vibrate with excitement as celebrities, celebrity spotters and wannabes crowd the sidewalk bars to revel in the unique glitzy atmosphere.

The Lowdown
The Strip is a sinuous, sexy, utterly unique stretch of street where paparazzi stalk coy celebrities and everyone else turns out to watch the hunt.

The Strip lies just outside of the Los Angeles city limits and beyond the authority of the Los Angeles Police Department. In the 1920s it became a magnet for casinos and nightclubs, where alcohol was served in back rooms. When prohibition ended, The Strip grew glamorous as movie stars, moguls and politicians came to dance at such legendary venues as the Garden of Allah, Mocambo, Ciro's and the Trocadero. Things started to become a bit shabby in the 1960s as the stars and movie moguls sought new playgrounds, and the clubs became home to local bands. A youthful, energetic new vibe began to grow, and The Strip reinvented itself as a centre for rock. New clubs arrived, such as the Whisky a Go Go (8901 Sunset Boulevard; 310 652 4202), where The Doors got their start as the house band, and The Roxy (9009 Sunset Boulevard; 310 276 2222), where Bruce Springsteen's career started. In later decades, the two were home to Metallica, Van Halen and Guns N' Roses.

The Good
The sidewalk cafes, bars and music venues are people-watching paradise.

The Strip today is no longer a cradle of emerging music but the scene lives on in clubs such as The House of Blues at 8430 (323 848 5100; www.hob.com) and The Viper Room at 8852 (310 358 1881; www.viperroom.com), formerly owned by Johnny Depp, and where River Phoenix died of a drug overdose in 1993. A few blocks down and across the street is the Chateau Marmont (p.18). Built in 1929 based on the design of an existing Parisian chateau, it has been host to many major stars and visiting celebrities from all over the world. It was here that actor John Belushi died of a drug overdose. Just down the street is the Cajun Bistro at 8301 (323 656 6388). Its sidewalk cafe was the location for the final scenes of the Woody Allen film *Annie Hall*.

The Bad
The crowds at the sidewalk cafes, bars and music venues can be overwhelming at times.

At 8440 Sunset Boulevard is the famed Mondrian (323 848 6025), which contains The Sky Room, one of the hottest nightspots in LA. The legendary Hollywood meeting spot Schwab's Drug Store used to reside at 8024. Recently the site was occupied by a Virgin Megastore, but it closed early in 2008 – a victim of soaring rents and online music-buying. The Comedy Store at 8433 (p.358) is the best venue for stand-up in LA. Richard Pryor and Jay Leno got their big breaks here. Sunset Tower (p.20) at 8358 was previously known as The Argyle and almost every star in Hollywood has stayed there at one time or another. Completely renovated in the late 80s, this 13 storey landmark is today one of the best examples of the architecture of Hollywood's 'golden era'. Sunset Plaza at 8600 features trendy boutiques, outside cafes and cosy bars – you're almost guaranteed to see a celebrity if you sit here long enough. Le Dome at 8720 (310 659 6919) is *the* restaurant of the rich and famous, and features a mammoth circular bar. The Rainbow Bar & Grill at 9015 (310 278 4232) was in former days The Villa Nova restaurant, where Vincente Minnelli (Liza's father) proposed to Judy Garland and Marilyn Monroe had a blind date with baseball legend and future husband Joe DiMaggio.

The Must-Dos
Have a drink at the Sky Bar at the Mondrian, check out the Standard or drop in on Johnny Depp's old place, the infamous Viper Room. You are now officially cool.

The compact area is packed with more than 400 furniture and clothing designers, graphic artists and architects. It is also the centre of one of the largest gay communities on the west coast and the site of an annual gay, lesbian and transgender rights parade. The parade, on Santa Monica Boulevard in early June, is one of the best of its kind in the world and an unforgettable spectacle for all sexes (www.westhollywood.com).

Area P p.144
See also Map 4

Westside

LA's trendy Westside is a cosmopolitan network of neighbourhoods that stretch from the Wilshire Corridor to Brentwood. The area grew rapidly after the Great Depression, when many Angelenos moved to the area from Downtown, attracted by the Westside's distinctly village-like atmosphere. It's really more a collection of distinct communities, each with its own unique character, than a single slice of LA. The main areas are Brentwood, Westwood and Century City. Although Beverly Hills is technically part of Westside, it is generally recognised as a separate entity.

The Lowdown
Brentwood is one of the most exclusive and expensive communities in LA and Westwood, where UCLA is located, is one of the most sophisticated college towns in the world.

Brentwood

Brentwood is overshadowed by the Santa Monica Mountains and includes most of the exclusive Bel-Air Estates. It is locally famous for its many Italian eateries. Originally part of a Spanish land grant and later an agricultural district, Brentwood is now one of the wealthiest neighbourhoods in Los Angeles. The term 'upscale' is an understatement for this community of spectacular multi-million dollar homes and celebrity residents, among them 'Der Governator', Arnold Schwarzenegger. It is also home to The Getty Center (p.172), the fabulous museum complex perched high on a ridgeline above the 405 freeway. Since it opened in 1997, The Getty has been recognised as one of the greatest museums in the world, and although its reputation was tarnished recently in scandals involving the museum's acquisition of looted antiquities, its collection of Greek and Roman sculpture is among the best in the world.

The Good
The Tuscan restaurants in Brentwood and the movie premiers in Westwood.

The Bad
The worst traffic in the city.

Westwood

Westwood is UCLA's college town, located directly adjacent to the campus. It offers all the amenities you would expect to find next to a world-class university: excellent bookstores, coffee shops and affordable eateries in a pedestrian friendly warren of boutique-lined streets. Just east of Brentwood, Westwood is perhaps most well known for its movie palaces that have been host to major premiers covered by newsreels and TV over the decades. Among them, the Crest (www.westwoodcrest.com) with its distinctive art deco tower and the former Fox Theatre – now the Mann Village (961 Broxton Av; 310 248 6266). Many of Hollywood's brightest stars are buried at the Westwood Village Memorial Park Cemetery (1218 Glendon Av; 310 474 1579), including Marilyn Monroe, whose grave is graced with a single red rose every day, paid for by the estate of Joe DiMaggio. A museum endowed by Occidental Petroleum mogul and philanthropist Armand Hammer (and named for him) is one of Los Angeles' trendiest cultural attractions. The Hammer (p.171) has an excellent permanent collection of impressionist art, and regularly hosts cutting edge modern and post-modern exhibitions. The museum also houses the Billy Wilder Theater, run by the UCLA Film and Television Archive.

The Must-Dos
Go to the Getty Museum. Have lunch there. Take in one of the best collections in the world.

On the downside, Westwood has some of the worst traffic congestion in Los Angeles. Even with the opening of numerous municipal parking structures in recent decades, finding a parking spot in Westwood Village is notoriously difficult.
The Los Angeles California Temple (www.ldschurchtemples.com/losangeles), the second-largest temple operated by The Church of Jesus Christ of Latter-day Saints (LDS), is just south of the campus area, where it looms monumentally above Santa Monica Boulevard. A visitors' centre is open to the public. The temple grounds are home to the Los Angeles Regional Family History Center

> **Traffic Alert!**
> When Century City was built it was with the understanding it would be served by the Beverly Hills Freeway and a rapid transit corridor. However, these transportation improvements were never completed and so Century City is a source of traffic irritation for visitors and residents alike.

(LARFHC), which is open to the public. It is the second-largest branch in the Family History Library system of the LDS Church, and contains more than 100,000 microfiche and 30,000 books.

Century City

Century City's 176 urbanised acres jut up from between Westwood, Beverlywood, Ranch Park and Beverly Hills like a giant silver thumb. Its towering skyscrapers, the first built in the region after earthquake safety-height restrictions were modified in the early 1960s, are its dominant feature. It almost looks like a big chunk of the future that fell out of the sky and landed on the recent past. One of the most recognisable buildings on the former 20th Century Fox backlot is Fox Plaza, familiar to movie goers as Nakatomi Plaza in the movie *Die Hard*. One of the best big-screen theatres is here, in the Century City Mall, right next to one of the most upscale foodcourts in the city.

Whisky a Go Go club

Sunset Boulevard

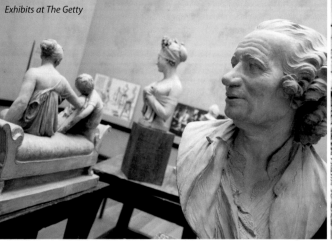
Exhibits at The Getty

Viper Room

Babywear p.98
Bank Loans p.22

Written by residents, the New York Explorer
is packed with insider info, from arriving
in the city to making it your home and
everything in between.

New York Explorer Residents' Guide
We Know Where You Live

Area ❼ *p.144* ◀
See also Map 7

The Lowdown ◀
*To travel the length of
Wilshire is to journey across
the social, cultural and
physical landscape of LA.*

The Good ◀
*Greenery, culture and
shopping – there's
something for everyone.*

The Bad ◀
*The Metro subway only
goes so far.*

The Must-Dos ◀
*Museum Row includes
the Los Angeles County
Museum of Art (LACMA),
the Page Museum and
the Peterson Automotive
Museum. Just up the street
and around the corner is
the Farmers Market for
lunch and The Grove, a
temple to retail sales*

Farmers' Market

Wilshire Corridor

Heading west from the slick skyscrapers of Downtown, Wilshire Boulevard passes through Westlake, perhaps best well-known as the home of MacArthur Park, where, in the Jimmy Webb song of the same name, someone left a cake out in the rain. The park is divided in two by Wilshire. The area south of the boulevard is dominated by a palm-fringed lake with a geyser-like fountain fed by natural springs. The northern half includes an amphitheatre and a bandstand that hosts jazz, big band, salsa and world music concerts. In the 1890s, the park was a vacation destination surrounded by luxury hotels. By the early part of the 20th century, the area became known as the Champs-Élysées of Los Angeles. In the 1980s and 90s the park was notorious as a centre of gang activity, but an aggressive campaign by community leaders and the LAPD in recent years has encouraged the re-emergence of small businesses and visitors have begun to flock to the area once again. The views of Downtown across the lake make it a great urban picnic spot.

Continuing west, Wilshire Boulevard crosses Vermont and enters Koreatown, roughly bounded by 8th Street to the north, 12th Street to the south and Western Avenue to the west. In the 1970s, South Korean emigrants, displaced by the heavy-chemical industry drive, settled in the area (which already had a small Korean population) and it was christened Koreatown. The growing community soon became famed for its Korean BBQ, tofu houses, noodle shops and a wide selection of excellent restaurants. At that same intersection is the Wiltern Theatre (213 388 1400) which is, along with the neighbouring Pellissier Building, a stunning landmark clad in glistening aquamarine terracotta tile and regarded as one of the finest examples of art deco architecture in the country. It is also one of finest concert venues in LA.

A mere 20 blocks westward, Wilshire crosses Highland, marking the eastern boundary of the Miracle Mile, so dubbed because of the rapid development of the area from sleepy rural community to high-rise urban density in the mid 1920s. Twenty blocks up the Mile is Museum Row, one of the densest museum complexes in the world. It is here that the vast Los Angeles County Museum of Art (LACMA, p.174) compound nestles up against the reconstructed woolly mammoths of the Page Museum and La Brea Tar Pits (p.177) across the boulevard from the Peterson Automotive Museum (323 930 2277; www.petersen.org). LACMA is the largest

encyclopaedic museum west of Chicago, with more than 250,000 works of art from antiquity to the present. The museum also features film and concert series throughout the year. The Page Museum's meticulously constructed dioramas offer startlingly realistic windows onto the prehistoric past. Artefacts are gleaned from the bones of creatures that still bubble up from the tar pits now ringed by walkways. The Peterson's exhibits

Miraculous Congestion

Miracle Mile's famous developer, AW Ross, planned the area to be car friendly. He included many innovations to ease the flow of traffic, including dedicated left-turn lanes and mandatory carparks for new buildings. Even the architecture was designed for fast-moving eyes. The dream could only last so long – today Miracle Mile has some of the worst traffic in the city.

of rare and classic cars explore the impact the evolution of the automobile had on our culture and society. Kids love it. Finally, at the corner of Wilshire and Fairfax, is the old May Company building, a marvel of modern architecture salvaged by LACMA and now its architectural annex.

The area around the corner up Fairfax to the north is the Fairfax District, long a centre for the city's Jewish community. There were four synagogues here in 1935. Ten years later, there were twelve. After the second world war, many more Jewish emigrants, among them Holocaust survivors, settled in the area. From the 1950s to the 1970s, the Fairfax District was the centre of Jewish life in Los Angeles. Of the many kosher delis and shops that once lined Fairfax Avenue, only a few remain. Thankfully, one of the best delicatessens this side of New York survives, the famous Canter's (www.cantersdeli.com).

The Farmers Market at Third and Fairfax was created in 1934 by farmers who offered their locally grown produce from the tailgates of their pickup trucks. It was an instant success and the dusty lot was transformed into a bustling marketplace and remains so to this day, with fresh fruit and vegetable stalls crowded together with chic little eateries and icecream vendors (www.farmersmarketla.com). This is a favourite among Angelenos and visitors and has become even more successful with the development of The Grove (p.308), an innovative, upscale mall designed to vaguely resemble a European marketplace and featuring high-end restaurants and high-tech cinemas.

CBS Television City was built in 1952 at Fairfax Avenue and Beverly Boulevard. This is where the network records *The Young and the Restless*, the *Late Late Show*, and *The Price is Right*. Tickets for shows are available at the box office on the corner but it's wise to call in advance (323 575 2458).

A bit further up, Fairfax intersects with Melrose Avenue. In the late 1970s, Melrose became known as a street of funky shops and a youthful street scene; LA's version of Haight-Ashbury in San Francisco. Like that famous locale, the area has had its ups and downs but today it is a fashion district celebrated for its eclectic and independent designers and chic bistros.

LACMA

Amusement Parks

Other options **Theme Parks** p.186

Santa Monica Pier
Santa Monica
Map 3 C4 **1**

Pacific Park

310 260 8744 | www.pacpark.com

Pacific Park is a family amusement park on the Santa Monica Pier. It features lovingly restored attractions that nostalgically recall amusement parks of yore, such as the famed Looff Hippodrome and its 1920s carousel, now a National Historic Landmark. The park also has more up-to-date rides, in particular, the west coaster, the only west coast steel roller coaster built on a coastal pier. The Coaster rises to five storeys and offers spectacular views of Santa Monica Bay before plunging back down towards the water in the salt sea breeze. There's also the Pacific Plunge, a soaring nine-storey tower that drops riders on a weightless

Pacific Park's iconic ferris wheel

plunge more than 150 feet, and the Pacific Wheel, a 30 foot tall solar-powered ferris wheel. There are also plenty of rides for little kids. Pacific Park is a wonderful afternoon diversion within walking distance of downtown Santa Monica and beachfront restaurants along Ocean Front Walk.

Art Galleries

Other options **Art** p.260, **Art & Craft Supplies** p.261

354 N Bedford Dr
Beverly Hills
Map 4 E2 **7**

Anderson Galleries

310 858 1644 | www.andersongalleries.com

The Anderson Galleries exhibits barbizon, academic, impressionist and post-impressionist works. It specialises in late 19th and early 20th century European art. Open Monday to Saturday from 11:00 to 18:00.

102 W 5th St
Downtown
Map 9 D1 **2**

Bert Green Fine Art

213 624 6212 | www.bgfa.us

Bert Green is one of the pioneers of the Downtown arts scene and his gallery, located at the centre of Gallery Row, features some of the most exciting and challenging works by local artists. Visit in the early evening of the second Thursday of the month, when all the galleries in the area offer extended hours for the Gallery Row Art Walk (www.galleryrow.org). Open Tuesday to Saturday, 12:00 to 18:00 (until 21:00 on Thursday). Closed between scheduled exhibitions.

110 Winston St
Downtown
Map 10 D3 **3**

Crewest

213 627 8272 | www.crewest.com

This small gallery tucked just off Main Street in Gallery Row showcases some of the most vital young artists in Los Angeles. The focus is almost exclusively on those who have emerged from the graffiti scene, bringing with them a new visual vernacular that is to the visual arts what rap and hip-hop are to music. The work is fresh, original and fun, even when charged with an edginess that can be surprisingly complex. This is a required stop on the Downtown Art Walk. Open Tuesday, Wednesday and Thursday 12:00 to 18:00; Friday and Saturday 12:00 to 20:00; and Sunday 12:00 to 18:00 (and until 21:00 on the second Thursday of each month). Closed Mondays.

Gagosian Gallery

456 N Camden Dr
Beverly Hills
Map 4 E2 4

310 271 9400 | www.gagosian.com
Renowned art dealer Larry Gagosian has galleries in London, Rome and New York, and ever since this Beverly Hills gallery opened in 1995 it's become a significant player in the LA art scene. The 8,000 square foot gallery is a showcase for modern and post-modern artists, among them Richard Serra, Cy Twombly, Julian Schnabel and Ed Ruscha. Open Tuesday to Saturday 10:00 to 17:30.

Galerie Michael

430 N Rodeo Dr
Beverly Hills
Map 4 E2 5

310 273 3377 | www.galeriemichael.com
Galerie Michael's speciality is European paintings, drawings and prints from the 17th century to the present. The extremely upscale Rodeo Drive gallery exhibits works by artists of the barbizon school, Chagall, Matisse, Picasso, Rembrandt and Renoir. Open Monday to Saturday 10:00 to 19:00 and Sunday 12:00 to 18:00.

Hamilton-Selway Fine Art

8678 Melrose Ave
West Hollywood
Map 5 A4 6

310 657 1711 | www.hamiltonselway.com
This is one of the largest wholesale dealers of contemporary and pop art in the United States. It specialises in the works of Andy Warhol and also features works by his contemporaries Robert Rauschenberg, Roy Lichtenstein, Keith Haring and others of that colourful ilk. Open Monday to Saturday, 09:00 to 17:00.

I-5 Gallery

The Brewery 2100 N Main St
Downtown
Map 2 D2

323 342 0717 | www.the-brewery.net
A former industrial space that was once home to the Angeles Brewery is now the largest art colony in the world. It is a world unto itself that has to be visited to be truly appreciated. The Brewery Art Community comprises a dozen or so galleries and hundreds of working artists' lofts, and the I-5 Gallery is a showcase for their work. A visit during one of the twice-yearly Art Walk weekends is particularly recommended. Gallery hours are Friday and Saturday, 12:00 to 16:00 or by appointment.

L2Kontemporary

990 N Hill St
Chinatown
Map 8 E4 8

323 225 1288 | www.l2kontemporary.com
Chinatown is emerging as a hotspot for galleries, with several excellent little venues surfacing in recent years as intriguing showcases for experimental work. One of the most consistently discerning is L2K, located on the second floor of a building just a block or so from Chung King Road, where you'll find half a dozen or more galleries. Check the website for openings, drop by for a look-see and then walk down the street to Hop Louie on the first floor of a neon-encrusted pagoda (you can't miss it) for a drink with the local bohemian crowd.

Museum of Design Art and Architecture (MODAA)

8609 Washington Blvd
Culver City
Map 7 A4 9

310 558 0902 | www.modaagallery.com
Culver City is becoming known for its red-hot gallery scene, with a raft of new venues opening near the intersection of Washington and La Cienega. With more than two dozen to choose from, it's hard to recommend any one, but the MODAA is an anchor institution that serves well as an initial destination. The museum hosts exhibitions that tread the fine line between art and architecture. MODAA is open Monday to Friday, 12:00 to 18:00.

Pharmaka

101 W 5th St
Downtown
Map 10 D3 **10**

213 689 7799 | *www.pharmaka-art.org*
Located just across the street from Bert Green Fine Art (p.168), Pharmaka presents the works of a diverse group of painters embracing many styles. The collective is united by a belief in the power of painting as a visual and emotional language that serves a myriad of social, political, religious, and even mystical purposes. And it's also a lot of fun. Open Wednesday to Saturday 12:00 to 18:00 (18:00 to 21:00 on the second Thursday of every month).

Pomona Galleries & Art Walk

S Garey Ave
& E 2nd St
Pomona

909 261 5004 | *www.metropomona.com*
Another arts area that has emerged recently is downtown Pomona, about a 40 minute drive from Downtown. More than a dozen galleries stay open late on the second Saturday of each month and several have become significant venues for local artists, a few of whom have organised buses to transport jaded urban Angelenos to this cheery suburban outpost.

Track 16

Bergamot Station
2525 Michigan Ave
Santa Monica
Map 3 C2 **12**

310 264 4678 | *www.track16.com*
Former television writer-producer Tom Patchett has atoned for inflicting *Alf* on American culture by opening this vital and exciting gallery. It was originally intended (at least in part) to house his immense collection of kitschy pop culture memorabilia (he is rumoured to have bought a condo in Santa Monica just to house his ashtray collection). A passionate supporter of the city's arts community, Patchett has fashioned Track 16 into one of the most intriguing display and performance spaces in LA. The gallery often hosts lectures, readings and live music. There are about 30 other galleries at Bergamot station, a former train station which has become an epicentre of the city's exploding arts scene. Regular hours are Tuesday to Saturday 11:00 to 18:00. Check the website for openings and other special events.

Historic Houses

Hearst Castle

750 Hearst Castle Rd
San Simeon

800 444 4445 | *www.hearstcastle.com*
Hearst Castle is 400 kilometres (250 miles) from Los Angeles, but that didn't stop Hollywood's elite from regularly making the five hour drive to the palatial coastal estate of newspaper magnate William Randolph Hearst. The main residence, a meticulous reproduction of a 16th century Spanish cathedral, dominates the hilltop and from its wide steps there is a sweeping view of the Californian coast. The original compound was really a small, self-sustaining city with its own airport, dairy farm, 127 acres of gardens, swimming pools, tennis courts, a movie theatre and a private zoo. Hearst's instructions to San Francisco architect Julia Morgan in 1919 were simply: 'Miss Morgan, we are tired of camping out in the open at the ranch in San Simeon and I would like to build a little something' In its vast hall, Hearst's paramour, Marion Davies, presided over lavish formal dinners attended by the likes of Charlie Chaplin, Cary Grant, the Marx brothers, Calvin Coolidge, Charles Lindbergh and Winston Churchill. There are half a dozen towns in the immediate area where you can find lodgings. Hearst Castle is open to visitors every day, March to September from 08:00 to 18:00, and October to February, Monday to Friday 09:00 to 17:00 and on weekends 09:00 to 15:00. Reservations are recommended.

Museums
Other options **Art** p.260

10899 Wilshire Blvd
Westside
Map 4 B3 **14**

Armand Hammer Museum of Art and Culture
310 443 7000 | www.hammer.ucla.edu
The Armand Hammer Museum was built by Occidental Petroleum Chairman Armand Hammer, and opened its doors in 1990 to less than enthusiastic reviews (writing for *Time* magazine, Robert Hughes called it a 'monument to vanity'). However, neighbouring University of California at Los Angeles has since assumed management and it has lately emerged as an innovative and energetic centre of contemporary art, creating and hosting exhibits and a wide range of educational activities, including film series, readings and musical performances. In the cultural ecology of Los Angeles, the Armand Hammer occupies the niche reserved for cutting-edge research in post-modern art. Most importantly, the Hammer has become a significant venue for displaying the work of emerging artists. The permanent collection includes impressionist and post-impressionist paintings by Monet, Pissarro, Sargent and Van Gogh. The Daumier collection, consisting of more than 7,500 of the artist's works, is truly remarkable. The real draw, however, is the ever-changing calendar of special exhibits and events. Check the website for a current schedule. The opening hours are Tuesday, Wednesday and Friday from 11:00 to 19:00, Thursday from 11:00 to 21:00, and Sunday from 11:00 to 17:00.

Exposition Park 700
State Dr
Downtown
Map 9 B4 **15**

California Science Center
323 724 3623 | www.californiasciencecenter.org
Here, you and your children can get messy and play games that educate about the environment, the body and earthquake-proof structures. The museum is home to a myriad of cool activities, such as 'life tunnel,' which teaches children (and adults who fell asleep in biology class) about life cycles of tiny cells and large creatures. For budding architects there is also an exhibit that allows you to construct a building with blocks and see if it can withstand an earthquake. The centre is open daily from 10:00 to 17:00, but recommends arriving after 13:30 to avoid large crowds. Parking is $6 per car.

Various Locations

Children's Museum of Los Angeles
818 686 9280 | www.childrensmuseumla.org
While the Children's Museum of Los Angeles is temporarily closed due to relocation, it has expanded the minds of more than five million young Angelenos in its 25 year history. The museum is moving to Hansen Dam Recreation Area, where the city is constructing a new state-of-the-art building. In the meantime, the organisation is still serving the community by sponsoring a variety of mobile educational programmes. For more information, consult its website.

152 N Central Ave
Little Tokyo
Map 10 F4 **17**

Geffen Contemporary at MOCA
213 626 6222 | www.moca-la.org
In 1983, this former hardware store, warehouse and police car garage in Little Tokyo opened as the temporary site of the Museum of Contemporary Art (MOCA), following renovation by famed LA architect Frank Gehry. The city extended the lease to MOCA, even after its permanent home on Grand Avenue was completed in 1986. A decade later, the temporary Contemporary became the Geffen Contemporary, when the David Geffen Foundation gave $5 million to the museum. The vast space is perfect for large-scale shows, such as Richard Serra's 'Torqued Ellipses': massive steel slabs (each 13 feet high and weighing more than 40 tons) twisted in spirals

and long, sinuous curves creating walls, canyons and womb-like enclosures. Free jazz concerts in the courtyard beneath a lacework of steel girders enliven Thursday nights throughout the summer. The opening hours are Monday 11:00 to 17:00, Thursday 11:00 to 20:00, Friday 11:00 to 17:00, Saturday and Sunday 11:00 to 18:00. The museum is closed Tuesdays, Wednesdays, New Year's Day, Independence Day, Thanksgiving, and Christmas Day.

1200 Getty Ctr Dr ◄   ## The Getty
Brentwood   *310 440 7300* | *www.getty.edu*
Map 2 C1   More than 14 million visitors have taken the tram ride up to the Getty Center's mountain-top museum complex since it opened in 1997. Endowed by the J Paul Getty Trust, it has become one of the leading cultural institutions in the world, supporting restoration efforts, arts education, and a broad spectrum of arts-related activities in 174 countries. The Getty Center is its showcase and features one of the finest collections of antiquities in the US (if not the world), along with a continuously growing collection of art, sculpture and photography from Europe and the US. It hosts a variety of theatre, music, dance and other events, making it easily one of the most significant destinations for cultural tourism in the US. It also boasts one of the finest art research libraries in the world, with more than 26 miles of shelving. One of the strangest items in the research collection is a lock of Auguste Rodin's hair.

The Getty's location (with great views of the mountains and coast), stunning architecture and an excellent cafeteria would be enough to recommend a visit, even without some of the finest art in the world. Admission is free but parking costs $8. Visitors are whisked up the hillside from the carpark by an electric tram. The opening hours are Tuesday, Wednesday, Thursday and Sunday from 10:00 to 18:00, and Friday and Saturday from 10:00 to 21:00. It is closed on Mondays, Independence Day, Christmas Day and New Year's Day. Check the website for special events, of which there are many.

6764 Hollywood Blvd ◄   ## Guinness World Records Museum
Hollywood   *323 463 6433* | *www.guinnessattractions.com*
Map 6 B1 **19**   After you tire of gazing at the dummies in the Hollywood Wax Museum (p.174), head across Hollywood Boulevard to find out who holds the world record for 'highest jump by a pig' (70cm by Kotetsu, a potbellied pig from Japan) or 'most cockroaches eaten' (Ken Edwards of Glossop, Derbyshire – 36 roaches in one minute, topping his 47 rats-down-the-trousers trick). Just like its waxwork sister museum over the road (both are operated by the same company), the Guinness Museum is open daily from 10:00 to 24:00.

3800 Homer St ◄   ## Heritage Square
Mt Washington   *323 225 2700* | *www.heritagesquare.org*
Map 2 D1   Eight historic structures dating back to the Victorian era have been meticulously restored at this unusual museum of architecture and social customs. From grand, opulent homes to humble, functional dwellings of the hoi polloi (and with a carriage house and church thrown in for good measure), Heritage Square invites visitors to experience 19th century California life. This is an excellent family adventure easily accessed by the Gold Line. Heritage Square Museum is open every Friday, Saturday, Sunday and most holiday Mondays from 12:00 to 17:00. Opening hours between November and March are from 11:30 to 16:30. On Saturday and Sunday, guided tours of most of the structures depart hourly from 12:00 to 15:00 from the Palms Depot. No admittance after the final tour has departed. The museum is closed Thanksgiving, Christmas Day and New Year's Day.

Getty foyer

Pacific Design Center

Step back in time at The Getty

Heritage Square

Gardens at The Huntington

Hollywood Wax Museum

6767 Hollywood Blvd
Hollywood
Map 6 B1 **21**

323 462 8860 | *www.hollywoodwax.com*

It wouldn't be Hollywood without a certain amount of kitsch and you'll find all you want (and probably a lot more!) at the Hollywood Wax Museum. Here, you can depend on the stars to look just like you expect them to, from Humphrey Bogart with that world-weary expression to Arnold Schwarzenegger with his face peeled back to reveal a machine (no surprise to California voters). For added authenticity, some of the sculptures are dressed in the stars' actual clothes, including Michael Jackson's *Bad* jacket and Hugh Hefner's pyjamas. It really is fun (and a little spooky). Open daily from 10:00 to 24:00.

The Huntington

1151 Oxford Rd
San Marino
Pasadena
Map 2 E1

626 405 2100 | *www.huntington.org*

The Huntington is a genteel retreat set amid 120 acres of breathtaking and well-groomed gardens. The library features a vast collection of works, including an original Gutenberg Bible and Chaucer's *Canterbury Tales*. Private collections, stored in temperature, humidity and light-protected vaults, are also available to scholars from around the world. Three art galleries showcase 18th and 19th century British and French masterpieces, including Gainsborough's *Blue Boy* and Lawrence's *Pinkie*. Fifteen gardens, including a fanatically maintained Japanese garden and a vast cactus collection, feature 14,000 species of plants. High tea is served daily in a light and airy space that overlooks the gardens stretching into the distance. You must make a reservation for this, and you should. It is surprisingly affordable, and the teas, cucumber sandwiches and various sweets are on a par with what you would expect at a top hotel. If you only have time to visit one attraction in the Los Angeles area, this should be very near the top of your list. Open Monday, Wednesday, Thursday, Friday 12:00 to 16:30. Saturday and Sunday 10:30 to 16:30. Closed Tuesday.

Japanese American National Museum

369 E 1st St
Little Tokyo
Map 10 E4 **23**

213 625 0414 | *www.janm.org*

Just down the street from the Japanese American National Museum on 1st Street near Central is a brass line drawing of a suitcase set in the pavement. This is where the population of Little Tokyo lined up to be shipped off to detention camps during the second world war. Many of these ill-treated citizens were bussed through Owens Valley to Manzanar, a bleak, windy, high-desert camp ringed with fences and guard towers. One of the Manzanar barracks has been carefully reconstructed in the Japanese American National Museum, a sad monument to intolerance brought to vivid life with personal accounts, letters and contemporary artefacts. The rest of the exhibits are given over to shows featuring Japanese and Japanese American artists, artisans and designers. The quality of the shows and curation has made this a regular destination for the LA arts crowd. Open Tuesday, Wednesday, Friday, Saturday and Sunday from 11:00 to 17:00, Thursday from 11:00 to 20:00. Closed Mondays, Independence Day, Thanksgiving Day, Christmas Day and New Year's Day. Final visitor admissions take place 30 minutes before closing.

Los Angeles County Museum of Art (LACMA)

5905 Wilshire Blvd
Wilshire
Map 7 B2 **24**

323 857 6000 | *www.lacma.org*

The Los Angeles County Museum of Art, or LACMA as it is known locally, houses the largest and most encyclopaedic collection of art west of Chicago. At 20 acres, the complex is big, and both its holding and display space grew dramatically in 2007 when it acquired a masterpiece of modernist architecture, the former May Department Store on the corner of Wilshire and Fairfax. It also received as a gift the remarkable collection of Janice and Henri Lazaroff. This collection includes well-regarded works by Picasso, Klee, Kandinsky, de Kooning, Miro, and Arp, sculpture by Moore and Barncusi, and a number of pieces by Alberto Giacometti. The museum is also in the midst of a six-year makeover (which will be complete in 2010) under the direction of renowned architect Renzo Piano. LACMA's dynamic new director, Michael Govan, has generated a new sense of excitement in the Los Angeles art scene that was only slightly dampened by a scandal involving the museum's acquisition of possibly looted Asian artworks. Plan to spend the better part of a day here. Open every day except Wednesdays, Thanksgiving and Christmas Day 12:00 to 20:00 weekdays, until 21:00 Fridays and 11:00 to 20:00 on weekends. Check the website for openings and special events.

250 S Grand Ave
Downtown
Map 10 E2 **25**

Museum of Contemporary Art (MOCA)

213 626 6222 | *www.moca.org*

Ever since the Arata Isozaki-designed Museum of Contemporary Art opened it doors in 1986, it has been a hub for the chic, black-shirted art crowd that gathers here on warm summer Saturday nights for the 'night vision: MOCA after dark' series. Here, visitors can explore the galleries late into the evening and groove to live DJs. When the permanent collection was unveiled, *The Los Angeles Times* crowed: 'There isn't a city in America… where a more impressive museum collection of contemporary art can be seen'. Artists represented in the permanent collection include David Hockney, Roy Lichtenstein, Jackson Pollock and Mark Rothko, to name a few. The temporary exhibits, usually major retrospectives of an important artist or works connected by a theme, are a major draw, and the gift shop and cafe, the Patinette, are destinations in themselves. Above the museum is an urban park with reflecting pools and a pedestrian boulevard that opens onto the fountains of California Plaza, the site of weekly summer evening concerts. Open on Mondays from 11:00 to 17:00, Thursdays from 11:00 to 20:00, Fridays from 11:00 to 17:00, Saturday and Sunday from 11:00 to 18:00. The museum is closed Tuesdays, Wednesdays, New Year's Day, Independence Day, Thanksgiving and Christmas Day.

9341 Venice Blvd
Culver City
Map 2 C2

Museum of Jurassic Technology

310 836 6131 | *www.mjt.org*

This is undoubtedly one of the most unusual and fascinating attractions in Los Angeles. It resembles the cabinets of curiosities that emerged in renaissance Europe and persisted throughout the 19th century. These proto-museums gathered all manner of fossils, mineral formations, stuffed animals and anything else remarkable, strange or inexplicable, and grouped the items in their displays by whimsy. The purpose was less to link and explain, as modern museums of natural history do, than to thrill and mystify. The proprietors of the Museum of Jurassic Technology certainly achieve this effect. Before you dismiss this as just another wacky roadside attraction, you should know that curator

MOCA

David Wilson is the recipient of a prestigious MacArthur Grant and the museum has a branch in the well-regarded Karl Ernst Osthaus Museum in Germany. Is this some form of conceptual art or an attempt to evoke the sense of wonder inspired by museums of yore? There's only one way to find out. Open Thursday from 14:00 to 20:00 and Friday, Saturday and Sunday from 12:00 to 18:00.

Museum of the American West

4700 Western
Heritage Way
Griffith Park
Map 2 D1

323 667 2000 | www.autrynationalcenter.org
Created by Gene Autry, America's favourite singing cowboy and the only person with five stars on Hollywood's Walk of Fame, this museum in Griffith Park explores the diverse and dynamic history of the American West and how it has affected the rest of the world. The artfully contrived collections of artefacts, photographs and paintings offer visitors a detailed glimpse of life in the old west. This is an excellent family adventure. Open from 10:00 to 17:00, Tuesdays to Sundays and Thursdays till 20:00 in the summer. Closed Mondays, New Year's Day, Independence Day, Thanksgiving and Christmas Day.

Museum of Tolerance

9786 W Pico Blvd
Westside
Map 4 E4 28

310 553 8403 | www.museumoftolerance.com
A visit to the Museum of Tolerance can be a life-altering experience. Anyone who has visited the Anne Frank House in Amsterdam or Auschwitz in Poland, will understand. Although the exhibits focus primarily on the Holocaust, the message is that intolerance takes many forms and persists around the world in every aspect of daily life. The stories of individuals caught up in the horrors of modern history are fascinating, compelling and frightening, and are brought vividly to life through artefacts, photos and documents that connect the visitor directly to some of the most horrific and momentous events of the 20th century. Families looking for experiences that will help expand their understanding of the human experience will find much to contemplate here. Open weekdays from 10:00 to 17:00 (closes at 15:00 on Fridays from November to March) and Sundays from 11:00 to 17:00. Closed Saturday.

Natural History Museum of Los Angeles County

900 Exposition Blvd
Exposition Park
Map 9 B3 29

213 763 3466 | www.nhm.org
Founded in 1913, the Natural History Museum is the crown jewel of Exposition Park and one of the leading institutions of its kind in the world. It has amassed one of the world's largest and most comprehensive collections – more than 35 million objects, some as old as 4.5 billion years. The museum also curates new, immersive exhibitions presented with cutting-edge digital technology. Permanent displays include dramatic collections of fossils and dinosaurs, exquisite gems and minerals, grand animal dioramas and an ancient Latin American hall. The insect zoo presents live insects from around the world. The insects are cool, but it's worth a visit just to step into the grand foyer where the celebrated 'duelling dinosaurs' (complete skeletons of a tyrannosaurus rex and triceratops) are posed in mortal combat. This is a great family destination and is highly recommended. Open Monday to Friday 09:30 to 17:00 and Saturday, Sunday and holidays 10:00 to 17:00.

Norton Simon Museum of Art

411 W Colorado Blvd
Pasadena
Map 2 E2

626 449 6840 | www.nortonsimon.org
The Norton Simon houses one of the most comprehensive collections of Picasso prints in the world, illustrating the quintessential 20th century artist's long and winding career. The permanent collection also features some of the best paintings of the four leading Blaue Reiter artists (Kandinsky, Feininger, Klee and Jawlensky) to be seen

outside of Munich. A haunting and wide-ranging collection of Buddhist statuary from throughout south-east Asia is also on permanent and dramatic display. The garden is inspired by Monet's beloved Giverny. Best of all the museum is a five-minute walk from the bistros and shops of Pasadena's Old Town. The opening times are Mondays, Wednesdays, Thursdays, Saturdays and Sundays from 12:00 to 18:00, Fridays from 12:00 to 21:00. Closed Tuesdays. The museum is also closed on New Year's Day, Thanksgiving and Christmas Day.

46 N Los Robles Ave
Pasadena
Map 2 E2

Pacific Asia Museum

626 449 2742 | *www.pacificasiamuseum.org*

The Pacific Asia Museum offers a quiet and elegant respite from the urban sprawl that swirls around it. The collection of more than 14,000 works spanning five millennia offers a rare opportunity to grasp the breadth, depth and complexity of Asian and Pacific cultures. It is particularly noted for its jade carvings and Tibetan Buddhist art and artefacts. A research library of more than 7,000 volumes is available to scholars. Built in the 1920s and based on a typical Chinese Qing mansion, it is where Marcel Duchamp presided over a travelling exhibition of his works in the 1960s and where he famously played a game of chess with the beautiful (and quite naked) chronicler of Hollywood, Eve Babitz. Despite the distraction, he won. With its shimmering koi pond, the garden is an excellent place for quiet contemplation, and the gift shop offers some of the most interesting knick knacks in all LA. Open Wednesday to Sunday, 10:00 to 18:00. Closed Thanksgiving, Christmas Day and New Year's Day.

8687 Melrose Ave
West Hollywood
Map 5 A4 **32**

Pacific Design Center

310 289 5223 | *www.pacificdesigncenter.com*

The Pacific Design Center is the third component of the cultural family that also includes the Museum of Contemporary Art (MOCA, p.175) and the Geffen Contemporary (p.171). Angelenos often refer to it as the 'blue whale' because of the brilliant blue-glass exterior of its largest building, which looms dramatically over the modest structures around it. The enormous facility (1.2 million square feet) is really a kind of convention centre for interior design. Its 130 showrooms offer more than 2,100 product lines to interior designers, architects, decorators and dealers. There is also a beautifully designed MOCA extension, two restaurants operated by Wolfgang Puck, the SilverScreen Theater, a frequent site of premiere screenings, and a 200 seat conference centre. The whole 14 acre campus was designed by architect Cesar Pelli, and is worth a visit, particularly for the MOCA extension that offers shows that are hard to classify. The Center is open Tuesdays, Wednesdays, Fridays from 11:00 to 17:00, Thursdays from 11:00 to 20:00, Saturdays and Sundays from 11:00 to 18:00. Closed Mondays and public holidays.

5801 Wilshire Blvd
Wilshire
Map 7 C2 **33**

Page Museum at the La Brea Tar Pits

323 934 7234 | *www.tarpits.org*

Around 40,000 years ago, sabre-toothed tigers and enormous mammoths roamed throughout an area now dominated by Starbucks and starlets. Some of them got sucked into the sticky ooze of the ancient tar pits where they were preserved across millennia, much to the delight of palaeontologists and children. The museum features the reassembled skeletons of the mighty prehistoric beasts and outside are the pits themselves, surrounded by full-sized replicas of mammoths and long-toothed tigers, where you can watch researchers as they delicately tease out newly discovered remains. This is another great family destination located directly adjacent to the Los Angeles County Museum of Art (p.174). Open from Mondays to Fridays 09:30 to 17:00 and Saturdays, Sundays and public holidays 10:00 to 17:00. Admission is free on the first Tuesday of each month. The museum is closed on Independence Day, Thanksgiving Day, Christmas Day and New Year's Day.

6780 Hollywood Blvd
Hollywood
Map 6 A1 **34**

Ripley's Believe It or Not! Museum

323 466 6335 | www.ripleys.com

Robert Ripley's collection of oddities might once have filled what used to be called cabinets of curiosities. The popularity of his syndicated cartoons and the museums he built around the world suggest we share a need to contemplate the strange and inexplicable, whether it is the story of the Russian boy raised by birds (he chirps and waves his arms a lot) or plans to build a real Jurassic Park with robotic dinosaurs (in Dubai, of course). The updated, digitised museum is filled with fascinating titbits, but the vast collection of Ripley's illustrated columns (which he drew upside down) is worth a visit alone. Open Sunday to Thursday 10:00 to 22:00 and Friday and Saturday 10:00 to 23:00.

234 Museum Dr
Mt Washington
Map 2 D1

Southwest Museum of the American Indian

323 221 2164 | www.autrynationalcenter.org

The oldest museum in Los Angeles is housed in a beautiful mission-style structure dramatically perched high above the gully that runs through Highland Park. It's worth a trip just to visit the building and enjoy the Maxfield Parrish view. The extensive collections of Native American artefacts and 19th century photos of thriving communities are dramatic proof of the country's rich Native American heritage, as well as a sad reminder of what has been lost. The galleries were closed in 2007 for extensive and much-needed repairs, so check the website before planning a visit. Parts of the museum building and the gift store are open weekends from 12:00 to 17:00. A great way to visit is by the Gold Line Tram which stops at the Southwest Museum.

6505 Wilshire Blvd
MidWilshire
Map 7 B2 **35**

Zimmer Children's Museum

323 761 8984 | www.zimmermuseum.org

The museum has a socially conscious bent and is ideal for those wishing to learn more about Jewish culture. It features fun exhibits such as a giant interactive pinball machine, a replica plane where children can play pilot and a replica of the Kotel in Jerusalem. During the holiday season, the museum sponsors a variety of fun activities such as art studios for little ones, a Maccabean fashion show where children make costumes that would be worn in 185BC and a card-making drive for the Children's Hospital. Admission is $8 for adults, and $5 for children aged 3 to 12.

La Brea Tar Pits

Natural Attractions

401 Hillcrest Dr
Thousand Oaks
Map 2 A1

Santa Monica Mountains National Recreation Area

818 597 9192 | *www.nps.gov/samo*

One of the best things about living in Los Angeles is the proximity of vast wilderness areas that can be reached in a short drive. If you feel the need to embrace Mother Nature, just head for the 150,000 acres of the Santa Monica Mountains National Recreation Area where you'll find rugged mountains, rolling hills and more than fifty miles of ocean shoreline between Santa Monica and Point Mugu. There is also a string of state parks and beaches offering opportunities for camping, fishing, surfing, hiking, mountain biking, horseriding, birdwatching or archaeological explorations into the remains of Chumash villages or the set from the TV series *MASH*. Outdoor enthusiasts can find plenty of information online courtesy of the National Park Service (website listed above), Santa Monica Mountains Conservancy (www.smmc.ca.gov), Santa Monica Mountains Trails Council (www.smmtc.org), Resource Conservation District of the Santa Monica Mountains (www.rcdsmm.org) and Los Angeles County Department of Beaches & Harbors (www.beaches.co.la.ca.us).

Other Attractions

1000 Elysian Park Ave
Chavez Ravine
Map 8 E3 **38**

Dodger Stadium

866 363 4377 | *www.dodgers.mlb.com*

In an odd way, Dodger Stadium is a monument to the Cold War mentality that darkly coloured the political and cultural landscape of the United States in the post-war decades of the 20th century. Back in the 1940s, a progressive LA administration proposed tearing down the old, ramshackle (and primarily Mexican American) neighbourhood in Chavez Ravine and building a gleaming new housing development featuring all the modern conveniences. The project got as far as the tearing down phase and was halted a decade or so later. In place of public housing, a stadium was erected and the Dodgers were imported from Brooklyn. The stadium is today a classic example of 1960s modern architecture and is also home to the 'Dodger Dog', the eponymous sausage beloved by Angelenos of every cultural ilk. Go see a game if you can and enjoy the breathtaking views of Downtown. A particularly good game is when the hated San Francisco Giants are the opposition.

6712 Hollywood Blvd
Hollywood
Map 6 B1 **39**

Egyptian Theatre

323 466 3456 | *www.egyptiantheatre.com*

In October of 1922, one month before archaeologist Howard Carter discovered the treasure of King Tut, Grauman's Egyptian Theatre illuminated its silver screen for the first time with the world premiere of Douglas Fairbanks's *Robin Hood*. As *Vanity Fair* reported: 'The theatre was its own kind of kaleidoscope, a riot of hieroglyphs and cenotaphs, animal-headed gods and winged scarabs, bas-relief sphinx heads and a gilded sun-disk ceiling'. A $15 million dollar rehabilitation has restored The Egyptian to its full splendour. It is now the biggest and most beautiful independent movie theatre in town, screening classics, independent and foreign films under the able aegis of the non-profit American Cinematheque. If you only have time to see one movie in Hollywood – see it here (or across the street at Sid Grauman's other great cinema palace, the Chinese Theatre, p.181).

Exposition Blvd
Exposition Park
Map 9 B3 **40**

Exposition Park

www.nhm.org/expo/

The 130 acre Exposition Park, which dates back to 1909, is urban LA's grand old area of museums, vast manicured lawns, gardens and sports facilities. It is home to the Coliseum, which is the only stadium in the world to have hosted two Olympiads (the 10th and the 13th), two Superbowls (the 1st and the 7th) and a World Series (in 1959). Both the Pope and the Rolling Stones have appeared here (though not at the same time). The Park is adjacent to the University of Southern California and the Coliseum today plays host to the USC Trojans (American football). The Park also includes the California African American Museum (which celebrates the rich contributions of African Americans to American culture), a swimming stadium (with programmes and facilities open to the public), the California Science Center (p.171) and the Natural History Museum of Los Angeles County (p.176). On 4 July, a sizable chunk of the city's population gathers with picnic baskets to enjoy one of the most spectacular annual firework displays in Southern California, and on any given day it is the park of choice for Frisbee-throwing USC students.

6333 W 3rd St
Park La Brea
Map 7 C1 **41**

Farmers Market

323 933 9211 | *www.farmersmarketla.com*

The classic 1934 Three Stooges feature, *Three Little Pigskins*, was shot in Gilmore Stadium, on the property now occupied by CBS's Television City, adjacent to the Farmers Market at 3rd and Fairfax. This is the hallowed ground where the Hollywood Stars played to sell-out crowds. The stadium and the midget-car racetrack are gone, but the Farmers Market lives on, looking pretty much as it did in its 40s heyday with its wooden clocktower and shaded arcades. It is still one of the most popular destinations in town, despite the mammoth Grove shopping mall that looms next door (p.308). This is the source for fabulous and exotic fresh produce, meats, sausages, fish and even dried goods and speciality items from Europe. Best of all are the many restaurant stalls that feature everything from Frank Sinatra's favourite west coast pasta to the best icecream floats west of the Mississippi. The market tends to get a bit crowded around lunch and dinner time. You're advised to come early and stay late. Open Monday to Friday from 09:00 to 21:00, Saturday from 09:00 to 20:00 and Sunday from 10:00 to 19:00. Some merchant hours may vary. Check the website for details.

2580 Cahuenga Blvd
Hollywood Hills
Map 2 C1

Ford Amphitheatre

323 461 3673 | *www.fordtheatres.org*

The Ford Amphitheatre is tucked among towering cypresses across the Cahuenga Canyon from the Holiday Bowl. It was built in 1920 by playwright Christina Wetherill Stevenson for her *Pilgrimage Play*, which depicted the entire life of Christ. Until the trees grew between the two venues, concert goers at the Bowl were occasionally disconcerted by the sudden appearance, at the climactic moment in the play, of Christ on his cross picked out by a blazing spotlight. The current 1,200 seat outdoor stage, inspired by the ancient gates of Jerusalem, was built after a fire in 1929 destroyed the original wooden structure. It is host to music, dance, theatre and film events from May to October. A separate 87 seat indoor theatre is home to the well-regarded Ensemble Theater Collective. As good as the theatre is, locals

*Coliseum,
Exposition Park*

prize this venue most for the excellent 'box dinners' that are among the best dining bargains in town. After checking the menu on the website, call the caterers in advance (310 652 3797) to place your order.

Forest Lawn Memorial Park

1712 S Glendale Ave
Glendale
Map 2 D1

800 204 3131 | *www.forestlawn.com*

Evelyn Waugh's dark, satiric novel *The Loved One* was inspired by what is perhaps America's most well-known cemetery, Forest Lawn Memorial Park. Although it has been criticised for having a theme-park feel with its various 'lands' (Babyland, Vesperland, Graceland), it has also been hailed for radically redefining traditional ideas about funerary landscapes. Dr Hubert Eaton, the primary architect of this 100 year-old cemetery, insisted on broad, open spaces, breathtaking views, inspiring art and uplifting architecture. He firmly believed in a glorious afterlife and wanted visitors to focus on the living rather than dwelling on death. The idea has been well received in Los Angeles, as indicated by the number of weddings (35,000, according to a recent count) conducted at the various quaint chapels or among the well-groomed gardens. Among the artworks are a vivid stained-glass reproduction of Da Vinci's *The Last Supper* in the memorial court and various full-size reproductions of renaissance sculpture, such as Michelangelo's *David*. There are half a dozen Forest Lawns in the Los Angeles area, but the oldest and most well-known is the 300 acre park in Glendale, just a 10 minute drive from Downtown. A gallery at Glendale Park offers regular exhibitions of travelling shows. Check the website for a current schedule. Open to the public daily from 08:00 to 17:00 (18:00 during Daylight Saving Time).

Grand Central Market

317 S Broadway
Downtown
Map 10 E3 **42**

213 624 2378 | *www.grandcentralsquare.com*

The oldest open-air market in Los Angeles, this is an excellent place for a multicultural lunch in a colourful, bustling market just a short walk but a world away from the temples of high culture on Bunker Hill. Forty vendors offer produce, dry goods and delicacies from around the globe. Whether you crave over-stuffed pupusas, Cuban sandwiches, chow mein or fresh-squeezed fruit juice (and if the sight of skinned goat heads don't discourage your appetite), you'll love this place. This is a favourite lunch spot for many locals. Look for the most crowded stands and get in line. Open daily from 09:00 to 18:00.

Grauman's Chinese Theatre

6925 Hollywood Blvd
Hollywood
Map 6 A1 **43**

323 464 8111 | *www.manntheatres.com*

Undoubtedly the most well-known movie palace in the world, Grauman's Chinese Theatre is Hollywood's most enduring icon. This is where the hand and footprints of the stars are preserved in the pavement – the first to stomp in the wet cement were Sid Grauman and his partners, Douglas Fairbanks and Mary Pickford. It opened in 1927, a few years after the only slightly less spectacular Egyptian (another Grauman theatre). The courtyard features lotus-shaped fountains, copper-topped turrets and curving, 40 foot high walls that embrace a pair of giant stone heaven dogs imported from China. Determined to make the opening a memorable event, Grauman worked the publicity mill and a huge crowd turned out to watch the red-carpet arrival of the stars at the premier of Cecil B DeMille's *The King of Kings*. The police failed to anticipate the size and excitability of the crowd and in the crush the shoving became violent and a riot broke out. Now the crown jewel in the Mann Theatre chain, it is the second-best place to see a movie in Hollywood. The best is Grauman's other theatre, The Egyptian (p.179), just down the street.

Griffith Observatory

2800 E Observatory Rd
Griffith Park
Map 2 D1

213 473 0800 | *www.griffithobs.org*

Perched on a hilltop in Griffith Park and overlooking the Los Angeles Basin, Griffith Observatory is second only to the Hollywood sign as a beloved and highly visible icon of LA. It has been featured in dozens of films and television shows from *Rebel Without A Cause* to *Transformers*. James Dean is even memorialised there with a bust on the lawn opposite the entrance. The main attractions are the recently renovated Samuel Oschin Planetarium and, of course, the telescope. The planetarium has been completely redesigned and features a 300 seat theatre. The new Zeiss star projector and a computer-controlled light and sound system guarantee visitors will have an experience that is truly out of this world. Since opening in 1935, more than seven million people have peered into space through the 12 inch Zeiss refracting telescope, making it the most popular and accessible telescope in the world. Located in the rooftop dome on the building's east end, the Zeiss telescope is used mainly for night time viewing of the moon, the planets and other bright celestial objects. It's always a popular public destination when special events occur – more people viewed Halley's Comet and comets Hale-Bopp and Hyakutake through the Observatory's telescope than through any other on the planet. Food and drink is available at The Café at the End of the Universe. Parking is extremely limited so check the website or call for information about bus service. Open six days a week. Tuesdays to Fridays 12:00 to 22:00, Saturdays and Sundays from 10:00 to 22:00. Closed Mondays and on Thanksgiving Day and Christmas Day.

Hollywood Bowl

2301 N Highland Ave
Hollywood
Map 2 D1

323 850 2000 | *www.hollywoodbowl.com*

The Beatles performed here. Leonard Bernstein conducted here. Judy Garland sang, Abbot and Costello fooled around and President Franklin Delano Roosevelt stirred the Hollywood crowd to dig into its collective pockets and support the war effort. One of the largest natural amphitheatres in the world and the summer home of the Los Angeles Philharmonic and another on the list of iconic LA landmarks, the Hollywood Bowl is an experience no one should miss. On star-filled warm summer nights, the bowl fills with picnickers toting wine coolers for one of the most magical experiences in town. There are locals who go a dozen times each summer and never tire of it. If there's something vaguely familiar about the white marble statues that grace the entrance, it's because they were carved by George Stanley, the artist who created the most sought-after figure in Hollywood, Oscar. Check the website for a concert schedule.

Hollywood Forever Cemetery

6000 Santa
Monica Blvd
Hollywood
Map 6 D3 44

323 469 1181 | *www.hollywoodforever.com*

This is the final resting place of Cecile B DeMille, Douglas Fairbanks, Rudolph Valentino, Jayne Mansfield and dozens of other stars who were immortalised, at least on the silver screen. The white marble tombs and mausoleums are surrounded by 60 scenic acres of palms and lily-filled ponds. Appropriately, the property backs onto Paramount Studios, one of oldest working movie lots in Hollywood. The grounds have recently undergone a thorough restoration and the cemetery has been opened on summer nights for outdoor film festivals on the lawn, drawing a young crowd of picnickers and film enthusiasts attracted by some of the greatest titles in filmdom. Vampire movies and classics of the suspense genre are favourites. The screening season starts in May; check out www.cinsepia.org for the schedule. The cemetery is open daily until sunset and on screening evenings.

244 S San Pedro St
Little Tokyo
Map 10 E4 **45**

Japanese American Cultural and Community Center
213 628 2725 | www.jaccc.org

At the centre of the plaza that fronts the Japanese American Cultural and Community Center one of the largest and most dramatic works of public art in the city, a megalithic sculpture by Isamu Noguchi, looms against the Los Angeles skyline. It's an apt symbol for an institution that is a vigorous venue for traditional and modern Japanese theatre, music, dance, film and the plastic arts. The plaza is the heart of community festivals, most notably Nisei Week and the annual Tofu Festival in August. The theatre hosts excellent live performances of bunraku (puppet theatre), noh (musical drama), as well as taiko drumming and an annual festival of anime. The popular pop group, Hiroshima, regularly performs here (and regularly announces that each concert is its last). Exhibits in the centre's main building feature everything from a history of Japanese armour to the traditional decorative arts and crafts. Tucked in the back, around the corner, is one of LA's best kept secrets: a beautiful Japanese garden with delicate bridges arching over a burbling stream – all shoehorned into a space of less than half an acre. Hours vary depending on what's happening. The garden alone is worth a visit if you are in the neighbourhood. Just around the corner is a Pinkberry icecream shop, if you crave the latest food fad.

6801 Hollywood Blvd
Hollywood
Map 6 A1 **46**

Kodak Theatre
323 308 6333 | www.kodaktheatre.com

The Kodak Theatre, in the Hollywood & Highland Center, is a glorious architectural reverie inspired by the great cinema palaces of yore (and by Michelangelo's Campidoglio in Rome and Busby Berkeley's choreography, according to the architects). It is the new and permanent home of the Academy Awards, the most glittering annual event in the capital of glitter. Broadway shows, concerts and a host of award shows fill the Kodak's calendar, but the 3,400 seat venue is open for tours, which are recommended. The theatre cost almost $100 million, and from the luxurious five-storey lobby, wrapped in a grand staircase and festooned with photos of filmdom's brightest stars, to the enormous, looping oval audience chamber, it is a truly (and appropriately) dramatic space. Due to the constantly changing performance schedule, you need to check the website for tour availability.

**2701 N
Sepulveda Blvd**
Westside
Map 2 C1

Skirball Cultural Center
310 440 4501 | www.skirball.org

Just up Sepulveda from the J Paul Getty Museum is The Skirball, a cultural centre dedicated to exploring 'the connections between four thousand years of Jewish heritage and the vitality of American democratic ideals', with special emphasis on 'vitality'. This is an extremely lively cultural centre (and a beautiful piece of architecture), featuring world-class museum exhibits, film screenings and a variety of performing arts. A new interactive exhibit for kids, Noah's Ark, was five years in the making and is reportedly one of the most popular draws for children in LA that does not involve explosions or vertigo. Open Tuesday to Friday, 12:00 to 17:00 and Saturday and Sunday, 10:00 to17:00. Extended hours for all exhibitions (except Noah's Ark) on Thursdays until 21:00. Closed Mondays and holidays.

1111 S Figueroa
Downtown
Map 10 B2 **47**

Staples Center
213 742 7340 | www.staplescenter.com

This is the premier sports arena in Los Angeles. It's the home of the National Basketball Association's LA Lakers and LA Clippers, the National Hockey League's Los Angeles Kings, the WNBA's Los Angeles Sparks, and Jack Nicholson, who often supplements the work of the Lakers' coaching staff from his courtside seat. If you're a basketball fan and you're in town when a Lakers' game is scheduled, go. It's also the largest special event venue in LA and has hosted concerts by the likes of U2, Madonna, Justin Timberlake and the Rolling Stones. The Staples Center is adjacent to the Convention Center and the new Nokia Theater (p.360) in an area of intense development from which a vast and shiny group of bars and restaurants is emerging. The Hotel Figueroa (p.20), just down the street, has a poolside bar decorated in Spanish tile work and palms, and is a terrific place to decompress with a martini after a game.

111 S Grand Ave
Downtown
Map 10 E2 **48**

Walt Disney Concert Hall

323 850 2000 | *www.laphil.com*

Designed by Frank Gehry, the metal-clad structure on the summit of Bunker Hill on Grand Avenue at First Street became an instant city icon when it was completed in October 2003. The architecture provoked some controversy but the hall itself, designed to be one of the most acoustically sophisticated concert venues in the world, has been praised by audiences, musicians and music critics. It is the fourth hall of the Los Angeles Music Center and seats 2,265 people. It serves, among other purposes, as the home of the Los Angeles Philharmonic Orchestra and the Los Angeles Master Chorale. Beneath the structure, and accessible only around the corner, is the Redcat, a performance space dedicated to experimental, even subversive work that challenges traditional notions of music and peformance art forms. The smallest state park in California wraps around much of the building, featuring sculpture and two small amphitheatre performance spaces. Admission to the park is free.

1765 E 107th St
Watts
Map 2 D2

Watts Towers

213 847 4646 | *www.wattstowers.org*

This splendid example of outsider or 'folk' art is a true icon of Los Angeles. Built between 1921 and 1955 by Italian immigrant Simon Rodia as a tribute to his adopted country, the towers consist of 17 structures rising to 99 feet. Rodia worked without a scaffold, welding rebar, iron pipes and metal mesh together while swinging from a window-washer belt. The city sought to condemn the towers in 1959, but vigorous protests by fans of the work from around the world eventually saved the day, and in 1978 the site was handed over to the State of California. The Watts Towers Arts Center is host to concerts, dance performances and other events. Check the website for a schedule. Open Tuesday to Saturday 10:00 to 16:00 and on Sunday 12:00 to 16:00.

Religious Sites

555 W Temple St
Downtown
Map 10 F2 **49**

Cathedral Of Our Lady Of The Angels

213 680 5200 | *www.olacathedral.org*

In 1994, an earthquake severely damaged St Vibiana's, Los Angeles' old cathedral on Main at 2nd Street, and rather than restore the 19th century structure, Cardinal Roger Mahony decided that Los Angeles' growing population of Catholics needed a new cathedral. The lavish, imposing, post-modern Cathedral Of Our Lady Of The Angels, sitting high atop Bunker Hill, was consecrated in 2002 to mixed reviews. It cost just under $200 million, including $5 million for a single slab of marble that serves as the altar. The oddly lump-like exterior (there are no right angles) was criticised. The interior, however, has generally been prized as a truly inspirational space and the artwork, particularly the vivid tapestries depicting a communion of the saints by painter John Nava, is well worth a pilgrimage. One of its most appealing features (to Angelenos) is the carefully and deliberately calculated length of the main sanctuary: 100 metres (or 333 feet) – exactly one foot longer than St Patrick's Cathedral in New York. There

Hollywood Forever Cemetery

Hollywood Bowl

Cathedral Of Our Lady Of The Angels

Walt Disney Concert Hall

Griffith Observatory

are free guided tours at 13:00, Monday to Friday. Mass is held in Spanish and English, Monday to Friday at 07:00 and 12:10, and on Sundays at 08:00 and 10:00 (and in Spanish only at 12:30). St Vibiana's, meanwhile, was saved from the wrecking ball by a coalition led by visionary Downtown developer Tom Gilmore and has been lovingly restored as a venue for special events (www.vibianala.com).

Self-Realization Fellowship Lake Shrine

17190 Sunset Blvd
Pacific Palisades
Map 2 B1

310 454 4114 | *www.yogananda-srf.org/temples/lakeshrine*

Just up a winding stretch of Sunset Boulevard from the Pacific Ocean in the Pacific Palisades is a truly wonderful spot that represents, perhaps, all the best in the western romance with eastern religion and philosophy. This is the site of the Mahatma Gandhi World Peace Memorial, where some of Gandhi's ashes are modestly enshrined. There's also a faithful replica of a Dutch windmill, which houses a popular chapel for meditation (and was the site of George Harrison's memorial service) and a gift shop with textiles, incense and arts and crafts from India. But what really draws visitors to the 10 acre site are the beautifully tended and exotic gardens that surround the natural spring-fed lake, filled with vibrant life including turtles, swans, ducks, koi and lotus flowers. At intervals off the surrounding pathway are five shrines, each dedicated to one of the world's five great faiths. A slow stroll around the lake is a soul-refreshing experience. Visiting hours are 09:00 to 16:30 Tuesday to Saturday and 12:30 to 16:30 on Sunday. Closed on Mondays, Thanksgiving, Christmas Day and in rainy weather.

Theme Parks

Other options **Amusement Parks** p.168

Disneyland Park

1313 S Harbor Blvd
Anaheim
Map 2 F3

714 781 4565 | *www.disneyland.disney.go.com*

Disneyland, the 'Magic Kingdom' and 'Happiest Place on Earth', has been the most well-known theme park in the world since it first opened its gates in Anaheim, a 20 minute drive south from LA, in 1955. It features eight themed 'lands', ranging from the traditional, nostalgic (and some might say mythical) Main Street, USA, to the innovative, high-tech 'Finding Nemo Submarine Voyage'. This is the ultimate California family destination. Its most iconic attraction (and the Disney logo) is Snow White's castle. It was aptly inspired by Neuschwanstein, the fanciful architectural confection built by Mad King Ludwig of Bavaria that was itself inspired by the myths and fictions of an idealised, romanticised past that might be more appropriately situated in Neverland. Not even the most cynical and jaded can resist the charms conceived by Uncle Walt. Surrounded by hotels and a Disney-themed village (Downtown Disney – accessed by monorail). Open daily, hours vary, so check the website for details.

Disneyland's California Adventure Park

1313 S Harbor Blvd
Anaheim
Map 2 F3

714 781 4565 | *www.disneyland.disney.go.com*

Celebrating the history of the Golden State from the gold rush to the golden age of Hollywood, Disneyland's California Adventure Park (located conveniently adjacent to Disneyland) features an array of traditional rides such as a huge ferris wheel and log flume. The nostalgic view of California did hot have the draw the designers had hoped for, so more marketable attractions have been added to spice things up, such as a supernatural free-fall ride 'The Twilight Zone Tower of Terror' in a haunted elevator. A Disney animation workshop for kids is worth the visit alone. Open daily, hours vary, so check the website for details.

Knott's Berry Farm

8309 Beach Blvd
Buena Park
Map 2 F3

714 220 5200 | *www.knotts.com*

Knott's Berry farm bills itself as 'America's first theme park,' and with good reason. In 1920 it was, well, a berry farm featuring a small roadside stand on Route 39 in the sleepy agricultural town of Buena Park. Owner Walter Knott added a small restaurant at which he served his wife's fried chicken on their wedding china. As traffic along the highway increased, Walter built a ghost town to entertain the diners who were lining up and waiting an hour or more for their chicken dinner. Today it is a 160 acre theme park of eight villages more or less based on western themes. It features rides such as the narrow-gauge ghost town and calico railway (using original historic equipment from Rocky Mountain narrow-gauge lines), the butterfield stagecoach ride and the silver bullet (the longest inverted roller coaster on the west coast). The Bigfoot Rapids, particularly recommended on hot and humid summer afternoons, shoots riders down California's longest man-made white-water river on a spinning, bouncing, splashing and extremely wet ride.

Raging Waters

111 Raging Waters Dr
San Dimas
Map 2 F1

909 802 2200 | *www.ragingwaters.com*

When it gets hot, head for Raging Waters in San Dimas (the home of Bill and Ted from *Bill and Ted's Excellent Adventure*), about half an hour's drive from Downtown. It is California's largest water park and is ranked the third best water park in the nation by the Travel Channel. Thirty six slides and a variety of other wet attractions are spread over 50 acres. In addition to water slides of varying degrees of intimidation, visitors can take a white water raft ride, float down a replica of the Amazon River or hang out in the huge wave pool. For younger children there's kid's kingdom and splash island.

Six Flags Magic Mountain

26101 Magic
Mountain Parkway
Valencia
Map 2 C1

661 255 4100 | *www.sixflags.com*

Located in Valencia, a half-hour's drive north of Los Angeles, Six Flags Magic Mountain, the self-described 'thrill capital of the world', is indeed a mecca for adrenaline junkies. It has some of the most awesome, gut-wrenching high-tech roller coasters in the country, the newest of which is the X2, which sends riders screaming in terror around a 3,600 foot steel track maze on wing-shaped trains in seats extending off the track to the sides, rotating head over heels, to and fro, befuddling the senses. If that wasn't enough, riders are plunged into tunnels where they are stunned by light effects designed to dazzle and daze. This is a ride best experienced on an empty stomach. There are 13 other rollercoasters in the park, with names such as ninja, dive devil, scream, goliath and revolution. Six Flags also features more moderate rides and has recently developed attractions for younger children to make it a more family-friendly experience. Open daily from mid-March to August and on weekends the rest of the year, 10:30 to 22:00 weekdays and 10:00 to on 22:00 weekends.

Universal Studios Hollywood

100 Universal
City Plaza
San Fernando Valley
Map 2 C1

800 864 8377 | *www.universalstudioshollywood.com*

Just over the Cahuenga Pass from Hollywood, the 415 acre Universal Studios Hollywood sprawls along the edge of the foothills, beckoning visitors and locals with some of the most popular attractions in LA. The studio tour is a backstage journey through real working sets and recreated scenes from your favourite mega-hits. Attractions include Jurassic Park: The Ride; War of the Worlds (the real Spielberg set featuring the smouldering wreckage of a 747); Revenge of the Mummy and a dozen other rides and shows that will exhaust parents and whip children into a frenzy of delight. Afterwards, there's CityWalk (www. citywalkhollywood.com), a sort of miniature LA, featuring a Hard Rock Cafe, BB King's Blues Club & Restaurant (p.317) and a Wolfgang Puck Cafe. There is also a multiplex movie theatre and an amphitheatre that has become a popular concert venue. There's a host of ticket options for the park, including a 'front of line' pass, a 'VIP experience,' and annual passes. See the website for full details and prices. The core opening hours are 10:00 to 18:00 weekdays and 09:00 to 18:00 weekends, but these are extended during the summer. CityWalk venues are open though the evening, some until 02:00.

Zoos, Wildlife Parks & Open Farms

5333 Zoo Dr
Griffith Park
Los Feliz
Map 2 D1

Los Angeles Zoo & Botanical Gardens

323 644 4200 | *www.lazoo.org*
With its special animal-themed climbing exhibitions and petting zoo, the Los Angeles Zoo & Botanical Gardens has enough activities to tire even the most energetic youngsters. Add to that an interactive story time and an entertaining bird show, and you've got a great place to learn about the animal kingdom. Visitors will also have the chance to see elephants, tigers, and the crowd-favourite chimpanzees and koalas. The zoo is open every day from 10:00 to 17:00, and costs $10 per adult and $5 per child. Be sure to get there before 16:00, as the zookeepers start putting the animals to bed soon after.

15500 San Pasqual
Valley Rd
Escondido

San Diego Wild Animal Park

760 747 8702 | *www.sandiegozoo.org/wap*
The 1,800 acre San Diego Wild Animal Park is one of the largest and most impressive tourist attractions in Southern California. Short of an actual safari, it is as close as you will ever get to seeing hundreds of species in habitats approaching their natural environments. The park is centred on an exquisite, traditional Nairobi-style village, and there are miles of trails. However, the best way to see the elephants, giraffes, cheetahs, antelopes, lions, rhinoceros, bonobo and other species is to take the skyfari aerial tram; a ride that would have thrilled Earnest Hemingway. The night moves animal courtship tour is recommended (it's particularly popular around Valentines' Day). The park is open from 1 September to 20 June 09:00 to 16:00, and 21 June to 1 September 09:00 to 20:00.

2920 Zoo Dr
San Diego

San Diego Zoo

619 234 3153 | *www.sandiegozoo.org*
It is no exaggeration to say that this is one of the finest zoos in the world and well worth the two-and-a-half hour journey from Los Angeles. Occupying about 100 acres in lush Balboa Park, the zoo features large, beautifully landscaped enclosures where you can encounter creatures rarely seen outside their native habitat (such as giant pandas, mountain gorillas and koalas) and actually interact with some of the friendlier species (the walk-through hummingbird enclosure is particularly recommended). The zoo is a world leader in the conservation of endangered species and has led a heroic and largely successful effort to bring the giant condor back from the brink of extinction. If you do get to the zoo or its sister institution, the San Diego Wild Animal Park (p.188), be sure to catch one of the birds of prey shows and see a condor or bald eagle close up – it is an unforgettable experience. The zoo is open daily, including all holidays 09:00 to 16:00, and until 20:00 in the summer.

Beaches
Other options **Swimming** p.238

From Malibu in the north to Redondo in the south, there's a beach in LA for everyone. Many of them are part of a unique community and each has its own feel. Most have public facilities such as bathrooms and cafes. Check www.beaches.co.la.ca.us for details on each specific beach. See also beach cities on p.152.

Playa Del Rey
Map 2 C2

Dockweiler State Beach
Dockweiler, just south of Playa del Rey, has five kilometres (three miles) of shoreline and generous picnic areas. The wide white sand beach lies directly beneath the Los Angeles Airport flight path, which is either a blessing or a curse, depending on how fond you are of watching jetliners roar out over the Pacific. The beach is conveniently located on the coastal bike path and it is one of the few along this stretch of coast with fire pits. There are more than 2,000 parking spaces.

El Segundo
Map 2 C2

El Segundo Beach
El Segundo Beach is Dockweiler's southern neighbour. Its wide beaches topped with tufted dunes would easily make it one of the best sunbathing beaches in the area if it weren't for the enormous oil refinery just across the coastal road. However, as long as there is an on-shore breeze (which is most of the time), this is an excellent playground that is usually empty, even on the warmest days of summer.

Hermosa Beach
Map 2 C3

Hermosa Beach
Just to the south of Manhattan Beach is Hermosa Beach, a charming little beach city with a plaza featuring eateries and boutiques. In December, crowds gather for an annual snowman sand sculpture contest. Many of the contestants come back year after year, and their works are true marvels.

Huntington Beach
Map 2 E4

Huntington Beach
Huntington Beach, with its many hotels, is one of the favourite destinations for visitors travelling to Disneyland in nearby Anaheim. Renowned as a birthplace of the surfing industry, Huntington's major attraction is its broad beaches that are ideal for surfing. There are two small museums dedicated to local history, a quaint Main Street featuring casual bistros and surfer shops and a long pleasure pier that offers a vantage point from which to watch the surfers and the sunset. There's also an outstanding music venue, Perq's (714 960 9996), a former brothel that now features blues, jazz and rock and roll. Just down Main Street is Korn's, owned by a member of the band of the same name and featuring copies of their platinum records on the walls.

Long Beach
Map 2 E4

Naples
Naples, a region of Long Beach (see p.151), was built as a vacation paradise in the early 20th century. During prohibition rum-runners used the canals to smuggle booze to the many local speakeasies. Today you can explore the waterways in a rented kayak or book a romantic ride in a Venetian-style gondola.

Playa Del Rey
Map 2 C2

Playa del Rey
Just south of Marina del Rey lies this laid-back community. Its location next to the mouth of Ballona Creek gives it a bit of an isolated feel, but the beaches are quite wide and are a great break from the much more popular Venice and Santa Monica.

Echo Park Lake

Rancho Palos Verdes

Rancho Palos Verdes

Just inland, Rancho Palos Verdes is a coastal paradise of rolling hills furred with native grasses, parks, horse, hiking and bicycle trails and few, if any, industrial businesses. At Los Serenos de Point Vicente guides conduct guided tours of the Ocean Trails Project. The walks begin at the public parking lot at the end of La Rotonda Drive off Palos Verdes Drive South. The area also features excellent surf spots (310 373 0202; www.pvplc.org).

Redondo Beach

Redondo
Map 2 C3

Redondo Beach, with its excellent surfing, is host (along with the neighbouring Hermosa Beach and Manhattan Beach) to the annual International Surf Festival held each August, featuring surfing, sand soccer, volleyball, body surfing, paddleboarding and the inevitable sand castle contest (www.surffestival. org). Fishing is hugely popular and King Harbor is one of the best bonito fisheries in California.

Santa Monica Beach

Santa Monica
Map 3 B4 **50**

www.smgov.net/osm/beach_info.htm

Santa Monica Beach's main feature is the fun and fishing pier built in 1909 that once packed in the crowds for dancing at the La Monica Ballroom or for a rollicking ride on the blue streak wooden roller coaster. Today the famed Pacific Park (p.168) is a huge attraction for both tourists and visitors. The beach itself is one of the most crowded in the city, so if you choose to make this your regular, be sure to get there early.

Sunset Beach

Sunset Beach
Map 2 E4

Sunset Beach is located a few miles south of Seal Beach (p.153). The 100 year-old community is another quirky seaside town that has preserved its folksy charm. It features wide, sandy beaches and a little bay, ideal for launching kayaks. The television soap opera, *Sunset Beach,* was supposedly inspired by this classic California surf spot.

Parks & Gardens

Echo Park Lake

751 Echo Park Ave
Echo Park
Map 8 D3 **51**

323 640 6449 | *www.laparks.org*

Tucked between the 101 freeway and Angelus Temple, Echo Park Lake, encircled by towering palms and dotted with lotus blossoms, is a true urban oasis. At the centre of the lake a geyser-like fountain shoots a veil of spray 80 feet into the air. Originally a city reservoir, the lake and the surrounding property were acquired as a city park in the 1890s. Just minutes from the centre of Downtown, the lake is an excellent urban escape on hot summer days. Paddle boats are available for rent on the weekends and the view of downtown, framed by the palm trees and the great plume of the fountain, is unique. Icecream and tamale vendors frequently ply their trade on the winding pathways. The annual Lotus Festival in July celebrates the flowering of that aquatic plant and, if you're in town around the middle of the month, it's definitely worth checking out. The lake is open year round, weekdays from 12:00 to 17:00 and weekends from 11:00 to 18:00. To reserve a paddle boat, contact Aquatics (323 906 7953).

Elysian Park

835 Academy Rd
Chavez Ravine
Map 8 E2 52

213 485 5054 | www.laparks.org

Elysian Park is in Chavez Ravine, just above Chinatown and in the shadow of Dodger Stadium. It is the city's oldest park (the land was set aside when the city was incorporated in 1781) and at almost 600 acres, is second only in size to Griffith Park. The Los Angeles Police Department's Academy is here, and jogging cadets are a common and reassuring presence. An arboretum, man-made lakes, barbecue pits, hiking trails that ascend to breathtaking views of the city, and play areas designed specifically for small children make this an ideal family picnic destination. The victory memorial grove, a first world war memorial, evokes a sense of a gentler, bygone era and is a particularly pleasant spot for the visitor seeking to escape the urban hurly-burly. The park is open from 05:00 to 22:00.

Griffith Park

4730 Crystal
Spring Dr
Los Feliz
Map 2 D1

323 913 4688 | www.lacity.org/rap/dos/parks/griffithPK/index.htm

Griffith J Griffith, the benefactor who donated 3,015 acres to the City of Los Angeles in 1896 (thus creating the largest municipal park in the world), was not a likable character. He was vain, arrogant and a boor: 'a midget egomaniac' is how one acquaintance described him. He was also immensely wealthy. A self-taught geologist, he made a fortune in mining. He moved to Los Angeles in the early 1880s and made another fortune speculating in real estate. He married a wealthy heiress and grew even richer. But what he really wanted was to be accepted among the city's elite. But not even the gift of the park could persuade LA's leading lights to invite the obnoxious Griffith into their parlours. The temperance movement was in vogue at the time so he became an ardent supporter, hoping to win friends, while secretly consuming at least two quarts of bourbon a day. Inevitably, his grasp on reality loosened. He became convinced his wife was plotting with the Pope to poison him… so he shot her. She had the good sense to dive out of a window just as he fired and escaped with her life, although the bullet grazed her skull and she lost an eye (at Griffith's trial she was described by the press as 'the society wife who wouldn't die'). In what would become a legal tradition in Los Angeles, Griffith mounted an expensive defence and got off with a two year sentence, claiming temporary alcoholic insanity. When he got out, he offered Los Angeles $150,000 (which was a lot of money in 1903) to build an observatory and a Greek Theatre in the park. Absence had engendered no fondness for Griffith among Angelenos, who rejected the offer. He put the money in a trust and the city accepted it only after his death. Today, the vast park, with its network of cycling, hiking, equestrian and jogging trails, the Greek Theatre (p.360), a miniature railway, the Los Angeles Zoo (p.188), The Autry Center (aka the Museum of the American West, p.176), the observatory (p.182), an equestrian centre and acres of tree-shaded lawns where you can picnic and play, is the city's most treasured asset. You can't possibly explore it in a single day, but you can certainly try.

Will Rogers State Historic Park

1501 Will Rogers
Park Rd
Pacific Palisades
Map 2 B1

310 454 8212 | www.parks.ca.gov

One of the best things to do for free in Los Angeles is take a picnic to Will Rogers State Historic Park on any Saturday or Sunday afternoon from April to October and catch a polo match. Will Rogers' house is also here, and it is open for tours. His remarkable living room, decorated in opulent, early 20th century cowboy, features the stuffed heifer that Rogers used to keep his lasso techniques sharp until he wore the ears clean off. A looping three-mile trail leads hikers up to the aptly named Inspiration Point. This is also the starting point for a much longer trail for hearty hikers, mountain bikers and equestrians, leading all the way to Point Mugu. Open daily, 08:00 to sunset. Ranch House tours are offered Tuesday to Sunday at 11:00, 13:00 and 14:00.

Tours & Sightseeing

When it comes to exploring and sightseeing, LA offers pretty much everything to see and do under the sun. Given the city's sprawling expanse, a tour is a great way to tick off some of the multitude of possibilities. If shuffling on to a bus with a crowd of camera toting tourists and a droning guide is not your idea of a good time, don't be put off. Sightseeing tours in Los Angeles range from the overwhelmingly energetic (up for a run, anyone?) to the downright creepy. And with the right guide, you can see things that you didn't even know existed. Even if you are a long-time resident, take a tour and immerse you in the city's unique history and culture. From walking tours of Hollywood's most famous movie studios to whirlwind bus tours that will take you from the city to the beach and everywhere in between, there is something here for most tastes. Many of the larger sightseeing companies offer numerous bus and walking tours covering different aspects of LA and its surrounding areas. If you want to cover a lot of ground in one go or don't have a lot of time to spare, combination tours will save you some money and allow you to pack a lot of punch into your day of sightseeing.

The following is an overview of the different types of tours available and some of the companies that offer them. For more information on local tours and tour operators, contact the Los Angeles Convention and Visitors Bureau (213 624 7300, www.seemyLA.com).

Activity Tours

Various Locations ◀ Amazing LA Tours

866 778 7979 | *www.amazinglatours.com*

For a tour that is truly unique to Los Angeles, saddle up with Amazing LA Tours for a two-hour horse riding expedition under the Hollywood sign and through Griffith Park. In case you were in any doubt as to what it's all about, the tour is called 'be a cowboy for a day!'. You don't have to be an experienced rider, but it wouldn't hurt to have your chaps broken in – the outing lasts seven hours.

Various Locations ◀ Off 'N Running Tours

310 246 1418 | *www.offnrunningtours.com*

Combine seeing the sights with a great workout with this company. Off 'N Running livens up a challenging fitness walk or jog by throwing in an exciting sightseeing tour as well. There are four themed programmes that can be customised for any fitness level, including an ocean-view run through Santa Monica or the popular 'marvelous mansions' tour, which takes joggers past the Playboy Mansion and other breathtakingly luxurious estates. Tours cost $60 and include a T-shirt, snacks, fruit and water.

Boat Tours & Charters

A boat tour of Los Angeles Harbour – the largest port in the country – is an interesting way to spend an afternoon, if close-up views of container ships coming, going, loading and unloading are your thing. Contact the Port of Los Angeles (310 732 7678; www.portoflosangeles.org) for more information. For a more idyllic boating experience, many companies offer sport-fishing excursions, dinner cruises and private charters.

13755 Fiji Way ◀ Hornblower Cruises & Events
Marina del Rey
Map 2 C2   *888 467 6256* | *www.hornblower.com*

Operating out of the beautiful seaside town of Marina del Rey, Hornblower Cruises offers a variety of boat tours every weekend, including sunset and Sunday brunch options, plus dinner dances every Friday and Saturday night. Prices range from about $50 to $72 – not bad when you consider it includes champagne, a buffet meal, and hours of entertainment and ocean breezes. Hornblower also has private yacht charters available for weddings and other special events.

Berth 77
San Pedro
Map 2 E4

Spirit Cruises

310 548 8080 | www.spiritdinnercruises.com

Spirit Cruises offers a variety of boat tours, dinner cruises, and whale watching excursions. One of its most popular options is its super circle cruise, a two-hour trip through Long Beach and LA harbours, taking in the Queen Mary, Terminal Island, and the Port of Los Angeles. You can also arrange private charters.

Dolphin & Whale Watching

Dolphin and whale watching tours are popular options for people who want to experience Southern California's thriving aquatic life. For the most part, dolphin and whale watching tours run through the winter months (January to March) when there is the greatest chance of seeing these migrating animals in action. Although you may have more of a drive to get to the docks of some of the following companies, these excursions are fun for the whole family.

Berth 36
Cabrillo Marina
San Pedro
Map 2 D4

22nd Street Landing

310 832 8304 | www.22ndstreet.com

Although this company specialises in deep sea fishing charters and day trips, whale watching tours are offered during the winter season. Tickets are $14 for adults and $11 for children, and tours depart twice a day. There is a nice restaurant on site too, which makes the most of the supply of fresh seafood. Charters are available. See the website for more information and times.

3720 Stephen M
White Dr
San Pedro
Map 2 D4

Cabrillo Marine Aquarium

310 548 7563 | www.cabrilloaq.org

The Cabrillo Marine Aquarium, located near the Port of Los Angeles in San Pedro, offers whale watching tours during the annual migration of the Pacific grey whale from December to March. As well as day tours, the aquarium runs longer marine expeditions. While you're there, check out the aquarium's exhibit hall for a crash course on Southern California's marine habitats.

34451 Ensenada Pl
Dana Point
Map 2 F4

Capt. Dave's Dolphin Safari

949 488 2828 | www.dolphinsafari.com

For a closer inspection of the life aquatic, try Capt. Dave's Dolphin Safari tours. This firm's trips are aboard a catamaran designed specifically for dolphin tours, allowing passengers to get close-up views of the animals. This two-and-a-half-hour safari costs $49 for adults and $35 for children. Private charters are available.

34675 Golden
Lantern
Dana Point
Map 2 F4

Dana Wharf

949 496 5794 | www.danawharfsportfishing.com

Offering daily whale watching tours in season, Dana Wharf is a popular option. The tours operate out of Dana Point Harbor, a charming waterfront village with numerous restaurants, shops, icecream parlours, that's a pleasant place to spend a day. Adults pay $29 for a half-day outing, children 12 or under go for $19.00. Private charters are available, and the company has several other boat-related options, including fishing and sailing trips.

4375 Admiralty Way
Marina del Rey
Map 3 F4 `53`

Malibu Dolphin Tours

310 467 6898 | *www.malibudolphintours.com*

Though the company's name is Malibu Dolphin Tours, don't be confused – it's actually based in Marina del Rey. Though it's a little more expensive than other dolphin tours ($60 for a two-hour tour), a smaller boat makes this a more personalised experience than some. Private charters are available.

Helicopter & Plane Tours

961 W Alondra Blvd
Compton
Map 2 D3

Celebrity Helicopters

877 999 2099 | *www.celebheli.com*

Celebrity stuntman Robin Petgrave runs this company, which offers a wide range of tours all over LA. The flights offer the usual famous sights, including a 'celebrity homes' tour so you can try to spot your favourite star from the sky. For special occasions try the 'deluxe night tour', which offers pick-up and drop-off from your hotel in a limousine, dinner at a selected restaurant, and a bottle of bubbly during the flight.

Van Nuys Airport
Van Nuys
Map 2 C1

Group 3 Aviation

818 994 9376 | *www.group3aviation.com*

If you fancy behaving like a real Angel in the City, there is no better way than with a helicopter tour. Group 3 aims to show visitors the best LA has to offer but from a slightly different perspective. The company has tours dedicated to the Hollywood sights or the beach communities, plus the option to combine the two. The 'grand' tour gives passengers the sights from all the tours, plus some fantastic scenery over the Malibu canyons.

Torrance Airport
Torrance
Map 2 C3

JJ Helicopters

310 257 8622 | *www.jjheli.com*

This company offers a number of tours. Most last approximately 30 minutes, which is plenty of time to take in sights such as the Getty Museum, or the crowded beaches. JJ also offers sunset flights; recommended if you're out to impress. Alternatively you could opt for the VIP tour and fly over the Playboy Mansion.

Novelty Tours

Go on, admit it. Even if you scoff at those who come to LA in the hope of catching a glimpse of movie stars, you know you secretly want to see one, too. A good way to track them down is tour of the stars' homes. And if you don't get to see a star in person, at least you can sneak a peak at their manicured front lawns and the flashy cars parked in their driveways. Many operators run such tours, a notable one being the hollywood movie dtars' homes tour through Hollywood Tours (800 789 9575; www.hollywoodtours.us). It has one of the most comprehensive itineraries, boasting drive-bys of more than 40 celebrity homes and stops at Rodeo Drive and the Hollywood sign, all in about two hours. If it's movie landmarks rather than modern-day star stalking you're interested in, try Red Line Tours' Hollywood Behind the Scenes walking tour. There are other unusual tours on offer in LA too, including a chance to get up close to the macabre sights and the offbeat Esotouric (p.195).

6741 Hollywood Blvd
Hollywood
Map 6 B1 `56`

Dearly Departed Tours

323 466 3696 | *www.dearlydepartedtours.com*

If you crave the macabre, then don't miss this tour of LA's most notorious deaths, scandals and crime scenes. This three-hour tour, in the dearly departed tomb buggy (aka a van), will take you past nearly 100 points of interest, including the site of the

Manson murders and the bathroom where George Michael was caught with his pants down in 1998. If you have kids, it's probably a wise choice to leave them behind for this one. Dearly Departed is owned and operated by one guy, and has only one vehicle that departs once a day (although private tours can be arranged for groups of four or more), so make reservations in advance.

Various Locations

Esotouric

323 223 2767 | *www.esotouric.com*

Esotouric's bus and walking tours offer real insights into the quirky character of Los Angeles, with routes that take you off the beaten path. Tour themes include crime and social history, rock and roll and architecture, literature and film, fine art and urban studies, brought to life by a slick, entertaining commentary. The unconventional angle even extends to the food stops, which include Chinese dumplings in a garden of concrete sea monsters, home-made lemonade and cookies at the site of the first UFO sighting in the Southland, and nicotine-flavoured gelato in East Hollywood. Private and solo tours are also available, as are season passes and gift certificates.

6773 Hollywood Blvd
Hollywood
Map 6 A1 **55**

Red Line Tours

323 402 1074 | *www.redlinetours.com*

Red Line Tours offers daily walking tours through Hollywood, and its Hollywood behind the scenes tour is one that shouldn't be missed. See and learn the history and insider's scoop on many of Hollywood's most famous landmarks, including Grauman's Chinese Theatre, the El Capitan, and the Hollywood Walk of Fame. What makes this tour worthwhile is that you won't just cruise by the outside of these buildings, you'll get to explore the inside of many too.

1660 Ocean Ave
Santa Monica
Map 3 C4 **56**

Segway Los Angeles

310 395 1395 | *www.segway.la*

There are only so many bus tours you can do without feeling that LA has passed you by through the windows of your air-conditioned coach. Segway Tours offers a fun and unusual alternative. For two hours you can whiz through Venice Beach and Santa Monica in the sunshine on a motorised Segway. The experienced guides offer an introductory lesson to get you started, and you can extend your tour to explore on your own. Tours start throughout the day, and booking is recommended. Please note that there is a minimum weight requirement for under 18s.

Private Tours

If you are willing to shell out a little extra cash, private tours are the ultimate way to enjoy the places you want to see, when you want to see them. Many companies specialise in this service, and there are some that offer private tours in addition to their regularly scheduled sightseeing tour options. If you like the idea of being able to ask a lot of questions or are looking for a fantastic way to impress your out of town visitors, this just might be the way to go.

Most of the larger sightseeing companies are able to tailor tours to suit; some, such as Starline Tours (323 463 3333; www.starlinetours.com) cater for larger groups and trips as well – it can lead you and up to 50 of your friends on a tour of LA and its environs, adding in overnighters in Las Vegas, Laughlin, Palm Springs San Francisco, should you wish.

There are stylish options on offer too: Hollywood Tours (800 789 9575; www. hollywoodtours.us) offers a four-hour private ride for up to five people in a classic 1960s red convertible Cadillac, including an experienced tour guide and driver.

Various Locations ◀ Take My Mother Please

323 737 2200 | *www.takemymotherplease.com*

As the name suggests, this company offers to take your visiting relatives off your hands for a while, and show them parts of LA they want to see at the same time. It's open to anyone though, not just mothers, and although it's pricey (around $350 for a half day for up to three people, or $550 for a full day), it has an excellent, intimate reputation. You (or your mother) can design a personalised itinerary and go just about anywhere in or around the city.

Pub Crawl Tours

Various Locations ◀ Destination Nightlife

310 575 5693 | *www.destination-nightlife.com*

Experience LA's party scene like a true VIP. This trendy service allows you to customise your nightlife itinerary, and combines safe transportation and exclusive access (meaning no waiting in queues to get in) to LA's premier hotspots for a truly memorable (alcohol consumption levels permitting), personalised night on the town. The website lets you put together your programme from a pick of the city's top venues.

Various Locations ◀ Party Bus Los Angeles

800 881 6323 | *www.partybuslosangeles.com*

Disco lights, a state-of-the-art sound system, room to mingle, and an onboard full-service bar define the Party Bus, where getting to the bars on this weekly pub crawl tour is half the fun. Party buses can also be rented for private outings, with customised itineraries. Either way, you'll be picked up from your home or hotel so you don't have to worry about drinking and driving.

Shopping Tours

Several of the major LA tour companies pass through the main shopping areas of the city on their trips. Hollywood Tours (800 789 9575, www.hollywoodtours.us) offers a number of combinations that visit the most popular shopping districts along the way, including Rodeo Drive, the Beverly Center and the Third Street Promenade in Santa Monica. For the more dedicated shopper, the two companies listed below can help you focus your purchasing prowess.

Various Locations ◀ The Shopanista

310 696 6055 | *www.shopanista.com*

With more than 20 hotspots available for you to choose from, The Shopanista will transport you to the trendiest shopping neighbourhoods, malls and outlet centres, as well as the little-known boutiques and sample sales in LA. It's a little pricey, so bring a friend or two to justify the cost, which is the same for one to four people.

Various Locations ◀ Urban Shopping Adventures

213 683 9715 | *www.urbanshoppingadventures.com*

Led by experienced guides, Urban Shopping Adventures offers five different packages to a variety of locations in and around LA, as well as the option to create a custom shopping experience. The guides not only show shoppers where to go, but give tips on how to find the perfect garment.

Sightseeing Tours

A tour is a great way to see a city as sprawled out as Los Angeles. Most tours that visit multiple locations will take place on a bus or shuttle van. There are many reputable

We're all over the world

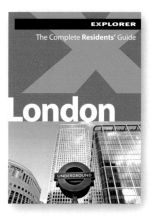

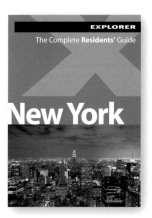

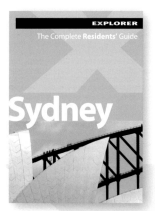

When it's time to make the next stop on your expat adventure, be sure to pack an Explorer Residents' Guide. These essential books will help you make the most of your new life in a new city.

Explorer Residents' Guides – We Know Where You Live

sightseeing companies in town, and most offer multiple itineraries (some with hundreds of different tour options). Most of the larger companies offer combo deals, where you can enjoy two or more tours in one day at a reduced price. In addition, most of these larger companies offer hotel pick-up, so if you don't have a car you can still enjoy the sights. The following are three of the major sightseeing organisations in LA.

Various Locations ◄ ## Hollywood Tours

800 789 9575 | *www.hollywoodtours.us*

If it's in Southern California and you want to see it, chances are Hollywood Tours can find a place on a tour for you. From helicopter rides high above the city to boat trips across the ocean to Catalina Island, and from architecture tours of Downtown to excursions to San Diego's most popular attractions, Hollywood Tours has hundreds of fun and informative tours to choose from.

Various Locations ◄ ## LA Tours

323 460 6490 | *www.latours.net*

Choose from 15 fun and fascinating sightseeing and combo tours in and around LA, as well as daily trips to local theme parks, beaches and museums. LA Tours operates comfortable shuttle buses, and smaller groups mean these tours are a little more informal and cosy.

6541 Hollywood Blvd ◄ ## Starline Tours
Hollywood
Map 6 A1 **57**

323 463 3333 | *www.starlinetours.com*

One of the oldest tour operators in Los Angeles (it's been around since 1935), Starline Tours offers a variety of popular sightseeing options. Its hop-on, hop-off bus tour allows you to take in the sights at your own pace, with unlimited chances to get on and off at 17 locations in Hollywood and Beverly Hills. Other popular tours include the Hollywood trolley tour, movie stars' homes, and grand tour of LA, where you'll see all of the city's most famous landmarks and neighbourhoods in just over five hours.

Studio Tours

If Los Angeles is famous for one thing, it's for being the home of the silver screen. No wonder then that so many people want to see the bright lights of the showbiz industry. If you're interested in checking out some working studios and Hollywood backlots, there are no shortage of opportunities.

You can do more than just sneak a peek at some of the studios too – if you time it right you can even stay for the show. Audiences Unlimited (818 753 3470) provides free tickets to dozens of programmes taped in different locations throughout LA. You can also contact individual television studios to ask about tickets or becoming a contestant on one of the many game shows filmed in the area. Just be sure to make your reservations well in advance.

In addition to the studio tours listed below, you can also take a look behind the scenes at Universal Studios Hollywood, which is both a theme park and working movie studio (see p.187).

3000 W Alameda Ave ◄ ## NBC Studio Tour
Burbank
Map 2 D1

818 840 3537 | *www.nbc.com*

See the home of *The Tonight Show With Jay Leno*, along with many other working television sets on the NBC Studio Tour. It's a simple, no-frills indoor walking tour that takes less than an hour and a half, but you'll get a nice taste of what goes on behind the scenes of one of TV's top working studios (and at less than $10 per person, the price is right too).

Paramount Pictures Studio Tour

5555 Melrose Ave
Hollywood
Map 6 D4 **58**

323 956 1777 | *www.paramount.com*

Led by knowledgeable guides both on foot and by trolley, this entertaining tour will take you inside current working movie and TV stages (*Entertainment Tonight* and *Dr Phil* are just two of the television shows that are currently shot here) and past some spots of historical significance (*I Love Lucy* called Paramount home in the 1950s). Free tickets to television show tapings are also available.

Sony Pictures Studios Tour

10202 W Washington Blvd
Culver City
Map 2 C2

310 244 3695 | *www.sonypicturesstudios.com*

Cameras rolled here in the 1930s while Dorothy followed the Yellow Brick Road to Oz. Today, Sony Pictures Studios is still one of LA's busiest working television and movie studios, and for $25 you can see it for yourself. On this walking tour, expert guides share historical anecdotes and shed light on the wonders of modern filmmaking technology as you explore working sets and behind-the-scenes areas.

Warner Bros Studios Tour

3400 Riverside Dr
Burbank
Map 2 C1

818 972 8687 | *www.wbstudiotour.com*

This two-hour tour of Warner Bros Studios' working soundstages truly immerses you in the inner workings of a TV and movie studio. Explore both on foot and by motorised cart, and learn how sets are configured, how special effects are made, and how costumes are designed and stored. The tour includes a stop at the studio's museum, where you will see scripts, costumes, and props from the sets of many Warner Bros productions. There's a good cafe adjacent to the studio where you can grab some lunch before or after your tour, and maybe even catch a glimpse of a celebrity taking a break at the next table.

Walking Tours

Los Angeles Conservancy

Various Locations

213 623 2489 | *www.laconservancy.org*

For a very modest fee, you can join the Los Angeles Conservancy on one of 14 weekly guided walking tours, led by local guides brimming with fun facts and information. Tours range from 'art deco' to 'Downtown's evolving skyline' – a look at how architecture has changed over the years, and where it is headed in the future. You can also make reservations for a tour specialising in one of several unique neighbourhoods, as well as visiting City Hall, Union Station, or the legendary Biltmore Hotel. Most tours last around two-and-a-half hours and cover up to 1.5 miles of ground, but with frequent stops and lots of interesting historical anecdotes you'll hardly notice if your feet start to hurt. If you'd rather go at your own pace, you can download a free self-guided walking tour map with comprehensive descriptions for Downtown.

Red Line Tours

6773 Hollywood Blvd
Hollywood
Map 6 A1 **55**

323 402 1074 | *www.redlinetours.com*

Red Line Tours offers a number of walking tours through Hollywood and Downtown LA, including the Hollywood behind the scenes tour, inside contemporary Downtown LA, and inside historic Downtown LA. This dedicated walking tour company also offers 'assisted audio' technology so that you'll be sure to hear the guide (live, not pre-recorded) amplified over city noise and traffic.

*Colorado Street
Bridge, Pasadena*

Tours Outside Los Angeles

There's fun to be had in all directions out of the city, and a host of tour companies ready to take you there. Taking a trip out of LA is a great way to see parts of the western US without having to venture out on your own or worry about driving. Overnight packages usually include hotel accommodation and admission to certain tours and attractions.

One of the most popular short trips away is a visit east to the bright lights of Las Vegas and the natural beauty of Big Bear and Lake Arrowhead. These two prime visitor hotspots can be combined on a three-day tour from LA, or companies can simply shuttle you to Vegas and leave you to it. For more information on things to see and do in Vegas, see the entry under Weekend Breaks on p.204

San Francisco and San Diego are also both regular destinations for tour companies. For a small slice of Mexico, you can hop on an organised daytrip just across the border to Tijuana. A high cultural experience it may not be, but it's an interesting spot for an afternoon of shopping. Be prepared to haggle for a good deal, and be sure to bring a valid passport to cross the US-Mexico border. Starline Tours (323 463 3333; www.starlinetours.com) and LA City Tours (888 800 7878; www.lacitytours.com) both offer trips out of town.

Tour Operators

With so many things to do and see, sightseeing tours are a good way to let the experts do the talking while you sit back and take it all in. Los Angeles has an extraordinary number of reputable tours and tour operators from which to choose. Take some time to check out their various websites for comprehensive descriptions of the tours and the places they stop; many also offer discounts for booking online. The Los Angeles Convention and Visitors Bureau is a good place to start if you need a little help deciding what's what. You can call them at 213 624 7300 or visit www.seemyLA.com. It also has a terrific annual visitors' guide.

Tour Operators		
Adventure Helicopter Tours	818 612 3676	www.adventurehelicoptertours.com
All Star Showbiz Tours	888 908 3311	www.showbiztours.com
Amazing LA Tours	866 778 7979	www.amazinglatours.com
Dearly Departed Tours	323 466 3696	www.dearlydepartedtours.com
Go West Adventures	310 216 2522	www.gowestadventures.com
Guideline Tours	213 385 3004	www.guidelinetours.com
Hollywood Tours	800 789 9575	www.hollywoodtours.us
LA Tours	323 460 6490	www.latours.net
Red Line Tours	323 402 1074	www.redlinetours.com
Starline Tours	323 463 3333	www.starlinetours.com

Daytrips

There's an old adage that says Southern California is the only place in the world where you can spend the morning swimming at the beach and the afternoon skiing in the mountains. Take advantage of this unique versatility by venturing out of the city for a day excursion to one of many nearby destinations.

To the south of Los Angeles lie the coastal communities of Orange County, home of some of the best beaches in California, and its more famous theme park landmarks, Disneyland (p.186) and Knotts Berry Farm (p.187). A short drive north will take you to yet another Southern California theme park, Six Flags Magic Mountain (p.189) in Valencia, as well as Santa Barbara (p.202) and the quaint Danish-themed village of Solvang. To the east lie the mountains and the desert, each offering several daytrip possibilities.

There is limited train service to some of these destinations, and you can catch a ride to the theme parks by bus from Los Angeles or as part of a sightseeing tour, but to really see the sights it's best to have your own car.

Orange County

Although millions of people flock to Orange County (www.anaheimoc.org) each year to experience its theme parks, there's more to the place than Mickey Mouse. Beach bums shouldn't miss Huntington Beach (www.surfcityusa.com), home to the International Surfing Museum, an iconic pier and some of the best stretches of sand around. Follow the Pacific Coast Highway south, and you'll hit the upscale city of Newport Beach (www.visitnewportbeach.com) and the neighbouring town of Costa Mesa, a true shopper's paradise where you'll find upscale shopping centres, including Fashion Island and South Coast Plaza. A bit further down the coast is Laguna Beach (www.lagunabeachinfo.com). Best known for its numerous art galleries, Laguna Beach is home to artsy types who enjoy sipping wine and strolling through the seaside side streets lined with upscale craft and clothing stores. At the tip of Orange County, just before it meets San Diego County, is Dana Point (www.danapointvisitorcenter.com), a lovely area packed with beaches, golf courses, restaurants and a lovely fishing village where you can catch a boat to Catalina (p.160) or go on a fishing or whale watching adventure.

Solvang

Blooming flower boxes, Scandinavian bakeries and gift shops, cobblestone streets and charming old world architecture make this a destination not to be missed. More than 70 wineries and tasting rooms dot the region, so if wine is your thing, this is sure to be paradise. The quaint village of Solvang is easy to explore on foot, or you can take a 20 minute tour in the 'Hønen', a 1915 streetcar replica drawn by two Belgian draft horses. For contact details and hotel options, visit www.solvangusa.com.

Big Bear & Lake Arrowhead

You'll feel like you're in a foreign Alpine country when you visit the mountain towns of Lake Arrowhead and Big Bear in the San Bernardino Mountains. Perched about 7,000 feet above sea level, the area is a great place to visit in the summer. During the winter, the mountains are a popular spot for ski and snowboard enthusiasts, with a number of ski resorts in Big Bear (www.bigbear.com) and Snow Valley (www.snow-valley.com). There is a pristine lake and endless forest for year-round recreational adventures. There is also the usual variety of tiny shops, restaurants and some lovely bed and breakfasts. Check out Big Bear Mountain Brewery for hand-crafted beers, and don't miss Lake Arrowhead Village (www.lakearrowhead.net) for outlet shops and a wonderful lakeside meal.

Weekend Breaks

LA's fame as a holiday destination means two things. First, there is always plenty to do in and around the city. Second, there is a constant stream of outsiders and tourists invading your home turf. Getting out of town for a weekend is a must and you might be surprised at the possibilities that lie within a few hours' drive.

Summer, Christmas and spring break (usually around Easter) are always the busiest times of year for most American travellers. If you are looking for a quiet escape, consider travelling during the shoulder seasons of spring and autumn, when school is in session. If you must take your holiday during the busier months, be sure to make your travel arrangements well in advance or you may find yourself out of luck when it comes to booking a hotel room.

Travel Agencies

American Express Travel Agency	310 659 1682	www.americanexpress.com/travel
Carlson Wagonlit Travel	800 335 8747	www.carlsontravel.com
Concordia Travel	323 341 5820	www.concordiatravel.com
Corniche Group	310 854 6000	www.corniche.com
Melrose Travel	323 655 4400	www.melrosetravel.com
Picasso Travel	310 645 4400	www.picassotravel.com
Silverlake Travel	323 661 1171	na
Town & Country Travel	323 464 1214	na
Travel Landing USA	323 932 1222	www.travellanding.com
Wilshire Travel Center	213 380 2880	na

Baja California, Mexico

As long as you have a passport, travelling to Mexico from Los Angeles is easy and there are several destinations to choose from once you get there. For a quick trip and a true border town experience, Tijuana (www.tijuanaonline.org) is a great place for bargain shopping and tequila shooting. Further down the coast you'll find the more relaxed beach resort towns of Rosarito (www.rosarito.org) and Ensenada (www.enjoyensenada.com), both known for their sports fishing, restaurants and seemingly endless string of snack bars and nightclubs. If you don't mind things a little rough around the edges, there are some great deals to be found at hotels right on the beach; you'll never find an ocean facing room at these prices in California. However, if it's luxury that you're seeking, cruise a little further down the peninsula to Cabo San Lucas (www.cabo.com). This paradise is known for its high-end mega resorts, endless beaches, restaurants, spas and golf courses.

Baja California, Mexico

Cabo Dolphins	800 745 2226	www.cabosanlucasdolphins.com	Visitor attraction
Cabo San Lucas	888 760 2226	www.cabo.com	Tourist office
Ensenada Tourism Board	800 310 9687	www.enjoyensenada.com	Tourist office
Playa Grande Resort Hotel	800 344 3349	www.playagranderesort.com	Hotel
Pueblo Bonito Las Cabos Hotel	800 990 8250	www.pueblobonito.com	Hotel
The Rosarito Beach Hotel	866 767 27486	www.rosaritobeachhotel.com	Hotel
Rosarito Tourism Bureau	800 962 2252	www.rosarito.org	Tourist office
Sancho Panza Wine Bistro & Night Club	na	www.sanchopanza.com	Restaurant
Tijuana Convention & Visitors Bureau	664 6073097	www.tijuanaonline.org	Tourist office

Santa Barbara

There is a reason Santa Barbara is known as the 'American Riviera'. It's blessed with an idyllic location, where beaches, mountains and vineyards made famous by the movie *Sideways* all come together. It has one of the largest and busiest piers in Southern California, jutting out into the Pacific from an expansive beach. It's the perfect place for a fresh seafood lunch or an icecream cone while taking in the views. A short walk from the beach is State Street, the hub of Santa Barbara, where you'll find a crafty array of shops, coffee shops and sidewalk eateries. All in all, Santa Barbara's relaxed atmosphere is a welcome change from Los Angeles.

Santa Barbara

Bacara Resort & Spa	877 422 4245	www.bacararesort.com	Hotel
Brisas del Mar, Inn at the Beach	805 966 2219	www.brisasdelmarinn.com	Hotel
Endless Summer Café	805 564 4666	www.endlesssummerbarcafe.com	Restaurant
Harbor Restaurant	805 963 3311	www.harborsb.com	Restaurant
Inn by the Harbor	805 963 7851	www.innbytheharbor.com	Hotel
Pepper Tree Inn	805 687 5511	www.bestwesternpeppertreeinn.com	Hotel
Santa Barbara Shellfish Company	805 966 6676	www.sbfishhouse.com	Restaurant
The Santa Barbara Conference & Visitors Bureau	805 966 9222	www.santabarbaraca.com	Tourist office

Temecula

Temecula is a town of contrasts. On one hand it is known for upscale wineries, inns and restaurants, and pricey activities such as hot-air ballooning, hang-gliding and golf (the Temecula Valley area has eight golf courses, seven of them championship standard). On the other hand, there's Old Town Temecula – a historic strip, with wooden boardwalks, rustic architecture and more than 600 antique shops. While Temecula has preserved its 120 year-old history in Old Town, its tremendous recent growth can be witnessed by the residential neighbourhoods and shopping centres that have seemingly sprung up overnight, as well as the towering Pechanga Resort and Casino. Its proximity to Los Angeles (about 90 minutes by car) makes this a great place for a romantic weekend of wine tasting and relaxation.

Temecula

Hot Air Balloon Rides	800 510 9000	www.hotairadventures.com	Visitor attraction
South Coast Winery Resort & Spa	951 587 9463	www.wineresort.com	Hotel
Temecula Creek Inn Golf Resort	760 728 9100	www.temeculacreekinn.com	Hotel
Temecula Valley Convention and Visitors Bureau	888 363 2852	www.temeculacvb.com	Tourist office
Temecula Wine Country	800 801 9463	www.temeculawines.org	Visitor attraction
The Pinnacle Restaurant at Falkner Winery	951 676 8231	www.falknerwinery.com	Restaurant
The Vineyard Rose	951 587 9463	na	Restaurant

California's Indian Casino Resorts

If you wanted to go gambling a few years ago, you'd have had to hop on a plane or drive five hours to Las Vegas. These days, you can try your luck at any of the Vegas-style casino resorts in Southern California, many within one to two hours

California's Indian Casino Resorts

Barona Valley Ranch Resort & Casino	888 722 7662	Lake Side (San Diego County)	www.barona.com
Fantasy Springs Resort Hotel & Casino	800 827 2946	Palm Springs	www.fantasyspringsresort.com
Harrah's Rincon	760 751 3100	Valley Center (San Diego County)	www.harrahsrincon.com
Morongo Casino Resort & Spa	888 667 6646	Cabazon (Near Palm Springs)	www.morongocasinoresort.com
Pala Casino Spa and Resort	877 946 7252	Pala (San Diego County)	www.palacasino.com
Pechanga Resort & Casino	951 693 1819	Temecula	www.pechanga.com
Spa Resort Casino	888 999 1995	Palm Springs	www.sparesortcasino.com

of Los Angeles. Thanks to laws passed by local voters in February 2008, many of the casinos are expanding their premises and increasing the number of slot machines they operate – sometimes by several thousand. With their sprawling casino floors, posh hotel rooms, top notch entertainment options and first-class restaurants and nightclubs, there's no doubt California's Indian Casinos will soon be giving Las Vegas resorts a run for their money.

Cruises

The port of Los Angeles is home to several cruise lines, making cruises an easy and relatively inexpensive holiday option. With three, four or seven-day itineraries, cruises are a popular choice for locals who want a low maintenance, fun and all-inclusive break, without the hassle of having to take a flight. Most cruise lines departing from LA (the port is actually located in nearby San Pedro) travel south to Mexico, visiting ports such as Puerto Vallarta, Mazatlan and Cabo San Lucas. The shorter itineraries usually sail to Ensenada and Catalina Island (p.160), just off the coast of Southern California.

Cruises		
Carnival Cruise Lines	888 227 6482	www.carnival.com
Holland America Line	206 281 3535	www.hollandamerica.com
Norwegian Cruise Line	866 234 0292	www.ncl.com
Princess Cruises	800 774 6237	www.princess.com
Royal Caribbean International	866 562 7625	www.royalcaribbean.com

With competition heating up among the cruise lines, you can get a great deal – especially during the non-peak winter months – and fabulous amenities on par with what you might find at an exclusive resort.

Hawaii

If you read enough gossip magazines it won't take long to notice that when celebrities escape from LA, it is usually to Hawaii. With its sandy beaches, myriad of activities and alluring culture, it begs you to slow down and enjoy its exotic ambience (and a Mai Tai or two). Six dramatically different islands offer something for everyone, whether you are looking to experience a quiet and romantic getaway or a holiday packed with action and adventure.

Hawaii		
Hawaii's Big Island Visitors Bureau	808 961 5797	www.bigisland.org
Kaua'i Visitors Bureau	808 245 3971	www.kauaidiscovery.com
Lanai Visitors Bureau	800 947 4774	www.visitlanai.net
Maui Visitors Bureau	800 525 6284	www.visitmaui.com
Molokai Visitors Association	800 800 6367	www.molokai-hawaii.com
Oahu Visitors Bureau	na	www.visit-oahu.com

Las Vegas

For a city that started as a barren stretch of desert just under a century ago, Las Vegas is now one of the busiest and most glamorous resort destinations in the world, with nearly 40 million visitors descending upon it each year.

Seventeen of the 20 biggest hotels in the United States are located here. You'll find most of the major and popular resorts centred on 'The Strip', but in recent years mega casino resorts have begun popping up in the outskirts of town, along with golf courses, upscale shopping centres and other attractions. With A-list entertainment, expansive casino gaming floors and tropical pool areas that will make you feel like you're in paradise, Vegas has plenty to do 24 hours a day, seven days a week.

Las Vegas is about a six-hour drive from Los Angeles (there are frequent bus services if you don't have a car), but flying is the way to go if you want to really leave your cares behind. It's only a 50 minute flight from LA, and almost every airline offers direct flights

Las Vegas

Caesar's Palace	702 731 7110	www.caesarspalace.com	Hotel & casino
Green Valley Ranch Resort	866 782 9487	www.greenvalleyranchresort.com	Hotel & casino
Las Vegas Convention & Visitors Authority	702 892 0711	www.visitlasvegas.com	Tourist office
MGM Grand	877 880 0880	www.mgmgrand.com	Hotel & casino
Red Rock Casino, Resort and Spa	702 797 7777	www.redrocklasvegas.com	Hotel & casino
The District	877 564 8595	www.thedistrictatgvr.com	Shopping
The Luxor	888 777 0188	www.luxor.com	Hotel & casino
The Venetian	702 414 1000	www.venetian.com	Hotel & casino
Wynn Las Vegas	702 770 7000	www.wynnlasvegas.com	Hotel & casino

at reasonable fares. Once there, getting around is easy, and most hotels offer a shuttle service from the airport directly to the check-in counter.

Palm Springs

Long regarded as a playground for Hollywood's elite, Palm Springs has been a favourite escape from Los Angeles for decades. Today, you can experience the oasis of Palm Springs for yourself as a daytrip, weekend or extended holiday.

Accommodation ranges from inexpensive hotels to luxurious full-service resorts, and there is no shortage of either. The region is blessed with year round sunshine, although summer days can reach as high as 45°C (110° F) or hotter. Cool off in the pool, or for a unique experience, take a ride on the Palm Springs Aerial Tramway. The tram rises over two and a half miles into Mt San Jacinto State Park, where you can enjoy beautiful vistas, outdoor activities and even some snow in winter.

Palm Springs is about 160 kilometres (100 miles) east of Los Angeles, and easy to reach thanks to a straight drive on the 10 freeway.

Palm Springs

Azul Restaurant	760 325 5533	www.azultapaslounge.com	Restaurant
Blue Coyote Grill	760 327 1196	www.bluecoyote-grill.com	Restaurant
Hotel Zoso	760 325 9676	www.hotelzoso.com	Hotel
Miramonte Resort & Spa	760 341 2200	www.miramonteresort.com	Hotel
Palm Springs Aerial Tramway	760 325 1391	www.pstramway.com	Visitor attraction
Palm Springs Desert Resort Communities Convention & Visitors Authority	800 967 3767	www.giveintothedesert.com	Tourist office
Wyndham Palm Springs Hotel	760 322 6000	www.wyndham.com	Hotel

San Diego

San Diego is known for its sun-kissed beaches and family-friendly array of activities. Sprawling from the Mexican border to the southern tip of Orange County, it boasts miles of beach considered among the country's best; from the hip and happening Mission Beach to the quiet sands of Carlsbad and Oceanside. The city of San Diego won't leave you disappointed if you are looking for nightlife; downtown and the

San Diego

Balboa Park	619 239 0512	www.balboapark.org	Visitor attraction
Hard Rock Hotel San Diego	619 702 3000	www.hardrockhotelsandiego.com	Hotel
Hotel Del Coronado	800 468 3533	www.hoteldel.com	Hotel
San Diego Convention & Visitors Bureau	619 232 3101	www.sandiego.org	Tourist office
Seaport Village	619 235 4014	www.seaportvillage.com	Visitor attraction
Sea World	800 257 4268	www.seaworldsandiego.com	Visitor attraction
W San Diego	619 231 8220	www.whotels.com	Hotel

Gaslamp District offer dozens of choices when it comes to restaurants, bars and clubs. Don't miss its famous attractions in the daytime. Sea World, Legoland and the San Diego Zoo attract tourists from all over the world. Shopping enthusiasts will enjoy Horton Plaza and the city's many other retail hotspots. San Diego is an easy two-hour drive from LA, but you can also get there by train or bus.

San Francisco

Alcatraz	415 981 7625	www.alcatrazcruises.com	Visitor attraction
Aquarium of the Bay	415 623 5300	www.aquariumofthebay.com	Visitor attraction
Fisherman's Wharf	na	www.fishermanswharf.com	Shopping & restaurants
Ghirardelli Square	415 775 5500	www.ghirardellisq.com	Visitor attraction
Orchard Hotel	888 717 2881	www.theorchardhotels.com	Hotel
San Francisco Convention & Visitors Bureau	877 665 9673	www.onlyinsanfrancisco.com	Tourist office
Union Square	415 781 7880	www.unionsquaresf.net	Shopping

San Francisco

San Francisco may not have the Hollywood glamour for which LA is known, but this stunning city by the bay offers some of the most scenic and historic sights on the west coast. From the gorgeous Golden Gate Bridge to the notorious island of Alcatraz, there is never a shortage of things to do, with many interesting, ethnic neighbourhoods to discover. The Union Station area is known for its fabulous shopping, and just happens to be where you'll likely end up if you take the obligatory trolley ride. The drive along the coast from LA is one of the great wonders of the United States. Once there, tour the compact city either by foot or bicycle, and don't forget to take a trolley ride up one of the steep streets.

San Francisco sights

Life in the fast lane?

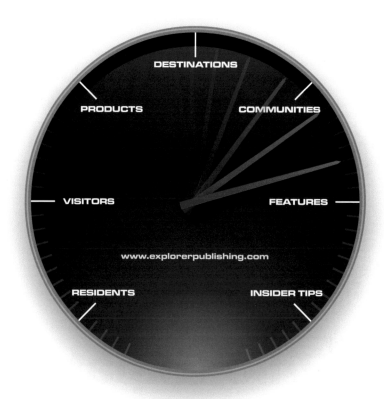

Life can move pretty quickly so make sure you keep in the know with regular updates from **www.explorerpublishing.com**

Or better still, share your knowledge and advice with others, find answers to your questions, or just make new friends in our community area

www.explorerpublishing.com – for life in real time

Activities

Sports & Activities

Southern California is a paradise for outdoor activity enthusiasts. Throughout the year, residents can enjoy hiking, running and biking in the Santa Monica Mountains or along the pristine Pacific coast without having to venture far from their homes. Skiers and snowboarders are also in luck. Big Bear, Mammoth and Mt Baldy are within driving distance and have all the ingredients for a winter weekend of fun in the snow. Visit one of the city's many public parks or beaches and you'll be sure to find an informal 'pick-up' game of beach volleyball or basketball. Those with a more competitive bent can also take advantage of the leagues that organise games of American football, soccer (football) and baseball. Additionally, recent arrivals to the city should be able to find sports popular in their native countries, like rugby, cricket and netball.

The city is known for being fitness conscious, and there are several gyms and fitness centres. Many of which have extensive free-weight and cardiovascular equipment and offer aerobics classes like boxing, dancing and step. There are also several martial arts and boxing studios dedicated to keeping you fit while teaching you self-defence. Dancers will have no trouble finding a studio and dance form of their liking, be it salsa, belly dancing or swing.

As the home of the television and film industry, there is a vibrant artistic and thespian community here. Indulge your creative side by enrolling in a beginner's acting class, taking a painting class, 'throwing' your first pottery bowl or scrapbooking with your friends. An extensive public library system can round out your education, as they offer an amazing collection of books and classes for adults and youngsters.

Some organisations are nebulous, offering a way to informally get together and meet people in your field of interest, while others, such as city-run sports leagues, offer organised sports seasons. A good way to find out about these groups is to visit their websites and sign up for their mailing lists or newsletters.

Activity Finder

Acting Classes

Los Angeles is full of actors, so it's no surprise that there are many great classes and workshops for budding thespians. In addition to 'straight' acting, there are also programmes to help people hone their comedy craft. Many of these acting and comedy classes have a showcase at the end of the course where talent agents will be invited to come and watch.

5508 Cahuenga Blvd
North Hollywood
Map 2 C1

The Acting Corps
818 753 2800 | www.theactingcorps.com

The Acting Corps offers a four-week intensive 'boot camp' teaching acting basics through techniques from Meisner and Chekhov. The school believes in improving by doing, so you will actually be acting for at least 90 minutes in each class. There are classes on specific aspects of the profession, such as how to audition on camera and how to prepare for a 'cold reading.' Classes meet every day, so this wouldn't suit someone with a nine-to-five job. Famous alumni from the Acting Corps include Rainn Wilson from the sitcom *The Office*.

7307 Melrose Ave
West Hollywood
Map 5 F4 **1**

The Groundlings
323 934 4747 | www.groundlings.com

World-famous for its improv comedy instruction, The Groundlings is a fertile training ground for future comedy stars. Alumni include former *Saturday Night Live* stars Will Ferrell, Phil Hartman and Maya Rudolph. The improv workshops, which are open to anyone, are suitable for beginners. After getting a grasp of the improv 'rules', students can audition for a higher-level class in order to continue studying at the theatre.

7936 Santa Monica Blvd
West Hollywood
Map 5 D3 **2**

Lee Strasberg Theatre & Film Institute
323 650 7777 | www.strasberg.com

The Strasberg Institute is famous for its dedication to the 'method' style of acting, by which actors draw inspiration from experiences in their own lives to create a realistic character. This has worked for several former students including Robert De Niro, Al Pacino and Angelina Jolie. The coursework offered here is best suited to the aspiring professional actor, and there is a rigorous application process.

5919 Franklin Ave
Hollywood Hills
Map 2 D1

Upright Citizens Brigade
323 908 8702 | www.ucbtheatre.com

Though fairly new to the city, the UCB is quickly gaining a reputation as the hottest place in LA for offbeat improv comedy. Several classes are offered throughout the year teaching long-form improv known as 'the Harold,' and are open to beginners and aspiring professionals alike. At the end of each course there is a performance at the theatre. There are no auditions to advance to the higher-level classes, but you will have to audition if you'd like to be on one of the 'house teams' that perform weekly.

The Groundlings

Aerobics & Fitness Classes

LA is known for being a physically fit city, and there's no shortage of places to work out. In fact, Santa Monica even claims to be the birthplace of the physical fitness movement in the United States. So whether you are looking for a class on Pilates, yoga, spinning, or even strip aerobics, you should have no trouble finding it. Classes are often grouped by fitness level, so there is something for everyone. These classes can usually be found at the many gym chains throughout the city and are generally free to attend with a gym membership. Many classes at the gyms do not require you to sign-up. You can simply come as often (or as little) as you please. But because there are usually several classes throughout the week, the excuse of 'being too busy' doesn't hold up. Personal trainers who offer private one-on-one instruction are also available for hire at these gyms.

For those without gym memberships, there are several speciality dance studios throughout the city, such as Heartbeat House in Atwater Village (323 669 2821; www.heartbeathouse.com), which offers fun aerobic classes like '1980s Dance Party' to help you sweat out the calories.

Aerobics & Fitness Classes

24 Hour Fitness	866 819 7414	www.24hourfitness.com	Abs, Cycling, Hip-Hop, Mixed Impact Aerobics, Step, Yoga, Kickboxing, and many more.
Bally Total Fitness	800 515 2582	www.ballyfitness.com	Kwando, Cardio, Cycling, Pilates, Yoga, Step, Rebounding, Hip-Hop, and many more.
Bodies in Motion	323 933 5875	www.bodiesinmotion.com	Abs, Cycling, Pilates, Yoga, Sculpting, Step, Boxing and many more.
Crunch	323 654 4550	www.crunch.com	Abs, Sculpting, Cardio, Rebounding, Boxing, Bootcamp, Pilates, Yoga, Spinning, and many more.
Equinox	310 289 1900	www.equinoxfitness.com	Abs, Sculpting, Cardio, Cycling, Pilates, Boxing, and many more.
Gold's Gym	213 688 1441	www.goldsgym.com	Abs, Cycling, Pilates, Yoga, Sculpting, Step Hip-Hop and many more.
LA Fitness	888 889 0984	www.lafitness.com	Abs, Cycling, Sculpting, Pilates, Yoga, Hip-Hop, Step, Kickboxing, Tai Chi and many more.

American Football

Despite not having a professional football team in the city, Angelenos love the pigskin. For those residents wishing to be more than armchair quarterbacks, however, finding enough players to field an 11 player team can be difficult. Fortunately, the city runs a flag football league at several parks throughout the city. The 10 game seasons offer residents a chance to emulate their favourite players while experiencing the thrill of victory. For more information on joining, visit www.laparks.org.

Art Classes

Other options **Art & Craft Supplies** p.261, **Art Galleries** p.168

5905 Wilshire Blvd
Wilshire
Map 7 C2 3

Los Angeles County Museum of Art
323 857 6000 | www.lacma.org

The Los Angeles County Museum of Modern Art offers five-week courses on topics such as drawing and landscape painting. Students in these 20 person classes often study the masterpieces in the museum for inspiration while learning the basics under the tutelage of their artist-instructors. Classes are open to all skill levels and tend to sell out quickly. Prices range from about $145 to $230 for non-museum members.

10995 Le Conte Ave
Westwood
Map 4 B3 4

UCLA Extension
310 825 9971 | www.uclaextension.edu

The UCLA Extension offers a variety of art studio classes, including beginners' drawing classes, watercolours and even jewellery making. The breadth of the course offerings is impressive and students with all skills levels should find something to meet their needs. Beginners can take introductory classes on the basics of a particular discipline, whether it be drawing or oil painting, while more advanced artists can take higher level classes with a more specific focus. The classes are scheduled to meet one night or weekend day per week for several months and are usually led by trained artists. Classes change each semester, so consult the website for the course catalogue.

Astronomy

2800 E
Observatory Rd
Griffith Park
Map 2 D1

Griffith Observatory

213 473 0800 | *www.griffithobservatory.org*

Visitors to the newly renovated observatory can star-gaze through gigantic Zeiss and solar telescopes while knowledgeable guides explain what you are seeing. The interactive exhibits feature many buttons and dials. Visiting the observatory is free and reservations are not required, but those wishing to take in a show in the planetarium must pay $7 per person or $3 for children aged 5 to 12. The observatory is open from Tuesday to Friday, 12:00 to 22:00, and 10:00 to 22:00 on weekends.

Ballet Classes

Other options **Dance Classes** p.220

18138 Sherman Way
Reseda
Map 2 B1

Los Angeles Ballet Academy

818 780 6126 | *www.laballet.com*

The Los Angeles Ballet Academy offers several ballet classes for children, as well as supplementary classes in Pilates, hip-hop and tap to round out the training. The instructors here are professional dancers themselves and have received teaching certification from the Royal Academy of Dance in London, so they have much to offer in the instruction of this art. And for those who have secretly wanted to learn to pirouette but have never found time, it's not too late. Adults, both male and female, are also welcome to attend the specially designed adult tap and ballet classes.

Baseball

Various Locations

City of Los Angeles Municipal Baseball League

888 527 2757 | *www.laparks.org*

The Los Angeles Dodgers recently hired the legendary manager Joe Torre, and excitement about baseball has reached a new level. For children there are several local Little Leagues in communities throughout Los Angeles. For the more 'mature' players, the Department of Parks and Recreation runs an adult baseball league with two seasons per year. The winter league plays from September to March and the spring league plays from April to September, allowing Angelenos to play America's pastime year-round. There are three divisions based on skill level, ranging from average to semi-pro. Some travelling is required as the teams play on several fields throughout Los Angeles.

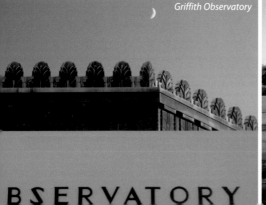

Griffith Observatory

Baseball in Elysian Park

Basketball

As the home to two professional basketball teams (LA Clippers and LA Lakers) and a collegiate team that is a perennial championship contender (UCLA), Angelenos can't seem to get enough of basketball. Luckily, there are plenty of outdoor public courts where you can find a good pick-up game. You can show up alone or with friends, but it is a good idea to bring along your own ball to warm-up. The winning team generally stays on the court while challenging teams get to play on a first-come, first-serve basis. In the warmer months these courts are crowded after 17:00 and mid-morning on weekends. Particularly popular courts for competitive streetballers include the beachfront courts in Venice (Ocean Front and Windward Avenue), which have been featured in several movies, and the Poinsettia Courts on Willoughby and Poinsettia in Hollywood. For a list of public courts, check www.laparks.org. The city also runs an organised adult league that plays its games throughout Los Angeles. After-work, company-sponsored adult leagues, such as the Memorial Park League in Santa Monica (www.smgov.net), are also popular and surprisingly competitive.

Belly Dancing

Other options **Dance Classes** p.220

Aisha Ali Belly Dancing

3270 Kelton Ave
West LA
Map 2 C2

310 474 4867 | www.aisha-ali.com

Specialising in Middle Eastern and North African dances, instructor Aisha Ali offers belly dancing classes every Tuesday. Ali has been recognised internationally for her work in dance. Classes cover several forms of dance, such as Raqs Sharqi, Jar and Zar. The earlier sessions on Tuesday evenings are best for the beginner, while the more advanced dancers should attend the later session. Reservations are recommended and each class costs $15. Private sessions are also available by appointment.

Belly Dance Classes with Amara

17550 Burbank Blvd
Encino
Map 2 B1

818 906 1947 | www.amaradances.com

Amara, a dancer who has performed all over the world, shares her mastery of several Middle Eastern dances with beginners and professionals alike. Her students can learn Egyptian and Turkish cabaret, Middle Eastern folk dances and even finger cymbal work. Aspiring dancers who are just starting out can join her Wednesday class at any time. She also offers private instruction and specialised workshops for groups (by appointment).

Birdwatching

Other options **Environmental Groups** p.221, **Birdwatching** p.214

Los Angeles Audubon Society

7377 Santa
Monica Blvd
West Hollywood
Map 5 F3

323 876 0202 | www.laaudubon.org

Though it is certainly overdeveloped in places, Southern California is home to a wide array of bird species. Los Angeles boasts several good birding parks, such as Ernest Debs Park and Griffith Park (p.191). The Los Angeles Audubon Society organises bird walks throughout the year to help beginners identify species. These walks are also a good way to socialise and meet people similarly interested in birds and nature. Be sure to sign up early on the website as the walks tend to fill quickly. A good way to stay abreast of any unusual bird sightings is the Rare Bird Alerts section on the website, where society members list the species and location of birds they've identified.

Bowling

Lucky Strike

6801 Hollywood
Blvd Ste 143
Hollywood
Map 6 A1 6

323 467 7776 | www.bowlluckystrike.com

This 12 lane hipster hangout is as good a place to bowl as it is to people watch. Trendy twentysomethings come to this 'bowling lounge' to knock over a few pins in a modern upscale setting that features large TV screens and sometimes a live DJ. Its location in the heart of Hollywood is great for bar hopping after a few games. It can get quite crowded on Friday nights and weekends. You should also consult the website for more information on the dress code. Game fees are $4.75 to $7.95 per person per game, and $3.95 for shoe rental.

PINZ

12655 Ventura Blvd
Studio City
Map 2 C1

818 769 7600 | www.pinzbowlingcenter.com

Pinz has billiards tables, Jerry's Famous Deli, a nightclub and 32 lane bowling alley all under one roof. The bowling alley features state-of-the-art lanes and their famous 'Rock N' Roll' bowling four times a week. During Rock N' Roll bowling, the lanes are lit by strobe lights and disco balls while punters try to dance and bowl at the same time. If you are bowling with a large group, it is a good idea to call ahead to reserve a group of lanes. Game fees are $4 to $7 per person per game, and $4 for shoe rental.

Shatto 39 Lanes

3255 W 4th St
Koreatown
Map 8 A4 7

213 385 9475 | www.shatto39lanes.com

Shatto 39 offers affordable bowling without the bells and whistles of the new breed. It is also the home to a bowling league with several teams. There are billiards, old school arcade games, a coffee shop and a bar for those just looking for a place to relax. The neighbourhood isn't great so it is recommended you park in the underground carpark. Game fees are $3.25 to $4.95 per person per game and $2.50 for shoe rental.

Boxing

For many amateur athletes and exercisers, the sport has been recognised as a great way to lose weight, improve cardiovascular health and agility, and perhaps most importantly, get a more defined body. To that end, most gyms in Los Angeles, such as Bodies in Motion (www.bodiesinmotion.com) and Crunch (p.246), now offer some derivation of a group boxing class. These classes usually involve running and punching a heavy bag while an instructor shouts over upbeat hip-hop songs. The emphasis in these group classes is often on fitness, as opposed to boxing technique, making them good for anyone who wants to break a sweat.

For those interested in learning more advanced boxing technique, it might be a good idea to take a private one-on-one class at your gym or at a gym specifically dedicated to boxing. These boxing gyms, such as Wild Card Boxing Club (www.wildcardbc.com), Boxing on the Boulevard (www.boxingontheboulevard.com), and Boxing Academy Los Angeles (www.boxingacademyla.com), often have aspiring professionals working out and offer one-on-one classes taught by former professional or up-and-coming boxers. These private sessions are a great way to learn about boxing strategy, to perfect your jabs and upper cuts, and to get in shape – all at the same time. Watch out Rocky…

Feeling Left Out?

If you run a club or take part in an activity that deserves a mention in these pages, let us know and we'll share the news in the next edition. Log on to www.explorerpublishing.com and click on 'feedback'. Give us your details, tell us what you do and we'll try to squeeze you in next time around.

Camping

Other options **Outdoor Goods** p.289

140 miles east of
Los Angeles
Map 2 C2

Joshua Tree National Park
760 367 5500 | www.nps.gov/jotr

This is one of the more well-known desert parks in the country. About 225km (140 miles) outside of Los Angeles, Joshua Tree is known for its brutally hot summers and devastatingly beautiful rock formations. Sometimes it might feel as if you have ventured into a Georgia O'Keefe painting. But for a desert setting there is plenty to do, from rock climbing to hiking and exploring abandoned mine shafts. This a great place for an adventurous family. The park is open year-round, but because of the extreme heat during the summer, it is best to go camping in the cooler winter months. The park offers nine campsites, only some of which require reservations.

35000 W Pacific
Coast Hwy
Malibu
Map 2 A2

Leo Carrillo State Park
818 880 0363 | www.parks.ca.gov

Leo Carrillo State Park offers a close escape from the city's congestion. This park features 3,000 acres and 127 campsites along the Pacific Coast, allowing you to sleep under the stars while listening to the breaking waves of the Pacific. A beautiful public beach is only a short walk away and if you really can't afford to leave it all behind for a weekend, there is Wi-Fi access in the park.

Catalina Island
Map 2 D4

Two Harbors
310 510 0303 | www.visitcatalinaisland.com

Only a short distance from Los Angeles, this pristine island is home to several coastal campgrounds. If you are looking for an even more secluded campsite, there are special 'boat-in' areas that are reachable only by private boat or kayak. For children who get bored there are also several eco-tourist activities like glass-bottomed boat trips and hiking excursions to keep them occupied. A wildfire devastated parts of Catalina Island in 2007, but most of the campsites are now operating normally. Also, because there are several plant species indigenous only to Catalina, there are strict rules about bringing pets. Permits are required and can be purchased at the Two Harbor Visitor Center. See p.160 for more information on the island.

Canoeing

Other options **Outdoor Goods** p.289

There are several lakes in and around Los Angeles where you can go canoeing. These lakes like Hansen Dam, Echo Park Lake, MacArthur Park Lake, and Hollenbeck Lake (www.laparks.org) probably won't satisfy the boater seeking a wild outdoor adventure, but are great for families with younger children looking for an affordable, day-long excursion. These public lakes usually allow other activities like swimming, fishing and the use of remote control boats, so little ones shouldn't have time to get bored. Not all of the lakes around Los Angeles are open year-round, so it's a good idea to call ahead of time to find out. For those interested in a more scenic trip, there are several canoeing options further outside of the city. Mono Lake (www.monolake.org), for instance, is about a five and a half hour drive from Los Angeles, and is one of the oldest lakes on the continent. There are guided canoe tours available in the summer.
The large population of South Pacific peoples in LA has influenced many to take up competitive outrigger canoeing. The Southern California Outrigger Racing Association (www.socaloutrigger.org) organises several competitive events each year and maintains a list of clubs in the region.

Chess

3665 South Vermont Ave
Exposition Park
Map 9 A3 8

Exposition Park Library

323 732 0169 | http://chess.expoparkla.com

Every Sunday from 13:00 to 16:30, players gather at the Exposition Park Library to do battle on the chess board. The games are open to everyone and free. There are also periodic tournaments. The library provides the game pieces and there is a section of chess-related books and magazines so you can brush up on the latest trends in the game. All you need to bring is a master strategy.

11514 Santa Monica Blvd
West LA
Map 4 B4 9

LA Chess Club

310 559 5551 | www.lachessclub.com

This club offers several classes teaching novices the basics of chess such as movements and openings. It also holds tournaments for more experienced players. The club hosts more advanced lectures that delve into particular aspects of the game in depth, ensuring that even the grandmasters out there learn a thing or two. It's open at the weekend and on Tuesday evenings.

Various Locations

Southern California Chess Federation

www.scchess.com

This organisation is the Southern California branch of the United States Chess Federation and serves as a clearinghouse of sorts for the local chess clubs around Los Angeles. The Federation is a good source of information about upcoming tournaments and local chess meeting places. It also publishes *Rank and File*, which is a bi-monthly magazine that details upcoming chess events and new strategies. Membership costs $14 per year and includes a subscription to *Rank and File*.

Climbing

11866 La Grange Ave
West LA
Map 3 C1 10

Rockreation

310 207 7199 | www.rockreation.com/lahome.html

This climbing gym boasts over 9,000 square feet of indoor climbing paths. Rockreation also has more traditional exercise equipment to stay in shape for the next big climb. Their 'Fight Gravity' climbing classes are good for novice cliffhangers of all ages as they teach basics such as knot tying and belaying. There are also activities for young climbers and you can even have birthday parties here.

Various Locations

Southern California Mountaineers' Association

www.rockclimbing.org

This is a great place to meet other climbers and participate in organised trips to the Palisades, Yosemite, and Joshua Tree. The organisation has over 200 members and sponsors safety courses for beginners. It supplies the ropes but not other equipment such as harnesses. The group also holds monthly speaker events and slideshows in Griffith Park. The meetings are open to all, but yearly membership fees are $45. This includes a subscription to the newsletter.

Intersection of the 118 & Topanga Canyon Blvd
Chatsworth
Map 2 B1

Stoney Point

818 756 8060 | www.sowr.com

This historic training ground of many of the sport's greats is the best spot to climb near Los Angeles. The boulders feature caves and difficult climbing routes, making it a popular destination for climbers year-round. Note that because the boulders are sandstone, it is not advisable to climb in or after a rain storm, as the wet rock is very difficult to grasp.

Cookery Classes

642 Moulton Ave
Downtown
Map 2 D1

Hipcooks
323 222 3663 | www.hipcooks.com
Located in an artists' loft, Hipcooks offers popular classes with a 'don't sweat the details' approach. That means things like measuring cups and teaspoons aren't always used. The thorough three-hour hands-on classes offer lessons in subjects such as cooking for a surprise guest, preparing a romantic dinner, and hosting a dinner party. Take a class alone or go with a partner. Classes start at $55 per session and are offered several times per week.

4643 Lakeview Canyon Rd
Westlake
Map 2 A1

Let's Get Cookin'
818 991 3940 | www.letsgetcookin.com
This school is great for aspiring chefs and those who just want to prepare some good home-cooked meals. The classes are taught by knowledgeable professionals, including chefs at some of Los Angeles' top restaurants. While they offer advanced classes on specific foods, particularly good for newcomers are the 'Basic Technique' series. These courses teach general rules and basic skills, from poaching to braising to making your own stock, giving you the building blocks to get more adventurous in your own kitchen. Classes range from $55 to $85 per session.

8690 Washington Blvd
Culver City
Map 2 C2

The New School of Cooking
310 842 9702 | www.newschoolofcooking.com
With tons of classes in specific culinary skills like roasting and cutting as well as courses in preparing ethnic cuisine from all over the globe, you should have no problem finding a class or series of classes that meets your needs. The six-class basic series offers tips to the beginner on how to pick out good ingredients, while also giving you hands-on opportunities to improve knife handling and cooking. A beginner series is also offered for vegetarian cooking. Classes cost around $85 per session.

6333 W 3rd St
West Hollywood
Map 7 B1 11

Sur La Table
323 954 9190 | www.surlatable.com
While some come just to purchase high-end kitchenware, many flock to Sur La Table to learn how to actually use the high-end kitchenware. Experienced instructors, many of whom are professional chefs, offer classes nearly every night of the week teaching would-be Wolfgang Pucks the culinary arts, like knife skills, mastering the wok, and baking. Sur La Table offers both cooking demonstrations and hands-on classes, which cost about $65. To enrol and to see a full schedule of classes, consult the website.

Cricket
While cricket does not enjoy the popularity of baseball, there are plenty of opportunities to defend the wicket in Los Angeles. The city is the home to a large population of expatriats who have formed cricket clubs and leagues. The majority of games are played in Woodley Cricket Complex and Erwin Park (13100 Erwin St, Van Nuys).

Various Locations

The Corinthian Cricket Club
www.corinthiancricketclub.com
As one of the oldest cricket clubs in Southern California, this club features members hailing from across the globe and remains one of the region's premier cricket clubs. It offers several teams, grouped by skill levels. The Corinthians and the Casuals are for more advanced players and play in the Southern California Cricket Association League, while the Corinthian Occasionals play in the more relaxed Los Angeles Social Cricket Alliance. Membership fees are $300 per year.

Various Locations

Los Angeles Social Cricket Alliance
www.lasca.org

The LASCA was founded with the mission to provide as many people as possible the opportunity to play cricket. Decidedly more casual than the Southern California Cricket Association, the LASCA organises a recreational league for eight to 10 teams every year. The league is perhaps best-known for one of those teams, the Compton Homies, and the Popz, a club formed by former gang members as a way of teaching ethics and manners through the game of cricket. Consult the website for schedules and individual club information.

Various Locations

Southern California Cricket Association
www.sccacricket.org

Established in 1935, the Southern California Cricket Association (SCCA) is the leading cricket organisation in Southern California and is recognized by the USA Cricket Association. Each year the SCCA organises a four-division league with 46 teams from all over Southern California. It also hosts annual tournaments that field teams from all over the world. Logging on to the website is a great starting point to learn more about the current teams, schedules, and public cricket facilities in the region.

Cycling
Other options **Sports Goods** p.295, **Mountain Biking** p.229, **Bicycle** p.263

Cycling in a city known for its aggressive drivers can be hazardous. Cycling commuters are rare, but that is not to say there aren't cycling opportunities in Los Angeles. Whether cyclists are pedalling as a way to be more environmentally friendly, to become the next Lance Armstrong, or simply to meet new friends, there are plenty of organisations and riding paths to help you reach your goals. The Santa Monica Bike Path, for instance, has a slew of bike rental shops and is great for casual riders, while the famed Pacific Coast Highway near Malibu offers a scenic ride for more serious riders. If you plan to ride on the street, make sure to purchase a helmet and equip your bicycle with a flashing white light, a legal requirement for using a bicycle at night. For additional information on cycling groups and a comprehensive list of current and developing bike routes throughout the city, contact the Los Angeles Department of Transportation (213 972 4962; www.bicyclela.org).

18400 Avalon Blvd
Carson
Map 2 D3

ADT Event Center Velodrome
www.lavelodrome.org

The nation's only indoor velodrome is the training ground for aspiring Olympians and novice riders alike. Riders wishing to sample the track can schedule a one-off ride, which costs $20 plus equipment rental charges. All other riders must be approved by the director of the track before attempting to break any world records. But if at first you don't succeed, the Los Angeles Velodrome also offers a variety of weekly classes that cover riding basics and etiquette costing $225.

Cruising the beach

Bicycle Kitchen

706 Heliotrope
Koreatown
Map 8 A2 **12**

323 662 2776 | www.bicyclekitchen.com

In a crowded city like Los Angeles it can be hard to find the necessary space to work on your bicycle. Luckily, the Bicycle Kitchen provides all the space and tools necessary to give your bike that tune-up it needs. For a small donation, you can use the Kitchen's tools and pick the brains of the volunteer staff about anything bicycle related. You can also build your own bike from scratch using old parts available in the garage. The Kitchen also hosts workshops teaching skills like wrenching and wheel building. The Kitchen is open from 12:00 to 18:00 from Saturday to Monday, and 18:30 to 21:30 the rest of the week. It is closed on Fridays.

Encino Velodrome

17301 Oxnard St
Encino
Map 2 B1

818 881 7441 | www.encinovelodrome.org

Aspiring racers can challenge their friends at Adult Open Training nights on Wednesday from 17:00 to 20:00. For more advanced riders, the venue offers a Tuesday night training session from 17:00 to 21:00. Each session costs $7 and an additional $5 to rent a bicycle. Personal bicycles must be approved before they are allowed on the track.

Los Angeles Wheelmen

Various Locations

www.lawheelmen.org

The Los Angeles Wheelmen is a recreational bicycling group open to people of all skill levels. It sponsors weekly rides on Sundays throughout Los Angeles County and Orange County, which can range from 25 miles (40km) to over 55 miles (89km). Throughout the year, the Wheelmen also participate in multiple day trips that can be up to 400 miles. There are also regular rides throughout the week, starting from places like Griffith Park and the San Fernando Valley. The group allows non-members to ride with them before joining, which is a good way to figure out if the Wheelmen are right for you. All riders are required to wear a helmet.

San Fernando Valley Bicycle Club

Woodland Hills
San Fernando
Map 2 B1

www.sfvbc.org

Founded in 1978, the San Fernando Valley Bicycle Club has over 500 members. The club sponsors a variety of weekly rides during the week and at weekends. The rides range from 15 miles to 100 miles and each ride caters to a different skill level. The site provides a legend outlining the obstacles in each course. Membership fees are $18 per year and membership entitles you to discounts at several bicycle shops in the San Fernando Valley.

Dance Classes

Other options **Salsa Dancing** p.234, **Music Lessons** p.229, **Belly Dancing** p.214

3rd Street Swingers

3rd St Promenade
Santa Monica
Map 3 B4 **13**

www.geocities.com/thirdstreetswingers

This group gets together several times a month to dance the day away at the 3rd Street Promenade in Santa Monica. Anyone is welcome to join the group as they lindy hop, jitterbug and swing, but you should have some experience of dancing socially. Dances are on the first, third and fifth Sundays of the month and there is a $10 participation fee.

Dance Arts Academy

731 S La Brea Av
MidWilshire
Map 7 D2 **14**

323 932 6230 | www.danceartsacademy.com

The massive 10,000 square foot studio offers classes in almost every dance form, including flamenco, tango, jazz, Irish step, hip-hop and ballet. There are classes specifically designed for adults, including ballet and flamenco, though they also offer many classes for young dancers, aged 5 through 18. More experienced dancers can sign-up for the master classes, which often feature special guest instructors.

1941 Westwood Blvd
Westwood
Map 4 C4 **15**

LA Dance Experience

310 475 1878 | www.ladanceexperience.com

This company offers group classes in ballroom dance, salsa, swing, and tango. Individuals without a partner are welcome, as they will be paired with a partner who has similar skills. There are monthly dance parties where people of all skill levels can strut their stuff. Classes run for six weeks and cost $85 for new students.

Environmental Groups

Other options **Voluntary & Charity Work** p.52

Hardly a minute in conservation goes by in Los Angeles without a mention of what it means to be 'green.' Los Angeles is a very environmentally conscious city, as you'll see from its vocal 'green' celebrities and the many hybrid automobiles on the roads. As such, there are many groups dedicated to making the world more environmentally friendly. These groups range in focus from local to national issues, and vary in the ways that volunteers can get involved. Some organisations simply seek donations to create awareness, while other groups need active volunteers to support their causes in the field.

Environmental Groups

California Coastal Coalition	www.calcoast.org	Beach Erosion
Californians Against Waste	www.cawrecycles.org	Recycling
Coalition for Clean Air	www.coalitionforcleanair.org	Clean Air
Environment California	www.environmentcalifornia.org	Conservation, Water Quality Oceans, Energy, Global Warming
Nature Conservancy	www.nature.org	Conservation
Santa Monica Baykeeper	www.smbaykeeper.org	Ocean Water Quality
Santa Monica Conservancy	www.smconservancy.org	Conservation
Sierra Club	http://angeles.sierraclub.org	Conservation, Outdoor Education
Surfrider Foundation	www.surfrider.org	Ocean Water Quality

First Aid

11355 Ohio Ave
West LA
Map 4 B4 **16**

American Red Cross of Greater Los Angeles

310 445 9900 | www.redcrossla.org

The American Red Cross offers training to help you become adept at handling any emergency. Classes on topics like CPR, babysitters' training, pet first aid and sport safety training are available at local Red Cross chapters throughout Los Angeles. These classes are particularly useful for a parent with small children, a sports coach, or anyone who engages in outdoor activities. For those who can't travel to attend a course, there are several safety courses available online. The courses are generally under $100 and many are even free. To find a Red Cross chapter near you and to enrol in a course, simply visit the website.

Fishing

Other options **Boat Tours & Charters** p.192

There are plenty of public freshwater lakes open year-round and stocked with fish frequently, giving you a better chance of hauling in your record catch. The California

Echo Park fishing

Department of Fish and Game (DFG; www.dfg.ca.gov) maintains an interactive map on its website where you can search for fishing spots by specific types of fish. It is best to bring your own equipment, and everyone older than 16 needs to get a fishing licence from the DFG. Most licences require an annual fee for renewal, but you can also purchase a one-day or two-day licence if you are planning a short trip. Licences can be purchased from many sporting goods stores throughout Los Angeles.

Saltwater fisherman can try their luck on the many public piers by the ocean, such as the Santa Monica Pier. It is important to pay attention to the size requirements for certain species of fish, as you can be fined for keeping undersized fish.

For those anglers seeking an ocean adventure, your best bet is to head to Marina Del Rey or the Long Beach area. Several charter boats offering half-day or full-day trips in the Pacific are based in these harbours and operate throughout the year. These large boats usually have all the fishing equipment you need to land 'the big one.' Marina Del Rey Sport Fishing (800 822 3625, www.marinadelreysportfishing.com) and 22nd Street Landing in San Pedro (310 832 8304, www.22ndstreet.com), for instance, offer daily trips for gamefish like halibut, barracuda and yellowtail, in addition to whalewatching tours from January to March. If you prefer fishing with a smaller party, private charters are available too. Companies such as Chubasco Sportfishing in Long Beach (818 345 3154; www.chubasco3.976-tuna.com) also offer smaller fishing excursions for up to six people.

Flower Arranging
Other options **Flowers** p.275, **Gardens** p.277

Various Locations

Flower Duet
310 792 4968 | www.flowerduet.com

At Flower Duet, you can learn all you need to know to make the perfect floral arrangement for any occasion, from a birthday party to a memorial service. The two owners running Flower Duet offer group lessons as well as private lessons at your home, where you can tell them exactly what you want to learn. Lessons start at $75 and Flower Duet provides all the supplies you need to work on your arrangements, including the flowers.

Flying
Despite its crowded airspace, the area around Los Angeles has several places to launch small aircraft, such as Long Beach, Hawthorne, Santa Monica, and Van Nuys. Many of these schools offer classes for the casual aviator seeking a trial flight, and for the more serious pilot who wants to get a licence.

The A&E Flying Club, for instance, is a non-profit club based out of Hawthorne Airport where members co-own the club's four Cessna aircraft. Members with the appropriate qualifications can take them up in the sky by scheduling their flights on the website (www.aandeflyingclub.org).

Hollywood Aviators (www.hollywoodaviators.com), based out of Van Nuys Airport, offers trained pilots the chance to rent a single-engine or multi-engine aircraft, while also offering lessons for first-time flyers. For those not quite ready to take the controls, you can take an aerial tour of Los Angeles with an instructor.

Los Angeles Helicopters (www.lahelicopters.com), based out of Long Beach, offers aerial tours of Los Angeles in a helicopter. It also provides training to aspiring helicopter pilots and the opportunity to man the controls of a helicopter.

Golf

When the Northern Trust Open (formerly the Los Angeles Open and Nissan Open) stops in Los Angeles in February, many fans flock to the Riviera Country Club (310 454 6591, www.therivieracountryclub.com) to watch their favourite professionals compete for the $6.2 million purse. For those playing simply for bragging rights, there are plenty of opportunities to tee-off all year long. Many of the most prestigious courses in the area, such as Bel-Air Country Club (310 472 9563, www.bel-aircc.org) and Los Angeles Country Club (310 276 6104) are private and require an invitation from a member to play. But there is also a good variety of public courses available for those looking to work on their stroke at affordable prices. Visit www.laparks.org for a full rundown of the courses operated by the Department of Recreation & Parks.

4730 Crystal Springs Dr
Los Feliz
Map 2 D1

Griffith Park
323 664 2255 | www.laparks.org

There is some great golf to be had in the heart of Griffith Park: two 18 hole, par 72 courses, two nine-hole courses, a driving range, and a pro shop. Along with Rancho Park, these courses are widely regarded as some of the best public courses in the area. The 18 hole, 6,942 yard Wilson course is a few hundred yards longer than the Harding course, making it a favourite with big hitters. The shorter Harding course, on the other hand, is more of a finesse player's course. Regardless of which you pick, be prepared to wait as they get extremely crowded. Lessons are available through the pro shop. Reservations are required and can be made by calling 310 216 2626. To make a reservation, you first must get a city golf card, which can be done by calling 818 291 9980. Greens fees range from $24 to $31 with additional fees for cart rental.

901 Encinal Canyon Rd
Malibu
Map 2 A1

Malibu Country Club
818 889 6680 | www.malibucountryclub.net

Set in the tranquil Malibu Canyons, this public course is great for leisurely weekends. A reasonably short drive from the congestion of Los Angeles, the club is the home to a 6,740 yard, par 72 Bermuda grass course. Call to reserve a tee time. Greens fees are $70 to $95 per round and you can rent clubs for $40.

10460 W Pico Blvd
West LA
Map 4 E4 **17**

Rancho Park Golf Course
310 839 9812 | www.laparks.org

This is one of the most popular public golf courses in the city. Featuring a nine-hole course and an 18 hole, 6,628 yard par 71 yard course, it's great for beginners and anyone who wants to play at a high-quality course for a reasonable price. Because of its well-maintained bluegrass fairways and affordability, it can get quite crowded, so be prepared to wait after your shots. There is also a driving range and a pro shop offering lessons. Reservations are required and can be made by calling 310 216 2626. To make a reservation, you first must get a city golf card, which can be done by calling 818 291 9980. Greens fees range from $24 to $31 with additional fees for cart rental.

Hiking

Other options **Outdoor Goods** p.289

With its pleasant year-round climate and over 55,000 acres of public parkland, Los Angeles is a hiker's paradise. The Santa Monica Mountains conveniently run directly through Los Angeles, making hiking one of the city's most popular outdoor activities. Whether you are looking for a strenuous workout or a casual walk, the 114 public facilities throughout the city have trails suitable for all interests and skill levels. There are many parks to choose from, but Griffith Park, the city's largest public park, remains one of the city's most popular hiking destinations with over 53 miles of trails. There are plenty of panoramic views of downtown Los Angeles to be had. The trail from Griffith Park Observatory to Mount Hollywood in particular is not to be missed. For hikers who also love film, Malibu Creek State Park offers the chance to walk through famous movie filming locations, like Planet of the Apes and MASH. Back in Hollywood, Runyon Canyon Park offers incredible views of the city and the famed Hollywood sign, and is great for jogging, dog walking, and perhaps Los Angeles' most popular pastime: celebrity gazing. But if you are looking for solitude on your hike, it is probably best to go as early as possible. No matter what park you choose, remember that they are all smoke free due to the dry climate and the fire hazard smoking poses. While self-directed hikes are the norm, many of the parks also sponsor group activities throughout the year. A list of these events and a great resource featuring interactive trail maps is www.lamountains.com.

Ice Hockey

Other options **Ice Skating** p.224

Southern California is home to two professional hockey teams, the Los Angeles Kings and the 2007 Stanley Cup winners, the Anaheim Ducks. Amateurs can practise their hip checks and slap shots with the several adult leagues in Los Angeles. Games can be found at the local ice rinks, like Culver Ice Arena (p.224) and Pickwick Gardens (p.225). Culver Ice Arena, for instance, offers pick-up hockey games at lunchtime during the week and on Sundays. LA Hockey (www.lahockey.com) provides a list of some adult ice and roller hockey leagues in the area. These leagues generally have games at night during the week, so people with day jobs can still participate. The leagues are comprised of several teams, some of which hold try-outs for new team members. To find a team you might want to play for, it is a good idea to attend some of their games to get a feel for their style and attitude.

Ice Skating

Other options **Ice Hockey** p.224

4545 Sepulveda Blvd
Culver City
Map 2 C2

Culver Ice Arena

310 398 5719 | www.culvericearena.com

Serious skaters of all ages or couples looking for a romantic date flock to Culver Ice Arena to glide around the ring while music plays. The arena offers classes such as Mommy and Me skating, figure skating, as well as an adult hockey league. There are more informal pick-up hockey games on Sunday, which are open to anyone and cost $20 to participate. The public skating sessions are open to all. From Thursday to Sunday there are night time public skating sessions from 20:00 to 22:30 in addition to the daytime public sessions. Each session costs $8 per adult and $3 for skate rental.

Pershing Square Ice Skating

532 S Olive St
Downtown
Map 10 D3 **18**

213 847 4970 | *www.laparks.org*

For the last 10 years the city has turned Pershing Square into a downtown winter wonderland. Starting in mid November and running to the last week of January, Pershing Square offers ice skating from 12:00 to 22:00 every day. Cover bands and up-and-comers play concerts near the ice, making for a great holiday treat. It costs $6 per session and $2 for skate rental.

Pickwick Gardens

1001 W Riverside Dr
Burbank
Map 2 D1

818 845 5300 | *www.pickwickgardens.com*

Visitors of all ages can take figure skating lessons, participate in hockey leagues, or simply skate around the rink at their own pace. There is also an 800 seat spectator area, so there will be several people to witness your graceful skating. Public skating sessions occur throughout the week and the night time skating sessions on Wednesdays and Saturdays from 20:30 to 22:00 are particularly good for people who work during the day. There is even an arcade and a 24 lane bowling alley in Pickwick Gardens in case you've had enough falls on the ice for one day. Each session costs $7 per adult and $3 for skate rental.

Kids' Activities

As the world's entertainment capital, Los Angeles has enough activities to keep people of all ages having fun. The summer in particular is great for free or inexpensive outdoor activities like Shakespeare plays in the park (www.independentshakespeare.com) or world music festivals at the Hollywood Bowl (p.182). During the rest of the year, the city's wide array of museums with interactive exhibits and art studios designed for children should provide a good outlet for your little one's boundless energy. In addition to the venues listed below, parents looking to entertain their kids should consider the California Science Center (p.181), the Children's Museum of Los Angeles (p.171), Disneyland (p.186), Los Angeles Zoo (p.188) and the Zimmer Children's Museum (p.178).

American Girl

189 The Grove Dr
West Hollywood
Map 7 C1 **19**

1877 247 5223 | *www.americangirl.com*

This hybrid retail and restaurant destination is a unique and fun environment for little girls to play and dine with their favourite dolls. Visitors can style their dolls' hair, pose for pictures with their inanimate friends, and even enjoy a meal together. Lunch is $22 per person while dinner is $24 per person. Be sure to call for reservations. The shop is located in the Grove Shopping Center (p.308), which also has plenty of stores for grown-ups too.

Build-A-Bear

Various Locations

1877 789 2327 | *www.buildabear.com*

With several locations throughout the city, this retail chain allows children and their parents to make their own stuffed bears. Children can choose their new friend's stuffing, clothing, names and can even insert a microchip with pre-recorded messages of their choosing. Prices range from $10 to $25 per bear. Build-A-Bear is also a popular destination to host birthday parties.

Kitesurfing

Other options **Beaches** p.189

Thanks to gusty breezes and large public beaches, there are many places to kiteboard in the LA area. But for beginners it is sometimes difficult to know where to start your drags. The Southern California Kiteboarding Association (www.scka.org) fosters a community dedicated to safe kiteboarding and hosts events throughout the year where you can meet people with similar interests. It is recommended that you never kiteboard alone for safety reasons, so this may be the place to meet a partner. If you are a beginner, Zuma in Malibu is a good place to practise in the off-season, especially if there is no one in the water. Lessons are nearly a must and the SCKA lists several schools on its site. Note that many kiteboarding areas like Zuma and Leo Carrillo Beach get very crowded in the summer and kiteboarders can only practise when the waters are clear of bathers, or with the approval of lifeguards.

Language Schools
Other options **Education** p.124

With its close proximity to Mexico and a large population of immigrants from all over the globe, Los Angeles is a multi-lingual city (area names such as Little Armenia, Little Ethiopia, and Koreatown give some clue). Proficiency in English and an additional language, especially Spanish, is helpful when living here. Knowing multiple languages is also a major advantage when searching for a job.

Various Locations

Berlitz
www.berlitz.us
The ever-popular Berlitz has several locations throughout the city, and teaches a myriad of languages, from Spanish to Mandarin. Berlitz uses an immersive approach where all conversation during class time is in the language you would like to learn, so some previous study of the language is helpful. Several curriculums are available, and there is a choice of one-to-one tuition or small classes.

439 N Canon Dr
Beverly Hills
Map 4 E2 20

Beverly Hills Lingual Institute
310 858 0717 | www.bhlingual.com
Boasting over 1,300 students per term, the institution offers over 25 languages and has classes to fit even the busiest schedule. The instruction here is first class, as is apparent from the institute's inclusion on the 2005 'Best of LA' list compiled by *Los Angeles Magazine* and the fact that several major corporations, such as Honda and Giorgio Armani, have sent their employees here. Classes are small and generally meet once a week, so discipline is needed to practise and complete your assignments out of class.

10995 Le Conte Ave
Westwood
Map 4 B3 4

UCLA Extension
310 825 9971 | www.uclaextension.edu
This programme is great for those wishing to learn a language in a university setting. Most of the classes are at night to accommodate the working schedules of students. There are several languages to choose from, and because the instructors are often affiliated with UCLA, the teaching is top notch. The courses are taught in small classes and often assign homework. The extension programme offers new courses every semester, so be sure to check its website to avoid missing registration deadlines.

Libraries
Other options **Second-Hand Items** p.293, **Books** p.263

Various Locations

Los Angeles Public Library
213 228 7000 | www.lapl.org
The Los Angeles Public Library has over 70 branches throughout the city and several million books in circulation, making it one of the largest public library systems in

the world. The central library is located downtown (213 228 7000; 630 W 5th St) and is the home to the rare book collection and several special exhibits. For those who can't make it to the downtown location, the library also maintains a robust website which offers the ability to search the extensive databases of articles, book titles and photographs of Southern California. The branch libraries maintain extensive collections and even have a section for audio books, which are especially popular for commuters. Most branches feature activities to promote literacy for children, such as homework sessions or storytimes. The libraries also have public computers and wireless internet so you can bring your laptop. It is recommended that you reserve a computer through the website. You must have a library card before using the facilities, but it's free and there are no residency restrictions. Simply take your photo ID to the nearest library and it will issue you one. To find the closest branch, log on to the website.

Martial Arts

912 1/2 S Robertson Blvd
West LA
Map 7 A3 **21**

Beverly Hills Jiu-Jitsu Club
310 854 7664 | www.bhjjc.com
This club offers classes almost every day of the week in a variety of fighting styles, such as Muay Thai, Kickboxing, Brazilian Jiu-Jitsu, Wrestling and Judo. There are programmes for every skill level and several fighters training here have gone on to fight in international events like the Pan-Am games. These group classes are great for people looking to get in shape, to learn self-defence, or to fight competitively. Private lessons are also available.

1723 Hillhurst Ave
Los Feliz
Map 8 B1 **22**

Sifu Buck Sam Kong
323 664 8882 | www.bucksamkongkungfu.com
Sifu Kong, a member of the Black Belt Hall of Fame, taught the US Army hand-to-hand combat techniques before he opened his own martial arts school in Hollywood in 1977. Today students of all ages can learn from this master kung-fu artist nearly every day of the week. The beginner hung gar kung-fu classes are particularly good for someone who hasn't attempted a fingertip thrust or crane pose before.

Various Locations

United Studios of Self-Defense
www.ussd.com
With several locations throughout the city, you should have no trouble finding a studio to sharpen your self-defence skills. Specialising in Shaolin Kempo, a combination of several fighting styles, United Studios of Self Defense features classes for men and women of all ages. The instructors all have at least 10 years of training and will make sure that you leave the class tougher than when you arrived. It also offers a one-time free guest pass so you can see if it's right for you.

10610 Culver Blvd
Culver City
Map 2 C1

West Los Angeles Seido Karate
323 731 2820 | http://westlaseido.com
This is a great place for children and adults to learn the Japanese martial art of Seido Karate. It offers evening adult classes that are focused on helping you improve your cardiovascular fitness and concentration skills. Using Seido Karate, the kyoshi also teaches techniques to help control aggression. Students looking for a challenge can fight in a safe environment. It is recommended that you observe a class before enrolling.

Mini Golf

Other options **Golf** p.223

Arroyo Seco Mini-Golf

1055 Lohman Lane
South Pasadena
Map 2 E1

323 257 0475 | www.arroyoseco.com

Next to the nine-hole par three golf course is a traditional mini golf course with a windmill and other fun obstacles that will make you feel like a kid again. Afterwards you can head to the lighted driving range to hit a couple of buckets or go to the restaurant to grab a bite. This is a great low-key date spot and it only costs $2 per round.

Putting Edge

6081 Ctr Dr
Culver City
Map 2 C2

310 348 9770 | www.putting-edge.com

This isn't the mini golf you played as a kid, this is glow-in-the-dark, sensory overload golf. The darkness and bright lights might be too intense for very young children, but it is a good place for older children and adults to try to make par. There is also an arcade in the facility. It costs $9.35 per round for adults and $8.35 for children who are 7 to 12 years old. You can book a tee time online to avoid a long wait.

Mother & Toddler Activities

From the free outdoor playgrounds, to the spas that allow mum to relax while watching her children play, Los Angeles has no shortage of activities for mothers and their toddlers to do together. Not surprisingly, the health-conscious city has a particularly robust offering of establishments that allow mothers to exercise alongside their young children.

Boogie Mama's

Electric Lodge
1416 Electric Ave
Venice
Map 3 E4 23

310 428 7308 | www.madamechocolate.com/boogie.html

For those mothers who feel like dancing, Boogie Mamas offers an intense but light-hearted dance workout. Mothers can dance the morning away as their toddlers 'dance' beside them. Don't worry if you are tone deaf, there is no judgement here, only a good time. Classes run from 10:45 to 11:45 every Friday morning.

Circus training at Focus Fish

Focus Fish

Various Locations

323 691 5747 | www.focusfish.com

For many parents the last thing you want to hear is your child telling you they're running away to join the circus. But at Focus Fish you can do it together. Parents and their toddlers can take a variety of classes that teach coordination through circus acts, such as developing mini-trapeze, rings, and hoop skills. There are several classes grouped by age and they run at several times and locations throughout the city.

Motorsports

Auto Club Speedway

9300 Cherry Ave
Fontana

909 429 5000 | www.californiaspeedway.com

Just an hour from Los Angeles, the California Speedway hosts several NASCAR Cup Series events and seats over 92,000 racing fans. Those who want to get fast and furious themselves have the opportunity to take driving lessons from the many schools that practise there. Classes for all levels of drivers are available from schools that bear the names of driving greats like Richard Petty (www.1800bepetty.com) and Mario Andretti (www.andrettiracing.com). Motorcycle lessons are available too. There is also an adjacent dragway which hosts amateur and youth driving events.

AV Motoplex

2551 W Av H
Lancaster

661 723 0773 | www.avmotoplex.com

For motocrossers looking for a place to jump and get muddy, this complex hosts public practices every Sunday from 09:00 to 15:30, as well as a variety of races throughout the year. There is also a pee-wee track, so young bikers can practise too. Mini-bikes, quads and motorbikes are welcome on the course. It costs $25 per person per session to ride. Another good source for motocrossing is www.socalmotocross.com, which provides a list of motocross tracks and clubs in the area.

Irwindale Speedway

500 Speedway Dr
Irwindale
Map 2 E1

626 358 1100 | www.irwindalespeedway.com

With the 2007 closing of the Los Angeles County Raceway dragstrip (www.lacr.net), Irwindale is a good option for those wishing to drag race legally. Here, anyone with a valid driver's licence and a vehicle that meets certain requirements can race anything from a snowmobile to a car on the 1/8 mile drag strip. The Irwindale Speedway also hosts many professional racing events throughout the year that are sanctioned by NASCAR.

Mountain Biking
Other options **Cycling** p.219

With a vast supply of public parkland, Los Angeles has plenty of trails to keep diehard mountain bikers satisfied. Several of the parks that are good for hiking, like Malibu Creek State Park, Coldwater Canyon Park and Griffith Park, also have specific trails for mountain bikers. Most of these trails close at dark and can get crowded when the weather is nice. A good resource for finding biking trails in the Santa Monica Mountains near your home is www.lamountains.com, which provides a biking trail locator in which you input your zip code and the trails closest to you are displayed. For those looking for a group to ride with, www.bicyclela.org is a good place to start your search. Over The Bars Mountain Bike Club (www.otbmbc.com) sponsors weekly group rides that are free to attend and open to anyone with an interest in mountain biking.

Music Lessons
Other options **Music, DVDs & Videos** p.287, **Dance Classes** p.220

Whether you want to learn music to express yourself or simply to get ready for that upcoming *American Idol* audition, finding lessons in a city full of aspiring musicians isn't hard to do. Telephone poles throughout the city are covered with adverts for guitar lessons, but for a more reliable start to your search, check out www.craigslist.org or www.privatelessons.com, or a local music training centre. Those options should return plenty of results when searching for an instructor in your area of interest.

Hollywood Academy of Music

7469 Melrose Ave Suite 34
Hollywood
Map 5 E4 **24**

323 651 2395 | www.hollywoodacademyofmusic.com

Offering private vocal and various instrumental lessons, Hollywood Academy can take both the beginner and advanced musicians to the next level. Particularly interesting are their group music lessons, like School of Rock 101, which let you jam with fellow students to experience what it's like to be in a rock band. You might want to wait a few classes before quitting your day job. Private lessons cost $29 per 30 minute session and group sessions are $35 per class, in addition to a yearly registration fee of $30. There is a second location in North Hollywood (818 760 7740).

Ron Anthony Guitar Lessons

Burbank

818 848 8192 | www.ronanthonyjazz.com

Having played with George Shearing and Frank Sinatra in his 50 year career, jazz guitarist Ron Anthony knows a thing or two about music. Fortunately, he is willing to share this knowledge. Anthony has taught at several colleges over the years and now offers private jazz guitar lessons at his Burbank studio. This is great for anyone wishing to learn the fundamentals of jazz guitar from a pro.

Silverlake Conservatory of Music

3920 Sunset Blvd
Silver Lake
Map 8 B2 **25**

323 665 3363 | www.silverlakeconservatory.com

Founded by Flea of the rock band Red Hot Chili Peppers, the Silverlake Conservatory offers lessons for adults and children at affordable prices. Choose any instrument you'd like to learn and it'll do its best to find an instructor. Offering free lessons to those who can't afford them, the conservatory was founded with the mission to help all children in the community learn music. Adults seeking to learn an instrument are welcome too. Lessons cost $25 for a 30 minute session in addition to a yearly $20 registration fee.

Netball

Los Angeles Waves Netball Club

Victoria Park 419 E 192nd St
Carson
Map 2 D3

www.wavesnetball.com

Though netball is not well known by Americans, expats looking for some competitive yet friendly netball action are in luck. The Los Angeles Waves Netball Club was founded in 2002 and is now the largest netball club in California with over 40 members. The group sponsors tournaments as well as year-round Saturday morning practices, which are open to anyone. The club is predominantly female, but men are welcome to attend. Yearly membership fees are $95 per adult or $45 for children under 16 years of age.

Orchestras & Bands
Other options **Music Lessons** p.229

The Association of Concert Bands of America (ACBA)

Various Locations

www.acbands.org

This association is dedicated to helping adult musicians and community bands. Its licensing deals with ASCAP and BMI allow member bands to perform music at reasonable costs, and its magazine is a great resource to keep abreast of new developments in the community concert band scene. The website is a great way to find groups in your area.

Burbank Community Band

Gross Park 2814 W Empire Ave
Burbank
Map 2 D1

www.burbankband.org

With the goal of educating the public about music, this community concert band plays throughout Los Angeles, including events at local schools. The Burbank Community

Band rehearses every Friday morning and is open to any musician with an instrument and a desire to play. There are no auditions or fees charged to play with the band.

6201 Winnetka Ave
Woodland Hills
Map 2 B1

LA Winds Music Department Pierce College

www.lawinds.org

Founded in 1983, this 100 piece band is comprised of professional and amateur musicians. The band has released albums and toured the world while putting on five concerts per season at the Pierce College campus in Woodland Hills. The group rehearses one night per week and holds auditions for newcomers wishing to join the band. Rehearsals are open to the public and are a good way to find out if the band's sound is something that appeals to you.

216 N Brand Blvd
Glendale
Map 2 D1

Los Angeles Chamber Orchestra

213 622 7001 | www.laco.org

Founded in 1968 as a meeting place for film studio musicians, the 40 member Los Angeles Chamber Orchestra performs 15 concerts per season. This small ensemble of expert musicians performs both new and old compositions, from pieces written in the baroque period to those composed in the 20th century. It has received several awards for its masterful performances, and some fans regard the Chamber Orchestra as one of the best small orchestras in the country.

Paintballing

210 & Osborne Exit
San Fernando
Map 2 D1

Conquest Paintball

818 503 7627 | www.conquestpaintball.com

So remote it doesn't even have a street address, Conquest Paintball offers the chance to attack your friends on a course deep in the San Fernando Valley. Based on a 700 acre horse farm, there are plenty of trees and bushes to hide behind in this wooded course. It's only open at the weekend and costs $20 per person to play all day. Rental equipment is also available. Players must be over 10 years of age, and those under 18 must be accompanied by an adult.

33500 Ridge
Route Rd
Castaic

Warped Paintball Park

310 966 1100
www.warpedpaintballpark.com

Musician on Colorado Boulevard, Pasadena

This paintball park has four fields on over 40 acres of land. With a trench field, pork chop hill, spool field and jungle field, you can play Rambo with your friends in the setting of your choice. The course is open during the week to parties of 30 or more people, and at the weekend for walk-on players. Half-day afternoon sessions are also available. The cost is $15 for a full day session and rental equipment is available for an extra fee. Again, players must be over 10 and those under 18 must be accompanied by an adult.

Photography

Various Locations

Los Angeles Underwater Photographic Society
www.laups.org
LAUPS sponsors several boat trips throughout the year as well as monthly photography contests. Beginners and more experienced photographers are invited to join. There are several tiers of membership available and annual fees generally run from $15 to $30.

Various Locations

Southern California Council of Camera Clubs
www.s4c-photo.org
Founded in 1939, Southern California Council of Camera Clubs (S4C) is an umbrella organisation for several photography clubs, and is a good starting point to find local photography chapters in your neighbourhood. S4C sponsors outings and photography events throughout the year – great for meeting fellow enthusiasts. The organisation also sponsors frequent photography competitions in areas such as colour, nature and photojournalism.

10995 Le Conte Ave
Westwood
Map 4 B3 4

UCLA Extension
310 825 9971 | www.uclaextension.edu
The UCLA Extension offers a variety of courses on digital photography, dark room techniques and lighting. These courses are a good way for novices to get acquainted with photography basics under the instruction of a professional. More advanced students can delve into specific areas of study in one-day workshops (such as Photoshop tricks) or longer courses covering subjects like portraiture. Courses generally run several weeks and you must bring your own camera and film.

Polo

501 Will Rogers
State Park Rd
Pacific Palisades
Map 2 B1

Will Rogers State Park
310 573 5000 | www.willrogerspolo.org
For those wishing to re-enact their favourite scene from *The Great Gatsby*, head to Will Rogers State Park for a game of polo. This is the only place in Los Angeles to catch a game and it is completely free to watch. Even if you don't understand the sport or have a clue what a chukker is, these games are fun and a great way to spend a weekend. The polo season runs from April to September and games are played on Saturdays from 14:00 to 17:00 and Sundays from 10:00 to 13:00.

Pottery

2856 S Robertson Blvd
West LA
Map 2 C2

Echo Ceramics
310 815 1525 | www.echoceramics.com
Echo Ceramics provides a great environment for both expert sculptors and first-time potters. Advanced sculptors can become members of the studio for $135 per month, which entitles them to use equipment like wheels, tables and kilns at their convenience. Beginners can take weekly classes on subjects such as basic wheel techniques. Classes generally run eight weeks and cost $285. Echo Ceramics will also glaze and fire pottery in its kilns for a fee.

3795 Boise Ave
Mar Vista
Map 3 F2 26

Peach Tree Pottery
310 567 2708 | www.peachtreepottery.com
This pottery gallery sells the work of emerging ceramics artists, while offering classes for all ages and skill levels. Classes teach beginners the basics of working with a wheel,

and generally run four weeks at a cost of $135, though single classes are available. After completing four classes, you may qualify for self-directed study where you can use Peach Tree's equipment without any formal instruction. The gallery also offers several classes tailored to children.

Public Speaking

Various Locations

Toastmasters
www.toastmasters.org

Toastmasters has over 220,000 members in 11,300 clubs internationally. The organisation is dedicated to helping people become better public speakers through practising in front of a group of other like-minded individuals. Weekly sessions consist of giving speeches and receiving critiques from your peers. There are plenty of Toastmasters clubs in Los Angeles, all of which are listed on the website. New members must pay a $20 registration fee and $27 every six months.

Rowing

Marina Del Rey is the best bet for those interested in sculling or testing themselves on the 'erg'. Located on a harbour, Marina Del Rey is the home to The Los Angeles Rowing Club (www.larowing.com) and Lions Rowing Club (www.lionsrc.com). These clubs operate out of boathouses near the water and have several top-of-the-line boats available to members of all abilities. Instruction is available for novice rowers and boats are divided by skill level. Both clubs practise very early every morning, and prospective members can attend a trial row before deciding whether to join.

Rugby

Various Locations

Southern California Rugby Football Union
www.scrfu.org

Established in 1937, this is the main rugby league in Los Angeles. The SCRFU sponsors league play with several divisions based on age, gender and skill level. Competition is fierce and the SCRFU is thought by some clubs to be the toughest league in the country. The Santa Monica Rugby Club (www.santamonicarugby.com), a member of the league, for instance, was national club champion in 2005 and 2006. If you want to hone your skills or just get some exercise, the SCRFU offers clinics. Many teams in the league also offer weekly practices throughout the year. Attending a practice or two is a good way to learn if the team is a good fit for you before forking out your registration fees to join. If you do decide to join a club or to start your own, you must register with USA Rugby (www.usarugby.org) which costs $35 per year for first-time members.

Running

Like most major cities, every gym in Los Angeles features a large treadmill section for those wishing to run indoors. But Southern California's warm climate, extensive mountain trails and proximity to the ocean make it the perfect place for year-round outdoor running. To be sure, running in the city can be difficult due to the busy streets and limited space on sidewalks, but there are plenty of public parks with mountain trails or beachfront paths that offer a distinctly Los Angeles running experience.

1450 Ocean Ave
Santa Monica
Map 3 A4 27

The Los Angeles Leggers
310 577 8000 | www.laleggers.com

Boasting over a thousand members throughout Southern California, the Los Angeles Leggers is a group dedicated to helping you prepare for the Los Angeles Marathon.

Jogger in Santa Monica

The group meets every Saturday morning starting approximately 30 weeks before the Los Angeles Marathon in March. The programme features weekly runs in pacing groups, mentor programmes and even inspirational speakers. Runners of all speeds are encouraged to join. Membership costs $75 per year.

Downeworth ◄

Los Angeles Marathon

310 444 5544 | www.lamarathon.com

Every year 25,000 runners compete in the marathon, which is the biggest and most talked about running event in the city. The route weaves through several of Los Angeles' most historic neighbourhoods, including Rossmore and Leimert Park, providing some interesting architectural sights along the 42.2km (26.2 mile) journey. The marathon takes place in March of every year and registration is usually around $100, but jumps to $115 as the race approaches. For those not quite ready for the marathon, there is also a 5k run.

Santa Monica ◄
Map 3 C4

Santa Monica Bike Path

This path along Santa Monica beach is one of the most popular in Los Angeles as it provides a great way to catch some rays while working up a sweat. Because of its close proximity to the Santa Monica Pier, wandering tourists often crowd the path by midday, so start your run early in the morning. There is ample street parking and the beach has several public carparks nearby.

4th St & Adelaide Dr ◄
Santa Monica
Map 2 B2

Santa Monica Stairs

Santa Monica's worst kept 'secret' is a set of steep concrete and wooden stairs. The stairs, set against the gorgeous backdrop of the Pacific Ocean, offer an intense lower body workout, and two or three trips up and down is enough for most. In the mornings and at weekends the stairs can get quite crowded with throngs of beautiful people and sometimes even a movie star.

Pacific Palisades ◄
Map 2 B2

Trail Runners Club

www.trailrunnersclub.com

The Trail Runners Club meets in the Pacific Palisades and organises weekly Sunday morning runs on trails through the tranquil Santa Monica Mountains. The runs usually range between eight and 12 miles, and can accommodate runners of all skill levels. If you are worried that you are too slow, the group lets slower runners start earlier to allow everyone to finish together. Membership fees are $45 per year.

Salsa Dancing

Other options **Belly Dancing** p.204, **Dance Classes** p.220

8558 W 3rd St ◄
Beverly Hills
Map 7 A1 **28**

3rd Street Dance

310 275 4683 | www.3rdstreetdance.com

Offering frequent classes in all types of dance including tango, ballroom, and salsa, this is a great place to pick up some new moves. Students with no previous dance experience are welcome to attend the beginner salsa classes, which pair up similarly skilled dancers. The studio also offers Salsa Workshops at the weekend which are open to dancers with at least an intermediate skill level.

The Salsa Box Studios

1877 W Adams Blvd
West Adams
Map 7 F4 **29**

323 931 9285 | *www.thesalsaboxstudios.com*

The Salsa Box has classes to fit any skill level and schedule. The classes are small and pair you with a similarly skilled partner, so there is no need to be embarrassed when stepping on your partner's toes. For those with a busy schedule, the weekend bootcamps are a good way to learn salsa basics quickly. The studio also hosts practice mixers, where you can strut your stuff in front of other dancers.

Scrapbooking

Scrapbook Safari

20660 Ventura Blvd
Woodland Hills
Map 2 B1

818 227 9704 | *www.scrapbooksafari.com*

With classes almost every day of the week, Scrapbook Safari is an excellent place to learn how to crop. Scrapbookers taking the '5 and 10' classes are eligible for a coupon for scrapbooking materials. Scrapbook Safari carries a wide array of everything you need to scrapbook, including a large supply of acid free photo materials. Keep an eye out for special events throughout the year like the all-night cropping fests, which include dinners, coffee and massage.

Sweetpeas & Snapshots

11726 W Pico Blvd
West LA
Map 2 C2

310 479 2444 | *www.sweetpeasandsnapshots.com*

The store is run by artists who can guide you to materials right for you, such as the wide selection of rubber stamps and vintage decorations. There is even a section with fun gifts and furniture available for purchase. Sweetpeas also hosts scrapbooking workshops, offering tips on presenting your favourite pictures. It will also help you plan birthday and tea parties for kids, as well as baby showers.

Skiing & Snowboarding

Big Bear

43101 Goldmine Dr
Big Bear Lake

909 866 5766 | *www.bearmountain.com*

Just two and a half hours outside Los Angeles, Big Bear is perfect for a quick trip out of the city. With over 435 acres of skiable land, Bear Mountain has something for skiers and snowboarders of all skill levels. The mountain features a 1,665 foot vertical drop

Waiting for the snow at Mt Baldy

and several areas with half-pipes, jumps, and jibs for snowboarders. Bear Mountain gets about 100 inches of snow per year, but also has the ability to produce artificial snow.

Mammoth Mountain

1 Minaret Rd
Mammoth Lakes

800 626 6684 | www.mammothmountain.com

About a five and a half hour drive from Los Angeles, Mammoth Mountain offers 3,500 skiable acres and 150 trails. The mountain gets over 400 inches of snow each year and offers areas for snowmobiles, snowshoeing, skiing and snowboarding, ensuring that all winter sports enthusiasts are satisfied. For snowboarders, the mountain boasts a 'Super-Pipe' and other areas with jumps and obstacles. For beginners, there is also a ski and snowboarding school offering lessons.

Mt Baldy

End of Mt Baldy Road
Mt Baldy

909 982 0800 | www.shopbaldy.com

The closest resort to LA, Mt Baldy offers steeper terrain than elsewhere in the county, and is more suited to experienced skiers and boarders. The resort has 28 runs covering 500 skiable acres, and a vertical drop of 2,100 feet. There are four chair lifts. Lessons are available and equipment can be rented. The chair lift from the carpark up to the restaurant at 7,800 feet keeps running even when there's no snow, meaning visitors can access kilometres of hiking trails and enjoy the stunning views. There is a lodge in Mt Baldy village (www.mtbaldylodge.com) with a restaurant, and six cabins for rent.

Soccer

Although David Beckham's debut soccer season for the Los Angeles Galaxy created more headlines in the gossip magazines than in sports pages, soccer remains a popular sport in the city. In addition to the countless youth leagues in the greater Los Angeles area, there are several organised adult leagues running throughout the year. If you just can't wait until next season to bend it like Beckham, you can easily find more informal games on public fields. A comprehensive list of these fields can be found at www. laparks.org/dos/sports/soccer.htm.

Los Angeles Premier League

Crossroads School
1715 Olympic Blvd
Santa Monica
Map 3 C3 30

www.lapremierleague.com

Founded in 2002, the over 30 Premier League has 12 men's teams, including one founded by singing star Robbie Williams. The league offers two seasons per year, and is not for novices or casual players. The competition is fierce and features former college and semi-professional players. Individual players interested in joining should fill out the 'Free Agent' form on the website.

Municipal Soccer League

Various Locations

818 246 5613 | www.laparks.org/dos/sports/soccer.htm

The Department of Recreation and Parks runs two soccer seasons per year for adult men and women. There are eight different leagues, depending on a player's skill level. While it is best to sign up as part of a team, the league is open to individual players. Simply fill out a 'Free Agent' form on the website and you will be called when needed.

Social Groups

Other options **Support Groups** p.123

Los Angeles' size can make it difficult to socialise with people of similar backgrounds. Fortunately, there are several organisations for expatriates looking to reconnect with fellow countrymen. The clubs vary in purpose; from casual cocktails and social events, to business networking opportunities. Most of these clubs are inexpensive to join. A valuable resource for expatriates of all nationalities is www.meetup.com, which allows you to search for online groups with members in Southern California. You can then communicate with members via an online forum. Also have a look at the various publications targeted towards specific communities. The *L'Italo-Americano* weekly newspaper (www.italoamericano.com), for instance, is a good way for Italians and Italian-Americans to find out about upcoming cultural activities. Canadians Abroad (www.canadiansabroad.com) sponsors fun social events like going to hockey games and is an easy way to find fellow canucks. For British newcomers, The Council of British Societies (626 966 9178; www.cobsinfo.com) sponsors several charitable and social events throughout the year. The Mayflower Club (818 769 9805; www.mayflowerclub.com) is another old British club. Located in North Hollywood, the group sponsors a variety of entertainment nights, dances, banquets and card games. AustraUSA (www.australaevents.com) helps Australians find their niche in the city with an events calendar packed with everything from garden tours to Aussie Rules viewing parties. For those wanting to mingle in exclusive circles, the Jonathan Club (213 624 0881; www.jc.org) is the most prestigious and exclusive in LA, and caters to the business and social elite. Membership is only extended by invitation.

Squash

Other options **Sports & Leisure Facilities** p.245

Though squash is not the city's most popular sport, squash lovers need not fret. Residents looking for the optimal squash facility can start their search with the Southern California Squash Racquets Association at www.socalsquash.com. The club maintains a list of several squash courts in the area and links to several other squash sites. The US Squash Organization also has a handy search feature on their website, www.us-squash.org, which allows you to search for courts near your zip code. For the more advanced players, the famed Los Angeles Athletic Club (p.245) located in downtown Los Angeles, sponsors tournaments that are sometimes open to non-members.

Surfing

Other options **Beaches** p.189, **Kitesurfing** p.225

Surfin' USA

There is a reason why Southern California is depicted in the media as a sun-soaked, surf-obsessed culture: because it actually is. There are many places to catch waves around Los Angeles, such as Zuma and Surfrider Beach in Malibu and Huntington Beach, also known as 'Surf City'. On any given morning, the Pacific Coast Highway is lined with pick-up trucks, cars with roof-racks, and surfers putting on their wetsuits for an early session. The water can be quite cold, even in the summer. There are plenty of places to rent boards and wet suits. Any surf shop in a beach city generally has equipment available, especially in areas that attract tourists like Santa Monica. For those just starting out, it is a good idea to start with a longer board, as these provide more stability when trying to stand up for the first time. A great resource for newcomers to the Los Angeles area is www.surfline.com. This website features surfing videos and pictures, weather and condition updates and live webcam feeds of many of the area's most popular surfing spots. If you want more formal training, there are several surf schools, such as Learn to Surf LA (www. learntosurfla.com), Surf Academy (www.surfacademy.com), Aqua Surf School (www. aquasurfschool.com), Corky Carroll's Surf School (www.surfschool.net) and Blue Rider (www.blueridersurf.com). Each provides hands-on lessons for all ages and skill levels covering the basics – from surfing techniques to surfing etiquette. Private lessons for adults, community classes and intensive surf camps are available. Many of these schools also offer special surfing events for companies seeking a uniquely SoCal way to bond with their staff.

Swimming
Other options **Sports & Leisure Facilities** p.245, **Beaches** p.189

With the Pacific Ocean and 59 municipal swimming pools, there are plenty of places to swim in Los Angeles. Many stretches of the coastline and all of the public pools are guarded during the summer, giving you the peace of mind that professionals are watching. The pools often have designated times allotted for swimming laps, so check the schedule at www.laparks.org. Most of them close in September and the Pacific Ocean gets surprisingly chilly, even in the summer. The city and surrounding communities keep several indoor and heated outdoor pools open all year round. There are also many private gyms with indoor pools to get you through cooler times. Those looking for more organised swimming workouts or private adult swimming lessons should consult Southern California Aquatics (www.swim.net), the largest masters swimming programme in the country.

Tennis
Other options **Sports & Leisure Facilities** p.245

While the Countrywide Classic (formerly the Mercedes Benz Cup) brings some of the biggest names in professional tennis to Los Angeles in August, amateurs practise their forehands all year at the city's many outdoor courts. It is a good idea to check www.laparks.org/dos/sports/tennis.htm to see which courts have lighting. Most courts are free and operate on a first-come, first-serve basis. There are, however, a handful of fee courts, which range in price from $5 to $8 per hour, and require a $15 reservation card. Reservation cards can be purchased by calling 323 644 3536. To reserve a court you must call 213 625 1010 or 323 644 3536, which are both answered 24 hours a day. Finding a partner is perhaps the hardest part about tennis in LA, but there are several clubs and leagues to help.

325 S La Cienega Blvd
Beverly Hills
Map 7 A1 **31**

La Cienega Tennis Center
310 550 4765 | www.beverlyhills.org
This public complex in the heart of Beverly Hills offers 16 beautiful, lit courts. With four courts dedicated to lessons, this is also a great spot to learn the sport. The cost to non-residents of Beverly Hills is $8.50 to $9.75 per hour depending on the time of day, and reservations are possible with the purchase of a reservation card for $14.25.

Various Locations ◄ Los Angeles Tennis Association
www.lataweb.com

With over 600 members, the Los Angeles Tennis Association claims it is the largest gay and lesbian tennis organisation in the world. The association is well organised and offers many social events, hosts tournaments, and offers 'Team Tennis', a system which enables you to easily find tennis partners and competitors. To become a member, you simply have to fill out a form on the website and pay $35 per year.

Various Locations ◄ Tennis Los Angeles
www.tennislosangeles.com

Tennis Los Angeles offers leagues in four different areas of the city: Westside, Hollywood, the San Fernando Valley and San Gabriel. Players are then grouped into divisions with six or more people and introduced via email. People then schedule their matches at mutually convenient times and locations. Membership costs $29.95 for the year and applications can be filled out on the website.

Volleyball

As home to the Manhattan Beach AVP Tournament, dubbed 'The Wimbledon of Beach Volleyball', it is no surprise that the coast is peppered with bronzed amateurs practising their sets and spikes on the area's public beach volleyball courts. Beaches from Zuma to Huntington Beach have beach volleyball courts open to everyone, and pickup games are common. Play is on a first-come, first-serve basis, and the courts can get quite crowded in the summer. According to the courts' rules, you can always challenge the winning team to a game, even if you are alone.

For a list of the public beach volleyball courts, consult the Los Angeles County Department of Beaches and Harbors website (http://beaches.co.la.ca.us). The California Beach Volleyball Association (www.cbva.com) is also a good place to learn more about organised beach volleyball play.

Weightlifting

Other options **Aerobics and Fitness Classes** p.211

There are plenty of gyms, and most feature a large area of free weights and machines, which are good for building muscle mass (p.245). These gyms usually have personal

Volleyball in Santa Monica

Muscle Beach, Venice

trainers and nutritionists available who can design workout regimes and diets specifically for you. Many also have juice bars located on the premises so you can slam a healthy protein shake after a workout. Perhaps the most well-known gym for bodybuilders is the outdoor Muscle Beach in Venice (1800 Ocean Front Walk, Venice), a place made famous by California Governor Arnold Schwarzenegger in the

Rad pectos

1970s. This is not for the modest, as crowds often gather to watch the exhibitionist lifters work out. For serious bodybuilders who seek competition, a good organisation to contact is the National Physique Committee (www.nationalphysiquecommittee. com), which is one of the nation's largest amateur bodybuilding organisations. Its website provides information about upcoming competitions, several of which are held in the Los Angeles area.

Wine Tasting

Various Locations

Bristol Farms

310 233 4700 | www.bristolfarms.com

Upscale grocer Bristol Farms offers a reasonably priced wine tasting dinner every week. While a sommelier discusses the merits of each bottle, participants enjoy a small but delicious three-course meal and 'study' the different wines, making this a great place to bring a date. These dinners cost around $25 per person and tend to fill up quickly, so definitely make reservations.

737 Lamar St
Downtown
Map 8 F4 32

San Antonio Winery

323 223 1401 | www.sanantoniowinery.com

Founded in 1917, San Antonio Winery remains the only operating winery in Los Angeles. It even remained open while most of the other wineries in the area shut down during Prohibition. While early in its history the grapes came from the Los Angeles River basin, it now gets its grapes from farms in Napa and Monterey. The winery offers many types of California coastal wines to sample at its weekend tasting seminars, which start at $50. There is also an Italian restaurant in the winery.

2395 Glendale Blvd
Silver Lake
Map 8 D1 33

Silver Lake Wine

323 662 9024 | www.silverlakewine.com

This Silver Lake wine shop is known and loved by hipsters for its knowledgeable staff and affordable, thrice-weekly tastings. The store features a hand-picked selection of wines from smaller vineyards across the globe. The tasting sessions are an opportunity to treat your palate to something new. Sessions are held on Mondays, Thursdays and Sundays and can get pretty crowded, but in this laid-back atmosphere, reservations are only required for the Sunday session. Each session costs from $8 to $20 per person.

Spectator Sports

Los Angeles has a long sporting history, hosting the summer Olympics in both 1932 and 1984. The city's love affair with sports continues today, as celebrities and common folk alike turn out in droves for the city's many sporting events. With several professional sports clubs, including soccer, basketball, baseball and hockey, there is no shortage of events to attend throughout the year. The city is also home to a professional tennis tournament, golf tournament and frequent horse races at nearby tracks. LA lacks a professional American football team, and The University of Southern California Trojans are the most popular football team in the city. USC's cross-town rivals, the UCLA Bruins, play home games in the Rose Bowl in Pasadena, famous as the home of several Super Bowls, the NCAA Rose Bowl and Rose Parade. Tickets to events can be purchased in person, on the official team websites, or through ticket brokers like www.ticketmaster.com. Popular events such as the USC-UCLA football game and Lakers games will often sell out, so be sure to purchase your tickets as soon as they go on sale. It's a good idea to sign up for a team's email list to find out about upcoming ticket sales and special offers. Though there are reputable third-party ticket brokers (such as eBay's www.stubhub.com) where you can purchase tickets to sold-out events, exercise caution when shopping for tickets online or on the street.

American Football

Qualcomm Stadium
9449 Friars Rd
San Diego
Map 2 C1

San Diego Chargers
www.chargers.com

Located about 125 miles to the south, the San Diego Chargers are the closest professional football team to Los Angeles. Many Angelenos, feeling spurned by the departure of the LA Rams to St. Louis in 1994 and the LA Raiders to Oakland in 1995, have turned their allegiance to the Chargers. Over the last few seasons, the Chargers have transformed into perennial playoff contenders under the leadership of former NFL MVP LaDainian Tomlinson.

1001 Rose Bowl Dr
Pasadena
Map 2 E2

UCLA Bruins
http://uclabruins.cstv.com

After a few disappointing seasons, the UCLA Bruins have hired a new coach in the hope of turning themselves around. But no matter how poorly a season may be going, the Bruins always bring out their best for the game against rival USC. In fact, UCLA often relish spoiling USC's national championship hopes. They play their home games in the famous Rose Bowl in Pasadena, the site of the Rose Bowl game and four Super Bowls.

Rose Bowl 3911 S
Figueroa St
Exposition Park
Map 9 B4 **34**

University of Southern California Trojans
http://usctrojans.cstv.com

Without a professional football team in the city, the Trojans are the next best thing. The legendary football team has sent several players to the NFL and usually has a Heisman Trophy contender on its squad. The team has enjoyed success over the last decade, winning two national championships in 2003 and 2004. They play in the 92,000 seat Los Angeles Coliseum and games tend to sell out quickly. The game against cross-town rival UCLA is not to be missed.

Battle Chess

Those who grew up watching rugby may be surprised at the popularity of American football. Don't let the pads and helmets fool you, this sport is not for the faint of heart. Hard, open field tackles and intricate strategies combine to create what many consider the perfect sport for television.

Baseball

Angel Stadium 2000 E
Gene Autry Way
Anaheim
Map 2 F3

Los Angeles Angels of Anaheim
www.angels.mlb.com

After a surprise victory in the 2002 World Series, the Los Angeles Angels of Anaheim have been a powerhouse in Major League Baseball. The team is especially popular with residents of Orange County, which is where the stadium is located. The Angels are owned by the controversial Arturo Moreno, the first Hispanic owner of a major league franchise. He has sought to bolster the team's image and playoff chances by making some big free-agent acquisitions in the last few seasons, like superstar outfielder Vladimir Guerrero.

Dodger Stadium 1000
Elysian Park Ave
Echo Park
Map 8 E3

Los Angeles Dodgers
www.dodgers.mlb.com

With the recent hiring of legendary Yankees skipper, Joe Torre, Dodgers fans were swept up by a new feeling of excitement. The team has a storied past starting from its days in Brooklyn, and is famous for baseball greats like manager Tommy LaSorda. Though they haven't won a World Series since 1988, this is Los Angeles' team and many throughout the city 'bleed Dodger blue'.

Basketball

Staples Ctr 1111 S
Figueroa St
Downtown
Map 10 B2 35

Los Angeles Clippers
www.nba.com/clippers

Long known as the other basketball team playing in Los Angeles, the Clippers showed signs of life after winning their first playoff game in 13 years in 2006. The team is decidedly less glamorous than the Lakers and boasts fewer celebrity fans, but after their strong 2006 season, people around the city started to take notice. Comprised of a bunch of budding young stars like Elton Brand and Corey Maggette, this team is fun to watch.

Staples Ctr 1111 S
Figueroa St
Downtown
Map 10 B2 36

Los Angeles Lakers
www.nba.com/lakers

Basketball greats like Magic Johnson, Kareem Abdul-Jabbar, Shaquille O'Neal and Kobe Bryant have all worn the purple and gold uniform of the Los Angeles Lakers, one of the most eminent franchises in professional basketball. With 14 league championships and a slew of celebrity fans at every home game (like actor Jack Nicholson), the Lakers are also perhaps the most glamorous team in the league. The ever-popular team is now anchored by future Hall of Famer Kobe Bryant and legendary coach Phil Jackson, who uses Zen philosophy to calm his players. Recently, rumours have swirled around star Bryant, making many fans worried (or excited) about the prospect of a major roster change.

Golf

Riviera Country Club
1250 Capri Dr
Pacific Palisades
Map 2 C2

Northern Trust Open
www.northerntrustopen.com

Every year in February the game's top professionals convene in the Pacific Palisades for the $6.2 million Northern Trust Open, a PGA Tour Event. Spectators turn out in droves to follow their favourite players around the 6,987 yard course. The tournament is also televised on the Golf Channel and CBS.

Spectator Sports

Horse Racing

Hollywood Park

1050 S Prairie Ave
Inglewood
Map 2 C2

310 419 1500 | www.hollywoodpark.com

Founded in 1938 by several Hollywood luminaries, Hollywood Park is still the place to go if you feel like 'playing the ponies'. This racetrack features live horse races or simulcasts nearly every day of the week. Races occur at the track from April through July and from October through December. There is also a full casino and upscale restaurant on the premises. General admission is $7.

Santa Anita Park

285 W Huntington Dr
Arcadia
Map 2 E2

www.santaanita.com

The Santa Anita track hosts horse races from Thursday to Monday. The official season starts in December and runs to April. The track also hosts major events, like the Breeders Cup World Championships in October 2008 and 2009. Betters can also place money on races that are simulcast. General admission to the park starts at $5.

Ice Hockey

Anaheim Ducks

Honda Ctr 2695 E
Katella Ave
Anaheim
Map 2 F3

www.anaheimducks.com

Despite being only 14 years old, the Anaheim Ducks are the National Hockey League's reigning Stanley Cup champions. The Walt Disney Company founded the team as the 'Mighty Ducks', after a movie with the same name. Since then, the team has grown out of its cute name. The Ducks play in Anaheim in the Honda Center, and their main local rivals are the Los Angeles Kings.

Los Angeles Kings

Staples Ctr 1111 S
Figueroa St
Downtown
Map 10 B2 **37**

www.lakings.com

The Kings have been Los Angeles's hockey team since the 1960s. Since then they have had several players elevated to the Hall of Fame, including 'The Great One', Wayne Gretsky. While hockey doesn't enjoy the popularity of other professional sports in the city, thousands of diehard fans flock to every home game at the Staples Center.

Soccer

Chivas USA

Home Depot Ctr 18400
Avalon Blvd Suite 200
Carson
Map 2 D3

http://chivas.usa.mlsnet.com

A recent member of Major League Soccer, Chivas USA also plays in the Home Depot Center in Carson. Though only founded in 2004, the team is quite popular. Its parent club, Club Deportivo Guadalajara, is the most popular soccer club in the Mexican professional leagues. The team won the Western Conference in the 2007 season and its goalkeeper was named best in the league. Games are televised by the Fox Sports Network and broadcast in Spanish on KTNQ.

Los Angeles Galaxy

Home Depot Ctr 18400
Avalon Blvd
Carson
Map 2 D3

www.lagalaxy.com

The arrival of David Beckham in 2007 brought international headlines national attention to the Los Angeles Galaxy, which play in a stadium designed specifically for soccer in Carson. Following the superstar signing, the team actually had a sub-par season, but it is generally considered to have one of the top squads in the league, making the playoffs for 10 consecutive seasons and winning league championships in 2002 and in 2005. Games are televised by the Fox Sports Network and tickets to home games are reasonably priced.

Speedway

500 Speedway Dr
Irwindale
Map 2 E1

Irwindale Speedway

626 358 1100 | www.irwindalespeedway.com

Just 30 minutes outside the city, Irwindale Speedway offers an intimate 6,000 seat setting to watch auto races. The short half-mile oval track hosts a variety of races with cars such as late models, super trucks and mini-stock cars. The racing season starts in March, and Irwindale has other family-friendly events like a Demolition Derby (where cars smash into one another) and a 'drifting' competition. There is also a dragstrip to watch racers put the pedal to the metal.

Auto Club Speedway
9300 Cherry Ave
Fontana
Map 2 E2

NASCAR

800 944 7223 | www.californiaspeedway.com

NASCAR is the most popular spectator sport in America. Races routinely pack in over 100,000 spectators, each with a strict loyalty to a particular driver. The California Speedway has been the centre of NASCAR events in Southern California since 1997. The two-mile D-shaped oval track sees racers break speeds of 200 miles per hour. The racing season runs from February to September. The track recently added a FanZone, where fans can shop, listen to live music, or dine at a Wolfgang Puck restaurant.

Tennis

LA Tennis Ctr 555
Westwood Plaza
Westwood
Map 4 B2 **38**

Countrywide Classic

www.countrywideclassic.com

Since 1927, some of the best professional male tennis players have visited Los Angeles for the Countrywide Classic (formerly the Mercedes Benz Cup) in August, a tournament in the US Open series. The players compete for over $500,000 in prize money in front of the 10,000 fans. Past champions include Andre Agassi, Arthur Ashe, Rod Laver and John McEnroe. For those who can't make it in person, the tournament is broadcast on ESPN 2.

UCLA Bruins recover a fumble

Big serve at the Countrywide Classic

Sports & Leisure Facilities

Los Angeles' proximity to all kinds of natural exercise and adventure is often overlooked. Oceans, lakes, mountains and flatlands; all are within a two-hour radius. Working 50 hours a week, managing to sustain a significant other and keeping your body and mind in fine-tuned shape is all made possible by the city's remarkable sports and leisure facilities. They bend for every budget and innovate to make your working-out routine as painless as possible.

Luxury Health Clubs

431 W 7th St
Downtown
Map 10 D3 **41**

Los Angeles Athletic Club
213 625 2211 | www.laac.com

Founded in 1880, the LAAC has a storied history as the gathering place of Hollywood legends. An air of mystery and old bourgeoisie lingers, and is reinforced by the presence of local politicos. Besides every top-shelf exercise machine, sports court and a heated pool, this club has two restaurants, two bars and a poolside continental breakfast. You can also rent a room at the sports club's own hotel located next door.

Various Locations

The Spectrum
877 278 3787 | www.spectrumclubs.com

The Spectrum maintains a resort feel through its comprehensive workout amenities, full-service spa and salon and healthy cafe. Cardio equipment with individual TVs, a cycling studio, kid and teen zones, a martial arts programme and on-staff dieticians set the Spectrum above the standard gym pack.

1835 Sepulveda Blvd
West LA
Map 4 B4 **42**

The Sports Club LA
310 473 1447 | www.thesportsclubla.com

This is the most prestigious and indulgent sports club the city has to offer. High ceilings that rival a Gothic church, valet parking, a driving range, outdoor sun deck, and luxury cafe (with a complete wine list and full bar), only offer a hint at this club's expansiveness. So expensive they don't dare to advertise enrolment prices, this club has everything you need for exercise and well-being in spades, and a fully staffed salon and spa to boot.

Community Centres

Various Locations

YMCA
213 380 6448 | www.ymcala.org

The closest thing to a public health club you can get, the city's YMCAs provide all sorts of amenities for prices you can afford. The 'Y' emphasises well-being on all levels and for all ages. For an average of $50 a month you get unlimited access to indoor basketball courts, group exercise classes, lap pools and other gym essentials. An added bonus of the YMCA is its diverse assortment of artistic workshops and classes (see p.212), as well as free internet access and free childcare services, and a non-competitive atmosphere for personal growth.

Gyms

For the guy who's trying to lose his college beer gut, the girl who needs to blow off some post-work steam, or someone competing in the world's strongest man competition, there is a gym here for you. Bare bones machinery, free weights or a cardio workout from a group class of striptease, gyms are sparred none of LA's wonderful eccentricities.

Various Locations

24 Hour Fitness
866 819 7414 | www.24hourfitness.com

This massive chain has locations close to your home or office no matter where you live. 24 Hour constantly offers attractive sign-up deals, reasonable monthly rates, and innovative aerobics classes. With pools, saunas, tennis, basketball and racquetball courts, and free group classes, the economy of this gym is just the icing on the accessible cake.

Various Locations

Bally Total Fitness
800 515 2582 | www.ballyfitness.com

Only second to 24 Hour when it comes to locations, Ballys is consistently innovative and challenging. It offers state-of-the-art cardio and weight-training equipment as well as classes like 'Kwando' (a hybrid of Karate and Tae kwon do) and 'Cardio Hoops' (hula-hooping for grown-ups). The gym offers a 30 day free trial membership.

2516 Hyperion Ave
Silver Lake
Map 8 C1 39

Bodybuilder's
323 668 0802 | www.bodybuildersgym.com

This classic gym makes getting in shape the high point of your day. The boutique pricing is well worth it considering the immense two-storey facilities. Bodybuilder's amazing assortment of magazines, friendliest of patrons, and comprehensive list of cardio and strength-training machines makes it this neighbourhood's best kept secret.

Barry's Bootcamp

This trendy programme is 30 minutes of treadmill cardio, free weights and actual military exercises are combined into one hour of concentrated, no-nonsense fitness. Each programme is a month long and five days a week. Each 'enlistee' must pay $290 and reserve an entire month. (www.barrysbootcamp.com)

8000 Sunset Blvd
West Hollywood
Map 5 C2 40

Crunch
323 654 4550 | www.crunch.com

Nestled in trendy WeHo, this multi-storey gym hosts hardbodies from across the city. There are more than enough cardio and weight-training machines, and unconventional exercise classes like Nap-time, Kama Sutra Yoga and Cardio Striptease offer enticing variations from humdrum exercise. Crunch heavily emphasises the use of its well-trained personal trainers. Beware of your pocketbook, it's not cheap.

Various Locations

LA Fitness
888 889 0984 | www.lafitness.com

With a group class schedule consisting of Basic Yoga and Cycling, Mat Pilates, Boot Camp Conditioning, Hip-Hop Dance and Kickbox Cardio, there is something to get your blood pumping from 05:30 in the morning until 20:00 at night. Racquetball and basketball courts are available, and some branches also organise competitive events.

Gyms

24 Hour Fitness	Various Locations	866 819 7414
Absolution	West Hollywood	310 657 7878
Bally Total Fitness	Various Locations	800 515 2582
Bodies in Motion	Wilshire	323 933 5875
Body Maxx	Downtown	323 655 8365
Bodybuilder's	Silver Lake	323 668 0802
Century Sports Club	West LA	323 954 1020
Crunch	West Hollywood	323 654 4550
Equinox	West Hollywood	310 289 1900
Gold's Gym	Downtown	213 688 1441
Hollywood Gym	Hollywood	323 845 1420
LA Fitness	Various Locations	888 889 0984
Train	West Hollywood	310 657 4140
Ultra Body Fitness	West Hollywood	323 464 5300
Vert Fitness	Santa Monica	310 264 8385

Great things can come in small packages…

Perfectly proportioned to fit in your pocket, these marvellous mini guidebooks make sure you don't just get the holiday you paid for, but rather the one that you dreamed of.

Explorer Mini Visitors' Guides
Maximising your holiday, minimising your hand luggage

Well-Being

There's a reason LA is known for its fad diets or off-the-wall exercise routines. Traffic, stress and relentless work ethic need measured ways to relieve anxiety. If a health practice can relieve stress while helping shed pounds, LA has thought of it. Working hard leads to playing hard, and for many that means spa treatments and deep breathing exercises like yoga, Pilates or meditation. The looks and mental well-being of LA's city-goers are well catered to, and the city is always one step ahead of the game when it comes to beauty enhancements.

Hairdressers

1541 Echo Park Ave
Echo Park
Map 8 D2 **43**

Lucas

213 250 7992 | www.lucasechopark.com

Lucas represents Echo Park's renaissance, sandwiched between a coffee shop of bohemian proportions and an artist-owned women's boutique that makes clothes worthy to hang in the Louvre. Hair styling is skilled and ingenious, so while prices are a little steep, with women's cuts starting at $75 and men's at $55, the quaint intimacy of this studio-sized salon puts you at ease. An extra perk? There is an on-staff aesthetician who can perform oxygenisation, enzyme therapy or anti-bacterial facials.

1724 N Vermont Ave
Los Feliz
Map 8 A1 **44**

Purple Circle

323 666 2965 | www.purple-circle.com

Tired of your old hairstylist interpreting 'crazy' to mean extra layers? Purple Circle will give you dreads, extensions, pink hair or just an innovative cut, depending on your preference. Staffed by the friendliest bunch of eclectics this side of Hollywood Boulevard, there are rumours of cupcake offerings upon arrival and full refunds if for some reason you are not happy with your haircut. Creative minds lead to creative hands, and this salon has both.

Various Locations

Rudy's Barber Shop

323 661 6535 | www.rudysbarbershop.com

Don't let the hipster vibe of this warehouse barber shop intimidate you; Rudy's is the worst kept secret in the neighbourhood. With a retro paint job and no-frills decor consisting of concrete floors and basic black pillars, Rudy's is cheap, good, and requires no appointment. Drop in and wait for your name to be called by any one of the trendily clad employees. This is one of the few places in Los Angeles where a girl can get an amazing haircut for $25 and not leave crying.

321 Santa
Monica Blvd
Santa Monica
Map 3 B3 **45**

Vidal Sassoon Hair Academy

310 255 0011 | www.sassoon.com

Normally 'surprise' isn't a word you want anywhere near your haircut, but this highly qualified, student-staffed hair salon does styling justice. With a grab bag element that comes with the learning curve, this salon is all about the basics. Usually the price is $15 a head, making the experience financially accessible, but it's slightly more costly when it comes to pre-cut anguish and wait time. As scary as it sounds, these are not novices running around with scissors and clippers, but trained hair stylists on their way to employment.

Pricey Perms

For some, even the hippest hairdos are wothless if they aren't accompanied by a celebrity name drop. For a cut with kudos, make an appointment with Cristophe (www.cristophe.com), Jose Eber (www.joseeberatelier.com) or Prive (www.privesalon.com) and prepare to unload that wad of cash that's been weighing you down.

Health Spas

Other options **Massage** p.250, **Sports & Leisure Facilities** p.245

Various Locations

Burke Williams Spa

866 239 6635 | www.burkewilliamsspa.com

Paying for a bath has never made so much sense! Herbal, seaweed, and milk baths for less then $40 are the best deal at this boutique spa. Although massage sessions average $125 per hour, they're thorough, professional, and diverse roots (Thai, Shiatsu, and even Lymphatic massages are offered). Consider it a personal investment. Manicures and pedicures, exfoliating facials, and detox body wraps are spa standards and allow you to combine them in a speciality entitled 'A Day at the Spa'. Although the price tag is steep at $500, these entire day packages allow you or someone you love, to indulge in every category of physical and spiritual treatment the spa offers.

8253 Santa Monica Blvd
West Hollywood
Map 5 C3 46

Euphoria

323 656 9944

With a narrowed focus, Euphoria day spa focuses on massage therapy, skin care and waxing. Thorough in all areas, the shortest massage time available is 75 minutes, requiring a purchase price of $110 but ensuring you leave satisfied. Facials begin with an aesthetician consultation, picking from the array of specialised skin products to find what is best suited to your needs. Taking into account your work and social habits, living situation and average diet, a routine for home use will also be recommended free with your facial. Waxing prices are modest, and employ top-of-the-line European waxes to make an already uncomfortable situation slightly less so.

331 N Larchmont Blvd
Larchmont Village
Map 7 E1 47

Le Petite Retreat Day Spa

323 466 1028 | www.lepetiteretreat.com

Specialising in couples' treatments including hot stone massages, rejuvenating facials, and champagne bubble baths, this tasteful island-themed resort makes even bill time relaxing. Nestled in the boutique neighbourhood of Hollywood known as Larchmont Village, Le Petite was designed by a Feng Shui master and blessed by Tibetan monks. The atmosphere of spirituality saturates the aroma-soaked air. While complete hour massages can run a tab of almost $200, speciality treatments like hydro therapeutic 'Green Tea Escape' are only $45, an economy price for five-star relaxation.

Le Petite Retreat Day Spa

Murad Medical Spa

2141 Rosecrans Ave
El Segundo
Map 2 C3

310 726 2040 | www.murad.com/spa

Murad products have become a well-known health and beauty commodity through its appearances in multiple TV infomercials. Founded by Dr Murad himself, the Murad Medical Spa in the south bay has a level of science and professionalism that many other spas lack. With competitive prices, this spa merges a clinical outlook with pampering, and uses factual research to conceive of spa procedures that maximise your enjoyment and health benefits.

Ona Spa

7373 Beverly Blvd
West LA
Map 7 C1 48

323 931 4242 | www.onaspa.com

Practicality and outlandish LA luxury come together in this popular Westside spa. If a simple massage is what you need, it's available, but not without sorting through wades of other women awaiting medical cosmetic procedures from Botox to laser hair removal, collagen implants and Brite Smile teeth-whitening treatments. While not exactly the poster child for simplicity and Zen, this spa knows its audience and appeals to beauty concerns across the board.

Trilogy Day Spa

1301 Manhattan Ave
Hermosa Beach
Map 2 D3

310 318 3511 | www.trilogyspa.com

The first thing to know about this spa, and probably its greatest asset, is its proximity to one of Southern California's most beautiful beaches. The spa encompasses the beach community's air of simplicity, offering spa staples at reasonable prices, such as an hour-long massage for $85. Make a day out of a Trilogy procedure, and take the coastal route from the city. Leave some time after your paid relaxation appointment to enjoy all the free relaxation the city has to offer: a clean beach, downtown boutiques and a temperature that never drops below 20°C (70°F).

Massage

Other options **Health Spas** p.249, **Sports & Leisure Facilities** p.245, **Reflexology & Massage Therapy** p.120

An ancient art now enhanced with scientific progress, massage in LA has become commonplace. A concentration of Thai and Chinese massage parlours dominate much of the Eastside as well as some of Hollywood. Most specialise in culture-specific massage techniques and often exclude additional spa treatments that many Americanised massage parlours have adopted. While hiring a masseuse is still common practice, especially for those in the upper economic tier, massage is now for the masses, ranging from $50 per hour steals to $125 per hour indulgences, complete with champagne and ridiculously high thread count sheets.

dtox Day Spa

3206 Los Feliz Blvd
Los Feliz
Map 2 D1

323 665 3869 | www.dtoxdayspa.com

Organic. Zen. Minimalist. Put these three things in a suburb of LA that more closely resembles a ghost town, and the recipe for peace of mind is undeniable. Prices are higher as you pay for the atmosphere; an atrium, a waterfall, chaise lounges, skylights to harness the natural soothing of the sun, and a giant centrepiece Buddha give this massage parlour more flavour than most. Dtox's Friday 'Happy Hours' are the 21st century's hybrid of self-healing. $39 will purchase music, hors d'oeuvres, wine, and a choice of any 20 minute spa service, including anything from a custom facial to a Reiki session.

Various Locations
Healing Hands Massage and Wellness Center
323 782 3900 | www.healinghandswc.com

While current trends have turned massage parlours into boutique spas with outlandish prices and unnecessary adornments, Healing Hands sacrifices none of its professionalism and tranquillity while still maintaining drastically lower prices. Paying a low $55 for an hour massage, there are on-staff specialists in Shiatsu, Sport, Reflexology, and even pre and post-natal massage. Chiropractors are also on site, ensuring that if recreational massage isn't effective enough the professionals are there to step in.

Meditation

Los Angeles has learned to hybridise everything. In other places, it might be near impossible to work a full-time job while maintaining a spiritually settled life, but not here. LA uses its melting pot status to enhance all facets of life, and spiritual enhancement is no exception. Meditation is now accessible in your car, home or even at work, as the contemporary meditation gurus shape enlightenment in the city's favourite format; to go.

Buddha takes many forms as he surfaces in your local chain gym, your 'Meditation for Dummies' guidebook, and your car audio-led pursuit of chakra location. Learning to use downtime, no matter how brief, allows one to keep a balanced mind even in the busiest of circumstances.

928 S New Hampshire Blvd
Map 8 A4 **49**
International Buddhist Meditation Center
213 384 0850 | www.urbandharma.org/ibmc/

Founded almost 40 years ago by a Vietnamese Zen Master and professor at the insistence of his UCLA students, this meditation centre is legitimate and respects Buddhism's historical routes. Zen meditation sessions twice a week, training for monks and Dharma teachers, traditional Buddhist celebrations, and even a residency programme that rents out unfurnished rooms to small groups of individuals so that they can feel the spiritual benefits of facilitated community, this meditation forum is thorough to say the least.

963 Colorado Blvd
Eagle Rock
Map 2 D1
Shambhala Meditation Center
323 255 5472 | www.la.shambhala.org

An organisation founded around Shambhala Buddhism, this instructional centre for Shambhala practice has two locations: on the Eastside in Eagle Rock and the Westside in ocean side Santa Monica. Drop in any Thursday for a free introductory lesson and learn more about this meditation centre that is also a school of art and Buddhism. Four days a week the centre offers public 'sittings' for two to three-hour blocks, where questions are accepted and guidance happily given on how to improve your meditation techniques and overall spiritual life.

1845 S Bundy
West LA
Map 3 C1 **50**
Siddha Meditation Center
310 207 9909 | www.symcla.org

Siddha is considered a new age concept of religion and yoga practice, based on certain strains of Hindu spiritualism. Siddha yoga is a physical facilitator to help the individual realise divinity within, and the Siddha Meditation Center revolves around that concept. Every Saturday there is an orientation for newcomers that is interesting to attend even if actual class attendance will be minimal. Hatha Yoga classes are Mondays, Wednesdays, Fridays, and Family Satsang on Saturday is where public gathers to discuss scriptures and relate them intimately to contemporary life.

Pilates

5225 Wilshire Blvd
Fairfax
Map 7 D2 **51**

Core Pilates NYC
323 939 6333 | www.corepilatesnyc.com
Core Pilates trains future Pilates teachers and teaches public classes at reasonable rates. Sessions are comprehensive and conducive to getting beginners happily hooked. The instructor training programme builds upon classical Pilates to incorporate the teacher's unique strengths and methods. Although the comprehensive training package might be too financially steep for a mere Pilates enthusiast, the educational seminars pursue specific Pilates niches like pregnancy or diet and nutrition.

1947 ½ Hillhurst Ave
Los Feliz
Map 8 D1

Mind Body Fitness
323 661 2711 | www.mind-bodyfitness.net
Pilates for the dedicated, Mind Body Fitness takes the spiritual and physical act of Pilates seriously. Eight private or small group sessions are required for all beginners to ensure a proper start. Although these introductory classes are fairly expensive at up to $65 each, if you plan on continuing down the Pilates path you may consider it an investment, as standard mat classes are only $15 and have well-rounded, heartfelt instructors.

1512 N Gardner St
West Hollywood
Map 5 E2 **52**

Pilates By The Park
323 845 9744 | www.pilatesbythepark.com
A simple, airy, window-framed room with views of expansive park trees and blue skies is the perfect setting to increase the productivity of a Pilates session. Group classes cost $25, and single and semi-private sessions are available – often for bargain deals if you book five or more at a time. Whether you are after a perfect dancer's body, looking for a change of pace from your gym rat workout routine, or merely want to try a low-impact high result workout method, this studio is a great way to ease yourself in.

215 N Larchmont Blvd
Larchmont Village
Map 7 E1 **53**

Studio B Pilates
323 461 8663 | www.studiobpilates.com
An exercise in strength and toning, Studio B instructors combine choreography and kinesiology to develop lean muscles and adjust skeletal alignments to benefit the patron. Group sessions are $15 per person, or $120 for 10 sessions.

Reiki

2016 Hillhurst Ave
Los Feliz
Map 2 D1

Being In LA
323 665 9355 | www.beinginla.com
This wellness centre is unique in its emphasis on understanding, compassion, and individual help. Offering professional hair styling and multiple forms of massage in addition to Reiki, you can heal your spiritual ailments, relax your wound-up muscles, and make yourself feel beautiful at the same time. Leaving the wellness centre with a happy heart and haircut is worth the $75 Reiki session and $100 haircut.

808 Manhattan Ave
Manhattan Beach
Map 2 C3

Body in Balance
310 406 1910 | www.bodyinbalancedayspa.com
Located in pristine Manhattan Beach, where the pavements are clean and the air smells like the ocean, Body in Balance is one of the top holistic healing centres in Southern California. Reiki is performed by specialists who transfer energy between themselves and the patron, cleansing what we'd commonly think of as 'bad vibes' in order to provide peace and a sense of sanctuary. More relaxing than massage and longer lasting than a facial, Reiki at Body In Balance is $55 for 30 minutes and $75 for an hour.

Tai Chi

While Tai Chi seemed to peak in mainstream popularity in the early 1990s, historic Tai Chi academies, as well as new wave outdoor group Tai Chi programmes, still penetrate the city with a peaceful vengeance. Often combined with Karate or Tae Kwon Do, this slow-movement martial art is a very particular niche, so classes are usually welcoming. Gyms like 24 Hour Fitness (p.246) often offer Tai Chi classes later in the evening, presenting them in the same category as yoga or meditation.

1433 2nd St
Santa Monica
Map 3 B4 **54**

Beijing Tai Chi & Kung Fu Academy

310 396 8482 | www.beijingkungfu.com

Founded upon the historical Chinese Guoshu Institute that was destroyed during the second world war, this academy aims to resurrect the institute's wishes of preserving the art of Kung Fu. With an emphasis on the delicate balance between fighting and dance, Kung Fu themes permeate the Tai Chi programme. The level of class you choose to attend is entirely up to you, allowing for personal growth within a set structure.

1723 Hillhurst Ave
Los Feliz
Map 8 B1 **55**

Buck Sam Kong Kung Fu

323 664 8882 | www.bucksamkongkungfu.com

Originally from Hong Kong, Sifu Kong began studying Kung Fu at the tender age of 6. His dedication to the finer forms of martial arts has continued through his move to Los Angeles and the creation of his own martial arts school in Los Feliz. While Kung Fu classes at all levels of expertise dominate weekdays, Tai Chi reserves its contemplative position every Saturday morning at 09:00.

Yoga

700 W 1st St
Downtown
Map 10 E2 **56**

Bikram Yoga Downtown LA

213 626 9642 | www.bikramyogadowntownla.com

Bikram is a particular style of yoga that's done in a temperature-controlled studio of up to 46°C (115°F). While completing a routine of familiar yoga stretches and poses, the excessive temperature expedites bodily cleansing by completely cycling the bodies oxygenated blood, stimulating every organ and gland, and even aiding in weight loss. This intensified form of yoga comes at a reasonable price of $15 per session, and the studio offers incentives to commit to more classes.

2809 W Sunset Blvd
Echo Park
Map 8 C2 **57**

Urth Yoga

213 483 9642 | www.urthyoga.com

This yoga studio built entirely out of natural products (made with no toxins) brings environmental friendliness to whole new heights. Going the extra mile to purify the highly spiritual yoga space, Urth Yoga caters to all levels of yoga-ers, and conveniently holds one and a half hour classes all day every day. Proving that East LA corners the market in forward thinking, classes are only $15 a session, and if it's your first time you may purchase unlimited monthly access for only $49.

Various Locations

YogaWorks

323 464 1276 | www.yogaworks.com

YogaWorks' studios are strategically placed around Los Angeles, conveniently nestled among popular shopping and dining areas. The most cutting edge and contemporary in yoga, these studios have four levels of student difficulty, organised retreats, corporate yoga, and even 'mommy and me' sessions where you and your young one can harness your chakras.

Thinking about a career overseas?

Working abroad already?

Join the Expat Network
The organisation that can't do enough for its people.
We can help in your jobsearch, or assist you in every aspect of your life abroad.
We have already helped thousands of expatriates since our inception in 1989.
Talk to other expats on our forums, read expat-related features in our monthly magazine Nexus. Go to
www.expatnetwork.com
to find out what you are missing.

We can help you find work overseas, advise about most aspects of working and living in another country, introduce you to others doing the same thing, you can even talk to them on the expat network forums. We can send gifts to your people at home, link you to key clients and recruiters or even act on your behalf like your own virtual P.A. You get a great magazine every month AND a list of 500 contacts every year*.
You can call us for answers or a shoulder if something goes wrong.
Oh! and you get to talk to real human beings - we are definitely not computers and we absolutely DO NOT work from any kind of script.

* free publication if you join for a minimum of twelve months as a result of reading this advertisement. Cannot be used with any other offer.

Shopping

Shopping

Shopping

New York may be the headquarters for high couture magazines, but Los Angeles usually gets the credit for the trendy fashions worn by celebrities. With paparazzi feverishly working high-profile streets like Melrose, Montana Ave and Robertson Boulevard, it's no wonder that some of the hottest boutiques on the west coast wind up in the pages of *In Style*, *People* and *Entertainment Weekly*. When the stars are photographed in hip new clothes, the styles soon trickle down to the masses, if only in knockoff versions.

LA is the birthplace of the business casual look. It boasts more bikini boutiques than any other state, and it definitely had a big hand in starting the whole premium denim craze. It's where you'll notice a woman pairing a vintage sweater with a Dolce & Gabbana skirt, or a guy looking movie star handsome in just a plain white tee and jeans. There is a certain edginess to LA fashions: a touch of fake fur on a jacket collar, a jean that's cut daringly low, and a shirt that sparkles all have an unmistakable west coast charm. Part of the fun of shopping on Melrose Avenue or Rodeo Drive is the coolness factor, but mostly shopping in this city is an adventure. Every neighbourhood offers something different and you never know what you'll discover around the next corner.

Online Shopping

Shopping from home has become a favourite pastime for many people and you'll find an increasing number of stores in Los Angeles with an internet presence. Some stores allow you to order merchandise online and pick it up at the store closest to your location. Store policies vary as far as international shipping. Many stores like Lands End charge additional fees for shipping items to Canada, while others ship packages strictly in the United States to avoid dealing with customs regulations. Internet purchases from international locations are subject to customs inspection and some items are prohibited from entering the country, such as animal products on the endangered species list and plants that could be harbouring insects. The Home Shopping Network and competitor QVC allow shoppers to view apparel, jewellery and home decor items on television and place their order online or by phone. Amazon.com is the most well-known online shopping site. Offering a plethora of merchandise, often at deep discounts, it combines a vast merchandise selection with the convenience of shopping from home and low shipping charges. Many online retailers offer free shipping if you purchase a minimum amount. Albertsons and Vons offer grocery shopping online with a small charge for delivery service.

Online Shopping

www.albertsons.com	Select groceries online and get them delivered to your home.
www.amazon.com	Apparel, books, CDs, DVDs, tools, small appliances, and gifts.
www.bluefly.com	Close-out prices on a wide variety of trendy and designer fashions.
www.ebay.com	Auction site with new and used items up for bids.
www.fandango.com	Order movie tickets in advance and pick up at your local theatre.
www.fragrance.net	Popular fragrances available for purchase with dollars, pounds and euros.
www.hsn.com	View a variety of products on TV and order online.
www.landsend.com	Moderately priced casual apparel for the whole family.
www.netflix.com	Choose movies online and receive rental videos by mail.
www.overstocks.com	Deep discounts on apparel, bedding, home decor, electronics, rugs.
www.qvc.com	Order products online after seeing items shown on TV.
www.sephora.com	Beauty product superstore with international sites.
www.vons.com	Choose food and beverages for home delivery.

Clothing Sizes ◄

Figuring out your size isn't rocket science, just a bit of a pain. Firstly, check the label – international sizes are often printed on them. Secondly, check the store – they will often have a helpful conversion chart on display. Otherwise, a UK size is always two higher than a US size (so a UK 10 is actually a US 6. To convert European sizes into US sizes, just subtract 32 (so a European 38 is actually a US 6). To convert European sizes into UK sizes, a 38 is roughly a 10, but some countries size smaller so you'll have to try clothes on to be sure. Italian sizing is different again.

Refunds & Exchanges

Store policies vary regarding refunds and exchanges, but most will provide a full refund if an item is returned in good condition with a receipt. Many stores allow refunds for up to 30 days with a receipt, and some with more liberal policies (like Nordstrom, p.305) will accept merchandise returned up to 90 days later even without a receipt. Returns regarding electronics and software vary, so it's best to check the store policy and the warranty before you purchase an expensive item. If a clothing or home decor item still has tags and you lose the receipt you can still get a refund as long as it's a line the store carries. If the item appears to have been worn or damaged, you will probably be out of luck. Many stores have strict policies that evening gowns, cocktail dresses and expensive men's suits may not be returned if the tags are missing. Some stores have begun keeping track of what they call chronic returns. If a person returns more than six items within a two-month period, for example, they might be denied a refund the next time.

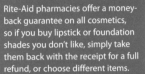

Beauty Insurance

Rite-Aid pharmacies offer a money-back guarantee on all cosmetics, so if you buy lipstick or foundation shades you don't like, simply take them back with the receipt for a full refund, or choose different items.

Consumer Rights

The sales staff at most stores will approach to ask if you need assistance. Smile, be polite and let them know if you need help or if you want to continue browsing on your own. Most will respect your wishes but if an associate seems too aggressive or pushy, ask for more time alone to shop. Sometimes you may encounter uncooperative or rude salespeople when you have a complaint or need to return an item. Ask to speak with the supervisor and attempt to resolve the issue. For larger companies you may file a complaint with the company headquarters by phone, letter or email. Most major retailers have corporate offices listed on their websites. If you paid for a defective item with your credit card, contact the issuer and file a complaint. They can put a hold on payment to the retailer until the situation is resolved or credit funds back to your account if fraud or deception is involved. If you encounter poor service, faulty merchandise or rude treatment at a store you can file a complaint with the Consumer Affairs Department (www.consumeraffairs.com) or the Better Business Bureau (www.labbb.org). The State Attorney General's office (http://ag.ca.gov/consumers) also keeps consumer complaints on file and looks into shady practices. Most stores and shopping malls have security personnel on staff. If you feel that you are being harassed, followed or feel uneasy about a fellow shopper's behaviour, find a security person and alert them to the problem.

Shipping

Most stores will arrange for shipping. Fees vary regarding international shipments. Depending on the size and destination of the item, it's smart to compare prices among different shippers. UPS and DHL are used most often for international shipping, but the United States Postal Service also ships to hundreds of international destinations. Costs of shipping generally depend on the weight, distance and urgency of delivery.

Shipping		
DHL	800 225 5345	www.dhl.com
FedEx	800 463 3339	www.fedex.com
UPS	800 742 5877	www.ups.com
United States Postal Service	800 275 8777	www.usps.com

Visiting the websites of the major shippers can give you an idea of prices, delivery ranges and other services available such as shipment tracking and delivery confirmation. You may also be able to view and print necessary customs forms for your shipment.

How To Pay

Most stores accept cash, credit cards, ATM cards and debit cards. American Express, MasterCard and Visa are the most widely accepted cards, with Discover, Carte Blanche and Diners Club cards accepted in fewer places. Many stores also accept personal cheques and traveller's cheques with proper identification. Most farmers market vendors and flea market merchants only accept cash. The increasing ease of using ATM and debit cards has resulted in people carrying less cash and using their bank cards to pay for purchases. However, be aware that sometimes the machines that process the cards in the store can be out of order, so it's wise to always carry some cash with you.

Bargaining

Bargaining is not that common in the United States, although there are exceptions. Typically buyers haggle over the price of new and used cars and some big-ticket items like furniture, electronics and appliances. Many electronics stores and car dealers will meet or beat the price of a competitor if you show them an ad with a price published in a newspaper. Bargaining is also acceptable with street vendors and at flea markets where the merchant is more likely to give you a quantity discount. Many vendors will also lower their prices at the end of the day so they will have fewer items to pack up and move. Bartering over produce tends to be frowned on at farmer's markets since the prices are already low.

Flashy storefront on Melrose Avenue

Even the road sign is posh

Don't Drink And Drive
There are stiff penalties for driving while intoxicated, and driving with an open container of beer, wine or liquor will also net you a big fine.

Alcohol

Other options **Drinks** p.343, **On the Town** p.343

Finding a place to buy alcohol in California is easy, but you must show valid ID proving you are over 21. Alcohol may only be sold between the hours of 06:00 and 02:00. Supermarkets, pharmacies and convenience stores sell a variety of beer and wines, often at sale prices. Those seeking a broader selection will find much to choose from at Trader Joe's, known for its award winning and inexpensive Charles Shaw label. Cost Plus carries an impressive selection of discounted domestic and imported wines, plus hard-

Wine for sale

to-find beers. Many neighbourhoods have liquor stores that also carry deli foods and snacks. Depending where you shop and the brand, a six pack of beer will run around $8.99, a bottle of basic white wine around $12 and a bottle of vodka around $15. Buying liquor from duty free shops at LAX is more trouble than it's worth due to strict security and customs regulations.

7100 Santa Monica Blvd
West Hollywood
Map 6 A3 **1**

Beverages and More

323 882 6971 | www.bevmo.com

Known by the nickname BevMo, this beverage warehouse store specialises in booze of all kinds at discount prices. Whether you are buying in quantity for holiday gifts or stocking up for a party, you'll find an impressive selection of wine, beer and spirits, plus glassware, cheeses and gourmet gift baskets. Prices tend to be cheaper than liquor marts, and the store regularly schedules tastings and educational lectures by wine experts. Club Bev, the free store membership card features special discounts each month, a newsletter and other perks. Other locations include Burbank, Pasadena, Van Nuys, Glendale, Torrance, Northridge and Long Beach.

Alcohol

7-11	na	Various Locations	800 255 0711	www.7eleven.com
Beverages and More	7100 Santa Monica Blvd	West Hollywood	323 882 6971	www.bevmo.com
Bottle Rock	3747 Main St	Culver City	310 836 9463	www.bottlerock.net
Colorado Wine Co	2214 Colorado Blvd	Eagle Rock	3234 781 985	www.cowineco.com
Cost Plus	na	Various Locations	877 967 5362	www.worldmarket.com
K&L Wine Merchants	1400 Vine St	Hollywood	323 464 9463	www.klwines.com
Red Carpet Wine	400 E Glenoaks Blvd	Glendale	8182 475 544	www.redcarpetwine.com
Silver Lake Wine	2395 Glendale Blvd	Silver Lake	323 662 9024	www.silverlakewine.com
Trader Joe's	na	Various Locations	800 746 7857	www.traderjoes.com
Wally's Wine & Spirits	2107 Westwood Blvd	Westwood	310 475 0606	www.wallywine.com

K&L Wine Merchants

1400 Vine St
Hollywood
Map 6 C2 **2**

323 464 9463 | www.klwines.com
One of the most highly rated wine shops on the west coast, this 9,000 square foot shop has earned praise from *Wine Spectator, Gentleman's Quarterly, The Wall Street Journal* and *Time*. Offering highly experienced staff and a selection from the top wine regions of the world, it's the kind of shop where wine enthusiasts can discover new labels and beginners can learn much from talking to fellow shoppers. Prices span the gamut from under $25 to pricey vintages sought after by connoisseurs. Tastings are held on Thursdays from 17:00 to 19:00 and Saturdays from 14:00 to 17:00.

Red Carpet Wine & Spirits

400 E Glenoaks Blvd
Glendale
Map 2 D1

818 247 5544 | www.redcarpetwine.com
Featuring an impressive choice of domestic and imported labels, this speciality shop offers wine and spirits to fit every budget plus a good selection of high-end liquors for special occasions. The friendly staff are knowledgeable enough to meet the demands of wine snobs and very kind and helpful to those who need guidance. Beer lovers will find domestic and imported brands as well as micro brews. A wine tasting bar is open on Tuesdays from 16:00 to 19:00. The walk-in humidor with a selection of more than 150 premium brands is a favourite with cigar fans.

Art

LA Art Show

Other options **Art Classes** p.212, **Art Galleries** p.168,
Art & Craft Supplies p.261

The LA Art Show
(310 822 9145, www.
LAArtShow.com)
takes place in late
January each year at
Santa Monica's Barker
Hangar. Exhibits
from more than
125 internationally
renowned artists are
on display, and a
variety of educational
seminars take place
during the five-
day event. Show
admission is $20 and
catalogues are $10.

The art community in Los Angeles is not confined to one or two neighbourhoods. You will find the upscale gallery Martin Lawrence at Universal Citywalk and Fashion Island, plus hundreds of small to medium-sized galleries spread throughout the city. The Jan Kesner Gallery in West Hollywood showcases the works of international photographers, and the Gagosian Gallery in Beverly Hills, designed by famous architect Richard Meier, is a work of art in itself. Inside you'll find high priced canvases from a variety of contemporary artists. Chinatown's galleries seem to come and go but China Art Objects maintains a loyal following and continues to promote the works of new talent. Gallery Row in downtown Los Angeles offers several interesting spaces to explore including Gallery 727 and Infusion Gallery. Santa Monica is home to Adamm's Gallery featuring the works of more than 100 of America's top glass artists. Displays include breathtaking vases, wall art, and

Art			
Adamm's	Santa Monica	310 451 9390	www.adammsgallery.com
Bergamot Station	Santa Monica	310 453 7535	www.bergamotstation.com
Blum & Poe	Culver City	310 836 2062	www.blumandpoe.com
China Art Objects	Chinatown	213 613 0384	www.chinaartobjects.com
Corey Helford	Culver City	310 287 2340	www.coreyhelfordgallery.com
Gagosian Gallery	Beverly Hills	310 271 9400	www.gagosian.com
Gallery 727	Downtown	213 627 9563	www.gallery727losangeles.com
Infusion Gallery	Downtown	213 683 8827	www.infusiongallery.com
Jan Kessner Gallery	West Hollywood	323 938 6834	www.jankesnergallery.com
Martin Lawrence	Various Locations	818 508 7867	www.martinlawrence.com
Pageant of Masters	Laguna Beach	949 494 1145	www.foapom.com
Sawdust Festival	Laguna Beach	949 494 3030	www.sawdustartfestival.org
Susanne Vielmetter	Culver City	323 933 2117	www.veilmetter.com
Z Gallerie	Various Locations	800 908 6748	www.zgallerie.com

jewellery all created from glass. Bergamot Station, also in Santa Monica, features more than 30 galleries spread among an arts complex that includes a charming outdoor cafe. Culver City has become a hot spot for art in recent years. Among the must-see galleries are Blum & Poe, Susanne Vielmetter and Corey Helford. Art festivals in communities like Pasadena, Malibu and Manhattan Beach provide a good opportunity to see works from many local and regional artists all in one place. The Sawdust Festival and Winter Fantasy Festival held each January and July in Laguna Beach showcase everything from paintings and photography to ceramics, glass and sculptures. Pageant of the Masters (p.260), the premier event of the summer in Laguna Beach, employs a legion of costumed volunteers to bring famous paintings to life onstage at its outdoor amphitheatre. The pageant runs from July to August and tickets are quite reasonable. For those who love fine art but can't afford to buy originals, Z Gallerie offers a large selection of affordable prints featuring the works of art icons. Many are already mounted and framed but you may also select from custom frames and mats in the store.

Art & Craft Supplies

Other options **Art** p.260, **Art Classes** p.212, **Art Galleries** p.168

Art & Craft Supplies			
Aaron Brothers	Various Locations	888 372 6464	www.aaronbrothers.com
Blick Art Materials	Various Locations	800 723 2787	www.dickblick.com
Blue Rooster	Hollywood	323 661 9471	www.blueroosterartsupplies.com
Joann	Various Locations	800 525 4951	www.joann.com
Lyon Art Supply	Long Beach	562 435 5383	www.lyonsartsupply.com
Michaels	Various Locations	800 642 4235	www.michaels.com
Pudgy Beads	Long Beach	562 427 0018	www.pudgybeads.com
Scrap Session	West LA	310 204 3883	www.scrapsession.com
Swain's Art Supplies	Glendale	818 243 3129	www.swainsart.com
Utrecht Art Supplies	Santa Monica	310 478 5775	www.utrechtart.com
Walser's	Torrance	310 891 3325	www.walsers.com

Whether you are a professional artist or delve into art as a hobby, you'll find a variety of art supply stores throughout the city. All are well stocked with watercolour paper, canvases, brushes, and speciality items like airbrushing tools and drafting equipment. Most also offer gift items like greeting cards, journals and art books. Hobbyists flock to Michaels and Joann for scrapbooking tools, floral accessories, and a huge selection of knitting and crocheting yarns. Aaron Brothers is a great spot to pick up frames for photos or art. Be sure to stock up when they have their annual 'buy one, get another for one cent' sale. The popularity of beading has created a demand for stores selling beads and jewellery making supplies. Pudgy Beads in Long Beach is a good place to find vintage and gemstone beads from exotic locales. They also offer beading classes for beginners. Scrap Sessions in Glendale caters to scrapbookers with a wide assortment of binders, acid-free papers, unique scissor designs, stickers, photo sleeves, and other accessories. Sign up for mailing lists online or in the store and receive advance notice of sales and news of upcoming special events.

Baby Stores

Baby clothing, furniture and accessories are widely available at department stores, discount chains and speciality shops. Babies R Us is a one-stop-shop for everything you could possibly need to outfit a nursery and care for a child, including baby bottles, formula, diapers, cribs, strollers, car seats, diaper bags and room decor. Some major department stores and many baby shops offer registry services so that expectant parents may select a list of items they would like to receive at a baby shower. Others provide a convenient checklist of items new parents can consult to

Baby Stores

Auntie Barbara's Kids	310 285 0873	www.auntiebarbaraskids.com
Babies R Us	800 869 7787	www.babiesrus
Baby Ant	818 609 0410	www.babyant.com
Bellini	310 859 7133	www.bellini.com
Kids Land	213 487 9090	www.kidslandusa.com
La La Ling	323 664 4400	www.lalaling.com
Petit Tresor	310 659 3970	www.petittresor.com
Swanky Blanky	323 478 9306	www.swankyblankykids.com
Toluca Tots	818 509 2900	www.tolucatots.com
Wonderland	310 440 9970	www.childrenswonderland.com

make sure they have everything they need before a child's arrival. Bellini has been designing baby furniture for more than 25 years and has gained a devoted following for its high-quality designs that are built to last for years. Many of its cribs convert to toddler beds, and matching chests have sliding changing tables that may be conveniently removed later. Upscale shops like Petit Tresor specialise in high dollar clothing like cashmere sweaters for babies, while Auntie Barbara's Kids is known for handpainted furniture, accessories and custom gift baskets. Many baby stores like La La Ling, Toluca Tots and Swanky Blanky offer a more colourful selection of infant clothing and bedding than the traditional pastels of years past, and they are well-stocked with bed linens, bathing accessories, and popular items like photo albums and baby spoons. Supermarkets carry a wide selection of baby foods, diapers, and basic accessories like bibs, wipes and pacifiers. Health food stores offer organic baby food lines and books on making your own organic baby foods at home. Discount stores like Target (www.target.com) and Wal-Mart (www.walmart.com) generally offer better prices on basic baby supplies, undershirts, diaper shirts, booties and gear like strollers and car seats.

Save Money

Swimwear is available all year in Los Angeles but you'll find the biggest markdowns in late summer and autumn as shops make way for back to school, skiwear, and holiday merchandise.

Beachwear

Other options **Clothes** p.266, **Sports Goods** p.295

Shopping for a swimsuit in Los Angeles is easier than in many parts of the country. Beachside communities offer a plethora of bikini stores and surf shops, while most malls have at least one beach-themed shop with suits for men, women and children. Department stores and discount chains offer suits for the whole family, and if you hit the stores during clearance sales, you may snag a huge discount. Women of all sizes will find the hottest styles and colours at Diane's, where mix-and-match tops and bottoms are available in cup sizes from AA to E. Surf shops carry hip and trendy board shorts for guys along with a full selection of wetsuits, surfboards, fins and beach towels. For those seeking high-performance brands, Sports Authority is a good choice for Speedos, Nike and other athletic-inspired designs. Loehmann's is a great spot to score a designer suit for a bargain price if you're lucky enough to find your size. Pacific Sunwear caters to the teen set with styles from Paul Frank, Roxy and Quiksilver.

Beachwear

Becker Surfboards	310 320 5736	www.beckersurf.com
Canyon Beachwear	310 459 5070	www.canyonbeachwear.com
Diane's	310 224 1900	www.dianesbeachwear.com
Everything But Water	310 289 1550	www.everythingbutwater.com
Loehmann's	310 659 0674	www.loehmanns.com
Pacific Sunwear	877 372 2786	www.pacsun.com
Quiksilver	323 933 9373	www.quiksilver.com
Sports Authority	800 901 0795	www.sportsauthority.com
Turtle Beach Swimwear	310 652 6039	www.turtlebeachswimwear.com
Val Surf	888 825 7873	www.valsurf.com

Bicycles

While cars still rule the roads in California, cyclists are gaining more ground as communities in Los Angeles continue to add more bike paths to roads and parks. Bicycles are allowed on metro rail trains except between 06:30 and 08:30 and 16:30 and 18:30 on weekdays (most train stations have free bike racks and rental lockers). MTA buses are equipped with bike racks for those travelling distances too far to bike the entire way (www.mta.net). Single-speed bikes known as beach cruisers are very popular in oceanside areas like Hermosa Beach and Santa Monica, while mountain bikes and all-terrain hybrids are popular in inland areas where bike riders explore parks and trails. Cycling enthusiasts tend to favour bicycle speciality shops for higher end models, cycling attire and accessories like baby trailers. Single-speed bikes (known as beach cruisers) cost between $125 and $300 depending on the model, while mountain bikes start at $200, while upscale brands can cost as much at $3,000 depending on added features. Racing bikes command even higher prices with some luxury models retailing at $4,000 or more. Children's bicycles available at Target and chain sports stores average between $60 and $200. By California law anyone under 18 must wear a bicycle helmet, and many adults wear them for enhanced safety protection. Children's helmets typically sell for $15 to $40, while adult models range from $40 to $90. Bike accessories are available at major chain stores, speciality shops and even some pharmacies. Locks are a necessity in Los Angeles, with basic cable models selling for $14 and maximum-security models costing $95 and up. Most major bike shops provide preventive maintenance services and repairs. Bike shops sell a variety of moderate to high-end models from brands like Trek, LeMond and Cannondale, and many offer used bikes for sale. Shoppers on a budget may also find used bikes listed in newspaper classifieds, on college bulletin boards and on websites like Craig's List (www.craigslist.com).

Bicycles		
Beverly Hills Bike Shop	310 275 2453	NA
Big 5 Sporting Goods	800 898 2994	www.big5sportinggoods.com
Bike Attack	3105 818 014	www.bikeattack.com
Helen's Cycles	310 453 8396	www.helenscycles.com
Jax Bicycles	562 421 4646	wwwjaxbicycles.com
REI	800 426 4840	www.rei.com
Sport Chalet	888 801 9162	www.sportchalet.com
Sports Authority	800 901 0795	www.sportsauthority.com
Target	800 591 3869	www.target.com

Books

Other options **Second-Hand Items** p.293, **Libraries** p.226

Borders and Barnes & Noble are the leading book chains in Los Angeles, and their well-organised stores with coffee cafes and free internet access please the masses with frequent sales, book signings and live entertainment. As the big chains have expanded, many independent neighbourhood bookshops have closed, finding it almost impossible to compete, but a few diehards remain thanks to their specialised inventories and loyal fans who prefer smaller shops with a unique ambience. For those who love browsing used bookshops, Acres of Books in Long Beach is the largest in California. The landmark building offers more than one million

Books		
Acres of Books	562 437 6980	www.acresofbooks.com
Barnes & Noble	800 843 2665	www.barnesandnoble.com
Bodhi Tree Bookstore	310 659 1733	www.bodhitree.com
Book Soup	310 659 3110	www.booksoup.com
Borders	888 812 6657	www.borders.com
Brand Bookshop	818 507 5943	www.abebooks.com
Dutton's	310 476 6263	www.duttonsbrentwood.com
Equator Books	310 399 5544	www.eqautorbooks.com
Imix Book Store	323 257 2512	www.imixbooks.com
Skylight Books	323 660 1175	www.skylightbooks.com
Storyopolis	818 509 5600	www.storyopolis.com
Vromans Bookstore	626 351 0828	www.vromansbookstore.com

books on topics from A to Z in a wondrous maze of stacks and adjoining rooms that seem to stretch on endlessly. It's a fun place to spend an afternoon, and chances are you'll leave with half a dozen books for less than $40. *Los Angeles Times* Festival of Books, held on the UCLA campus in mid-April showcases upcoming titles and offers a plethora of special events including appearances by famous authors and celebrities. (213 237 6365, www.latimes.com/extras/festivalofbooks).

8818 Sunset Blvd
West Hollywood
Map 5 A3 **3**

Book Soup

310 659 3110 | www.booksoup.com

A landmark on the Sunset Strip, this eclectic, independent bookseller is a fun place to browse and a great place for people watching. Over the last 31 years it has cultivated a quirky image while also serving loyal clientele with mainstream fiction and non-fiction, a large selection of art, film and music books, as well as titles from little-known writers and publishers. Stars from films, TV and the literary world often drop in for book signings but you'll also spot them browsing among the stacks if you come on a regular basis. Hours: Daily 09:00 to 22:00

1818 N Vermont Ave
Los Feliz
Map 8 A1 **4**

Skylight Books

323 660 1175 | www.skylightbooks.com

Situated in Los Feliz long before the area became a favourite hangout for trendsetters, this cosy bookshop is independently owned and known for its vast selection of alternative literature, literary fiction and titles on Los Angeles, cinema and theatre. Book signings are held frequently and autographed copies are often available from prior events. The helpful staff keep tabs on local reading groups and often post news about upcoming literary events in the area. Hours: Daily 10:00 to 22:00

12348 Ventura Blvd
Studio City
Map 2 C1

Storyopolis

818 509 5600 | www.storyopolis.com

Offering a colourful atmosphere and an energetic vibe that is a far cry from typical bookstores, this family-friendly shop offers an incredible selection of contemporary and classic children's books. Regular story time readings are held throughout the week and

Book Soup

Borders

presented in such an entertaining format that adults seem to enjoy them as much as the tots. One of the more popular gift items in the store is Books by the Bushel: handpicked titles chosen to match the recipient's age and tastes. Available for both children and adults, they are packaged in colourful cardboard suitcases, attractive baskets or whimsically decorated hatboxes and range in price from $75 to $200. Hours: Sun 11:00 to 16:00, Mon: Closed, Tue to Sat 11:00 to 17:00

Camera Equipment
Other options **Electronics & Home Appliances** p.274

In a city where paparazzi hang around trendy restaurants, and teenagers routinely take photos with their mobile phones, it's no surprise that camera equipment is easy to come by. Chain stores like Best Buy and Circuit City frequently have sales on digital cameras, camcorders and accessories. Since there are so many places to buy photographic equipment, prices are quite competitive, so it's wise

Camera Equipment		
Best Buy	888 237 8289	www.bestbuy.com
Calumet Photographic	323 466 1238	www.calumetphoto.com
Canoga Park Camera	818 346 5506	www.canogacamera.com
Circuit City	800 843 2489	www.circuitcity.com
DVR Camera Supply	800 607 4145	www.dvrcamerasupply.com
Frank's Camera Store	323 255 5151	www.frankscamera.com
Paul's Photo	310 375 7014	www.paulsphoto.com
Ritz Camera	877 690 0099	www.ritzcamera.com
Samy's Camera Outlet	323 939 4566	www.samyscamera.com
Target	800 591 3869	www.target.com

to shop around. Speciality camera stores cater to pros with filters, lenses, tripods, lighting kits and darkroom supplies, but many shops, like Ritz Camera, also offer training classes for novices eager to improve their skills. Disposable cameras and film are available at most local pharmacies, supermarkets and gift shops catering to tourists. Some pharmacies and greeting card stores offer film processing and the option of having your photos transferred to CD. Some stores also have photo machines on site that allow customers to make instant copies and enlargements. If you don't mind buying used equipment, check pawnshops, Craig's List (www. craigslist.com) and newspaper classifieds, where you can find great deals from professional photographers and hobbyists who have upgraded their equipment and want to unload their old gear.

Car Parts & Accessories
The automobile is king in LA, and some people take better care of their cars than their living spaces. Car washes are easy to find in most neighbourhoods. Some offer drive-through automated systems, while others are coin operated or employ a host of workers to clean, shine and deodorise your vehicle. Most major car dealers

Give A Hoot – Don't Pollute

Los Angeles requires a biennial smog test at an authorised inspection station, which means vehicle owners must submit evidence of smog inspection every other registration renewal period. Currently, smog inspections are required for all vehicles except diesel-powered, electric, natural gas powered vehicles over 14,000 lbs, hybrids, motorcycles, trailers, or vehicles 1975 and older. Santa Monica Smog Check and Test (310 450 9316) will test your car in 15 minutes or less while you relax in the comfy waiting room.

Car Parts & Accessories		
American Tire Depot	626 709 3375	www.americantiredepot.com
AutoZone	800 288 6966	www.autozone.com
Beverly Hills Auto Service	323 463 2361	www.volvoautorepair.com
Distinctive Automotive	818 704 9252	www.distinctiveautomotive.com
Fashion Square Car Wash	818 981 2333	www.fashionsquarecarwash.com
Five Star Tires	323 876 1033	www.lafivestartires.com
Jiffy Lube	800 344 6933	www.jiffylube.com
Kragen Auto Parts	877 808 0698	www.partsamerica.com
Midas	800 621 8545	www.midas.com
Pep Boys	800 737 2697	www.pepboys.com
Santa Monica Smog Check	310 450 9316	www.santamonicasmogcheck.com

offer car repairs, but LA also boasts many auto repair shops that specialise in imports or classic models. Motor oil and basic accessories like car mats or window visors are available at chain stores like Target and Wal-Mart, but for more specialised gadgets and a larger selection, stores like Pep Boys and Auto Zone are a good bet. Distinctive Automotive in Woodland Hills specialises in audio and video installations and also offers window tinting and car detailing.

Carpets	
American Home	888 973 6635
Banner Carpet	310 451 8836
Carpet Wagon	866 204 8060
David Alan Flooring	310 838 2278
Discover Flooring	323 436 6298
Empire Today	800 588 2300
Home Depot	800 553 3199
IKEA	800 434 4532
Linoleum City	323 469 0063
Lowe's	800 445 6937
Marble & Tile Depot	818 764 2254
Powers Hardwood	213 457 9677

Carpets

Independently owned and franchise stores offer wall-to-wall carpet, padding and installation in a range of prices to suit any budget. Over the last few years homeowners have been clamouring for hardwood floors, marble, tile and easy to maintain surfaces like vinyl and linoleum. Many stores have transformed their showrooms into flooring galleries to make it easier for shoppers to envision how different surfaces will look in the home. Some companies, like Empire Today, bring carpet and flooring samples to your home, take measurements and install the new floors at your convenience. Chain stores like Home Depot and Lowe's offer a large assortment of flooring samples on display and have experts on hand to give you a quick estimate of how much new flooring or carpet will cost. Do-it-yourself types will find floor and carpet tiles, floor laying kits, liners and a variety of laminated and wood floors to choose from at IKEA. They also stock a large selection of room size and area rugs at reasonable prices.

Fashion Finder ◀ ## Clothes

Within this Clothes category there are three tables to help you find a suitable outfit for any occasion. Moderate Apparel on p.270 lists stores selling stylish yet affordable clothes, Trendsetters on p.273 contains shops on the cutting edge of fashion, and on p.268 you'll find a selection of Rodeo Drive's designer boutiques.

Other options **Tailoring** p.296, **Shoes** p.294, **Lingerie** p.284, **Beachwear** p.262, **Sports Goods** p.295

From the hub of the fashion district downtown, where designers concoct new trends, to the sprawling suburbs surrounding the city, there are endless opportunities to literally shop till you drop. Typically you will find a wider range of sizes in mall stores and department stores than in trendy boutiques. While many actresses may fit into a size 0, the truth is the average woman shopper is more likely to be several sizes larger. Most department and discount stores now offer plus sizes and speciality stores like Avenue and Lane Bryant cater to women from size 14 and up. Big and tall men can be assured of finding sizes that fit at Kohl's, JC Penney, Casual Male and Big Dog Sportswear.

Rodeo Drive in Beverly Hills, Melrose Avenue in West Hollywood and Montana Avenue in Santa Monica have long been the shopping hotspots for high-end apparel, but in recent years other areas like Eagle Rock, Manhattan Beach, Pasadena and Los Feliz have also attracted chic boutiques.

The LA Fashion District (www.fashiondistrict.org) is a 90 block treasure hunt where the bounty is brand name and designer clothing at 40% to 70% off retail prices. The Downtown area includes over a thousand stores selling wholesale and retail apparel. Many stores are open Monday to Sunday from 10:00 to 17:00, but some wholesalers only sell to the public on Saturdays. The gigantic shopping district includes 700 stores for women, 360 for men, and 169 specialising in children's clothing. You'll find everything from discounted bridal gowns and premium women's jeans to men's suits and children's school uniforms at prices way below retail. Many wardrobe designers for movies and TV shows shop at the textiles stores for unusual trims, fabrics and jewellery. Along Santee Alley (12th Street to Olympic Boulevard between Santee Street and Maple Ave) street vendors entice shoppers with designer knockoff handbags, men's

Endless shopping opportunities

belts, children's T-shirts and a plethora of other apparel and accessories. Along this stretch of downtown the quality of the merchandise may be irregular or slightly flawed, and sizes are hit or miss. There are no dressing rooms and you won't be able to make exchanges, so it's best to be absolutely sure before you fork over cash for anything. Use Metro bus or rail transportation to reach Downtown (www.mta.net), and then board the DASH bus D and E lines that cross the Fashion District (25 cents per ride). The closest Metro stops are Pico and San Pedro stations.

280 E Colorado Blvd
Pasadena
Map 2 E1

A Snail's Pace Running Shop
626 568 9886 | www.runasnailspace.com
Known as one of the best shops for runners in California, this athletic store stocks walking and running shoes by brands like Adidas, Mizuno, Saucony and Etonic. Plus it has a wide array of fitness clothing from Asics, Nike, Brooks and Champion. Accessories include gloves, sports bras, hats, insoles and several products for treating injuries. Novice runners won't feel intimidated here as the staff go out of their way to treat beginners with the same respect they show long-time customers. The store also sponsors a running club that gives people of all athletic levels a chance to meet, mingle and participate in fun activities. Training programs are offered for beginning runners and those preparing for marathons. Additional locations are in Fountain Valley (714 842 2337), Laguna Hills (949 707 1460) and Brea (714 529 6313).

8500 Beverly Ctr
Dr Suite 725
Westwood
Map 7 A1 **5**

Ben Sherman
310 657 3400 | www.benshermanusa.com
Credited with inventing the Oxford button down shirt in 1963, and known worldwide for setting trends, Ben Sherman is one of the largest menswear brands in the UK. The Los Angeles store features the familiar whimsical decor – chairs covered in Union Jack flags, bookcases jammed with shoes and antiques, and hardwood floors sporting the trademark target logo. The walls are a fascinating collage of images, fabric samples and collectibles paying homage to London and the artists and icons who influenced music and fashion. Moderately priced apparel for men and women merges classic looks with a modern twist on bomber jackets, mini skirts, low-rise skinny jeans and shirts with a slim or extra slim fit. Accessories include messenger bags, belts, hats and retro-inspired footwear.

7368 Melrose Ave
West Hollywood
Map 5 F4 **6**

Blowout Mens
323 653 7530 | www.blowoutmens.com
Walking into this upscale men's boutique is a far cry from what you'll experience on Rodeo Drive. The atmosphere is relaxed and unpretentious, the staff greet everyone like an old friend, and the displays are hip without being garish. Buyers Gila and Johnny stay a step ahead with the latest looks from American and European runways. In the

Rodeo Drive Designer Boutiques

Chanel	400 North Rodeo Drive	3102785500	www.chanel.com
Christian Dior	309 North Rodeo Drive	3108594700	www.dior.com
Dolce & Gabbana	312 North Rodeo Drive	3108888701	www.dolcegabbana.it
Giorgio Armani	436 North Rodeo Drive	3102715555	www.giorgioarmani.com
Gucci	347 North Rodeo Drive	3102783451	www.gucci.com
Prada	343 North Rodeo Drive	3102788661	www.prada.com
Ralph Lauren	444 North Rodeo Drive	3102811500	www.ralphlauren.com
Valentino	360 North Rodeo Drive	3102470103	www.valentino.com
Versace	248 North Rodeo Drive	3102053921	www.versace.com
Yves St Laurent	326 North Rodeo Drive	3102714110	www.ysl.com

business long enough to know a thing or two about style and up and coming trends, they often supply clothes for television shows and special events. Jackets are casually sophisticated with details like embroidery, studs or velvet trim to give them a touch of rock star coolness, and jeans are from premium lines like True Religion and Antik. For a dressier look, you'll find silk shirts from Roberto Cavalli and Ted Baker. Styling consultations are available for men who need guidance for a special event or who want to totally revamp their wardrobes.

Beverly Ctr 8500
Beverly Blvd
West Hollywood
Map 7 A1 **7**

Burberry

310 657 2424 | *www.burberry.com*

Although the name still conjures up images of trench coats, umbrellas and rain hats, this upscale outpost of the famous British brand features a spacious gallery-like shop, brimming with contemporary dresses, sophisticated sportswear and a fragrance collection that is as modern as the brand's updated new image. Shoes and handbags featuring the signature plaid are hot sellers along with a new line of watches and sunglasses.

400 S Baldwin Ave
Arcadia
Map 2 E1

Charlotte Russe

626 446 8019 | *www.charlotterusse.com*

A popular haunt for teenage girls, college students and young working women who like to dress trendy on a budget, Charlotte Russe is a great place to find stylish skirts, tops and dresses for a fraction of the price you will pay in boutiques. The store layout is huge, and a backdrop of blaring music and bright colours give it a youthful energy and raucous feel that at times can be frenetic. Less expensive than Forever 21 or Express, it offers a wide choice of fashions that don't cost a bundle. Accessories including jewellery, bags and belts mimic higher priced lines in styling but aren't built to last. Sizing tends to run small, so with many styles it's best to choose one size larger than normal for a better fit.

420 Broadway 4th St
Santa Monica
Map 3 B4 **8**

Fred Segal

310 458 9940 | *www.fredsegalfun.com*

As much a place to see and be seen as it is to shop, this pricey Santa Monica superstore boasts many celebrities as patrons and it's not unusual to spot one or two having lunch at the cafe after a shopping foray. Renowned for its inventory of cutting edge lines, the store frequently supplies the wardrobes for TV shows aimed at the young and trendy. There's another branch on Melrose Avenue that is a paparazzi magnet, but the Santa Monica store offers multiple boutiques under one roof, in close proximity to Third Street Promenade. Service tends to be super-attentive or non-existent depending on the crowds. Can't afford the high price tags? Shop early during the annual sale in late September and snag a bounty of tees, accessories and beauty products at deep discounts.

Block at Orange
20 City Blvd W
Orange
Map 2 F3

Hilo Hattie

714 769 3255 | *www.hilohattie.com*

Featuring one of the largest selections of Hawaiian resort wear in the United States, this 20,000sq ft Orange County store offers tropical apparel and accessories in a wide range of sizes for men, women, children and babies. Choose from aloha shirts, swimwear with matching sarongs, cute sets for kids, and a ton of accessories from sandals and towels to tote bags, jewellery, beach mats and sunglasses; all moderately priced. Be sure to check out the window displays for the world's largest aloha shirt – size 400XL (recorded in the Guinness Book of Records). The store also carries an extensive selection of food items including Kona coffee, chocolate-covered macadamia nuts and other island delicacies.

It's A Wrap

3315 W
Magnolia Blvd
Burbank
Map 2 D1

818 567 7366 | www.itsawraphollywood.com
Situated in a building resembling a soundstage and spanning 7000sq ft, this film-buff paradise is loaded with clothes and props discarded by the wardrobe departments of movie and television studios. Owner Janet Dion has been working with Paramount, NBC, Warner Brothers and other studios since 1992. A huge array of framed costumes and photos line the walls, giving the place a Hollywood museum ambience. Prices vary from inexpensive to pricey depending on the item, but you can expect to pay 30% to 50% off retail. Designer apparel from names like Armani, Dolce & Gabbana and Chanel are displayed on the second floor, while the first floor houses clothes worn by actors from TV shows and movies like *Mission Impossible, Miami Vice* and *Star Trek*. All clothes are tagged with the show or movie they were used in and specify which actor or actress wore them. Another location is at 1164 South Robertson (310 246 9727).

Jacqueline Jarrot

8500 Beverly Blvd
Suite 601A
West Hollywood
Map 7 A1 🄨

310 659 2094 | www.jacquelinejarrot.com
Frequently featured in fashion magazines, this ultra-hip store offers all the latest trends in women's clothing and accessories. With labels like Betsey Johnson, Hale Bob and Bailey, it's a terrific place to try on glamorous dresses for a special occasion. Women's fashions and handbags are on the pricey side, but the amazing selection of jewellery ranges from $30 to $300, with many of the more affordable pieces looking much more expensive than they are. Men will find a limited selection of jackets, denim and T-shirts from names like Diesel , Raw 7, and Chip+Pepper. The gift area offers a wide array of affordably priced items like mirrored compacts, cosmetic bags, and phone cases. There is another location at Sherman Oaks Fashion Square, 14006 Riverside Drive (818 501 2056).

Jennifer Croll

7942 E Pacific
Coast Hwy
Newport Beach
Map 2 F4

949 494 4773 | www.jennifercroll.com
Featuring everything from sought-after Rachel Pally dresses and Nicole Miller bridal gowns to sporty menswear from Ted Baker and Hugo Boss, this Orange County boutique is worth the drive. Women tired of the styles in department stores will find this shop offers some of the most talked about lines in fashion circles including Nanette LePore, Sue Wong and Frankie B. Taking your time to try on outfits is encouraged, and friends who are tagging along can catch a game on the plasma TV or play a game of pool in the sports lounge.

Jos A Bank

345 S Lake Ave
Suite 104
Pasadena
Map 2 E1

626 666 5878 | www.josbank.com
Offering the service and attention to detail of a fine menswear boutique without the sky-high prices, this highly regarded brand has been around for over 100 years. With

Moderate Apparel		
Avenue	800 441 1362	www.avenue.com
Banana Republic	888 277 8953	www.bananarepublic.com
Casual Male	800 767 0319	www.casualmale.com
Gap	800 427 7895	www.gap.com
JC Penney	800 322 1189	www.jcpenney.com
Kohl's	866 887 8884	www.kohls.com
Loehmann's	310 659 0674	www.loehmanns.com
Nordstrom Rack	888 282 6060	www.nordstromrack.com
Off Fifth	714 769 4200	www.saksincorporated.com
Sears	800 549 4505	www.sears.com

a reputation for traditional styling, and offering an unconditional guarantee on everything in the store, it's a no-risk shopping experience for men who need to upgrade their wardrobe. Business Express suit separates are among the bestsellers, giving men a chance to mix and match jackets and trousers in different sizes, fabrics and styles for a more custom look. An on-site tailor makes sure the fit is perfect. The popular Traveller's Collection includes wrinkle-free dress shirts in a large selection of colours and collar styles, and a stay cool suit, designed to keep men comfortable in warm climates.

Kitson

115 S Robertson Blvd
West Hollywood
Map 7 A1 **10**

Kitson

310 859 2652 | www.shopkitson.com

Located near the entertainment industry's popular lunch hangout, The Ivy, this ever-expanding store includes the main showroom on Robertson Boulevard, Kitson Men and Kitson Studio next door, and a Kitson Kids across the street. Featuring an interesting mix of clever T-shirts, accessories and flirty dresses for women, it also offers denim from Victoria Beckham, fitted jackets from Paris Hilton, and lines from a lengthy designer roster including Alexander McQueen, Betsey Johnson and Diane von Furstenberg. Men's shirts, hoodies and jeans are all equally expensive, and kids' clothes are way beyond the budget of most parents, but part of the fun is braving the crowds to catch a glimpse of a movie star on a shopping spree.

1409 3rd St
Promenade
Santa Monica
Map 3 B4 **11**

The Levi's Store

310 393 4899 | www.levisstore.com

Fed up with spending a month's paycheque on designer denim? This gargantuan store sells nothing but Levi's brand merchandise. It's the largest Levi's store in California and revered for its wide selection of sizes and styles for men, women and boys. Staff are experts at using the Levi's Jeanfinder, a quick question and answer screening process that can assess which style is likely to fit best. The store also carries a vintage line with reproductions of iconic designs and an eco-friendly jean made from organic cotton. Along with denim in various washes and cuts, you'll find shirts, jackets and accessories, all at down-to-earth prices.

10250 Santa
Monica Blvd 185
Century City
Map 4 D3 **12**

Martin + Osa

310 785 7924 | www.martinandosa.com

An offshoot of American Eagle Outfitters, this apparel store for men and women was named for Martin and Osa Johnson, husband and wife adventurers who travelled to distant lands and photographed their adventures. Casual sportswear in easy care fabrics are the heart of the line along with jeans and jackets that can take you from the airport to dinner and still look crisp and modern. You'll find a wide range of shirts and slacks that are great for packing light. Accessories include casual shoes, hiking boots, backpacks and totes.

Westfield Century City 10250
Century City
Map 4 D3 **13**

MNG By Mango

310 282 0632 | *www.mangoshop.com*

With over a thousand stores in 89 countries, MNG by Mango is an internationally known Spanish brand that offers women a relaxed shopping environment combined with attentive service. After signing acclaimed actress Penelope Cruz as its new spokesperson the store has updated its image with an even more diverse selection of youthful and urban styles. Cruz and her sister Monica designed a new line exclusively for Mango featuring jeans, shirts, dresses, jackets and accessories that reflect current European trends at more reasonable prices. Other collections include tailored mix and match separates for office wear, lifestyle casual pieces, and pretty dresses for evenings out. Other locations are at Topanga Plaza, Canoga Park and South Coast Plaza, Costa Mesa.

Various Locations

Old Navy

800 653 6289 | *www.oldnavy.com*

A lifesaver for growing families, young singles on a budget and fans of retro-inspired clothing, this popular chain store has branches at most major shopping centres in the Los Angeles area. Stocking a huge selection of basic T-shirts, tank tops, khaki pants and classic collared shirts, it offers seasonal selections of trendy skirts, hoodies, jackets and shorts, plus a large stock of basics like socks, belts, hats and gloves. Jeans are available in several styles including high and low waist designs. The shoe selection is mostly inexpensive flip-flops and slip-on sneakers for men, and cute ballet flats and wedges for women. Fashionable maternity tops and pants are available in sizes from XS to XXL and are a good buy if you don't want to spend a fortune on clothes you'll only wear for a few months. Don't miss the Dog Supply, a collection of sweaters, polo shirts and rain jackets for dogs. All orders placed online for US delivery qualify for $5 shipping.

4637 Hollywood Blvd
Hollywood
Map 8 A1 **14**

Ozzie Dots

323 663 2867 | *www.ozziedots.com*

One of the city's largest suppliers of adult costumes, Ozzie Dots is your best bet when you need costumes for a party or want to plan a fantasy night with that special someone. Offering a selection far more expansive than the seasonal Halloween stores or shops that sell costumes as a sideline, the choices here range from Frankenstein and Wonder woman to London bobbies, samurai warriors, mermaids and saloon girls. A huge array of wigs include Carmen Miranda, dreadlocks, witch hair and afros in a rainbow of colours. Accessories span the gamut from nerd glasses to elf shoes and angel wings. The store also stocks a large variety of

Prices

Prices for apparel, shoes and accessories vary widely depending on the shopping area. You'll pay top dollar on Rodeo Drive, mid-range prices at department stores and sometimes get up to 75% off at outlet malls and flea markets. The sales tax in Los Angeles is 8.25%. It's smart to read local newspapers to stay informed about upcoming promotions. Many department stores seem to have constant sales but in the weeks just prior and right after the winter holidays, you'll get the best markdowns. A new law just implemented in California requires that all stores are required to give cash for all gift cards with balances of less than $10.

vintage costumes and novelties like severed fingers, eerie eyes and chattering teeth, perfect for Halloween decorating.

Various Locations ◄

Quiksilver

www.quiksilver.com

Long established as a frontrunner in the surf-inspired apparel market, Quiksilver expanded beyond distribution to surf shops and department stores to create its own stand-alone stores. Featuring spacious layouts with lots of wood and walls covered with huge posters of surfers and skateboard pros, the stores have a party-like ambience with music blaring, and clothes displayed around eye-catching props like surfboards and fake palm trees. The board short and T-shirt selections are huge, and fans of the line will also find lots of hoodies, hats, watches and jeans with the signature logo.

8428 Melrose Ave ◄
West Hollywood
Map 5 B4 **15**

Theory

323 782 0163 | *www.theory.com*

Taking a minimalist approach with its sleek and modern decor, this clothing shop for men and women features large white cubes and circular seating in the centre of the store while racks of clothes for men and women line each wall. Best known for its tailored pants and jackets in designs and fabrics that stretch with the body, the brand has made business casual comfortable again. Both men and women will find more than enough outfits suitable for office wear, and many can be dressed up for a night out by simply changing accessories or adding an accent piece like a flirty blouse or striking tie. Prices are on the high side but if you call ahead to ask about clearance sales, you will find many pieces that are quite affordable. The store's Icon Project donates a pair of shoes to children in need for each pair of TOMS shoes purchased.

8595 W Sunset Blvd ◄
West Hollywood
Map 5 A2 **16**

Tracey Ross

310 854 1996 | *www.traceyross.com*

This trendy boutique located in Sunset Plaza gets tons of publicity from the celebrity clients who frequently pop by. Decorated in a contemporary motif with cosy chairs, attractive wall art and fragrant candles, it features racks of carefully chosen dresses, separates, shoes and accessories from some of the fashion industry's biggest names including Stella McCartney, Derek Lam, Vanessa Bruno, Helmut Lang and Rebecca Taylor. The prices are steep but it doesn't cost a penny to take a peek, and browsing is encouraged. Whether you need a dazzling dress for a special event or shoes to match an outfit you already own, the staff are extremely patient and helpful. Several pampering beauty products from Loree Rodkin and Reverence de Bastien are offered, and there is an eclectic gift section featuring everything from art and books to iPod cases and cashmere throws.

Trendsetters

Chloe	Costa Mesa	714 481 0308	www.chloe.com
Curve	West Hollywood	310 360 8008	www.shopcurve.com
John Varvatos	West Hollywood	310 859 2791	www.johnvarvatos.com
Juicy Couture	Various Locations	888 908 1160	www.juicycouture.com
Lisa Kline	Beverly Hills	323 297 0490	www.lisakline.com
Madison	Beverly Hills	310 275 1930	www.madisonlosangeles.com
Marc Jacobs	West Hollywood	323 653 5100	www.marcjacobs.com
Michael Kors	Beverly Hills	310 777 8862	www.michaelkors.com
Nanette LePore	Beverly Hills	310 281 0004	www.nanettelepore.com
Tory Burch	Beverly Hills	310 248 2612	www.toryburch.com

Computers
Other options **Electronics & Home Appliances** p.274

Computers		
Apple Store	800 692 7753	www.apple.com
Best Buy	888 237 8289	www.bestbuy.com
CAM Technologies	310 777 0316	www.cambusinesssolutions.com
Circuit City	800 843 2489	www.circuitcity.com
CRE Rentals	877 266 7725	www.computerrentals.com
Fry's	877 688 7678	www.outpost.com
MacMall	310 353 7443	www.macmall.com
Melrose Mac	888 728 5038	www.melrosemac.com
Office Depot	800 463 3768	www.officedepot.com
Office Max	800 661 5931	www.officemax.com
PC Warehouse	310 347 3370	www.pcwarehouse.com
Staples	800 378 2753	www.staples.com
Wal-Mart	800 925 6278	www.walmart.com

Buying a computer in Los Angeles has never been easier. Major office supply chains like Staples, Office Max and Office Depot carry PCs, laptops and accessories, as do electronics superstores like Best Buy and Circuit City. For comparison shopping, check newspaper ads in the *Los Angeles Times* and neighbourhood newspapers. Sales on PCs are very competitive and you'll even find a decent selection of laptops at Wal-Mart. Prices on Macs are fixed by Apple but you will find deals at warehouse outlets like MacMall that may include free printers, software or other incentives. Sleek and flashy Apple Stores are popping up all over the city with locations at major hot spots like Hollywood & Highland, Third Street Promenade and other popular shopping districts. Boasting highly trained staff, Genius Bars for repairs and on-site help, plus many interactive displays, they have set the bar for other stores by making computer shopping more fun and exciting. For PC experts Fry's offers all the components and gadgets necessary to build your own computer system as well as popular models from major manufacturers including Sony, Toshiba, Compaq and Hewlett Packard. Computer repair centres authorised by the major manufacturers include Fry's, Melrose Mac and CAM Technologies.

Computer SOS
If you need to lease a desktop or laptop computer for short-term use, or while yours is being repaired, CRE Rentals offers daily, monthly and longer term rates for individuals and businesses. (877 266 7725, www.computerrentals.com)

Electronics & Home Appliances
Other options **Camera Equipment** p.269, **Computers** p.274

Big-ticket items like washers, refrigerators and televisions are available at chains like Best Buy and Sears as well as local speciality dealers like Friedman's and Howard's. You'll also find a good selection and frequent sale prices on appliances at home improvement centres like Home Depot and Lowe's. Pacific Sales offers deeply discounted prices on major appliance brands and high-end home entertainment items. Sears, well known for its Kenmore line of washers and dryers, also offers electronics items at affordable prices. Unless you plan to load and setup the new appliance yourself, ask about delivery charges. Some stores offer free delivery while others charge

Electronics & Home Appliances		
Best Buy	888 237 8289	www.bestbuy.com
Circuit City	800 843 2489	www.circuitcity.com
Friedman's	562 989 7756	www.friedmansappliancecenter.com
Fry's	877 688 7678	www.outpost.com
Home Depot	800 553 3199	www.homedepot.com
Howard's	888 246 9273	www.howards.com
Lowe's	800 445 6937	www.lowes.com
Pacific Sales	818 391 2800	www.pacificsales.com
Rent-A-Center	800 422 8186	www.rentacenter.com
Sears	800 349 4358	www.sears.com

anywhere from $25 to $75. If shelling out big bucks for an appliance or TV doesn't fit your current budget, Rent-A-Center offers monthly leasing and rent-to-own plans. Buying used is another option. Check out local newspaper classifieds and Craig's List (www.craigslist.com) online to see what's available in nearby neighbourhoods. People who are moving long distances or divorcing often sell good quality items at very low prices.

Eyewear
Other options **Sports Goods** p.299

Sunglasses are a must in sunny Los Angeles. You'll want at least one good pair to protect your eyes from glare, and another to achieve that ultracool look made famous by film and rock stars. Stylish shades are available from optometrists, speciality optical shops, discount chains and department stores. Many stores like Target and Wal-Mart offer basic eye exams (in the $50 range), and you can have prescriptions filled or buy contact lenses at their vision centres. Designer frames from names like Gucci, Prada, and Dolce & Gabbana are the speciality of upscale optical shops like Oliver Peoples, Eyes on Main and Eyetailor. Knockoffs of designer sunglasses are available at flea markets for ridiculously low prices (two for $15), but keep in mind you get what you pay for. Laser eye surgery is offered at many vision centres throughout Los Angeles. The going rate is $1,000 to $2,400 per eye but specials as low as $500 per eye are often available.

Eyewear		
Eyes On Main	310 399 3302	www.eyesonmain.com
Eyetailor	323 664 2020	www.eyetailor.com
Laser Eye Center	800 805 2737	www.lasereyecenter.com
LensCrafters	310 360 8220	www.lenscrafters.com
Oakley	323 962 9285	www.oakley.com
Oliver Peoples	310 657 2553	www.oliverpeoples.com
Pearle Vision	877 486 6486	www.pearlevision.com
Sunglass Hut	800 786 4527	www.sunglasshut.com
Target Optical	800 591 3869	www.target.com
WalMart	800 925 6278	www.walmart.com

Flowers
Other options **Gardens** p.277

Neighbourhood supermarkets like Vons carry simple floral bouquets, vases and houseplants. Many nurseries and home improvement centres like Home Depot have prearranged floral bouquets, or you can create your own from available flowers. Local farmers markets are a good place to pick up fresh cut flowers for your home. Shops like Romance Etc in Long Beach offer beautiful flowers along with chocolates, jewellery, body lotions and other gifts. Most florists provide delivery service within a specified local area, and many will wire flowers to another city or state through services like Teleflora or FTD. If you are sending flowers internationally, phoning a local flower shop

Flowers		
Conroy's	800 356 9377	www.1800flowers.com
Home Depot	800 553 3199	www.homedepot.com
House of Petals	310 289 2700	www.houseofpetalsla.com
Jacob Maarse	626 449 0246	www.jacobmaarse.com
LA Flower District	213 622 1966	www.laflowerdistrict.com
La Premier	310 276 4665	www.lapremier.com
Manhattan Beach Nursery	310 379 3634	www.marinagardencenter.com
Mark's Garden	818 906 1718	www.marksgarden.net
Romance Etc	562 439 5372	www.romanceetc.com
Scentiments	310 399 4110	www.scentimentsflowers.com
Tic Tock Couture	800 893 6688	www.tictock.com
Vons	866 619 9106	www.ftdfloristsonline.com/vons

in the country where you seek delivery and charging it to your credit card is often less expensive than using a wire service. Full-service florists handle wedding decorations and funeral sprays, while some upscale shops like Tic Toc Couture and La Premier cater to businesses and celebrities with exotic arrangements and elaborate gift baskets.

LA Flower Market

The LA Flower Market in downtown Los Angeles features a spectacular assortment of flowers, plants, dried and silk flowers and floral supplies. Serving the wholesale and retail flower trade, it is located along 8th Street between Wall and San Pedro Streets in Downtown Los Angeles. A $2 admission fee is charged to the general public during special hours (Mon, Wed and Fri, 08:00 to midday, and Tues, Thurs, Sat., 06:00 to midday. Admission on Saturday is only $1.) Florists and wholesale flower dealers get first pick since they arrive well before 06:00, so the earlier you go, the better selection you will have.

Food

Other options **Health Food** p.281, **Supermarkets** p. 309

Boasting hundreds of delis, markets and gourmet shops, plus a plethora of caterers, chocolatiers, icecream parlours and bakeries, Los Angeles has plenty to offer foodies and those who enjoy the simple pleasure of a gourmet cupcake or a slice of artisan bread with perfectly aged cheese. The city's many ethnic neighbourhoods from Hispanic and Asian to Russian and Jewish offer an incredible array of authentic foods from savoury handmade tamales to dim sum, borscht and blintzes. Many delis also stock speciality foods, cheeses, wines and breads that are difficult to find in supermarkets. Upscale markets like Bristol Farms (www.bristolfarms.com) and Gelson's (www.gelsons.com) cater to those with champagne tastes, while Trader Joe's (www.traderjoes.com) provides a bounty of healthy and speciality foods and wines at budget prices. Candy shops selling confections by the pound are found in popular shopping districts, while upscale areas like Beverly Hills and Brentwood are home to some of the most decadent truffles in town.

3849 Torrance Blvd
Torrance
Map 2 C3

Giuliano's

310 540 2500 | www.giulianostorrance.com

Wander into this deli and market any time of day and you're likely to hear accents from Brooklyn and Philadelphia. East coast transplants and Italian food enthusiasts come here to stock up on pasta, sauces, balsamic vinegars, imported olive oils and tasty meats like pepperoni, salami and prosciutto. The crumbled meatball sandwiches and Sicilian sausage and pepper subs bring in throngs of office workers at lunchtime, and the dessert section is worth a trip just for the authentic New York cheesecake and spumoni.

8350 W 3rd St
Park La Brea
Map 7 B1 **17**

Joan's On Third

323 655 2285 | www.joansonthird.com

The sidewalk patio is usually jammed with locals feasting on sandwiches, healthy salads breakfast pastries or veggie omelettes, but it's worth winding your way past the crowd to view the deli shelves inside filled with cheeses, pastas, olives, premium deli meats and desserts. A large selection of prepared dinners, freezer meals and picnic boxes are available, and catering may be arranged for parties and weddings. Elegant food baskets are available for gifts.

624 S La Brea Ave
Hancock Park
Map 7 D3 **18**

La Brea Bakery

323 939 6813 | www.labreabakery.com

When chef Nancy Silverton sought out bread for her restaurant Campanile, she couldn't find the type of loaves she wanted to serve with the food. After a few experiments with bread recipes, she developed a bread starter that still serves as the foundation for the bakery's best-loved artisan-style baguettes. Whether you pick up a sourdough roll and Normandy rye loaf to take home, or you choose to enjoy french toast or a panini sandwich at the cafe, you will leave a new appreciation for bread making artistry.

6333 W 3rd St
West Hollywood
Map 7 B2 **19**

Monsieur Marcel Gourmet Market

323 939 7792 | *www.mrmarcel.com*

Located in the world famous Farmers Market, this gourmet French grocer specialises in artisan, gourmet and imported cheeses, and offers a variety of deli meats, wine, and private label food items. Dozens of enticing condiments are on display, including balsamic vinegars and a selection of different mustards, glazes and meat sauces. Wines from the world's top vineyards are featured and wine tastings led by regional experts are scheduled frequently. A cheese tasting class is held once a month on Monday at 19:00 for $25. Call 323 939 7792 for more information.

9635 S Santa
Monica Blvd
Beverly Hills
Map 4 E2 **20**

Sprinkles Cupcakes

310 274 8765 | *www.sprinklescupcakes.com*

Forget about the pint-sized cupcakes your mom used to bake for school functions. These elegant beauties are works of art and taste as good as they look thanks to premium ingredients like imported Madagascar bourbon vanilla and decadent chocolate sprinkles from France. Fans line up every day to view the rotating menu of enticing little cakes displayed in trays. The red velvet chocolate cupcake is a bestseller but you'll also find ginger lemon, peanut butter chip, carrot and strawberry varieties depending on the season. Prices are $3.25 each or $36 per dozen, but the indulgence is worth it according to regulars who love to sit at the coffee bar and enjoy a cupcake with a tasty cappuccino.

Cultivate Your
Green Thumb
The LA County
Arboretum (626 821
3222, www.arboretum.
org) and Huntington
Botanical Gardens
(626 821 3222,
www.huntington.
org) provide year-
round inspiration
for gardeners. In
addition to awesome
landscaping displays,
both have gift shops
filled with helpful
gardening books,
gadgets and tools.
Their frequent plant
sales are great spots
to find unusual
specimens you won't
often see in nurseries.

Gardens

Other options **Hardware & DIY** p.280, **Flowers** p.275

Gardening is a year-round activity in Los Angeles thanks to the mild climate and the abundance of well-stocked garden centres. Over the last few years homeowners have been transforming basic patios into lavish outdoor living areas complete with high-end barbecues, fireplaces, fountains, and upscale furniture that rivals what some people have in their living rooms. Whether you're in the market for a palm tree or a few flowers to fill a window box, you'll find a variety of nurseries and home improvement centres to meet all your landscaping and home patio needs. Many will come to your home and provide stunning

Plants for sale in Koreatown

garden makeovers, or you can take advantage of in-store consultations and seminars if you're the do-it-yourself type. Local gardeners available through the phone book (or by word of mouth through your neighbours) will provide lawn mowing, weed pulling and shrub trimming services for a weekly, bi-weekly or monthly fee from $40 and up. Prices vary according to services provided and the size of your yard.

216 S Rosemead Blvd
Pasadena
Map 2 E1

California Cactus Center

626 795 2788 | *www.cactuscenter.com*

Located just a 10 minute drive from the Los Angeles County Arboretum, this spacious nursery specialises in cacti and succulents from around the world including exotic specimens, hardy varieties for Southern California landscaping, and unusual plants like bromeliads. The store carries a large assortment of pottery in all sizes as well as planters, baskets, barrels and other unique containers for displaying cacti. Natural and coloured stones, outdoor sculptures and birdbaths are popular accessories for enhancing cactus and succulent gardens. The helpful staff are great at taking the time to explain how to care for different varieties and often post news about upcoming cactus shows and sales in the area.

13198 Mindanao Way
Marina Del Rey
Map 2 C2

Marina Del Rey Garden Center

310 823 5956 | *www.marinagardencenter.com*

Specialising in plants that thrive in the Southern California climate, this popular neighbourhood nursery offers a large selection of perennials, cactus and succulents, plus shrubs and trees that can tolerate strong sun and long periods of drought. Spread over two acres, the garden centre is conducive to browsing, with paths that wind past fountains, pottery and outdoor ornaments to suit both small and large spaces. The knowledgeable staff can help you choose plants that will work best for your yard size and soil type. Delivery service is available seven days a week.

2301 San Joaquin
Hills Rd
Corona del Mar
Map 2 F4

Roger's Gardens

949 640 5800 | *www.rogersgardens.com*

This seven-acre nursery is considered one of the finest garden centres in Southern California and it's well worth the drive to nearby Orange County whether you're on a mission to buy plants or just want to wander through the gorgeous grounds. Renowned for its huge variety of roses and diverse indoor and outdoor plants, it's the kind of place you can poke around for a couple of hours and spend far more money than you intended. Whether you are landscaping a backyard or creating an indoor garden, you'll find a spectacular array of premium quality flowers, trees, and horticulture accessories as well as high-end outdoor furniture. The artfully arranged

Gardens			
Armstrong Garden Center	Various Locations	818 761 1522	www.armstronggardens.com
California Cactus Center	216 S Rosemead Blvd	626 795 2788	www.cactuscenter.com
Green Thumb Nursery	Canoga Park	818 340 6400	www.supergarden.com
Home Depot	Various Locations	800 553 3199	www.homedepot.com
Huntington Botanical Gardens	1151 Oxford Rd, San Marino	626 405 2100	www.huntington.org
LA County Arboretum	301 N Baldwin Av, Arcadia	626 821 3222	www.arboretum.org
Lowe's	Various Locations	800 445 6937	www.lowes.com
Annie's Manhattan Beach Nursery	207 N Sepulveda Blvd	310 379 3634	na
Marina Del Rey Garden Center	13198 Mindanao Way	310 823 5956	www.marinagardencenter.com
Roger's Gardens	2301 San Joaquin Hills Rd	949 640 5800	www.rogersgardens.com
Sperling Nursery	24460 Calabass Rd	818 591 9111	www.sperlingnursery.com
Sunflower Farms	17609 S Western Av, Gardena	310 527 8371	na

gift gallery spans several rooms and features everything from magnificent rare orchids and topiary to elegant picture frames, unique candles, pottery, and collectible holiday ornaments. Gardening classes led by experts are held frequently.

Gifts

Finding a gift shop in LA is easy, but narrowing down the seemingly endless choices is a challenge. Whether you prefer the broad variety of the big shopping malls or the quaint little boutiques on side streets, there's a shop waiting for you with must-have treasures. Department stores like Macy's and Bloomingdale's, discount stores and home decor outlets like Crate and Barrel offer a huge array of gift items for all occasions and maintain wedding registry services. Children's stores La La Ling and Babies R Us are great for personalised keepsakes and traditional gifts like silver spoons and cups for baby showers and christenings. Jacqueline Jarrot has an irresistible selection of women's apparel and accessories from some of the hottest designers around, and 5001 in Long Beach displays everything from martini shakers to handcrafted jewellery boxes and classy writing pens. A gift from Tiffany is always in good taste, whether it's a classic silver keychain or a gold cross to mark a religious occasion like holy communion. Things Remembered specialises in engraved gifts perfect for anniversaries, bar mitzvahs and other special events. Z Gallerie, well known for its affordable candleholders and home accessories, also offers framed wall art. For adults and children of all ages, Puzzle Zoo features a huge assortment of games, collectibles, stuffed toys and dolls. Lemon Tree Bungalow arranges custom gift baskets for celebrity clients and ordinary folk who need help with gift ideas. If you need a last minute present, pharmacies and supermarkets carry racks full of gift cards from major chains and online shopping merchants. All you have to do is decide on the shop, choose the dollar amount and have the card validated. Most larger department stores and speciality shops provide gift wrapping and shipping services.

> ### Star Gazing
>
> Head over to Malibu Country Mart (3835 Cross Creed Road) and you'll see more stars than you're likely to find at trendy Beverly Hills restaurants. Many celebrities have homes in the area or friends who live nearby, so they often drop into chic boutiques like Lisa Kline and Crush before having dinner at Nobu.

Gifts		
5001	562 439 1875	na
Babies R Us	800 869 7787	www.babiesrus
Bloomingdale's	310 772 2100	www.bloomingdales.com
Crate and Barrel	800 967 6696	www.crateandbarrel.com
Jacqueline Jarrot	818 501 2056	www.jacquelinejarrot.com
La La Ling	323 664 4400	www.lalaling.com
Lemon Tree Bungalow	310 657 0211	www.lemontreebungalow.com
Macy's	800 289 6229	www.macys.com
Puzzle Zoo	310 393 9201	www.puzzlezoo.com
Things Remembered	866 902 4438	www.thingsremembered.com
Tiffany	310 273 8880	www.tiffany.com
Z Gallerie	800 358 8288	www.zgallerie.com

Handbags

Shopping for a handbag depends primarily on your lifestyle and how much you're willing to empty your bank account for the sake of fashion. For those in the market for stylish purses in the moderate price range, department stores like Macy's, Bloomingdale's and Nordstrom carry an enormous selection from names like Kate Spade, Burberry and Kenneth Cole. Barney's and Neiman Marcus offer pricier brands like Marc Jacobs, Dolce & Gabbana and Prada. Hitting any of the department stores during clearance sales could net you a fabulous purse from Dooney & Bourke, Guess or Calvin Klein for up to 50% off. Those who can't afford the trendy bags toted by celebrities will find budget priced knockoffs for sale

Handbags

Handbags		
Barneys	9570 Wilshire Blvd	310 276 4400
Bloomingdale's	8500 Beverly Blvd	310 360 2700
Bottega Veneta	457 N Rodeo Dr	310 858 6533
Coach	Various Locations	888 262 2664
Louis Vuitton	6801 Hollywood Blvd	323 962 6216
Macy's	750 W 7th St	213 628 9311
Marc Jacobs	8400 Melrose Pl	323 653 5100
Nordstrom	Various Locations	888 282 6060
Old Navy	Various Locations	800 653 6289
Orange County Marketplace	88 Fair Dr	949 723 6616
Santee Alley	Santee St & Maple Av	213 488 1153
Target	Various Locations	800 591 3869

at outdoor markets like the Orange County Marketplace (see p.307) and from numerous vendors along Santee Alley in the Fashion District (see p.266). Stores like Target and Old Navy cater to the teen crowd with cute styles that won't make mom and dad flinch at the price tags. Shoppers on a quest for the best will find chic designer bags at shops along Robertson, Melrose, Rodeo Drive and Montana Ave. Local vintage and resale shops are purse heaven for those who appreciate classic designs from the past.

Hardware & DIY

Other options **Outdoor Goods** p.289

Professional contractors and do-it-yourselfers flock to Home Depot for everything from lumber and paint to plumbing supplies, kitchen sinks, and nails. With stores in most major neighbourhoods throughout Los Angeles, the chain offers a huge selection, friendly service, and expert help if needed. Frequent in-store workshops cover topics like building a deck or choosing paint colours. Professional installation is available on a wide range of products from kitchen cabinetry and countertops to flooring and plumbing fixtures. Other large hardware chains include Lowe's and Orchard. Some shoppers may find smaller neighbourhood stores less intimidating, and they're a good choice for basic needs like drain plugs, replacement screws and the like. Speciality lumber supply outlets and paint stores often carry higher quality products and more choices than the chains. Sears is well known for its Craftsman line of tools and is a good place to stock up on accessories and organiser cabinets for a home workshop. Restoration Hardware offers retro chic tools, gadgets, paints, unique drawer pulls, doorknobs and lighting, among other items.

Hardware & DIY		
B&B Lumber	818 983 1645	na
Dick's True Value	310 397 3220	www.dickstruevalue.com
Home Depot	800 553 3199	www.homedepot.com
Koontz Hardware	310 652 0123	www.koontzhardware.com
Lowe's	800 445 6937	www.lowes.com
Orchard Hardware	888 674 4438	www.osh.com
Restoration Hardware	800 910 9836	www.restorationhardware.com
Sears	800 349 4358	www.sears.com
Tashman Screens	323 656 7028	www.tashmanscreenshardware.com
Vista Paint	310 474 7229	www.vistapaint.com

Hats

In many areas of the country hats are a necessity for coping with cold weather, wind, and rain, but in Los Angeles, they are mostly worn for recreational sports, casual weekend wear, or to make a fashion statement. Stores like Hat World/Lids carry baseball caps in a rainbow of colours with logos for sports teams, TV shows, beer brands, rock groups and cartoon characters. True hat fanatics will be in heaven at Goorin's on Melrose. Featuring a huge selection of styles for men and women including everything from newsboy caps and duckbills to straw cowboy hats and fedoras, there's something for everyone priced from $18 to $100. Fun grab bags contain four or more clearance hats in a variety of styles for $80. Bucket hats, popular with all ages, can be found at upscale stores like Burberry and numerous department stores, speciality shops and flea markets. Knit caps, a favourite with the hip-hop crowd, skateboarders and skiers, are available at chain stores like REI,

Hats	
Burberry	310 657 2424
Goorin Hat Shop	323 951 0393
HatWorld/Lids	310 360 9518
Old Navy	800 653 6289
REI	800 426 4840
Roger Dunn	888 216 5252
Sports Authority	888 801 9164
Urban Outfitters	800 282 2200
Val Surf	818 225 8177
Virgin Megastore	323 769 8520

Sports Authority and Old Navy as well as youth-focused shops like Val Surf and Urban Outfitters. Roger Dunn offers a full range of golf hats and visors from Adidas, Calloway and Nike as well as the popular Kangol driving cap worn frequently by Tom Watson and other pro golfers. Music stores and trendy vintage shops are your best bet for caps with classic rock band logos.

Health Food
Other options **Health Clubs** p.245, **Food** p.276

Los Angeles is a mecca for health food devotees, vegetarians and those seeking to eliminate unhealthy products from their lifestyle. Along with supermarkets specialising in health foods like Whole Foods Market and Trader Joe's, there are numerous vitamin and nutrition stores like GNC and Lindbergh Nutrition, which cater to dieters and athletes with supplements, protein powders,

Health Food	
All Pro Health Foods	310 454 7457
Crescenta Canada Health Foods	818 249 8886
Erewhon Natural Foods	323 937 0777
Follow Your Heart	818 438 3240
Full O'Life Foods	818 845 7411
GNC	877 462 4700
Jamba Juice	866 473 7848
Lindburgh Nutrition	310 372 1028
Trader Joe's	800 746 7857
Whole Foods	323 848 4200

energy bars and juices. Many of the stores offer an array of products that are gluten, dairy and wheat free for those with dietary restrictions. Speciality stores like Jamba Juice and some juice bars adjacent to fitness centres blend fruit and juices with powder boosters that can boost energy, enhance immunity or soothe the soul with various vitamins, proteins and herbs. Chain grocery stores like Ralphs and Vons have enlarged their health food inventory with aisles full of organic, all-natural and sugar-free foods. Follow Your Heart Market and Café sells its own line of vegan products, plus organic produce. Whole Foods is celebrated for its tasty salad bar, takeout foods, and large selection of all-natural personal care products.

Stay Healthy
Many health food stores like Lindburgh Nutrition (310 372 1028, www.nutritionexpress. com) offer consultations with a nutritionist who can help you determine which vitamins, supplements and foods will work best for your individual needs. Some stores also offer occasional low-cost health screenings for high cholesterol, elevated blood pressure, and other conditions. Sign up for newsletters and check bulletin boards and flyers for information on upcoming events.

Home Furnishings & Accessories
Other options **Hardware & DIY** p.280

Decorating your home or apartment is limited only by your space and budget since home furnishings and accessories stores seem to be everywhere. Eclectic retailers like Anthropologie and the Home Grown Store effortlessly mix

Home Furnishings & Accessories

Anthropologie	800 543 1039	www.anthropologie.com
Bed, Bath and Beyond	800 462 3966	www.bedbathandbeyond.com
Big Daddy's Antiques	310 769 6600	www.bdantiques.com
Bloomingdale's	310 360 2700	www.bloomingdales.com
California Closets	800 274 6754	www.californiaclosets.com
Container Store	888 266 8246	www.containerstore.com
Cost Plus	877 967 5362	www.worldmarket.com
Crate and Barrel	800 967 6696	www.crateandbarrel.com
Home Grown Store	323 933 5400	www.homegrownstore.com
IKEA	818 842 IKEA	www.ikea.com
Lamps Plus	800 782 1967	www.lampsplus.com
Macy's	310 694 3333	www.macys.com
Pasadena Antique Center	626 449 7706	www.pasadenaantiquecenter.com
Pier One Imports	800 245 4595	www.pier1.com
Pottery Barn	888 779 5176	www.potterybarn.com
Restoration Hardware	800 910 9836	www.restorationhardware.com
Rose Bowl Flea Market	323 560 7469	www.rgcshows.com
Sit and Sleep	888 506 1059	www.sitandsleep.com
Sur La Table	310 395 0390	www.surlatable.com
Wickes Clearance Center	818 780 2244	www.wickes.com
Z Gallerie	800 358 8288	www.zgallerie.com

apparel, rustic furniture and eclectic accessories in settings that invite browsing. Pottery Barn and Z Gallerie offer contemporary and retro inspired furnishings and accessories for every room in the home with prices ranging from $4 plates to $1200 sofas. Crate and Barrel and Sur La Table primarily offer dinnerware and linens, but you'll also find interesting gadgets, cookware, serving pieces and much more. Bed, Bath and Beyond stocks everything from sheets and towels to showerheads and blenders. Bloomingdale's and Macy's have home galleries filled with mid-range to upscale furniture, designer linens, lamps,

Sleep On It ◄

and accessories, while speciality furniture stores like Wickes offer a wide selection of affordably priced furnishings for every room. Antique buffs will find home, garden and architectural treasures at Big Daddy Antiques and malls like Pasadena Antique Center. The Rose Bowl Flea Market, held the second Sunday of each month, attracts celebrities and early bird shoppers who clamour for retro furniture and unique collectibles. Great deals on bookcases, accent tables, lamps and accessories can be found at IKEA and world import stores Pier One and Cost Plus. Interior decorating services are available from upscale furniture stores and licensed contractors in most areas of the city. Prices vary from low-cost hourly consultations to expensive home makeovers. If organising clutter is your goal, the Container Store offers many low-cost options, or splurge on a custom-built closet organising system from California Closets. Reupholstery shops will give your favourite chair a new lease on life, or you can cover stains and worn spots with handsome slipcovers available at department stores and discount outlets.

Serta, Sealy and Simmons market mattresses under different names at department stores and independent dealers so comparison-shopping is tricky. Lie down on several mattresses at two or three stores and compare features, comfort and prices. Beware of warehouse mattress outlets hawking little-known brands at cheap prices. The discount beds probably aren't built to last. Expect to pay between $600 and $900 for a quality mattress set. Most dealers provide free delivery, setup and disposal of your old mattress, while department stores may charge a small fee.

Jewellery & Watches

Rodeo Drive in Beverly Hills is the haven for internationally acclaimed jewellers. Along the posh streets you'll find Cartier, De Beers, Tiffany and Bvlgari among other revered gem specialists. Ever wonder where celebrities get the jewels they wear on the red carpet? Harry Winston and Van Cleef & Arpels supply many of the diamonds adorning the necks, wrists and earlobes of A-List stars. Their luxurious boutiques decorated with sumptuous fabrics, sparkling chandeliers and glimmering gold are a little intimidating for first timers, but the museum-worthy jewels and elegant displays are fun to look at even if you can't afford to buy. For shoppers seeking more down-to-earth prices, Inta Gems, Diamonds and Jewelry located in the Jewelry District downtown specialises in diamond engagement rings and custom-made gemstone jewellery at wholesale prices. Robbins Brothers, a chain with multiple locations, offers one of the largest selections of engagement rings in the area. Kay Jewelers, found at numerous shopping malls, also offers moderately priced diamonds. Those who prefer more contemporary pieces will like TeNo, an avant garde boutique featuring jewellery and watches constructed in stainless steel and teamed with gemstones, wood, ceramics and pearls. Fine timepieces from Movado, Rolex and Omega can be found in Beverly Hills boutiques and at South Coast Plaza in Orange County. Upscale department stores (see p.304) carry designer watches from Dolce & Gabbana, Fendi and Marc Jacobs, while mid-range stores are well stocked with Seiko, Tissot and Swiss Army. Second Time Around Watch Company buys and sells used luxury and vintage watches including brands like Longines, Rolex, Cartier, and Patek Phillippe. All come with a one-year warranty and prices considerably lower than if you bought them new. Fossil and Swatch stores offer a wide variety of affordably priced watch designs, replacement bands and gift items appropriate for all ages.

Jewellery & Watches

Bvlgari	310 858 9216	www.bulgari.com
Cartier	310 275 4272	www.cartier.com
DeBeers	310 228 1900	www.debeers.com
Erica Courtney	323 938 2373	www.ericacourtney.com
Fossil	800 449 3096	www.fossil.com
Geary's	310 887 4250	www.gearys.com
Harry Winston	310 271 8554	www.harrywinston.com
Inta Gems, Diamonds & Jewelry	213 689 9650	www.intagems.com
Kay Jewelers	800 527 8029	www.kayjewelers.com
Moondance	310 395 5516	www.moondancejewelry.com
Movado	800 810 2311	www.movado.com
Omega	310 860 9990	www.omegawatches.com
Robbins Brothers	800 295 1543	www.robbinsbros.com
Second Time Around Watch Co.	310 271 6615	www.secondtimearoundwatchco.com
Swatch	800 879 2824	www.swatch.com
TeNo	323 464 6566	www.teno.com
Tiffany	310 273 8880	www.tiffany.com
Van Cleef & Arpels	310 276 1161	www.vancleef-arpels.com

Kids' Items

Children's clothes and shoes are available at major department stores, mid-range stores and discount stores like Target and Wal-Mart. There are many children's speciality shops throughout LA. Some cater primarily to babies and toddlers, while others offer sizes for infants, toddlers and pre-teens. This Little Piggy Wears Cotton features both European and American labels, plus a private-label line for infants and children up to age 12. The store also carries a good selection of toys, books, accessories and gift items. Old Navy is a great place to stock up on essentials like T-shirts, socks, pants and shorts. Fabrics are easy care, and you'll find a large selection of styles and sizes at very affordable prices. Gap Kids, Children's Place and Gymboree are in the mid-range as far as pricing, and offer a good selection of tops and bottoms, swimwear, hats and shoes. Kitson Kids and Lola Rouge Kids offer trendy fashions for parents who don't mind paying higher prices for designer labels. Tough Cookies Children's boutique provides a safe play area for kids to have fun while mom and dad shop. American Girl Place, themed around the American Girl doll line, combines an apparel and accessories boutique with a youth-oriented cafe, beauty salon and live entertainment. Birthday packages are available, and there is a photo

Kids' Items

American Girl Place	877 247 5223
Childrens Place	877 752 2382
Gap Kids	800 427 7895
Girl Mania	949 721 5709
Gymboree	877 449 6932
Kitson Kids	310 246 3829
Kohl's	866 887 8884
Lola Rouge Kids	949 719 1919
My Diva Girls	818 470 8168
Old Navy	800 653 6289
Pottery Barns Kids	800 993 4923
Sanrio	800 759 6454
This Little Piggy Wears Cotton	310 260 2727
Tough Cookies Children's Boutique	818 990 0972

studio on site for souvenir pictures. Girl Mania offers apparel and accessories, costumes and a fun makeup area where kids can try on costumes or have a party with friends. IKEA and Pottery Barn Kids feature a large assortment of reasonably priced children's furniture, bedding and accessories. Sanrio stores, located in major shopping malls, are a fun place to take the kids for Hello Kitty merchandise including school supplies, scrapbooks, stuffed toys, costumes, backpacks and cell phone cases.

Lingerie

Other options **Clothes** p.266

Show up at any nightclub in LA and it may seem than most women are wearing lingerie and little else. Even on the street the underwear as outerwear trend is going strong with lacy bra straps accenting body-hugging tank tops and sexy camisoles peeking out from tailored suit jackets. Whether you are shopping for a romantic honeymoon nightie or a curve-enhancing body briefer to smooth out the bumps and bulges under a clingy dress, Los Angeles offers an array of lingerie shops to please everyone from hopeless romantics to temptresses who dress to thrill. A visit to Nordstrom Rack may net you hot lingerie from Hanky Panky, Elle MacPherson or Le Mystere at discounted prices. Lane Bryant Cacique caters to fuller figures with sizes from 32B to 42F. Trashy Lingerie and Agent Provocateur live up to their monikers with provocative crotchless panties, see-through bras, fantasy costumes, and kinky accessories like fur-trimmed handcuffs.

1406 Micheltorena St
Silver Lake
Map 8 C2 **21**

Bittersweet Butterfly

323 660 4303 | *www.bittersweetbutterfly.com*
The atmosphere at this quaint little shop is as romantic as it gets with deliciously scented soaps and potpourri, beautiful perfume bottles, and a gallery filled with exotic flowers, sparkling jewellery and irresistible chocolate confections. The upscale lingerie line includes both sexy and demure designs as well as comfy pyjamas and slippers for lounging. Jewellery and gift items range from moderate to expensive. Whether you are shopping for yourself, your spouse or a friend, the staff are experts at choosing gifts that make women feel pampered and adored.

6751 Hollywood Blvd
Hollywood
Map 6 B1 **22**

Frederick's of Hollywood

323 957 5953 | *www.frederickshollywood.com*
Although branches of Fredericks Hollywood are found in malls around the city and throughout the country, the Hollywood Boulevard store features a small lingerie museum that pays tribute to celebrities who have been photographed in sexy lingerie. Frederick's claims to be the first to introduce thongs and pushup bras among other notable designs, and they were producing provocative women's underwear and sleepwear long before Victoria's Secret entered the scene. Among the hottest sellers are the maribou trimmed stilettos that make any woman feel like a movie star. Lingerie sizes range from petite to plus size, and prices are moderate.

433 N Rodeo Dr
Beverly Hills
Map 4 E2 **23**

La Perla

310 860 0561 | *www.laperla.com*
Countless models and actresses have graced the pages of fashion magazines in sexy and luxurious La Perla lingerie. The lavish Rodeo Drive boutique exudes elegance with displays that showcase the Italian lingerie designs like fine jewels. Along with exquisite bra and bikini sets in the $150 and up range, the store carries silk pyjamas, swimwear too gorgeous to get wet, glamorous nightgowns, and a selection of camisoles and bustiers perfect for turning heads on a night of clubhopping. While the pricey

garments are a splurge for most women, fans rave the quality is outstanding, and the sensuous fabrics feel marvellous against the skin.

Lingerie

Agent Provocateur	323 653 0229	www.agentprovocateur.com
Bittersweet Butterfly	323 660 4303	www.bittersweetbutterfly.com
Faire Frou Frou	818 783 4970	www.fairefroufrou.com
Frederick's of Hollywood	323 957 5953	www.frederickshollywood.com
La Perla	310 860 0561	www.laperla.com
Lane Bryant Cacique	800 888 4163	www.lanebryant.com
Nordstrom Rack	310 641 4046	www.nordstrom.com
Only Hearts	310 393 3088	www.onlyhearts.com
Sara's Lingerie	818 990 1270	www.saraslingerie.com
Trashy Lingerie	310 652 4543	www.trashy.com

Posh Leather

Premium leather brands are available at upscale department stores, but if you want to shop in a more luxurious setting, check out these designer boutiques in Beverly Hills: Bottega Veneta (457 N Rodeo Dr, 310 858 6533) Fendi (355 N Rodeo Dr, 310 276 8888) Gucci (347 N Rodeo Dr, 310, 278 3451) Hermes (434 N Rodeo Dr, 310 278 0890) Prada (343 N Rodeo Dr, 310 278 8661) Louis Vuitton (295 N Rodeo Dr, 310 3601506)

Luggage & Leather

There's a certain cool factor to wearing leather in LA, and apparel is easy to find all year round. Trendy boutiques and department stores like Bloomingdale's and Macy's carry moderate to high priced styles of jackets and trousers, while Harley Davidson shops are your best bet for fringed jackets, lace-up vests and leather caps. Union War Surplus store stocks a good selection of budget motorcycle jackets for men and women, plus belts, gloves, and wallets. Jo Ann Page Leather Studio is known for unique handbags and backpacks handcrafted in premium leather and exotic skins. If you salivate over the trendy handbags carried by models and celebrities but can't afford the high prices, a trip to the Orange County Marketplace will get you a bargain knockoff of any brand you can name. It's also a great place for inexpensive luggage. From wheeled garment bags and carry-on styles in every size, shape and colour to children's suitcases with cartoon logos, you'll pay way below retail. Wilson's Leather stores found in many area shopping malls, feature leather apparel for men and women, briefcases and accessories, plus a large inventory of luggage. Department stores stock a wide assortment of moderately priced luggage from names like Samsonite, Tumi and Kenneth Cole. Target is the place to go for budget models in lightweight, durable fabrics, while travel speciality store Distant Lands features high quality bags for everything from backpacking to touring Europe. Lazar's Luggage Superstore carries a wide assortment of computer cases, plus wheeled backpacks for students, leather agendas, organisers and money clips.

Luggage & Leather

Bloomingdale's	310 360 2700	www.bloomingdales.com
Distant Lands	626 449 3220	www.distantlands.com
Harley Davidson	818 754 6200	www.hollywoodharley.com
Jo Anne Page Leather Studio	323 037 7406	www.joannpageleather.com
Lazar's Fine Leather Goods	818 784 1355	www.lazarsluggage.com
Macy's	213 628 9311	www.macys.com
Orange County Marketplace	949 723 6616	www.ocmarketplace.com
Target	800 440 0680	www.target.com
Union War Surplus Store	310 833 2949	www.unionwarsurplus.com
Wilson's Leather	818 841 7789	www.wilsonsleather.com

Maternity Items

Expectant mothers no longer have to trade fashion for comfort during pregnancy. Liz Lange was one of the first designers to transform maternity clothes from dowdy

Maternity Items	
Babystyle	877 378 9537
JC Penney	800 322 1189
Liz Lange	310 273 0099
Moms the Word	866 435 6667
Motherhood Maternity	800 466 6223
Nordstrom	888 282 6060
Pancia Maternity	310 392 2867
Pea in the Pod	877 273 2763
Pump Station	310 998 1981
Target	800 591 3869

to dazzling, and her Beverly Hills boutique is a favourite of celebrity mothers-to-be. Can't afford her high end line? Target carries a line of maternity wear designed by Liz that is stylish and quite affordable. Moms the Word in Santa Monica is known for its trendy maternity fashions including embellished jeans, swimwear and office separates that are smart looking without being uncomfortable. Pancia in Venice stocks premium denim in maternity sizes and a large selection of flattering tops that can help carry you through the last months of pregnancy in high style. Chains like Motherhood Maternity, Babystyle and Pea in the Pod are found in major malls and carry maternity wear in a range of styles and prices including casual separates, evening wear, lingerie, and pyjamas. The Pump Station in Santa Monica rents and sells hospital grade breast pumps and features everything from nursing bras and support belts to baby slings, breastfeeding books, and developmental baby toys. Department stores JC Penney and Nordstrom are great spots for stocking up on maternity fashions, diaper bags, and cute gifts for baby showers.

Medicine

Other options **General Medical Care** p.110

Pharmacies are so widespread in Los Angeles you won't have to go far to find one. Many hospitals and doctor's offices also have pharmacies, but they are often more expensive. Discount chains Target and Wal-Mart offer more than 100 common generic drugs for only $4. Many pharmacies

Medicine		
CVS	888 607 4287	www.cvs.com
Ralphs	888 437 3496	www.ralphs.com
RiteAid	800 748 3243	www.riteaid.com
SavOn	877 728 6655	www.savon.com
Target	800 591 3869	www.target.com
Walgreens	800 925 4733	www.walgreens.com
WalMart	800 925 6278	www.walmart.com

also reduce prices if you have an insurance-issued prescription drug card. Over-the-counter medicines for common ailments like headaches, stomach upsets and heartburn are widely available at pharmacies, supermarkets and in limited quantities at convenience stores. Since the ingredient pseudoephedrine is used as a component in methamphetamines, restrictions on all medicines containing it have made it necessary to request cold and sinus pills from the pharmacist. No prescription is required, but you must show an ID and sign for the purchase. Many pharmacies in Los Angeles are open 24 hours and some have drive-thru windows for fast and easy pickup of prescriptions. The following chains have multiple locations throughout LA. Check their websites for the branch closest to you. Some are open 24/7.

Mobile Phones

Other options **Telephone** p.106

Mobile Phones		
Apple Store	800 692 7753	www.apple.com
AT&T	800 331 0500	www.wireless.att.com
Sprint	888 211 4727	www.sprint.com
Target	800 591 3869	www.target.com
T-Mobile	800 937 8997	www.tmobile.com
Verizon	800 922 0204	www.verizonwireless.com
WalMart	800 925 6278	www.walmart.com

Mobile phones have become so common it's rare to walk down the street without seeing several people using them. Major providers have stores located throughout LA and many have kiosks in shopping malls. Most electronic retailers also carry mobile phones and accessories. Phone service providers like AT&T, T-Mobile, Sprint, Nextel and Verizon continuously offer promotions featuring a choice of deeply discounted phones. The catch is the consumer must sign up for a one or two year contract that includes a specified number of minutes and features for a monthly fee. Prices for cell phones range from free (with a commitment for a minimum number of months) to $50 and up. Monthly service rates average $39.99 to $69.99 depending on usage and extras. Apple's iPhone is a must have and combines music, video and internet access, it's a pricey piece and service can only be had through AT&T. Several companies offer family plans where two phones connected to one service plan share minutes and calling features for a monthly rate of $60 to $100. Adding additional lines is extra. Most contracts include an early termination fee, so switching providers can be costly. Applying for a contract involves a credit check, but some providers offer automatic payment plans through checking accounts or debit cards for those with poor credit.

Unlike many countries where shoppers can buy phones without being locked into service from one provider, mobile phone users in the United States have had to contend with phone

Spoilt for choice at Amoeba Music

service providers that lock phones so they will only work on their own network. Some mobile phone users have discovered their phones don't work if they travel to other countries or if they do work, they end up paying expensive roaming charges. Services like Unlock to Talk (800 891 0522, www.unlocktotalk.com) provide unlocking codes for a fee to consumers who want to use their phones with a different service provider. Unlocked phones are also available for purchase at www.amazon.com. An unlocked phone offers the convenience of using the device with any GSM network carrier that uses SIM cards. For those who don't want to commit to a contract, inexpensive pre-paid phones and refill cards in amounts from $10 to $100 are widely available at pharmacies, supermarkets and discount chains like Target and Wal-Mart. California legislation effective in July 2008 bans the use of a wireless phone while driving unless a hands-free apparatus is installed in the vehicle. Anyone under 18 is prohibited from using a cell phone while driving.

Music, DVDs & Videos

6400 Sunset Blvd
Hollywood
Map 6 C2 **24**

Amoeba Music
323 245 6400 | *www.amoeba.com*
This popular independent shop catering to music and movie buffs quickly earned a devoted Los Angeles fan base. Offering a diverse selection of new and used titles from classic rock and country to British imports, world music, classic jazz, hip-hop and electronica, it's the kind of record store that seems to be disappearing in most parts of the country. For first timers, stepping through the door is a little like being in a wall to wall candy store, only here the sweet surprise is reasonably priced music and movie titles, classic posters and all sorts of unique collectibles. You can easily spend hours poking through used record bins, chatting with the friendly staff, and listening to the live bands who often drop by to play. The buy and trade fees vary depending on the title and

condition, but you can expect to be well rewarded for hard to find items. Parking is free with validation at the underground garage or in the lot behind the store.

6801 Hollywood Blvd
Hollywood
Map 6 B1 **25**

Virgin Megastore

323 769 8520 | www.virginmega.com

Sandwiched between The Kodak Theatre and Grauman's Chinese Theatre, the Hollywood and Highland branch of Virgin Megastore is well known for its impressive selection of music imports, and is a good place to look when you're trying to locate an obscure movie title. The store provides a large number of listening stations, giving you a chance to try before you buy. Along with movies, music, and accessories for storing and cleaning CDs, you'll find a fascinating array of books on film, television and pop culture, electronic gadgets from Mp3 players and headphones to digital cameras, plus a gigantic selection of video games. Be sure to check out the apparel boutiques for men and women featuring cool hats, bags and a collection of rock, punk and retro T-shirts.

Music, DVDs & Videos

Amoeba Music	323 245 6400	www.amoeba.com
Barnes and Noble	800 843 2665	www.barnesandnoble.com
Blockbuster	310 659 8366	www.blockbuster.com
Borders	888 812 6657	www.borders.com
Eddie Brandt's Saturday Matinee	818 506 4242	www.ebsmvideo.com
Fingerprints	562 433 4996	www.fingerprints.com
Second Spin	818 986 6866	www.secondspin.com
Suncoast	310 921 3640	www.suncoast.com
Target	800 591 3869	www.target.com
Video West	818 760 0096	www.videowest.net
Vidiots	310 392 8508	www.vidiotsvideo.com
Virgin Megastore	323 769 8520	www.virginmega.com

Musical Instruments

Other options **Music, DVDs & Videos** p.287, **Music Lessons** p.229

Whether you are a professional musician in an orchestra or a beginner longing for your first guitar or piano, LA boasts plenty of music stores catering to all skill levels. Fields Pianos in West Los Angeles specialises in new and used models with an impressive selection including Steinway, Kohler & Campbell, Boston, Essex, and Kawai. Used pianos are serviced and restored before they are put on sale. The store also offers an institutional department and maintains a concert and artist division for professional musicians. Rock and Roll Emporium in Huntington Beach is worth the drive for its cool collection of custom component guitars, memorabilia, pedals, and accessories. Hollywood Piano Company in Burbank offers a staff comprising musicians, teachers and piano technicians. Their clientele includes the LA Chamber Orchestra and Burbank Philharmonic. Guitar Center, with several area locations, is a music lover's paradise with one of the largest and most reasonably

Musical Instruments

Fantastic Instruments	626 794 7554	www.gotofmi.com
Fields Pianos	310 207 2400	www.fieldspianos.com
Guitar Center	866 498 7882	www.guitarcenter.com
Hollywood Piano Co.	800 697 4266	www.hollywoodpiano.com
Krell Piano/Instrument	310 470 6602	na
Rock and Roll Emporium	714 960 4040	www.rockandrollemporium.com
Sam Ash Music	323 850 1050	www.samashmusic.com
String Instrument Repair	323 851 9998	www.violuthier.com
Voltage Guitars	818 762 3411	www.voltageguitars.com
West Coast Drum Center	877 923 7867	www.westcoastdrums.com

priced selections of instruments for beginners and professionals. Along with keyboards, drum sets and guitars from major names like Fender and Gibson, the store carries recording and lighting equipment and a huge array of accessories from picks and guitar straps to drumsticks and instrument cases. Voltage Guitars in West Hollywood is known for its vintage bass, electric and acoustic guitars from names like Fender and Stratocaster. Co-owner Lloyd Chiate played with a few Motown bands in the 70s and has sold guitars to many well-known musicians. Sam Ash Music, with locations in Hollywood and Torrance, offers a full complement of band instruments including brass, woodwinds, percussion and strings, plus a large inventory of instructional and music books. Rentals are available by the day, the week or the month at most stores with prices varying according to the brand, quality and instrument. Local pawnshops are a great place for beginners to pick up used instruments at bargain prices.

Outdoor Goods
Other options **Hardware & DIY** p.280, **Sports Goods** p.295, **Camping** p.216

Outdoor enthusiasts have a wide choice of sports-focused dealers to choose from. General merchandisers like Target, Sears and Wal-Mart carry limited selections of sports gear, but they also have seasonal sales with great deals. REI and Sport Chalet sell equipment for everything from hiking and rock-climbing to skiing, kayaking and camping. Along with trekking poles, car racks and lanterns, they offer snowboards, bikes, helmets and top brands of skiwear, boots and hats. REI is also known for its eco-friendly apparel made from recycled fibres, hemp and bamboo. Sport Chalet's speciality is ski equipment and clothing, but they carry apparel and accessories for a huge array of sports from boxing and in-line skating to tennis and watersports. Surfboards and wetsuits are the main attraction at Becker Surfboards, but you'll also find backpacks, sunglasses, swim fins and tote bags. ZJ Boarding House in Santa Monica specialises in equipment for surfers, snowboarders and skateboarding. Union War Surplus, a fixture in San Pedro since 1946, sells discounted military gear perfect for camping, hiking and other outdoor pursuits. Stocking everything from thermal underwear and camouflage pants to tents, sleeping bags, knives and firearms, it's also a great place to buy flashlights, canteens and first-aid kits. Turners Outdoorsman is a favourite of fishermen, who appreciate the extensive selection of rods, lures and accessories. Hunting and fishing licences are sold at all store locations, and they offer firearms training courses. Roger Dunn is one of the major suppliers of golf equipment and apparel with products from Calloway, Nike, Ben Hogan and Cobra among many others.

Outdoor Goods		
Becker Surfboards	310 320 5736	www.beckersurf.com
REI	800 426 4840	www.rei.com
Roger Dunn	888 216 5252	www.worldwidegolfshops.com
Sears	800 349 4358	www.sears.com
Sport Chalet	888 801 9162	www.sportchalet.com
Target	800 591 3869	www.target.com
Turner Outdoorsman	818 996 5033	www.turners.com
Union War Surplus Store	310 833 2949	www.unionwarsurplus.com
Wal-Mart	800 925 6278	www.walmart.com
ZJ Boarding House	310 392 5646	www.zjboardinghouse.com

Party Accessories
Chuck E Cheese is a popular venue for children's birthday parties. After sharing pizza and cake the birthday celebrants get to enjoy a stage show featuring costumed characters and visit the arcade filled with video games. Once Upon A Princess supplies costumed characters like Cinderella and The Little Mermaid for children's parties. The event package includes face painting, games, songs and other activities. LA Pinata Party Supply is one of the best sources in town for inexpensive candy-filled piñatas. Styles range from comic book super heroes to a variety of animals and

Creepy costumes

cartoon characters. Balloons On The Run rent inflatable jumpers and bouncers, a great solution for keeping noisy children outside. Vine American Party Supply is headquarters for balloon bouquets, party hats, noisemakers, disposable tableware, and seasonal decorations. They also offer personalised favours, gift-wrapping and a balloon delivery service. DJs and karaoke machines are widely available for adult parties and most party supply stores also rent fog machines and decorations for Halloween. Baskin Robbins is a crowd favourite for its delicious icecream filled cakes, and The Torrance Bakery is renowned for personalised birthday cakes. Offering a huge selection of cleverly decorated theme cakes for children, they also scan photos onto cakes for adult parties and other occasions. Inexpensive birthday cakes are available at most supermarket bakeries and you'll find a large assortment of decorative icings, birthday candles and sprinkles in the baking aisle. Supermarkets and delis also offer many types of affordably priced food trays including sandwiches, fruits, hors d'oeuvres and desserts. Most restaurants provide catering menus for parties.

Mini Explorer

Don't let the size of this little star fool you – it's full of insider info, maps, contacts, tips and facts for visitors. From shops to spas, bars to bargains and everything in between, the Mini Explorer range helps you get the most out of your stay in the city, however long you're there for.

Party Accessories		
Balloon Celebrations	888 522 5566	www.ballooncelebrations.com
Balloons On The Run	323 578 6300	na
Baskin Robbins	800 859 5339	www.baskinrobbins.com
California DJs	714 751 3322	www.californiadjs.com
Chuck E. Cheese	888 778 7193	www.chuckecheese.com
Hallmark Gold Crown	800 425 5627	www.hallmark.com
Herman's Party Supply	310 530 7735	www.hermansparty.com
LA Pinata Party Supply	310 306 3348	na
Michaels	800 642 4235	www.michaels.com
Once Upon A Princess	626 622 1220	na
Ralphs	888 437 3496	www.ralphs.com
Target	800 591 3869	www.target.com
Torrance Bakery	310 326 1944	www.torrancebakery.com
Vine American Party Store	323 467 7124	www.vineamericanparty.com

Perfumes & Cosmetics

Department store beauty counters in Los Angeles showcase all the major cosmetic brands like Elizabeth Arden, Estee Lauder, Lancome and Prescriptives along with popular fragrance lines like Calvin Klein, Ralph Lauren and Liz Claiborne. Feel free to spritz away until you find the scent that's just right among the endless perfume bottles on display. The helpful salespeople can also guide you to makeup and skin care products that will work best for your skin type and colouring. Neiman Marcus and Barney's carry higher-end cosmetics and perfumes as well as pricey skin care lines like ReVive and La Mer. Macy's is great for scoring bonus gifts from manufacturers particularly during the holiday season. Caswell Massey and Bath and Body Works specialise in fragrant soaps, shower gels, colognes and boxed sets designed for both sexes. Speciality supply stores like Ulta feature a full range of personal care products from tweezers and makeup sponges to hair colouring kits.

Various Locations ◄ ## Bath and Body Works
800 756 5005 | *www.bathandbodyworks.com*
You can smell this store from half a block away, and enticing aromas like coconut, cinnamon and vanilla inevitably lure you in. Before you know it you're holding a basket and loading it up with two-for-one specials on heavenly smelling shower gels, body lotions and soaps. The staff are friendly without being pushy, and the line of products keeps expanding with signature skin care lines for men, women and teens. In addition to body care products in scents like plumrose, cucumber melon and pearberry, the store offers a line of aromatherapy products for the home called Wallflowers. Reasonably priced gift sets are big sellers during major holidays and scents like pumpkin pie and winter candy apple are only offered seasonally.

Fashion Island ◄ ## Caswell Massey
Suite 205 *949 640 6750* | *www.caswellmassey.com*
Newport Beach With a colourful history that stretches back to 1752, this renowned manufacturer of
Map 2 F2 fragrances and lotions boasts several former presidents and first ladies as fans. The classy shop located above the Fashion Island foodcourt features hardwood floors, neutral walls and a sophisticated uncluttered layout to perfectly showcase the displays of soaps, lotions and gift sets. Moderately priced items for men include old fashioned shaving kits, and Newport, a fresh, citrusy scent that is clean and masculine without being overpowering. Top sellers for women include Freesia, Damask Rose and English Lavender. Sampler sets are available for those who like to try different fragrances before buying larger sizes.

8327 Beverly Blvd ◄ ## Scent Bar
West Hollywood *323 782 8300* | *www.luckyscent.com*
Map 7 B1 **26** What started as a successful online perfume business expanded to include this West Hollywood boutique. The Scent Bar is a favourite with women and men who like to take their time in choosing a new fragrance. The owners designed the shop with a long white bar and comfy stools to give customers a place to relax and sip a cup of tea as they choose samples from the long list of sought-after scents. Shelves full of gorgeous perfume bottles line the walls, and an extensive collection of candles and aromatherapy items for the home are also available. Fragrances are selected by name, or clients may choose according to type such as aquatic, earthy, citrus, or masculine. Sample vials of any scent are $3 to $4, and full sizes are $50 and up. Browsing is encouraged, and free samples are included with every purchase.

Various Locations ◄ ## Sephora
800 737 4672 | *www.sephora.com*
A beauty fanatic's dream come true, and possibly a man's worst nightmare, this store filled with endless displays of makeup and fragrances carries products from the biggest names in cosmetics, perfumes and skin care along with indispensable gadgets like eyelash curlers, tweezers, professional brush sets and hair styling tools. Try samples from upscale brands like Stila, Benefit, Vincent Longo and Smashbox, or check out the latest cleansers and moisturisers from Philosophy, Perricone and Kinerase. Reasonably priced Sephora Brand items include cosmetics, bath and body products, and a variety of accessories. If you're shopping for a new fragrance for women or men, it's one of the

best places in town to try before you buy. Free in-store makeup consultations include product samples to try at home.

7100 Santa ◀
Monica Blvd
West Hollywood
Map 6 A2 **27**

Ulta

323 878 2524 | *www.ulta.com*

If you took the cosmetics section of a major pharmacy, combined it with a department store fragrance counter, and added a hair salon, you would have Ulta, the latest wave in beauty supply stores. Offering moderately priced lines of skin care and makeup, the shop is best known for its great deals on hair care products from names like Paul Mitchell and Nexxus. The hefty sizes, designed for hair salon use, will last most people several months for an investment of less than $20. Popular fragrance lines from Sarah Jessica Parker and Liz Claiborne among other brands, are showcased alongside the store's own affordably priced line of cosmetics and makeup kits in a variety of convenient sizes and styles. Ulta has four other locations throughout the city.

Perfumes & Cosmetics

Aveda	800 644 4831	www.aveda.com
Barneys New York	310 276 4400	www.barneys.com
Beauty Box	310 659 3802	www.thebeautybox.com
Caswell Massey	949 640 6750	www.caswellmassey.com
Fresh	800 373 7420	www.fresh.com
Mac Cosmetics	800 588 0070	www.maccosmetics.com
Macy's	213 628 9311	www.macys.com
Neiman Marcus	800 289 6229	www.neimanmarcus.com
Second Street Beauty	562 493 6000	www.2ndstbeauty.com
Sephora	800 737 4672	www.sephora.com

Pets

Other options **Pets** p.103

The most humane way to acquire a pet in LA is through adoption. The SPCA has pet shelters located throughout the city, and many animal rescue groups work with local pet stores to set up adoption days for dogs and cats. You will pay a fee of between $50 and $90 at the time of adoption to cover the cost of vaccinations, licensing and neutering or spaying. Dogs in Los Angeles must be licensed, (www.cityofla.org/ANI), and many vet clinics offer microchip implantations for identification if your pet is lost or stolen. If you have your heart set on a particular breed, the American Kennel Club website (www.akc.org) has a directory with information on local breeders and a list of clubs that may be able to help you find the perfect pooch. The American Cat Fanciers Association provides information on pedigreed cats (www.cfainc.org). Reptile Depot is the place to go for more exotic pets like iguanas, boa constrictors and unusual lizards. Once you've acquired a new pet, you'll find no shortage of supply shops, groomers, kennels and even pet spas. From Wags To Whiskers offers doggy daycare and cage-free overnight boarding. Speciality stores like Wiskers and Dog Pet Boutique stock a huge assortment of bowls, feeders, drinking fountains and fresh-baked treats. Muttropolis in Orange

Pets

Chateau Marmutt	West LA	323 653 2062	www.chateaumarmutt.com
Dog Pet Boutique	West Hollywood	310 424 5807	www.dogpetboutique.com
From Wags To Wiskers	Culver City	310 202 9247	www.fromwags2whiskers.com
Muttropolis	Newport Beach	949 717 6888	www.muttropolis.com
PetCo	Various Locations	877 738 6742	www.petco.com
PetsMart	Various Locations	310 390 5120	www.petsmart.com
Reptile Depot	Chatsworth	818 576 1508	www.reptiledepot.com
SPCA	Various Locations	323 730 5000	www.spcala.com
Wagville	Eagle Rock	323 222 4442	www.wagville.com
Wiskers	Long Beach	562 433 0707	www.wiskers.com

County is worth the drive for designer carriers, fancy collars and lots of whimsical toys. Big chains like PetsMart and Petco sell birds, fish, lizards and small animals like mice and hamsters. They typically offer the best deals on premium food and pet supplies. PetsMart has an on-site veterinary clinic for vaccinations, checkups, and preventive care. Wagville, a holistic pet store, offers herbal treatments, massage, acupressure and organic foods.

Portrait Photographers & Artists

There are many portrait studios in a wide variety of price ranges throughout Los Angeles. The least expensive option is a chain store that offers family portraits. You will find them at stores like K-Mart, Target, Sears and JC Penney. In most cases a series of photos will be taken and you will be offered a set of proofs to choose from. Depending on the studio you may receive an assortment of sizes as part of a package deal. Many families take advantage of seasonal backgrounds at these studios to have photos made for holiday cards. Clipping coupons from local newspapers may enable you to save money on sitting fees or receive a certain number of photos free. If you have something more artistic than a standard portrait in mind, Linnea Lenkus specialises in maternity and couples photos, infant photography, creative children's portraits and family photos. She maintains studios in Pasadena, Irvine and Long Beach with prices starting at $199. Lilhearts Photography in Pasadena is known for capturing endearing images of children in candid moments. Focusing on a more natural approach, they create photos that become family keepsakes. Family Portrait Fun goes on location to beaches, amusement parks and other areas to shoot images of families at play. Kevyn Major Howard is a pro at shooting head shots for actors but he also works with professionals in many industries to provide image-enhancing photos for business use. If you would like to commission a portrait of your pet, Wiskers can connect you with a professional artist who creates charming paintings of animals based on photos you provide. Commissioning oil paintings of people tends to be quite expensive, but if you have your heart set on it, visit local art galleries and ask the dealers if they can recommend a portrait artist in your area.

Portrait Photographers & Artists

Family Portrait	310 322 5502	www.familyportraitfun.com
JC Penney	800 322 1189	www.jcpenney.com
Kevyn Major Howard Photography	323 664 9564	www.headshot-photography.com
Lilhearts Photography	626 441 8803	www.lilhearts.com
Linnea Lenkus	562 981 8900	www.linnealinkus.com
Olan Mills K-Mart Studios	818 764 5986	www.olanmills.com
Sears Portrait Studio	888 767 8724	www.sears.com
Target Portrait Studio	888 887 8994	www.target.com
Wiskers	562 433 0707	www.wiskers.com

Second-Hand Items

Other options **Books** p.263

Whether you love poking through vintage clothing shops or you're in the market for used furniture, there are plenty of stores throughout Los Angeles where you can score second-hand items at great prices. Many churches and charities operate thrift shops where you'll find everything from glasses and cookware to toys, rugs and sports equipment. Goodwill and Salvation Army have trucks picking up donations all over the city, and depending on how much time and patience you have for perusing the racks, it's possible to find amazing merchandise in their thrift stores. Resale shops near upscale neighbourhoods in Beverly Hills, Santa Monica and the San Fernando Valley are where rich ladies clean out their closets and savvy shoppers pick up gently used designer fashions for a fraction of the original price. Buffalo Exchange is a hip store where in-the-

Second-Hand Items

Aardvark's	310 370 6500	www.aardvarks.com
AdDress	310 394 1406	www.theaddressboutique.com
Buffalo Exchange	323 938 8604	www.buffaloexchange.com
Decades	323 655 1960	www.decadesinc.com
Goodwill Store	323 223 1211	www.goodwillsocal.org
Lily et Cie	310 724 5757	www.lilyetcie.com
Maggie Rose	818 763 5150	www.maggierosecouture.com
Ozzie Dots	323 663 2867	www.ozziedots.com
Salvation Army	213 389 6774	www.salvationarmysocal.org
Wasteland	323 653 3028	www.thewasteland.com

know guys and gals trade their castoffs for someone else's, and Army-Navy surplus stores offer everything from watch caps and pea coats to camouflage pants and camping gear. Garage sales and estate auctions offer incredible deals on everything from cameras and lawn mowers to antique vases, art and jewellery. Craig's List (www.craigslist.com) and local newspaper classifieds are good places to check for used furniture, appliances, and computers.

Fab Footwear For A Song
Barneys' (310 276 4400, www.barneys.com) semi-annual warehouse sale at Barker Hanger in Santa Monica (February and August) is the place to scoop up coveted Marc Jacobs boots, Giuseppi Zanotti ballet flats and other designer goodies at huge markdowns.

Shoes

Other options **Sports Goods** p.295, **Clothes** p.266, **Beachwear** p.262

Stilt-like stilettos, buttery leather boots and sexy sandals are the footwear of choice for Hollywood starlets, career women and young hipsters who haunt the city's nightclubs. Luxury department stores and shoe boutiques cater to them with designer names like Manolo Blahnik, Jill Sander, and Stella McCartney. Fancy footwear fanatics also flock to Jimmy Choo and Barneys in Beverly Hills, but Nordstrom is legendary for its enormous women's shoe selection in a wide pride range. For those who prefer retro looks, ReMix offers reproductions of pump, platform and sandal designs from the 40s-90s. Famous Footwear features a vast inventory of popular brands like Aerosoles, Nine West and Steve Madden, and Kohl's has a huge stock of women's and men's athletic shoes at sale prices. Payless is a favourite of budget minded families for its frequent buy-one, get-one free promotions. Urban cowboys will find that Boot Barn is stocked to the rafters with affordably priced western designs from Nocona, Tony Lama and Dan Post. Heavy-duty work shoes and motorcycle boots are the speciality of Red Wing Shoes, while REI stocks comfy hiking, running and climbing shoes.

Shoes

Barneys	310 276 4400
Boot Barn	888 440 2668
Famous Footwear	888 869 1053
Jimmy Choo	310 860 9045
Kohl's	866 887 8884
Nordstrom	888 282 6060
Payless	877 474 6369
Red Wing Shoes	800 733 9464
REI	800 426 4840
ReMix	323 936 6210

Souvenirs

Other options **Gifts** p.279

Venice Beach shops

Gift shops at Los Angeles International Airport offer lots of souvenir items from shot glasses and key chains to tee shirts and LA Dodger caps, but the prices aren't cheap, and in most cases you will get a better deal if you shop elsewhere. Ocean Front Walk in Venice Beach is a great place to people-watch and you'll find wonderful souvenirs like plastic margarita glasses, toy cars, palm tree salt and pepper shakers, and lots of wild and wacky hats. Universal

Citywalk has several shops worth exploring including the Universal Studios store just outside Universal Studios Hollywood. On Hollywood Boulevard souvenir shops are jammed with T-shirts, posters, photos of celebrities, and logo merchandise from popular TV shows. Wacko features an eclectic mix of gift items, souvenirs, gag gifts and oddities you won't see in mainstream stores. The Third Street Promenade in Santa Monica is the place to find street artists doing caricatures, and cart vendors selling everything from scarves and jewellery to incense and candles. Sports fans can pick up licensed merchandise for the Dodgers, LA Kings, Clippers and LA Galaxy at Team LA located at Staples Center. Some of the best quality souvenirs in the city are found at popular attractions like the LA Zoo and Museum of Natural History. The gift shops at the Getty Museum (p.172) and the Huntington Library and Gardens (p.174) have many fascinating art and California history books as well beautiful stationery and fun toys for kids.

Souvenirs

Book City Collectibles	818 767 5194	www.bookcity.net
Geffen Museum of Modern Art	213 626 6222	www.moca.org
Hollywood Book and Poster Co.	323 465 0413	www.hollywoodbookandposter.com
Huntington Botanical Gardens	626 405 2100	www.huntington.org
Los Angeles Zoo & Botanical Gardens	323 644 4200	www.lazoo.org
Museum of Natural History	213 763 3466	www.nhm.org
Team LA	213 742 7852	www.teamlastore.com
The Getty	310 440 7300	www.getty.edu
Universal Studios Store	818 622 8000	www.citywalkhollywood.com
Wacko	323 663 0122	www.soapplant.com

Sports Goods

Other options **Outdoor Goods** p.289

Sports gear is easily accessible in fitness-conscious Los Angeles. Shops like Adidas, and Niketown offer athletic shoes and apparel for a wide range of sports, plus fashionable casual wear in the moderate to high price range. Lululemon features workout clothes popular with yoga enthusiasts, cyclists and runners. Designed with light, breathable fabrics and seam-free construction, they move easily with the wearer and won't chafe during strenuous gym or outdoor workouts. Champs stores, located in shopping malls throughout the area, are known for their huge selection of fan clothing including tees, jerseys and sweatshirts for major US teams, NASCAR and the Major League Soccer. Chain stores like Big 5 Sporting Goods and Sports Authority stock athletic apparel and footwear plus equipment and accessories for team and individual sports. Workout equipment like weights, dumbbells and resistance bands are available at the sports chain stores along with stationary bikes, treadmills, tennis rackets, bowling balls and boxing gear. Target, Sears and Wal-Mart also stock a wide array of fitness apparel and equipment, and they frequently offer sales on home gym machines. For those with space for a pool table, AAA Billiards sells new and antique models in four sizes, plus cue sticks, lighting, and a variety of accessories.

Sports Goods

AAA Billiards	888 667 3508	wwwaaabilliards.com
Adidas	800 448 1796	www.adidas.com
Big 5 Sporting Goods	800 898 2994	www.big5sportinggoods.com
Champs	800 991 6813	www.champssports.com
Lululemon	877 263 9300	www.lululemon.com
Niketown	310 275 9998	www.nike.com
Sears	800 349 4358	www.sears.com
Sports Authority	800 901 0795	www.sportsauthority.com
Target	800 591 3869	www.target.com
Wal-Mart	800 925 6278	www.walmart.com

Stationery

Stationery enthusiasts don't have to go far to stock up on crisp new writing paper, envelopes and greeting cards. Discount chains, pharmacies and supermarkets carry a variety of inexpensive pens, writing tablets and envelopes for chores like recordkeeping and bill paying. Staples and other office supply stores are stocked to the rafters with labels, templates for making your own business cards, sticky notes, and paper in every size, shape and colour. They carry a wide variety of writing instruments, binders, clips, packing supplies and business envelopes. Franklin Covey is an upscale store specialising in personalised organisers, handsome notebooks, calendars and tote bags. They also offer time management workshops based on the book *Seven Habits of Highly Effective People*. Michaels is primarily an arts and crafts store but they stock an extensive array of coloured papers, gel pens, scrapbook pages, stickers and gift wrap supplies. Hallmark Gold Crown Stores offer a huge selection of greeting cards, note cards, invitations and journals, plus unusual ribbons, bows and gift bags. Upscale paper stores like Papyrus and Urbanic Paper Boutique specialise in elegant stationery, custom printed invitations and desk accessories. Carmody and Company has graphic artists on staff to help you create custom-designed invitations, or you can shop for fine stationery and gifts from Crane, Vera Wang and Kate Spade. Those who love exotic handmade papers will find an impressive international selection at Soolip Paperie and Press. Bookstores have also expanded their stationery departments. Vroman's, Barnes and Noble, and Borders all stock a huge selection of journals, address books, greeting cards, writing instruments and calendars.

Stationery		
Barnes and Noble	800 843 2665	www.barnesandnoble.com
Borders	888 812 6657	www.borders.com
Carmody & Co.	626 795 2924	www.carmodynco.com
Franklin Covey	310 727 0720	www.franklincovey.com
Hallmark Gold Crown	800 425 5627	www.hallmark.com
Michaels	800 642 4235	www.michaels.com
Papyrus	800 789 1649	www.payrusonline.com
Soolip Paperie and Press	310 360 0545	www.soolip.com
Staples	800 378 2753	www.staples.com
Urbanic Paper Boutique	310 401 0427	www.urbanicdesigns.com
Vroman's Bookstore	626 449 5320	www.vromansbookstore.com

Tailoring

Other options **Textiles** p.297, **Clothes** p.266, **Tailors** p.100

Thanks to the wide availability of clothing in every price range it has become less common in the United States to have suits and special occasion dresses custom made. Upscale department stores like Neiman Marcus and Barneys have tailors on staff to handle alterations for men's and women's suits and designer clothing. Some menswear stores, like Men's Wearhouse, offer same day and 24 hour service on trouser hemming and minor alterations at very affordable prices. P&J European Tailoring provides expert alterations on bridal and evening gowns, with prices from $50 and up. Most salons and stores that sell bridal gowns also provide alterations. Fees vary depending on the complexity of the adjustments. Some upscale speciality shops can also refer you to experienced seamstresses who specialise in adding beads, lace and other embellishments to wedding gowns. Most neighbourhood dry cleaners offer basic alterations like hemming pants, shortening jacket sleeves and replacing zippers. Prices range from $10 to $35 for simple repairs. If you have lost weight and need seams taken in, most reputable tailors will provide an estimate for altering a large number of garments. Dr. Blue Jeans in Sherman Oaks specialises in alterations on premium and

Tailoring	
Dr. Blue Jeans	818 986 8047
Elevee	818 908 0900
First Class Tailors	310 207 0080
Four Season Tailor Shop	323 656 3553
International Custom Tailors	818 509 9032
Lizon Tailors	310 558 8611
Lorenzo Tailors	714 772 8570
Mens Wearhouse	877 986 9669
Novex Custom Tailors	310 855 1770
P&J European Tailoring	310 475 8089

vintage denim. Whether you need the waistband lowered, holes repaired, or the legs tapered, the staff will give your jeans a custom look with prices starting at $20. Novex Custom Tailors in Beverly Hills sells a large collection of Brioni suits for men and has specialised in expert alterations for more than 50 years.

Textiles

Other options **Tailoring** p.296

Take A Guided Tour
Urban Shopping Adventures (213 683 9715, www. urbanshoppingadventures.com) offers fun and informative tours of the Textiles district. The combination bus and walking tour will give you an insider's look at some of the district's most fascinating shops.

The LA Fashion District downtown is a must for those who love textiles and notions. As the bustling centre of the apparel industry on the west coast, the district offers more than 200 wholesale and retail vendors selling fabrics and exquisite trims for apparel, home decor and crafts. Prices range from $2 for a bag full of buttons to hundreds of dollars per yard for luxurious fabrics. Textile and notion stores are centred primarily in a four-block area between Maple Avenue and San Julian Street from 8th Street to Olympic Boulevard. A new multi-level parking structure at 636 South Maple Avenue provides convenient parking, or use Metro bus or rail transportation to reach downtown (www.mta.net), then hop on the DASH bus D and E lines that traverse the Fashion District (25 cents per ride). Many vendors are open seven days a week (10:00 to 17:00) but some only sell to the public on Saturdays and others close on Sundays.

For those who prefer to shop for fabrics and trims closer to their own neighbourhood, F&S Fabrics, featured on the TV show Project Runway, offers a high-end mix of textiles and unique accessories. Calico Corners, a popular chain specialising in moderately priced fabrics, patterns and notions, frequently offers in-store sewing classes. Wal-Mart and IKEA carry a large variety of fabrics for crafts and home decor, while specialists like Quilt Emporium and That Yarn Store accommodate quilting and knitting fans.

Textiles

Alen's Fabric	213 622 4454	www.alensfabric.com
Ashanti Fabrics	213 689 9337	www.ashantifabrics.com
Calico Corners	800 213 6366	www.calicocorners.com
F&S Fabrics	310 475 1637	www.fandsfabrics.com
IKEA	818 842 IKEA	www.ikea.com
Pavilion Fabric	323 256 9276	www.pavilionfabric.com
Quilt Emporium	818 704 8238	www.quiltemporium.com
That Yarn Store	3232 569 276	www.thatyarnstore.com
WalMart	800 925 6278	www.walmart.com

Toys & Games

Toys and games are available at an amazing variety of stores in Los Angeles. Colouring books, crayons, toy cars and inexpensive plastic toys are even available at supermarkets and pharmacies. Major bookstores like Borders and Barnes and Noble carry crossword puzzle books, travel-sized portable games for adults and children and a variety of jigsaw puzzles and board games. Typically they carry a larger selection during the holiday season. Toy speciality stores like Puzzle Zoo in Santa Monica stock a wide variety of dolls including Barbie, Hannah Montana and upscale lines like Madame Alexander. Many antique stores sell collectible dolls, toys and games priced according to their age and condition. Toys R Us and KB Toys are chain toy stores selling all the current toy lines plus trains, sports equipment, dolls, action figures, interactive games and stuffed toys. The Disney Store specialises in costumes and apparel for kids, plus a wide variety of toys based on Disney movies and television shows. Sparky's is a great place to find retro toys and boasts the

Toys & Games

Disney Store	800 328 0368	www.disneyshopping.go.com
EB Games	800 883 8895	www.ebgames.com
KB Toys	877 452 5437	www.kbtoys.com
Puzzle Zoo	310 393 9201	www.puzzlezoo.com
Sanrio	800 759 6454	www.sanrio.com
Sparky's	818 622 2925	na
Target	800 591 3869	www.target.com
Toy Boat, Toy Boat	949 729 9800	www.tbtbtb.com
Toys R Us	800 869 7787	www.toysrus.com
Wound & Wound Toy Co	818 509 8179	www.thewoundandwound.com

largest inventory of Pez dispensers in the city, while Wound & Wound Toy Company specialises in new and collectible windup toys. EB Games is paradise for video game enthusiasts and comic book fans. They carry all the current Nintendo and Playstation games plus a large selection of books, comics and electronics accessories. Toys R Us is a delight for children and adults with its vast inventory including bikes, balls, wagons, inflatable pools and virtually every kind of toy currently being manufactured. Discount stores Target and Wal-Mart stock a more limited selection of toys but generally offer better prices than the speciality shops.

Wedding Items

Getting married in Los Angeles is a little easier thanks to the hundreds of experts who plan weddings each year. BrideWorld Expo, held at the Los Angeles Convention Center in mid-January, is one of the largest bridal shows in Southern California. Admission is $10 but all participants receive planning guides, current copies of wedding magazines and a plethora of other helpful information as part of the registrant package. Local newspapers and many bridal shops also carry listings of upcoming bridal shows. If you're in need of wedding planning services, Bring Something To The Party can help you with everything from the reception decor and coordinating equipment rentals to overseeing florists, caterers and entertainment.

Papyrus and Folklore Eye are great sources for custom and printed invitations. David's Bridal is the largest bridal retailer in the United States, with several locations in the LA area. They carry a broad range of styles at budget, mid-range and upscale prices. Renee Strauss offers a gorgeous selection of bridal gowns priced from $1,200 to $4,000 and up. An entire second floor is devoted to bridesmaid

Wedding Items		
Barneys	310 276 4400	www.barneys.com
Bridal Bar	310 858 0119	www.bridalbar.com
BrideWorld Expo	800 600 7080	www.brideworld.com
Bring Something To The Party	310 392 9487	www.bringsomethingtotheparty.com
David's Bridal	877 923 2743	www.davidsbridal.com
Floral Creations	818 921 3490	www.floralcreations.com
Folklore Eye	818 404 2301	www.folkloreye.com
KLS Limousine Service	310 247 0804	www.klsla.com
La Soie Bridal	310 921 1198	www.lasoiebridal.com
Mr. Tuxedo	310 477 8633	www.mrtuxedo.com
Neiman Marcus	310 550 5900	www.neimanmarcus.com
Nordstrom	888 282 6060	www.nordstrom.com
Papyrus	800 789 1649	www.payrusonline.com
Paris 1900	310 396 0405	www.paris1900.com
Party Central Event Rentals	818 951 7998	www.partyrentals4u.com
Renee Strauss For The Bride	310 657 1700	www.reneestrauss.com
Richard Tyler Boutique	626 799 9961	na
Saks Fifth Avenue	310 275 4211	www.saks.com
Tiffany & Co	800 843 3269	www.tiffany.com
Vermont Bridal and Tuxedos	213 739 9739	www.vermontbridal.net

dresses, and the helpful staff maintain a referral service for photographers, reception venues and other needs. Neiman Marcus, Saks and Barneys also carry wedding gowns from top American and European designers. Paris 1900 is known for its fully restored vintage gowns, romantic veils and lacy lingerie. Nordstrom offers a spectacular selection of shoes, plus tuxedos for the groom and outfits for children in the wedding party. Mr. Tuxedo features a wide selection of tuxedo styles for grooms, best men and ushers who prefer to rent. For those planning a backyard wedding or reception in a park, Party Central Event Rentals can provide everything from tables and canopies to punch bowls, dishes, dancefloors and lighting. All major department stores carry gift registries. (See p.304).

Dry Cleaners p.74
Divorce Lawyers p.108

Written by residents, these unique guidebooks are packed with insider info, from arriving in a new destination to making it your home and everything in between.

Explorer Residents' Guides
We Know Where You Live

Areas To Shop

Shopping districts in Los Angeles are extremely spread out, so it's best to limit yourself to one or two areas each time to fully experience each neighbourhood. Beverly Hills, Robertson Boulevard and Montana Avenue are areas where you may want to dress up a bit to fit in with the style-conscious crowd, but in most communities you can dress as casually as you like. Malls and shopping centres tend to be huge and require lots of walking, so it's smart to wear comfortable shoes. On quick trips to one specific store at a large mall, call ahead to see where the store is located and park as close to that entrance as possible. Most malls and shopping centres have directories posted near the front. Take a few moments to view the list of stores and jot down the locations of those that interest you. The larger shopping centres have an information desk or concierge to assist you with directions, getting oversized packages to your car and other needs like strollers or shopping carts. At shopping centres in the suburbs parking is usually free. In more congested areas like Beverly Hills, West Hollywood, Pasadena and Santa Monica, you will have a choice of metered street parking, valet parking, or parking structures that charge by the hour. At many parking structures connected to malls, the first two hours are free with validation, and there is a maximum rate charged after five or six hours.

Plan Ahead
If you're planning a shopping trip using public transportation, visit www.mta.net and use the handy trip planner to see whether the bus, Metro rail, or a combination of the two works best for your destination.

West Side

The west side of Los Angeles is a shopper's delight with malls like the Beverly Center (p.307) and The Grove (p.308) within a short drive. The Beverly Center, located between La Cienega and San Vicente Boulevards near Beverly Hills, is a multi-storey shopping complex with Bloomingdale's, Macy's and more than 160 other shops including H&M, Ben Sherman, Jacqueline Jarrot and Burberry. The Grove is home to Barney's Co-Op, Anthropologie, Nordstrom and American Girl Place. A free trolley takes shoppers to the nearby Farmers Market. West 3rd Street is filled with eclectic gift shops, home decor accessories and women's boutiques featuring the newest creations from up and coming designers. The streets of Westwood near the UCLA campus offer a plethora of hip boutiques, bookstores and speciality shops that stay open late on Fridays and Saturdays.

Orange County

Huntington Beach, located along scenic Pacific Coast Highway, is known for its surf and bikini shops, vintage stores, T-shirt shops, and jewellery retailers. South Coast Plaza in Costa Mesa is located at the Bristol Parkway exit of the 405 Freeway. Filled with boutiques from some of the world's most famous designers, including Chloe, Christian Dior, Valentino and Dolce & Gabbana, it's designed for those with a taste for luxury (See p.309). Fashion Island, located in Newport Beach, is an open-air style shopping centre with a wonderfully casual ambience (they even allow dogs), and a huge selection of stores including Tommy Bahama, Juicy Couture, Caswell Massey and Bloomingdale's. Laguna Beach, about 30 minutes further south, is well worth the drive. Located off Pacific Coast Highway, the beachside community is known for its quaint shops selling everything from pricey artwork and ceramics to the latest fashions from hip new designers.

Beverly Hills

The Beverly Hills shopping district called the Golden Triangle is located between Crescent Drive, Wilshire Boulevard and Little Santa Monica Boulevard. Rodeo Drive is the most famous of the shopping streets, and it's where you'll find the biggest names in the fashion world – Gucci, Armani, Yves St. Laurent, Valentino, Chanel. Wilshire Boulevard, north of Rodeo Drive, boasts Neiman Marcus, Barneys New York and Saks

Fifth Avenue all within a few blocks. Wilshire is also home to St. John Knits, Burberry and Niketown. Canon Drive, to the east, is lined with a variety of small boutiques, while Beverly Drive offers home decor retailers like Pottery Barn, Williams Sonoma and Crate and Barrel. A few blocks further east, Robertson Boulevard (between West 3rd and Beverly Boulevard) offers some of the most talked about shops in town. You won't find many bargains, but you just might spot a celebrity or two at Kitson (p.271).

The city of Beverly Hills has 12 parking facilities offering one to three hours of free parking. Five others offer three-hour metered parking. Second hour rates are $1 per half hour and $1.50 thereafter. The daily maximum is $13.50. There is a flat rate of $2 for parking after 18:00.

Community Shopping
The Communities section of the Explorer Publishing website (www. explorerpublishing.com) is a great place to share some of your favourite tips and learn a few secrets from fellow shopaholics.

West Hollywood & Melrose

Melrose Avenue is the haven of trendsetting designers like Marc Jacobs and Paul Smith. There's an outpost of the hipster hangout Fred Segal, and interspersed between the chic boutiques you'll find high-priced hair salons, European-inspired sidewalk cafes, and a mixture of unique shops selling everything from Ugg boots and jewellery to stationery and hand painted sneakers. Be sure to check out Decades Two (www. decadestwo.com), where used designer frocks and accessories look brand new. Sunset Plaza (8600 Sunset Boulevard) on the Sunset Strip between La Cienega and San Vicente Boulevards is home to the upscale Tracey Ross boutique (p.273), and other designer shops like Armani A/X and Nicole Miller. Several restaurants in the complex serve lunch and dinner alfresco.

Santa Monica

Third Street Promenade is a pedestrian-friendly area just three blocks west of the Santa Monica Pier. Along with retailers like Old Navy, Urban Outfitters and a Levi's store, it offers numerous cart vendors, restaurants, multiplex cinemas, and a constantly rotating array of street performers. Santa Monica Place, at the south end of Third Street Promenade, is an indoor shopping mall anchored by Macy's with stores like Ann Taylor, Forever 21, Gymboree and Sunglass Hut. It also offers a large foodcourt and a reasonably priced parking structure. Nearby Montana Avenue (between 6th and 17th Street) is full of chic boutiques for men, women, children and pets. Check out the Blues Jean Bar, a shop featuring more than 40 brands of designer denim in a setting complete with a wooden bar and barstools. (310 656 7898, www. thebluesjeanbar.com).

Hollywood & San Fernando Valley

The Hollywood and Highland (see p.308) shopping complex has given a huge boost to the Hollywood Boulevard area, once known primarily for tacky souvenir shops. The mall is easily reached on the Metro red line. Get off at the Hollywood/Highland stop. Universal Citywalk (www.citywalkhollywood.com) in North Hollywood is more than just a tourist hangout. The youth oriented collection of stores includes Sparky's, a retro toy shop, Guess, Quiksilver, and the Universal Studios Store. Get there on the Metro red line and disembark at the Universal City/North Hollywood stop. Ventura Boulevard in Sherman Oaks is lined with vintage shops and trendy boutiques including actress Lisa Rinna's store Belle Gray (www.bellegray.com). The fashionista favourite carries Michael Stars tees, Rachel Pally dresses and jeans from names like Paige and Citizens of Humanity. Westfield Fashion Square (www.westfield.com/fashionsquare) offers Bloomingdale's, and a host of other popular retailers including Abercrombie & Fitch and Sephora. Burbank Town Center (www.burbanktowncenter.com), a shopping mall with more than 300 boutiques and an AMC Theater, is located at Burbank Boulevard and Interstate 5.

San Gabriel Valley

Pasadena provides a variety of shopping experiences from upscale jewellery and clothing boutiques to high-tech speciality shops like the Apple store. Colorado Boulevard, where the famous Rose parade takes place on New Year's Day, is lined with an eclectic variety of upscale shops, houseware favourite Sur La Table, and Vroman's, known for its terrific book and gift selection. Paseo Colorado located at Los Robles and Colorado Boulevard is an open-air mall featuring stores like Tommy Bahama, Cole Haan, Loehmann's and Lucky Jeans. ARTS buses take shoppers to prime areas like Old Pasadena, South Lake Avenue and Paseo Colorado, or you can park at one of the many parking garages located throughout the area.

Downtown

The fashion district Downtown offers a large concentration of fashion retailers and wholesalers within a 90 block area. Over a thousand retailers and wholesalers sell to the public at discounted prices that range from 30% to 75% off. Many stores are open daily from 10:00 to 17:00 but some only sell to the public on Saturdays – the busiest day of the week in the district. Santee Alley (12th Street to Olympic Boulevard between Santee Street and Maple Avenue) is a bustling bazaar where hundreds of vendors sell deeply discounted clothing and accessories. Take the Metro blue line to Pico station and walk east to reach the fashion district or board DASH shuttle bus E, at the San Pedro Station.

Chinatown

Chinatown, located north of the 101 Freeway and east of the Pasadena Freeway is easily reached from the red line Union Station stop and Dash bus line B. Along the streets of this fascinating area you'll find a variety of shops selling silk fashions and accessories, footwear, toys, and home decor items like tea sets, pillows, and rugs. The enticing aromas wafting from the many restaurants will tempt you to abandon your shopping for a Chinese feast, but most shops stay open until at least 17:00, so you'll have time to enjoy your egg rolls and savoury noodles and resume shopping later.

The Beach Cities

The beach cities in Los Angeles offer many shopping opportunities. Malibu Country Mart located at the Malibu Civic Center is full of trendy boutiques and a great place for spotting celebrities. Venice Beach boasts trendy Abbot Kinney Boulevard for upscale home decor shops and hip clothing boutiques. The shops along the boardwalk are a bit more eclectic with vendors selling everything from tie-dyed skirts and floppy hats to beaded bracelets, incense and candles. Manhattan Beach, further south, is where you'll find Diane's Swimwear, chic women's boutiques, and a True Religion denim shop. The Belmont Shore area of Long Beach runs along 2nd Street south of Ocean Boulevard. It offers a variety of popular stores like Gap, Banana Republic and The Children's Place, plus gems like the 5001 gift store and Luna, a speciality shop featuring candles, hand-blown glass, jewellery and other treasures.

Tax Facts

In Los Angeles County, sales tax is currently set at 8.25%. This tax generally applies, but is not limited, to alcoholic beverages, books and publications, cameras and film, carbonated soft drinks and water, clothing, dietary supplements, hardware, household goods, ice, medicated gum, over-the-counter medicines and cosmetics, pet food and supplies, petrol (gasoline), soaps and detergents, sporting goods, tobacco products and toys.

Places To Shop

Everyone loves Chinatown

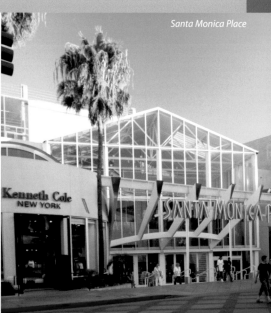
Santa Monica Place

Funky Venice Beach

Welcome to Rodeo Drive

Grand Central Market

Department Stores

Department stores are the anchors of most shopping centres in LA. Upscale stores include Bloomingdale's, Barneys, Neiman Marcus, Nordstrom, and Saks Fifth Avenue. The high-end stores tend to offer more amenities like free gift wrapping, and some have on-site cafes or coffee bars. Targeting shoppers with mid-range prices are Macy's, Kohl's, Mervyn's, Sears, and JC Penney. Competition between stores is fierce, and local newspapers have ads promoting sales every week. The mid-range stores frequently advertise early-bird sales offering selected products at deeply discounted prices before 13:00. Others promote buy one, get one half price specials, or place coupons in newspapers that entitle shoppers to 25% off their purchases. Most stores offer a wide selection of apparel for the whole family along with home decor items, linens and small kitchen appliances. Macy's and Bloomingdale's operate separate home stores in larger shopping centres. Sears is known for its Kenmore appliances and impressive selection of tools and home maintenance supplies, in addition to clothing, furniture and household accessories. It also serves as a delivery and return outpost for online retailer Lands End. JC Penney offers reasonably priced clothing for the whole family, including plus sizes for women, and big and tall sizes for men. Kohl's, notable for its large housewares department, also features a well-priced selection of brand name athletic shoes. Two chain stores with somewhat misleading names are Linens and Things, and Bed, Bath and Beyond. Both offer a huge selection of sheets, towels and bath accessories, but they also sell a broad range of products for the entire home including dishes, rugs, kitchen gadgets and storage organisers.

9570 Wilshire Blvd
Beverly Hills
Map 4 E2 **28**

Barneys New York

310 276 4400 | *www.barneys.com*

Barneys began as a men's store in New York offering good deals on suits, but evolved over the years into an upscale fashion emporium with an eye for new designers. Currently the haunt of trendsetters who like to dress fabulously without trying too hard, it has a devoted following among shoppers who appreciate cutting edge lines displayed with savvy and humour. The women's collection includes designs from Kate Moss, Helmut Lang and Juicy Couture as well as Barneys private label. Men will find a large selection of premium denim brands including Citizens For Humanity, 7 For All Mankind and Rogan, plus a unique collection of accessories called Barneys Obsessions. The twice-yearly warehouse sale at Santa Monica's Barker Hangar offers designer apparel at huge discounts and attracts fashion hounds in droves. Have breakfast or lunch at the on-site restaurant Barney Greengrass and you're almost guaranteed to spot a celebrity.

8500 Beverly Blvd
Beverly Hills
Map 7 A1 **29**

Bloomingdale's

310 360 2700 | *www.bloomingdales.com*

The Bloomingdale brothers got their start selling hoop skirts on New York's Lower East Side in the 1860s and the venerable retailer has been at the forefront of trendsetting fashions ever since. Fashionistas in LA breathed a sigh of relief when Bloomies headed west. With locations in Beverly Hills, Newport Beach, Sherman Oaks and Costa Mesa, the upscale department store seems intent on cementing its west coast presence. Offering an impressive selection of fashion labels like Marc Jacobs, Ralph Lauren and John Varvatos to choose from, both men and women can feel confident Bloomingdale's will keep them clothed in high style. If you're redecorating a room the home galleries are great for inspiration. The store also offers a wedding registry service, and you'll find all the latest fragrances and cosmetics in the beauty department.

Macy's

750 W 7th St
Little Tokyo
Map 10 C2 **30**

213 628 9311 | *www.macys.com*

While the Herald Square store in New York City gets most of the publicity thanks to its annual televised Thanksgiving parade, Macy's expanded across the United States many years ago and beefed up its west coast profile even further when it acquired the popular Robinsons May stores. Now found in almost every major shopping mall in Southern California, Macy's offers a broad selection of apparel and accessories for the whole family across several price ranges. The store ambience and layout isn't as elegant as Nordstrom or Bloomingdale's, but you'll find sales on popular lines like DKNY, Liz Claiborne, Kenneth Cole and Ralph Lauren. The first floor of each store is a giant maze of fragrance and cosmetic counters with the rest of the floors devoted to shoes, accessories and menswear. Home furnishings, kitchenware, women's and children's apparel are spread among the upper floors. Several malls offer separate Macy's Home and Macy's Men's Stores. Sales are held frequently throughout the year, but the biggest markdowns are usually in December and January.

Neiman Marcus

9700 Wilshire Blvd
Beverly Hills
Map 4 E3 **31**

310 550 5900 | *www.neimanmarcus.com*

Neiman Marcus got its start in Dallas selling high-end end goods to wealthy oil barons. Today the store enjoys worldwide popularity for its holiday catalogue featuring wildly extravagant and unusual gifts. The biggest draw at the Beverly Hills branch is the shoe department featuring fancy footwear from Gucci, Prada, Yves St. Laurent and Christian Louboutin. The designer apparel roster is like a who's who of the fashion industry with price tags to match, but smart shoppers take advantage of the last call racks for deep discounts on fancy frocks, sophisticated sportswear and enticing undies. The jewellery and watch collection will take your breath away, and the haute collectibles from Baccarat, Faberge and Lalique are perfect for gift giving. After your shopping spree, have a martini at Bar on 4, the hip lounge located near the men's department, or enjoy a tasty lunch at the chic FreshMarket cafe.

Nordstrom

Various Locations

888 282 6060 | *www.nordstrom.com*

From its humble beginnings as a Seattle shoe store, Nordstrom has evolved into an upscale nationwide chain that sets the bar for others when it comes to customer service. One of the forerunners of the lifestyle merchandising concept, the store is organised into fashion departments that are elegant without being stuffy. A live pianist playing a grand piano has become the store's trademark, along with an in-house cafe offering tasty sandwiches, salads and irresistible desserts. Renowned for its shoe department, which hosts a wide selection of styles and sizes, the store also features a popular juniors department, stylish suits for businesswomen, adorable children's clothing, home decor, and a men's area with sophisticated business and casual wear for any occasion. The biannual anniversary sales are legendary, and throngs of customers line-up for big discounts on designer clothes and accessories.

Saks Fifth Avenue

9600 Wilshire Blvd
Beverly Hills
Map 4 E3 **32**

310 275 4211 | *www.saks.com*

The flagship New York store was founded by Horace Saks and Bernard Gimbel in 1924 and became a legend for its classy shopping environment combined with attentive service. Today the fashion giant has grown to 54 stores in 25 states. From the beginning Saks incorporated speciality boutiques into its layout to showcase designer fashions for men and women. The company acquired four I Magnin stores on the west coast in 1994 and opened the Beverly Hills Saks in 1995. Today it's the largest speciality store in Beverly

Hills. Women will find a long list of designer fashions to choose from including Chloe, Diane von Furstenberg, Zac Posen and Versace. The men's store is equally impressive with lines from Armani, Dolce & Gabbana, Ralph Lauren and Ermenegildo Zegna. Children get outfitted in style with pint-sized designs from Burberry, Lily Pulitzer and Ralph Lauren. There is an additional location on South Coast Plaza (3333 Bristol Street, 714 540 3233).

Department Stores		
Bed, Bath and Beyond	800 462 3966	www.bedbathandbeyond.com
JC Penney	800 322 1189	www.jcpenney.com
Kohl's	866 887 8884	www.kohls.com
Linens and Things	866 568 7378	www.lnt.com
Mervyns	800 637 8967	www.mervyns.com
Sears	800 549 4505	www.sears.com

Hypermarkets

Referred to as hypermarkets, superstores or big box stores, these warehouse-like spaces are divided into different departments offering something for everyone. Wares include affordably priced clothing for the whole family, home decor, sports equipment, personal care items and gardening supplies. There's often a vast area devoted to electronics, books, CDs and videos. Target and Wal-Mart have pharmacies and some locations also offer vision centres, groceries, and portrait studios. Anna's Linens is known for inexpensive bedding, curtains, pillows and other home decor. Ross, Marshall's and TJ Maxx are best known for drastic reductions on brand name apparel but they also offer home furnishing and gift items. Big Lots and 99 Cent stores offer deep discounts on a range of items from toys and car accessories to clothing, toiletries and seasonal decorations.

Hypermarkets		
99 Cent Only Store	323 980 8145	www.99only.com
Anna's Linens	866 266 2728	www.annaslinens.com
Big Lots	310 391 5905	www.biglots.com
K-Mart	866 562 7848	www.kmart.com
Marshall's	323 951 0402	www.marshallsonline.com
Ross	800 335 1115	www.rossstores.com
Target	800 591 3869	www.target.com
TJ Maxx	800 926 6299	www.tjmaxx.com
Wal-Mart	800 925 6278	www.walmart.com

Markets

Los Angeles offers a growing number of markets where residents can purchase fresh fruits, locally grown produce, nuts and speciality items. Neighbourhood farmers markets held on specified days of the week are located throughout Los Angeles and they are very pleasant to wander through. Most merchants are friendly, offer free samples and will happily engage in conversation. Visit the Farmer Net website (www.farmernet.com) for a complete list of locations and times. Grand Central Market, at 317 South Broadway, Downtown and the Farmers Market, at 3rd Street and Fairfax Avenue, have permanent stalls open daily with vendors selling meats, tortillas, fresh flowers, cheeses and bakery items in addition to produce. These two venues are worth a visit even for non-shoppers, so you'll find separate reviews in the Exploring chapter – p.181 and p.180, respectively. The Orange County Marketplace in Costa Mesa is a giant flea market open on Saturday and Sunday from 07:00 to16:00. It features more than 1,100 merchants selling new clothing, home decor, toys, produce, electronics and handbags at deeply discounted prices. The Rose Bowl Flea Market, held the second Sunday of each month, is a paradise for antique-buffs, with more than 2,500 vendors selling novelties, foods, household products and clothing. The Long Beach Antique Market is held the third Sunday of each month and offers everything from sofas and rugs, to hats, vintage clothing and collectable toys. Saugus Speedway's Sunday marketplace

Markets

Farmers Market	6333 W 3rd St	Park La Brea
Grand Central Market	317 S Broadway	Downtown
LA Area Farmers Markets	NA	Various Locations
Long Beach Antique Market	5000 Lew Davis St	Long Beach
Orange County Marketplace	88 Fair Dr	Costa Mesa
Rose Bowl Flea Market	1001 Rose Bowl Dr	Pasadena
Saugus Swap Meet	22500 Soledad Canyon Rd	Saugus

offers more than 600 merchants, live entertainment, and a variety of food vendors and is a family-friendly outdoor bazaar.

Many of the markets open early and close by mid-afternoon. It's best to arrive early for the best selection and be prepared with your own bag or cart in case vendors are running low on plastic bags. Also be aware that some vendors only accept cash while others will take credit cards.

Shopping Malls

LA residents seek out malls for major shopping sprees and when they want to spend a day window shopping or socialising with friends. In many Downtown communities, areas have given way to antique stores and speciality shops, while major shopping centres tend to be located near freeways, housing developments and farther away from the town centre. Over the last few years many of the older malls have undergone dramatic makeovers and transformed into open air structures with pleasing architectural elements, gardens and outdoor seating areas to reflect the west coast lifestyle. Restaurants and entertainment options have become a major part of the mall experience with many shopping centres offering a wide choice of upscale, mid-range and fast food eateries. As the competition for shoppers has intensified, malls have also begun offering more amenities such as valet parking, hotel and restaurant reservations, and improved facilities for children that include play areas, arcades, carnival-like rides, and interactive exhibits. While it may seem that most malls have the same roster of stores, it's smart to check the directories for exclusive boutiques and unique speciality stores.

8500 Beverly Blvd
West Hollywood
Map 7 A1 **33**

Beverly Center
310 854 0071 | www.beverlycenter.com

Bloomingdale's and Macy's are the largest tenants at this popular mall standing eight stories high and boasting more than 160 retailers. The landmark structure has appeared in countless movies and television shows, giving many out of town visitors the eerie sensation that it's strangely familiar. Conveniently located between Beverly Hills and West Hollywood, the mall has undergone several makeovers to keep up with the times including the addition of neon escalators and a rooftop restaurant used for private parties and special events. Shops range from upscale boutiques like Gucci, Christian Dior and Louis Vuitton to mid-range stores like Ann Taylor and Nine West, plus a wide selection of speciality retailers including Montblanc, Brookstone and Papyrus. Among the newest additions are H&M, Ben Sherman, Calvin Klein and Coach. For those seeking entertainment, the Beverly Cinema offers 13 movie screens. Other conveniences include an on-site auto spa, valet parking, complimentary strollers and wheelchairs, translation services, and an ATM machine. Restaurants include Grand Lux Café, California Pizza Kitchen, PF Chang's, and an impressive variety of fast food eateries.

401 Newport Ctr Dr
Newport Beach
Map 2 F4

Fashion Island
866 331 0595 | www.shopfashionisland.com

One of the first Californian malls constructed with an open-air layout. This upscale centre, set among palm trees, fountains and koi ponds, is designed around a Mediterranean village theme. Dogs are welcome, and there's an amusing parade of breeds walking on leashes, peeking from tote bags or drinking from the many water bowls set out by store employees. The centre offers more than 200 stores including

Bloomingdale's, Neiman Marcus, Macy's, and name brand retailers like Apple, Kenneth Cole, Pottery Barn and Sharper Image. Shoppers will find a good mix of upscale apparel and speciality shops for the whole family and even a seven-screen movie theatre. Restaurants scattered throughout the complex include Cheesecake Factory, PF Chang's, California Pizza Kitchen, Fleming's Steakhouse and Blue Coral Seafood, among the more popular choices. The centre's summer concert series presents a variety of live music acts performing in Bloomingdale's courtyard on Wednesday evenings. Admission is free, with preferred seat tickets available for $20. Other amenities include free parking, a carousel for children, complimentary strollers and wheelchairs, restaurant reservations and free brochures on other Orange County attractions.

189 Grove Dr
West Hollywood
Map 2 F1

The Grove
323 900 8080 | *www.thegrovela.com*

Located in West Hollywood, this extremely popular outdoor shopping plaza attracts a steady stream of tourists, locals and celebrities who drop in to enjoy the warm ambience and diverse array of shops. An old-fashioned trolley takes shoppers from the mall to the historic Farmers Market next door, and decorative elements like water fountains and street lamps give the walkways an unexpected touch of charm. The family-friendly complex features a 14 screen movie theatre with comfortable stadium seating, and an entertainment stage used frequently for fashion shows and concerts. Recent additions include a Michael Kors lifestyle store and Barney's New York Co-Op. Other popular retailers include American Girl Place, J Crew, Banana Republic, Anthropologie and Pacific Sunwear. On-site restaurants range from The Cheesecake Factory and Maggiano's Italy to Morel's French Steakhouse and Wood Ranch BBQ and Grill.

6801 Hollywood Blvd
Hollywood
Map 6 A1 **34**

Hollywood & Highland
323 817 0200 | *www.hollywoodandhighland.com*

Hollywood & Highland attracts more than 15 million visitors each year and provides a fun spot for locals to unwind. Offering more than 60 retailers including American Eagle Outfitters, H&M, Polo Ralph Lauren, Sephora and Lucky Brand Jeans, the shopping area is an interesting mix of upscale and moderately priced stores on four levels. Build A Bear

The Grove

Hollywood & Highland

Shopping Malls

7+Fig	Downtown	213 955 7150
Bella Terra	Huntington Beach	714 897 2534
Brentwood Country Mart	Brentwood	310 451 9877
Del Amo Fashion Center	Torrance	310 542 8525
Glendale Galleria	Glendale	818 240 9481
Lakewood Center	Lakewood	562 531 6707
Long Beach Towne Center	Long Beach	562 938 1722
Los Cerritos Mall	Cerritos	562 402 7467
Malibu Country Mart	Malibu	310 826 5635
Manhattan Village	Manhattan Beach	310 546 5555
South Bay Galleria	Redondo Beach	310 371 7546
Westfield Century City	Century City	310 277 3898
Westfield Fashion Park	Santa Anita	626 445 6255
Westfield Fashion Square	Sherman Oaks	818 783 0550
Westfield Topanga	Canoga Park	818 594 9740

Workshop is one of the more family-friendly attractions, offering kids and their parents the chance to build stuffed bears from scratch at a series of assembly stations. Virgin Megastore is open until midnight daily with hundreds of titles to choose from, plus a fascinating array of trendy T-shirts, books, gifts and collectibles. Watch collectors will find plenty of timepieces to drool over at Swatch or Fossil, and beauty fanatics have a field day at Sephora and Mac Cosmetics. Entertainment choices span the gamut from movies at the Mann Chinese 6 Theater to bowling at Lucky Strike Lanes. For a special night out take in the spectacular views at Highlands nightclub. The centre offers a free shuttle to the Pantages Theater for visitors who dine at The Grill, Koji's Shabu Shabu or Trastevere Ristorante. Other amenities include validated parking up to four hours for $2, valet parking for $5, and easy accessibility to the Metro Red line station. Guided tours of the famous Kodak and Grauman's Chinese theaters are available several times daily.

3333 Bristol St
Santa Ana
Map 2 F4

South Coast Plaza

800 782 8888 | www.southcoastplaza.com

Located approximately a one hour drive from Beverly Hills, this gigantic shopping complex is known as the premier luxury shopping centre in America and it is one of the largest malls on the west coast. A glitzy structure on one side houses boutiques from the world's most sought-after luxury brands, and a second wing connected by a bridge offers more mid-range retailers. Anchored by major department stores Bloomingdale's, Saks Fifth Avenue, Nordstrom and Macy's, the massive mall features more than 300 upscale boutiques including several that are exclusive to the west coast. With annual sales of $1.5 billion, the centre constantly reinvents itself with the addition of new stores and restaurants. Next on the horizon is the first Rolex flagship store in the United States. Award-winning restaurants include Morton's Steakhouse, Turner New Zealand and Pinot Provence. Casual eateries are scattered throughout the complex. Guest amenities accessible from four concierge locations include valet parking, custom gift wrapping, translation assistance, money exchange, hotel and restaurant reservations, and information on airport shuttles, taxis and limousines. Self parking is free at lots and enclosed structures.

Supermarkets

Many foreign visitors to the United States are amazed at the huge size of supermarkets and the wide array of non-food products they carry. Increasingly food stores are becoming lifestyle centres where you can shop for groceries, buy greeting cards, pet food, toys for children and tickets to amusement parks. Some major supermarkets have small bank branches inside and most offer customer service centres that handle wire transfers and sell postage stamps and money orders. The larger supermarkets have bakeries and delis on site where you can purchase a wide variety of prepared entrees, side dishes and desserts. Many also offer catering services and sell precooked family dinners for holidays. Along with produce and food aisles, most supermarkets feature a wide array of household cleaning supplies, cosmetics, toiletries and paper goods. Some stores also have pharmacies on site. Vons and Albertsons offer online ordering and delivery services for a small charge. Gelson's and Bristol Farms are food speciality stores focusing on gourmet items and higher quality produce and meats. They tend to be located in upscale neighbourhoods where shoppers aren't overly concerned with higher prices. Mitsua caters to the high Asian population of Los Angeles with Japanese-style stores selling everything from toys and dishes to sushi, T-shirts and a variety of groceries. Many neighbourhoods have 99 cent stores, known for their everyday bargains on canned goods, spices, common household items and beverages.

> **Membership Stores**
> Costco (www.costco.com, 800 955 2292) and Sam's Club (www.samsclub.com, 888 746 7726) are wholesale warehouse stores offering huge discounts on everything from groceries and clothing to electronics, toys, home maintenance supplies and kitchenware. Members pay a fee of approximately $50 per year to shop for a broad assortment of products at discounted prices. They are a good value option for large families and those who like to buy in bulk sizes.

Various Locations

Ralphs
888 437 3496 | www.ralphs.com
Ralphs, a branch of the Kroger Company, is one of the largest grocery chains in southern California. Designed as lifestyle stores with bakeries, delis, pharmacies, on-site banks, and customer service centres, they are one-stop shops for many families who stock up on everything from groceries and cleaning supplies to precooked foods for a party. Stores are large, clean and well stocked with wide aisles and easily accessible restrooms. Some branches also offer convenient picnic areas for customers who want food from the deli to eat outside. Ralphs is popular for its double coupon policy, which means any food coupon you clip from a newspaper is automatically doubled. The store also offers a free membership card, which entitles shoppers to lower club prices.

Various Locations

Trader Joe's
800 746 7857 | www.traderjoes.com
Trader Joe's began as Pronto Markets in the 50s and has expanded to more than 280 stores in 23 states. Still privately owned, the popular chain is known for buying in bulk from a variety of wholesalers and passing on reduced prices to customers. Offering a wide selection of both common and gourmet items, the store specialises in health foods and hormone-free meats and offers many choices for vegetarians. Featuring a wide choice of affordably priced organic produce, cheeses and a huge selection of nuts, the store is also well known for its vast collection of wines including the bargain-priced Charles Shaw line. The selection of canned goods and meats is not as large as major grocery stores but many shoppers prefer the friendly, more intimate ambience to the bigger chains.

Various Locations

Whole Foods Market
512 477 4455 | www.wholefoodsmarket.com
Founded in Texas in 1980 as a natural foods store with a supermarket format, Whole Foods Market has expanded across the country by buying out numerous other natural food stores. Specialising in high quality natural and organic products, the store is known for its commitment to preserving the environment through recycling programmes and for its superior customer service. Offering a huge selection of natural foods and hormone-free meats, the store is famous for its bounteous deli featuring a variety of tasty vegetarian entrees, salads, soups and breads. The personal care section offers a large selection of vitamins and herbs, all-natural shampoos, face creams, cosmetics, and organic cleaning products. Shoppers will also find a nice collection of home trimmings including candles, placemats, and fresh flowers.

Other Supermarkets

99cent stores	323 980 8145	www.99only.com
Albertsons	877 932 7948	www.albertsons.com
Bristol Farms	310 233 4700	www.bristolfarms.com
Food 4 Less	888 437 3496	www.food4less1.com
Gelson's	818 906 5700	www.gelsons.com
Mitsua	626 457 2899	www.mitsua.com
Pavilion's	877 723 3929	www.pavilions.com
Stater Brothers	909 733 5000	www.staterbros.com
Von's	877 723 3929	www.vons.com

Fashion Boutiques p.123
Financial Advisors p.95

Written by residents, the Tokyo Explorer is packed with insider info, from arriving in the city to making it your home and everything in between.

Tokyo Explorer Residents' Guide
We Know Where You Live

EXPLORER

Going Out

Going Out

Going Out

Going out is an integral part of the Los Angeles lifestyle. And if you have patience, curiosity, and a full tank of petrol, there are endless hidden gems to discover.

The second largest city in the USA, Los Angeles is vast – spanning more than 1,200 square kilometres – so the social and cultural scene you'll encounter will greatly depend upon the region. In general, the Eastside (Silver Lake, Echo Park and Los Feliz) caters to a younger crowd of up-and-coming artists and musicians, while the Westside (Beverly Hills, West LA and Santa Monica) tends to feature more upscale establishments geared towards industry professionals. Obviously this is an oversimplified generalisation, but a helpful one nonetheless. As you explore the city firsthand, you'll get a feel for the subtle nuances of each neighbourhood and gradually find your personal areas of preference.

Read It And Eat

The number of eating and drinking venues in Los Angeles is simply staggering. To help you in your search there are a number of worthy online resources, including the perennially popular Zagat *guide (www. zagat.com), and* Citysearch *(www. losangeles.citysearch. com). You should also keep tabs on the comprehensive restaurant section of the* Los Angeles Times *(www.calendarlive. com/dining).*

Wedged between the Eastside and the Westside is Hollywood, an eclectic mix of tourists, misfits and locals. While this historic area is primarily known for its tourist attractions, locals flock here at the weekend for the many concert and performance venues, clubs and special events.

Nightlife in Los Angeles is as varied as the residents themselves and is primarily fuelled by drinking. Meeting friends at a bar or club is common practice, but not quite the all-night affair that is customary in other international cities. In LA the bars close at 02:00.

As you would imagine, the city's arts and entertainment scene is extensive and varied, with concert halls, theatres, museums and art galleries peppered throughout every region of the city. A fantastic resource for what's on where is *LA Weekly*, a free weekly newspaper found on street corners across the city (www.laweekly.com).

When it comes to eating out, you can find just about anything your heart desires. The distinct cultural influences on the local cuisine within each neighborhood make for a richly diverse dining experience.

Most cafes are open all day, but when dining at night it's better to get an early start; restaurants generally don't tend to stay open past 22:00 on weeknights, midnight at weekends. Reservations are always recommended for fine dining establishments.

The public transportation system is limited and not easily navigated, so you'll most likely be driving yourself to any given destination. That means you should be prepared for the infamous LA traffic. Keep in mind that it can take anywhere from 25 minutes to over an hour to get from one side of town to the other. Consult the California Department of Transportation's website to assess traffic conditions (www.dot.ca.gov).

Eating Out

If it can be eaten, it can be found in Los Angeles. Each borough brings its own unique culinary take to the table. Whether you're searching for kosher cuisine in the Fairfax District, sushi in Little Tokyo, or Mexican food in Echo Park, the perfect dish is right around the corner. You can find something to suit any appetite or budget, from a $3 meal off a taco truck to a $100 plus multi-course meal at a fine dining restaurant. While the average meal will cost between $8 and $25, it's good to remember that alcoholic drinks can often dramatically increase the bill, and that lunch is usually cheaper than dinner. Restaurant hours vary, but generally speaking they are 11:00 to 15:00 for lunch and 18:00 to 22:00 for dinner (sometimes later at weekends). Cafes are typically open from 08:00 to 23:00.

Friday and Saturday nights are the busiest times, so it's good to make reservations whenever possible. Note that many restaurants are closed on Sundays and/or Mondays. Late-night dining in LA can sometimes be a challenge. After 23:00 you may have to find a 24 hour joint – but fear not, there are many. *LA Weekly* (www.laweekly. com) is a wonderful resource for restaurant listings and reviews. When choosing a place to dine, always note the restaurant rating posted in the window (A, B or C) and try to stick to As and Bs (see below).

Local Cuisine

While Los Angeles features culinary delights from all corners of the globe, the city is famous for serving up ingredient-driven Californian cuisine, which highlights the bounty of fresh foods grown locally, especially fruits and vegetables. The diverse array of agricultural products found in Southern California is made possible by a temperate climate and a long growing season – factors that encourage a light, summery approach to cooking.

Avocados, citrus fruits, tomatoes, lettuces and herbs are just a small sample of what you'll find in local dishes. This abundance of local ingredients is what inspired chefs to create California cuisine.

The melting-pot culture of LA has contributed to the rise of California fusion: the integration of distinct cooking styles from various cultures and geographical regions with freshly prepared local ingredients to create a wholly new kind of cuisine. For a selection of venues serving Californian cuisine, see p.321.

Online Communities

Log on to www. explorerpublishing. com and click on the Communities link. Here you'll be able to connect with like-minded residents, join forums, pose questions and maybe even learn about hot new bar and restaurant discoveries.

Delivery & Takeaways

Pizza and Thai food are popular delivery and takeaway choices, but there are a number of options. Call your restaurant of choice to find out if it offers either of these services. Drive-thru restaurants are also very popular – and usually open late, if not 24 hours – but are primarily limited to fastfood such as burgers and tacos.

There are delivery services such as LAbite.com (310 441 2483; www.labite.com) that will deliver food from a number of restaurants for an additional fee, and supermarket delivery services such as Pink Dot (800 746 5368; www.pinkdot.com) for your grocery needs.

Hygiene

All restaurants in Los Angeles are regularly inspected by the Department of Public Health's Environmental Health Division (626 430 5200; www.lapublichealth.org/eh). Upon completion of inspection, each restaurant is given a letter rating of A, B or C (A being the highest) and are required to post this in plain view of the customer. Be wary of eating at establishments below a B rating, or worse, no posted rating at all.

Special Deals & Theme Nights

Many bars and clubs have special nights or theme nights that offer discounts, karaoke, trivia, guest DJs or comedy acts. As theme nights tend to change weekly or monthly, it's best to contact the establishment directly or consult its website for the most up to date information. Some notable nights include: 80s Tuesdays at Little Cave (p.348), King Trivia Night Monday and Wednesdays at The Fox and Hounds (p.347), Karaoke Mondays at The Bigfoot Lodge (p.344) and Comedy Mondays at Tiger Lily (323 661 5900; www. tigerlilyrestaurant.com).

Tax & Service Charges

When dining and drinking in Los Angeles, a sales tax of 8.25% will be added to the food portion of your restaurant bill and clearly noted as such. Taxes on alcohol are typically already incorporated into the listed beverage price. Some restaurants that do not sell wine will allow you to bring your own for a corkage fee – anywhere from $5 to $20 per bottle.

Tipping

It is customary to leave a 15% to 20% tip for service at restaurants, coffee shops, cafes and bars. Many restaurants will automatically include the gratuity for parties of six or more. When dining in a large group, ask your waiter if the tip is included in the bill.

Restaurant Listing Structure

To review every eating and drinking venue in LA would be a lifetime's work and would fill countless volumes, so this Going Out section presents a cross section of the city's recommended outlets. Restaurants have been categorised by cuisine, and are listed in alphabetical order. Following on from restaurants you'll find a selection of cafes and coffee shops starting on p.340.

Vegetarian Food

While many restaurants in Los Angeles offer some sort of vegetarian starter, the selection can be quite limited and often repetitive. After all, how many mixed green salads can one eat?

Vietnamese and Thai restaurants consistently offer the most vegetarian-friendly options, but there are a number of restaurants that specialise solely in vegetarian and vegan cuisine. Try the quaint and cosy Elf Cafe (p.336) for an intimate bite, or the more spacious Fatty's & Co. (p.337), both delicious vegetarian options. Vegans should definitely sample the menus at Flore (p.337), the macrobiotic M Cafe in Hollywood (323 525 0588; www.mcafedechaya.com), Native Foods (p.342), and the crown jewel of Los Angeles vegan restaurants, Real Food Daily (p.337).

Bar Marmont (p.344)

The Yellow Star

The natty yellow star seen to the right highlights places that merit extra praise. It might be the atmosphere, the food, the cocktails, the music or the crowd, but any review that you see with the star attached marks somewhere that's a bit special.

Street Food

Street vendors in all shapes and forms crop up in various locations across Los Angeles, from hand-made pushcarts to full mobile kitchens. During the day you might see them selling everything from corn to icecream, especially around city parks and on street corners. While it's not unusual to find a vendor selling bacon-wrapped hot dogs to patrons outside a bar or club late in the evening, the most common form of street food is the taco wagon: a mobile stand or vehicle that usually features a limited Mexican menu with traditionally prepared tacos, such as al pastor (spit-fired) or al carbon (charcoal-grilled). This food might be some of the most authentic and delicious Mexican cuisine the city has to offer, but keep in mind that these vendors are rarely regulated by the health department, so be circumspect.

American

4616 Eagle Rock Blvd
Eagle Rock
Map 2 D1

Auntie Em's Kitchen

323 255 0800 | www.auntieemskitchen.com

This popular breakfast and lunch spot has quickly earned a reputation for having some of the best breakfasts around, with favorites like open faced egg and bacon sandwiches or biscuits and gravy. The real treats here though are the specials that change daily, such as French toast or buttermilk pancakes with fresh fruit. Auntie Em's is also known for its baked goods and has had its famous red velvet cupcakes featured on the food network. Be prepared to wait however, although there is plenty of seating the restaurant fills up quickly. Luckily you can grab a cup of coffee and hang out outside while you wait.

Top Dog

Los Angeles has long taken pride in its hot dogs, and the two most famous restaurants for meatsticks are Pink's in Hollywood (www.pinkshollywood.com) and Carney's in West Hollywood (www. carneytrain.com). Locals have debated for ages about which serves the better weiner, but you'll just have to find out for yourself.

Universal City Walk
1000 Universal Ctr Dr
Universal City
Map 2 D2

B.B. King's

818 622 5464 | http://la.bbkingclubs.com

Locals and tourists come here both for hearty southern cooking and the live music that's inspired by its owner, blues great B.B King. Upstairs at busy Universal City Walk, the bar and restaurant is packed with food lovers and partygoers who follow the large neon sign for their taste of the south, LA style. There's nothing fancy about the menu, with spinach artichoke cheese dip, BBQ wings or cheese and sausage platter. Those on a health kick will want to steer clear of the fried peanut butter and jelly, served with fries or vanilla ice cream. Live music can be heard from B.B's on any given night and come summer, guests line up to attend the B.B King style gospel brunch and patio barbecue.

2903 Rowena Ave
Silver Lake
Map 2 D1

Blair's

323 660 1882 | www.blairsrestaurant.com

One of the few eateries in Los Angeles which serves an upscale lunch and dinner. Blair's prides itself on an affordable menu of classic dishes influenced from around the world, and has an extensive wine and beer list. There is no need to worry about reservations, just show up and sit down at the ample bar and relax until your table is ready. Blair's is also a great place to stop in for lunch at the weekends as it is usually less crowded than many of the other spots in the neighbourhood. The food is on the lighter side too, with many vegetarian items available.

4211 Riverside Dr
Burbank
Map 2 D1

Bob's Big Boy

818 843 9334 | www.bigboy.com

This Californian icon is much more than just a burger joint; the menu's stacked full of hearty American favourites – from the stuffed potato pancake breakfast to the all you can eat soup, salad and fruit bar dinner. Well known for its Big Boy burger, you can't miss the florescent sign that welcomes drivers and passers-by who have shopped up a storm at the nearby Burbank city centre. Not too far from the entrance stands the famous Big Boy character holding a replica of the famed burger, with its two meat patties, cheese and lettuce. Don't leave without trying one of the Big Boy icecream shakes and malts, topped with whipped cream. You can also take home a memento of your visit, from the restaurant's selection of Big Boy merchandise.

Cinespace

6356 Hollywood Blvd
Hollywood
Map 6 C1 **1**

323 817 3456 | *www.cinespace.info*

There's something always happening at this Hollywood hangout, where movies and meals come together to create a novel dining experience. The inconspicuous entrance with its narrow staircase leads to a large loft which is divided into the restaurant, screening area and nightclub, where you can work off your meal with a dance or two after dinner. While reservations here are recommended, there is plenty to do while waiting for a table, such as kicking back in the cosy cocktail lounge with film shorts to distract you. Once seated in a sleek Cinespace booth, tuck into a fire grilled pizza (such as the roast chicken, tomato, scallion, pesto and mozzarella) as you catch film scenes in between bites. Finish up with a slice of white chocolate cheesecake or the lavender crème brule.

Duke's Malibu

21150 Pacific
Coast Hwy
Malibu
Map 2 A2

310 317 0777 | *www.dukesmalibu.com*

You don't have to travel to Hawaii to experience restaurant dining aloha style. Duke's Malibu, which was established with the islands very much in mind, is perched on one of the most expansive ocean fronts on the west coast, yet dining here won't leave you with an empty wallet. In fact, this restaurant, with its many dining rooms and two bar areas, is quite casual with surfboard-lined walls and chilled-out, attentive waiting staff. Dishes such as Honolulu favourite huli huli chicken are on the menu, but there's also plenty here for red meat lovers, such as prime teriyaki sirloin and herb roasted prime rib. Locals and tourists frequent the Barefoot Bar to enjoy a more casual eating experience and the occasional spray from the Pacific Ocean.

Eclectic Wine Bar & Grille

5156 Lankershim Blvd
North Hollywood
Map 2 C1

818 760 2233 | *www.eclecticwinebarandgrille.com*

From its homely burgundy and brick walls to the fresh, hearty meals and extensive wine menu, it's easy to see why those in the know book ahead to secure a seat here. The wine bar is a popular spot for after dinner drinks, while the dim lighting and heavy leather banquettes attract an eclectic crowd, just as the restaurant's name suggests. One visit will never be enough, thanks to the menu that caters for any taste and appetite, from the garlic penne broccoli to the crab cake sandwich. Set in the heart of the NoHo arts district, the restaurant's walls reflect the nearby art galleries, with art work and photographs adorning the walls. Value for money here is guaranteed.

Edendale Grill

2838 Rowena Ave
Silver Lake
Map 2 D1

323 666 2000 | *www.edendalegrill.com*

A perfect place to meet people, Edendale is frequented by both straight and gay crowds. It's equally good for a romantic dinner or for a large group of friends, or you can just hang out at the bar and eye the locals. The food is a bit of an afterthought but the atmosphere is second to none. Originally an old fire station, the building has kept much of its charm, with room for large parties. The Edendale is also perfect for a quiet dinner on the large patio adjacent to the bar, where you can dine, drink and smoke – an unusual luxury in any American city.

Father's Office

1018 Montana Ave
Santa Monica
Map 3 A3 **2**

310 393 2337 | *www.fathersoffice.com*

Despite the name, Father's Office is strictly for those over 21, thanks to its well stocked bar of national and imported beers and wines. A local favourite for over 50 years, this popular hangout has earned its reputation through cheerful service, great brews and food that's worth writing home to dad about. One of the greatest temptations is The

Office Burger that can be ordered straight from the 'Big Food' section of the menu. With its patty of dry aged beef and toppings of caramelised onion, applewood bacon compote, gruyeye, matag blue cheese and arugula, this is one meal that deserves a beer accompaniment. Private parties are also a speciality here.

1535 Ocean Ave
Santa Monica
Map 3 B4 **3**

Ivy At The Shore
310 393 3113

If the name of this restaurant sounds familiar, you're not mistaken. Sister to the Robertson Boulevard celebrity haunt, The Ivy, this restaurant on Santa Monica's oceanfront features the same charm and equally top-notch cuisine. Here, celebrity sightings are almost as common, but the menu very much reflects its location, with ample servings of fish and chips, freshly caught shrimp and calamari. The crowds flock here for Sunday brunch, thanks to its upmarket, yet chilled surroundings. Equally popular come the evening, the well-stocked bar makes this an ideal spot for a casual drink. Be warned: as the crowd rolls in, the noise levels rise. Also, expect your bill to be higher than average.

8590 Sunset Blvd
West Hollywood
Map 5 B2 **4**

Ketchup
310 289 8510 | www.dolcegroup.com/ketchup

You don't have to like ketchup to experience and enjoy everything about this ultra-modern take on America's favourite: the diner. Sitting on the famous Sunset Boulevard in West Hollywood, everything about this restaurant is contemporary, from the slick white floors and white leather booths to the menu with such delights as the 'shake 'n' bake' (pistachio-crusted chicken breast, raspberry Dijon sauce, baby vegetables and garlic mash). Finding a dish that comes with the restaurant's namesake is easy too, with the menu clearly marked 'ketchup' on traditional favourites such as the 'barking dogs' and 'BBQ chick'. Dinner over, the leather-clad bar stools make for a comfortable invitation to the bar, with its ruby red countertop and red ambient lighting – a sexy match for the rest of this cleverly thought-out and executed restaurant.

Restaurant Timings

Restaurant hours can vary wildly in Los Angeles. In general, restaurants that are open for both lunch and dinner tend to have business hours from 11:00 to 15:00, then close briefly and reopen from 17:00 to 22:00, usually later on Fridays and Saturdays. Many restaurants are closed on either Sunday or Monday, or both. Cafes are usually open from 08:00 to 23:00. Some bars are open during the day, but most open in the early evening, around 17:00. Various establishments adjust their schedules for public holidays, so it's best to call ahead.

Ketchup

Musso & Frank Grill

4348 Fountain Ave
Silver Lake
Map 8 B1 5

The Kitchen

323 664 3663 | www.thekitchen-silverlake.com

With menu and decor as simple as its name, the kitchen has kept a low-profile in a neighbourhood reputed for being loud. What the Kitchen lacks in flair they make up for in a straightforward and delicious menu serving simply good food which is also good for you. Featuring old standbys like macaroni cheese and chicken pot pie, you cannot go wrong when in the mood for delicious food at prices everyone can appreciate. Be forewarned that they do not serve alcohol so if you like wine with your dinner, stop up the street at Cap n Cork which has a huge selection.

6667 Hollywood Blvd
Hollywood
Map 6 B1

Musso & Frank Grill

323 467 7788

This old-school grill has been serving Hollywood's elite since it opened in 1919. Local legend has it that Raymond Chandler wrote most of *The Big Sleep* from one of the red leather booths. Orson Welles dropped by in 1939 and pretty much moved into a corner table for three decades. The steaks, chops and Welsh rarebit are good (as are the eleven potato dishes) but it is the martinis for which this venerable establishment is greatly prized. Grab a seat at the wood and lead-glass bar and watch as an ancient, red-jacketed attendant juggles a chilled pedestal glass and a carafe, and builds the generous tipple with fine gin and just the faintest whisper of vermouth. It is quite definitely stirred and *not* shaken (why on earth would anyone expect a Scottish spy to know how to make a proper martini?). Open Tuesday to Saturday, 11:00 to 22:00.

414 N Beverly Dr
Beverly Hills
Map 4 E2 6

Nate 'N Al

310 274 0101 | www.natenal.com

For 62 years Nate 'n Al's have been serving up American favourites to locals and tourists who drop by the restaurant for its famous staple of lox (smoked salmon), bagels and cream cheese. Open from 07:00 to 21:00, this charming, family-owned delicatessen has always been a draw for celebrities and mere mortals alike, with no one exempt from lining up to secure a seat in one of the leather booths. Television talkshow host Larry King is one of many who can be found perusing the packed menu for a morning treat. While meat is very much on the menu with such dishes as pastrami, corned beef and tongue, vegetarians are well catered for with an extensive range of hearty salads.

1001 N Alameda St
Chinatown
Map 2 D2

Philippe The Original

213 628 3781 | www.philippes.com

This is a Los Angeles institution, which claims to have invented the French dip sandwich. Although there are a few other establishments in LA that also claim this title, there is no arguing that customers come from all over the city to enjoy the sandwich that has kept this restaurant in business for 100 years. The atmosphere has not changed much over the years either with sawdust on the floors and food served on paper plates. You can get a French dip featuring beef, turkey, pork or even lamb. Phillipe's has become a destination for baseball fans because of its close proximity to Dodger Stadium, not to mention the dirt cheap prices and famous hot mustard that is available in take home jars as well. Open 06:00 to 22:00 daily.

913 E California Blvd
Pasadena
Map 2 E1

Pie 'n Burger

626 795 1123 | www.pienburger.com

Having stayed pretty much the same since it opened in 1963, Pie 'n Burger has become a favourite among children and adults alike. The burgers are cooked on the grill and served simply with lettuce tomatoes and cheese as well as Pie 'n Burger's secret sauce. The secret is probably the thousands of burgers that have shared the same grill since opening. It's the type of flavour not found in a chain restaurant or anywhere using high-tech machinery to cook food. The hamburgers here are handmade and there's just about every type of pie you could imagine; all are delicious. Breakfast is served as well as various types of sandwiches and dinner plates. The name pretty much says it all and people come from all over to try these classic American dishes.

8020 Beverly Blvd
West LA
Map 7 B1 **7**

Swingers

323 653 5858 | *www.swingersdiner.com*

Not much is taken seriously at this popular LA diner, where the menu pokes fun at celebrity, and patrons share a laugh with the happy-go-lucky staff. What is taken seriously is the food – and there's plenty of that – from the sky-high stack of buttermilk pancakes to a classic American burger. Out-of-work actors and other Hollywood hopefuls fill the red vinyl booths and perch on swivel chairs at the service counter, nodding in agreement over the affordable menu prices and generous servings. For those who remember *Happy Days* and want to feel the 'Fonz' vibe, there's a jukebox at the ready, filled with tunes to encourage a toe tap or two, no matter what your musical taste. Swingers can also be found at 802 Broadway in Santa Monica (310 393 9793).

Brunch

Brunch in Los Angeles tends to be less about the menu selection and more about the hours it's served. Most restaurants simply utilise their breakfast menu and extend their breakfast hours to accommodate a brunch crowd, but some restaurants have specific brunch menus – typically at weekends, and most commonly on Sunday. The menu offered will vary depending upon the type of cuisine served, and is usually a la carte, but some restaurants feature all-inclusive meals that are often referred to as a 'Champagne Brunch' as they are served with a glass of bubbly. An inclusive brunch tends to be more expensive, anywhere from $25 to $60 per person.

Brunch			
Alcove Cafe & Bakery	Wilshire	323 644 0100	www.alcovecafe.com
Campanile	Hollywood	323 938 1447	www.campanilerestaurant.com
The Castaway	Burbank	818 848 6691	www.castawayrestaurant.com
Geoffrey's Malibu	Malibu	310 457 1519	www.geoffreysmalibu.com
The Griddle Cafe	Hollywood	323 874 0377	www.thegriddlecafe.com
Grub	Hollywood	323 461 3663	www.grub-la.com
Joe's	Venice	310 399 5811	www.joesrestaurant.com
Maison Akira	Pasadena	626 796 9501	www.maisonakira.com
The Rose Cafe	Venice	310 399 0711	www.rosecafe.com
Whist	Viceroy Santa Monica	800 670 6185	www.viceroysantamonica.com

Californian

8022 W 3rd St
West Hollywood
Map 7 B1 **8**

A.O.C.

323 653 6359

The French take on tapas at A.O.C in Los Angeles' trendy west is ever popular, thanks to its innovative eats and cosy, minimalist interior. Booths that seat up to four line the walls of what used to be the LA Trattoria, with ambient lighting casting a glow over well-aged cheeses and bites of patés. The clink of wine glasses and merry chatter can be heard around the room and into the adjoining bar, as waiting staff busy themselves nearby filling orders from the wood oven. After dinner, the bar is home to patrons who appreciate fine wine in surroundings that are a far cry from the city's young bar scene. To secure a seat at A.O.C it's imperative to book.

624 S La Brea Ave
Hollywood
Map 7 C2 **9**

Campanile

323 938 1447 | *www.campanilerestaurant.com*

Hollywood history buffs will love Campanile because Charlie Chaplin built it, yet there's much more to this majestic, award-winning restaurant than trivia. The Tuscan-style building, which was erected in 1928 as Chaplin's office space, is home to a Californian Mediterranean menu, with specialties like peeky toe crab salad with jalapeño ramoulade and sautéed trenne. The faultless food is even more enjoyable thanks to the calm, airy surroundings enhanced by a skylight, which gives diners a clear view of the bell tower. Campanile was the recipient of the James Beard Outstanding Restaurant Award, the *Nation's Restaurant News* Restaurant of North America and the Los Angeles Culinary Master of the Year for chef Mark Peel. The restaurant also does catered private events.

8155 Melrose Ave
West Hollywood
Map 5 C4 **10**

Chocolat Restaurant & Bar

323 651 2111 | *www.chocolatrestaurant.com*

While chocoholics will be tempted to skip the dinner menu and jump straight to dessert, it's worth noting there's more to this restaurant than its delectable chocolate sweets. Once the home of the popular Moustache Café, father and son David and Kia Illulian have created a dining experience that guarantees you'll need to book ahead to get in on the action. Food here is packed with flavour, with fresh ingredients presented on the plate like a sophisticated work of art. While menu prices are above average, it's worth every penny for dishes such as the chicken monte carlo and the Chilean sea bass. Come dessert; opt for one of the speciality soufflés – Chocolat, Grand Marnier or a combination of both. Finish your night at the bar with a Chocolat or espresso martini.

734 E 3rd St
Downtown
Map 10 E4 **11**

E3rd Steakhouse and Lounge

213 680 3003 | *www.eastthird.com*

Decorated in urban-loft chic and located in a former warehouse, E3rd's long, sleek interior features a slate wall where local artists create a new mural every few months. But as nice as the art is, it is the food that is the huge draw here. Owner Jason Ha has designed a menu that offers traditional steakhouse staples with an Asian flair. The slow-cooked ribs marinated in pear juice are truly remarkable and the filet mignon, ribeye and New York strip steaks are as good as you would find at the best steakhouses in town (for a much higher price). The appetisers are also creative interpretations of traditional dishes. There's a full bar, a charming bamboo-enclosed patio and a decent wine list. E3rd doesn't deserve just one star, it deserves a galaxy. Open for lunch Monday to Friday, and dinner daily, with late night dining until 01:00 on Thursday, Friday and Saturday.

4375 Admiralty Way
Marina Del Rey
Map 3 F3 **12**

Jer-Ne Restaurant + Bar

310 823 2403 | *www.ritzcarlton.com*

Arrive early to enjoy a cocktail at the Ritz Carlton bar before being ushered to a prime seat overlooking one of the world's largest marinas. Jer-Ne Restaurant is class all the way with a menu of regional Californian cuisine and impeccable service that you'd expect from any Ritz Carlton experience. Popular for brunch, the restaurant also dishes up breakfast favourites such as fluffy buttermilk pancakes and eggs benedict. Come lunchtime, the menu is extensive and features superb offerings including the tender salmon with lobster and fennel brandade, watermelon radish and blood orange vinaigrette. The cannelloni bean fondue with Gorgonzola, eggplant chips and garlic naan is a must for dinner. The wine list is ample and many wines are available by the glass.

Pete's Cafe & Bar

400 S Main St
Downtown
Map 10 E3 **13**

213 617 1000 | *www.petescafe.com*

A favourite among locals and visitors to the nearby galleries, museums and theatres, Pete's serves fare that runs from innovative Californian cuisine to elegant dinner dishes. This cafe and restaurant has a prime spot in Downtown's Gallery Row, and features dark wood panelling, floor-to-ceiling windows and a historic mosaic tile floor. An added bonus is the bistro-style pavement seating. Pete's is open for lunch and dinner seven days a week, and is particularly popular for weekend brunch. The menu and wine list are available on the website. There's valet parking and a free shuttle service to the Ahmanson, Disney Hall and, when the Lakers play, Staples Center.

Warung Café

118 W 4th St
Downtown
Map 10 E3 **14**

213 626 0662 | *www.warungcafela.com*

This hip and cosy cafe sits in the heart of Gallery Row in the new Downtown. The menu focuses on inexpensive tapas-sized dishes. At only $5 or $6 each, you'll want to try as many as possible. The dim lighting makes for an intimate evening and the tiny floor plan begs patrons to sit for hours exploring the menu in what feels like their own private discovery. This is one of those places that you only tell your close friends about, always asking them not to tell anyone else. Open for lunch and dinner Monday to Friday and dinner only on Saturday. Parking Downtown can sometimes be a turnoff if you're coming from afar, but Pete's Café (p.323) is close and offers valet parking.

Whist

Viceroy 1819
Ocean Ave
Santa Monica
Map 3 C4 **15**

800 670 6185 | *www.viceroysantamonica.com*

Named as one of the top 50 hotel restaurants by Food & Wine magazine, Whist is a breath of fresh ocean air. Tucked inside the Viceroy Hotel, Santa Monica, the restaurant, which was named after an English card game, is as loved for its mix of plush modern and vintage furnishings as for its contemporary take on traditional American cuisine. Slide into one of the intimate, curved blue leather booths, and take in some of the dramatic interior touches by designer Kelly Wearstler. Alternatively, impress your date by booking one of the poolside cabanas. The extensive menu offers fresh seafood and tender meat dishes such as roasted elk tenderloin. Whist's kitchen also takes its diners on a trip around the world, with a section of the menu dedicated to eats from around the globe, such as the seafood *ceviche* from Mexico, *Chuu chili gung* from Thailand, *moule a la marinere* from France and *patlican musakka* from Turkey.

Chinese

Bamboo Cuisine

14010 Ventura Blvd
Sherman Oaks
Map 2 C1

818 788 0202 | *www.bamboocuisine.com*

Chinese food lovers are spoiled for choice at Bamboo Cuisine, with a menu packed with dishes from every major region of China. Ingredients here are fresh and the flavours abundant, and can be enjoyed in one of the restaurant's booths or tables. If you like to spice things up, there's plenty of hot dishes to please, from the pork-fried rice to the hot braised scallops. While reservations aren't always necessary, this popular place can fill up fast, with seats taken by those who've heard Bamboo serves the best Chinese food in The Valley. Parties are also popular here, with a banquet room available on request. Bamboo Cuisine also caters and delivers.

206 S Garfield Ave
Monterey Park
Map 2 D2

Chun King Restaurant

626 280 7430

As one of the New York Times most highly regarded Chinese restaurants in the western hemisphere, Chun King may serve some of the best, or possibly the worst food you will ever eat. The dishes are so hot from the Szechuan peppercorns, that at some point during the meal you will most definitely notice a general numbness throughout your face. For fans of spice this can be quite an added experience, but other less adventurous eaters may feel overwhelmed to the point of panic. The fried chicken cubes with chili peppers are one of the most simply satisfying dishes ever created. And dirt cheap to boot. Cash only.

685 N Spring St
Chinatown
Map 8 E4 16

Mayflower

213 628 0116

Located deep in the heart of Chinatown, Mayflower is popular with local Chinese families as well as east side hipsters who like traditional and exotic Chinese cuisine. The restaurant easily seats large parties and the wait is generally short for dining in or pick up. With a menu as long and complicated as Chinese history, it is best to stick with the chef's recommendations at the beginning of the book. Fans of duck will feel right at home with roast ducks that are much more appetising than the ones seen traditionally hanging in window displays. There is no alcohol served so bring your own if you like beer with your fried rice. Cash only.

Contemporary

**20356 Pacific
Coast Hwy**
Malibu
Map 2 A2

Moonshadows

310 456 3010 | *www.moonshadowsmalibu.com*

Once home to beach-loving surfers back in the 70s, Moonshadows has in recent times been transformed into a sophisticated version of its former self. Its sleek Japanese-style interior, impressive menu from executive chef Joachim Weritz and water views bring in the hip and the hungry from Malibu and well beyond. While those after a cocktail or two head to the Moonshadows Blue Lounge, you can't beat the restaurant for an upmarket, yet pleasantly casual dining experience. Seafood lovers shouldn't miss the sweet Maine lobster caesar salad with its smoked applewood bacon and avocado focaccia croutons. Another treat is the dried black mission fig salad with prosciutto, toasted pinenuts and fig-balsamic vinaigrette.

**8279 Santa
Monica Blvd**
West Hollywood
Map 5 C3 17

O-Bar & Restaurant

323 822 3300 | *www.obarrestaurant.com*

Once discovered, it's easy to understand why this inviting restaurant and bar is a much-loved LA dining and drinking destination. Its interior, with a striking combination of elements – stone, water, wood and fire – has attracted countless A-list celebrities, who share cocktails inside under the flicker of votive candlelight or on one of the patio areas, with nearby fountains that really calm the mood. The menu here is filled with classic eats, from burger and fries to meatballs and mashed potatoes. Yet, there's plenty to keep the more discerning of diners happy with dishes such as the *mahi-mahi ala ratatouille* from the kitchen of executive chef, Aaron Robbins. The dessert menu is worth saving room for: the pumpkin cheesecake served with orange and cranberry sorbet is a must.

**2930 Beverly
Glen Circle**
Bel-Air
Map 2 C1

Vibrato Grill Jazz

310 474 9400 | *www.vibratogrilljazz.com*

Vibrato Grill Jazz, the brainchild of Grammy Award-winning musician Herb Alpert, marries contemporary American cuisine and jazz in classy, yet relaxed surroundings.

Restaurants

E3rd Steakhouse and Lounge

Pete's Cafe & Bar

Warung Café

Poolside cabana at Whist

Vibrato Grill Jazz

Despite its location, perched above famous Mulholland Drive in swanky Bel-Air, this restaurant is not exclusive to the rich and famous. Arrive early to enjoy a martini at the bar, before retreating to a linen-clothed table to order a tender petite filet mignon or perfectly prepared coriander, basil and mint crusted ahi tuna. While the menu at Vibrato is worth revisiting more than once (desserts here aren't forgotten easily), it's the cool tunes played by some of the jazz industry's finest that keep adoring patrons coming back.

French

3219 Glendale Blvd
Atwater Village
Map 2 D1

Canele

323 666 7133 | *www.canele-la.com*

Located in the hip, up and coming area of Atwater Village, Canele offers classic French dining in an area most associated with coffee shops and cheap Mexican food. The menu is scrawled onto a chalkboard and the decor is something that you might find in a friends house, warm and inviting without pretense. Simple dishes like asparagus with soft cooked egg, and roast lamb with scalloped potatoes are on offer and the wine list is extensive including local, organic and French wines. Be sure to try the restaurant's name sake on your way out. The Canele is a small French pastry in the shape of a cylinder with a crusty outside and gooey inside filled with vanilla custard.

7458 Beverly Blvd
Park La Brea
Map 7 C1 **18**

Hatfield's

323 935 2977 | *www.hatfieldsrestaurant.com*

The Hatfield's tasting menu, with its seven courses, ensures even the fussiest diner returns. Chef-owners Quinn and Karen Hatfield opened the doors in June 2006, and soon build up a loyal following, keen to get their fill of a Californian take on French cuisine, cooked using fresh produce from local farmers' markets. Book ahead to be seated in the dining room, with its minimalist interior and polished cement floors, or take your time perusing the menu at a table for two on the timber-decked patio – also a top spot for sharing a cocktail. Desserts are a decadent treat, thanks to Karen Hatfield's time as a pastry chef in New York. A must try is the chocolate and peanut butter truffle cake with salted caramel ice cream and roasted peanut toffee.

10506 Santa Monica Blvd
Century City
Map 4 C4 **19**

La Cachete

310 470 4992 | *www.lacachetterestaurant.com*

From the escargots with mushroom lasagna to the more pricey osetra caviar with corn blinis, onions and sour cream, La Cachete takes a delightful menu beyond its traditional French heritage. Chef Jean Francois Meteigner, who is well known for his book *Cuisine Naturelle French Classics Redefined* and sold-out cooking classes, has, through his restaurant, changed the way Angelenos view French food. Known for removing much of the fat content – that is cream and butter – while retaining flavour, it's easy to see why health conscious LA can't get enough. The atmosphere here is light and airy, well suited to a great night out.

4724 Admiralty Way
Marina Del Rey
Map 2 C2

Le Marmiton Brasserie

310 773 3560 | *lemarmiton@hotmail.com*

As nervous daters share conversation over coq au vin, a family of four sit nearby sharing laughs over generous helpings of thick, homestyle soup. Le Marmiton Brasserie is a French restaurant that serves up traditional brasserie meals, from the kitchen of Jean Marc Kiffer, and has something for most tastes. For those unsure about French cuisine, head to the 'moderne' bistro night on Tuesdays from 17:00 until 22:00. For under $30 per person, you'll feast on a three-course meal of soup, salad composee, herb roasted chicken, Le Marmiton's famed bouillabaisse or café de Paris meatloaf. Finish off with a choice of desserts: baba au rhum, cherry-vanilla bread pudding or apple tartine with vanilla bean icecream. Le Marmiton also offers a take out option.

Melisse

1104 Wilshire Blvd
Santa Monica
Map 3 B3 **20**

310 395 0881 | www.melisse.com

Dining at Melisse is like being invited into someone's home, with a warm atmosphere and a friendly welcome. The cuisine is based on French American flavours and comes courtesy of chef Josiah Citrin, who trained under Wolfgang Puck after spending the early days of his culinary career in Paris. His travels are evident in the food he serves, from the Ris De Veau to the lobster bolognese. Melisse is also a favourite with vegetable lovers who come here for the vegetarian tasting menu, which often includes mandarin tomato soup, sweet white corn ravioli and roasted tofu. You can also have a private function at Melisse, with two dining rooms available.

Taix

1911 Sunset Blvd
Echo Park
Map 8 D3 **21**

213 484 1265 | www.taixfrench.com

A classic French style restaurant in the heart of Echo Park. Folks have been coming to Taix for the Steak Frites after a Dodgers game for over 40 years. Seating is available for large parties and Taix has become a destination for all walks of life and all ages. With large banquet halls available for sporting events, Taix is a perfect place to watch the Super Bowl or World Cup football (soccer). Taix offers a classic French menu with all your favourites like escargot or traditional salade nicoise. Centrally located close to many clubs and bars.

Greek

Zankou Chicken

5065 W Sunset Blvd
Hollywood
Map 2 D1

323 665 7842 | www.zankouchicken.com

Slightly between Greek and Mediteranean, Zankou Chicken's origin is hard to peg down. Regardless, the chicken here is delicious. An addiction to most people that have eaten it, Zankou has become a late night favourite for anyone remotely near Hollywood. Half chickens come with hummus, pita bread, pickled turnips and a garlic sauce that may be the most exciting thing about the meal. The chicken itself is crisp and juicy, but not fried. And that garlic sauce – it can't be beat. Tradional Greek sandwiches can be ordered as well, but almost everyone seen at Zankou with be hunkering down over a plate of the famous chicken.

Indian

Bollywood Cafe

11101 Ventura Blvd
Studio City
Map 2 C1

818 508 8400 | www.bollywoodcafela.com

Flavours abound at this Indian gem, tucked inconspicuously in the San Fernando Valley on busy Ventura Boulevard. As with many Los Angeles restaurants, bars and clubs, a glance at the exterior will give away nothing of what waits inside. From the timber bar that's stocked with a selection of wines and beers, to the small dining area, you can't help but feel transported well away from the traffic outside. Service here is friendly and fast and the menu extensive. The butter chicken and vegetable korma are a must to try with a side of garlic naan to soak up every last morsel. A second Bollywood Cafe can be found at 3737 Cahuenga Boulevard, also in Studio City. If ordering take-away, relax at the bar and enjoy a glass of imported Indian wine.

Italian

Other options **Mediterranean** p.333

4100 Caheunga Blvd
North Hollywood
Map 2 C1

Ca Del Sole

818 985 4669 | www.cadelsole.com

Dining at Ca Del Sole is like being welcomed by a large family into an authentic Venetian trattoria. The dark timbers and maroon, curved banquettes match perfectly the colour of the quality wine that flows here – to be enjoyed with generous portions of northern Italian cuisine. Freshness is never compromised, with handmade ravioli and tortellini among the kitchen favourites. Whether for lunch or dinner, a must order is the mezzelune with its half-moon shaped pasta stuffed with pumpkin and sautéed with butter, sage and parmesan cheese. Ca Del Sole is also popular among LA brunch lovers, who come to bask in the sunshine in the restaurant's courtyard, with its fountain and blooming flowers. Weddings and events, with up to 200 guests, are also catered for here in one of several private dining rooms.

1650 Colorado Blvd
Eagle Rock
Map 2 D1

Casa Bianca Pizza Pie

323 256 9617 | www.casabiancapizza.com

This is a real old school pizza joint, in business for over 50 years and still considered a local favourite. With red booths and checkered table cloths the joint feels like it could be straight out of a mobster movie. The walls are covered with photos of famous and not so famous guests and it can be fun to point out people you may recognise from TV or movies. The real star here is the pizza though. Big traditional style pies with a thin chewy crust. Be prepared to wait, as the restaurant is hugely popular. They serve beer and wine as well, just in case you cannot wait or burn the roof of your mouth biting into a steaming hot pizza slice.

9071 Santa Monica Blvd
West Hollywood
Map 4 F1 23

Dan Tana's

310 275 9444 | www.dantanasrestaurant.com

It's old-fashioned service and food all the way at Dan Tana's, an Italian restaurant that has been part of the Hollywood dining scene for more than 40 years. You instantly feel at home as you're welcomed to a checkered clothed table or one of their round, cosy booths where many a celebrity has sat before you (such as Hilton sister Nikki who has a salad named after her). Loyal patrons come for scallops with garlic toast and entrees of homemade ravioli with meat sauce or the chicken Tana followed by traditional Italian desserts. The Dan Tana bar is also a popular spot for a cocktail or two after dinner.

538 Palisades Dr
Pacific Palisades
Map 2 B2

Il Carpaccio

310 573 1411 | www.ilcarpaccioristorante.com

When a restaurant proudly offers cooking classes, you know you're onto something good. That something is Il Carpaccio from chef Antonio Mure, well known and loved in culinary circles from his time at Piccolo in Venice and La Botte, Santa Monica. Now operating on his own turf, Mure's passion for food has never been more apparent, with flavours abounding from dishes such as the grilled sea scallops on truffle parmigiano fondue and the semi-boneless quail, wrapped in pancetta and sage, served with just the right amount of white port and pomegranate sauce. Don't take finding a seat here for granted, as on any given night this Italian hotspot is bustling. Bookings can be made online or by phone.

9018 Burton Way
Beverly Hills
Map 4 F2 24

Il Cielo

310 276 9990 | www.ilcielo.com

You'd be forgiven for not wanting to leave this touch of Tuscany, in the heart of Beverly Hills, with its romantic Italian-inspired garden setting and twinkling lights.

Owner Pasquale Vericella got his wish when he set out, in 1986, to create a restaurant that was a home away from home for his guests. Regardless of whether you opt for a romantic dinner or a family get-together, the menu will take you straight to Italy without the cost. Start with fresh garden vegetable soup before ordering a main of flavour-filled homemade ravioli with porcini mushrooms and butternut squash. Wines at Il Cielo are well matched to each meal, with the friendly wait staff happy to suggest their top picks.

434 N Canon Dr
Beverly Hills
Map 4 E2 **25**

La Scala
310 275 0579
There's plenty of reasons why La Scala has been a Hollywood staple since the 1950s, even if it's not in its original location. Regulars know the gourmet chopped salads – with lashings of meat and mozzarella cheese – are a must to share, while nestled in the cosy red booths that line the walls. It's a place to see and be seen, with the celebrity set often dropping by to get a taste of a menu that has very much been tried and tested over the years. La Scala is proof that being the latest Tinseltown trend isn't always what keeps the customers happy. Lunch times here are busy and it's wise to book ahead for dinner.

2764 Rowena Ave
Silver Lake
Map 2 D1

Nicky D's Wood Fired Pizza
323 664 3333 | *www.nickydspizza.com*
With dine in, takeout or delivery, Nicky D's pizza can accommodate whatever dining mood you may be in. Nicky D's is pretty much the only available choice for Eastsiders who want to stay in and eat. Sure, there are other pizza places but LA is not known for its pizza and no other restaurant comes close to the quality and authenticity of Nicky D's New York style pizza. The place itself is cosy and inviting but parking is limited directly in front. Instead find parking nearby on the street. The service can be a bit slow and the pizza does take a while to cook, but bring your own bottle of wine as there is no fee for corkage.

641 N Highland Ave
Hollywood
Map 6 A4 **26**

Pizzeria Mozza
323 297 0101 | *www.mozza-la.com*
Pizza doesn't have to come in a box and be eaten on the floor – at Pizzeria Mozza, the Italian favourite is treated as a carefully thought out cuisine, to be enjoyed in classy surrounds. While you can expect the traditional offerings (think margarita), there's nothing ordinary about the menu, with delicious toppings such as squash blossoms, burrata and tomato, and Gorgonzola dolce, fingerling potatoes, radicchio and rosemary. Private events can be held in the Jack Warner Room with its wine cellar walls and ambient lighting created by strategically placed candles. Up to 14 guests can wine and dine here on gothic-style red leather thrones.

Japanese

913 S Vermont Ave
Koreatown
Map 9 A1 **27**

A-Won Japanese Restaurant
213 389 6764
The quality of sushi here is unparalleled, as are all the seafood dishes. With Korean favourites such as *albap* (fish eggs with rice) and steamed codfish in a spicy Korean broth, A-Won is the perfect combo of Japanese and Korean food not usually found on the same menu. One of the main favourites here is the HDB, basically a sashimi salad. The bowl is huge and loaded with generous pieces of raw fish and delicious greens. Tasting menus are available but quite expensive and should probably be experienced when you're boss is picking up the bill.

Geisha House

6633 Hollywood Blvd
Hollywood
Map 6 B1 **28**

323 460 6300 | www.dolcegroup.com/geisha
Modern Japanese design and cuisine meet at this slick Hollywood restaurant. Inspired by traditional Geisha houses, the space here is sexy in hues of red and earthy tones and the contemporary menu is innovative. The restaurant, sushi bar and sake lounge can cater to both large groups and a dinner for two, with service friendly and attentive. While prices here are a little loftier than in other LA Japanese restaurants, the Geisha House experience makes it worth every penny. The drinks menu is extensive and well thought out, with blended teas, sake and traditional wine and beer. Share in the fun here by ordering a Marilyn Monroll – a handroll with salmon tempura, light chile spices and avocado wrapped in rice paper. Bookings are a must.

Kouraku

314 E 2nd St
Little Tokyo
Map 10 E4 **29**

213 687 4972
Little Tokyo is known for its late night shops featuring Japanese toys and street fashion. And when the bars close and it's time to eat there are a couple options. One of the best is Kouraku which is open until 03:00 and features numerous types of Japanese diner food. Basically the idea is similar to American diners with plastic booths and countertop seating. But here you will find items that would never appear in any American styled diner. The *ramen* (traditional noodle dish) is the highlight and the selection of ingredients almost mind boggling. Another favourite is the Japanese curry which is different than Thai or Indian style curries and served with rice. Beer and sake are also available for those looking to keep the party going.

Mako

225 S Beverly Dr
Beverly Hills
Map 4 E3 **30**

310 288 8338 | www.makorestaurant.com
Discerning LA diners will recognise chef Makoto Tanaka from Spago and Chinois on Main, yet the dishes at Mako, his upmarket contemporary Asian restaurant, very much have a personality of their own. A Mediterranean influence is apparent in many of his dishes and is a pleasant surprise in such offerings as the bluefin tuna sashimi with jalapeño and soy olive oil dressing or the black angus prime filet mignon with its wasabi potato puree and cognac garlic sauce. A favourite is the Mako bento box – the reusable three-tiered box filled with appetisers, seafood, grilled meats and desserts. Those who can't get enough of Mako's flavours can return their box and have it refilled.

Mr. Ramen

341 1/2 E 1st St
Little Tokyo
Map 10 F4 **31**

213 626 4252
Located near lots of late night Japanese oddity stores, Mr. Ramen specialises in Japanese diner food. Basically a version of American diners post second world war, Japanese diners specialise in *ramen* and *udon* soups or other classics such as shrimp tempura or *gyoza*. With so many sushi restaurants and high-end Asian fusion restaurants out there, places like Mr. Ramen are a nice change. Japanese curry is different than its Indian brothers and is a common Japanese food that rarely finds itself on menus in America. The curry here is spectacular with a strong ginger bite that goes well with cooler weather. Beer, wine and sake are also available.

R23 Japanese Cuisine & Gallery

923 E 2nd St
Downtown
Map 10 F4 **32**

213 687 7178 | www.r23.com
R23 is a remarkable little culinary and cultural oasis, tucked off an alley in a former Santa Fe Railroad building in the post-industrial Arts District, just a few blocks from Little Tokyo. The decor is by famed architect Frank Gehry and features compressed cardboard furniture. The restaurant offers some of finest sushi in the city, although it is the truly outstanding

cooked items, such as Dungeness crab salad and grilled duck breast stuffed with Japanese scallions, that make R23 one of best-reviewed restaurants in Los Angeles. It can be pricey for dinner, but the more moderately priced lunch items are a genuine bargain for the gourmand. Lunch is served Monday to Friday, and dinner Monday to Saturday.

127 Japanese
Village Plaza Mall
Little Tokyo
Map 10 E4 **33**

Shabu Shabu House
213 680 3890

Lunch starts here from around 11:30, and you may even want to stick around until dinner as it's always heaving from open to close. It might be the fact that Shabu Shabu House is considered the best in the city. Shabu Shabu is basically very thinly sliced pieces of beef that are boiled with vegetables and then dipped in a variety of sauces. The meat is some of the freshest available, in part due to the high turnover and volume of customers passing through the doors. Be patient and prepare to have one of the most authentic Japanese meals in America.

11940 Ventura Blvd
Studio City
Map 2 C1

Teru Sushi
818 763 6201 | *www.terusushi.com*

While there are countless sushi restaurants in Los Angeles to keep the health conscious happy, it's unfortunate there's only one Teru Sushi. Forget wrestling with the Ventura

Geisha House

R23 Japanese Cuisine & Gallery

Geisha House

Boulevard traffic; hand your keys to the friendly valet before making your way past the trickling pond to a warm Japanese welcome. If the popular sushi bar is at capacity, join your party in one of the comfortable and semi-private timber booths or, better still, outside in the Japanese garden with its tranquil koi pond and waterfall. Teru Sushi's menu is comprehensive and ingredients are exceptionally fresh, from the yellowtail sashimi to the barbecued teriyaki chicken, washed down with hot sake. Those on a budget shouldn't look past a shared lunchtime treat of the sushi teriyaki combination, which comes with a rice noodle salad and miso for under $20.

Yamato

17200 Ventura Blvd 221
Encino
Map 2 B1

818 905 9920 | www.yamatorestaurants.com

Be sure to make a reservation at one of Yamato's four Los Angeles locations (there are also outlets in Agoura Hills, Valencia and Laguna Hills), as this restaurant chain is always bustling with hungry diners who've come to see what all the fuss is about. Yamato's reputation for fine food and service is well deserved, thanks to its attentive staff. Sushi chefs here double as entertainers as they skillfully dish up teppanyaki from a sizzling hot plate. Children are also catered for, with the Yamato kids menu featuring assorted tempura and chicken teriyaki ($8.95). Dishes such as the soft shell crab and salmon teriyaki are a must. While Yamato isn't the place for a quiet romantic date, its lively atmosphere and fresh menu will leave you wanting more.

Korean

Soot Bull Jeep

3136 W 8th St
Koreatown
Map 8 A4 34

213 387 3865

Filled with smoke and run by a staff of Korean waitresses who may or may not speak English and may or may not seem very friendly, Soot Bull Jeep has earned a reputation as a restaurant that is not for the faint of heart. That being said it offers up some of the best Korean barbecue available in Koreatown. Unlike most Korean barbecue places that use gas grills, Soot Bull Jeep relies on hardwood charcoal to infuse the meat with a delicious smoky flavour. More adventurous eaters will be pleased to find beef tongue on the menu, but if the site of raw meat upsets you then Soot Bull Jeep is not for you. Wash it all down with Korean Hite beer or yam vodka and don't forget the *kim chee*.

Latin American

Other options **Mexican** p.333

Fogo De Chao

133 N La Cienega Blvd
Beverly Hills
Map 7 A2 22

310 289 7755 | www.fogodechao.com

While it may be a relatively new addition to the Beverly Hills landscape, Fogo de Chao, is no culinary novice thanks to tried and true southern Brazilian recipes that date back more than three centuries. Meat lovers flock here, past a 27ft high wine cellar in the entryway, to indulge in a continuous service menu of fire-roasted meats, gourmet salads, Brazilian side dishes and tasty vegetables, served up in ambient surroundings. If traditional ordering isn't your style, ask your waiters about the entire menu sample option – highly recommended if it's your first visit to this family-owned restaurant. There's no rush at Fogo de Chao, with guests encouraged to control the pace of their service with a two-sided disc: green will bring waiters to the table, while red will give you time to recover before the next generous helping. Fogo de Chao Beverly Hills seats 280 guests. There's also a private dining section that seats up to 80 and a smaller room that caters for 20.

Mediterranean

Other options **Greek** p.327, **Italian** p.328

11720 Ventura Blvd
Studio City
Map 2 C1

Firefly

818 762 1833 | www.fireflystudiocity.com

For those who've dreamt of sharing a bathroom with the likes of Courtney Cox, this could be your kind of place. From the library-inspired bar interior to the dimly lit restaurant, Firefly is popular for dinner with friends, yet also accommodating if you choose to drink alone. Hidden behind a wall of ivy, only those in the know frequent this place where celebrity spotting is the norm. Booking ahead for dinner is a must, yet the outdoor patio awaits those who want to chill over some wine while sharing well-prepared Mediterranean snacks, such as the tasty crumbed olives. While the service can be lacking more often than not, it's easy to forgive when the food, ambience and company is this good.

11919 Ventura Blvd
Studio City
Map 2 C1

Jumpin' Java

818 980 4249

The servings at Jumpin' Java are as plentiful and as cheerful as the cafe's bright interior, where actor's headshots proudly hang – proof of a satisfied star clientele. The happy crowd of breakfast and lunch diners come for the fluffy pancakes or choose from a variety of homemade omelettes with sides of herb crusted potatoes and bread, enough to share if your appetite can't accommodate the serving size. While the coffee is hardly prepared Italian style, it's not a factor when the food is this satisfying and the menu prices so affordable. The staff also give you plenty of reasons to leave a sizeable tip, thanks to their friendly and efficient service.

8164 W 3rd St
Park La Brea
Map 7 B1 **35**

The Little Door

323 951 1210 | www.thelittledoor.com

Forget the LA traffic and take a peek through The Little Door. This romantic restaurant is authentically Mediterranean, from its vibrant blue seating and whitewashed walls to the vines that climb them and the mezze plates that are enjoyed in its surroundings. Touted as Hollywood's secret garden, this is an enchanting dining experience whether you lunch on the patio or share dinner with friends in the winter garden, piano or blue room. Wine lovers will also find this exotic retreat a must visit, with a bar that's well stocked with some of the world's finest vintages, many of which are served by the glass. The Little Door is also favoured by Angelenos who want a touch of the Mediterranean in their own backyard, thanks to a catering service which can be booked for corporate lunches, wedding receptions and cocktail parties.

Mexican

Other options **Latin American** p.332

3510 W Sunset Blvd
Silver Lake
Map 8 B2 **36**

Alegria

323 913 1422

With a nod to the Oaxacan region of Mexico, Alegria is known in east Los Angeles for having the best mole. The rich chocolate and herb infused sauce is used to flavour everything from grilled chicken to enchiladas. There is something for everyone on the menu here as Alegria strays from the typical Mexican fare to offer dishes that both meat eaters and vegetarians will love. The fresh fruit smoothies are also very popular. The restaurant is small and popular, so be prepared to wait. Weeknight dining is probably your best option. Also be sure to bring your own alcohol, as it is allowed, but not sold, on the premises.

El Cholo

323 734 2773 | www.elcholo.com

If *Gourmet Magazine* tells its readership it can't imagine Los Angeles without El Cholo, it's a sure bet this is one restaurant worth a visit. As much a part of the city's landscape as it's celebrities, El Cholo opened its doors in 1922 and continues to serve up authentic Mexican dishes, paired with perfectly prepared margaritas. Yet it's not just the menu that brings couples, families and large groups to this restaurant (which was a favourite of Bing Crosby's back in the day). Sandstone-coloured walls are adorned with brightly painted flowers above the fireplace and complemented by framed photographs that hang in the adjoining dining areas, while homely furnishings make it a great spot to relax in while slurping up the last drop of that authentic margarita. Be sure to order a Sonora style enchilada – a menu staple since 1923.

La Parilla

323 262 3434 | www.laparrillarestaurants.com

With a unique take on the normal Mexican restaurant, La Parilla attracts all walks of life. Whether it be Mexican families celebrating a birthday or local hipsters looking for authentic Mexican food without the normal bar crowd. The guacamole is fresh and delicious and the portions are more than generous. Molcajete's – dishes served in a heated stone pot and meant to be shared by two or more people – are ever present. As a bonus, some of the most flamboyant Mariachi singers in the city travel from table to table entertaining guests.

Leonor's

818 980 9011

Often touted as a vegetarian restaurant, Leonor's also caters to the meat lover. Whether you order the tacos with a faux-chicken filling or the soy cheese quesadilla with guacamole (servings are almost bigger than the plate they're served on), you won't leave this place hungry. It's those generous portions and the well-prepared healthy take on Mexican food that has its customers returning regularly (including Barbara Streisand whose headshot hangs proudly on the wall). A favourite among The Valley's health conscious are Leonor's fresh juices, a prelude to selections from the Forever Young raw menu. Be warned, if you're hungry, it's wise to order ahead as service can be slow.

Malo

323 664 1011 | www.malorestaurant.com

Malo could probably be considered one of the hipper Mexican restaurants in LA. With a decidedly young crowd and a bar that's just as much of a singles scene as it is a place to wait for your table, Malo has become a destination for anyone wanting to familiarise themselves with the area. The food is also a little less than traditional compared to other Mexican restaurants in the immediate area. Beef and pickle or aubergine (eggplant) and potato tacos are some of the favourites and not nearly as weird as they sound. The bar offers a huge array of tequilas as well as other spirits and promises some of the best fresh margaritas in town.

Middle Eastern

Marouch

323 662 9325 | www.marouchrestaurant.com

You can smell the wood-fired pita bread as you walk into this charming restaurant, known for its authentic Lebanese, Armenian and Middle Eastern dishes. Small, yet large enough to accommodate a big family gathering, Marouch is often at capacity with the casual LA diner who comes here to get their fix of garlicky *baba ghanouge* or *shanklish*; a Lebanese aged cheese breaded with dry herbs and spices. Open for lunch and dinner, the restaurant also offers a full catering menu for those who want to bring a touch of the Middle East to their own gathering. If this is your first introduction to Middle Eastern cuisine, a great way to familiarise yourself is with a plate of assorted appetisers that will easily feed six.

Seafood

1535 Vine St
Hollywood
Map 6 C2 **41**

The Hungry Cat
323 462 2155 | www.thehungrycat.com

The Hungry Cat, at the famous intersection of Hollywood and Vine, may be small in stature (the restaurant seats at total of 75 in three separate areas) but not in taste. Diners can expect sleek, modern architecture incorporating white, silver and timber; and an ample menu of fresh seafood and meals from the raw bar – a big hit with health conscious Angelenos who eagerly fill the seats. Popular for brunch, The Hungry Cat also serves up impressive cocktails come evening, such as the hot tamale with tequila, lime, fresh orange juice and Fresno chilli maple syrup, which can be served alight if you choose. Prices here reflect the location and seafood menu, however, it's easy to enjoy dinner and drinks for two for under $100, plus tip.

1700 Ocean Ave
Santa Monica
Map 3 C4 **42**

Ocean & Vine
310 576 3180 | www.oceanandvine.com

Catch the ocean breeze at this sophisticated restaurant, tucked inside Loews Santa Monica Hotel. If the glow of the fire-pit bar doesn't grab you, cosy up in one of the plush booths with oversized pillows that make you feel right at home. Order an uncommon cosmopolitan or a red ruby cocktail at the sleek bar with its coloured lighting and padded bar stools, before settling in for a reasonably priced seafood dinner. The sauteed tiger shrimp with ricotta cheese cavatelli, squash and vermouth reduction is enough to make your mouth water, but it's the pan seared Alaskan halibut with caramelised onion polenta, sweet corn, morels and tomato coulis that really sings. While the setting, with its fireplace seating, beachfront patio and vibrant wall art is enough to make any guest feel right at home, it's what comes out of the kitchen that really makes Ocean and Vine a must visit.

1743 N Cahuenga Blvd
Hollywood
Map 6 C1 **43**

Ritual Restaurant & Nightclub
323 463 0060 | www.ritualsupperclub.com

Candle glow and ambient lights warm the earth-toned walls here, as guests enjoy cocktails on banquettes and industry types sip imported wine paired with fresh seafood as they close their business deals. Celebrities mix with the general public in a zen-like atmosphere – a great place to unwind after a week of office stress. The romantic-at-heart gravitate toward the candle-lit patio and if in the mood for a dance, head to the nightclub where the latest video mixes play continuously on wall-mounted flat screens. The young and the fabulous also come to listen to live bands after sharing health-conscious meals prepared by chef Andy Pastore, who is loved for his menu staple: the Mystical Chef Andy Cut Roll, overstuffed with crab, fried onion, albacore, gold flakes and caviar.

Steakhouses
Other options **American** p.317

224 S Beverly Dr
Beverly Hills
Map 4 F3 **44**

Ruth's Chris Steak House
310 859 8744 | www.ruthschris.com

Non-meat eaters can dine with their meat-loving friends at Ruth's, where seafood is just as popular as the slow-cooked porterhouse. For 20 years, this restaurant has been serving its dishes to A-list regulars, who come for the relaxed atmosphere, its many booths and linen-clothed tables, adorned with glistening silverware and wine glasses. Classy yet casual, the restaurant bar stocks fine wines and champagnes, as well as a selection of spirits that come together to make great cocktails to be shared at the bar or at your table. There's also the option of private dining at Ruth's with an elegant timber-panelled room, with a private bar, perfect for small weddings and special events. You can also find Ruth's in Anaheim, Irvine, Pasadena and Woodland Hills.

4420 W Lakeside Dr
Burbank
Map 2 D1

Smoke House

818 845 3731 | *www.smokehouse1946.com*

A Bob Hope favourite, Smoke House continues to attract star-studded clientele 60 years after it first opened its doors. Open seven days until 23:00 (21:00 on Sundays), the restaurant serves up tried and true American/Continental dishes such as crab stuffed mushrooms with crabmeat and béarnaise and the much-ordered Smoke House baby back ribs. Regardless of what you order, be sure to try a side of the Smoke House's famous garlic bread – a secret recipe developed there in 1959. While celebrity spotting here is usual, approaching your favourite star for an autograph is a no-no, as the restaurant has, over the years, become known as a dining haven for those who want privacy.

Thai

5900 Hollywood
Blvd Suite B
Hollywood
Map 6 D1 **45**

The Palms Thai

323 462 5073 | *www.palmsthai.com*

With tons of seating, authentic Thai food and LA's only Thai Elvis impersonator, The Palms Thai is one of those restaurants that could only exist in Los Angeles. A perfect place to bring out of town guests or to celebrate any special occasion. The food can be interesting: the 'Wild Things' section of the menu includes items such as 'raw' pork sausage and wild boar in green peppercorn sauce. If you're not feeling that adventurous, the more common dishes such as green curry with chicken or phad Thai are also top notch. Beer and wine are available. Be sure to tip your Elvis impersonator.

5257 Hollywood Blvd
Hollywood
Map 6 F1 **46**

Ruen Pair

323 466 0153

One of the best Thai restaurants in all of LA, and also one of the cheapest. Reun Pair is located in a small mall in the heart of Thai Town. Although quite popular there is ample seating and the decor is traditionally simple and Thai. The menu is extensive featuring Thai favourites such and green papaya salad and many different options for curries. The deep fried mussels are sweet, greasy and delicious. Also, the braised morning glories are a hit with everyone from staunch vegetarians to meat eaters who will find they can mix it with anything. Parking is a bit difficult but they offer a valet service for an additional $3.

Vegetarian

2135 W Sunset Blvd
Echo Park
Map 8 C3 **47**

Elf Cafe

213 484 6829

Nestled among the many tiny shops on Sunset in Echo Park, this itty-bitty cafe prepares Mediterranean-inspired vegetarian cuisine using organic, locally grown ingredients. The layout is intimate: a few small tables, some bar seating, and a couple of tables outside. Exposed brick and earthy tones coupled with the packed-in bohemian crowd give it a New York bistro feel. There is no alcohol served, but you're welcome to bring your own bottle of wine (you will be charged a $5 corkage fee). Because of its size and the proximity of the guests, the din of chatter can be a bit taxing at times, and the dishes are a little expensive for what they are, but you won't find anything else like it on the Eastside.

Fatty's & Co.

1627 Colorado Blvd
Eagle Rock
Map 2 B1

323 254 8804 | www.fattyscafe.com

Located on the Eastside in the blossoming Eagle Rock community, Fatty's is one of only a handful of restaurants in LA to feature a completely vegetarian menu. The gourmet dishes emphasise a number of vegetarian staples – chickpeas, lentils, tempeh, aubergine, fresh herbs – all expertly prepared and with careful attention paid to presentation. Flavourful and unique, these entrees will satisfy carnivores and herbivores alike. In addition to the delectable cuisine, the restaurant also features a substantial wine list. And vegans will be happy to know that most of Fatty's dishes can be prepared without dairy. The setting can feel a little cold and rigid, and the wait staff are a little hit and miss, but that's no reason to miss this Eagle Rock gem.

Flore

3818 W Sunset Blvd
Silver Lake
Map 8 B2 48

323 953 0611

Flore is a cute little organic vegan cafe and deli on Sunset in the hip Sunset Junction area of Silver Lake. It's a sit-down joint, but very low key – more utilitarian than eye-catching. The menu is diverse, from frittatas and tempeh melts to pizza and jicama taco, and very reasonably priced. The deli features a selection organic fruits, veggies, breads, sandwiches and various side dishes, all of which are perfect for those on the go. It also offers organic juices, coffees, teas and kombucha. The staff are friendly and the food is prepared with love, making it the ideal spot to grab a bite between retail therapy sessions.

Leaf Cuisine

11938 W Washington Blvd
Culver City
Map 2 C2

310 390 6005 | www.leafcuisine.com

As the world's first certified organic, vegan and raw restaurant, it's easy to see why the healthy flock to its two locations in Culver City and Sherman Oaks. Once inside, even the air feels healthier as you slide into the stark white booth seating. While the surroundings are sparse, the menu is anything but, with plenty of gourmet food to keep the hunger pangs at bay. Start with the hummus and flax seed crackers before ordering a Bedouin burrito wrap with sprouted chickpea hummus topped with tahini, mixed greens, tomatoes and sprouts. In between meals, the converted come to Leaf for the smoothies, bursting with fresh fruits and plenty of flavour – the blueberry bonanza with blueberries, banana, nut milk and dates is a must try.

Real Food Daily

414 N La Cienega Blvd
West Hollywood
Map 7 A1 49

310 289 9910 | www.realfood.com

Real Food Daily serves one of the only strictly vegan menus in the entire city, and is the best at it by far. None of their dishes contain meat or dairy, which is surprisingly rare in LA. But this doesn't mean you'll be choking down tasteless hippie chow – quite the opposite. What you'll find here is a full-flavoured celebration of natural ingredients crafted with care. The menu offers a vegan take on American classics and Eastern dishes alike, using only the freshest organic ingredients possible. With rotating monthly and weekly specials, the menu stays fresh week after week. The ambience is comfortable and cosy, with the added benefit of peaceful and friendly staff. If you know a special vegan or vegetarian someone, take them here for a meal they won't soon forget.

Vietnamese

Crustacean

9646 Little Santa Monica Blvd
Beverly Hills
Map 2 C1

310 205 8990 | www.anfamily.com

When Crustacean opened its doors in Beverly Hills in 1997, *Esquire* magazine named it one of the best new restaurants in the country. It has consistently been a favourite of critics and gourmands ever since, particularly for its roast Dungeness crab with garlic noodles, which is always prepared in a secret kitchen-within-the-kitchen by members of the owner's family. From the start, the remarkable cuisine and dramatic decor (including an 80 foot sunken aquarium that meanders through the dining area) attracted a star-studded crowd. But it is the food that is the real star here. Chef Helene An is credited with designing her own unique cuisine, drawing on her French/Vietnamese heritage leavened with European and nouveau flourishes. Whatever her secrets, she makes it work. Open for lunch, Monday to Friday 11:30 to 14:30, and dinner, Monday to Thursday 17:30 to 20:30, and on Friday and Saturday 17:30 to 11:30.

Gingergrass

2396 Glendale Blvd
Silver Lake
Map 8 D1 **50**

323 644 1600 | www.gingergrass.com

With an original take on Vietnamese food, Gingergrass has become a hotspot for anyone looking to try the unusual without fully immersing themselves into traditional and perhaps confusing food. Located near the Red Lion, Cha Cha and the Silverlake Wine Shop, Gingergrass has become a popular destination to grab a good meal before heading out. With classic dishes like Vietnamese pho soup or more exotic appetisers that change weekly, Gingergrass has something for everyone. Also featuring basil-lime elixirs, a popular street drink in Vietnam.

Pho 87

1019 N Broadway
Chinatown
Map 8 E4 **51**

323 227 0758

Pho, for the uninitiated is the traditional Vietnamese soup served for breakfast lunch and dinner. Almost scarily authentic Pho 87 features large bowls of noodles with ingredients such as tripe and tendon. For less adventurous eaters there are versions with cooked slices of beef or chicken. Also fresh spring rolls and dishes of grilled meat served on beds of cold rice noodles are a nice touch when most Pho restaurants only serve soup. The decor is slightly messy and unattractive but when eating a giant bowl of beef parts and drinking soda water mixed with preserved lemons, you won't have time to worry about the space surround you. For what it's worth Pho may just be the best in the city and as always, the portions are huge.

Little Temple (p.355)

Small but indispensable…

Perfectly proportioned to fit in your pocket,
this marvellous mini guidebook makes sure
you don't just get the holiday you paid for
but rather the one that you dreamed of.

Los Angeles Mini Visitors' Guide
Maximising your holiday, minimising your hand luggage

Cafes & Coffee Shops

Cafes and coffee shops abound in Los Angeles, and are overflowing with film industry hopefuls and professionals alike. Actors, writers, directors, agents – they all take meetings, often over a bite or a latte. Coffee shops typically have menus limited to baked goods and snacks, while cafes offer a much broader array. It's not unusual to spot a small army of hopefuls diligently pecking away at their laptops at these places. After all, where else can an up-and-coming writer work on their breakthrough screenplay?

While there are numerous fantastic local independent coffee houses, such as Intelligentsia (p.341) and Downbeat Cafe (p.341), coffee chains like Starbucks, The Coffee Bean & Tea Leaf, and Peet's Coffee & Tea are prevalent – with Starbucks winning the prize for most ubiquitous (there are over 150 in the greater LA area). Cafe styles are all over the map, but tend to lean towards Californian fusion, integrating various cooking styles while using freshly prepared local ingredients – salads being popular with the locals. Typical hours of operation are from 08:00 to 22:00. Coffee shops tend to open earlier and close later, some as early as 05:00 and as late as 02:00.

101 Coffee Shop

6145 Franklin Ave
Hollywood
Map 6 D1 **52**

323 467 1175

Adjoined to a Best Western hotel and located off the 101 freeway, the 101 Coffee Shop has been a longtime destination for actors and musicians staying in town for short periods of time. The food is traditionally American with items such as meatloaf with mash potatoes and gravy. But the 101 does offer up some different items for the 'Hollyweird' crowd that hang out here late at night or hungover at the weekends. Many vegetarian items and traditional Mexican plates are available. They also have an extensive beer list which you won't find on the menu of any family orientated diners. The decor is reminiscent of the late 60s and the general vibe of the place is just as debaucherous.

Aroma Café

4360 Tujunga Ave
Studio City
Map 2 C1

818 508 0677 | *www.aromacoffeeandtea.com*

On any given day, be it for breakfast, lunch or dinner, a queue of eager diners spills out the door and along the pavement by this bustling cafe in quaint Tujunga Village. Early risers with a healthy appetite shouldn't look further than the fluffy omelettes, served with a choice of fresh fillings. There's also something to be said for the coffee. In a city where an authentic cappuccino or latte can be hard to find, Aroma's barista is doing something right. The major draw besides the food, coffee and decadent cakes that fill the front glass display is the pleasant courtyard setting.

Clifton's Cafeteria

648 S Broadway
Downtown
Map 10 D3 **53**

213 627 1673 | *www.cliftonscafeteria.com*

No exploration downtown is complete without a trip to Clifton's. Located in what used to be a vibrant theatre district, this is a well-known (and treasured) local oddity. For five generations Clifton's has served a large cafeteria menu at low prices (and sometimes free to those who can't afford a meal). It draws a varied crowd with a blend of traditional and unusual meal options. The food however is not the main attraction. The full-wall forest mural and hand-carved wooden bear are just two examples of the unusual decor. Elderly folk and children tend to enjoy the atmosphere without thinking twice, while the rest of the diners wonder in amazement at how such a strange place still exists.

Delilah Bakery

1665 Echo Park Ave
Echo Park
Map 8 D2 **54**

213 975 9400 | www.delilahbakery.com

A coffee shop and bakery, Delilah has made a name for itself by serving up delicious classics such as red velvet cupcakes and German chocolate cake, as well as fine chocolate chip cookies. You might have to wait in a small queue at weekends, as folks from the surrounding neighbourhood pop in for their morning coffee or a post-jog treat. Sandwiches are also available for those in need of a quick bite. There is no seating inside, but outside are a couple of chairs and tables for when the weather's good. The cakes and cupcakes are perfect for parties and can be ordered ahead.

Downbeat Cafe

1202 N Alvarado St
Echo Park
Map 8 C3 **55**

213 483 3955 | www.thedownbeatcafe.com

Tucked away just off of Sunset on an old stretch of historic Route 66, this bohemian cafe caters to the young, hip and arty Echo Park crowd. The look is retro: 1950s kitchen tables and chairs mix with art deco touches, while local art and cool old covers of *Downbeat* jazz magazine pepper the walls. The coffee is fantastic – some of the best in the city – with an equally impressive menu that features breakfast selections, soups, salads, sandwiches and pastries, all packed with fresh, tasty ingredients. There are a few outdoor tables for smokers.

Intelligentsia Coffee & Tea

3922 W Sunset Blvd
Silver Lake
Map 8 B2 **56**

323 663 6173 | www.intelligentsiacoffee.com

If you're a coffee snob, this place is for you. It serves the best cup in town, hands down. Its blends are unique and robust, formed from beans roasted exclusively at Intelligentsia's own roasting plant and prepared by baristas who take pride in their work. You'll pay a premium, but if you're a bean fiend, it's worth it. The look here is clean, sparse and hip, with a cool, laid-back atmosphere. It's not unusual to find a queue trailing out the door at peak hours, but you won't be waiting long – service is quick and courteous. There's not a lot of seating inside, but plenty out front along Sunset in the area known as Sunset Junction; perfect for people watching.

Le Pain Quotidien

Various Locations

310 476 0969 | www.lepainquotidien.com

There's always a crowd filling the tables at one of the 11 Le Pain Quotidien stores dotted around Los Angeles. If you can get past the shock of being served real coffee in a town where the art of the barista is sadly lacking, you'll see there are plenty of reasons why they are popular. The aroma of bread is courtesy of the bakery shelves that are stocked high with fresh, organic offerings, while jars of delectable home-made spreads are within reach. But it's the cafe itself that really pleases, with an organic menu of fresh ingredients that can be ordered from a

Intelligentsia Coffee & Tea

table for two, or, for the more adventurous, at the communal table where guests are encouraged to dine with strangers.

1110 1/2 Gayley Ave
Westwood
Map 4 B3 **57**

Native Foods

310 209 1055 | www.nativefoods.com

In the thick of the university-centric community of Westwood you'll find this vegan cafe. The menu offers a vegetarian spin on American diner classics and ethnic cuisine, with a wide variety of options, all of which are meat and dairy free. A number of its dishes feature fresh *tempeh* (made from soybeans and rice) or *seitan* (made from wheat or gluten), which are made from scratch. The atmosphere leaves a bit to be desired, so you won't want to hang out all that long, but the food is fast, affordable and most importantly, tasty. The crowd is a mix of hippies and health nuts, and because of its proximity to UCLA, you'll most likely find a younger vegan crowd.

4150 Riverside Dr
Toluca Lake
Map 2 D1

Priscilla's Gourmet Coffee, Tea & Gifts

818 843 5707 | www.priscillascoffee.com

Just around the corner from Warner Bros Studios, Priscilla's supplies actors and film industry types with their daily caffeine fix. The quaint corner coffee shop features a good number of outdoor tables that are perfect for soaking up some afternoon sunshine while people watching. The interior has a simple, country cottage motif, with bucolic murals stretching along the walls. The shop features an impressive selection of gourmet coffee beans and loose leaf teas, both of which can be purchased in bulk. The gift shop, which seems like a bit of an afterthought, includes cards, little stuffed animals, and a surprising variety of mugs. There's internet access for a nominal fee.

2160 Colorado Blvd
Eagle Rock
Map 2 D1

Swork

323 258 5600 | www.swork.com

This goofy little coffee shop on Eagle Rock's main drag is as peculiar as its name. The interior is playful and childlike, balanced with a clean, Scandinavian modern look. Because of its proximity to Occidental College there's a collegiate vibe, but oddly enough, it's also very family oriented. Not many coffee shops are particularly kid-friendly, but this one actually encourages parents to bring their children. There's even a dedicated play area (Sworkland) in which kids can knock around. Swork offers free wireless internet access with any purchase, or you can buy time on an in-house computer. The coffee isn't as good as other independent places, but it's one of the few cafes in the area, and its parent-friendly atmosphere is a plus.

Le Pain Quotidien

On The Town

The nightlife scene in Los Angeles has so much to offer it's hard to do it justice in a few short paragraphs. A night on the town can be anything you want it to be – from a quiet intimate evening to a raucous all night affair. There are upscale cocktail bars where people dress to impress, hole-in-the-wall dive bars with drunken regulars, clubs with world-famous DJs, rooftop bars with incredible views, pubs with pints and trivia, karaoke bars, sports bars, you name it, LA's got it. The Eastside is known for its hipster bars, where the patrons pride themselves on looking like they just rolled out of bed. The Westside tends to have a more clean-cut, tucked in vibe. The Downtown scene has grown quite a bit in recent years and is a popular destination due to the high concentration of bars in relatively close proximity. If clubbing is your passion, Hollywood is the place to be, while West Hollywood (WeHo, as some call it) offers a ton of options for the gay and lesbian community.

Drinks
Other options **Alcohol** p.259

Drinking is heavily ingrained in the Los Angeles nightlife culture – a social lubricant found at nearly all after dark venues. Sit-down restaurants usually serve beer and wine, and some serve liquor, but your best bet for getting a drink is in an actual bar. Drink prices vary dramatically depending on the venue. In general, the Eastside and Downtown are cheaper than Hollywood and the Westside. Not all bars offer a 'happy hour', but at those that do you will find drink specials and discounts during a certain period of time, usually 16:00 to 19:00, Monday to Friday. Bars and clubs start to get crowded after 22:00 at the weekends, something to bear in mind if you're going out with a large group of people. Also, smoking is illegal in enclosed spaces in California, so all drinking establishments are smoke-free. Because of this, a number of venues offer outdoor smoking areas. Legally, bars, clubs and pubs must stop serving alcohol at 02:00, and many bars will set their clocks forward up to a half an hour, so don't expect to be able to get a drink past 01:45, which is usually your 'last call for alcohol'. Grocery stores, liquor stores (off-licences) and mini-marts are also prohibited from selling alcohol past 02:00. They do, however, resume selling it at 06:00 (depending on their hours of operation). To legally purchase alcohol, or to enter a bar or pub in California, you must be 21 years of age and provide legal proof (driver's licence, military identification or passport).

The Standard (p.350)

Bars & Pubs

4100 Sunset Blvd
Silver Lake
Map 8 B1 58

4100

323 666 4460

A popular Sunset Junction watering hole, 4100 has a thriving singles scene. Checking people out comes with the territory here, which can be challenging given the dim light cast by a few over-the-bar lamps and a handful of candles. There is a distinct far eastern vibe, with dragon patterns on the table tops, beads and tapestries on the walls, swooping draperies overhead, and a larger-than-life statue of Guan Yin, the bodhisattva of compassion, watching over all. The bar can accommodate a fairly large crowd, but it still manages to get packed at weekends (always good news for those on the prowl). Just don't expect to have a quiet conversation – the music will be blasting.

> ### Drinking & Driving
>
> Driving under the influence of alcohol is illegal in California. If you are caught operating a vehicle with a blood alcohol level of 0.08% or more, you will be arrested. The range of possible sentences for a conviction varies (see www.california-drunkdriving.org for more information). If you're planning on drinking, your best option is to travel by taxi. LA is a bustling metropolis, but it isn't known for its particularly prompt taxi service. Keep the telephone numbers of two taxi services handy, and allow up to 30 minutes for pick-up (Yellow Cab, 877 733 3305 and United Independent Taxi 800 822 8294).

8171 W Sunset Blvd
West Hollywood
Map 5 C2 59

Bar Marmont

323 650 0575 | *www.chateaumarmont.com*

This is the upscale bar at Chateau Marmont, one of LA's poshest hotels, famous for its celebrity guests and high-rolling clientele. Inside you'll find a mix of moneyed industry types, dealmakers, celebrities and wannabes – all knocking back fine wines, expensive champagne and high-priced drinks. The style of the bar is eclectic and vaguely Asian-themed, with multiple rooms and levels that make it feel more like the home of a Hollywood eccentric than a bar. The elegant menu features a wide variety of refined selections ranging from $5 to $30 (Oxtail Bruschetta anyone?). Valet parking will set you back $18, so look for street parking or a cheaper pay car park if possible. Reservations are recommended.

3172 Los Feliz Blvd
Atwater Village
Map 2 D1

The Bigfoot Lodge

323 662 9227 | *www.bigfootlodge.com*

There are a number of ornately themed bars in LA, but The Bigfoot Lodge is one of the best. The name itself conjures up images of a woodsy hideaway tucked back in the hills of some old forgotten American mountain town, and the bar does little to disappoint that vision. The interior walls and ceiling are comprised of rustic looking logs reminiscent of an Alpine cabin, with dark, grainy hues to set the mood. A fireplace, a rock-lined bar and horned creatures mounted on the walls complete the desired effect. The clientele varies depending on the night, as each night carries a different theme – from karaoke and bingo to Brit rock and rockabilly. Check the website for details.

*916 S San
Fernando Blvd*
Burbank
Map 2 D1

The Blue Room

323 849 2779

The Blue Room is, you guessed it, blue. Blue lights beam out from above the bar onto the blue walls and ceiling, blue diner-style booths and retro chairs and a blue tile floor. It's a dive bar that wants to be a hip and stylish lounge, but can't quite pull it off – and that's what's kind of cool and funky about it. The scene is casual, with a local mostly male Burbank crowd. The table service is a nice touch when the place gets packed at the weekends, and the drinks are cheap. A big-screen TV and electronic dartboard keep sports fans satiated, while smokers enjoy a decent-sized patio with seating out back.

6268 Sunset Blvd
Hollywood
Map 6 C1 **60**

The Bowery

323 465 3400 | www.theboweryhollywood.com

The Bowery draws inspiration from the neighbourhood of the same name in the borough of Manhattan. The pressed-tin roof, subway-style brick tiles, horizontal wood blinds and hardwood-panelled bar give off a distinctly New York vibe, and the multitude of full-length mirrors gives the diminutive room a sense of space. Bowery's food is classic American with a twist, and leaps and bounds ahead of traditional bar fare. If you're a burger fan, do yourself a favour and order the juicy sirloin. There is a well-rounded selection of wine and bottled beer (no draught beer, unfortunately).

1515 Abbot Kinney Blvd
Venice
Map 3 E4 **61**

The Brig

310 399 7537 | www.thebrig.com

Abbot Kinney Boulevard in Venice has experienced some serious gentrification over the last decade. What used to be a dumpy little strip in a dangerous part of town now has a clean, refined look, offering a myriad of shopping, dining and nightlife options. The Brig has stood there through it all, evolving from a neighborhood boxing-themed dive bar to a fashionable cocktail lounge. The decor is sparse and modern, with sleek wood-panelled walls and glowing orbs dangling from above. The vibe is casual, with DJs spinning music to match the mood of the room. Patrons are a mix of thirsty Venice locals and Westsiders who don't want to trek all the way to Hollywood for a loungy atmosphere.

830 S Broadway
Downtown
Map 10 C3 **62**

Broadway Bar

213 614 9909 | www.thebroadwaybar.net

This is a dark and classy watering hole smack in the middle of LA's historic theatre district. The exterior is gothic revival, while the interior has the flair of a 1940s supper club. The lavish circular bar with antique ceiling is the perfect centrepiece for the flock wallpaper, wood-panelled walls and period-inspired couches that wrap around the perimeter of the room. The upstairs has an additional bar and smoking terrace with views of Broadway and the rest of Downtown – an ideal partner for one of the many French champagnes available. Relatively hipster-free, the casual crowd is a mix from all over looking for a civilised night out on the town.

1819 Ocean Ave
Santa Monica
Map 3 C4 **63**

Cameo Bar

310 260 7500 | www.viceroysantamonica.com

Off the lobby of the Viceroy Hotel you'll find the swanky and sexy Cameo Bar, where vibrant colours mingle with mid-twentieth century style to form a striking, sophisticated cocktail lounge. The lighting is classy and subdued, with vintage and custom-designed furniture surrounding the intimate bar. Step out onto the sprawling patio sprinkled with white leather chairs, where you can wander between swimming pools and cosy cabanas with comfortable couches. The entire scene has a distinctly upper class vibe, with a clientele made up primarily of moneyed types and those looking to impress. The drinks are pricey and so is the valet parking, but street parking is available if you're willing to walk a couple blocks.

Broadway Bar

6530 Sunset Blvd
Hollywood
Map 6 B2 **64**

Cat & Fiddle

323 468 3800 | www.thecatandfiddle.com

The Cat & Fiddle is an English pub on Sunset in the heart of Hollywood. The historic building was once a studio commissary – some scenes from *Casablanca* were even shot here. The interior features stained glass windows and exposed brick, high-back wooden booths, a fireplace, a couple of dartboards and some televisions. The walls are a hodgepodge of images and beer adverts, a fairly typical American-style British pub look. What makes this place different is its sprawling garden patio. It's unlike anything else you'll find in Hollywood and the perfect place to sample a midday pint, or meet up with friends in the evening. There's a full menu of British pub standards and live jazz on Sunday nights.

2375 Glendale Blvd
Silver Lake
Map 8 D1 **65**

Cha Cha Lounge

323 660 7595 | www.chachalounge.com

This place is hipster heaven. The drinks are cheap, which is always a selling point for up-and-coming starving artists, and the look is Mexican restaurant meets eccentric lounge: dimly lit, with velvet paintings, sombreros and weird trinkets all over the walls. It has a musician vibe (the owners are from Seattle), so if you're in a band or follow the scene, you'll fit in pretty well. There is a photo booth to preserve the evening's events, and a couple of foosball (table football) tables to spill cheap beer on (Pabst Blue Ribbon being the poor man's beer of choice). Hipster music reigns supreme, with occasional karaoke and guest DJs spinning.

1630 Colorado Blvd
Eagle Rock
Map 2 D1

The Chalet

323 258 8800

Dark and cosy, this bar will whisk you away to a mountain chalet without ever leaving Los Angeles. The rock-lined walls, wood-panelled roof, and pastoral landscape paintings mingle with the warmth of a fire and the sounds from a well-stocked jukebox. A welcome addition to the burgeoning Eagle Rock nightlife scene, this ski-lodge themed bar is relaxing and intimate; the perfect place to kick back with friends and unwind after a long day of negotiating LA's notorious traffic. The comfy atmosphere lends itself to a romantic evening – but be forewarned, the bar is fairly small and tends to get crowded as the night stretches on, especially at weekends.

1760 N Vermont Ave
Los Feliz
Map 8 A1 **66**

The Dresden Room

323 665 4294 | www.thedresden.com

There's no better way to welcome someone to LA than by taking them to The Dresden, an old-school Vegas-style lounge bar. You won't find anything like it anywhere else in the city. Dark and cavernous, with corkboard and rockwork walls, old ball and chain chandeliers, and lounge seating, it's right out of another era. Crooning in the centre of the room you'll find Marty and Elayne (Monday to Saturday, 21:00 to 01:15). The beloved singers have been packing them in for more than 25 years. Skip the restaurant portion of the bar (unless you enjoy mediocre continental cuisine), but do take a peek at the awesome gaudy decor. Parking in the area can be tricky, but there's valet out back that is very reasonably priced.

108 E 2nd St
Downtown
Map 10 E3 **67**

The Edison

213 613 0000 | www.edisondowntown.com

Descending into The Edison is a lot like being transported into a Jules Verne novel. The huge subterranean space (you enter off an alley and go down a wide industrial stairway) is filled with Victorian-era electrical machinery and decorated

Discounts

Aside from 'happy hour' at bars, and posted menu specials at restaurants, discounts are not easily found. *LA Weekly* (www.laweekly.com) is your best bet for finding entertainment and dining specials.

with faded art-deco murals of the green absinthe fairy. The cracked 25 foot walls serve as giant screens onto which silent films are projected in ghostly luminescence. It is the kind of space that impels the visitor to utter 'wow' and really mean it. Originally an early 20th century power station, The Edison is now a bar, restaurant and nightclub that serves some of the best cocktails in town and features a delightful tipplers' menu ranging from Tesla fries to a lobster corndog. There's often live music, and the Thursday jazz happy hours are particularly recommended when martinis are offered at 1910 prices. Check the website for an entertainment calendar. This nightspot is highly recommended.

2702 Main St
Santa Monica
Map 3 D4 68

Finn McCool's

310 452 1734 | www.gerrigilliland.com/finn

Finn McCool's is a stylish and spacious Irish pub on a pedestrian-friendly stretch of Main Street. At every turn you will notice attention to detail: from Irish murals and classic Murphy's and Guinness ads to intricately carved wood and glasswork. The bar offers a well-rounded selection of beers on tap (served in imperial pints) and a wide variety of Irish and Scottish whiskys. There's an extensive menu of Irish fare, and live music and trivia nights on a regular basis. Loud and crowded at the weekends, the pub caters to locals by day and a mix of Main Street bar crawlers by night.

2640 N Figueroa St
Cypress
Map 8 F2 69

Footsies

323 221 6900

Footsies is a dive bar in Cypress Park that caters to the thirsty Eastside crowd. There's nothing fancy about the joint – it's not sexy or themed or a must-see by any means, but the drinks are cheap and strong, and it's got a laid-back hipster vibe. The style says 'who cares?', with kitschy paintings of nude women peering over black leather booths that dominate the room, and funky old lamps dangling from above. There's the requisite pool table and jukebox, with the addition of a patio out back for smokers. You'll often find patrons chomping on some of the greasy but tasty offerings from Taquerias El Atacor, the taco shop next door.

11100 Ventura Blvd
Studio City
Map 2 C1

The Fox & Hounds

818 763 7837 | www.thefoxandhounds.com

This English pub, on a popular stretch of Ventura Boulevard in Studio City, is short on style but long on sports and live music. With seven satellite dishes and plenty of televisions, the pub can accommodate sports fans from not only across the country, but from around the globe. There is some attempt at making the interior look like that of an actual English pub, with wood treatments and paintings of hounds and fox hunting here and there, but it doesn't quite pull it off. It does, however, have live music regularly, and 'king trivia night' every Monday and Wednesday. A covered outdoor patio with additional TVs is an added bonus for smokers who don't want to miss the game.

417 W 8th St
Downtown
Map 10 C3 70

Golden Gopher

213 614 8001 | www.goldengopherbar.com

Downtown has experienced a revival in the last few years. Old buildings have been refurbished and turned into lofts, retail spaces and galleries, which paved the way for a rejuvenated nightlife scene, of which Golden Gopher is part. Dimly lit by a legion of gopher-shaped lamps, the room features a lofted ceiling, exposed brick walls, studded leather furniture and wrap-around couches. The Gopher is ultra-spacious but a bit short on seating. At the weekend it can get pretty packed, so be prepared to stand, or explore the smoking patio, which offers a bit of additional seating. The crowd is your typical Downtown mix, everything from artists to lawyers. Due to a 1905 alcohol licence loophole, a concierge near the entrance legally sells booze to go.

1514 Hillhurst Ave
Los Feliz
Map 8 B1 **71**

Good Luck Bar
323 666 3524
This heavily themed Los Feliz bar specialises in Far East kitsch. Every inch has a touch of the Orient, right down to the matches on the bar. It is dimly lit, with Chinese lanterns casting a subtle glow on the red wood-panelled walls, tin-panel roof and velvet brocade wallpaper. There's a lounge off the main bar that's downright sultry – the perfect place to sip 'Singapore slings' in a dark corner. You'll find a myriad of speciality drinks with peculiar names such as 'Hong Kong bong', 'master min sing mah' and Good Luck's signature drink, a mysterious blue concoction named 'yee me loo'.

3000 Los Feliz Blvd
Atwater Village
Map 2 D1

The Griffin
323 644 0444
The Griffin is one of the newer additions to Atwater Village, and a welcome one at that. The style is gothic sexy, with brick arches and medieval chandeliers overhead, cool old period paintings, flickering fireplaces, hanging curtains and plenty of communal seating. The space is well planned and easy to navigate, and manages to feel roomy while still remaining intimate. There is a back room with a second bar to accommodate nights with larger crowds: primarily Eastsiders and Atwater locals, but drawing from points further west at the weekends. A covered and heated smoking patio with ample seating accommodates smokers.

2911 Main St
Santa Monica
Map 3 D4 **72**

Library Ale House
310 314 4855 | www.libraryalehouse.com
Library Ale House is more of a restaurant than a bar, but with 29 unique microbrews on tap and a winning selection of bottled beers from around the globe, it's definitely worth mentioning. Anchored on trendy Main Street, this Santa Monica-style public house features American Craftsmen architecture, with blonde wood walls and beams, old-fashioned library ladders, and a collection of beer bottles and cans from yesteryear. The pub menu offers everything from salads and sandwiches to burgers and substantial starters. The seating in the front is a little tight, but the back garden patio offers a more spacious and relaxed atmosphere. Library is perfect for an afternoon beer and a bite, or an evening of Main Street bar-hopping.

11780 W Pico Blvd
West LA
Map 3 D1 **73**

Liquid Kitty
310 473 3707 | www.thekitty.com
With lots of woody brown, and red and green hues, Liquid Kitty feels like the inside of a cigar box. It is dimly lit, with small pools of light highlighting the unique wooden walls and leather banquette seating. The bar features a number of speciality drinks with sassy names like 'The Diva' and 'The Low Life,' and its signature martini, 'The Liquid Kitty'. DJs spin throughout the week, and occasionally there are bands and other special events, but no entry charge. There is a steady stream of theme nights, such as 'iPod night', where patrons guest DJ. The crowd is a mix of Westsiders looking to groove, or possibly cosy up with some company in the back corner room.

5922 N Figueroa
East LA
Map 2 D1

Little Cave
323 255 6871 | www.littlecavebar.com
Yes, Little Cave does in fact resemble a little cave. The dark and cavernous room features a textured black ceiling, large glowing orbs, round red tables with matching carpet, and long horizontal mirrors against the wall. Illuminated light panels with shadowy bats hover above the bar, which is nicely complemented by additional brick and stone work. The crowd varies, but is usually a mix of Latino hipsters and neighbourhood locals. DJs spin an eclectic mix of sounds, from ska and punk to industrial and new wave. Call or

check the website for a current schedule. Patios can be found at the front and rear, both of which allow you to sip while you smoke.

Mandrake

2692 S La Cienega Blvd
Culver City
Map 7 A4 **74**

310 837 3297 | www.mandrakebar.com

Artists and art galleries have recently found their way to Culver City, creating a growing artist community and arts district. All those creatives need somewhere to whet their whistle, and that place is Mandrake. Its part art gallery, part bar, but feels more like a party at someone's loft. Art bars can sometimes have a pretentious air, but not this one – the vibe is low key and cool in all the right ways, with an eccentric, arty and fashion-forward crowd. The bar area is small and pretty basic, with wood-panelled walls, wood bench seating and log-slice tabletops. A DJ spins progressive tunes in the gallery, which features rotating art shows. Beyond the gallery there's a smoking patio with some seating.

Mixville Bar

2838 Rowena Ave
Silver Lake
Map 2 D1

323 666 2000 | www.edendalegrill.com

Mixville is the cocktail lounge within The Edendale Grill, a restaurant converted from a historic fire station. The bar has preserved the pressed-tin ceiling, hardwood floors and bay doors, and has restored a number of other features, adding a touch of class and a sense of nostalgia. The crowd is an even mix of artists and professionals, whose styles vary from dressy to casual. The large outdoor patio areas in both the front and rear of the bar make it an ideal watering hole during the summer months. In winter, the patio is covered and outdoor heaters are provided. Note that a good portion of the front patio is reserved for dining until the kitchen closes.

NoBAR

10622 Magnolia Blvd
North Hollywood
Map 2 D1

818 753 0545 | www.vintagebargroup.com/nobar

North Hollywood has had a facelift in recent years. The creation of the North Hollywood (NoHo) Arts District has attracted a younger, hipper crowd, resulting in a new wave of nightlife options, including NoBAR. The place has an intimate feel: dark and loungy, with wood-panelled and red felt brocade walls, retro glass lamps hanging in the corners, comfy communal seating, and touches of stained glass throughout the bar. The crowd is mostly hip locals from the North Hollywood and Burbank area who like to disappear into the shadows of the back corner room for a little privacy, or shoot some pool under the subdued light of the pool room.

The Prince

3198 W 7th St
Koreatown
Map 8 A4 **75**

213 389 2007

In the heart of Koreatown, at the base of the historic Windsor Hotel (now an apartment building), you'll find The Prince. Much of the interior dates from the early hotel days, with deep red leather booths, matching velvet brocade wallpaper, peculiar little lamps, and a mishmash of paintings and Tudor-style busts. The crowd is eclectic: a mix of Korean locals, Hollywood spillover and displaced hipsters. There's a full menu, featuring many Korean dishes, but the main draw is the novel

Sports Bars

Most bars in LA will have a TV showing the game, but some specialise in catering exclusively to the sports fan – with multiple big screens, drink specials, bar games and greasy snacks. Some of the most popular sports bars are Yankee Doodles in Santa Monica (310 394 4632; www.yankeedoodles.com), Barney's Beanery in West Hollywood (323 654 2287; www.barneysbeanery.com), Shark's Cove in Hermosa Beach (310 798 3932), Grand Avenue Sports Bar in Downtown (213 612 1205) and Hollywood Billiards in Hollywood (323 465 0115; www.hollywoodbilliards.com).

atmosphere; saddle up to the horseshoe-shaped bar, hunker down, and take in the scene. There's plenty of room for large groups, but forewarn your guests that the drinks are pretty pricey.

2366 Glendale Blvd
Silver Lake
Map 8 D1 **76**

Red Lion Tavern
323 662 5337

Here's a little taste of Bavaria. Everything about Red Lion screams Oktoberfest, from the architecture and costumed bar maids to the massive collection of beer steins and wiener-laden menu. The bar has an old-world country cottage feel and is awash with deep greens and browns. There's a vast selection of German beers as well as Bavarian wonders such as schnitzel and pickled herring. The main bar is downstairs, but there's also a small, cave-like room with a bar upstairs, and a covered beer garden, also with its own bar. The day crowd is full of hard-drinking regulars, while night draws a diverse mix of locals.

11938 Ventura Blvd
Studio City
Map 2 C1

The Sapphire
818 506 0777

The lighting in bars is notoriously dark, but minimalist lounge Sapphire takes darkness to new levels: it's lit only by a couple of chandeliers, a few wall lamps and a handful of tea lights. You can barely see your hand in front of your face, which is perfect if you're looking for a little privacy. Deep shades of green and brown add to the shadowy atmosphere, with dark-toned leather seating punctuated by colourful throw pillows. A cavernous hallway leads to a cosy back room with a brick fireplace reminiscent of a classic men's club – the perfect place to wind down with a whisky.

515 W 7th St
2nd Floor
Downtown
Map 10 D1 **77**

Seven Grand
213 614 0737 | www.sevengrand.la

Seven Grand is a must-see when exploring Downtown. It offers a mind-blowing 125 varieties of whiskeys, ryes and bourbons, with classy and extremely knowledgeable bartenders to help make sense of it all. Dark and seductive, it's the perfect environment for bookish creatures looking to disappear into the corners of the night. The hunting lodge meets boys' club aesthetic comes complete with a beautifully carved black walnut bar, leather couches, a 150 year-old pool table and a small army of mounted game. There's also a patio for those looking to enjoy a dipped-in-bourbon Maker's Mark cigar.

1455 W Sunset Blvd
Echo Park
Map 8 D3 **78**

The Short Stop
213 482 4942

This place gets its name from its proximity to Dodger Stadium, but it's a magnet for late-night hipsters looking for cheap drinks, dancing and company, not a sports bar. A hodgepodge of LA Dodgers team photos and random pictures pepper the walls. In the back room you'll find a pool table, a few video games, a photo booth, and oddly, a huge collection of police patches leftover from the days when it was the bar of choice for off-duty cops. The large dancefloor with seating around the perimeter makes it easy to get up and shake it when DJs are in the house. The alley in the back is an added bonus for smokers. There's no signage out front, so just look for the glowing 'cocktails' sign.

550 S Flower St
Downtown
Map 10 D4 **79**

The Standard
213 892 8080 | www.standardhotels.com

Head Downtown for an evening at one of the hippest hotels in the city. Start at the Lobby Lounge where the look is business meets playboy. Grab a drink and a seat, listen to the DJ, and watch the people come and go. If you're craving a meal, step into the space-age 24/7 Restaurant for some new American cuisine. For fantastic panoramic views of Downtown, take the lift up to the ultra-hip Rooftop Bar. This swanky perch looks like something out of *Clockwork Orange*, with odd little waterbed pods, sculpted topiaries, red Astroturf and a heated swimming pool. DJs spin nightly, and dancing follows when the mood suits. Note that drinks and parking here are anything but economical, and occasionally the Rooftop Bar is closed for private events. No entry charge.

Tom Bergin's Tavern

840 S Fairfax
Fairfax
Map 7 B2 **80**

323 936 7151 | *www.tombergins.com*

Near museum row in the Fairfax District you'll find Tom Bergin's Tavern, the oldest Irish pub in Los Angeles. Inside the quaint little cottage the first thing you'll notice are the thousands of inscribed paper shamrocks adorning the walls and ceiling – a testament to the faithful customers who have been frequenting the place for more than 70 years. Featuring a horseshoe bar with communal wooden benches and cavernous booths, the bar has a classic pub feel, with bartenders to match. There's a full menu with Irish specialties, which can be enjoyed in the bar or the dining hall, an elegant room with a stately wooden decor and flickering fireplace.

The Well

6255 W Sunset Blvd
Hollywood
Map 6 C2 **81**

323 467 9355 | *www.vintagebargroup.com/thewell*

Inside this hidden Hollywood lounge spotlights create small pools of light, gently illuminating the leather booths, ottomans and high-back banquettes that surround the room. A square bar occupies the centre of the space, with stools providing scenic views of the rest of the bar. An intimate corner room provides a bit of seclusion from the rest of the bar, which is usually filled with Hollywood vixens and lounge lizards. The bar menu is pretty standard, but there are some specialty drinks with curious names such as 'bloody matador' and 'hot and dirty'.

The Woods

1533 N La Brea Ave
Hollywood
Map 5 F2 **82**

323 876 6612 | *www.vintagebargroup.com/thewoods*

Formerly a historically dumpy dive bar in an uninspiring strip mall, this tiny space has been revamped big time. Befitting its name, you'll find plenty of timber at The Woods. A brief look around the room reveals a stone-stacked wall, tree-trunk tables, oaky wallpaper, long leather banquettes, a wall comprised of varying lengths of solid wood beams, and a ceiling embedded with twinkling stars. Above the bar hang two elk horn chandeliers – behind them, illuminated glass with intricately painted twigs. Try one of its many whiskeys, or take advantage of the later-than-usual happy hour specials from 20:00 to 22:00. Limited parking, but valet is available from Thursday to Saturday.

The York

5018 York Blvd
East LA
Map 2 D1

323 255 9675 | *www.theyorkonyork.com*

The York calls itself 'Highland Park's neighbourhood gastropub,' and it doesn't take long to understand why. It offers a large variety of beers, including unique imports, and an impressive selection of wines, as well as a fairly refined bar menu featuring items such as a good bruschetta and blackened catfish.

The space has an expansive New York loft vibe, with exposed brick walls and industrial looking bulbs dangling from the elevated ceiling. The lighting is subdued, but not dim, making it a good place to go if you actually want to see your date. The crowd is mostly locals during the week, but tends to be a magnet for a more tucked-in, cologne-friendly group at weekends. Note that because of the high ceilings it can get a little drafty in the winter months.

Gay & Lesbian
Other options **Gay & Lesbian** p.13

Unlike most cities, there is no real gay neighbourhood in Los Angeles. Of course, West Hollywood does come to mind when pinpointing the majority of LA's gay population, but there is not much this city hasn't seen in the way of human behaviour so people should feel very comfortable expressing their lifestyle here. The gay community is definitely one of the most culturally diverse in the country. LA and California in general have become a destination for people from all over the world and it is reflected in those you see. The only division seems to be East vs West, but that is also common in the straight scene and has more to do with the size of LA and distance between neighbourhoods than anything else.

692 N Robertson Blvd
West Hollywood
Map 5 A4 **83**

The Abbey
310 855 9977 | *www.abbeyfoodandbar.com*
Perfect for people-watching, the Abbey is frequented by gay Hollywood's in-crowd. Its outdoor patios and oversized couches are perfect for mingling and, with a delicious weekend brunch and nightly happy hours, the place is always packed with interesting people, both gay and straight. As with most bars in West Hollywood, the food and drinks can be quite expensive, making the Abbey best for an elegant night out rather than a few beers with friends.

4635 Sunset Blvd
Silver Lake
Map 8 B1 **84**

Akbar
323 665 6810 | *www.akbarsilverlake.com*
Akbar is one of the few dance clubs on the Eastside. It's primarily a gay and lesbian bar but the patrons are extremely straight-friendly, and open to anyone who's up for a night of dancing and debauchery. Much bigger than it looks from the outside, Akbar is split into two rooms – a bar room and a dance room – each with its own music. The decor has a slightly Indian influence, with a layout that accommodates the needs of dance enthusiasts and non-dancers alike. DJs spin throughout the week. Special evenings feature everything from live comedy to craft making. Entry is free at weekends.

4219 Santa Monica Blvd
Silver Lake
Map 8 B1 **85**

Eagle
323 669 9472 | *www.eaglela.com*
Leather daddies and tough guys flock from all over to experience The Eagle's rugged charm and stiff drinks. You'll also find quite a few uniform fetishists and curious onlookers. The bartenders are one of the main attractions, with each exuding their own style and personality. The bar is dark and the music is generally loud. Every night is different with theme parties based around various types of music or clothing. It's best to check the website for up-to-date information. Street parking is available but spots are few and far between so you're best off in a taxi.

4216 Melrose Ave
Hollywood
Map 8 A2 **86**

Faultline Bar
323 660 0889 | *www.faultlinebar.com*
The crowd here is mostly men who dress in leather and Levi jeans and like rock and roll, as opposed to the normal West Hollywood pretty boys. With live events such as a 'Mr Leather competition' and monthly art exhibits, the Faultine always has plenty to keep its large crowd of regulars entertained. Check its websites for updates as things change regularly. The Faultline is conveniently located right off the 101 freeway making it easily accessible form just about any part of the city. Open Wednesday to Sunday.

MJ's

2810 Hyperion Ave
Silver Lake
Map 2 D1

323 660 1503 | *www.mjsbar.com*

'No queens, no go-go boys, no attitude' is the motto for Trailer Trash Mondays at MJ's, a popular spot for men who want to listen to real rock and roll music while kicking back with a couple of cold beers. Tuesday is a popular night when you can expect the dancefloor to be packed. There is usually a small entry charge (no more than $5) at weekends. Parking is available on the street and next door at Trader Joe's after 22:00. Expect long queues on Fridays and Saturdays.

Rage

8911 Santa Monica Blvd
West Hollywood
Map 5 A4 87

310 652 7055 | *www.ragewesthollywood.com*

This popular place attracts a younger mix of boys and girls. There are two levels with dancefloors so be prepared to shake your stuff for all those above (and below) to see. If you're not feeling particularly adventurous you can always hang out up top where hip-hop is usually playing. The bar feels like one giant party with different theme nights. 'Gameboy' night features go-go dancers of both sexes dressed in outrageous costumes. Entry is usually more than $10, but worth the price if your night isn't complete without a high-energy dance party.

The Spotlight Bar

1601 N Cahuenga Blvd
Hollywood
Map 6 C1 88

323 467 2425

Just off Hollywood boulevard, The Spotlight is the place to be if you want to experience a true Hollywood dive bar. The drinks are cheap and very strong and the bar is dark and dingy. The cast of characters that frequent the place runs the gamut of transients and transvestites to the occasional old Hollywood star who would prefer not to be recognised. The bar is best experienced during the day as sporting events are broadcast and drink specials are readily available. One for adventurers only.

The Abbey

Golden Gopher (p.347)

Nightclubs

There's a nightclub for every walk of life in Los Angeles, and for every taste. You could go out for weeks without hitting the same club twice. Hip-hop, trance, industrial, lounge, swing, jazz – whatever you're into, you can find it. Styles range from gritty underground clubs to exclusive upscale spots thick with celebrity clientele. Then there are the LA institutions that you shouldn't really miss, including The Derby (p.355) in Hollywood. Most of the places listed below will charge a cover, usually $5 to $20. Drinks at nightclubs tend to be more expensive than those at a traditional bar or pub. Some clubs have specific dress codes such as no jeans or baseball caps, so it's always better to dress up a bit before going out. Many nightclubs feature the infamous 'red velvet rope', where club-goers must wait in line before entering. Sometimes this is just for show and sometimes the club is actually too packed to let more people in. When stuck behind the rope, three things will help you get in quicker: being with attractive women, being a celebrity or slipping the doorman some cash. You might struggle with the first two but the latter will always hold sway.

Dress & Door Policy

There is no specific dress code for going out in Los Angeles. In general, the smarter the establishment, the smarter you'll want to dress. Some nightclubs and bars have strict dress codes that prohibit baseball caps, jeans, T-shirts, shorts, or sandals. In the winter it can get chilly in the evening, so you might need a coat. The more upscale or customer-friendly establishments have cloakrooms, but they are not common. When waiting to gain entry to a club you may be asked to wait in some sort of line, often behind a red velvet rope. Though unfair, it is common for celebrities, people with connections, attractive women or those who slip the doorman extra money, to get in first.

Bordello

901 E 1st St
Downtown
Map 10 F4 **89**

213 687 3766 | *www.bordellobar.com*

This ornately themed club in an unassuming building on the border of Little Tokyo channels the look and feel of a 19th century brothel. Gothic-inspired high-back leather booths, black crystal chandeliers, satin curtains, and period chairs and sofas are all flooded with scarlet-red hues. Vintage photos of topless women adorn the walls, while gilded mirrors and busts frame the bar. The gritty neighbourhood and subterranean vibe draws a crowd eager to be entertained by the dancing girls, cabaret, burlesque shows and live music that frequent the opulent stage. Cover fees range from $5 to $15, but are well worth it. There's no signage out front, so look for the Little Pedro's sign – that's Bordello.

Circle Bar

2926 Main St
Santa Monica
Map 3 D4 **90**

310 450 0508 | *www.thecirclebar.com*

Circle Bar is one of the many stops that people make while bar-hopping down Main Street in Santa Monica. It's an unabashed meat market (it proudly announces it's been in the top five singles' bars in LA for the past five years). There's no entry charge, and there are DJs nightly, so if you want to shake your stuff on the strip, and attract someone at the same time, this is the place. A large oval bar fills the bulk of the room, with seating around the perimeter and a small dancefloor at the rear. Red lights and velour walls adorned with miscellaneous framed photos fill out the rest of the space, with mirrors over the dancefloor so people can check each other out on the sly. Be prepared to encounter a red velvet rop, some queues and a smarter dress code at the weekends.

Nightclubs

The Derby

4500 Los Feliz Blvd
Los Feliz
Map 2 D1

323 663 8979 | www.clubderby.com

The Derby is a piece of Hollywood history. It has gone through many incarnations in its 80 years, but is most fondly remembered as The Brown Derby, an upscale Hollywood hotspot owned between 1940 and 1960 by film pioneer Cecil B. DeMille. In 1992 the space was reinvented yet again, this time as The Derby, in homage to those early Hollywood days. The original exposed wood-beam domed roof was restored, and the roomy main hall revamped to invoke a classic Hollywood feel. The Back Bar, where DJs spin, puts out a much more modern club vibe. The Derby is credited for being a major influence in the revival of swing. The club primarily books bands and DJs now, but still features swing nights regularly.

Little Temple

4519 Santa Monica Blvd
Silver Lake
Map 8 B2 91

323 660 4540 | www.littletemple.com

Little Temple is a beat-driven lounge and dance club that throws down everything from soul, funk and reggae to hip-hop, dance and Latin rhythms. As the name suggests, the look is heavily inspired by the Far East, with bamboo walls, rock gardens, Chinese lanterns and dozens of candles, all creating a tranquil lounge awash with deep red and brown tones. A wide variety of urban DJs and live music graces the stage. The club draws people from all over LA – but primarily hip-hop fans. Get there early at the weekend as the place gets absolutely packed, with a queue out the door and down the street. Entry costs between $5 and $10.

The Mountain Bar

475 Gin Ling Way
Chinatown
Map 8 E4 92

213 625 7500 | www.themountainbar.com

Tucked away in Old Chinatown Plaza between Hill and Broadway you'll find the Mountain Bar. The interior is a sea of red. The stools, the lights, the pagoda-like bar, the paint dripping down the walls are all red, and framed by black, sloping ceilings, long Chinese curtains and a funky-coloured triangle tile floor. The split-level bar features a lounge downstairs with a DJ and space for dancing, with an additional lounge and club room upstairs. It's a hotspot at weekends, and usually cover-free. When trying to find the place note that Gin Ling Way isn't an actual street, it's a pedestrian walkway that leads to the Plaza and is located between Bernard Street and West College Street.

The Edison (p.346)   Liquid Kitty (p.348)

Cabaret & Strip Shows

4600 Hollywood Blvd
Silver Lake
Map 8 A1 93

Cheetah's

323 660 6733

Cheetah's is the type of relaxed strip club where your focus may or may not be on the girls. The crowd tends to be a mix of rockers, hipsters and hip-hop dudes whose main goal seems to be getting drunk and having a good time with their friends as opposed to ogling scantily clad women. It might also be because it's a non-nude bikini bar which means the girls are wearing bras and panties. The drinks are cheap, but lap dances are $25. There is generally a DJ playing music and live bands have been known to show up as Cheetah's was once a favourite hangout for 80s metallers.

5153 Hollywood Blvd
Hollywood
Map 8 A1 94

Jumbo's Clown Room

323 666 1187 | *www.jumbos.com*

Jumbo's is the type of place where, if your main focus is on the girls onstage, you may be a bit disappointed. Not because of the lack of quality (the girls are cute in a tattooed hipster sort of way) but the place is usually jam-packed with people drinking beer and socialising. With an equal ration of women to men in the audience you can feel comfortable bringing along your significant other when you feel like staring at half naked women. Jumbo's is a bikini bar so there is no nudity, but they do have a full bar with enough drinks that you can pretend the girls are naked.

1751 E Olympic Blvd
Downtown
Map 9 E3 95

Sam's Hofbrau

213 623 3989 | *www.samshofbrau.com*

Sam's Hofbrau is a classic joint reflecting the dinginess of Downtown. A perfect place to grab a beer after the Lakers game or any night for that matter when you feel like slumming it. The bouncers will search you for weapons at the door, which might seem a bit odd until you've entered the club. Then you'll actually be thankful that they're searching everyone. The crowd can seem a little unruly so it's best to keep to yourself and keep tipping the dancers. It's also best to park your car in the parking lot provided. The good thing is there's no cover charge and no drink minimum so all in all it's one of the cheaper strip clubs if not a little a dangerous. That's what makes it fun though, right?

2020 E Olympic Blvd
Downtown
Map 9 E3 96

Spearmint Rhino

213 629 9213 | *www.spearmintrhino.com*

Comparatively classy, Spearmint Rhino is a well known establishment with locations all over LA County. Featuring the types of girls that appear in Playboy and various porn stars, the Rhino is a favourite for the serious strip club enthusiast. It is very accommodating of large groups and sometimes discounts or coupons can be found in the *LA Weekly* newspaper. The club is spacious, clean and the girls are fully nude. The only drawback is that, as per the law, alcohol is not served. Lap dances are available, but be careful as the girls may request that you buy them expensive (soft) drinks to up their takings. Things can get pricey pretty quickly. It's best to hit the club earlier in the night. If you're feeling a bit too adventurous you might have trouble paying your cab fare home.

Cinemas

With such a storied history of film you would expect there to be a lot of cinemas in Los Angeles, and you'd be right. From old silent movie theatres to the newest in features such as IMAX and 3D, LA is a town that truly loves its film. It is not uncommon to see people standing in queues during the middle of day to catch movies that have just been released. You will also find many revival houses that cater to independent and foreign films. Midnight showings of outrageous horror movies or 1970s exploitation occur weekly and generally alcohol is encouraged as long as you wait until the lights go out to imbibe. The architecture of many theatres also harks back to the golden age of Hollywood and can be an experience in itself. Places such as Grauman's Chinese Theatre (p.181) and the Egyptian (p.179) are as famous as the stars that grace their screens, and for that reason are reviewed as attractions in the Exploring chapter.

6360 W Sunset Blvd
Hollywood
Map 6 C2 97

ArcLight

323 464 1478 | www.arclightcinemas.com

With a full bar, gift shop and a surrounding area full of bars, restaurants and the famous Amoeba Records, ArcLight has become much more of a night on the town as opposed to a simple theatre. Featuring at least 12 movies at a time, as well as a Cinerama dome, you'd have a hard time not being able to find something worth watching. With a parking lot attached and validated parking available it is also one of the easiest theatres in Hollywood to get to. Be sure to get there on time as they take films seriously at ArcLight and will not let in late moviegoers once the film has started. Your best bet is to buy tickets in advance via the phone, web or conveniently located kiosks at the theatre. You can even choose where you sit.

7165 W Beverly Blvd
West Hollywood
Map 7 C1 98

New Beverly Cinema

323 938 4038 | www.newbevcinema.com

One of the most popular revival houses in Los Angeles, the New Beverly specialises in showing classic films both new and old. The schedule changes almost daily so check the website or print edition so you don't miss anything. Tickets are generally cheap and the New Beverly allows audience members a chance to see films that may otherwise have been lost to the ages. Actors and directors usually stop by for Q&A sessions on the night of the film too. The atmosphere is light-hearted and it's not unusual for the audience to yell at the screen during some of the more ridiculous films. Parking is usually available on the street after 19:00 and most movies start late including midnight showings at the weekend.

611 N Fairfax Ave
Fairfax
Map 5 D4 99

The Silent Movie Theatre

323 655 2510 | www.cinefamily.org

Built in 1942, The Silent Movie Theatre ran for decades as the only fully functioning silent movie theatre in the country. Years later it has been fully restored to its original, vintage Art Deco design, along with a brand new screen and sound system. The name may be a bit misleading to some. Although they do sometimes screen original silent films, the majority are rare movies from the 50s, 60s and 70s. The theatre is programmed monthly with various themes based on genre, director or actor. The best bet to find out what's happening at the theatre is to look at their website or pick up a copy of the monthly newsletter. The theatre often plays films not found anywhere else so it's best to keep informed so you don't miss something truly spectacular.

4473 Sunset Dr
Los Feliz
Map 8 B1 100

Vista Theatre

323 660 6639

The Vista is a classicly designed theatre featuring a single screen in a remodelled Egyptian motif. During movie openings employees sometimes dress up as characters, adding to the kitsch factor of the space. The sound inside is spectacular and the seats are larger than normal. It should also be noted that there is more legroom available here than any other theatre in town. Taller patrons will appreciate that for sure. Be careful when parking as there is not a lot available and traffic cops are known to write tickets in the area. Be sure to read the signs. Also, the Vista tends not to advertise their films so your best bet would be to call ahead to find out what's playing.

Comedy

Los Angeles has a rich history of supporting comedy. Be it film and TV or stand up and improvisation, comedians come from all over the country and the world to perfect their act. One of the best features of the LA comedy scene is that because there are so many shows going on at once, you'll be able to experience headlining acts at a fraction of the price. Of course some of the larger chain clubs like the Laugh Factory can be expensive when factoring in drinks and food, but most keep costs down by utilising volunteers and doing as many shows per night as possible. The UCB theatre generally features three shows a night and almost all are under $10. It's best to visit the websites as the schedules change daily but with a little research there are some truly unique comedic performances to see.

Comedy			
Comedy Store	West Hollywood	323 650 6268	www.thecomedystore.com
Groundlings	West Hollywood	323 934 4747	www.groundlings.com
Improv	West Hollywood	323 651 2583	www.improv.com
IO Hollywood	Hollywood	323 962 7560	www.iowest.com
Laugh Factory	Hollywood	323 656 1336	www.laughfactory.com
UCB Theatre	Hollywood	323 908 8702	www.ucbtheatre.com
Ultimate Improv	Westwood	310 824 6566	www.ultimateimprov.com

Concerts & Live Music

Los Angeles' massive and diverse population makes it a guaranteed stop on any artist's US tour. The city's local offerings are often the most enjoyable to explore, and the LA Philharmonic is one of the most talented orchestras in the world. Summer concerts at the Hollywood Bowl (p.182) are a favourite for Angelenos and often feature major acts. Fans of the various underground scenes will get their fill at El Rey Theatre (www.theelrey.com) or the Music Box @ Fonda (www.henryfondatheater.com), which hosts quite an eclectic range of performances. The city has plenty of other venues and a visit to www.pollstar.com is a good way to keep up on the city's music schedule. Ordinarily, tickets to these concerts can be bought from the venue's box office, from their website or from Ticketmaster (www.ticketmaster.com).

1024 S Grand Ave
Downtown
Map 10 B3 **101**

Crash Mansion

213 747 0999 | www.crashmansionla.com

Since its opening early in 2008, Crash Mansion has established itself as a popular venue for live music in LA. The club occupies a building that was once the storied Myron Ballroom, a fabled 1940s swing club, now transformed into a state-of-the-art performance space with a 1,200 person capacity (by the same guys who brought you the Crash Mansion in New York's Bowery). The 10,000sq ft main room for headliners features lofted ceilings and a fully digital sound system, and the two adjacent rooms, the Crash Lounge and the Foyer Gallery, host more intimate performances. There are five bars to keep the party lubricated. Check the website for a schedule.

1822 Sunset Blvd
Echo Park
Map 8 D3 **102**

The Echo

213 413 8200 | www.attheecho.com

The Echo specialises in punk, indie, heavy rock and dance music. Part Time Punks is a popular Sunday night event where bands and DJs share the same bill and the over 18 crowd dances up a sweat to the beat. Beneath The Echo is a larger venue called the Echoplex so it's best to know which one you're supposed to be at. The Echoplex handles larger events and parties but still features a full bar and soundstage like it's older sibling upstairs. Be sure to check the calendar of events located on their website as there is something happening seven nights a week and, since both venues share a similar name, it can get confusing sometimes.

CRASH MANSION L.A.
1024 s. Grand Ave.
Los Angeles, CA 90015
Tel 213.747.0999
www.crashmansionla.com

RESTAURANT ● BAR ● LIVE MUSIC VENUE

CRASH MANSION L.A.
New York's Bowery Restaurant Group, known for New York City hot spots, Crash Mansion, BLVD., Opal and Village Lantern presents Crash Mansion L.A., downtown Los Angeles' premiere live music and event facility. Situated among the towering skyscrapers of South Park downtown, and literally steps away from the Nokia Theater, Staples Center, and Los Angeles Convention Center, this historic 14,000 sq. ft., 1200+ capacity venue is the ultimate entertainment destination. This location, style state-of-the-art sound and superior lighting systems, along with an upcoming artist calendar filled with world-renowned musical talent, singles out Crash Mansion as the consummate live music venue in Los Angeles.

RESTAURANT HOURS	MON - SAT 7:00PM - 12:00AM
BOX OFFICE HOURS	MON - SAT 10:00AM - 6:00PM

Visit our website for events and information
www.crashmansionla.com

2700 N Vermont Ave
Griffith Park
Map 2 D1

Greek Theatre

323 665 5857 | www.greektheatrela.com

A sylvan temple set in a wooded glen in Griffith Park, the 6,000 seat Greek Theatre is a classic outdoor entertainment venue that has hosted big name acts such as The Who, Sting, Elton John and Paul McCartney. Giant digital video screens and a state-of-the-art sound system are almost unnecessary enhancements. The Greek (as Angelenos simply call it) is a legacy of the park's annoying benefactor, Griffith J Griffith, who vainly envisaged it as a public stage where performances of the classics would enlighten the hoi polloi. Ha!

111 S Grand Ave
Downtown
Map 10 E2 **103**

Los Angeles Philharmonic

323 850 2000 | www.laphil.org

The world-famous Los Angeles Philharmonic performs in the futuristic Disney Concert Hall designed by Frank Gehry, ensuring that both architecture buffs and classical music lovers will have a memorable evening. The Philharmonic has over 100 musicians and is recognised as one of the best large orchestras in the world. Performances ranging from jazz, classical and contemporary music occur throughout the week. Particularly popular are their summer series in the Hollywood Bowl, and the concerts that pair the orchestra with popular recording artists such as Tony Bennett and indie rock favourite Bright Eyes. Sign up for the LA Phil 'Fast Notes' on their website so you don't miss any upcoming shows.

777 Chick Hearn Ct
Downtown
Map 10 B2 **104**

Nokia Theatre LA Live

213 763 6000 | www.nokiatheatrelalive.com

Nokia Theater LA Live is the new state-of-the-art performance arena that matches or surpasses its sister theatre in Times Square as one of the most audience-friendly performance venues in the US. Not one of the 7,100 seats is further than 220ft from the stage. The opening concert by The Eagles got high marks from the critics for the acoustics as well as the music. The theatre is the anchor of a $2.5 billion development that will include a Grammy museum, Club Nokia, a 2,500 seat live performance space, a Cineplex, the Conga Room, Lucky Strike Bowling Center, a broadcast studio, the offices of ESPN, luxury condos, a Ritz Carlton Hotel and many high-end restaurants. The complex is set to transform a formerly seedy area into a vibrant, upscale complex that will likely rival its New York counterpart as a national entertainment icon. Check out the glowing pillars and the neon-encrusted courtyard for yourself.

1717 Silver Lake Blvd
Silver Lake
Map 8 C2 **105**

Spaceland

213 985 4333 | www.clubspaceland.com

Spaceland currently enjoys the status of hippest rock club, only rivalled by The Echo in popularity for Eastsiders in LA. This club is spacious enough without feeling impersonal. The shows are generally packed with a mid 20s set looking to get drunk, hook up with one another, and see the hottest indie rock bands. Being a major tour stop, LA sees every band at least once, so generally the line up includes a headlining tour act with local bands opening. It's a good chance to see underground music in a non-threatening environment. There is a full bar and valet parking since parking on the street is very limited. If you do happen to find parking make sure to observe all street signs as Spaceland is located in a residential area and the rules change for parking based on the time of night.

9081 Santa Monica Blvd
West Hollywood
Map 4 F1 **106**

The Troubadour

310 276 6168 | www.troubadour.com

One of the most famous music venues in Los Angeles, the Troubadour has played host to countless legendary musicians as well as being a major hub for the hippy generation. The club is still going strong hosting shows or events seven nights a week.

The club itself features a great sound system and plenty of room on the main floor or upstairs to get a good view of the performers. There is a bar located in the main room but also in front of the club so, if the music is too loud or you find yourself wanting a breather, you can just relax out front while looking at all the autographed promotional photos of the countless musicians who have passed through the doors.

Theatre

As the heart of the film industry, LA has more than its share of actors. There are so many theatres in the city that it would be impossible to cover all of them here. In addition to those below, some of the city's theatres are attractions in their own right (such as The Kodak Theatre, p.183) so are covered in the Exploring chapter. For comprehensive theatre listings in LA, check out www.theatermania.com/la.

Ahmanson Theatre

135 N Grand Ave
Downtown
Map 10 F2 107

213 628 2722 | *www.centertheatergroup.org*

The 2,100 seat Ahmanson is *the* big ticket theatre in Los Angeles. Part of the Music Center Complex on Bunker Hill, the theatre hosts big-name musicals, dramas and comedies, including the sort of extravagant and lavish productions that are bound for (or coming from) Broadway. The season is year-round with a brief break in the autumn, and tickets are easier to come by than you might think. Although weekends, openings and holiday evenings are almost always sold out, there are frequently tickets available for weeknight performances. One caveat: if you have the slightest anxiety about heights, avoid the dramatically-raked balcony.

Dorothy Chandler Pavilion

135 N Grand Ave
Downtown
Map 8 D4 108

213 972 7211 | *www.musiccenter.org*

This is one of four venues that comprise the Los Angeles Music Center (the others being Walt Disney Concert Hall (p.184), the Mark Taper Forum (p.362) and the Ahmanson Theatre (p.361). The Chandler was often the site of the Academy Awards and although the Los Angeles Philharmonic has moved across the street to Disney Hall, it remains the home of the Los Angeles Opera and Music Center Dance. The Chandler is named for Dorothy Buffum Chandler, a visionary champion of the performing arts who spearheaded the creation of the airy, elegant, colonnaded pavilion, which opened in 1964. Her portrait hangs in the Founders' Room, a comfortable lounge lined with dark wood and strewn with overstuffed armchairs and giant Chinese vases filled with flowers. Directly opposite the portrait is a balcony featuring a single urn on a plinth. Although there's no plaque, and Music Center officials are (officially) sceptical, tradition and anecdotal evidence has it that the urn contains Dorothy's ashes. Whether it's true or not, the pavilion is certainly an apt memorial to one of Los Angeles' greatest benefactors. The Chandler is perched atop Bunker Hill and its fountain and reflecting ponds make it an elegant urban park. Check the website for a calendar of opera and dance.

Kirk Douglas Theatre

9820 Washington Blvd
Culver City
Map 2 C2

213 628 2772 | *www.centertheatregroup.org*

Located near the emerging arts quarter in downtown Culver City, the Kirk Douglas is the restrained rebel among LA's theatre companies, offering edgy but always entertaining fare and presenting works by local playwrights and featuring stellar casts. The artistic director is Michael Ritchie, who serves in the same capacity at the extremely well-regarded Mark Taper Forum (p.362), the sister company to the Kirk Douglas. The 317 seat theatre is a former Streamline Moderne movie palace, built in 1947, and now brilliantly restored and adapted for stage productions. The six-play season runs from February to August.

135 N Grand Ave
Downtown
Map 10 F2 **109**

The Mark Taper Forum

213 628 2772 | www.centertheatergroup.org

The circular Mark Taper Forum is located in the Music Center complex atop Bunker Hill and shares a colonnaded entrance with the Dorothy Chandler Pavilion. The 745 seat theatre is the home of one of the best resident companies in America and its productions have racked up an impressive number of Tonys and Pulitzer Prizes. Among the plays that have originated on its stage are *Angels in America* and *Children of a Lesser God*. Annette Bening and Kathleen Turner are among the luminaries who have trodden the boards in recent seasons. Currently undergoing extensive renovations which will make it a state-of-the-art stage, the Taper should re-open in the late summer of 2008. However, the Taper's sister stage, the Kirk Douglas Theater in Culver City (p.361) is up and running with a programme and star-studded casts to match the Taper's.

631 W 2nd St
Downtown
Map 10 E2 **110**

REDCAT (Roy & Edna Disney/CalArts Theater)

213 237 2800 | www.redcat.org

REDCAT is dedicated to artistic expression that challenges the boundaries of traditional genres. It is located underneath Disney Hall (p.184), an apt location for a venue that is essentially subversive to the cultural status quo. Experimental film, theatre and dance are accommodated in a high-tech theatre. One recent show was described as 'barrages of frantic avant-garde music (that) blend seamlessly with inventive Butoh-inspired movement and intense physical theatre in (a) rich, multilayered production from Seattle's high-octane experimental group'. You get the idea. The art displayed in the gallery is equally eclectic and experimental. This is highly recommended for connoisseurs of the cutting edge or anyone who just likes to dress in black and hang out in an elegant lounge (described as the best-kept secret in LA by the LA Times) and sip the house cocktail, the Cat-a-tonic. Open Tuesday to Friday, 09:00 to 21:00 or post-show; Saturday and Sunday, 12:00 to 21:00 or post-show.

Party Organisers & Caterers

Other options **Party Accessories** p.289

Los Angeles is a town that loves to throw a good party, which means that attendees often expect to have a fantastic time as well as experience something out of the ordinary. It's not unusual to give gift bags so that guests can take something away from the party as a souvenir. Good food and drinks are mandatory, as well as music either in the form of a live band or a DJ. With red carpet and corporate events happening nightly there is no shortage of work for party planners and caterers, so make sure that you book them well in advance in order to avoid a last minute disaster.

Party Organisers & Caterers

Name	Phone	Web	Speciality
Bright House Events	323 871 5879	www.brighthouseevents.com	Parties
Canter's Delicatessen & Restaurant	323 651 2030	www.cantersdeli.com	Catering
Carmelized Productions	954 599 6990	na	Catering
The Event	310 379 7568	www.eventsca.com	Special events
Jamaica's Cakes	310 478 1971	www.jamaicascakes.com	Catering
Langer's Deli	213 483 8050	www.langersdeli.com	Catering
Party Planners USA	310 979 3527	www.partyplannersusa.com	Parties
Susina Bakery & Café	323 934 7900	www.susinabakery.com	Catering
TACT Management	310 595 5659	na	Special events

LA Improv

Silent Movie Theatre

Dorothy Chandler Pavilion

Cameo Bar (p.345)

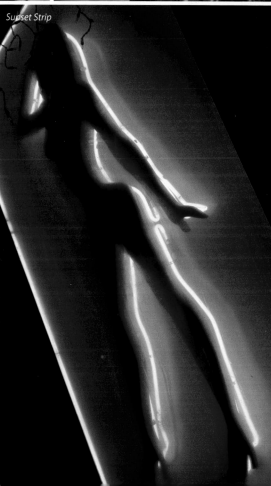

Sunset Strip

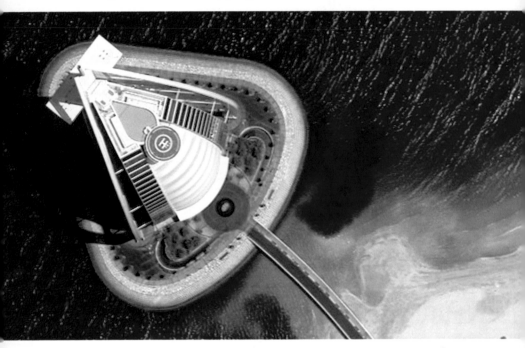

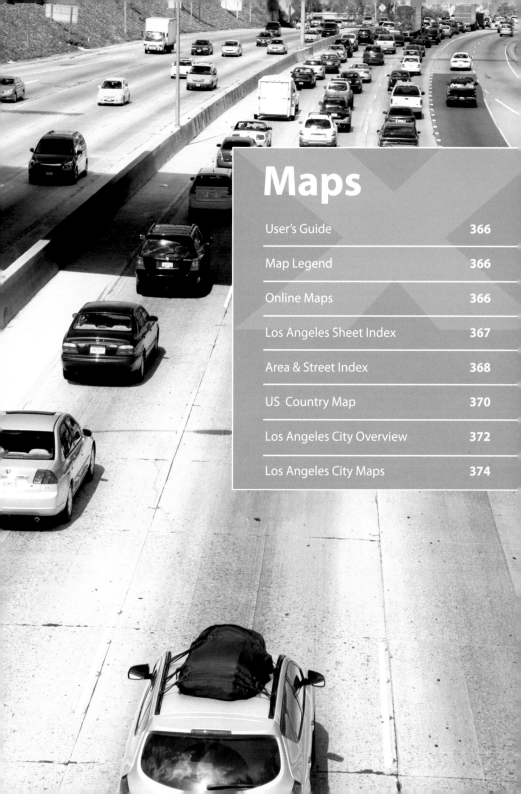

Maps

User's Guide

This section features detailed maps to help you get your bearings when you first arrive. It also gives you an idea of where we're talking about in the main chapters of the book. There's a map of the US on p.370 and an overview of Los Angeles on p.373. The maps in this section give detailed views of the LA areas that contain the most visitor attractions and points of interest. Most of the maps are at a scale of 1:30,000, while the maps of Downtown (Map 10), Hollywood (Map 6) and West Hollywood (Map 5) are more detailed, at a scale of 1:15,000. Turn to p.367 for a sheet index that shows the location of each map in relation to the rest of the city. Starting on p.368 there's an index of LA's main streets and areas, with a grid reference pointing to the right page.

We've included annotations for the main hotels (⬚⬚) starting on p.17, along with schools and hospitals (⬚⬚, p.113); museums, parks and other attractions (⬚⬚, p.168); activities (⬚⬚, p.212); shopping hotspots (⬚⬚, p.259); and popular bars, restaurants and clubs (⬚⬚, p.317).

We've included metro tracks and stations. Inside the back cover you'll find a metro map. Since driving is such an important part of LA life, there are parking icons on each of the maps to designate carparks.

More Maps ◀

Beyond these maps and our own very nifty LA Mini Map (see right for details) there are a number of street directories to be found in Los Angeles' bookshops and newsagents. Rand McNally publishes a massive, spiral-bound street guide called The Thomas Guide, which is considered an essential for any glove box. They also produce a detailed fold-out map. Any local bookshop will have a large selection, from 3D cartoon maps to geological maps with GPS points.

Need More?

We understand that the *Los Angeles Residents' Guide* is a pretty big book. It needs to be, to carry all the information about living in the city. But, unless you've got the pockets of a clown, it's unlikely to be carried around with you on daytrips. With this in mind, the *LA Mini Map* serves as a more manageable alternative. It packs the whole city into your pocket and, once unfolded, is an excellent navigational tool. It's part of a series of Mini Maps that includes cities as diverse as London, Dubai, New York and Tokyo. Visit www. explorerpublishing.com for details of how to pick up these little gems, or nip into any good bookshop.

Online Maps

Mapquest, Yahoo Maps and Google Maps are pretty similar in content. All three offer interactive maps, driving directions and live traffic updates. Google Maps also offers its 'street view' service for Los Angeles, which allows users to view 360° images of the addresses they are searching. Hardcore map fans tend to like Google Earth (download from http:// earth.google.com) for its satellite images, powerful search facility and incredibly detailed views.

Map Legend

🏨	Hotel/Resort	▬▬▬	Highway
	Education	▬▬	Major Road
	Park/Garden	▬	Secondary Road
✚	Hospital		Other Road
	Shopping	)═══(	Tunnel
🏛	Heritage/Museum	–O┤- - -	Purple Line
	Industrial Area	–O┤- - -	Blue Line
	Pedestrian Area	–O┤- - -	Green Line
	Built up Area/Building	–O┤- - -	Gold Line
	Land	–O┤- - -	Red Line
	Beach	–O┤- - -	El Monte Busway
✈	Airport	⊡─- - -	Light Rail

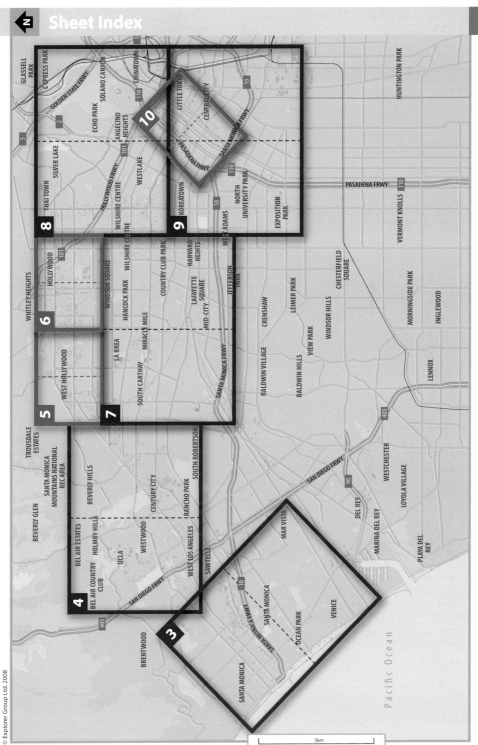

GLASSELL PARK

CYPRESS PARK

GOLDEN STATE FRWY

SOLANO CANYON

CHINATOWN

110

ECHO PARK

ANGELINO HEIGHTS

10

LITTLE TOKYO

CENTRAL CITY

10

SANTA MONICA FRWY

2

SILVER LAKE

HOLLYWOOD FRWY

WESTLAKE

PASADENA FRWY

5

101

THAI TOWN

WHITLEY HEIGHTS

WILSHIRE CENTRE

KOREATOWN

10

NORTH UNIVERSITY PARK

EXPOSITION PARK

PASADENA FRWY

110

8

WEST ADAMS

9

HUNTINGTON PARK

VERMONT KNOLLS

101

HOLLYWOOD

WINDSOR SQUARE

WILSHIRE CENTRE

HANCOCK PARK

COUNTRY CLUB PARK

HARVARD HEIGHTS

LAFAYETTE SQUARE

JEFFERSON PARK

CRENSHAW

LEIMER PARK

CHESTERFIELD SQUARE

MORNINGSIDE PARK

6

MID-CITY

MIRACLE MILE

LA BREA

WINDSOR HILLS

INGLEWOOD

WEST HOLLYWOOD

SOUTH CARTHAY

SANTA MONICA FRWY

BALDWIN VILLAGE

VIEW PARK

5

7

BALDWIN HILLS

LENNOX

TROUSDALE ESTATES

SOUTH ROBERTSON

405

WESTCHESTER

SANTA MONICA MOUNTAINS NATIONAL REC AREA

BEVERLY HILLS

CENTURY CITY

RANCHO PARK

SAN DIEGO FRWY

LOYOLA VILLAGE

BEVERLY GLEN

BEL AIR ESTATES

HOLMBY HILLS

WESTWOOD

WEST LOS ANGELES

90

DEL REY

MARINA DEL REY

PLAYA DEL REY

4

BEL AIR COUNTRY CLUB

UCLA

SAN DIEGO FRWY

SAWTELLE

MAR VISTA

405

BRENTWOOD

10

SANTA MONICA FRWY

SANTA MONICA

VENICE

3

SANTA MONICA

OCEAN PARK

Pacific Ocean

5km

Street Index

Street Name	Map Ref	Street Name	Map Ref
Glendale Blvd	8-D1	Penmar Ave	3-E3
Golden State Hwy	8-E2	Pickford St	7-B3
Gower St, North	6-D2	Pico Blvd, West	10-A2, 4-F3
Grand Ave, South	10-C2, 9-C3	Robertson Blvd, South	4-F4, 7-A3
Gregory Way	4-F3, 7-A2	Rodeo Dr	4-E2
Harbor Frwy	10-A1	Romaine St	5-E3, 6-C3
Hawthorn Ave	5-F1, 6-A1	Rossmore Ave, North	7-E1
Highland Ave, North	6-A2, 7-D1	Rossmore Ave, South	7-E2
Highland Ave, South	7-C4	San Diego Frwy	4-A3
Hill St, South	9-D1, 10-A4	San Fernando Rd, North	8-F2
Holloway Dr	5-A3	San Pedro St, South	9-D2, 10-B4
Hollywood Blvd	5-D1, 6-A1, 8-A1	San Vicente Blvd	4-A4, 7-C3
Hollywood Frwy	6-D1, 8-C3	San Vicente Blvd	4-A4, 7-C3
Hoover Blvd , South	9-B4	San Vicente Blvd, South	7-A1
Hope St, South	10-D2, 9-C1	Santa Fe Ave, South	9-F2
Hyperion Ave	8-B2	Santa Monica Blvd	4-A4, 5-A3, 6-A3, 8-A2
Jefferson Blvd, East	9-C4	Santa Monica Frwy	7-B4, 10-A4, 3-C2
Jefferson Blvd, West	9-C3	Santee St	10-C4, 9-D2
La Brea Ave, North	6-A2, 7-D2, 5-F1	Sepulveda Blvd, South	4-B4
La Brea Ave, South	7-C4	Silver Lake Blvd	8-C2
La Cienega Blvd, North	5-B2, 7-A1	Spring St, North	8-F3
La Cienega Blvd, South	7-A4	Spring St, South	10-E3
Laurel Dr, North	5-D2, 7-B1	Stone Canyon Rd	4-B1
Lexington Ave	6-C2, 5-E2	Sunset Blvd, West	4-A2, 6-B2, 8-C2
Lincoln Blvd	3-B3	Sycamore Ave, North	6-A2, 7-D1
Los Angeles St, South	9-D2, 10-A4	Temple St, East	10-F2
Main St, North	10-F3, 8-F4	Temple St, West	8-B3, 10-F1
Main St, South	9-D2, 10-E3	Venice Blvd	7-A4, 10-A1
Main Street, South	10-B3, 9-D2	Venice Blvd, North	3-F4
Mansfield Ave, North	6-A2, 7-D1	Venice Blvd, South	3-F4
Martin Luther King Junior Blvd, West	9-A4	Vermont Ave, North	8-A1
Melrose Ave	4-C1, 8-B2, 5-E4, 6-B4	Vermont Ave, South	8-A4, 9-A3
Montana Ave	4-A3, 3-A2	Vine St	6-C1
National Blvd	3-E1	Waring Ave	5-D4, 6-A4
Normandie Ave, South	9-A3	Washington Blvd	7-A4
Oakwood Ave	5-C1, 3-E3, 7-F1	Washington Blvd, East	9-D3
Ocean Ave	3-A4	Washington Blvd, West	7-B4
Ocean Park Blvd	3-D4	Western Ave, North	6-F1
Olive St, South	9-C3, 10-D3	Western Ave, South	7-F2
Olympic Blvd	3-D3	Willoughby Ave	5-D3, 6-A3
Olympic Blvd, East	9-E2	Wilshire Blvd	8-B4, 4-A4
Olympic Blvd, West	10-C3	Wilton Pl, North	6-E1, 7-F1
Olympic Blvd, West	10-B2, 7-E3, 10-B1		
Orange Dr, North	6-A2, 7-D1, 5-D3		
Palisades Beach Rd	3-A4		
Palms Blvd	3-E2		

Map 1   USA Country Map

CANADA

Prince George
Flin Flon
Edmonton
Saskatoon
Calgary
Winnipeg
Lethbridge
Regina
Vancouver
Victoria

Washington
North Dakota
Seattle
Bismarck
Olympia
Montana
Helena
Portland
Salem
Idaho
Boise
Oregon

South Dakota
Pierre

UNITED STATES OF
AMERICA

Wyoming
Great
Salt Lake
Salt Lake City
Cheyenne
Nebraska
Lincoln
Nevada
Denver
Carson City
Utah
Sacramento
Colorado
Kansas
Topeka
San Francisco
San Jose

California
Oklahoma
Santa Fe
Oklahoma City

Los Angeles
Arizona
San Diego
Phoenix
New Mexico
El Paso
Texas
Dallas
Heroica Nogales
Ciudad
Juarez
Austin
San Quintin
San Antonio

Guaymas
Chihuahua
Nuevo Laredo
Monclova
Loreto
MEXICO
Matamoros
Torreon
Saltillo
La Paz
Durango
Mazatlan
San Luis Potosi

Pacific Ocean

Irapuato

MEXICO CITY

© Explorer Group Ltd. 2008

Map **1**

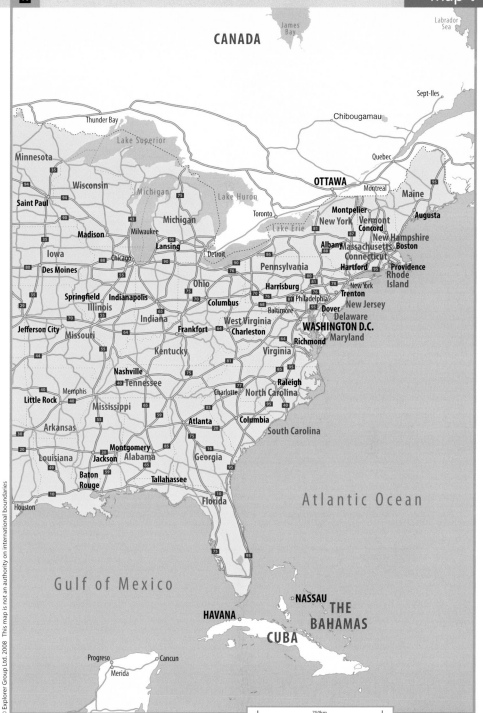

Map **2**   Los Angeles City Overview

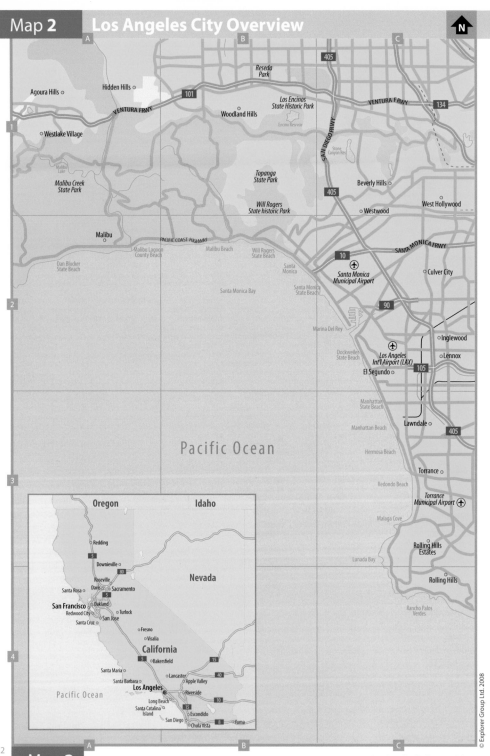

Map **2**
Los Angeles Explorer 1st Edition

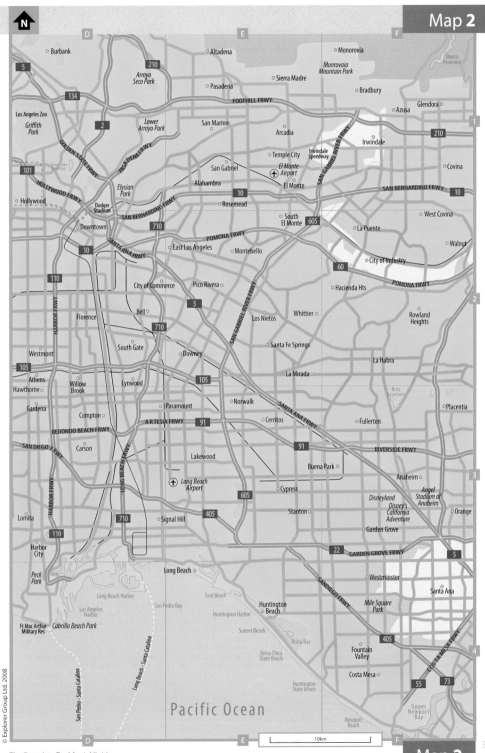

Map **2**

Pacific Ocean

10km

Map **3**

A

B

4

C

General Information p.17   Residents p.113   Exploring p.168   Activities p.212   Shopping p.259   Going Out p.317

N

S GRETNA GREEN WAY

GORHAM AVE

DOROTHY ST

DARLINGTON AVE

MAYFIELD AVE

KIOWA AVE

GOSHEN AVE

ARMACOST AVE

IDAHO AVE

S WESTGATE AVE

ARMACOST AVE

LA GRANGE AVE

MISSISSIPPI AVE

SAN VICENTE BLVD

S BUNDY DR

GRETNA GREEN WAY

MONTANA AVE

GORHAM AVE

DOROTHY ST

DARLINGTON AVE

ARIZONA AVE

S SALTAIR AVE

S BUNDY DR

SANTA MONICA BLVD

BROADWAY

S BUNDY DR

50

**Brentwood
Park**

WELLESLEY AVE

AMHERST AVE

WELLESLEY AVE

AMHERST AVE

NEBRASKA AVE

P

1

**Brentwood
Country Club**

S BRISTOL AVE

CENTINELA AVE

FRANKLIN ST

WILSHIRE BLVD

ARIZONA AVE

S CARMELINA AVE

S CENTINELA AVE

FRANKLIN ST

COLORADO AVE

FRANKLIN ST

2

W OLYMPIC BLVD

EXPOSITION BLVD

DELAWARE AVE

VIRGINIA AVE

P

P

S BURLINGAME AVE

MONTANA AVE

STANFORD ST

YALE ST

STANFORD ST

BERKELEY ST

YORKSHIRE AVE

SANTA MONICA FRWY

MORENO AVE

HARVARD ST

PRINCETON ST

YALE ST

HARVARD ST

STEWART ST

**Stewart
St Park**

26TH S T

PRINCETON ST

27TH ST

MICHIGAN AVE

VIRGINIA AVE

KANSAS AVE

PICO BLVD

25TH ST

ALTA AVE

25TH ST

25TH ST

ARIZONA AVE

SANTA MONICA BLVD

COLORADO AVE

CLOVERFIELD BLVD

12

2

24TH ST

MARGUERITA AVE

CHELSEA AVE

BROADWAY

10

23RD ST

WASHINGTON AVE

24TH ST

P

22ND ST

21ST ST

ALTA AVE

20TH ST

20TH ST

15

21ST ST

DELAWARE AVE

20TH ST

19TH ST

IDAHO AVE

20TH ST

SANTA MONICA

18TH ST

17TH ST

18TH ST

19TH ST

18TH ST

30

OLYMPIC BLVD

17TH ST

**Woodlawn
Cemetery**

16TH ST

**Santa
Monica-UCLA**

17TH ST

16TH ST

MICHIGAN AVE

14TH ST

GRANT ST

PACIFIC ST

15TH ST

MARGUERITA AVE

ALTA AVE

16TH ST

15TH ST

7

15TH ST

**Memorial
Park**

14TH ST

COLORADO AVE

OLYMPIC BLVD

PICO BLVD

S PICO PL

14TH ST

EUCLID ST

EUCLID ST

SANTA MONICA BLVD

3

12TH ST

CALIFORNIA AVE

12TH ST

12TH ST

11TH ST

SANTA MONICA

IDAHO AVE

20

WILSHIRE BLVD

11TH ST

11TH ST

PL CB BLVD

10TH ST

2

10TH ST

10TH ST

BAY ST

10TH ST

9TH ST

LINCOLN BLVD

WASHINGTON AVE

9TH ST

9TH ST

P

1

P

Joslyn Park

7TH ST

SAN VICENTE BLVD

**Goose Egg
Park**

MONTANA AVE

**Emerson
Reed Park**

7TH ST

LINCOLN BLVD

6TH ST

GEORGINA AVE

6TH ST

CALIFORNIA AVE

6TH ST

2

8

5TH ST

5TH ST

**Mary Hotchkiss
Park**

MARGUERITA AVE

5TH ST

4TH ST

**Edwards Comm
Centre**

4TH ST

4TH ST

PALISADES AVE

4TH ST

45

11 54

3RD ST

WILSHIRE BLVD

13

SANTA MONICA BLVD

P

23 15 63

2ND ST

H **Oceana**

13

Georgian

MAIN ST

4

OCEAN AVE

Palisades Park

27

CALIFORNIA INCLINE

PALISADES BEACH RD

6 H 3

1

56 42

**Casa
Del Mar**

H 8

**Crescent
Bay Park**

1

P

P

APPIAN WAY

P

21

P

**Santa Monica
State Beach**

50

17

**Santa
Monica
State Beach**

P a c i f i c   O c e a n

**Sanata
Monica Pier**

Explorer Group Ltd. 2008

Map **3**

Los Angeles Explorer 1st Edition

Map **3**

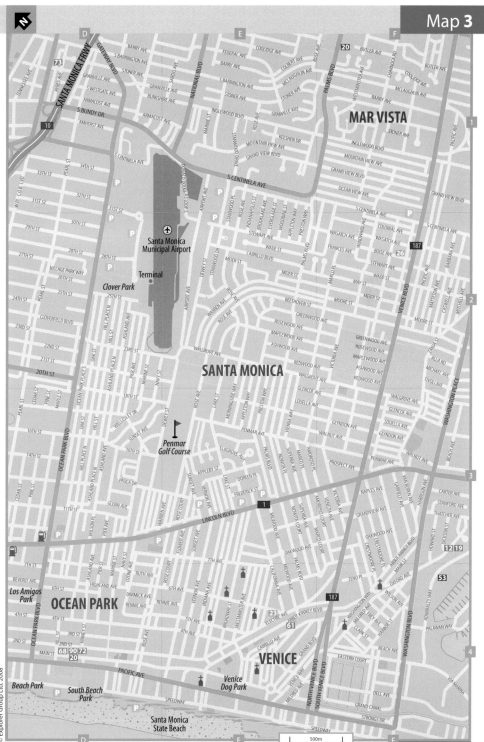

MAR VISTA

SANTA MONICA

Santa Monica
Municipal Airport

Terminal

Clover Park

Penmar
Golf Course

OCEAN PARK

Los Amigos
Park

VENICE

Venice
Dog Park

Beach Park

South Beach
Park

Santa Monica
State Beach

500m

Map **4**

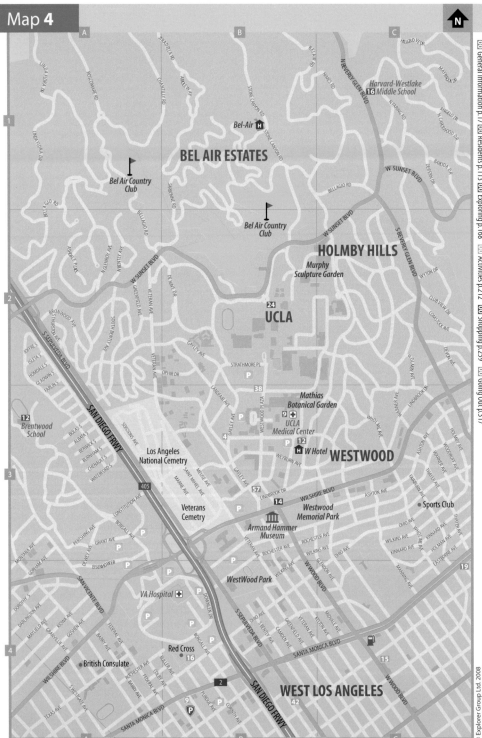

N

General Information p.17 ⬛ Residents p.113 ⬛ Exploring p.168 ⬛ Activities p.212 ⬛ Shopping p.259 ⬛ Going Out p.317

A · B · C

BEL AIR ESTATES

Bel-Air **H**

Harvard-Westlake
16 Middle School

Bel Air Country
Club

Bel Air Country
Club

HOLMBY HILLS

Murphy
Sculpture Garden

24

UCLA

STRATHMORE PL.

38

Mathias
Botanical Garden

9 +
UCLA
Medical Center

12
H W Hotel **WESTWOOD**

Brentwood
12
School

Los Angeles
National Cemetery

57

LINDBROOK DR.

14 WILSHIRE BLVD
Westwood
Memorial Park

• Sports Club

Veterans
Cemetry

Armand Hammer
Museum

WestWood Park

19

VA Hospital **+**

Red Cross
16

British Consulate

15

2

SAN DIEGO FRWY **WEST LOS ANGELES**

42

9
P

A · B · C

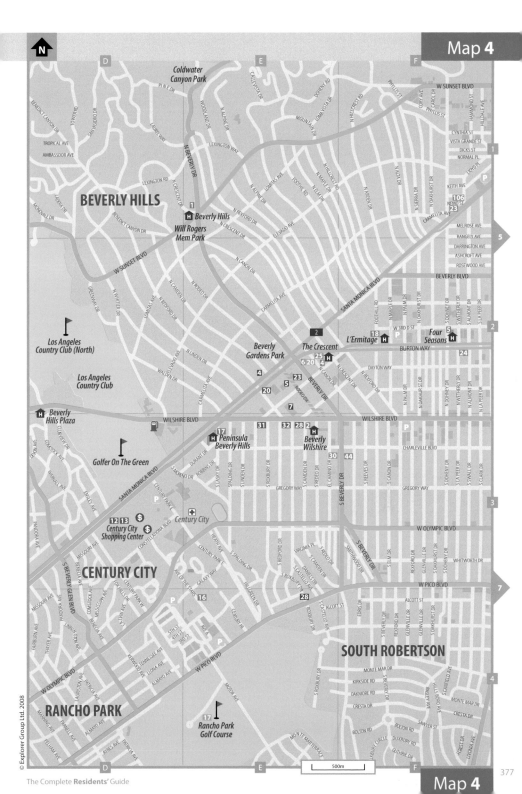

Map **4**

N

Coldwater
Canyon Park

BEVERLY HILLS

H Beverly Hills
Will Rogers
Mem Park

W SUNSET BLVD

Los Angeles
Country Club (North)

Los Angeles
Country Club

H Beverly
Hills Plaza

Golfer On The Green

WILSHIRE BLVD

Beverly
Gardens Park

The Crescent

L'Ermitage H

Four
Seasons H

BURTON WAY

2

25
6 20 H

23
5
4
20

7

31

32 28 2

24

H **17** Peninsula
Beverly Hills

H Beverly
Wilshire

30 **44**

WILSHIRE BLVD

CHARLEVILLE BLVD

SANTA MONICA BLVD

GREGORY WAY

GREGORY WAY

12 13 $
Century City
Shopping Center

$

Century City

W OLYMPIC BLVD

CENTURY CITY

W PICO BLVD

16

28

SOUTH ROBERTSON

W PICO BLVD

W OLYMPIC BLVD

RANCHO PARK

17
Rancho Park
Golf Course

500m

© Explorer Group Ltd. 2008

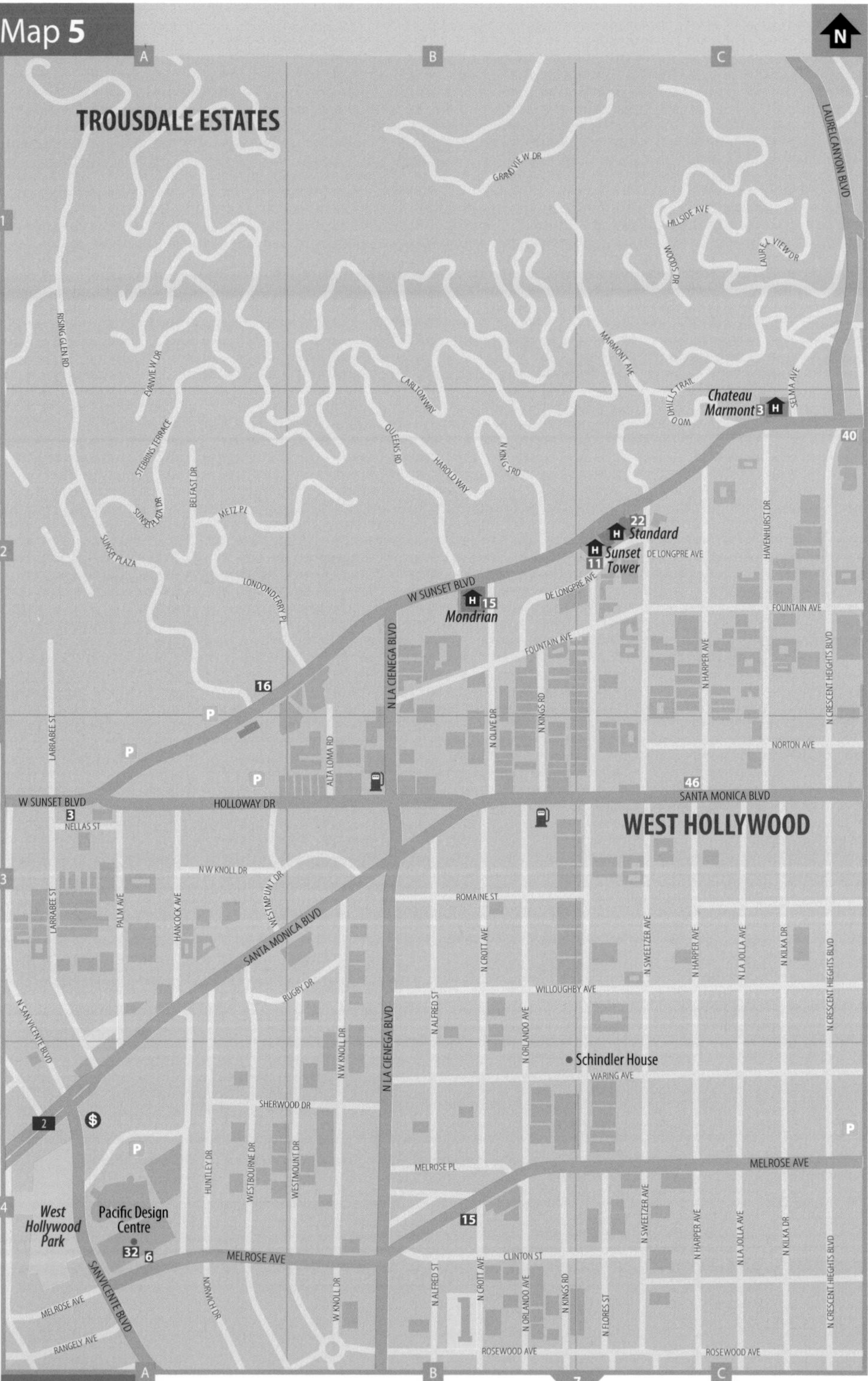

Map **5**

General Information p.17 | Residents p.113 | Exploring p.168 | Activities p.212 | Shopping p.259 | Going Out p.317

N

TROUSDALE ESTATES

A B C

RISING GLEN RD

GRAND VIEW DR

HILLSIDE AVE

WOODS DR

LAUREL VIEW DR

LAUREL CANYON BLVD

DAWNVIEW DR

CARLTON WAY

MARMONT AVE

HILLS TRAIL DOOM

STEBBINS TERRACE

BELFAST DR

SIMPSON DR

QUEENS RD

HAROLD WAY

N KINGS RD

SELMA AVE

Chateau Marmont ⬢ **H**

METZ PL

SUNSET PLAZA

LONDONDERRY PL

40

HAVENHURST DR

22 Standard

H

H **11** Sunset Tower

DE LONGPRE AVE

W SUNSET BLVD

H **15**
Mondrian

DE LONGPRE AVE

FOUNTAIN AVE

FOUNTAIN AVE

N LA CIENEGA BLVD

ALTA LOMA RD

N OLIVE DR

N KINGS RD

N CRESCENT HEIGHTS BLVD

16

P

LARRABEE ST

P

NORTON AVE

46

P

W SUNSET BLVD

HOLLOWAY DR

SANTA MONICA BLVD

3

NELLAS ST

⛽

⛽

WEST HOLLYWOOD

N W KNOLL DR

ROMAINE ST

N CROFT AVE

N SWEETZER AVE

N HARPER AVE

N LA JOLLA AVE

N KILKA DR

LARRABEE ST

PALM AVE

HANCOCK AVE

N W KNOLL DR

WEST MOUNT DR

SANTA MONICA BLVD

RUGBY DR

WILLOUGHBY AVE

N ALFRED ST

N ORLANDO AVE

N SWEETZER AVE

N HARPER AVE

N LA JOLLA AVE

N KILKA DR

N CRESCENT HEIGHTS BLVD

3

N SAN VICENTE BLVD

N W KNOLL DR

SHERWOOD DR

• Schindler House

WARING AVE

2

$

P

HUNTLEY DR

WESTBOURNE DR

WEST MOUNT DR

MELROSE PL

MELROSE AVE

P

4

West Hollywood Park

Pacific Design Centre

32 6

MELROSE AVE

N ALFRED ST

N CROFT AVE

CLINTON ST

N KINGS RD

N SWEETZER AVE

N HARPER AVE

N LA JOLLA AVE

N KILKA DR

N CRESCENT HEIGHTS BLVD

15

MELROSE AVE

NONNA CT R

W KNOLL DR

N FLORES ST

ROSEWOOD AVE

ROSEWOOD AVE

SAN VICENTE BLVD

RANGELY AVE

© Explorer Group Ltd 2008

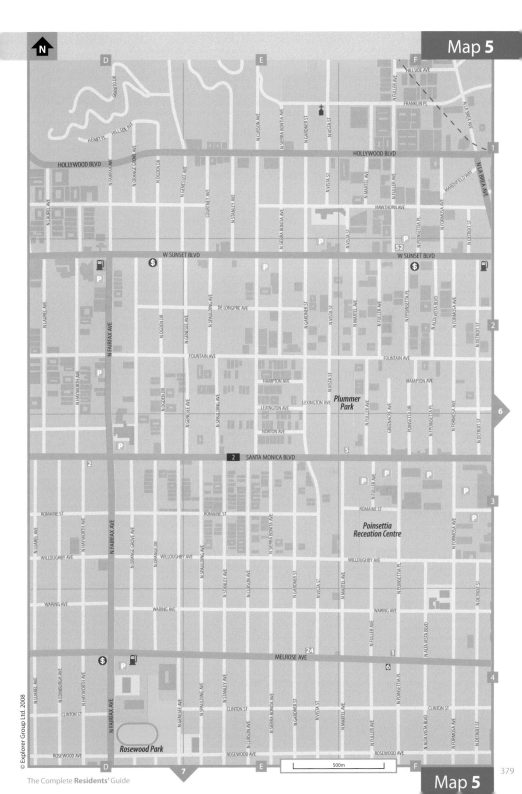

Map 5

Map 5

379

© Explorer Group Ltd. 2008

Map **6**

N

Hollywood
Franklin Park

FRANKLIN PL

**Kodak
Theatre** **46** **Hollywood
& Highland**

Chinese Theatre

43 **57** **34** 6

HOLLYWOOD BLVD

22
55 25 **54 21**

YUCCA ST

GRACE AVE

WILCOX AVE

N CAHUENGA BLVD

YUCCA ST

VINE ST

VAR AVE

VISTA DEL MAR AVE

N ARGYLE AVE

**Pantages
Theater**

**Radisson
Hollywood
Roosevelt** **7**

H

**Hollywood /
Highland Station**

34 **19** **39**

HOLLYWOOD BLVD

Hollywood / Vine Station

170

HAWTHORN AVE

N ORANGE DR

N HIGHLAND AVE

HAWTHORN AVE

N MCCADDEN PL

N LAS PALMAS AVE

N CHEROKEE AVE

SELMA AVE

SCHRADER BLVD

SELMA AVE

N CAHUENGA BLVD

VAR AVE

VINE ST

N ARGYLE AVE

**Hollywood
Medical Centre**

**Holly Wood
High School**

W SUNSET BLVD

27

N SYCAMORE AVE

N ORANGE DR

170

LELAND WAY

N MCCADDEN PL

LELAND WAY

N LAS PALMAS AVE

LELAND WAY

COLE PL

24

LELAND WAY

2

DE LONGPRE AVE

N MANSFIELD AVE

**De Longpre
Park**

DE LONGPRE AVE

N CHEROKEE AVE

DE LONGPRE AVE

HOMEWOOD AVE

VINE ST

1

DE LONGPRE AVE

AFTON PL

FOUNTAIN AVE

N ORANGE DR

FOUNTAIN AVE

N MCCADDEN PL

FOUNTAIN AVE

N LAS PALMAS AVE

FOUNTAIN AVE

N JUNE ST

WILCOX AVE

COLE AVE

LA MIRADA AVE

N CITRUS AVE

LEXINGTON AVE

N SYCAMORE AVE

N ORANGE DR

LEXINGTON AVE

LEXINGTON AVE

5

N LA BREA AVE

1

SANTA MONICA BLVD

N CITRUS AVE

2

SANTA MONICA BLVD

**Hollywood
Recreation
Center**

3

ROMAINE ST

N MCCADDEN PL

170

ROMAINE ST

WILCOX AVE

N CAHUENGA BLVD

ROMAINE ST

ELEANOR AVE

ROMAINE ST

BARTON AVE

BARTON AVE

WILLOUGHBY AVE

N SYCAMORE AVE

N MANSFIELD AVE

N CITRUS AVE

N HIGHLAND AVE

WILLOUGHBY AVE

N LAS PALMAS AVE

WILLOUGHBY AVE

N HUDSON AVE

COLE AVE

N CAHUENGA BLVD

WILLOUGHBY AVE

VINE ST

LILLIAN WAY

GREGORY AVE

WARING AVE

WARING AVE

WARING AVE

WILCOX AVE

WARING AVE

WARING AVE

CAMERFORD AVE

4

N LA BREA AVE

MELROSE AVE

MELROSE AVE

N MCCADDEN PL

MELROSE AVE

N CHEROKEE AVE

N JUNE ST

SEWARD ST

MELROSE AVE

COLE AVE

N CAHUENGA BLVD

MELROSE AVE

N ARDEN BLVD

N LUCERNE BLVD

CLINTON ST

N LA BREA AVE

CLINTON ST

N HIGHLAND AVE

CLINTON ST

N LAS PALMAS AVE

N CAHUENGA BLVD

CLINTON ST

LILLIAN WAY

CLINTON ST

**Wilshire
Country Club**

ROSEWOOD AVE

ROSEWOOD AVE

ROSEWOOD AVE

General Information p.17 — Residents p.113 — Exploring p.168 — Activities p.212 — Shopping p.259 — Going Out p.317

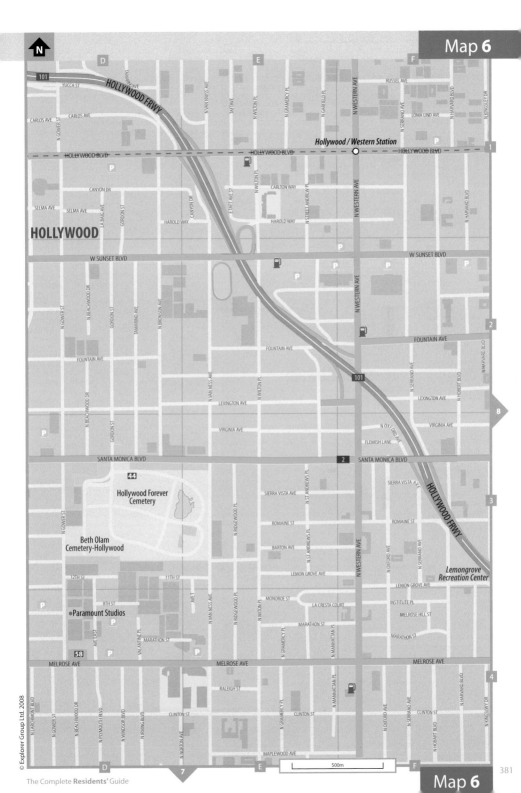

Map **6**

N

HOLLYWOOD

101

HOLLYWOOD FRWY

YUCCA ST

CARLOS AVE

CARLOS AVE

CARLOS AVE

SELMA AVE

SELMA AVE

CANYON DR

N GOWER ST

LA BAIG AVE

GORDON ST

CANYON DR

HAROLD WAY

W SUNSET BLVD

N GOWER ST

N BEACHWOOD DR

GORDON ST

TAMARIND AVE

N BRONSON AVE

FOUNTAIN AVE

N BEACHWOOD DR

GORDON ST

N VAN NESS AVE

LEXINGTON AVE

VIRGINIA AVE

SANTA MONICA BLVD

44

Hollywood Forever
Cemetery

**Beth Olam
Cemetery-Hollywood**

N GOWER ST

N RIDGEWOOD PL

12TH ST

11TH ST

8TH ST

•Paramount Studios

AVE

AVE EAST

VALENTINE PL

MARATHON ST

58

P

P

MELROSE AVE

N LARCHMONT BLVD

N GOWER ST

N BEACHWOOD DR

N PLYMOUTH BLVD

N WINDSOR BLVD

N IRVING BLVD

CLINTON ST

RALEIGH ST

N NORTON AVE

D

HOLLYWOOD BLVD

N VAN NESS AVE

TAFT AVE

N WILTON PL

E TAFT AVE ST

CANYON DR

N WILTON PL

CARLTON WAY

HAROLD WAY

N GRAMERCY PL

N STREET ANDREWS PL

Hollywood / Western Station

N WESTERN AVE

N WESTERN AVE

N GARFIELD PL

W SUNSET BLVD

P

P

N WESTERN AVE

FOUNTAIN AVE

FOUNTAIN AVE

N WILTON PL

LEXINGTON AVE

VIRGINIA AVE

N OXFORD AVE

FLEMISH LANE

2 SANTA MONICA BLVD

SIERRA VISTA AVE

N ST ANDREWS PL

ROMAINE ST

BARTON AVE

N ST ANDREWS PL

LEMON GROVE AVE

N WILTON PL

MONROE ST

N RIDGEWOOD PL

LA CRESTA COURT

MARATHON ST

N GRAMERCY PL

N MANHATTAN PL

MARATHON ST

MELROSE AVE

P

N GRAMERCY PL

CLINTON ST

CLINTON ST

MAPLEWOOD AVE

E

101

SANTA MONICA BLVD

SIERRA VISTA AVE

ROMAINE ST

LEMON GROVE AVE

INSTITUTE PL

MELROSE HILL ST

MARATHON ST

N OXFORD AVE

N SERRANO AVE

N SERRANO AVE

N SERRANO AVE

HOLLYWOOD FRWY

*Lemongrove
Recreation Center*

MELROSE AVE

N OXFORD AVE

N SERRANO AVE

N HOBART BLVD

N HOBART BLVD

CLINTON ST

N HARVARD BLVD

RUSSEL AVE

LOMA LIND AVE

N SERRANO AVE

N HARVARD BLVD

HOLLYWOOD BLVD

N HARVARD BLVD

P

P

N HARVARD BLVD

FOUNTAIN AVE

N HAVARD BLVD

LEXINGTON AVE

VIRGINIA AVE

N HARVARD BLVD

N KINGSLEY DR

N HARVARD BLVD

N KINGSLEY DR

F

HOLLYWOOD BLVD

1

2

8

3

4

500m

Map **6**

Map **7**

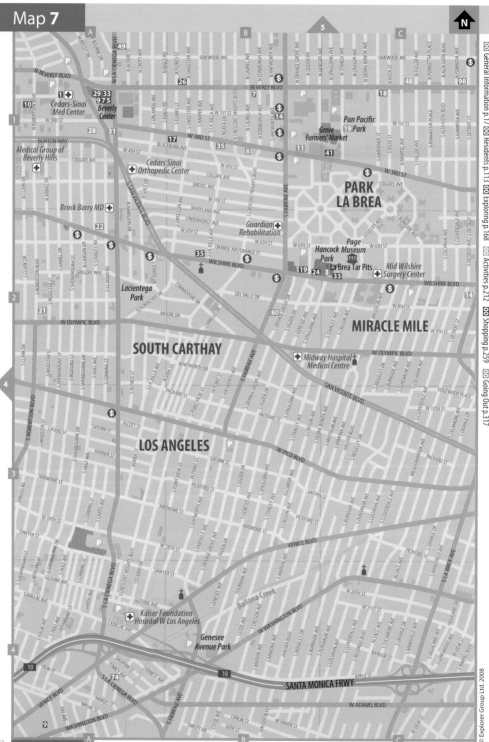

General Information p.17 | Residents p.113 | Exploring p.168 | Activities p.212 | Shopping p.259 | Going Out p.317

OAKWOOD AVE

BEVERLY BLVD

N BEVERLY BLVD

Cedars-Sinai
Med Center

Beverly
Center

W 3RD ST

BURTON WAY

Medical Group of
Beverly Hills

COLGATE AVE

Cedars Sinai
Orthopedic Center

BLACKBURN AVE

W 4TH ST

COLGATE AVE

DREXEL AVE

W 5TH ST

Brock Barry MD

MARYLAND AVE

LINDENHURST AVE

Guardian
Rehabilitation

W 6TH ST

ORANGE AVE/ORANGE ST

WILSHIRE BLVD

Lacientega
Park

DEL VALLE DR

MOORE DR

W OLYMPIC BLVD

Pan Pacific
Park

Grove
Farmers' Market

W 3RD ST

**PARK
LA BREA**

Page
Hancock Museum
Park

La Brea Tar Pits

Mid Wilshire
Surgery Center

WILSHIRE BLVD

W 8TH ST

MIRACLE MILE

W 9TH ST

SOUTH CARTHAY

WHITWORTH DR

PACKARD ST

W OLYMPIC BLVD

Midway Hospital
Medical Centre

SAN VICENTE BLVD

W 12TH ST

EDGEWOOD PLACE

PACKARD ST

LOS ANGELES

SATURN ST

HORNER ST

AIRDROME ST

W PICO BLVD

SATURN ST

PICKFORD ST

AIRDROME ST

W 18TH ST

SAWYER ST

VENICE BLVD

SAWYER ST

CADILLAC AVE

GUTHRIE AVE

Kaiser Foundation
Hospital W Los Angeles

CADILLAC AVE

W 20TH ST

W 21ST ST

Genesee
Avenue Park

SANTA MONICA FRWY

W WASHINGTON BLVD

Ballona Creek

APPLE ST

VENICE BLVD

WASHINGTON BLVD

W ADAMS BLVD

Map **7**

© Explorer Group Ltd 2008

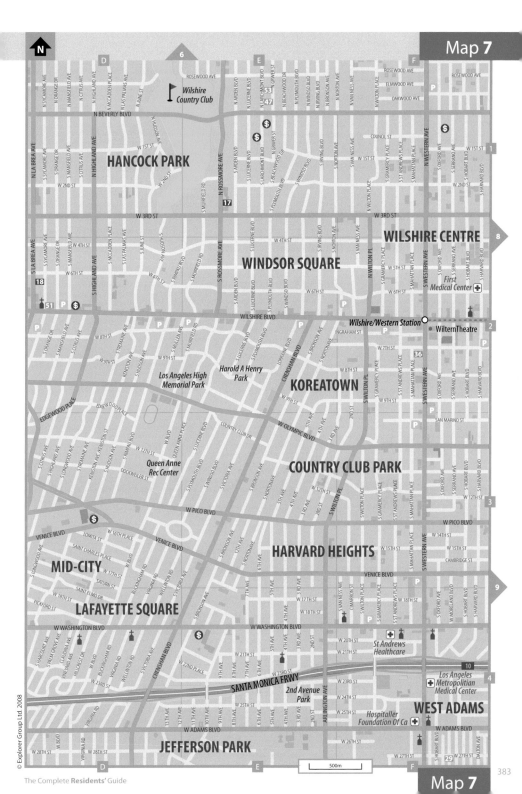

Map 7

N

Map 7

Wilshire
Country Club

HANCOCK PARK

WILSHIRE CENTRE

WINDSOR SQUARE

First
Medical Center

Wilshire/Western Station
Wiltern Theatre

Los Angeles High
Memorial Park

Harold A Henry
Park

KOREATOWN

Queen Anne
Rec Center

COUNTRY CLUB PARK

MID-CITY

HARVARD HEIGHTS

LAFAYETTE SQUARE

St Andrews
Healthcare

Los Angeles
Metropolitan
Medical Center

SANTA MONICA FRWY

2nd Avenue
Park

WEST ADAMS

Hospitaller
Foundation Of Ca

JEFFERSON PARK

500m

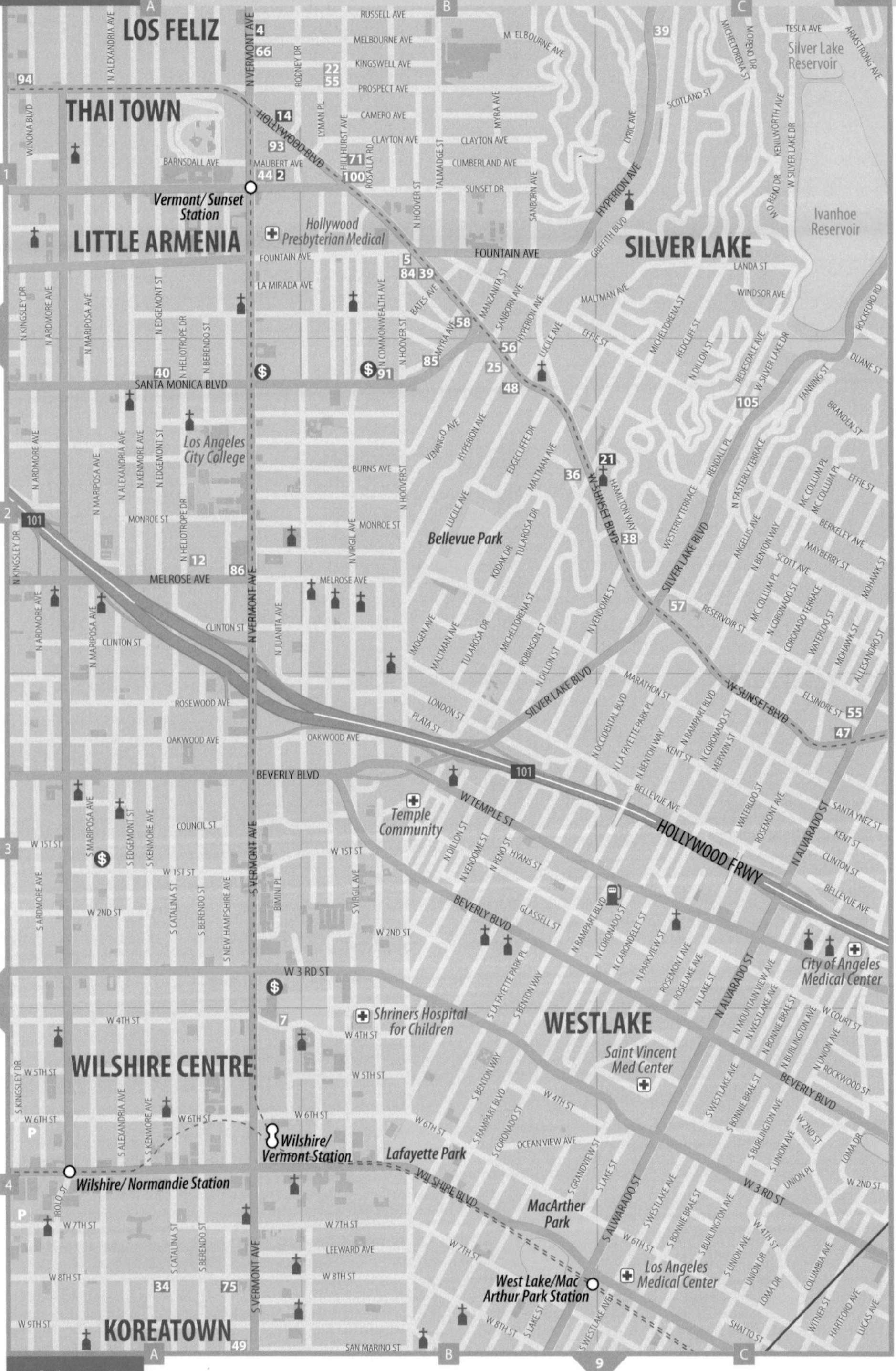

Map 8

N

General Information p.17   Residents p.113   Exploring p.168   Activities p.212   Shopping p.259   Going Out p.317

A   B   C

LOS FELIZ

RUSSELL AVE

MELBOURNE AVE

M ELBOURNE AVE

39

KINGSWELL AVE

22
55

TESLA AVE

Silver Lake
Reservoir

PROSPECT AVE

94

THAI TOWN

14

CAMERO AVE

SCOTLAND ST

CLAYTON AVE

CLAYTON AVE

93

71

CUMBERLAND AVE

100

Ivanhoe
Reservoir

1

44 2

SUNSET DR

SANBORN AVE

**Vermont/ Sunset
Station**

Hollywood
Presbyterian Medical

SILVER LAKE

HYPERION AVE

LITTLE ARMENIA

FOUNTAIN AVE

FOUNTAIN AVE

LANDA ST

5

84 39

WINDSOR CT

LA MIRADA AVE

MALTMAN AVE

MICHELTORENA ST

6

58

85

56

105

40

25

48

Santa Monica Blvd

91

**Los Angeles
City College**

BURNS AVE

36 21

57

2

101

MONROE ST

MELROSE AVE

12

86

MELROSE AVE

Bellevue Park

SILVER LAKE BLVD

38

CLINTON ST

55

ROSEWOOD AVE

SILVER LAKE BLVD

MARATHON ST

47

OAKWOOD AVE

OAKWOOD AVE

101

BEVERLY BLVD

W TEMPLE ST

HOLLYWOOD FRWY

3

Temple
Community

W 1ST ST

W 1ST ST

W 2ND ST

BEVERLY BLVD

**City of Angeles
Medical Center**

COUNCIL ST

W 2ND ST

WESTLAKE

7

W 3 RD ST

7

Shriners Hospital
for Children

**Saint Vincent
Med Center**

WILSHIRE CENTRE

W 4TH ST

W 4TH ST

W 5TH ST

W 5TH ST

P

W 6TH ST

W 6TH ST

Wilshire/
Vermont Station

Lafayette Park

4

Wilshire/ Normandie Station

WILSHIRE BLVD

**MacArthur
Park**

P

W 7TH ST

LEEWARD AVE

34
75

W 8TH ST

W 8TH ST

West Lake/Mac
Arthur Park Station

**Los Angeles
Medical Center**

KOREATOWN

49

SAN MARINO ST

A   B   9   C

Map 8

Explorer Group Ltd. 2006

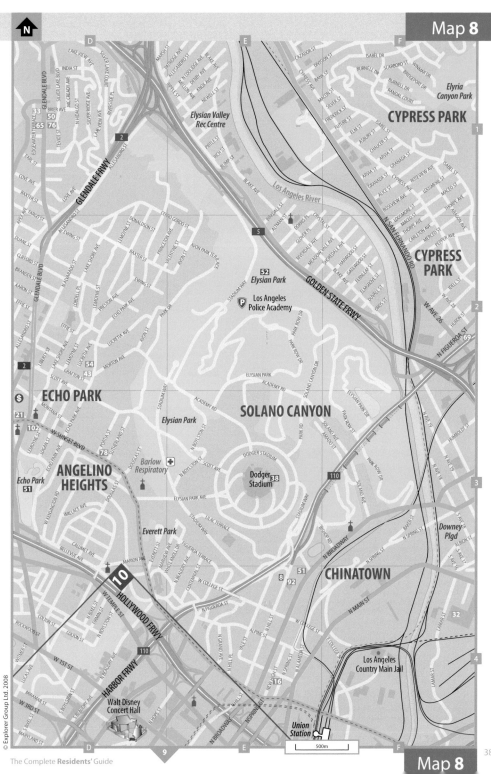

CYPRESS PARK

Elyria Canyon Park

Elysian Valley Rec Centre

Los Angeles River

CYPRESS PARK

GOLDEN STATE FRWY

52 Elysian Park

Los Angeles Police Academy

ELYSIAN PARK

SOLANO CANYON

ECHO PARK

Elysian Park

ANGELINO HEIGHTS

Barlow Respiratory

Echo Park

Dodger Stadium 38

Everett Park

Downey Plgd

CHINATOWN

Walt Disney Concert Hall

Los Angeles Country Main Jail

Union Station

500m

Map **9**

N

General Information p.17 ☐☐ Residents p.113 ☐☐ Exploring p.168 ☐☐ Activities p.212 ☐☐ Shopping p.259 ☐☐ Going Out p.317

KOREATOWN

Aromore Playground Park

W OLYMPIC BLVD

W OLYMPIC BLVD

W 12TH ST

W 14TH ST

Normandie Playground

Angelus Rosedale Cemetary

HARVARD HEIGHTS

VENICE BLVD

Pico Union Park

Terrace Park

L A Gospel Mission Church

West Wood Prep School

Toberman Play Ground

Staples Centre

HARBOR FRWY

Chick Hearn Court

California Hospital Medical

W 20TH ST

W 20TH ST

SANTA MONICA FRWY

SANTA MONICA FRWY

WEST ADAMS

W 22ND ST

W 23RD ST

W 24TH ST

W 25TH ST

W ADAMS BLVD

W ADAMS BLVD

James Park

W ADAMS BLVD

Grand Station

E WASHINGTON BLVD

W 27TH ST

W 28TH ST

W 29TH ST

W 30TH ST

W 35TH ST

W 35TH PL

W 36TH ST

W JEFFERSON BLVD

W 32ND ST

W 34TH ST

E JEFFERSON BLVD

W 37TH ST

W 37TH PL

W 37TH DR

EXPOSITION BLVD

Exposition Park

California Science Centre

Los Angeles Coliseum

Los Angeles Sports Arena

HARBOR FRWY

W MARTIN LUTHER KING JUNIOR BLVD

W 40TH PL

W 41ST ST

W 42ND ST

Martin Luther King Jr Mini Park

Theresa Lindsay Park

© Explorer Group Ltd. 2006

Map 9

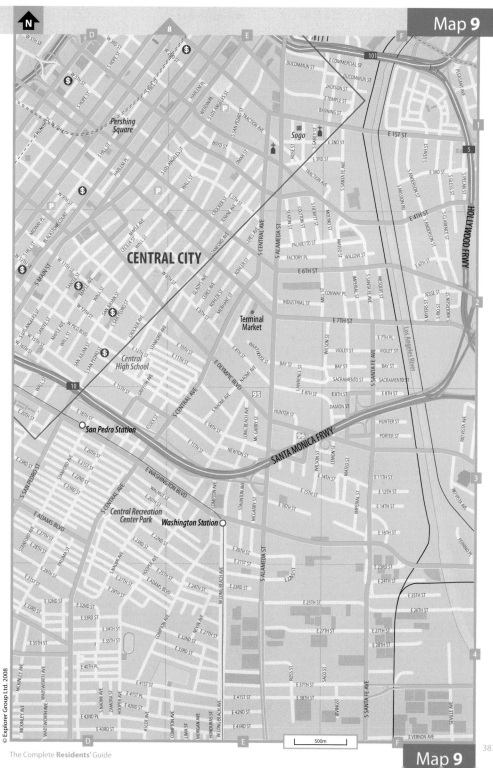

Map **10**

[M] General Information p.17 [M] Residents p.113 [M] Exploring p.168 [M] Activities p.212 [M] Shopping p.259 [M] Going Out p.317

W 14TH ST
S UNION AVE
S UNION AVE
W PICO BLVD
W 12TH PL
W 11TH PL
S UNION AVE
W 11TH PL
CONNECTICUT ST
GRATTAN ST
W OLYMPIC BLVD
VALENCIA ST
GREEN AVE
W 8TH ST
VALENCIA ST
COLUMBIA AVE
VALENCIA AVE
WITNER ST
W 10TH ST
ALBANY ST
WITMER ST
HARTFORD AVE
INGRAHAM ST
WILSHIRE BLVD

TOBERMAN ST
W 12TH PL
VALENCIA ST
W 11TH PL
W 11TH PL
BLAINE ST
GARLAND AVE

VALENCIA ST
W 14TH ST
W 9TH ST
S BIXEL ST

VENICE BLVD
W 15TH ST
OAK ST
HARBOR FRWY
110
HARBOR FRWY
FRANCISCO ST

BOND ST
CHERRY ST
CHERRY ST
CHERRY ST
W OLYMPIC BLVD
GEORGIA ST
Seventh Market
W 8TH PL

CHERRY ST
CHICK HEARN COURT
GEORGIA ST
FRANCISCO ST
FRANCISCO ST

CONVENTION CENTER DR
W PICO BLVD
W PICO BLVD
W 19TH ST
Figueroa
S FIGUEROA ST

W 12TH ST
Staples Centre
104
9
7th Street/ Metro Station
37 36 35
Holiday Inn City Centre
S FLOWER ST
30

W 15TH ST
S FIGUEROA ST
Convention Center/ Staples Center Station
47
Holiday Inn
S FLOWER ST
7TH ST

SANTA MONICA FRWY
LEBANON ST
S FLOWER ST
W 12TH ST
PEMBROKE LANE
S HOPE ST
W 9TH ST
S HOPE ST

S FIGUEROA ST
PEMBROKE LANE
S HOPE ST
Grand Hope Park
S GRAND AVE

W 18TH ST
California Hospital Medical
VENICE BLVD
W 15TH ST
S GRAND AVE
WEST OLYMPIC BOULEVARD
S OLIVE ST
W 8TH ST
70

S HILL ST
S HOPE ST
California Hospital
MARGO ST
W 12TH ST
101
MIDWAY PL
W 9TH ST
S HILL ST

S OLIVE ST
MIDWAY LANE
W PICO BLVD
S HILL ST
BLACKSTONE COURT
62

10
SOUTH BROADWAY
S MAIN ST

VENICE BOULEVARD
W 14TH ST
SOUTH MAIN STREET
S LOS ANGELES ST
SANTEE ST

SANTA MONICA FRWY
W 16TH ST
S LOS ANGELES ST
SANTEE ST
SANTEE ST
W 11TH ST
MAPLE AVE
CECILIA ST
WALL ST

S LOS ANGELES ST
MAPLE AVE
W PICO BLVD
MAPLE AVE
WALL ST
SAN JULIAN ST

MAPLE AVE
WALL ST
W 15TH ST
WALL ST
SAN JULIAN ST
SAN JULIAN ST

10
MYRTLE ST
W 15TH ST
SAN JULIAN ST
W 8TH ST

E 20TH ST
TRINITY ST
S SAN PEDRO ST
S SAN PEDRO ST
W 12TH ST
CROCKER ST
AGATHA ST

CENTRAL CITY

© Explorer Group Ltd. 2008

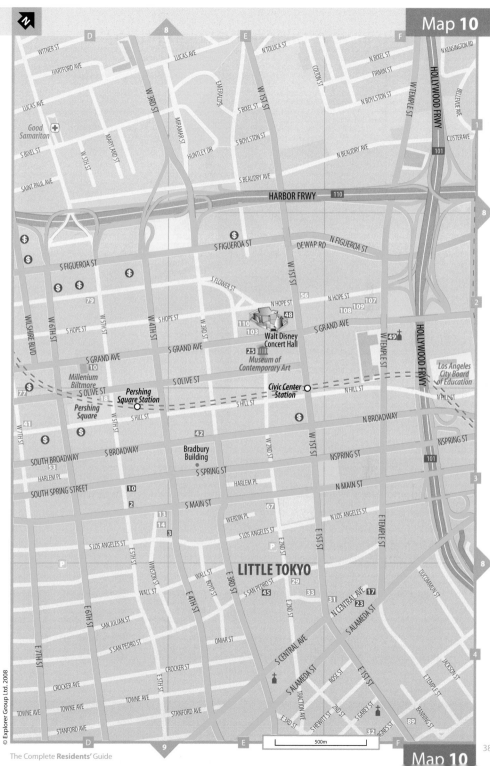

Map **10**

N

WITNER ST
HARTFORD AVE
LUCAS AVE
S BIXEL ST
W 5TH ST
MARYLAND ST
SAINT PAUL AVE

Good Samaritan

LUCAS AVE
EMERALD ST
MIRAMAR ST
HUNTLEY DR
W 3RD ST

N TOLUCA ST
N BIXEL ST
S BIXEL ST
S BOYLSTON ST
W 1ST ST
COTON ST
FIRMIN ST
N BOYLSTON ST
N BEAUDRY AVE
S BEAUDRY AVE

N KENSINGTON RD
HOLLYWOOD FRWY
W TEMPLE ST
BELLEVUE AVE
CUSTER AVE
101

HARBOR FRWY 110

WILSHIRE BLVD
S FIGUEROA ST
W 6TH ST
S HOPE ST
W 5TH ST
W 4TH ST
S HOPE ST
W 7TH ST
S GRAND AVE
79

S FIGUEROA ST
S FLOWER ST
S HOPE ST
S GRAND ST
S GRAND AVE

S FIGUEROA ST
DEWAP RD
N FIGUEROA ST
N HOPE ST
56
N HOPE ST
108 109 107
48
110
103
Walt Disney Concert Hall

S GRAND AVE
N TEMPLE ST
49
HOLLYWOOD FRWY

Los Angeles City Board of Education

25
Museum of Contemporary Art

S OLIVE ST
Millenium Biltmore
10
77
S OLIVE ST
18
Pershing Square Station
Pershing Square
W 5TH ST
S HILL ST
41
W 7TH ST
S HILL ST

Civic Center Station
N HILL ST
N HILL ST
N BROADWAY

SOUTH BROADWAY
53
HARLEM PL
SOUTH SPRING STREET
10
2
S BROADWAY

42
Bradbury Building
S SPRING ST
HARLEM PL
W 2ND ST
W 1ST ST
N SPRING ST
101
N SPRING ST

13
14
3
S LOS ANGELES ST
W 5TH ST
S MAIN ST
WINSTON ST
WALL ST
WALL ST
E 4TH ST
BOYD ST
E 6TH ST
SAN JULIAN ST
S SAN PEDRO ST
CROCKER ST
CROCKER AVE
TOWNE AVE
TOWNE AVE
STANFORD AVE
E 7TH ST
E 5TH ST
S 5TH ST

WERDIN PL
S LOS ANGELES ST
67
N MAIN ST
N LOS ANGELES ST

LITTLE TOKYO
29
45
E 2ND ST
33
E 3RD ST
31
23
17
N CENTRAL AVE
E 1ST ST
E TEMPLE ST

OMAR ST
S CENTRAL AVE
S ALAMEDA ST
S ALAMEDA ST
ROSE ST
S GAREY ST
E 1ST ST
DUCOMMUN ST
JACKSON ST
E TEMPLE ST
BANNING ST
89

TRACTION AVE
E 3RD ST
S HEWITT ST
2ND ST
32

500m

P

© Explorer Group Ltd. 2008

Are you always taking the wrong turn?

Whether you're a map person or not, these pocket-sized marvels will help you get to know the city – and its limits.

Explorer Mini Maps
Fit the city in your pocket

Index

Index

Index

Index

Index

Residents' Guides

All you need to know about living, working and enjoying life in these exciting destinations

Coming in 2008/9: Bangkok, Brussels, Mexico City, Moscow, San Francisco, Saudi Arabia and Taipei

Mini Guides
The perfect pocket-sized
Visitors' Guides

Mini Maps
Wherever you are,
never get lost again

Check out www.explorerpublishing.com/products

Photography Books
Beautiful cities caught through the lens

Calendars
The time, the place, and the date

Maps
Wherever you are, never get lost again

Activity and Lifestyle Guides
Drive, trek, dive and swim... life will never be boring again

Retail sales
Our books are available in most good bookshops around the world, and are also available online at Amazon.co.uk and Amazon.com. If you would like to enquire about any of our international distributors, please contact retail@explorerpublishing.com

Bulk sales and customisation
All our products are available for bulk sales with customisation options. For discount rates and further information, please contact corporatesales@explorerpublishing.com

Licensing and digital sales
All our content, maps and photography are available for print or digital use. For licensing enquiries please contact licensing@explorerpublishing.com

Check out www.explorerpublishing.com/products

Ahmed Mainodin
AKA: Mystery Man
We can never recognise Ahmed because of his constantly changing facial hair. He waltzes in with big lambchop sideburns one day, a handlebar moustache the next, and a neatly trimmed goatee after that. So far we've had no objections to his hirsute chameleonisms, but we'll definitely draw the line at a monobrow.

Andrea Fust
AKA: Mother Superior
By day Andrea is the most efficient manager in the world and by night she replaces the boardroom for her board and wows the pants off the dudes in Ski Dubai. Literally. Back in the office she definitely wears the trousers!

Ajay Krishnan R
AKA: Web Wonder
Ajay's mum and dad knew he was going to be an IT genius when they found him reconfiguring his Commodore 64 at the tender age of 2. He went on to become the technology consultant on all three Matrix films, and counts Keanu as a close personal friend.

Bahrudeen Abdul
AKA: The Stallion
Having tired of creating abstract sculptures out of papier maché and candy canes, Bahrudeen turned to the art of computer programming. After honing his skills in the southern Andes for three years he grew bored of Patagonian winters, and landed a job here, 'The Home of 01010101 Creative Freedom'.

Alex Jeffries
AKA: Easy Rider
Alex is happiest when dressed in leather from head to toe with a humming machine between his thighs – just like any other motorbike enthusiast. Whenever he's not speeding along the Hatta Road at full throttle, he can be found at his beloved Mac, still dressed in leather.

Ben Merrett
AKA: Big Ben
After a short (or tall as the case may have been) career as a human statue, Ben tired of the pigeons choosing him, rather than his namesake, as a public convenience and decided to fly the nest to seek his fortune in foreign lands. Not only is he big on personality but he brings in the big bucks with his bulk!

Alistair MacKenzie
AKA: Media Mogul
If only Alistair could take the paperless office one step further and achieve the officeless office he would be the happiest publisher alive. Wireless access from a remote spot somewhere in the Hajar Mountains would suit this intrepid explorer – less traffic, lots of fresh air, and wearing sandals all day – the perfect work environment!

Cherry Enriquez
AKA: Bean Counter
With the team's penchant for sweets and pastries, it's good to know we have Cherry on top of our accounting cake. The local confectioner is always paid on time, so we're guaranteed great gateaux for every special occasion.

Annabel Clough
AKA: Bollywood Babe
Taking a short break from her successful career in Bollywood, Annabel livens up the Explorer office with her spontaneous dance routines and random passionate outpouring of song. If there is a whiff of drama or a hint of romance, Annabel's famed vocal chords and nifty footwork will bring a touch of glamour to Al Quoz.

Claire England
AKA: Whip Cracker
No longer able to freeload off the fact that she once appeared in a Robbie Williams video, Claire now puts her creative skills to better use – looking up rude words in the dictionary! A child of English nobility, Claire is quite the lady – unless she's down at Rock Bottom.

Darwin Lovitos
AKA: The Philosopher
We are firm believers in our own Darwinism theory at Explorer – enthusiasm, organisation and a great sense of humour can evolve into a wonderful thing. He may not have the big beard (except on weekends) , but Darwin is just as wise as his namesake.

Hashim MM
AKA: Speedy Gonzales
They don't come much faster than Hashim – he's so speedy with his mouse that scientists are struggling to create a computer that can keep up with him. His nimble fingers leave his keyboard smouldering (he gets through three a week), and his go-faster stripes make him almost invisible to the naked eye when he moves.

David Quinn
AKA: Sharp Shooter
After a short stint as a children's TV presenter was robbed from David because he developed an allergy to sticky back plastic, he made his way to sandier pastures. Now that he's thinking outside the box, nothing gets past the man with the sharpest pencil in town.

Helen Spearman
AKA: Little Miss Sunshine
With her bubbly laugh and permanent smile, Helen is a much-needed ray of sunshine in the office when we're all grumpy and facing harrowing deadlines. It's almost impossible to think that she ever loses her temper or shows a dark side... although put her behind the wheel of a car, and you've got instant road rage.

Derrick Pereira
AKA: The Returnimator
After leaving Explorer in 2003, Derrick's life took a dramatic downturn – his dog ran away, his prized bonsai tree died and he got kicked out of his thrash metal band. Since rejoining us, things are looking up and he just found out he's won $10 million in a Nigerian sweepstakes competition. And he's got the desk by the window!

Henry Hilos
AKA: The Quiet Man
Henry can rarely be seen from behind his large obstructive screen but when you do catch a glimpse you'll be sure to get a smile. Lighthearted Henry keeps all those glossy pages filled with pretty pictures for something to look at when you can't be bothered to read.

Enrico Maullon
AKA: The Crooner
Frequently mistaken for his near-namesake Enrique Iglesias, Enrico decided to capitalise and is now a regular stand-in for the Latin heartthrob. If he's ever missing from the office, it usually means he's off performing for millions of adoring fans on another stadium tour of America.

Iain Young
AKA: 'The Cat'
Iain follows in the fine tradition of Scots with safe hands – Alan Rough, Andy Goram, Jim Leighton on a good day – but breaking into the Explorer XI has proved frustrating. There's no match on a Mac, but that Al Huzaifa ringer doesn't half make himself big.

Firos Khan
AKA: Big Smiler
Previously a body double in kung fu movies, including several appearances in close up scenes for Steven Seagal's moustache. He also once tore down a restaurant with his bare hands after they served him a mild curry by mistake.

Ieyad Charaf
AKA: Fashion Designer
When we hired Ieyad as a top designer, we didn't realise we'd be getting his designer tops too! By far the snappiest dresser in the office, you'd be hard-pressed to beat his impeccably ironed shirts.

Grace Carnay
AKA: Manila Ice
It's just as well the office is so close to a movie theatre, because Grace is always keen to catch the latest Hollywood offering from Brad Pitt, who she admires purely for his acting ability, of course. Her ice cool exterior conceals a tempestuous passion for jazz, which fuels her frenzied typing speed.

Ingrid Cupido
AKA: The Karaoke Queen
Ingrid has a voice to match her starlet name. She'll put any Pop Idols to shame once behind the mike, and she's pretty nifty on a keyboard too. She certainly gets our vote if she decides to go pro; just remember you saw her here first.

Johny Mathew
AKA: The Hawker
Caring Johny used to nurse wounded eagles back to health and teach them how to fly again before trying his luck in merchandising. Fortunately his skills in the field have come in handy at Explorer, where his efforts to improve our book sales have been a soaring success.

Joy Tubog
AKA: Joyburgh
Don't let her saintly office behaviour deceive you. Joy has the habit of jumping up and down while screaming 'Jumanji' the instant anyone mentions Robin Williams and his hair sweater. Thankfully, her volleyball team has learned to utilize her 'uniqueness' when it's her turn to spike the ball.

Ivan Rodrigues
AKA: The Aviator
After making a mint in the airline market, Ivan came to Explorer where he works for pleasure, not money. That's his story, anyway. We know that he is actually a corporate spy from a rival company and that his multi-level spreadsheets are really elaborate codes designed to confuse us.

Juby Jose
AKA: The Nutcracker
After years as a ballet teacher, Juby decided on mapping out a completely different career path, charting the UAE's ever-changing road network. Plotting products to illuminate the whole of the Middle East, she now works alongside the all-singing, all-dancing Madathil brothers, and cracks any nut that steps out of line.

Jake Marsico
AKA: Don Calzone
Jake spent the last 10 years on the tiny triangular Mediterranean island of Samoza, honing his traditional cooking techniques and perfecting his Italian. Now, whenever he returns to his native America, he impresses his buddies by effortlessly zapping a hot dog to perfection in any microwave, anywhere, anytime.

Kate Fox
AKA: Contacts Collector
Kate swooped into the office like the UK equivalent of Wonderwoman, minus the tights of course (it's much too hot for that), but armed with a superhuman marketing brain. Even though she's just arrived, she is already a regular on the Dubai social scene – she is helping to blast Explorer into the stratosphere, one champagne-soaked networking party at a time.

Jane Roberts
AKA: The Oracle
After working in an undisclosed role in the government, Jane brought her super sleuth skills to Explorer. Whatever the question, she knows what, where, who, how and when, but her encyclopaedic knowledge is only impressive until you realise she just makes things up randomly.

Kathryn Calderon
AKA: Miss Moneypenny
With her high-flying banking background, Kathryn is an invaluable member of the team. During her lunchtimes she conducts 'get rich quick' seminars that, she says, will make us so much money that we'll be able to retire early and spend our days reading books instead of making them. We're still waiting...

Jayde Fernandes
AKA: Pop Idol
Jayde's idol is Britney Spears, and he recently shaved his head to show solidarity with the troubled star. When he's not checking his dome for stubble, or practising the dance moves to 'Baby One More Time' in front of the bathroom mirror, he actually manages to get some designing done.

Katie Drynan
AKA: The Irish Deputy
This Irish lass is full of sass, fresh from her previous role as the four leaf clover mascot for the Irish ladies' rugby team. Katie provides the Explorer office with lots of Celtic banter and unlimited Irish charm.

Kelly Tesoro
AKA: Leading Lady
Kelly's former career as a Korean soapstar babe set her in good stead for the daily dramas at the bold and beautiful Explorer office. As our lovely receptionist she's on stage all day and her winning smile never slips.

Matt Farquharson
AKA: Hack Hunter
A career of tuppence-a-word hackery ended when Matt arrived in Dubai to cover a maggot wranglers' convention. He misguidedly thinks he's clever because he once wrote for some grown-up English papers.

Kiran Melwani
AKA: Bow Selector
Like a modern-day Robin Hood (right down to the green tights and band of merry men), Kiran's mission in life is to distribute Explorer's wealth of knowledge to the fact-hungry readers of the world. Just make sure you never do anything to upset her – rumour has it she's a pretty mean shot with that bow and arrow.

Mathew Samuel
AKA: Mr Modest
Matt's penchant for the entrepreneurial life began with a pair of red braces and a filofax when still a child. That yearning for the cut and thrust of commerce has brought him to Dubai, where he made a fortune in the sand-selling business before semi-retiring at Explorer.

Laura Zuffa
AKA: Travelling Salesgirl
Laura's passport is covered in more stamps than Kofi Annan's, and there isn't a city, country or continent that she won't travel to. With a smile that makes grown men weep, our girl on the frontlines always brings home the beef bacon.

Michael Samuel
AKA: Gordon Gekko
We have a feeling this mild mannered master of mathematics has a wild side. He hasn't witnessed an Explorer party yet but the office agrees that once the karaoke machine is out, Michael will be the maestro. Watch out Dubai!

Lennie Mangalino
AKA: Shaker Maker
With a giant spring in her step and music in her heart it's hard to not to swing to the beat when Lennie passes by in the office. She loves her Lambada… and Samba… and Salsa and anything else she can get the sales team shaking their hips to.

Mimi Stankova
AKA: Mind Controller
A master of mind control, Mimi's siren-like voice lulls people into doing whatever she asks. Her steely reserve and endless patience mean recalcitrant reporters and persistent PR people are putty in her hands, delivering whatever she wants, whenever she wants it.

Mannie Lugtu
AKA: Distribution Demon
When the travelling circus rode into town, their master juggler Mannie decided to leave the Big Top and explore Dubai instead. He may have swapped his balls for our books but his juggling skills still come in handy.

Maricar Ong
AKA: Pocket Docket
A pint-sized dynamo of ruthless efficiency, Maricar gets the job done before anyone else notices it needed doing. If this most able assistant is absent for a moment, it sends a surge of blind panic through the Explorer ranks.

Mohammed Sameer
AKA: Man in the Van
Known as MS, short for Microsoft, Sameer can pick apart a PC like a thief with a lock, which is why we keep him out of finance and pounding Dubai's roads in the unmissable Explorer van – so we can always spot him coming.

Najumudeen Kuttathundil
AKA: The Groove
If it weren't for Najumudeen, our stock of books would be lying in a massive pile of rubble in our warehouse. Thankfully, through hours of crunk dancing and forklift racing with Mohammed T, Najumudeen has perfected the art of organisation and currently holds the title for fastest forklift slalom in the UAE.

Rafi Jamal
AKA: Soap Star
After a walk on part in The Bold and the Beautiful, Rafi swapped the Hollywood Hills for the Hajar Mountains. Although he left the glitz behind, he still mingles with high society, moonlighting as a male gigolo and impressing Dubai's ladies with his fancy footwork.

Rafi VP
AKA: Party Trickster
After developing a rare allergy to sunlight in his teens, Rafi started to lose a few centimeters of height every year. He now stands just 30cm tall, and does his best work in our dingy basement wearing a pair of infrared goggles. His favourite party trick is to fold himself into a briefcase.

Noushad Madathil
AKA: Map Daddy
Where would Explorer be without the mercurial Madathil brothers? Lost in the Empty Quarter, that's where. Quieter than a mute dormouse, Noushad prefers to let his Photoshop layers, and brother Zain, do all the talking. A true Map Daddy.

Richard Greig
AKA: Sir Lancelot
Chivalrous to the last, Richard's dream of being a medieval knight suffered a setback after being born several centuries too late. His stellar parliamentary career remains intact, and he is in the process of creating a new party with the aim of abolishing all onions and onion-related produce.

Pamela Afram
AKA: Lady of Arabia
After an ill-fated accident playing Lawrence of Arabia's love interest in a play in Jumeira, Pamela found solace in the Explorer office. Her first paycheque went on a set of shiny new gleamers and she is now back to her bright and smiley self and is solely responsible for lighting up one half of the office!

Roshni Ahuja
AKA: Bright Spark
Never failing to brighten up the office with her colourful get-up, Roshni definitely puts the 'it' in the IT department. She's a perennially pleasant, profound programmer with peerless panache, and she does her job with plenty of pep and piles of pizzazz.

Pamela Grist
AKA: Happy Snapper
If a picture can speak a thousand words then Pam's photos say a lot about her - through her lens she manages to find the beauty in everything – even this motley crew. And when the camera never lies, thankfully Photoshop can.

Sean Kearns
AKA: The Tall Guy
Big Sean, as he's affectionately known, is so laid back he actually spends most of his time lying down (unless he's on a camping trip, when his ridiculously small tent forces him to sleep on his hands and knees). Despite the rest of us constantly tripping over his lanky frame, when the job requires someone who will work flat out, he always rises to the editorial occasion.

Pete Maloney
AKA: Graphic Guru
Image conscious he may be, but when Pete has his designs on something you can bet he's gonna get it! He's the king of chat up lines, ladies – if he ever opens a conversation with 'D'you come here often?' then brace yourself for the Maloney magic.

Shabsir M
AKA: Sticky Wicket
Shabsir is a valuable player on the Indian national cricket team, so instead of working you'll usually find him autographing cricket balls for crazed fans around the world. We don't mind though – if ever a retailer is stumped because they run out of stock, he knocks them for six with his speedy delivery.

Shan Kumar
AKA: Caped Crusader
Not dissimilar to the Batman's beacon, Explorer shines a giant X into the skies over Al Quoz in times of need. Luckily for us, Shan battled for days through the sand and warehouse units to save the day at our shiny new office. What a hero!

Steve Jones
AKA: Golden Boy
Our resident Kiwi lives in a nine-bedroom mansion and is already planning an extension. His winning smile has caused many a knee to weaken in Bur Dubai but sadly for the ladies, he's hopelessly devoted to his clients.

Shawn Jackson Zuzarte
AKA: Paper Plumber
If you thought rocket science was hard, try rearranging the chaotic babble that flows from the editorial team! If it weren't for Shawn, most of our books would require a kaleidoscope to read correctly so we're keeping him and his jazz hands under wraps.

Tim Binks
AKA: Class Clown
El Binksmeisterooney is such a sharp wit, he often has fellow Explorers gushing tea from their noses in convulsions of mirth. Years spent hiking across the Middle East have given him an encyclopaedic knowledge of rock formations and elaborate hair.

Shyrell Tamayo
AKA: Fashion Princess
We've never seen Shyrell wearing the same thing twice – her clothes collection is so large that her husband has to keep all his things in a shoebox. She runs Designlab like clockwork, because being late for deadlines is SO last season.

Tom Jordan
AKA: The True Professional
Explorer's resident thesp, Tom delivers lines almost as well as he cuts them. His early promise on the pantomime circuit was rewarded with an all-action role in hit UK drama Heartbeat. He's still living off the royalties – and the fact he shared a sandwich with Kenneth Branagh.

Sobia Gulzad
AKA: High Flyer
If Sobia's exam results in economics and management are anything to go by, she's destined to become a member of the global jet set. Her pursuit of glamour is almost more relentless than her pursuit of success, and in her time away from reading The Wealth of Nations she shops for designer handbags and that elusive perfect shade of lipgloss.

Tracy Fitzgerald
AKA: 'La Dona'
Tracy is a queenpin Catalan mafiosa and ringleader for the 'pescadora' clan, a nefarious group that runs a sushi smuggling operation between the Costa Brava and Ras Al Khaimah. She is not to be crossed. Rival clans will find themselves fed fish, and then fed to the fishes.

Sunita Lakhiani
AKA: Designlass
Initially suspicious of having a female in their midst, the boys in Designlab now treat Sunita like one of their own. A big shame for her, because they treat each other pretty damn bad!

Zainudheen Madathil
AKA: Map Master
Often confused with retired footballer Zinedine Zidane because of his dexterous displays and a bad head-butting habit, Zain tackles design with the mouse skills of a star striker. Maps are his goal and despite getting red-penned a few times, when he shoots, he scores.

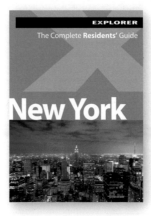

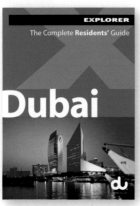

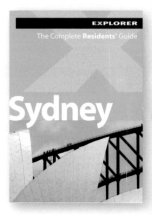

The *Los Angeles Residents' Guide* Team
Lead Editor David Quinn
Deputy Editor Jake Marsico
Editorial Assistant Grace Carnay
Designers Hashim Moideen, Rafi VP
Cartographers Noushad Madathil, Praseena Kunnummal, Raghunath Melethil, Ramlath Kambravan
Photographers Pete Maloney, David Quinn
Proofer Jo Holden-MacDonald

Publishing
Publisher Alistair MacKenzie
Associate Publisher Claire England
Assistant to Associate Publisher Kathryn Calderon

Editorial
Group Editor Jane Roberts
Lead Editors David Quinn, Katie Drynan, Matt Farquharson, Sean Kearns, Tim Binks, Tom Jordan
Deputy Editors Helen Spearman, Jake Marsico, Jenny Lyon, Pamela Afram, Richard Greig
Senior Editorial Assistant Mimi Stankova
Editorial Assistants Grace Carnay, Ingrid Cupido

Design
Creative Director Pete Maloney
Art Director Ieyad Charaf
Design Manager Alex Jeffries
Senior Designer Iain Young
Junior Designer Jessy Perera
Layout Manager Jayde Fernandes
Designers Hashim Moideen, Rafi VP, Shawn Jackson Zuzarte
Cartography Manager Zainudheen Madathil
Cartographers Juby Jose, Noushad Madathil, Sunita Lakhiani
Traffic Manager Maricar Ong
Production Coordinator Joy Tubog

Photography
Photography Manager Pamela Grist
Photographer Victor Romero
Image Editor Henry Hilos

Sales & Marketing
Media Sales Area Managers Laura Zuffa, Stephen Jones
Corporate Sales Executive Ben Merrett
Marketing Manager Kate Fox
Marketing Executive Annabel Clough
Marketing Assistant Shedan Ebona
Digital Content Manager Derrick Pereira
International Retail Sales Manager Ivan Rodrigues
Retail Sales Coordinators Kiran Melwani, Sobia Gulzad
Retail Sales Supervisor Mathew Samuel
Retail Sales Merchandisers Johny Mathew, Shan Kumar
Sales & Marketing Coordinator Lennie Mangalino
Senior Distribution Executives Ahmed Mainodin, Firos Khan
Warehouse Assistant Najumudeen Kuttathundil Ismail
Drivers Mohammed Sameer, Shabsir Madathil

Finance & Administration
Finance Manager Michael Samuel
HR & Administration Manager Andrea Fust
Admin Manager Shyrell Tamayo
Junior Accountant Cherry Enriquez
Accountants Assistant Darwin Lovitas
Administrators Enrico Maullon, Kelly Tesoro
Drivers Rafi Jamal, Mannie Lugtu

IT
IT Administrator Ajay Krishnan
Senior Software Engineer Bahrudeen Abdul
Software Engineer Roshni Ahuja

Contact Us
Reader Response
If you have any comments and suggestions, fill out our online reader response form and you could win prizes. Log on to **www.explorerpublishing.com**

General Enquiries
We'd love to hear your thoughts and answer any questions you have about this book or any other Explorer product. Contact us at **info@explorerpublishing.com**

Careers
If you fancy yourself as an Explorer, send your CV (stating the position you're interested in) to **jobs@explorerpublishing.com**

Designlab & Contract Publishing
For enquiries about Explorer's Contract Publishing arm and design services contact **designlab@explorerpublishing.com**

PR & Marketing
For PR and marketing enquries contact **marketing@explorerpublishing.com**
pr@explorerpublishing.com

Corporate Sales
For bulk sales and customisation options, for this book or any Explorer product, contact **sales@explorerpublishing.com**

Advertising & Sponsorship
For advertising and sponsorship, contact **media@explorerpublishing.com**

Explorer Publishing & Distribution
PO Box 34275, Dubai, United Arab Emirates
www.explorerpublishing.com

Phone: +971 (0)4 340 8805
Fax: +971 (0)4 340 8806

417

Emergency Numbers

Ambulance	911
Fire & Rescue	911
Police	911
National Poison Center	800 222 1222
CVS Pharmacy	888 607 4287
Sav-On Pharmacy	877 728 6655
Walgreens Pharmacy	800 925 4733
American Express	800 528 4800
MasterCard	800 627 8372
Visa	800 847 2911
M&M Towing	818 774 2233
Charlie's Towing	626 279 5530
AAA	800 400 4222

Landmark Hotels

Artists' Inn & Cottage	626 799 5668
Beverly Hills Hotel	310 276 2251
Beverly Wilshire	310 276 2251
Chateau Marmont	323 656 1010
The Crescent	310 247 0505
Four Seasons Beverly Hills	310 273 2222
Georgian Hotel	310 395 9945
Hollywood Roosevelt	323 466 7000
Hotel Bel-Air	310 472 1211
Hotel Casa Del Mar	310 581 5503
Hotel Figueroa	213 627 0305
Millennium Biltmore	213 624 1011
Queen Mary	562 435 3511
Sunset Tower	323 654 7100
W Los Angeles	310 208 8765

Embassies & Consulates

Argentina	323 954 9155
Australia	310 229 4800
Canada	213 346 2700
China	213 807 8088
Costa Rica	213 380 7915
Denmark	818 766 0003
France	310 235 3200
Germany	323 930 2703
Greece	310 826 5555
Israel	323 852 5500
Japan	213 617 6700
Mexico	213 351 6800
New Zealand	310 207 1605
Pakistan	310 441 5114
Philippines	213 639 0980
Poland	310 442 8500
Saudi Arabia	310 479 6000
South Africa	323 651 0902
Spain	323 938 0158
Sweden	310 445 4008
Thailand	323 962 9574
United Arab Emirates	202 243 2400
United Kingdom	310 481 0031
Switzerland	310 575 1145

Airport Information

LAX General Information	888 544 9444
Airport Police	310 646 7911
Lost & Found	310 417 0440
Bus Service Enquiries	800 266 6883

Airlines

British Airways	800 247 9297
Delta Airlines	800 221 1212
Emirates	800 777 3999
Northwest Airlines	800 225 2525
Quantas	800 227 4500
United Airlines	800 864 8331
US Airways	800 428 4322
Virgin	800 862 8621

Medical Services

Cedars Sinai	310 423 3277
Children's Hospital	323 660 2450
Encino-Tarzana Regional Medical Center	818 881 0800
Huntington Hospital	626 397 5000
Northridge Hospital Medical Center	818 885 8500
Saint Johns	310 829 5511
Sherman Oaks Hospital	818 981 7111
UCLA	310 825 9111
USC University Hospital	888 700 5700

City Information

www.culturela.org	LA Information
www.experiencela.com	LA Information
www.laist.com	Popular blog
www.lapdonline.org	LA Police
www.losangeles.citysearch.com	City info
www.latourist.com	Tourist Information
www.metro.net	Transportation
www.visitcalifornia.com	Tourism site

Public Holidays

New Year's Day	1 Jan
MLK Birthday	3rd Mon in Jan
President's Day	3rd Mon in Feb
Memorial Day	Last Mon in May
Independence Day	4 Jul
Labor Day	1st Mon in Sep
Columbus Day	2nd Mon in Oct
Veterans Day	11 Nov
Thanksgiving	Last Thurs in Nov
Christmas Day	25 Dec

Taxi Companies

Bell Cab	800 666 6664
Checker Cab	800 300 5007
City Cab	800 750 4400
Independent Taxi	800 521 8294
United Independent Taxi	800 411 0303
Yellow Cab	800 200 1085